U0920729

西安统计年鉴

XI'AN STATISTICAL YEARBOOK

2017

中英文对照 Chinese/English

中国统计出版社
China Statistics Press

西安市统计局
XI'AN MUNICIPAL BUREAU OF STATISTICS
国家统计局西安调查队
NBS SURVEY OFFICE IN XI'AN

图书在版编目（CIP）数据

西安统计年鉴. 2017 / 西安市统计局, 国家统计局西安调查队编. -- 北京 : 中国统计出版社, 2017.8
ISBN 978-7-5037-8282-4

Ⅰ. ①西… Ⅱ. ①西… ②国… Ⅲ. ①统计资料 - 西安 - 2017 - 年鉴 Ⅳ. ①C832.411-54

中国版本图书馆CIP数据核字（2017）第200710号

西安统计年鉴—2017

作　　者/ 西安市统计局 国家统计局西安调查队
责任编辑/ 陈越月
装帧设计/ 西安力天世纪品牌策划设计有限公司
出版发行/ 中国统计出版社
地　　址/ 北京市丰台区西三环南路甲6号 邮政编码/100073
电　　话/ 邮购（010）63376909 书店（010）68783171
网　　址/ http://csp.stats.gov.cn
印　　刷/西安一印制版有限责任公司
经　　销/ 新华书店
开　　本/ 890mm×1240mm 1/16
字　　数/ 1521千字
印　　张/ 44.5
版　　别/ 2017年8月第1版
版　　次/ 2017年8月第1次印刷
定　　价/ 260元

如有印装差错，由本社发行部调换。

《西安统计年鉴—2017》编辑部

XI'AN STATISTICAL YEARBOOK-2017
EDITORLAL STAFF

编者说明

一、《西安统计年鉴—2017》系统收录了全市、区县及开发区2016年经济、社会各方面统计数据，以及重要历史年份主要统计数据，是一部全面记载西安市国民经济和社会发展情况的大型连续性统计文献资料和重要工具书。

二、本年鉴正文内容分为二十二个篇章：（一）综合；（二）基本单位；（三）国民经济核算；（四）人口、从业人员与职工工资；（五）固定资产投资；（六）财政；（七）物价指数；（八）人民生活；（九）城市公用事业；（十）环境保护；（十一）农业；（十二）工业；（十三）能源；（十四）建筑业；（十五）运输邮电和信息化；（十六）国内贸易；（十七）对外经济贸易和旅游；（十八）服务业；（十九）金融业；（二十）教育和科技；（二十一）文化、体育、卫生、社会福利和其他；（二十二）企业调查。同时，为方便读者使用，各篇章前设有简要说明和主要统计指标，对本篇章的主要内容、资料来源、以及历史变动情况予以简要概述，篇末附有《主要统计指标解释》。

三、本年鉴统计资料的统计标准，按当时国家统计制度执行，有关指标的涵义、口径、范围、计算方法等，在不同时期可能有所不同，使用时请注意。如国民经济行业分类按GB/T4754—2011标准执行。

四、为便于国内外读者查阅，本年鉴全部内容均采用中英文对照编辑。

五、本年鉴中国民经济核算部分的2013年数据为全国第三次经济普查数据，2009—2012年数据为依据第三次经济普查修订数据；工业部分的2013年数据为第三次经济普查数据，依据第三次经济普查对2009—2012年规模以上工业增加值进行了修订。国内贸易部分的2009—2013年为依据第三次经济普查调整后数据。

六、本年鉴中的部分指标合计数或相对数由于单位取舍不同产生的计算误差均未作机械调整。

七、本年鉴所使用的计量单位均依据2016年相关统计报表制度。

八、本年鉴使用的符号说明：“空白”表示该项统计指标无数据或数据不详；“#”表示其中项；“*”表示另有注解。

感谢社会各界长期以来对《西安统计年鉴》的广泛关注和大力支持。为进一步做好工作，更好地为广大读者服务，希望社会各界提出宝贵意见。

PREFACE

I. *Xi'an Statistical Yearbook 2017* is a periodical statistic yearbook which record economic and social development of Xi'an all-around data in 2016 and some selected data series in historical important years. With its features of comprehensive and intensive information, this practically provides data covering the situation of social and economic developments in Xi'an.

II. The book contains twenty-two parts, 1.General Survey; 2.Basic Unit; 3.National Economic Account; 4.Population, Employment and Wages; 5.Investment in Fixed Assets; 6.Government Finance; 7.Price Indices; 8.People's Livelihood; 9.Urban Public Utilities; 10.Environmental Protection; 11.Agriculture; 12.Industry; 13.Energy; 14.Construction; 15.Transportation, Post Telecommunication Service and Informatization ; 16.Domestic Trade; 17.Foreign Trade; 18. Tertiary Industry; 19.Banking and Insurance; 20.Education, Science and Technology; 21.Culture, Sports, Public Health, Social Welfare Institutions and Other Social Activities; 22.Enterprises Investigation. As insert pages including statistical graphs and charts.Meanwhile, for the convenience of the reader, before each chapter, we make a brief description and the main statistical indicators, summarize the main contents of this charpter, sources of information and historical changes. At the end of the charpter, explanation of key statistical indicators are attached.

III. The data of various years in conformity to the statistical standards prescribed by national statistical system of the time. The meaning, scope and calculating method of indicators may have some difference in different periods, which readers must pay attention to. For example, national industries classification is carried out according to standard GB/T4754 -2011.

IV. For the convenience of being consulted by foreigners, the book is Chinese-English bilingual edition.

V. In this yearbook, data in 2013 at the part of National Economic Account and Industry is the results of Third National Economic Census, the data from 2009 to 2012 at the part of National Economic Account and data from 2009 to 2013 at the part of Domestic Trade have adjusted by Third National Economic Census, we also revised the industrial added value above designated size from 2009 to 2012.

VI. Statistical discrepancies due to rounding are not adjusted automatically in this yearbook.

VII. Unit of measurement is used in this yearbook according to 2016 statistics system.

VIII. Explanations on symbols used in this yearbook:

(Blank) indicates the data not available;

\# indicates the items of the total.

* indicates some other explanatory note.

Here we would like to express our sincere thanks to the people for their concerning and support to the Xi'an statistical yearbook. In order to do better and provide better service to readers, we hope that the whole society fields can propose constructive advices.

生产总值（亿元）
Gross Domestic Product(100 million yuan)

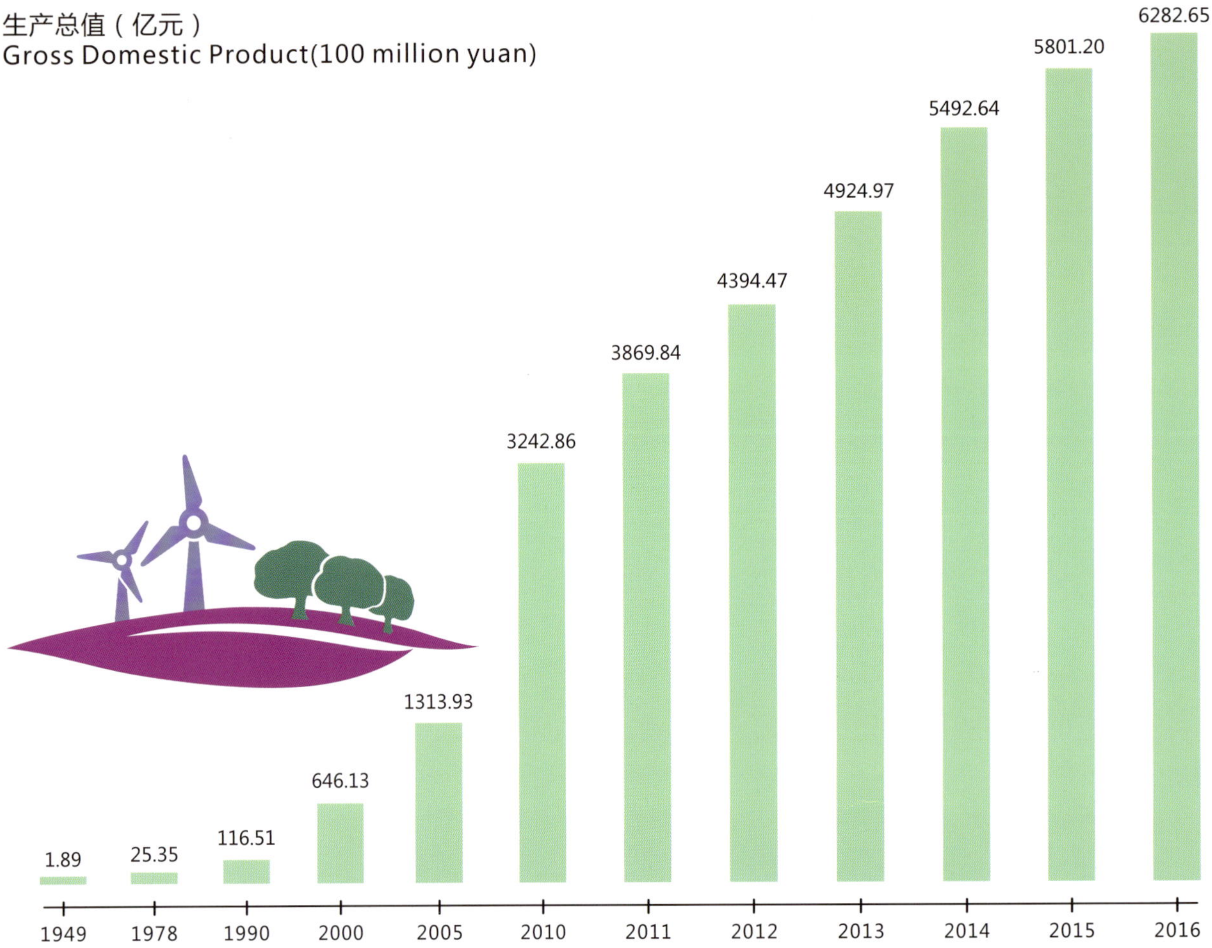

1.89
25.35
116.51
646.13
1313.93
3242.86
3869.84
4394.47
4924.97
5492.64
5801.20
6282.65
1949
1978
1990
2000
2005
2010
2011
2012
2013
2014
2015
2016

生产总值指数（以上年为100）
Indices of Gross Domestic Product (preceding year = 100)

100.0
108.4
103.6
126.1
122.0
103.8
101.7
111.5
112.6
105.2
110.0
113.0
114.0
114.5
113.5
112.2
111.1
109.9
108.2
108.6
1949
1950
1952
1965
1970
1975
1978
1980
1985
1990
1995
2000
2005
2010
2011
2012
2013
2014
2015
2016

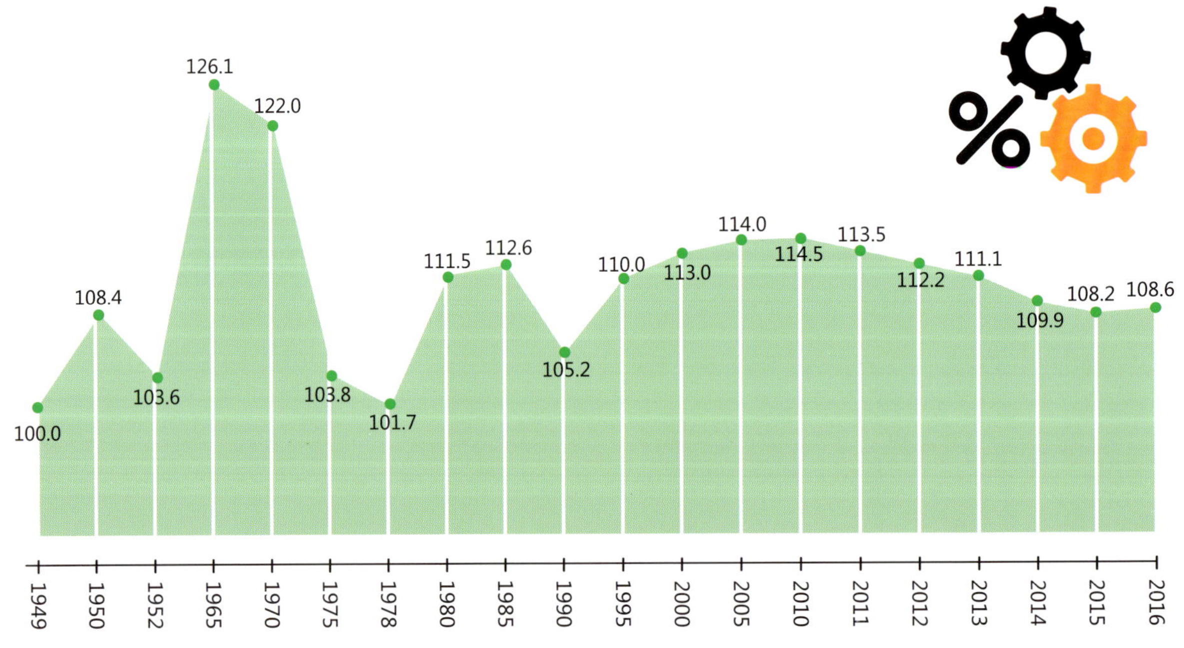

生产总值构成（%）
Composition of Gross Domestic Product (%)

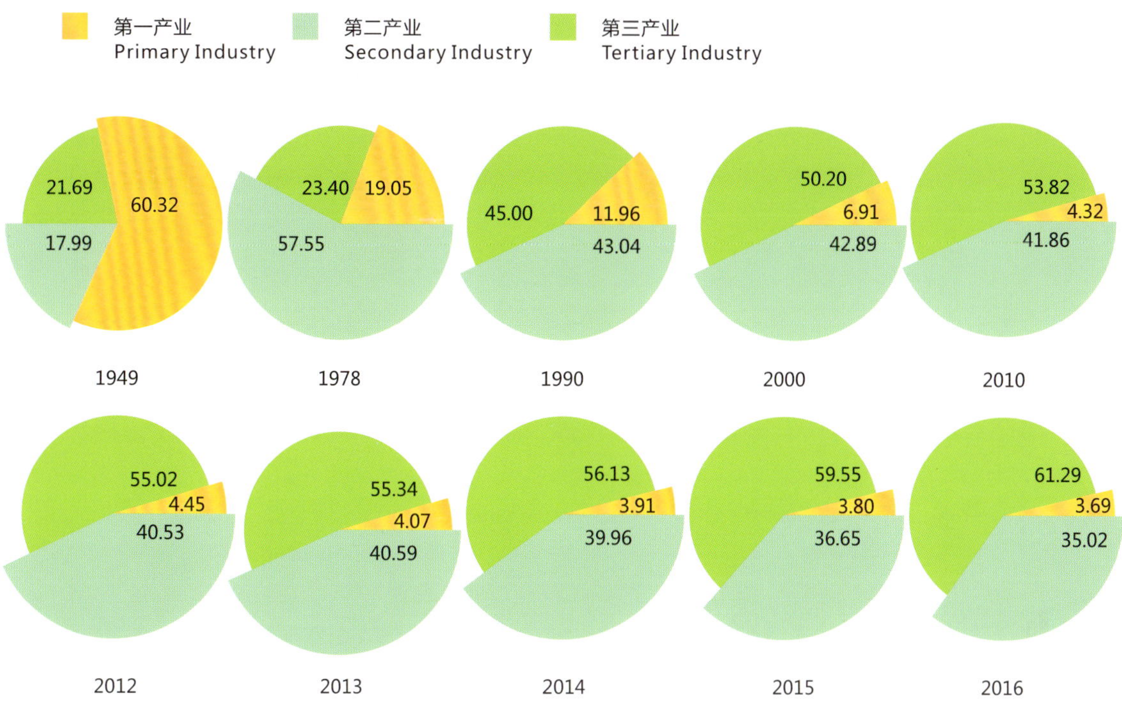

人均GDP（元/人）
Per Capita GDP(yuan/person)

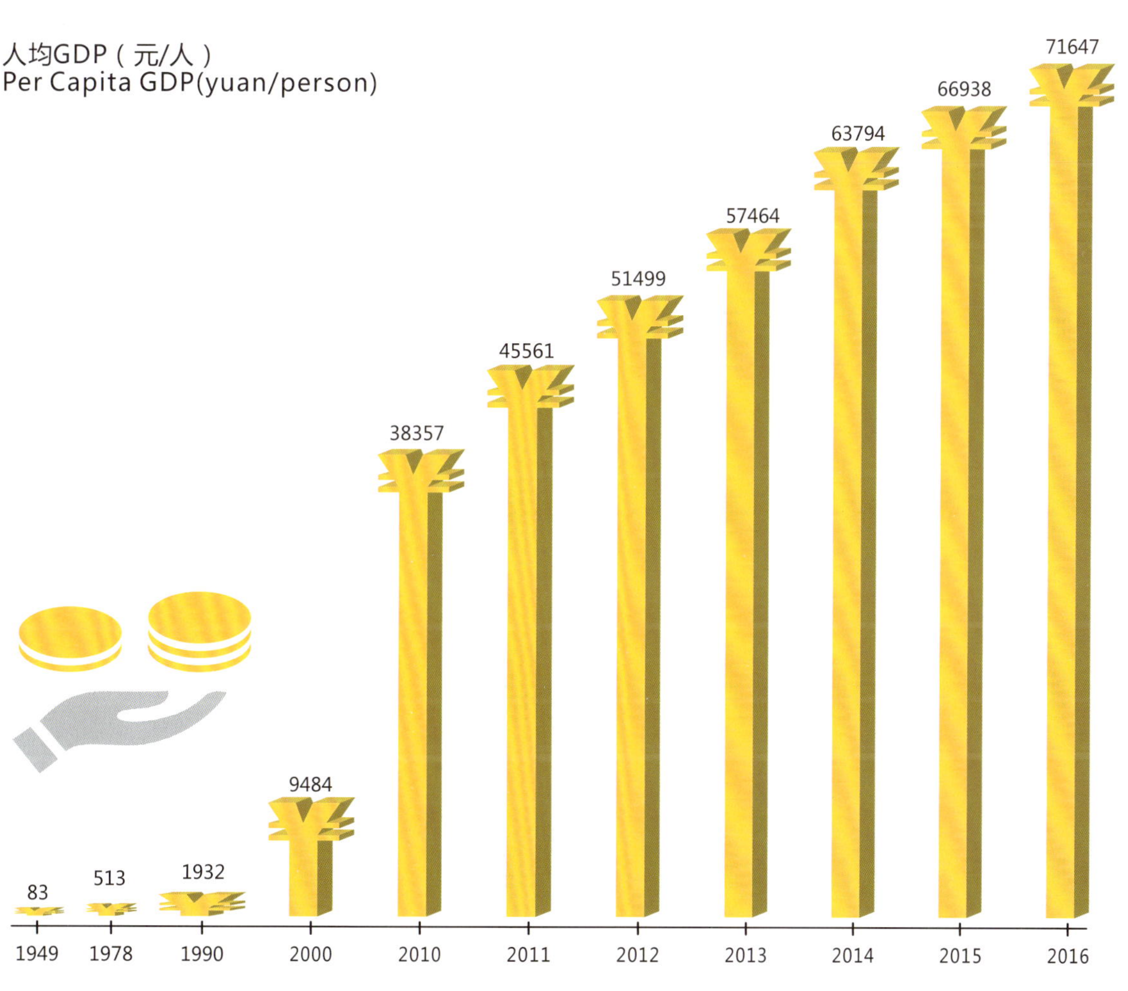

年末常住人口（万人）
Year-end Permanent population (10000 persons)

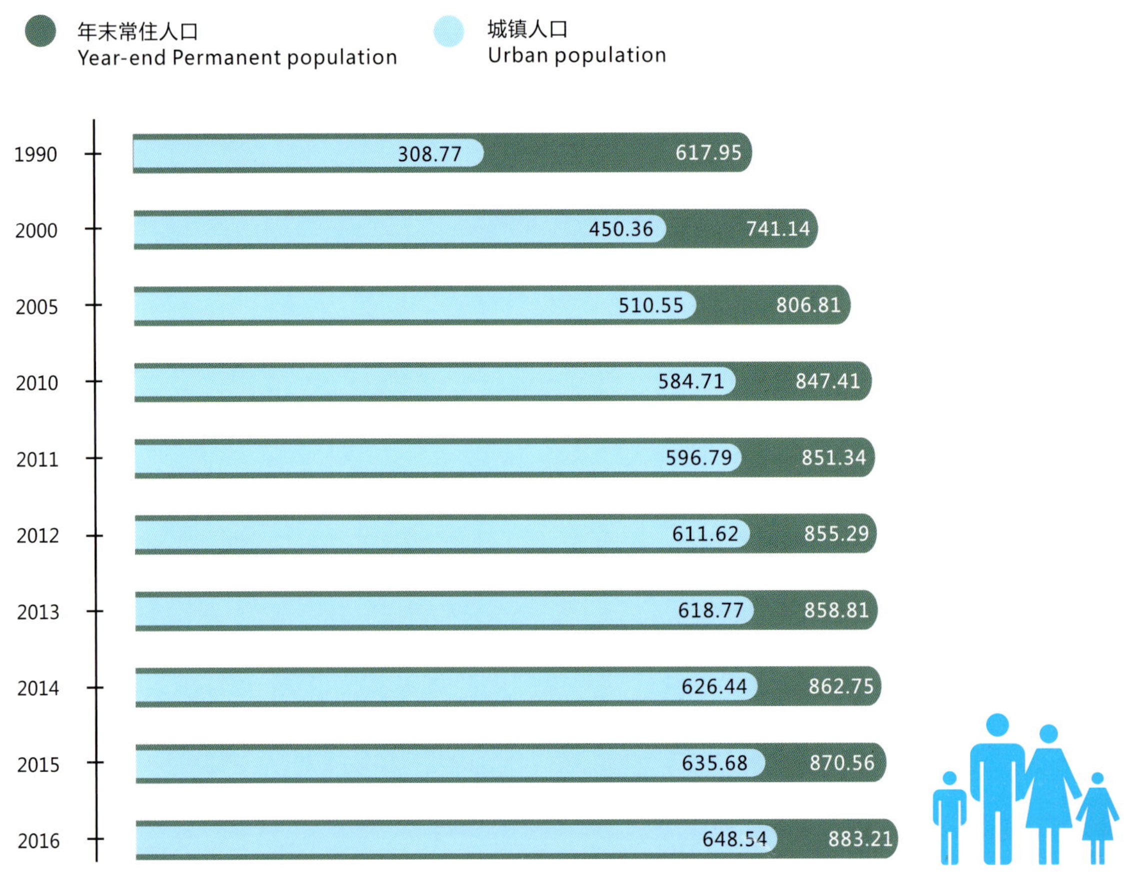

社会从业人数（万人）
Social Workers(10000 persons)

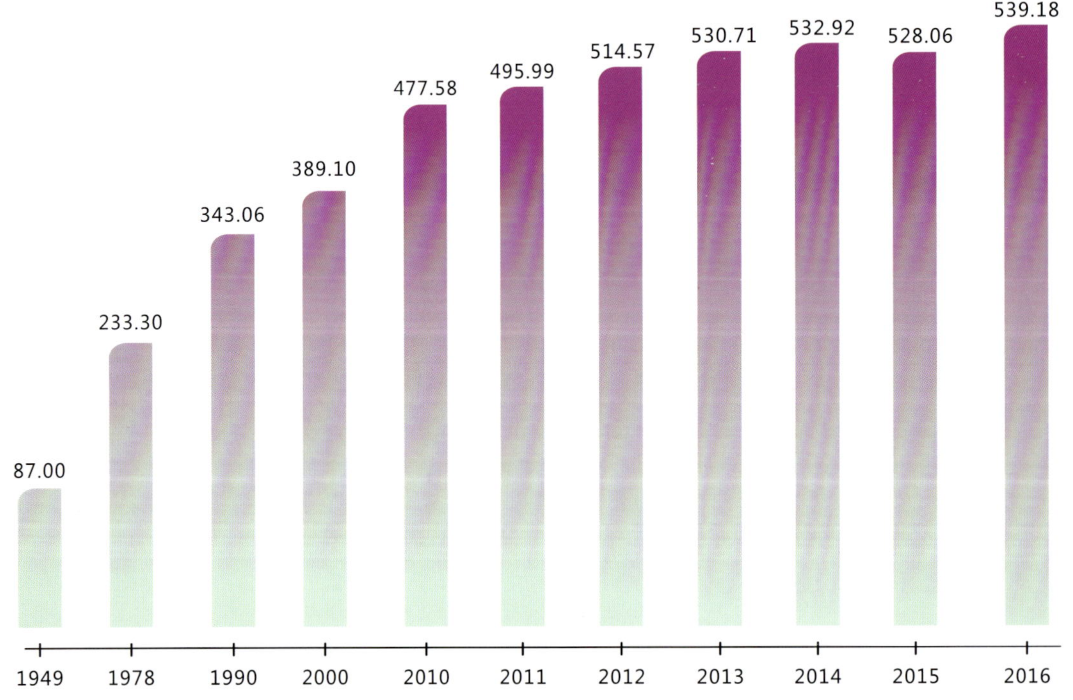

固定资产投资（亿元）
Investment in Fixed Assets(100 million yuan)

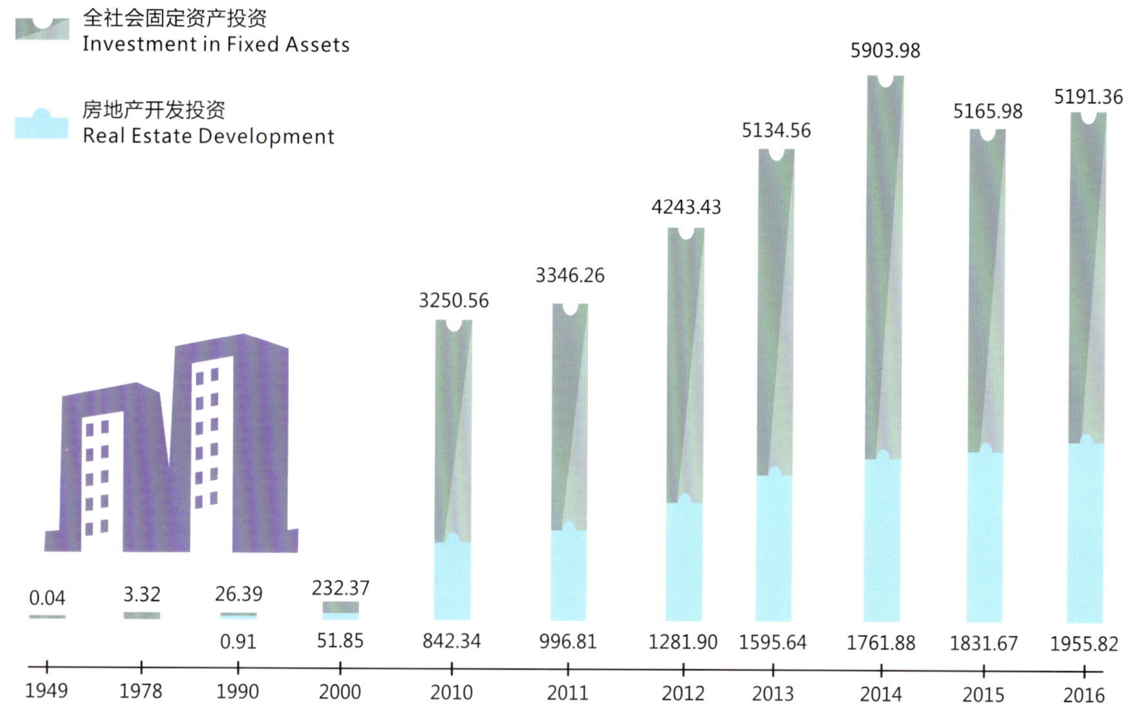

新增固定资产及住宅竣工面积
Newly Increased Fixed Assets and Residenctial Area of Completion

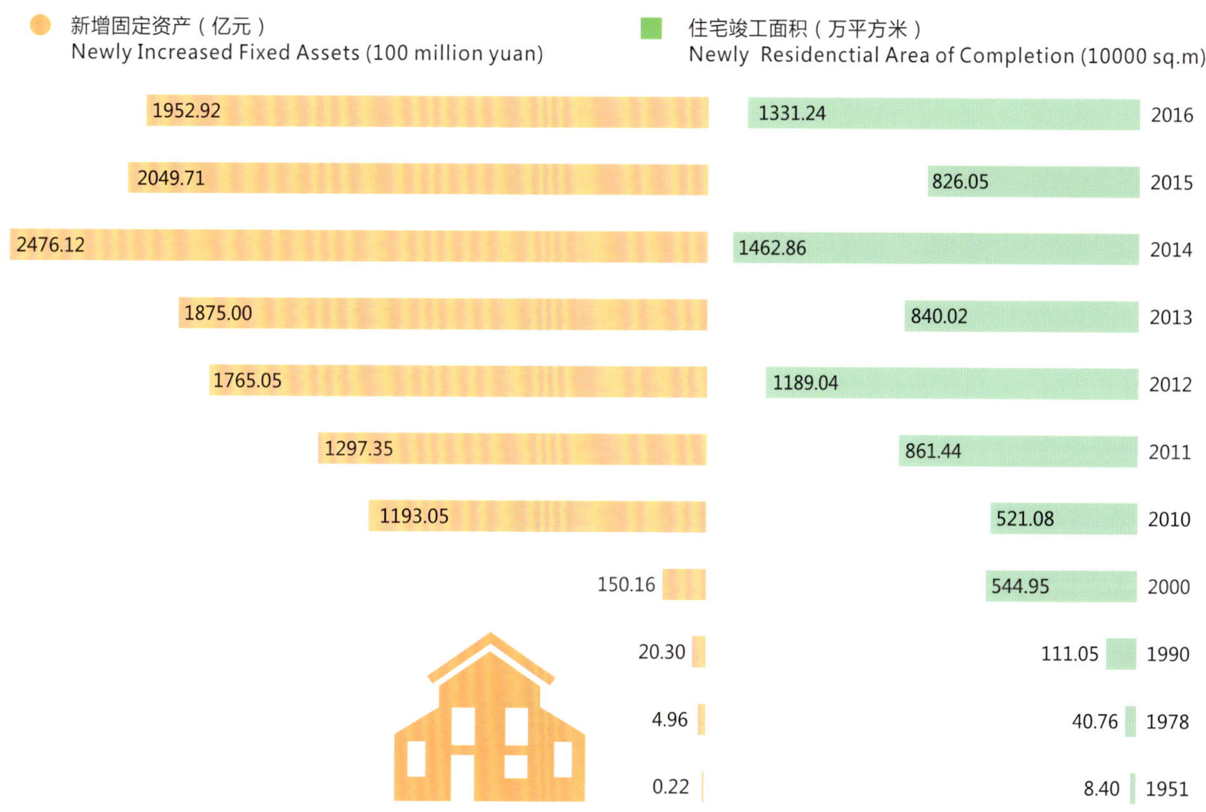

农林牧渔及服务业总产值（亿元）
Gross Output Value of Farming,Forestry, Animal Husbandry,Fishery and Service(100 million yuan)

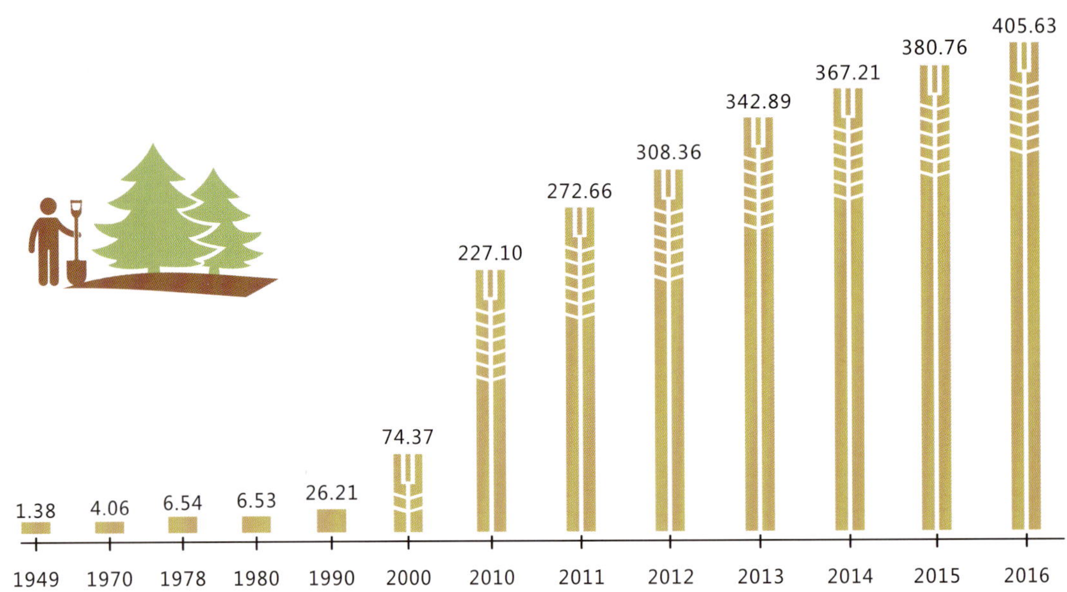

蔬菜产量（万吨）
Vegetables Product(10000 ton)

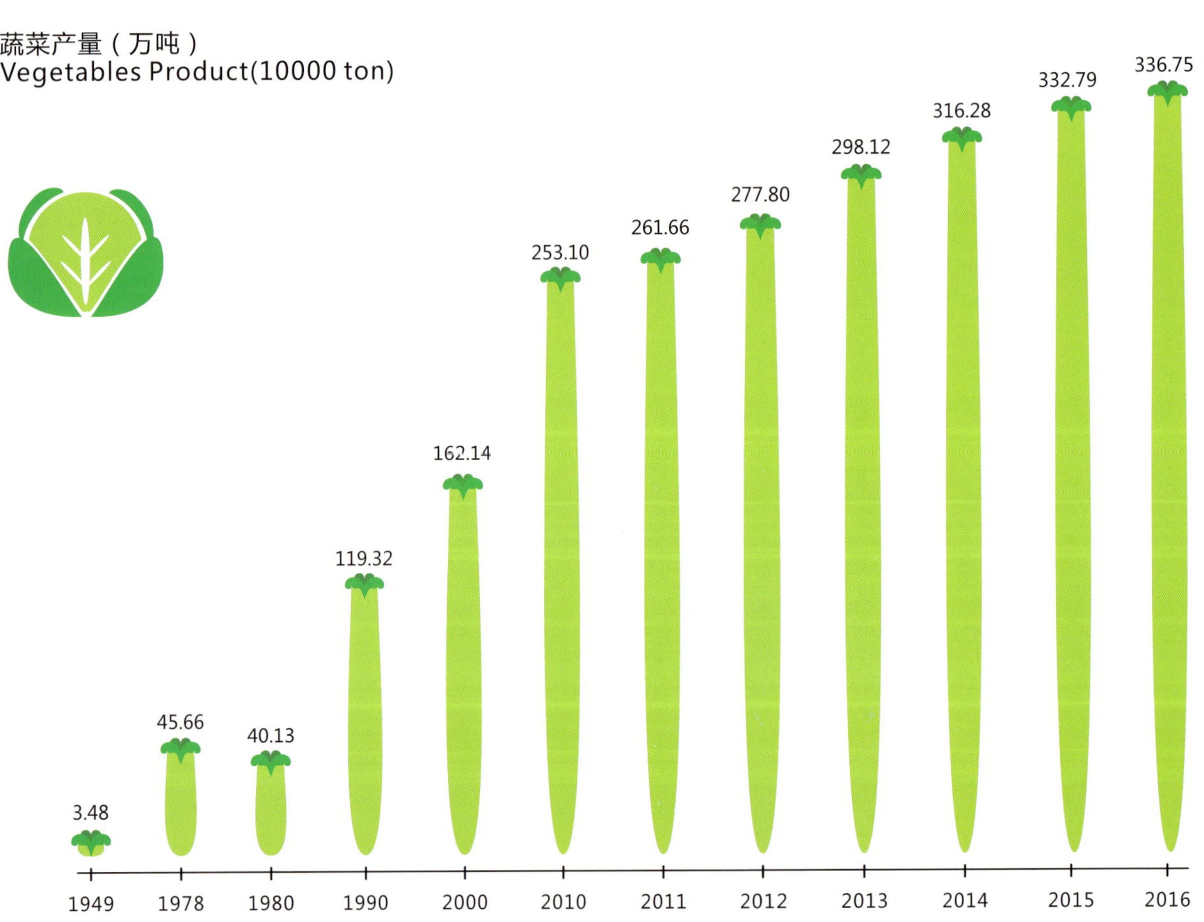

规模以上工业增加值（现价）（亿元）
Value Added of Industrial Enterprises Above Designated Size (100 million yuan)

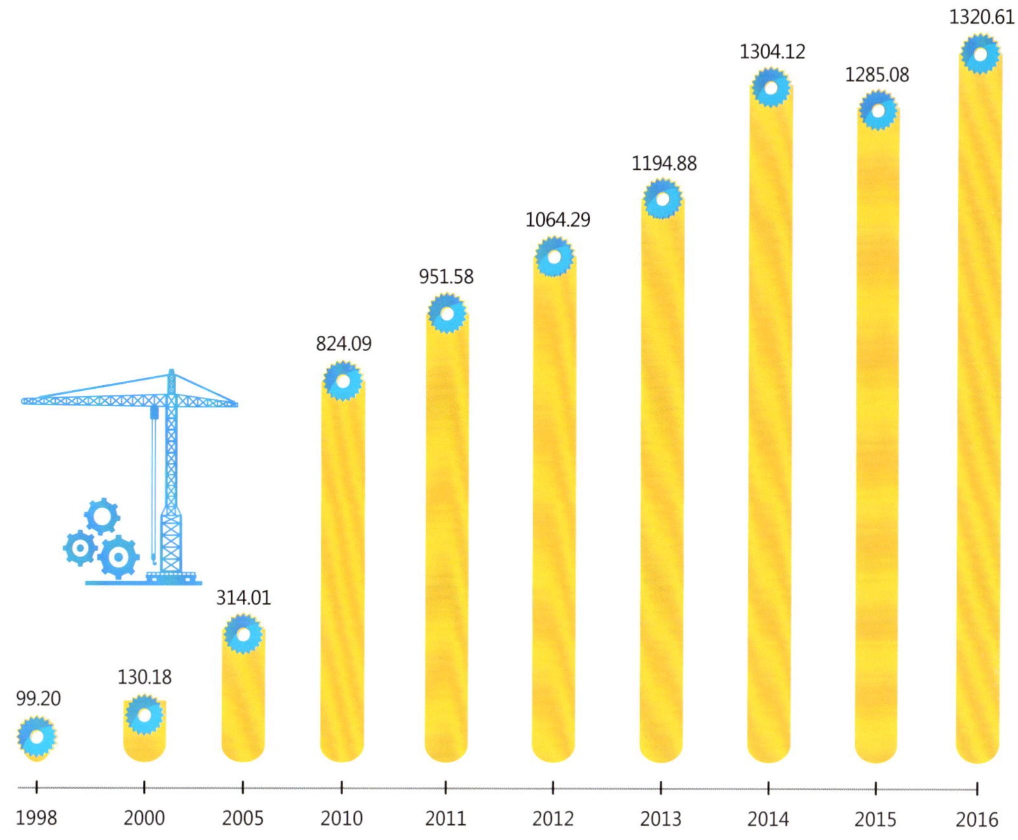

规模以上工业企业主要产品产量
Output of Major Industrial Products Of Enterprises Above Designated Size

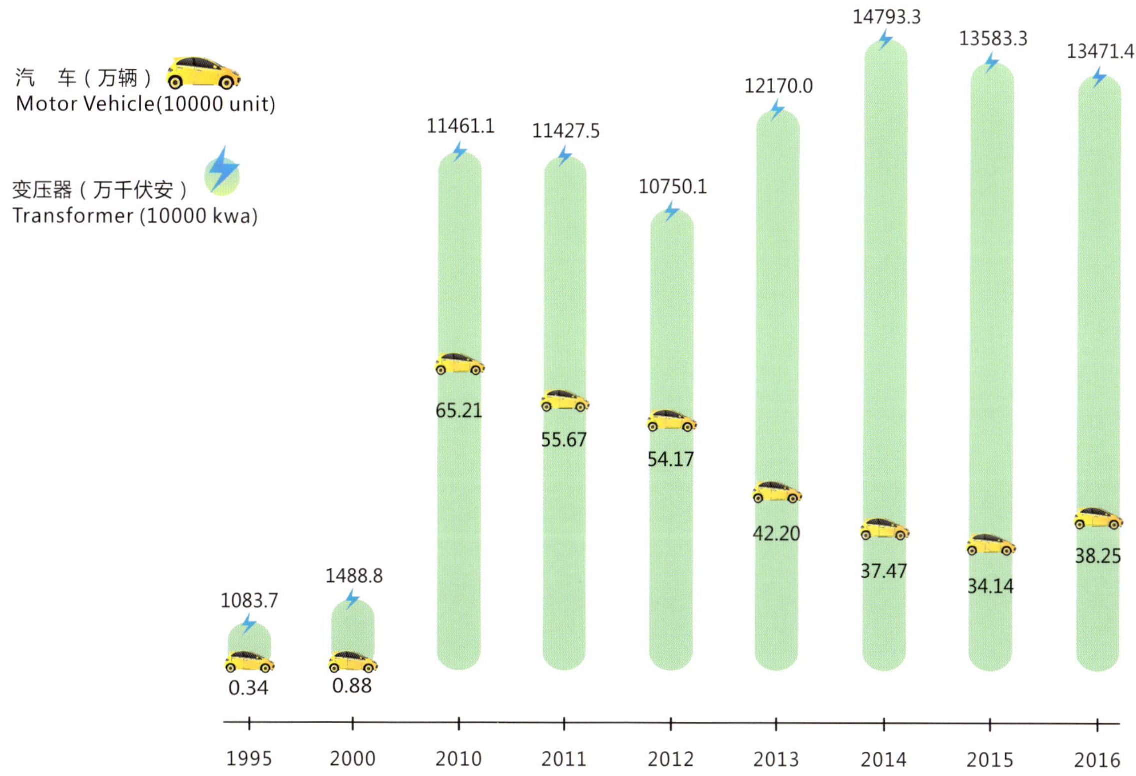

交通
Trafficed Size

等级公路（公里）
Expressways and Clas I to IV Highways(KM)

高速公路（公里）
Expressway(KM)

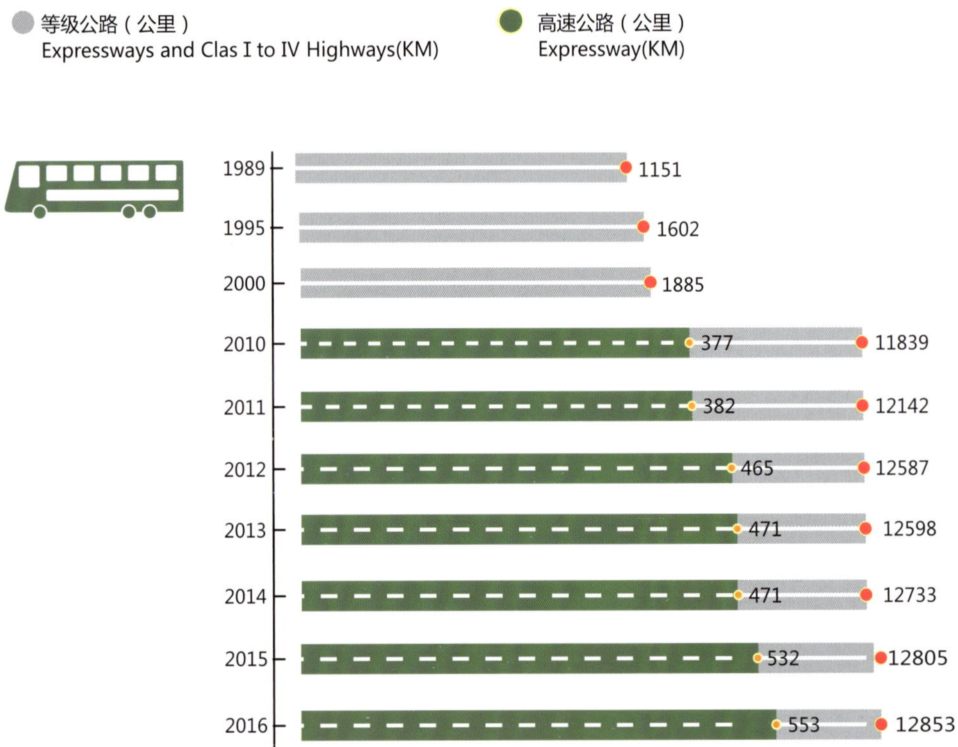

全社会车辆数（万辆）
Possession of Civil Vehicles(10000 unit)

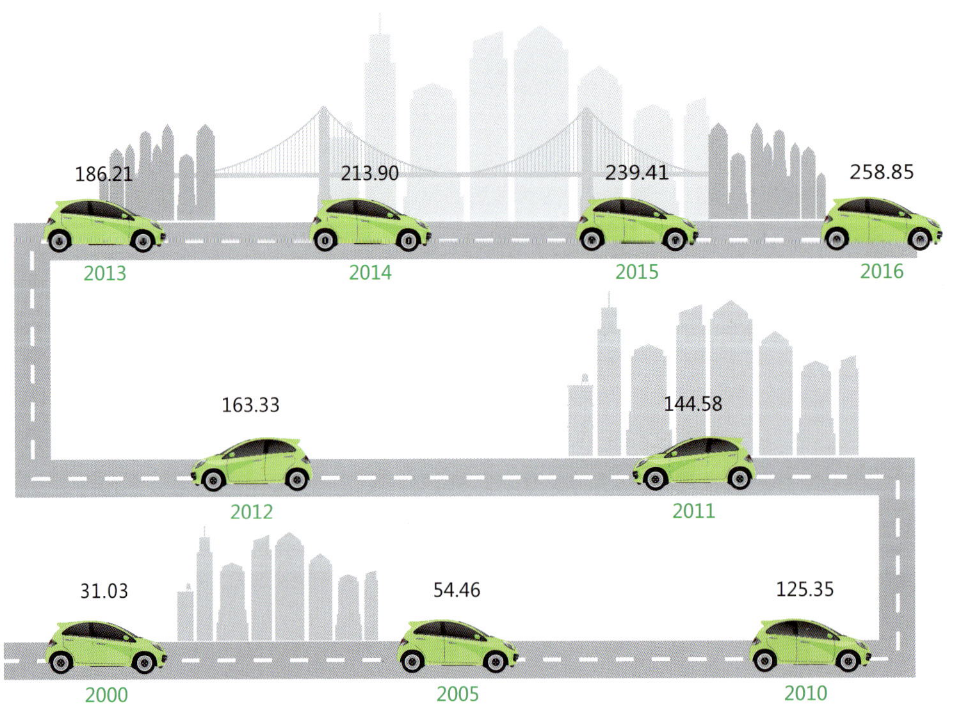

社会消费品零售总额（亿元）
Total Retail Sales of Consumer Goods(100 million yuan)

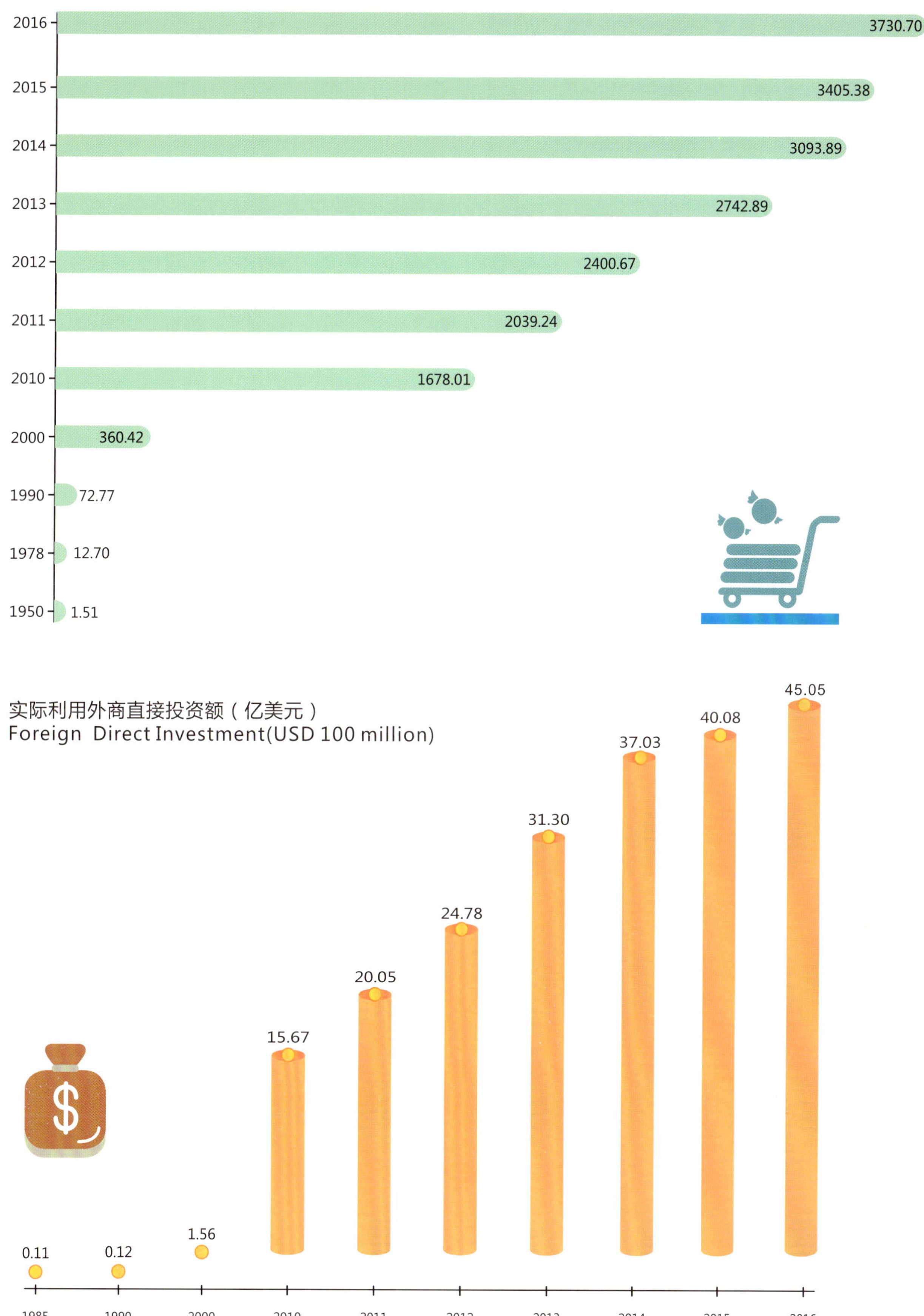

进出口总值（亿美元）
Total Value of Imports and Exports(USD 100 million)

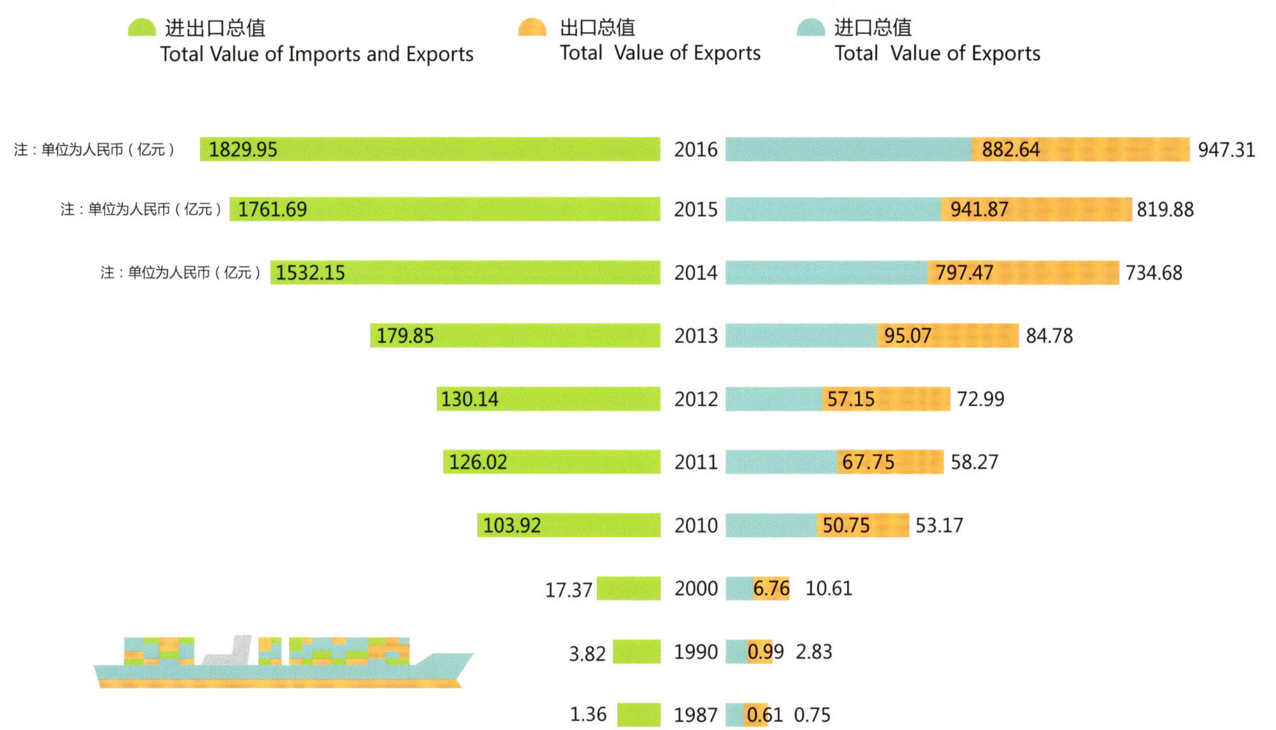

旅游人数及收入
Number of Tourists and Tourism Income

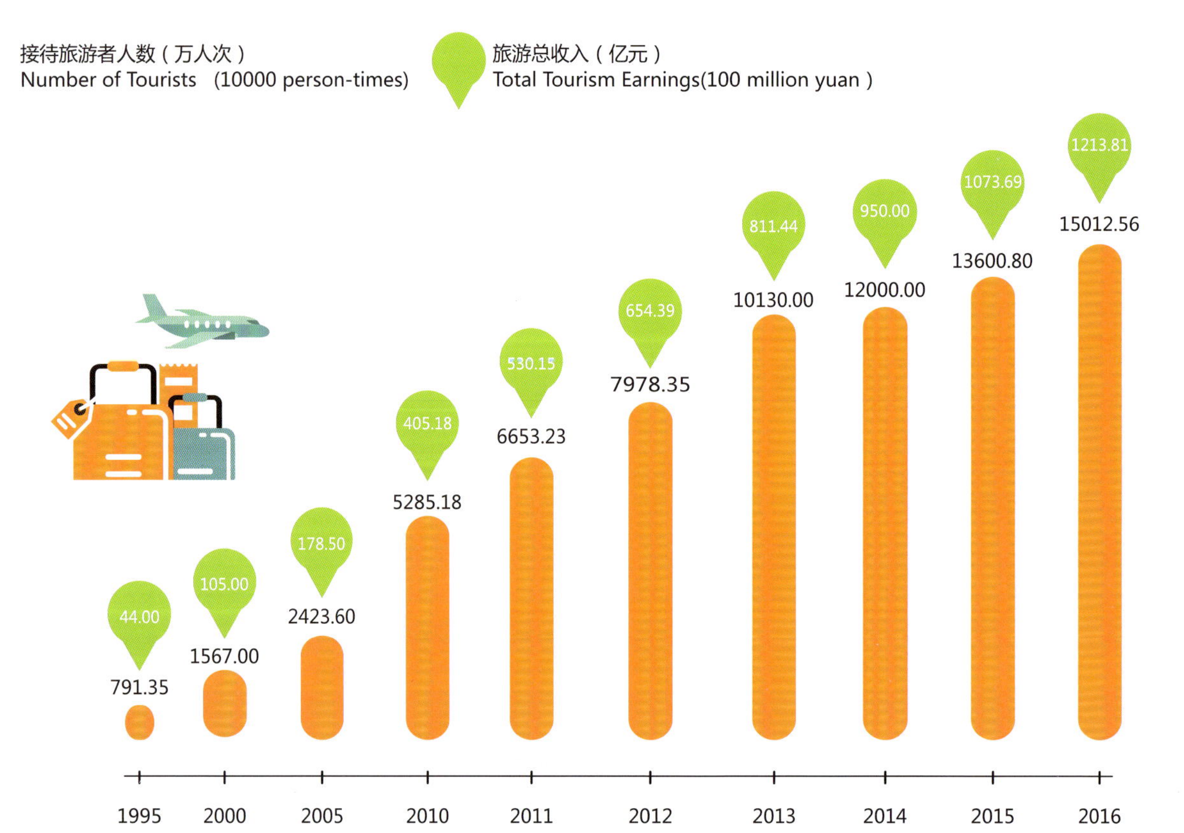

财政收支（亿元）
Government Revenue and Expenditure(100 million yuan)

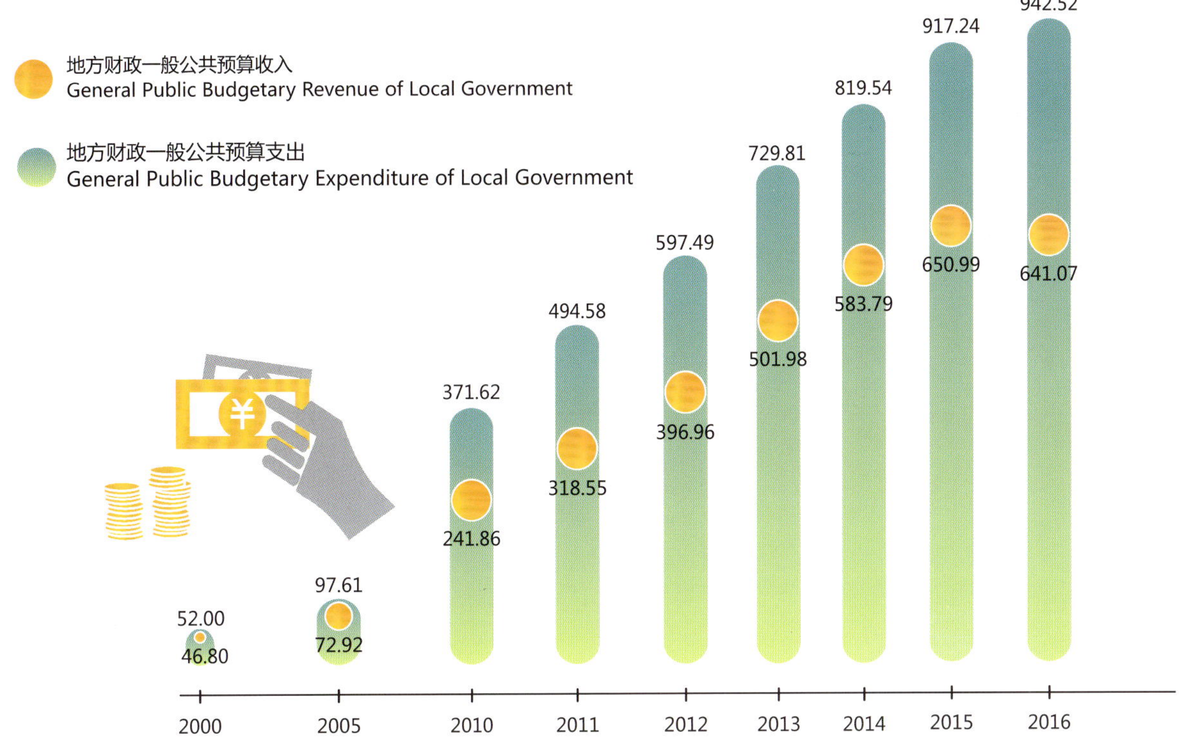

金融机构人民币存贷款年末余额（亿元）
Year-end Deposit and Loans in Financial Institutions (100 million yuan)

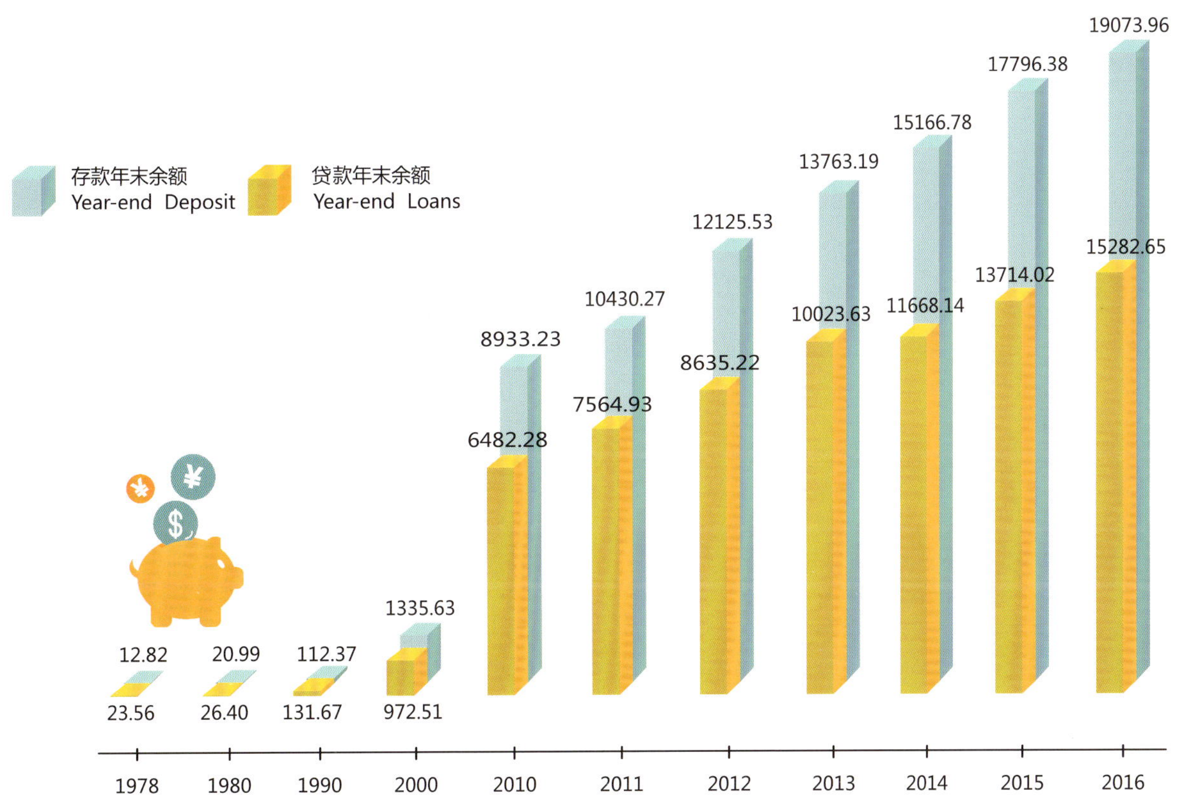

建成区面积（平方公里）
Area of Regions Built-up (sq.km)

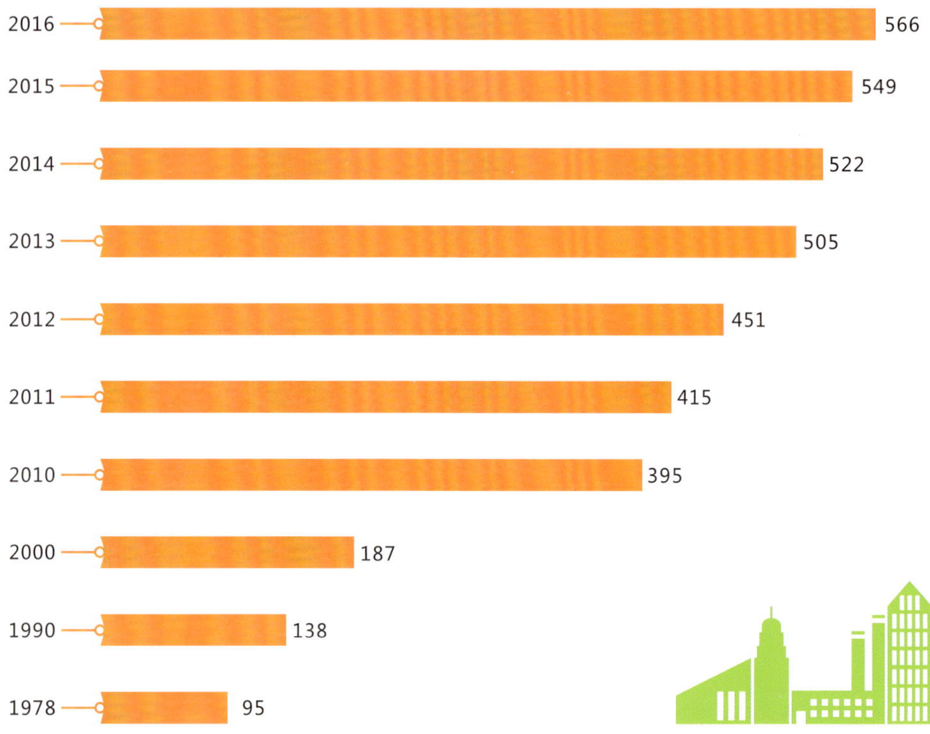

城市公共运营车辆（辆）
City Operating Vehicles(unit)

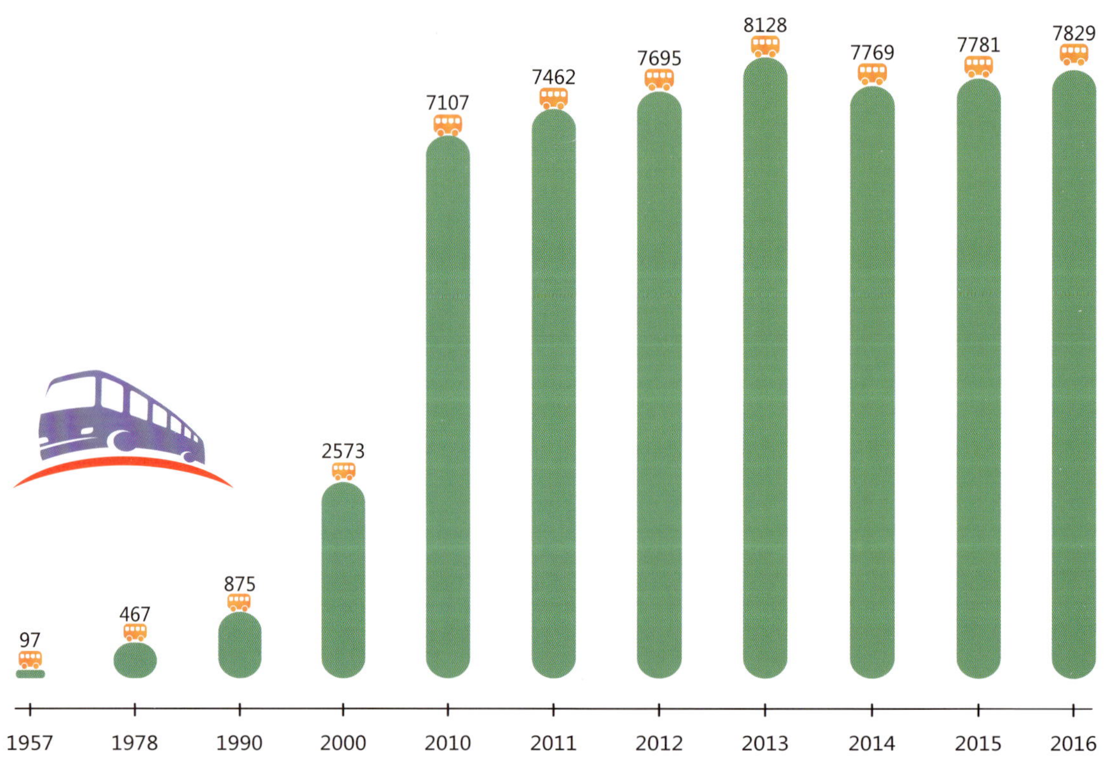

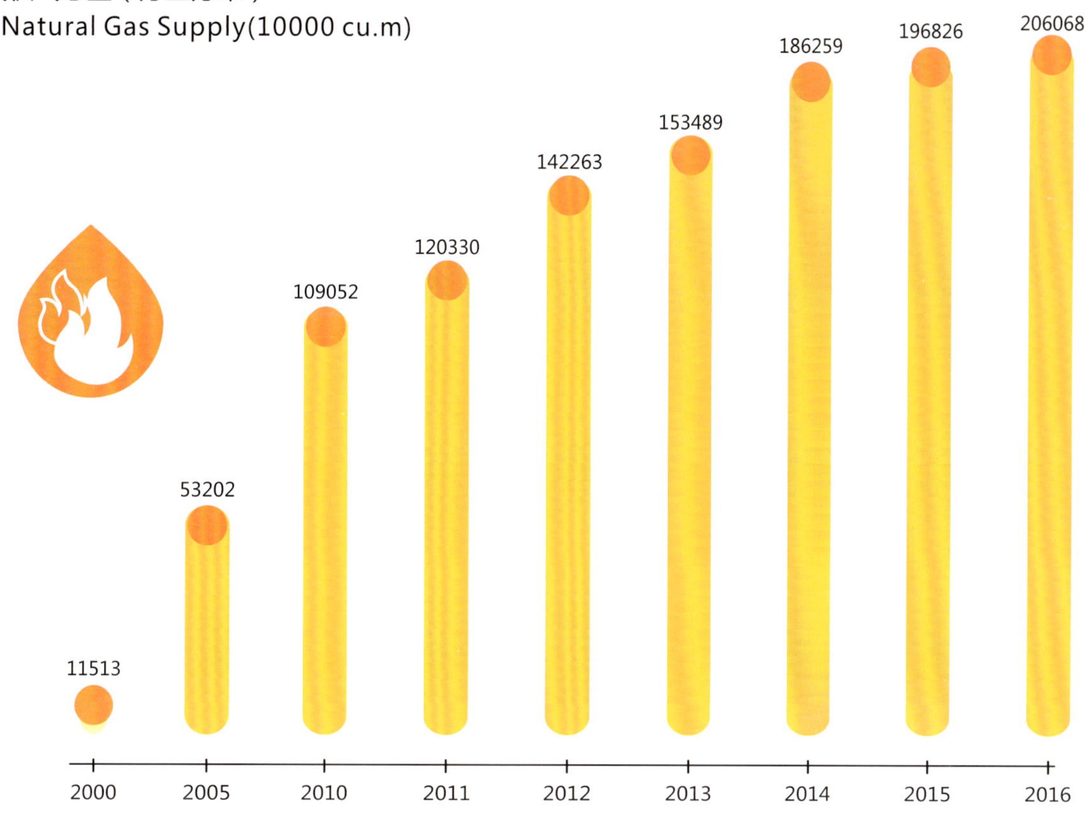
天然气供气总量（万立方米）
Total Natural Gas Supply(10000 cu.m)
11513
53202
109052
120330
142263
153489
186259
196826
206068
2000
2005
2010
2011
2012
2013
2014
2015
2016

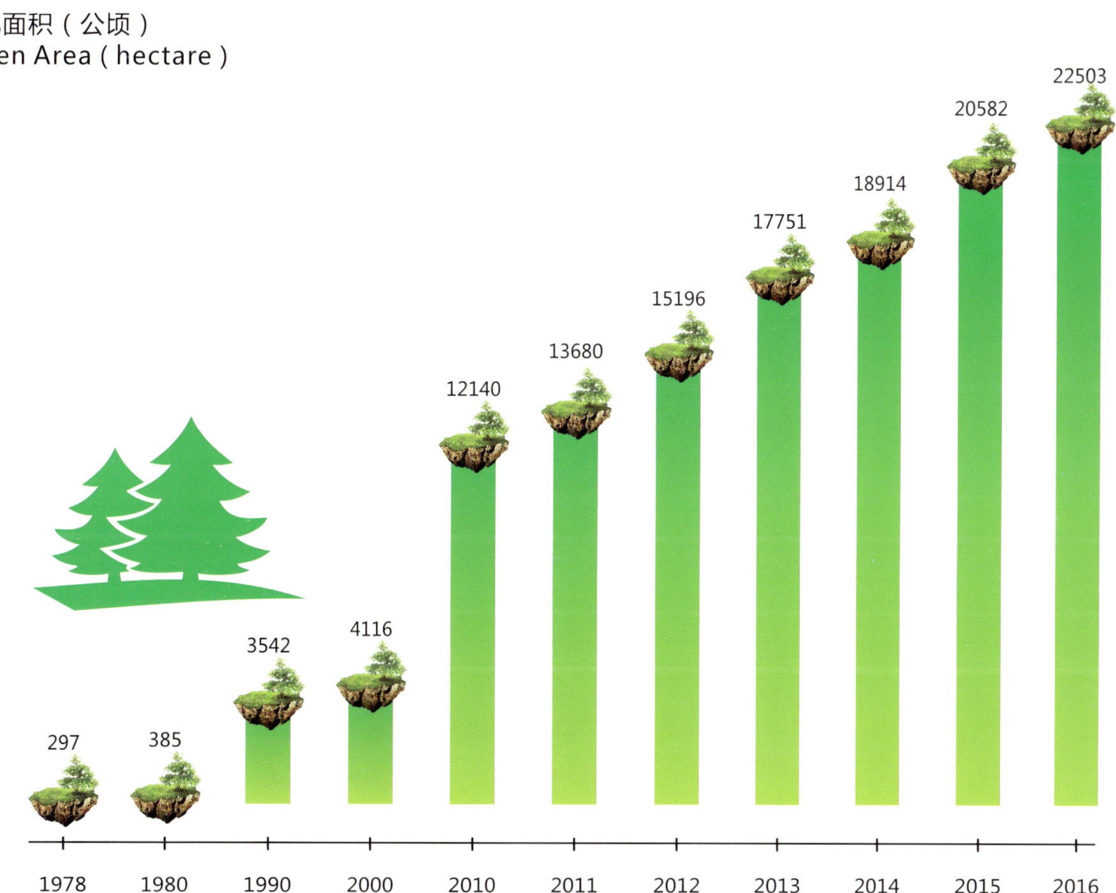
绿地面积（公顷）
Green Area (hectare)
297
385
3542
4116
12140
13680
15196
17751
18914
20582
22503
1978
1980
1990
2000
2010
2011
2012
2013
2014
2015
2016

专任教师（万人）
Full-time Teachers （10000 persons）

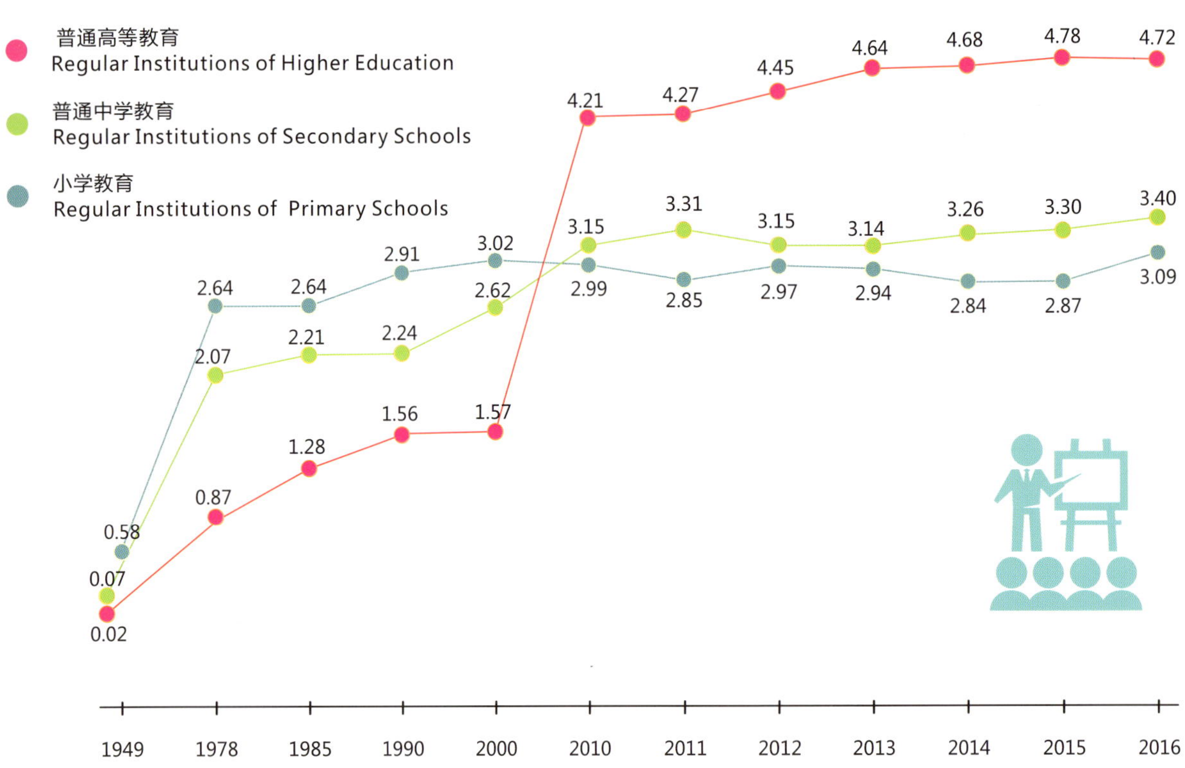

普通教育在校学生（万人）
Total Enrollment of Regular Education（10000 persons）

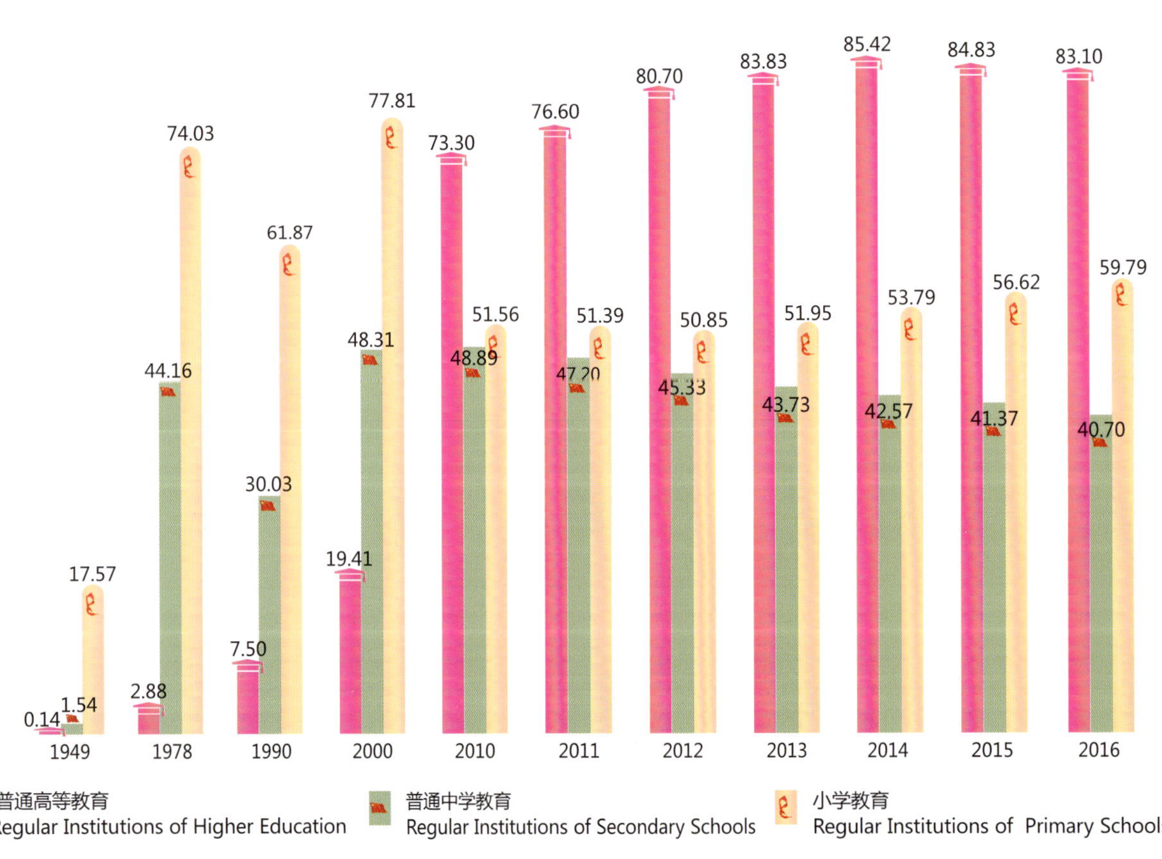

城乡居民收入（元）
The Income of Urban and Rural Residents (yuan)

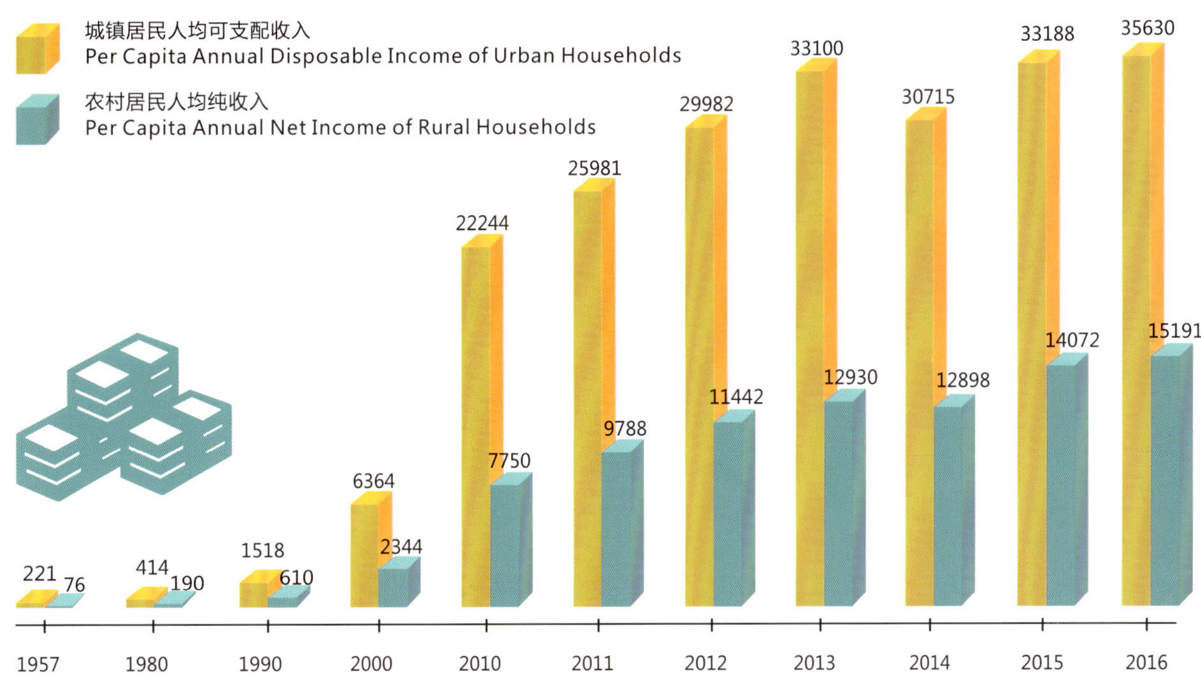

价格指数（以上年价格为100）
Price Indices(the price of preceding year=100)

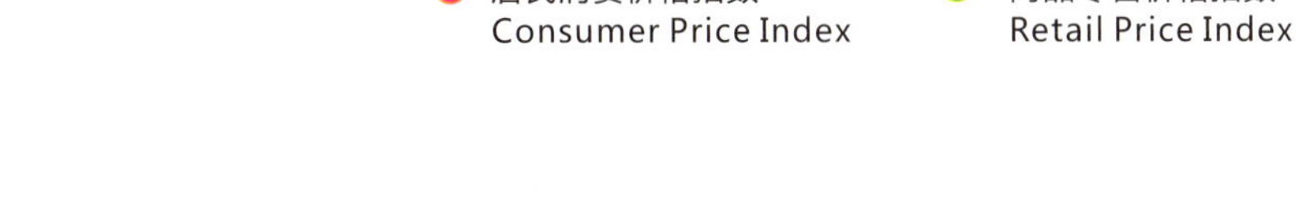

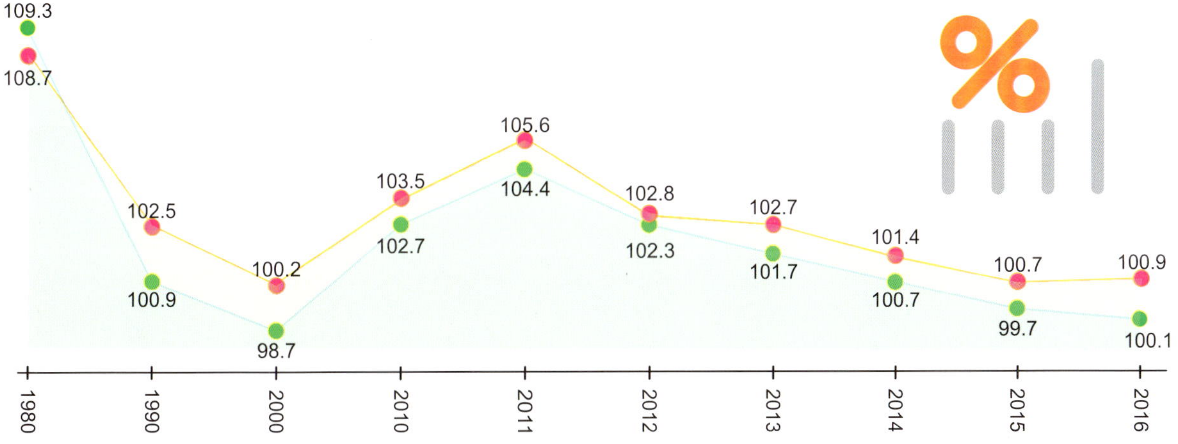

目　录

CONTENTS

一、综　合

GENERAL SURVEY

二、基本单位

BASIC UNIT

三、国民经济核算

NATIONAL ECONOMIC ACCOUNTS

四、人口、从业人员与职工工资

POPULATION，EMPLOYMENT AND WAGES

五、固定资产投资

INVESTMENT IN FIXED ASSETS

六、财　政
GOVERNMENT FINANCE

七、物价指数
PRICE INDICES

八、人民生活

PEOPLE'S LIVELIHOOD

九、城市公用事业

URBAN PUBLIC UTLITIES

十、环境保护

ENVIRONMENT PROTECTION

十一、农　业
AGRICULTURE

十二、工　业
INDUSTRY

十三、能　　源

ENERGY

十四、建筑业

CONSTRUCTION

十五、运输邮电和信息化

TRANSPORT，POSTAL TELECOMMUNICATION SERVICE AND INFORMATIZATION

十六、国内贸易

DOMESTIC TRADE

十七、对外经济贸易和旅游

FOREIGN TRADE AND ECONOMIC COOPERATION TOURISM

十八、规模以上服务业

TERTIARY INDUSTRY

十九、金融业

FINANCIAL INTERMEDIATION

二十、教育和科技

EDUCATION，SCIENCE AND TECHNOLOGY

二十一、文化、体育、卫生、社会福利和其他

CULTURE, SPORTS, PUBLIC HEALTH, SOCIAL WELFARE INSTITUTIONS AND OTHER SOCIAL ACTIVITIES

二十二、企业调查

ENTERPRISES INVESTIGATION

西安市2016年国民经济和社会发展统计公报[1]

西安市统计局　国家统计局西安调查队

2017年3月10日

2016年，是“十三五”和全面建成小康社会决胜阶段的开局之年，是深入推进结构性改革的攻坚之年。面对国内外形势深刻复杂变化，在党中央的坚强领导下，市委、市政府坚持稳中求进工作总基调，全面贯彻落实习近平总书记“追赶超越”定位和“五个扎实”要求，以推进供给侧结构性改革为主线，积极应对各种困难和挑战，全力稳增长、促改革、调结构、惠民生、防风险，经济社会保持平稳健康发展，实现了“十三五”良好开局。

一、综合

年末全市常住人口883.21万人，比上年末净增加12.65万人，其中，男性人口453.42万人，占51.3%；女性人口429.79万人，占48.7%，性别比为105.5（以女性为1，男性对女性的比例）。全年出生人口10.12万人，出生率为11.54‰；死亡人口4.74万人，死亡率为5.40‰；自然增长率为6.14‰。城镇人口648.54万人，占73.43%；乡村人口234.67万人，占26.57%。年末全市户籍总人口824.93万人，比上年增长1.14%。

初步核算，全年地区生产总值[2]（GDP）6257.18亿元，比上年增长8.5%。其中，第一产业增加值232.01亿元，增长3.8%；第二产业增加值2197.81亿元，增长8.6%；第三产业增加值3827.36亿元，增长8.8%。第一产业增加值占地区生产总值的比重为3.7%，第二产业增加值比重为35.1%，第三产业增加值比重为61.2%。全年人均生产总值71357元，比上年增长6.5%。

全年非公有制经济增加值3302.27亿元，占地区生产总值的比重为52.8%，占比与上年持平。

图1　2012-2016年生产总值及其增长速度

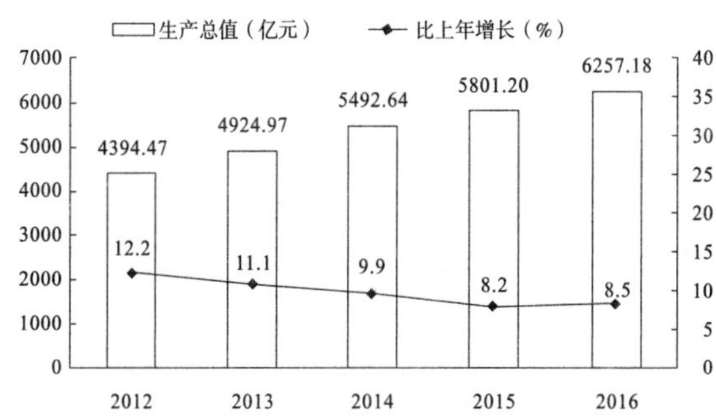

全年居民消费价格比上年上涨0.9%，其中，食品烟酒价格上涨2.8%。商品零售价格上涨0.1%。工业生产者出厂价格下降2.2%。工业生产者购进价格下降2.4%。固定资产投资价格持平。新建住宅销售价格上涨2.9%。

图2　2016年居民消费价格月度涨跌幅度（%）

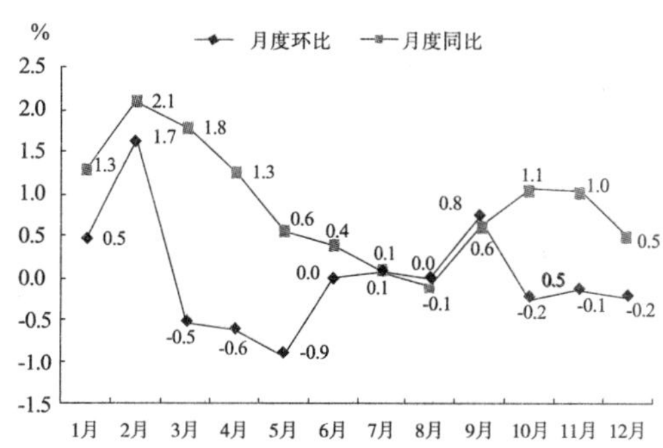

表1　2016年居民消费价格比上年涨跌幅度

指　标	涨跌幅度（%）
居民消费价格总指数	0.9
食品烟酒	2.8
衣着	2.1
居　住	0.6
生活用品及服务	-0.9
交通和通信	-2.7
教育文化和娱乐	-0.8
医疗保健	2.3
其他用品和服务	2.4

全年城镇新增就业12.92万人，城镇失业人员再就业6.03万人。年末城镇登记失业率为3.33%。

全年财政总收入1135.68亿元，比上年增长8.5%。全年地方财政一般公共预算收入641.07亿元，增长11.1%，其中税收收入370.56亿元，增长10.7%。全年地方财政一般公共预算支出942.52亿元，比上年增长2.8%。

二、农业

全年粮食播种面积527.74万亩，比上年下降1.8%；

油料播种面积6.18万亩，下降9.5%；蔬菜播种面积103.01万亩，下降0.5%；棉花播种面积0.27万亩，下降19.0%。全年粮食产量175.33万吨，比上年下降3.1%，其中，夏粮89.90万吨，下降3.5%；秋粮85.43万吨，下降2.6%。

表2　2016年主要农产品产量及其增长速度

产品名称	单位	产量	比上年增长（%）
粮食	万吨	175.33	-3.1
油料	万吨	0.86	-8.7
蔬菜	万吨	336.74	1.2
瓜果	万吨	55.21	1.6
园林水果	万吨	107.74	2.4
肉类	万吨	15.68	-2.8
奶类	万吨	56.20	-11.8
禽蛋	万吨	14.04	-3.5
大牲畜年末存栏数	万头	16.93	-15.1
#牛年末存栏数	万头	16.92	-15.1
猪年末存栏数	万头	89.53	-3.2
羊年末存栏数	万只	26.57	-6.2
家禽年末存栏数	万只	1125.25	-4.9

三、工业和建筑业

全年全部工业增加值1396.69亿元，比上年增长9.5%。规模以上工业增加值1178.39亿元，增长9.9%。在规模以上工业中，轻工业增加值255.70亿元，增长0.4%；重工业增加值922.69亿元，增长13.0%。

图3　2016年规模以上工业增加值增速（%）

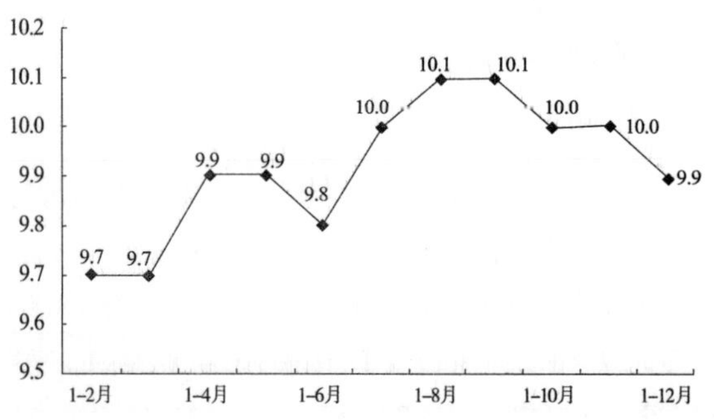

全年规模以上工业中，计算机、通信和其他电子设备制造业增加值增长36.0%，汽车制造业增长10.8%，电气机械和器材制造业增长15.9%。六大高耗能行业[3]增长9.9%，其中，非金属矿物制品业增长12.2%，化学原料和化学制品制造业增长27.5%，有色金属冶炼和压延加工业增长9.2%，黑色金属冶炼和压延加工业增长1.2%，电力、热力生产和供应业增长2.0%，石油加工、炼焦和核燃料加工业下降32.8%。装备制造业[4]增加值增长16.3%，占规模以上工业增加值的比重为55.5%。

2016年，规模以上工业高技术制造业[5]企业实现工业总产值1120.61亿元，占规模以上工业的比重为24.1%，比2015年提高6.0个百分点；同比增长35.8%，高于规模以上工业增速25.7个百分点。其中，电子及通信设备制造业实现工业总产值614.23亿元，占高技术产业的比重为54.8%，同比增长50.7%，增速高于规模以上工业40.6个百分点。

2016年，工业新产品产量快速增长。集成电路圆片127.00万片，同比增长79.1%；单晶硅7800.03吨，增长1.4倍；多晶硅357.35吨，增长20.0%；运动型多用途乘用车（SUV）6.83万辆，增长3.6倍；新能源汽车4.81万辆，增长46.9%；锂离子电池1851.24万只，增长81.9%；光缆501.91万芯千米，增长24.6%；光纤328.06万千米，增长9.4%；智能电视2.58万台，增长1.0倍。

表3　2016年主要工业产品产量及其增长速度

产品名称	单位	产量	比上年增长（%）
发电量	亿千瓦小时	161.01	2.1
软饮料	万吨	211.83	-19.5
小麦粉	万吨	87.64	-37.7
机制纸	万吨	13.45	10.1
配合饲料	万吨	6.69	-25.1
乳制品	万吨	88.42	-17.7
中成药	万吨	0.34	-10.5
钢材	万吨	43.92	18.3
交流电动机	万千瓦	318.23	-52.6
变压器	万千伏安	13471.36	-0.8
汽车	万辆	38.25	12.0
其中：载货汽车	万辆	10.99	32.3
轿车	万辆	19.59	-18.4
电力电缆	万千米	3.32	10.6
电子元件	亿只	3.58	18.0
单晶硅	吨	7800.03	140.6
集成电路圆片	万片	127.00	79.1

规模以上工业企业主营业务收入4207.80亿元，增长18.3%。实现利润总额248.90亿元，增长38.6%。

全年全社会建筑业增加值818.82亿元，比上年增长6.5%。全市具有资质等级的总承包和专业承包建筑业企业实现建筑业总产值2897.55亿元，增长9.3%，其中，国有及国有控股企业2288.23亿元，增长11.9%；签订合同额7666.69亿元，增长15.1%。

图4　2012-2016年建筑业增加值及其增长速度

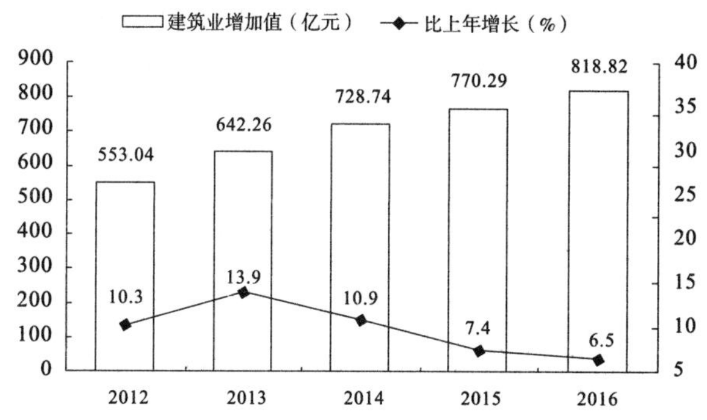

四、固定资产投资

全年全社会固定资产投资5191.36亿元，比上年增长2.0%。其中，固定资产投资（不含农户）5097.00亿元，增长3.4%。

图5　2012-2016年全社会固定资产投资（亿元）

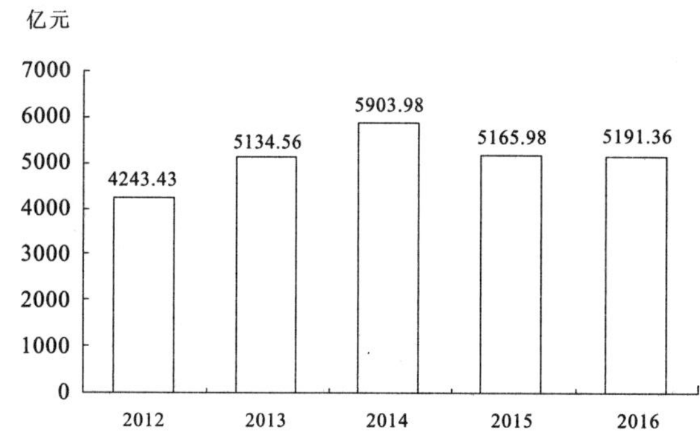

在固定资产投资（不含农户）中，第一产业投资89.70亿元，比上年下降10.1%；第二产业投资963.80亿元，下降12.3%，其中，工业投资949.27亿元，下降12.0%；第三产业投资4043.50亿元，增长8.3%。民间固定资产投资[6]2427.36亿元，下降6.1%，占固定资产投资（不含农户）的比重为47.6%。

表4　2016年分行业固定资产投资（不含农户）及其增长速度

行业	投资额（亿元）	比上年增长（%）
农、林、牧、渔业	101.15	-13.8
采矿业	0.70	7.2
制造业	780.45	-19.3
电力、热力、燃气及水的生产和供应业	168.13	49.9
建筑业	15.57	-22.3
批发和零售业	101.58	-29.8
交通运输、仓储和邮政业	322.37	16.0
住宿和餐饮业	31.84	-15.2
信息传输、软件和信息技术服务业	85.06	-21.4
金融业	6.98	0.1
房地产业	2468.05	5.1
租赁和商务服务业	92.05	104.2
科学研究和技术服务业	51.11	52.0
水利、环境和公共设施管理业	627.43	31.8
居民服务和其他服务业	5.79	-53.1
教育	75.81	-14.5
卫生和社会工作	57.42	-22.9
文化、体育和娱乐业	40.09	9.9
公共管理和社会组织	65.42	182.4

全年房地产开发投资[7]1955.82亿元，比上年增长6.8%。其中，住宅投资1342.05亿元，增长2.3%；办公楼投资172.19亿元，增长21.3%；商业营业用房投资290.25亿元，增长17.2%。房屋施工面积14727.10万平方米，增长10.0%；房屋竣工面积1560.18万平方米，增长59.7%。

表5　2016年房地产开发和销售主要指标及其增长速度

指　标	单位	绝对数	比上年增长（%）
房地产开发投资	亿元	1955.82	6.8
其中：住宅	亿元	1342.05	2.3
房屋施工面积	万平方米	14727.10	10.0
其中：住宅	万平方米	10468.80	7.1
房屋竣工面积	万平方米	1560.18	59.7
其中：住宅	万平方米	1259.24	64.3
商品房销售面积	万平方米	2047.67	16.1
其中：住宅	万平方米	1877.78	18.5
商品房销售额	亿元	1347.08	17.5
其中：住宅	亿元	1194.41	21.2

五、国内贸易

全年社会消费品零售总额3730.70亿元，比上年增长9.6%，扣除价格因素，实际增长9.5%。其中，限额以上企业（单位）消费品零售额2469.51亿元，增长4.5%。按经营地统计，城镇消费品零售额3598.73亿元，增长9.3%；乡村消费品零售额131.97亿元，增长17.3%。按消费形态统计，商品零售额3440.92亿元，增长9.4%；餐饮收入289.78亿元，增长11.9%。

2016年，限额以上企业（单位）消费品零售额中，通过公共网络实现的商品零售额[8]155.50亿元，占限额以上消费品零售额的6.3%，较上年提高2.3个百分点；同比增长65.9%，高于限额以上消费品零售额61.4个百分点。

图6　2016年社会消费品零售总额增速（累计同比）

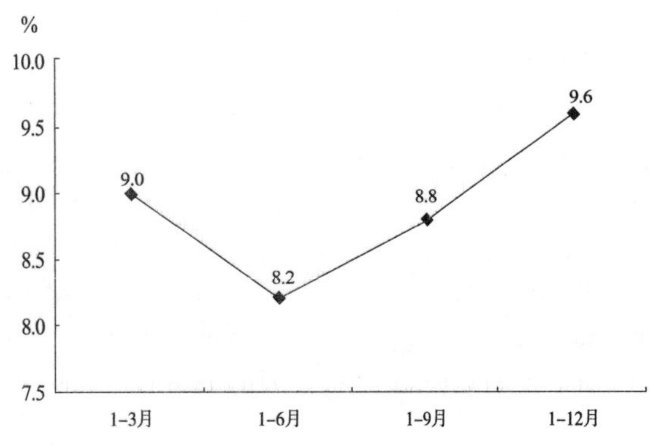

在限额以上企业（单位）商品零售额中，粮油、食品类零售额比上年增长14.8%，服装、鞋帽、针、纺织品类增长2.4%，化妆品类增长5.5%，金银珠宝类下降4.3%，日用品类增长16.8%，体育、娱乐用品类增长36.0%，电子出版物及音像制品类增长68.7%，家用电器和音像器材类增长13.4%，通讯器材类增长19.1%，家具类增长0.2%，石油及制品类下降0.8%，建筑及装潢材料类增长0.3%，汽车类增长2.6%。

六、对外经济

全年进出口总值1828.46亿元，比上年增长3.8%。其中，出口946.75亿元，增长15.5%；进口881.70亿元，下降6.4%。

在进出口总值中，加工贸易进出口1259.7亿元，增长20.2%，占进出口总额的68.9%；一般贸易进出口418.7亿元，增长7.0%，占进出口总额的22.9%。

主要进口商品有，机电产品进口693.3亿元，下降10.3%；精炼铜进口21.5亿元，下降54.7%；矿砂进口35.5亿元，增长56.8%；医药品进口16.1亿元，增长22.2%。主要出口商品有，机电产品出口828.2亿元，增长17.8%；单晶硅片出口22.4亿元，增长41.2%；农产品出口20.8亿元，增长5.0%；纺织服装出口11.3亿元，下降14.6%；矿产品出口14.6亿元，增长28.4%；有机化学品11.2亿元，增长1.8%。

全年吸收外商直接投资项目72个，批准合同外资10.21亿美元，比上年下降47.3%；实际利用外商直接投资45.05亿美元，增长14.0%。

七、交通、邮电和旅游

全年货物运输总量2.39亿吨，比上年增长5.1%；货物运输周转量552.13亿吨公里，增长5.1%。旅客运输总量2.37亿人次，增长2.5%；旅客运输周转量290.92亿人公里，增长7.9%。

表6　2016年各种运输方式完成货物运输量及其增长速度

指标	单位	绝对数	比上年增长（%）
货物运输总量	万吨	23888.03	5.1
公路	万吨	23011.00	5.2
铁路	万吨	853.66	0.7
民航（吞吐量）	万吨	23.38	10.5
货物运输周转量	亿吨公里	552.13	5.1
公路	亿吨公里	324.09	5.4
铁路	亿吨公里	227.05	4.6
民航	亿吨公里	0.99	24.6

表7　2016年各种运输方式完成旅客运输量及其增长速度

指　标	单位	绝对数	比上年增长（%）
旅客运输总量	万人次	23671.25	2.5
公路	万人次	15773.00	-0.2
铁路	万人次	4198.81	5.4
民航（吞吐量）	万人次	3699.44	12.2
旅客运输周转量	亿人公里	290.92	7.9
公路	亿人公里	90.84	-0.3
铁路	亿人公里	67.65	-0.8
民航	亿人公里	132.43	20.2

年末全社会车辆数258.85万辆，比上年末增长8.1%，其中，私人汽车拥有量222.14万辆，增长12.5%。

全年邮政业务总收入43.99亿元,比上年增长43.3%。电信业务总收入142.41亿元，增长9.1%。年末全市固定电话用户284.33万户。移动电话用户1919.39万户。固定互联网宽带接入用户[9]335.83万户。

全年接待国内外游客15012.56万人次，比上年增长10.4％；旅游业总收入1213.81亿元，增长13.1%。

八、金融

年末全市金融机构本外币存款余额19488.38亿元，比上年末增长8.0%；其中人民币存款余额19073.96亿元，增长7.2%，其中，住户存款余额7035.81亿元，增长7.1％。金融机构本外币贷款余额15542.39亿元，增长11.3%；其中人民币贷款余额15282.65亿元，增长11.4%。

全年证券市场各类证券交易总额28913.55亿元，比上年下降46.2%。年末全市拥有上市股份公司33家，上市总股本490.08亿股，总市值5474.22亿元。

年末全市共有保险公司55家，其中，财产险25家，人寿险30家。保险专业中介机构72家。全年保费收入352.35亿元，比上年增长30.7%，其中，财产险保费收入99.51亿元，增长10.9%；人身险保费收入252.84亿元，增长40.6%。全年支付各类赔款给付119.45亿元，比上年增长30.7%，其中，财产险业务、人身险业务分别为45.74和73.71亿元，分别比上年增长3.2%和56.8%。

九、教育、科技、文化和体育

全市普通高校63所，在校学生73.00万人，毕业生21.36万人，另有研究生培养单位43个，在学研究生9.47万人，毕业生2.48万人；普通中学422所，在校学生40.70万人，毕业生13.96万人；小学1190所，在校学生59.79万人，毕业生8.46万人。小学、初中学龄人口入学率分别为99.98%和99.86%。

全年实施市级科技计划项目116项。高新技术企业数1506家，重点扶持高新技术企业29家。全年技术市场交易额711.77亿元。申请专利量46103件，专利授权量38279件。

全市博物馆121座，公共图书馆13个，群众艺术馆2个，文化馆14个，文化站174个。地市广播电视台2座，县级广播电视台6座。

全年举办各类群众体育展示表演和竞赛活动共计260项次，体育社团举办和承办体育赛事315项次，其中，国际性和全国性赛事46项次。新建和更新社区全民健身路径150个。全市新增社会体育指导员1255名。已有晨晚练点1600个，健身气功站点276个，在册练功人数9505人。

2016年，我市培养输送运动员参加国际、国内各项比赛获得金牌23枚、银牌17枚、铜牌25枚。

十、卫生和社会服务

年末全市共有各类卫生机构5869个，其中，医院292个，社区卫生服务中心（站）215个，卫生院100个。各类卫生技术人员8.63万人，其中，执业（含助理）医师2.79万人。卫生机构床位5.63万张。

全市提供住宿的法定社会服务机构142个，床位2.6万张，年末收养人数1.4万人。年末城市低保对象2.7万户、4.7万人，发放低保金3.2亿元；农村低保对象3.3万户、9.7万人，发放低保金3.3亿元。5174人纳入农村五保供养，发放供养金3956万元。全年民政部门直接医疗救助2.5万人次。

十一、人民生活和社会保障

全年全市居民人均可支配收入30032元，比上年名义增长7.9％。其中，城镇常住居民人均可支配收入35630元，比上年名义增长7.4%；农村常住居民人均可支配收入15191元，比上年名义增长8.0%。

年末全市城镇基本医疗保险参保人数435.61万人；城镇企业职工养老保险参保人数330.50万人；失业保险参保人数152.73万人；工伤保险参保人数154.92万人；职工生育保险参保人数121.23万人。年末农村新型合作医疗参保人数381.45万人，实际参合率99.26%。

十二、城市建设、环境和安全生产

全年完成市政公用设施投资437.13亿元，增长11.3%。新建人行天桥及地下通道5座，新建改造绿地广场100个。年末建成区面积565.75平方公里，市区人均公园绿地面积11.87平方米，建成区绿化覆盖率43.15%。年末城市污水处理厂日处理能力261.1万吨，比上年末增长18.1%。

全年城市环境空气质量好于国家二级标准（良好）以上的天数192天。二氧化硫年平均浓度为19微克/标立方米，比上年下降20.8%；二氧化氮年平均浓度为53微克/标立方米，增长20.5%；可吸入颗粒物年平均浓度为136微克/标立方米，增长8.8%。全市集中式饮用水源地的水质达标率为99.72%。区域环境噪声等效声级均值为55.7分贝，道路交通噪声等效声级均值为71.2分贝。

全年共发生各类安全生产事故[10]1569起，死亡232人，受伤861人，直接财产损失3579.92万元。

注释：

［1］本公报数据为初步统计数，部分数据因四舍五入的原因，存在着分项与合计不等的情况。

［2］生产总值、各产业增加值和人均国内生产总值绝对数按现价计算，增长速度按不变价格计算。

［3］六大高耗能行业包括石油加工、炼焦和核燃

料加工业，化学原料和化学制品制造业，非金属矿物制品业，黑色金属冶炼和压延加工业，有色金属冶炼和压延加工业，电力、热力生产和供应业。

［4］装备制造业包括金属制品业，通用设备制造业，专用设备制造业，汽车制造业，铁路、船舶、航空航天和其他运输设备制造业，电气机械和器材制造业，计算机、通信和其他电子设备制造业，仪器仪表制造业。

［5］高技术制造业包括医药制造业，航空、航天器及设备制造业，电子及通信设备制造业，计算机及办公设备制造业，医疗仪器设备及仪器仪表制造业，信息化学品制造业。

［6］民间固定资产投资是指具有集体、私营、个人性质的内资企事业单位以及由其控股（包括绝对控股和相对控股）的企业单位建造或购置固定资产的投资。

［7］房地产业投资除房地产开发投资外，还包括建设单位自建房屋以及物业管理、中介服务和其他房地产投资。

［8］网上零售额是指通过公共网络交易平台（包括自建网站和第三方平台）实现的商品和服务零售额。其中，网上零售额包括的服务，以及少部分用于生产经营用或被转卖的商品不统计在社会消费品零售总额中。

［9］固定互联网宽带接入用户是指报告期末在电信企业登记注册，通过xDSL、FTTx+LAN、FTTH/0以及其他宽带接入方式和普通专线接入公众互联网的用户。

［10］2016年起，安全监管总局对生产安全事故统计制度进行改革，由于排除了非生产经营领域的事故，事故统计口径发生变化，数据同比按照可比口径计算。

资料来源：本公报中物价、居民人均可支配收入数据来自国家统计局西安调查队；城镇新增就业、登记失业率、社会保障数据来自西安市人力资源和社会保障局；财政数据来自市财政局；进出口数据来自西安海关；利用外资数据来自市商务局；铁路运输数据来自西安铁路局；公路运输数据来自市交通运输局；民航运输数据来自西安咸阳国际机场；机动车数据来自市车管所；邮政业务数据来自市邮政管理局；电信数据来自中国移动西安分公司、中国电信西安分公司、中国联通西安分公司；旅游数据来自市旅游局；货币金融数据来自中国人民银行西安分行营业管理部；证券数据、保险业数据来自市金融办；教育数据来自市教育局；科技数据来自市科技局；艺术表演团体、公共图书馆、文化馆、广播、电视数据来自市文化广电新闻出版局；博物馆数据来自市文物局；体育数据来自市体育局；卫生、新农合数据来自市卫计委；社会服务、低保和五保供养数据来自市民政局；城市建设数据来自市城乡建设委员会；环境监测数据来自市环境保护局；安全生产数据来自市安全生产监督管理局；其他数据均来自市统计局。

Statistical Communique of Xi'an City On 2016 National Economic and Social Development[1]

Xi'an Municipal Bureau of Statistics and NBS Survey Office in Xi'an

Mar.10th, 2017

The year of 2016 is not only the first year of the 13th Five-Year Plan and the decisive stage in finish building a moderately prosperous society in all respects, but it also is the significant year to push forward structural reforms. Faced with the complicated international and domestic situation, the Municipal Party Committee and Municipal Government of Xi'an insisted on the tone of maintaining stability of overall the work and fully implement the chairman Xi Jinping's "catch up and beyond" position and "five solid" requirements. Taking the structural reform of supply front as the main line, they respond to various difficulties and challenges actively, strove to promote the practice of plan on steady growth, promoting the reform, adjusting the structure, benefiting people's livelihood and risk prevention. The city's economic maintained a steady and fast growth while society maintained harmonious and steady, which made a good start on its 13th Five-Year Plan.

I. General Outlook

The resident population of Xi'an city at the end of 2016 was 8.8321 million, up by 126.5 thousand against the previous year, 4.5342 million male and 4.2979 million female, accounted for 51.3 percent and 48.7 percent respectively. The sex ratio was 105.5 (granted the female was 100). The born population in the whole year was 101.2 thousand, and the birth rate was 11.54‰; the death population in the whole year was 47.4 thousand, and the death rate was 5.40‰; the natural growth rate was 6.14‰. The urban population was 6.4854 million, accounted for 73.43 percent; the rural population was 2.3467 million, accounted for 26.57 percent. The total household population was 8.2493 million, up by 1.14 percent by previous year.

Based on the preliminary calculation, the gross domestic product[2] (GDP) preliminarily estimated was 625.718 billion Yuan, up by 8.5 percent against the previous year. Analyzed by different industries, the value added of the primary industry was 23.201 billion Yuan, up by 3.8 percent; the value added of the secondary industry was 219.781 billion Yuan, a rise of 8.6 percent; and the value added of the tertiary industry was 382.736 billion Yuan, up by 8.8 percent. The value added of the primary industry accounted for 3.7 percent of the GDP, that of the secondary industry accounted for 35.1 percent, the tertiary industry accounted for 61.2 percent. The per capita GDP of the year was 71.357 thousand, up by 6.5 percent against the previous year.

The value added of non-public sectors of the economy is 330.227 billion, accounted for the proportion of GDP is 52.8 percent, same as the previous year.

Table 1 The GDP and its Growth Rate Between Year 2012–2016

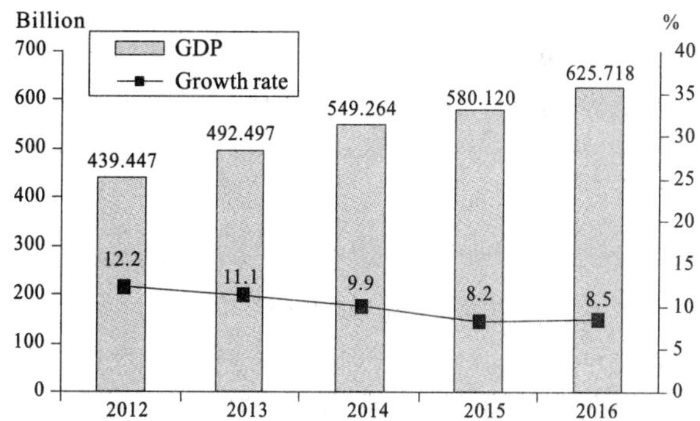

The general level of consumer prices in Xi'an was up by 0.9 percent against the previous year. Of this total, the prices of food, tobacco and liquor went up by 2.8 percent. The retail prices of commodities went up by 0.1 percent. The producer prices of manufactured goods went down by 2.2 percent. The purchasing prices of manufactured goods went down by 2.4 percent. The fixed asset investment price was the same and the price of newly founded house increased by 2.9 percent.

Table 2 The Rate of Increase and Decrease of CPI in 2016

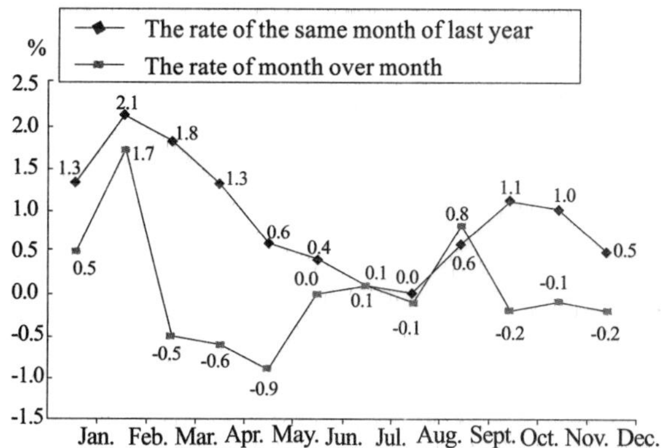

Sheet 1 Up and Fall Extent of Residents Consumer Price Indices against Previous Year（2016）

Item	2016(%)
Consumer Price Index	0.9
Food, tobacco and liquor	2.8
Clothing	2.1
Residence	0.6
Household facilities and maintaining services	-0.9
Transportation and Communication	-2.7
Recreation, Education and Cultural articles and Services	-0.8
Medical, Health and Personal Articles	2.3
Other supplies and services	2.4

In 2016, the number of newly increased employees in urban areas in Xi'an was 129.2 thousand. The number of reemployment of laid-off workers was 60.3 thousand， the urban unemployment rate through unemployment registration was 3.33 percent at the end of 2016.

The financial revenue totaled 113.568 billion Yuan, an increase of 8.5 percent compared with the previous year. The General Budget Revenue of Regional Finance reached 64.107 billion Yuan, up by 11.1 percent. Of this, tax revenue was 37.056 billion Yuan, an increase of 10.7 percent compared with the previous year. The General Budget Expenditure of Regional Finance totaled 94.252 billion Yuan, up by 2.8 percent.

II. Agriculture

In 2016， the sown area of grain was 5277.4 thousand mu, a decrease of 1.8 percent compared with the previous year; the sown area of oil-bearing crops was 61.8 thousand mu, a decrease of 9.5 percent; the sown area of vegetables was 1030.1 thousand mu, a decrease of 0.5 percent; the sown area of cotton was 2.7 thousand mu, a decrease of 19.0 percent. The total output of grain in 2016 was 1.7533 million tons, an decrease of 3.1 percent. Of this, the output of summer crops was 0.8990 million tons, went down by 3.5 percent, and that of the autumn grain was 0.8543 million tons, a decrease of 2.6 percent.

Sheet 2 Mail Product of Agriculture Production in 2016

Name of Product	Units	Output	Increase over the last year (%)
Grain	10,000 tons	175.33	-3.1
Oil	10,000 tons	0.86	-8.7
Vegetable	10,000 tons	336.74	1.2
Melon	10,000 tons	55.21	1.6
Fruit	10,000 tons	107.74	2.4
Meat	10,000 tons	15.68	-2.8
Milk	10,000 tons	56.20	-11.8
Poultry eggs	10,000 tons	14.04	-3.5
Year-end Cattle on hand	10,000 head	16.93	-15.1
#Year-end Ox on hand	10,000 head	16.92	-15.1
Year-end Pig on hand	10,000 head	89.53	-3.2
Year-end Sheep on hand	10,000 head	26.57	-6.2
Year-end Fowl on hand	10,000 head	1125.25	-4.9

III. Industry and Construction

In 2016, the value added by the industrial sectors was 139.669 billion Yuan, up by 9.5 percent over the previous year. The value added of industrial enterprises above the designated size was 117.839 billion Yuan, up by 9.9 percent. Of this, the value added of the light industry was 25.570 billion Yuan, up by 0.4 percent; that of the heavy industry was 92.269 billion Yuan, up by 13.0 percent.

Table 3 Growth of Above-Scale Industrial added Value in 2016

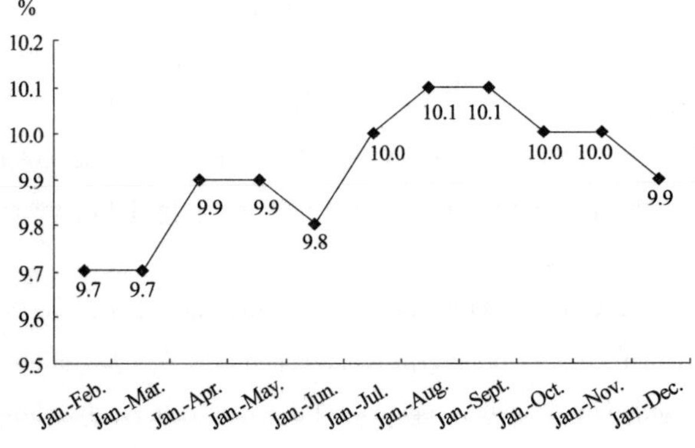

In 2016, of the industrial enterprises above designated size, the growth of value added for manufacture of computer, communication and other electrical devices was up by 36.0 percent over the previous year; for manufacture of car up by

10.8 percent; for manufacture of electrical machinery and equipment up by 15.9 percent. The growth of the value added for the major six high energy consuming industries[3] was 9.9 percent, of which, that of the manufacture of non-metallic mineral products was up by 12.2 percent, manufacture of raw chemical materials and chemical products up by 27.5 percent, smelting and pressing of ferrous metals up by 1.2 percent, smelting and pressing of non-ferrous metals down by 9.2 percent, production and supply of electric power and heat power up by 2.0 percent and 32.8 percent decrease for processing of petroleum, coking, processing of nuclear fuel. The growth of value added for equipment manufacturing industry[4] was up by 16.3 percent, accounted for 55.5 percent of the added value of industrial enterprises above designated size.

In 2016, the value of high technology industry industrial manufacturing enterprises above designated size[5]was 112.061 billion Yuan, accounted for 24.1 percent of the value for industrial enterprises above designated size, up by 6.0 percent over the previous year, soared by nearly 35.8% compared with last year, above scale industrial growth of 25.7 percentage points. Of which, the value of the electronic and communication equipment manufacturing was 61.423 billion Yuan, accounted for 54.8 percent of the value for high technology industry, soared by 50.7% compared with last year, above scale industrial growth of 40.6 percentage points.

In 2016, the output of new industrial products increased rapidly. The number of the integrated circuit wafer sums up to 1.27 million, soared by nearly 79.1% compared with last year; the number of monocrystalline silicon was 7.80003 thousand tons, up by 140 percent over the previous year; the number of polysilicon was 3.5735 billion tons, up by 20.0 percent over the previous year; the number of the Sport Utility Vehicle (SUV) was 68.3 thousand, up by 360 percent over the previous year; the number of the new energy vehicle was 48.1 thousand, up by 46.9 percent over the previous year; the number of the Lithium ion battery was 18.5124 million, up by 81.9 percent over the previous year; the length of the optical cable was 5.0191 billion core kilometers, up by 24.6% percent over the previous year; the length of the optical fiber was 3.2806 billion kilometers, up by 9.4 percent over the previous year; the number of Smart TV was 25.8 thousands, up by 100 percent over the previous year.

Sheet 3 Output of Major Industrial Products above Designated Size in Xi 'an (2016)

Name of Product	Units	Output	Increase over the last year (%)
Electricity	100 million kilo watt-hour	161.01	2.1
Soft Drink	10, 000 tons	211.83	-19.5
wheat meal	10, 000 tons	87.64	-37.7
Machine-made paper and Cardboard	10, 000 tons	13.45	10.1
Feed	10, 000 tons	6.69	-25.1
Dairy	10, 000 tons	88.42	-17.7
Proprietary Chinese Medicine	10, 000 tons	0.34	-10.5
Steel	10, 000 tons	43.92	18.3
AC motors	10, 000 Kilowatt	318.23	-52.6
Transformer	10, 000 kilovolt amperes	13471.36	-0.8
Motor vehicle	10, 000 units	38.25	12.0
# Truck	10, 000 units	10.99	32.3
#Car	10, 000 units	19.59	-18.4
Electric cable	10, 000 km	3.32	10.6
Electronic component	100 million units	3.58	18.0
Mono-crystalline silicon	ton	7800.03	140.6
Integrated circuit chip	10, 000 chips	127.00	79.1

The main business income of the industrial enterprises above designated size is 420.780 billion Yuan, up by 18.3 percent over the previous year. The profit was 24.890 billion Yuan, up by 38.6 percent.

In 2016, the added value of construction sector was 81.882 billion Yuan, increased by 6.5 percent over the previous year. The total output value created by qualified contractors and professional building contractor companies was 289.755 billion Yuan, increased by 9.3 percent. Of it, the output of State-owned and State holding Corporations was 228.823 billion Yuan, increased by 11.9 percent; contract amount was 766.669 billion Yuan, increased by 15.1 percent.

Table 4 The added Value of Construction and Growth Rate Between Year 2012–2016

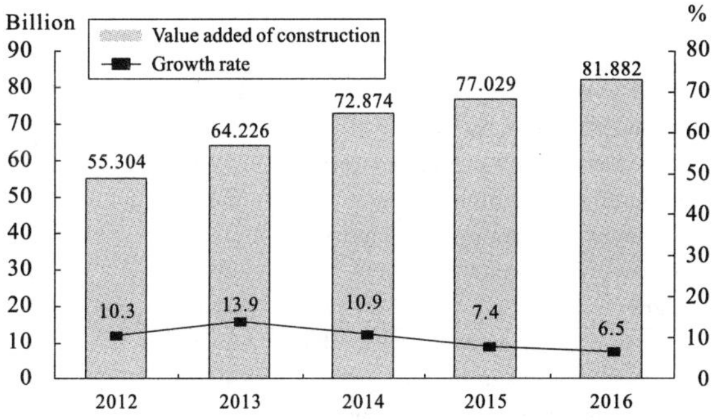

IV. Investment in Fixed Assets

The completed investment in fixed assets of the city in 2016 was 519.136 billion Yuan, up by 2.0 percent over the previous year. Investment in fixed assets (excluding farmers) was 509.700 billion Yuan, up by 3.4 percent.

Table 5 Fixed Asset Investment of Xi 'an Between Year 2012–2016

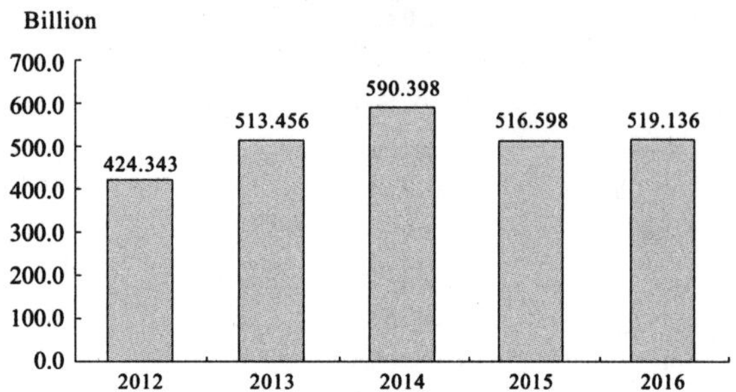

In whole investment(excluding farmers), the investment in the primary industry was 8.970 billion Yuan, down by 10.1 percent against the previous year; in the secondary industry, it was 96.380 billion Yuan, down by 12.3 percent, of which industrial investment was 94.927 billion Yuan, down by 12.0 percent; in the tertiary industry, it was 404.350 billion Yuan, up by 8.3 percent. Private investment in fixed assets[6] was 242.736 billion Yuan, down by 6.1 percent, accounted for 47.6 percent of investment in fixed assets.

Sheet 4 The Investment in Fixed Assets and Growth Rate in Main Industries in 2016

Industries	Investment (100 million Yuan)	Growth rate (%)
Agriculture, Forestry, Animal husbandry and fishery	101.15	-13.8
Mining industry	0.70	7.2
Manufacturing	780.45	-19.3
Electricity, heat, gas and water production and supply industry	168.13	49.9
Construction industry	15.57	-22.3
Wholesale and retail trade	101.58	-29.8
Transportation, storage and postal services	322.37	16.0
Hotels and catering services	31.84	-15.2
Information transmission, computer services and software industry	85.06	-21.4
Finance	6.98	0.1
Real estate industry	2468.05	5.1
Leasing and business services	92.05	104.2
Scientific research and technical service	51.11	52.0
Water Conservancy, environment and public facilities administration industry	627.43	31.8
Residential services and other services	5.79	-53.1
Education	75.81	-14.5
Sanitations, social security and social welfare	57.42	-22.9
Culture, sports and entertainment	40.09	9.9
Public administration and social organizations	65.42	182.4

In 2016, the investment in real estate development[7] was 195.582 billion Yuan, up by 6.8 percent. Of this, housing investment was 134.205 Yuan, up by 2.3 percent; office building investment was 17.219 billion Yuan, up by 21.3 percent; commercial and business building investment was 29.025 billion Yuan, up by 17.2 percent. Housing construction area was 147.271 million square meters, up by 10.0 percent; floor space of commercial houses completed was 15.6018 million square meters, up by 59.7 percent.

Sheet 5 Mail Indicators of Real Estate Development and Sales in 2016

Item	Units	Absolute Number	Increase over the last year(%)
Investment in Real Estate Development	100 million Yuan	1955.82	6.8
#Residential Building	100 million Yuan	1342.05	2.3
Building construction area	10,000 sq.m	14727.10	10.0
# Residential Building	10,000 sq.m	10468.80	7.1
Floor Space of Buildings Completed	10,000 sq.m	1560.18	59.7
# Residential Building	10,000 sq.m	1259.24	64.3
Commercial housing sales area	10,000 sq.m	2047.67	16.1
# Residential Building	10,000 sq.m	1877.78	18.5
Sales of commercial housing	100 million Yuan	1347.08	17.5
# Residential Building	100 million Yuan	1194.41	21.2

V. Domestic Trade

In 2016, the total retail sales of consumer goods reached 373.070 billion Yuan, a growth of 9.6 percent over the previous year or a real growth of 9.5 percent after deducting price factors. Of this, the total retail sales by wholesale and retail enterprises above designated size was 246.951 billion Yuan, up by 4.5 percent. An analysis on different areas showed that the retail sales of consumer goods in urban areas stood at 359.873 billion Yuan, up by 9.3 percent, and that in rural areas reached 13.197 billion Yuan, up by 17.3 percent. Grouped by consumption patterns, the income of retail sales of commodities was 344.092 billion Yuan, up by 9.4 percent; that of catering industry was 28.978 billion Yuan, up by 11.9 percent.

In 2016, the online sales by wholesale and retail enterprises[8] above designated size was 15.550 billion Yuan, accounted for 6.3% of retail sales of consumer goods above designated size, and increase 2.3 percentage points over the previous year, with year-on-year growth of 65.9%, 61.4 percentage points higher than the retail sales of consumer goods above designated size.

Table 6 The Total Retail Sales of Social Consumer Goods Growth Rate in 2016

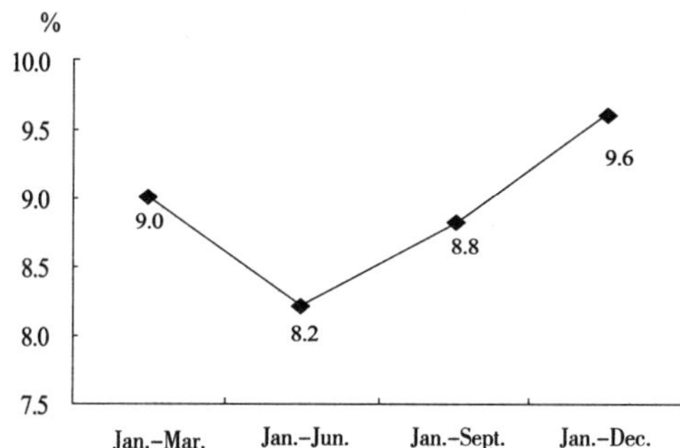

Of the total retail sales by wholesale and retail enterprises above designated size, the sales of food, beverage, wine and cigarette was up by 14.8 percent; clothing, shoes, hats and needle textiles up by 2.4 percent; cosmetics up by 5.5 percent; gold, silver and jewelry down by 4.3 percent ; daily necessities up by 16.8 percent; sports-recreation up by 36.0 percent; electronic appliances and audio-video productions up by 68.7 percent, household appliances and audio-video equipment up by 13.4 percent; telecommunication equipment up by 19.1 percent; furniture increased by 0.2 percent; oil and oil products down by 0.8 percent; building decoration materials up by 0.3 percent and motor vehicles up by 2.6 percent.

VI. Foreign Economic Relations

In 2016, the total value of imports and exports reached 182.846 billion Yuan, up by 3.8 percent over the previous year. Of this, the value of exports was 94.675 billion Yuan, up by 15.5 percent, and that of imports was 88.170 billion Yuan, down by 6.4 percent.

In total imports and exports, the value of processing trade was 125.97 billion Yuan, up by 20.2 percent, accounted for 68.9 percent of import and export whole value of Xi' an region. The value of imports and exports of general trade was 41.87 billion Yuan, increased by 7.0 percent, accounted for 22.9 percent of import and export whole value of Xi' an region.

Among the main import commodities, the value of imports of electromechanical products was 69.33 billion Yuan, down by 10.3 percent; the value of imports of refined copper was 2.15 billion Yuan, down by 54.7 percent; the value of imports of ore sand was 3.55 billion Yuan, up by 56.8 percent; the value of imports of medical products was 1.61 billion Yuan, up by 22.2 percent. Among the main export commodities, the value of exports of electromechanical products was 82.82 billion Yuan, up by 17.8 percent; the value of exports of agricultural product was 2.08 billion Yuan, an increase of 5.0 percent; the value of exports of textile products was 2.24 billion Yuan, an increase of 41.2 percent; the value of exports of mineral products was 1.46 billion Yuan, up by 28.4 percent; the organic chemicals was 1.12 billion Yuan, up by 1.8 percent.

In 2016, there were 72 foreign direct investment projects approved in Xi'an and the contracted foreign direct investment was 1.021 billion US dollars, a decrease of 47.3 percent compared with the previous year; the realized foreign direct investment was 4.505 billion US dollars, up by 14.0 percent.

VII. Transportation, Post, Telecommunications and Tourism

In 2016, the total freight traffic reached 239 million ton, up by 5.1 percent over the previous year. The total goods transportation turnover reached 55.213 billion ton-kilometers, up by 5.1 percent over the previous year. The Total passenger transport reached 237 million, up by 2.5 percent over the previous year. The passenger transport turnover reached 29.092 billion people-kilometers, up by 7.9 percent over the previous year.

Sheet 6 The Total Freight Traffic and Growth Rate created by Kinds of Transport Mode in 2016

Index	Unit	Amount	Growth rate (%)
The Total Freight Traffic	10,000 tons	23888.03	5.1
Highway	10,000 tons	23011.00	5.2
Railway	10,000 tons	853.66	0.7
Airway	10,000 tons	23.38	10.5
Goods Transportation Turnover	100 million ton-kilometers	552.13	5.1
Highway	100 million ton-kilometers	324.09	5.4
Railway	100 million ton-kilometers	227.05	4.6
Airway	100 million ton-kilometers	0.99	24.6

Sheet 7 The Total Passenger Traffic and Growth Rate created by Kinds of Transport Mode in 2016

Index	Unit	Amount	Growth rate (%)
The Total Passenger	1100 million people	23671.25	2.5
Highway	100 million people	15773.00	-0.2
Railway	100 million people	4198.81	5.4
Airway	100 million people	3699.44	12.2
The passenger transport turnover	100 million people -kilometers	290.92	7.9
Highway	100 million people -kilometers	90.84	-0.3
Railway	100 million people -kilometers	67.65	-0.8
Airway	100 million people -kilometers	132.43	20.2

The total number of motor vehicles for civilian use reached 2588.5 thousand by the end of 2016, up by 8.1 percent, of which private-owned vehicles numbered 2221.4 thousand, up by 12.5 percent.

The revenue of post services totaled 4.399 billion Yuan, an increase of 43.3 percent over the previous year. That of telecommunication services was 14.241 billion Yuan, up by 9.1 percent. At the end of 2016, there were 2.8433 million fixed telephone users; there were 19.1939 million mobile phone users. The number of fixed internet broadband access users[9] was 3.3583 million.

The annual domestic and foreign tourists count was 150.1256 million people, up by 10.4 percent. The revenue from tourism totaled 121.381 billion Yuan, up by 13.1 percent.

VIII. Finance

Savings deposit in RMB and foreign currencies in all items of financial institutions totaled 1948.838 billion Yuan at the end of 2016, an increase of 8.0 percent compared with the end of the previous year. The savings deposit in RMB stood at 1907.396 billion Yuan, an increase of 7.2 percent, of which the household deposit was 703.581 billion Yuan, up by 7.1 percent. Loans in all items of financial institutions in RMB and foreign currencies reached 1554.239 billion Yuan, an increase of 11.3 percent as compared with the end of the previous year. The loans in RMB stood at 1528.265 billion Yuan, an increase of 11.4 percent.

The trading volume of stock exchange market was 2891.355 billion Yuan in 2016, an decrease of 46.2 percent compared with the previous year. There were 33 listed companies in Xi'an at the end of 2016 of which the total capital stock was 49.008 billion shares, and the total market value was 547.422 billion Yuan.

By the end of 2016, there were 55 insurance institutions, of which the number of property insurance was 25, and that of life insurance was 30. There were 72 intermediary organs of insurance. The received by the insurance companies totaled 35.235 billion Yuan in 2016, up by 30.7 percent. Of this, the revenue from property insurance was 9.951 billion Yuan, up by 10.9 percent; that from life insurance was 25.284 billion Yuan, up by 40.6 percent. In total, insurance companies paid an indemnity worth of 11.945 billion Yuan, up by 30.7 percent over the previous year, of which the worth of property insurance and life insurance were 4.574 billion Yuan and 7.371 billion Yuan respectively, up by 3.2 percent and 56.8 percent respectively.

IX. Education、 Science & Technology、 Culture and Sports

There were 63 general universities and colleges, with 730.0 thousand general tertiary education enrollments, including 213.6 thousand graduates; there were 43 post-graduate training units, with 94.7 thousand students in school and 24.8 thousand graduates. There were 422 general middle schools and high schools, with 407.0 thousand junior high education enrollments and 139.6 thousand graduates; there were 1190 primary schools, with 597.9 thousand primary education enrollments and 84.6 thousand graduates. The enrollment rates for school-age population of primary school and junior high school were 99.98 percent and 99.86 percent respectively.

116 science and technology projects were carried out in 2016. The number of high-tech enterprises was 1506,and 29 high tech enterprises were supported especially. The turnover in technology market reached 71.177 billion Yuan. 46103 patents were applied in 2016, including of 38279 patents accredited.

By the end of 2016, there were 121 museums, 13 public libraries, 2 mass art museum, 14 cultural centers, 174 culture stations. There were 2 city radio and television stations and 6 county radio and television stations.

260 mass sports performances and competition activities were organized in 2016, and 315 sports competition were organized and host by sports associations, including 46

international and national sports competition. In 2016, there were 150 public national fitness paths of community built. The number of social sports instructors had increased 1255. There were 1600 sites for morning and evening exercise and 276 sites for fitness Qigong, with 9505 people taking part in fitness Qigong.

In 2016, the delegation of Xi'an won 23 gold medals、17 silver medals and 25 bronze medal in the National and international Games.

X. Health and Public Service

At the end of 2016, there were 5869 health institutions in Xi'an, including 292 general hospitals, 215 community health centers, and 100 health centers. There were all 86.3 thousand health care workers, including 27.9 thousand practicing (assistant) doctors. General health centers in Xi'an possessed 56.3 thousand beds.

There were 142 social welfare adoption class units, with a total of 26 thousand beds, and 14 thousand people adopted there at the end of 2016. There were 27 thousand of urban low-income households, with 47 thousand people, and 320 million Yuan were distributed to them. There were 33 thousand of village low-income households, with 97 thousand people, and 330 million Yuan were distributed to them. 5174 people were in the rural five guarantees and 39.56 million Yuan were distributed. 25 thousand people gained medical relief directly from civil affairs departments in 2016.

XI. Living Conditions and Social Security

In 2016, the annual per capita disposable income of all the city residents in Xi'an was 30032 Yuan, growth of 7.9 percent over the previous year. That of urban households was 35630 Yuan, growth of 7.4 percent over the previous year. And that of rural households was 15191 Yuan, growth of 8.0 percent over the previous year.

By the end of 2016, a total of 4.3561 million people participated in urban basic health insurance program; a total of 3.3050 million people participated in basic pension program for staff and workers of enterprises; a total of 1.5273 million people participated in unemployment insurance programs; a total of 1.5492 million people participated in work accident insurance; a total of 1.2123 million people participated in maternity insurance programs for staff and workers. The number of farmers taking part in the new cooperative medical care system in rural areas reached 3.8145 million, with a participation rate of 99.26 percent covered.

XII. Urban Construction, Environment and Work Safety

The total investment of municipal utilities was 43.713 billion Yuan, up by 11.3 percent. 5 pedestrian bridges, and 100 underground passages were newly built. By the end of the year, the built-up area was 565.75 square kilometers, and the per capita green space of the city was 11.87 square meters, with a green coverage rate of 43.15 percent in the built-up area. At the end of the year, the municipal wastewater treatment plant has a daily capacity of 2.611 million tons, an increase of 18.1 percent over the previous year.

In 2016, there were 192 days with air quality better than standard Grade II. The annual average sulfur dioxide concentration of 19 micrograms / m3, down by 20.8 percent over the previous year; the annual average concentration of nitrogen dioxide was 53 micrograms / m3, an increase of 20.5 percent; PM10 average concentration of 136 micrograms / m3, growth of 8.8 percent. The water quality compliance rate of centralized drinking water sources in the city was 99.72 percent. The average equivalent level of regional environmental noise is 55.7 decibels, and the average equivalent noise level of road traffic noise is 71.2 decibels.

In 2016, various kinds of work accidents[10] amounted to 1569. Of this, there were 232 people dead and 861 people injured, the property losses was 35.7992 million Yuan.

Notes:

1. All figures in this Communique are preliminary statistics.

2. The GDP, the added value of each industry and the absolute number of GDP per capita are calculated at current prices, and the growth rate is calculated at constant prices.

3. Six highly energy-consuming industries are: manufacture of raw chemical materials and chemical products, manufacture of non-metallic mineral products, smelting and pressing of ferrous metals, smelting and pressing of non-ferrous metals, oil processing, coking and nuclear fuel processing, and production and supply of electricity and heat.

4.Equipment manufacturing industry includes metal products industry, general equipment manufacturing industry, special equipment manufacturing industry, automobile manufacturing, railway, marine, aerospace and other transportation equipment manufacturing, electrical machinery and equipment manufacturing, computer, communications and other electronic equipment manufacturing, instrumentation manufacturing, metal products, machinery and equipment repair industry.

5.High tech manufacturing industry includes pharmaceutical manufacturing, aviation, aerospace and equipment manufacturing industry, electronics and communications equipment manufacturing, computer and office equipment manufacturing, medical equipment and instrument manufacturing, chemicals manufacturing information.

6.Private investment in fixed assets is the construction or purchase of fixed assets investment by collective, private and individual domestic enterprises or institutions and enterprise units by its holdings (including absolute holdings and relative holdings).

7.The real estate investment, in addition to investment in real estate development, also includes the construction of self-built housing units, as well as property management, intermediary services and other real estate investment.

8.Online sales by wholesale and retail enterprises above designated size are the wholesale and retail sales of consumer goods realized by enterprises above designated size through the public network trading platform (including self-built website and the third-party platform).

9.Fixed Internet broadband access users are people who have the registration of Telecom Enterprises at the end of the reporting period and access to the public Internet by xDSL、FTTx+LAN、FTTH/0 or other broadband access ways and common line access.

10.Since 2016, the General Administration of safety supervision had reformed the statistical system for production safety accidents. The accident statistics had changed due to the exclusion of accidents in the field of non-production and operation, and the figures were calculated on a comparable basis year by year.

Data Sources:

In this communiqu é , data of price are from NBS Survey Office in Xi'an ;data of newly increased employed people, unemployment rate through unemployment registration and social security are from the Xi'an Municipal Bureau of Human Resources and Social Security; financial data are from the Xi'an Municipal Bureau of Finance; data of imports and exports are from the Xi'an Customs; data of utilizing foreign capital are from the Xi'an Municipal Bureau of Business; data of railway transportation are from the Xi'an Municipal Bureau of Railways; data of highway transportation are from the Xi'an Municipal Bureau of Transport; data of air transport are from the Xi'an- Xian yang International Airport; data of motor vehicles for civilian use are from the Xi'an vehicle administration; data of post services are from the Xi'an Municipal Bureau of post; data of telecommunications are from Xi'an branch of China Mobile、China Unicom、China Telecom, and Shaanxi CTT; data of tourism are from the Xi'an Tourism Administration; data of monetary and financial are from business management department for Xi'an branch of the People's Bank of China; data of listed companies and insurance are from Xi'an Municipal Finance Office; data of education are from the Xi'an Municipal Bureau of Education; data of technology are from Xi'an Municipal Bureau of Technology; data of art-performing groups, public libraries, culture centers, radio and television are from the Xi'an Municipal Bureau of Culture, Radio, Press and Publication; data of museum are from Xi'an Municipal Bureau of Heritage; data of sports are from the Xi'an Municipal Bureau of Sport; data of health and new cooperative medical care system in rural areas are from the Xi'an Municipal Bureau of Health; data of central heating area and green area are from Xi'an Municipal Urban and Rural Construction Committee; data of sewage treatment in urban and environment monitoring are from the Xi'an Municipal Bureau of Environmental Protection; data of work safety are from the State Administration of Work Safety; all the other data are from Xi'an Municipal Bureau of Statistics.

1 综　合

GENERAL SURVEY

资料整理：李　芬
Data management：Li Fen
数据审核：陈　英
Data audit：Chen Ying

第一部分　综合

一、简要说明

本章资料主要包括西安市行政区划、自然地理、自然资源、气象、国民经济和社会发展等综合资料，由西安市统计局综合处根据局内各专业处及有关部门统计资料进行整理和编辑。

二、主要指标

生产总值（亿元）	6282.65	比上年增长	8.6%
农林牧渔及服务业总产值（亿元）	405.63	比上年增长	4.2%
规模以上工业增加值（亿元）	1320.61	比上年增长	9.6%
全社会固定资产投资额（亿元）	5191.36	比上年增长	2.0%
社会消费品零售总额（亿元）	3730.70	比上年增长	9.6%
财政一般公共预算收入（亿元）	641.07	比上年增长	11.1%
财政一般公共预算支出（亿元）	942.52	比上年增长	2.8%
进出口总值（亿元）	1829.95	比上年增长	3.9%
城镇居民人均可支配收入（元）	35630	比上年增长	7.4%
农村居民人均可支配收入（元）	15191	比上年增长	8.0%

1　GENERAL SURVEY

Ⅰ.Brief Introduction

This chapter consists of mainly unified data of administrative divisions, natural geography, natural resources, meteorology, national economy and social development of Xi'an city. It is compiled by Integration Division according to the reported data from other divisions of the Xi'an Bureau of Statistics and other departments of the municipal government.

Ⅱ. Major Indicators

		Increase over Preceding Year
Gross Domestic Product (100 mil. Yuan)	6282.65	8.6%
Gross Output Value of Farming, Forestry, Animal, Husbandry and Fishery (100 mil. Yuan)	405.63	4.2%
Added Value of Industrial Enterprises above Designated Size (100 mil. Yuan)	1320.61	9.6%
Total Investment In Fixed Assets (100 mil. Yuan)	5191.36	2.0%
Total Retail Sales of Consumer Goods (100 mil. Yuan)	3730.70	9.6%
Government General Public Budgetary Revenue (100 mil. Yuan)	641.07	11.1%
Government General Public Budgetary Expenditures (100 mil. Yuan)	942.52	2.8%
Total Value of Imports and Exports (RMB 100 mil.Yuan)	1829.95	3.9%
Per Capita Annual Disposable Income of Urban Households (Yuan)	35630	7.4%
Per Capita Annual Disposable Income of Rural Households (Yuan)	15191	8.0%

1-1 行政区划（2016年）

Administrative Division（2016）

单位：个 (unit)

地 区	Region	乡镇及街道办 Township and Urban Subdistrict Office	镇数 Town	街道办事处 Urban Subdistrict Office	村民委员会 Villagers' Committee	社区居委会 Neighbourhood Committee
西安市	**Xi'an**	**172**	**55**	**117**	**2005**	**913**
（一）市辖区	**Urban Area**	**114**	**5**	**109**	**1054**	**835**
新城区	Xincheng	9		9		101
碑林区	Beilin	8		8		100
莲湖区	Lianhu	9		9		131
灞桥区	Baqiao	9		9	209	51
未央区	Weiyang	10		10	68	124
雁塔区	Yanta	10		10	64	151
阎良区	Yanliang	7	2	5	73	24
临潼区	Lintong	23		23	226	41
长安区	Chang'an	22		22	328	98
高陵区	Gaoling	7	3	4	86	14
（二）三县	**Three Counties**	**53**	**50**	**3**	**851**	**53**
蓝田县	Lantian	19	18	1	337	9
周至县	Zhouzhi	20	19	1	260	18
户 县	Huxian	14	13	1	254	26
沣东新城	**Fengdongxincheng**	**5**		**5**	**100**	**25**

注：本表数据来源市民政局。

1-2 土地面积和常住人口密度（2016年）

Statistics on Land Area and Density of Permanent Population（2016）

地 区	Region	土地面积 Area 绝对数（平方公里）Absolute Value (sq.km)	比重（%）Proportion (%)	常住人口（万人）Total of Permanent Population (10 000 persons)	常住人口密度（人/平方公里）Density of Permanent Population (person/sq.km)
西安市	**Xi 'an**	**10096.81**	**100.0**	**883.21**	**875**
市区	**Urban**	**3866.24**	**38.2**	**714.41**	**1848**
新城区	Xincheng	30.13	0.3	60.91	20216
碑林区	Beilin	23.37	0.2	63.87	27330
莲湖区	Lianhu	38.32	0.4	72.23	18849
灞桥区	Baqiao	324.50	3.2	62.73	1933
未央区	Weiyang	264.41	2.6	85.08	3218
雁塔区	Yanta	151.44	1.5	123.11	8129
阎良区	Yanliang	244.55	2.4	29.08	1189
临潼区	Lintong	915.97	9.1	68.18	744
长安区	Chang'an	1588.53	15.7	114.11	718
高陵区	Gaoling	285.03	2.8	35.11	1232
三县	**Three Counties**	**6230.57**	**61.8**	**168.80**	**271**
蓝田县	Lantian	2005.95	19.9	52.86	264
周至县	Zhouzhi	2945.20	29.2	58.50	199
户 县	Huxian	1279.42	12.7	57.44	449

注：本表土地面积数据来源市国土资源局。

1-3 自然状况和资源（2016年）

Nature Conditions and Resources（2016）

指　标	Item	2016
一、自然状况	**Nature Conditions**	
土地总面积（平方公里）	Total Land Area (sq.km)	10096.81
#市区面积	Urban Area	3866.24
气候（市区）	Climate (Urban)	
年平均气温（℃）	Average Annual Temperature (℃)	15.8
年降水量（毫米）	Total Annual Precipitation (mm)	456.0
日照总时数（小时）	Total Sunshine Time (hour)	2140.3
平均风速（米/秒）	Average Wind-speed (m/sec.)	2.4
二、自然资源	**Natural Resources**	
年末实有耕地面积（千公顷）	Cultivated Area Year-end (1 000 hectare)	231.20
林业用地面积（千公顷）	Area of Forestry (1 000 hectare)	480.59
全市水面面积（千公顷）	Whole Water Area (1 000 hectare)	3.80
水资源总量（亿立方米）	Total Water Resource (0.1 billion cu.m)	21.56
#天然地表水资源总量	Total Savageness Surface Water Resource	14.15
地下水资源总量（亿立方米）	Total Ground Water Resource (0.1 billion cu.m)	14.27

注：全市水面面积包括湖泊、水库、鱼塘、城市段河流面积等。
本表数据来源市气象局、林业局、水务局等。

1-4 气象情况（2016年）

Climate Condition（2016）

地 区	Region	平均气温（℃）Average Temperature (℃)	日照时数（小时）Sunshine Time (hour)	降水天数（天）Raining days (day)	年降水量（毫米）Total Annual Precipitation (mm)	平均风速（米/秒）Average Wind-speed (m/second)
市 区	Urban	15.8	2140.3	73	456.0	2.4
临潼区	Lintong	15.2	2396.0	94	466.1	1.8
长安区	Chang'an	14.3	1754.2	98	830.3	1.3
高陵区	Gaoling	14.9	2241.2	86	462.0	2.1
蓝田县	Lantian	14.3	1710.9	109	667.6	1.5
周至县	Zhouzhi	14.5	1748.3	111	614.5	1.6
户 县	Huxian	14.7	2100.3	118	562.9	1.6

注：本表数据来源市气象局。

1-5 市区及县各月平均气温（2016年）

Average Temperature of Xi'an and the Districts of Each Month（2016）

单位：℃ (℃)

月 份	Month	市区 Urban	临潼区 Lintong	长安区 Chang'an	高陵区 Gaoling	蓝田县 Lantian	周至县 Zhouzhi	户县 Huxian
一月	January	0.3	-0.2	-1.3	-0.9	-1.7	-0.9	-0.8
二月	February	4.8	4.4	3.2	3.2	2.2	3.6	3.6
三月	March	11.5	10.9	10.2	10.5	10.1	10.4	10.1
四月	April	18.3	17.6	16.5	7.5	16.6	16.9	16.8
五月	May	20.2	19.5	18.6	19.5	18.9	18.8	18.9
六月	June	26.7	26.3	25.1	36.2	25.1	25.0	25.8
七月	July	28.3	28.0	27.1	28.0	27.2	27.1	27.4
八月	August	28.6	28.0	27.3	28.3	28.1	27.3	28.1
九月	September	22.6	21.7	20.9	21.6	21.2	20.9	21.5
十月	October	15.3	14.8	14.1	14.9	14.6	14.1	14.5
十一月	November	8.3	7.5	7.0	7.1	6.6	7.0	7.4
十二月	December	4.7	3.9	3.0	3.2	2.8	3.2	3.4

注：本表数据来源市气象局。

1-6 市区及县各月日照时数（2016年）

Sunshine Duration of Xi'an and the Districts of Each Month（2016）

单位：小时 (hour)

月 份	Month	市区 Urban	临潼区 Lintong	长安区 Chang'an	高陵区 Gaoling	蓝田区 Lantian	周至县 Zhouzhi	户县 Huxian
一月	January	111.9	158.8	112.6	159.0	120.8	125.0	142.2
二月	February	205.5	225.6	187.6	214.0	195.6	170.9	181.8
三月	March	168.8	176.8	154.0	169.1	166.1	148.7	162.2
四月	April	211.9	239.9	181.1	221.2	144.6	168.1	201.1
五月	May	200.7	228.6	162.8	209.0	153.6	154.8	198.0
六月	June	258.9	287.7	188.9	262.1	200.6	221.4	250.1
七月	July	231.6	268.8	225.3	259.6	203.4	220.4	257.4
八月	August	290.7	295.8	199.3	281.5	209.3	185.4	251.8
九月	September	141.5	148.1	104.5	129.4	100.6	118.7	139.0
十月	October	89.2	95.4	50.2	92.9	65.1	48.2	93.1
十一月	November	119.4	115.1	90.6	112.1	71.8	88.4	109.2
十二月	December	110.2	156.2	97.3	131.3	79.4	103.0	114.4

注：本表数据来源市气象局。

1-7 市区及县各月降水天数（2016年）

Precipitation Days of Xi'an and the Districts of Each Month（2016）

单位：天 (day)

月 份	Month	市区 Urban	临潼区 Lintong	长安区 Chang'an	高陵区 Gaoling	蓝田县 Lantian	周至县 Zhouzhi	户县 Huxian
一月	January	3	3	3	3	4	6	4
二月	February	2	3	3	3	4	4	5
三月	March	6	8	9	3	8	9	10
四月	April	5	8	9	10	13	12	12
五月	May	8	11	12	9	11	12	11
六月	June	7	9	9	13	11	10	10
七月	July	11	12	10	10	13	11	13
八月	August	3	3	8	2	7	4	7
九月	September	6	10	8	8	10	11	13
十月	October	13	15	17	15	17	18	17
十一月	November	4	6	5	5	6	6	8
十二月	December	5	6	5	5	5	8	8

注：本表数据来源市气象局。

1-8 市区及县各月降水量（2016年）

Amount of Precipitation of Xi'an and the Districts of Each Month（2016）

单位：毫米 (mm)

月 份	Month	市区 Urban	临潼区 Lintong	长安区 Chang'an	高陵区 Gaoling	蓝田县 Lantian	周至县 Zhouzhi	户县 Huxian
一月	January	8.9	4.2	26.4	3.7	7.1	4.8	8.3
二月	February	2.0	6.1	8.4	1.9	6.9	7.1	7.9
三月	March	5.9	3.9	12.3	2.9	6.1	8.1	5.7
四月	April	26.4	34.7	49.9	23.6	46.5	34.0	27.2
五月	May	53.7	63.4	90.8	55.5	111.4	64.4	74.1
六月	June	80.7	49.5	134.7	76.8	88.8	160.2	145.4
七月	July	104.8	100.7	217.2	111.6	156.4	81.3	68.7
八月	August	50.0	57.4	121.3	76.7	55.9	22.5	37.1
九月	September	13.3	40.9	41.3	11.9	34.7	116.1	73.6
十月	October	69.3	59.0	86.0	65.4	93.4	95.6	85.2
十一月	November	33.4	37.6	35.7	23.6	51.4	16.9	26.5
十二月	December	7.6	8.7	6.3	8.4	9.0	3.5	3.2

注：本表数据来源市气象局。

1-9 市区及区县各月平均风速（2016年）

Average Wind Velocity of Xi'an and the Districts of Each Month（2016）

单位：米/秒 (m/s)

月 份	Month	市区 Urban	临潼区 Lintong	长安区 Chang'an	高陵区 Gaoling	蓝田县 Lantian	周至县 Zhouzhi	户县 Huxian
一月	January	2.0	1.7	1.4	1.7	1.4	1.5	1.5
二月	February	2.3	2.0	1.5	2.1	1.6	1.6	1.7
三月	March	2.5	1.8	1.3	2.1	1.5	1.6	1.6
四月	April	2.3	1.9	1.4	2.1	1.6	1.8	1.7
五月	May	2.5	2.0	1.4	2.3	1.8	1.7	1.6
六月	June	2.5	1.9	1.2	2.4	1.5	1.9	1.9
七月	July	2.8	2.3	1.4	2.5	1.6	1.9	1.9
八月	August	3.3	2.2	1.3	2.7	1.8	1.6	1.7
九月	September	1.9	1.4	1.0	1.5	1.3	1.3	1.4
十月	October	2.1	1.7	1.1	2.0	1.5	1.3	1.4
十一月	November	1.9	1.5	1.1	1.6	1.2	1.2	1.3
十二月	December	2.1	1.6	1.3	1.7	1.5	1.4	1.5

注：本表数据来源市气象局。

1-10 主要年份国有土地使用权出让、划拨情况

The Transfer and Allocation of State-Owned Land Use Right in Representative Years

项目	Item	2008	2009	2010	2011	2012	2013	2014	2015	2016
国有土地使用权出让	**Lease of the Use Right of State-owned Land**									
出让地块(宗)	Land leased (item)	278	297	386	474	581	550	506	416	457
协议	Agreement	119	100	173	133	80	90	109	72	82
招标	Invitation for Bid	3		3						
拍卖	Auction	5	1	11						
挂牌交易	Listed Transaction	149	196	199	341	500	460	397	344	375
出让面积（公顷）	Area of Totally Leased Land (hectare)	809	1047	1364	1386	1853	2195	1789	1294	1599
土地使用权出让总收入（万元）	**Total Revenue from Leasing of the Use Right(10 000 yuan)**	**309181**	**284405**	**358098**	**334069**	**218817**	**292945**	**183901**	**109116**	**2832632**
国有土地使用权划拨	**Administrative Allocation of the Use Right of State-owned Land**									
划拨地块（宗）	Land Allocated (item)	102	79	108	253	154	234	152	141	132
划拨面积（公顷）	Area of Land Allocated(hectare)	455	1721	1027	1426	1617	1986	1739	1209	1135

注：1、本表数据来自市国土资源局。
2、2016年土地使用权出让总收入，现报表包括协议出让和招拍挂出让收入，原报表数据为协议出让收入。

1-11 主要年份国民经济和社会发展总量与速度指标

指 标	Item	总量指标 Total quantity index			
		1995	2000	2005	2010
人口与就业	**Population and Employment**				
人口	**Population**				
年底户籍总人口(万人)	Population at the Year-end (10 000 persons)	648.21	688.01	741.73	782.73
城镇人口	Urban Population	255.71	285.79	333.14	374.64
乡村人口	Rural Population	392.50	402.22	408.59	408.09
男性人口	Male Population	334.75	355.18	382.02	398.80
女性人口	Female Population	313.46	332.83	359.71	383.93
就业	**Employment**				
全社会从业人员数(万人)	Employment(10 000 persons)	372.60	389.10	415.83	477.58
#全部单位在岗职工人数	Number of Employed Staff and Workers	141.17	109.62	119.73	130.70
城镇登记失业人数	Registered Unemployed in Urban Areas	5.92	3.85	8.45	10.46
宏观经济	**Macroeconomic Indicator**				
国民经济核算(亿元)	**National Accounts(100 mil. yuan)**				
生产总值(亿元)	Gross Domestic Product(100 mil. yuan)	330.35	646.13	1313.93	3242.86
第一产业	Primary Industry	41.40	44.65	66.01	140.06
第二产业	Secondary Industry	135.33	277.13	540.50	1357.53
第三产业	Tertiary Industry	153.62	324.35	707.42	1745.27
工业	Industry	112.50	218.44	420.00	954.38
建筑业	Construction			120.50	403.15
在生产总值中：最终消费	Total Consumption	239.64	413.43	766.62	1598.51
资本形成总额	Total Investment	151.55	287.82	839.01	2835.42
固定资产投资	**Investment in Fixed Assets**				
全社会固定资产投资总额(亿元)	Total Investment in Fixed Assets(100 mil. yuan)	103.42	232.37	835.10	3250.56
按类别分：	By classification:				
固定资产投资（不含农户）	Investment in Fixed Assets (excluding farmers)	88.50	203.01	776.33	3104.92
#房地产开发投资	Real Estate Investment	21.65	51.85	225.23	842.34
农户投资	Farmer Investment	14.92	29.36	58.77	145.64
按经济成分划分:	By Economic Component				
国有单位	State-owned	69.08	159.60	373.70	1348.76
集体单位	Collective-Owned	9.78	14.65	59.23	326.44
个体经济	Self-employed Individual	11.13	24.40	79.04	54.73
其他经济	Other	13.43	33.72	323.13	1520.63
财政	**Public Finance**				
地方财政一般公共预算收入（亿元）	General Public Budgetary Revenue of Local Government (100 mil. yuan)	18.21	46.80	72.92	241.86
地方财政一般公共预算支出（亿元）	General Public Budgetary Expenditure of Local Government (100 mil. yuan)	18.42	52.00	97.61	371.62
物价指数(上年=100)	**Price Indices(preceding year=100)**				
商品零售价格指数	Retail Price Index	114.6	98.7	99.7	102.7
居民消费价格指数	Consumer Price Index	117.0	100.2	100.3	103.5
工业生产者出厂价格指数	Producer Price Indices (PPI) for Manufactured Goods	110.8	99.4	103.9	102.3
利用外资	**Utilization of Foreign Capital**				
利用外资签定协议额(万美元)	Amount of Foreign Capital for Utilization Through Signed Contracts or Agreements(USD 10 000)	28956	54123	121499	119689
外商实际直接投资额(万美元)	Amount of Foreign Capital Actually Utilized (USD 10 000)	18653	15633	57113	156653

注：国民经济核算2004—2008年为全国第二次经济普查修订数据。2009—2012年为三经普修订数据，2013年为全国第三次经济普查数据。2014—2015年为年报最终核实数。
2009年及以前年份财政收支为一般预算收支与基金预算收支之和。
由于2010年固定资产投资起报点的变化，指数和平均增长速度为可比口径计算。
2015年，市公安局提供户籍人口分类为“城镇人口”和“乡村人口”，2015年之前，分类为“非农业人口”和“农业人口”。
2015年，国家取消了城乡投资分组，“农户投资”2014年之前为原来的“农村投资”。

Total and Speed Index of National Economy and Social Development in Representative Years

					速度指标 （%）				Indices and Growth Rates （%）		
					指数（2016比以下各年） (2016 as percentage of the following years)				平均增长速度 Average Annual Growth Rate		
2012	2013	2014	2015	2016	2000	2005	2010	2015	2001-2005	2006-2010	2011-2015
795.98	806.93	815.29	815.66	824.93	119.9	111.2	105.3	101.1	1.5	1.1	0.8
398.40	409.82	418.16	545.95	552.21	193.1	165.7	147.3	101.1	3.1	2.4	7.8
397.58	397.11	397.13	269.71	272.72	67.8	66.7	66.8	101.1	0.3	-0.02	-7.9
403.94	408.78	412.46	412.23	416.54	117.3	109.0	104.4	101.0	1.5	0.9	0.7
392.04	398.15	402.83	403.43	408.39	122.7	113.5	106.4	101.2	1.6	1.3	1.0
514.57	530.71	532.92	528.06	539.18	138.5	129.7	112.9	102.1	1.3	2.8	2.0
155.28	183.60	183.22	181.86	184.93	168.7	154.5	141.5	101.7	1.8	1.8	6.8
9.60	10.13	10.84	10.74	11.29	293.2	133.6	107.9	105.1	17.0	4.4	0.5
4394.47	4924.97	5492.64	5801.2	6282.65	690.9	367.2	182.7	108.6	13.5	15.0	11.0
195.59	200.45	214.55	220.2	232.01	229.1	185.6	135.7	103.8	4.3	6.5	5.5
1781.09	1998.82	2194.78	2126.29	2200.36	723.3	356.6	179.2	108.5	15.2	14.8	10.6
2417.79	2725.7	3083.31	3454.71	3850.28	727.4	394.7	189.6	109.0	13.0	15.8	11.7
1228.05	1376.74	1488.02	1376.72	1397.25	674.0	337.8	179.7	109.2	14.8	13.4	10.5
553.04	642.26	728.74	770.29	818.82	911.5	424.0	178.0	106.5	16.5	19.0	10.8
2092.97											
3783.10											
4243.43	5134.56	5903.98	5165.98	5191.36	2863.3	796.7	204.7	102.0	29.2	31.2	14.9
4107.54	4982.25	5682.42	5086.93	5097.00	3313.5	886.5	216.6	103.4	30.8	31.9	15.9
1281.90	1595.64	1761.88	1831.67	1955.82	3773.0	868.6	232.3	106.8	34.1	30.2	16.8
135.89	152.31	221.56	79.05	78.65	268.0	133.9	54.0	99.5	14.9	19.9	-11.5
1661.22	1770.84	1916.31	1826.62	2332.08	1326.8	715.2	198.2	115.9	18.5	29.3	11.3
194.71	219.88	203.35	158.14	152.05	1124.3	278.1	50.5	82.5	32.2	40.7	-9.4
82.72	84.43	83.28	80.47	81.68	422.5	130.4	188.4	101.5	26.5	-7.1	13.2
2304.78	3059.41	3701.04	3100.75	2625.55	10795.3	1126.5	239.4	93.3	57.1	36.6	20.7
396.96	501.98	583.79	650.99	641.07	1545.4	991.8	299.1	111.1	9.3	27.1	21.9
597.49	729.81	819.54	917.24	942.52	1813.3	966.0	253.7	102.8	13.4	30.7	19.8
102.3	101.7	100.7	99.7	100.1					-0.2	2.5	1.7
102.8	102.7	101.4	100.7	100.9					0.3	3.1	2.6
100.5	99.5	99.5	98.5	97.8					1.1	2.2	0.1
360264	251874	255321	193684	102103	188.6	84.0	85.3	52.7	17.6	-0.3	10.1
247800	312994	370310	400833	450466	2881.9	788.8	287.6	112.4	29.6	22.4	20.7

1-11 续表1

指标	Item	总量指标 Total quantity index			
		1995	2000	2005	2010
产 业	**Industry**				
农业	**Agriculture**				
耕地面积(万亩)	Cultivated Areas(10 000 hectares)	463.97	443.37	400.17	383.32
农林牧渔及服务业总产值 (亿元)	Gross Output Value of Farming Forestry, Animal Husbandry and Fishery(100 mil yuan)	75.46	74.37	106.54	227.10
主要农产品产量(万吨)	Output of Major Farm Products(10 000 tons)				
粮 食	Grain	175.30	201.90	205.50	221.70
奶 类	Milk	13.29	24.59	42.22	63.37
油 料	Oil-bearing Crops	2.17	1.34	1.16	1.20
蔬 菜	Vegetables	133.60	162.14	195.70	253.10
水 果	Fruits	24.10	34.36	51.29	84.78
肉 类	Meat	12.78	14.76	18.20	13.65
水产品	Aquatic Products	0.85	1.14	0.94	1.19
工业	**Industry**				
全部工业总产值（亿元）	Gross Industrial Output Value(100 mil. yuan)	405.90	639.48	1308.56	3562.88
规模以上工业企业主要经济指标（亿元）	Main Economic Indicators of Industrial Enterprises above Designated Size				
工业增加值	Value Added of Industrial Enterprises above Designated Size		130.18	314.01	824.09
资产总计	Total Assets		958.05	1503.85	3592.13
主营业务收入	Revenue from Principal Business		420.42	980.97	3011.19
利润总额	Profits		16.11	28.72	245.37
从业人员年平均人数 （万人）	Annual Average Employees(10 000 persons)		43.25	37.92	47.11
主要工业产品产量	Output of Major Industrial Products				
布(亿米)	Cloth(100 mil.m)	3.03	2.48	2.70	2.38
机制纸及纸板(万吨)	Machine-Made Paper(10 000ton)	36.44	5.47	22.19	49.60
发电量(亿千瓦时)	Electricity(100 million kwh)	22.00	19.00	48.00	96.94
钢材(万吨)	Steel Products(10 000ton)	31.44	10.00	24.02	110.77
汽车(万辆)	Motor Vehicle (10 000 units)	0.30	0.90	4.10	65.21
建筑业	**Construction**				
建筑业企业从业人数(人)	Number of Employed Persons(person)		136718	158311	539000
建筑业总产值(亿元)	Gross Output Value(100 mil. yuan)	42.55	105.93	326.65	1334.00
房屋建筑施工面积 (万平方米)	Floor Space of Buildings under Construction (10 000 sq.m)	601.70	793.30	1801.20	4592.57
房屋建筑竣工面积 (万平方米)	Floor Space of Buildings Completed (10 000 sq.m)	177.15	336.80	569.01	1391.91

注：规模以上工业2013年为全国第三次经济普查数据。以前年份未做修订。
由于2010年规模以上工业起报点的变化，指数和平均增长速度为可比口径计算。

continued 1

2012	2013	2014	2015	2016	速度指标 (%)				Indices and Growth Rates (%)		
					指数（2016比以下各年） (2016 as percentage of the following years)				平均增长速度 Average Annual Growth Rate		
					2000	2005	2010	2015	2001-2005	2006-2010	2011-2015
369.91	366.23	360.73	356.89	346.80	78.2	86.7	90.5	97.2	-2.0	-9.0	-1.4
308.36	342.89	367.21	380.76	405.63	238.3	190.5	136.4	104.2	4.6	6.8	5.5
192.55	183.12	175.61	180.86	175.33	86.8	85.3	79.1	96.9	0.4	1.5	-4.0
66.64	65.77	65.80	63.73	56.20	228.6	133.2	88.7	88.2	11.4	8.5	0.1
1.02	1.00	0.98	0.95	0.86	64.2	74.1	71.7	90.5	-1.6		-4.6
277.80	298.12	316.28	332.79	336.75	207.7	172.1	133.1	101.2	3.8	5.3	5.6
93.21	95.19	99.66	105.2	107.74	313.7	210.0	127.1	102.4	8.3	10.6	4.4
15.17	15.74	16.19	16.13	15.68	106.2	86.1	114.8	97.2	4.2	-5.6	3.4
1.40	1.42	1.42	1.42	1.34	117.5	142.5	112.5	94.4	-3.9	5.7	3.6
4656.08	5042.64	5660.63	5159.91	5462.43	783.3	401.1	153.6	105.9	14.3	21.2	7.7
1064.29	1194.88	1304.12	1285.08	1320.61		435.1	194.5	109.6	15.9	16.2	10.9
4775.92	5127.69	6048.34	6740.26	7473.07	780.2	497.1	208.0	110.9	9.4	19.0	13.4
3758.56	4171.21	4566.20	4374.11	5028.28	1196.5	512.8	167.1	115.0	18.5	25.1	7.8
167.77	211.26	226.17	206.88	290.96	1805.6	1012.7	118.5	140.6	12.3	53.6	-3.4
49.23	44.27	49.53	50.59	49.55	114.5	130.6	105.1	97.9	-2.6	4.4	1.4
1.43	1.40	1.12	1.04	1.22	49.1	45.2	51.3	117.3	1.7	-2.5	-15.3
27.61	16.00	11.24	12.22	13.44	245.7	60.6	27.1	110.0	32.3	17.5	-24.4
99.48	184.50	179.58	158.68	161.00	847.7	335.6	166.2	101.5	20.4	15.1	10.4
31.29	54.30	42.87	37.03	43.92	439.2	182.9	39.6	118.6	19.2	35.8	-19.7
54.17	42.20	37.47	34.14	38.25	4248.5	932.6	58.7	112.0	35.4	73.9	-12.1
391199	577944	394070	596245	588418	430.4	371.7	109.2	98.7	3.0	27.8	2.0
1874.23	2228.41	2586.33	2650.41	2897.55	2734.7	886.9	217.2	109.3	25.3	41.0	14.7
7531.07	9753.45	11182.18	11979.16	11945.73	1505.5	663.1	260.0	99.7	17.8	20.6	21.1
1985.31	2229.97	2536.71	2712.01	2233.2	662.7	392.2	160.3	82.3	11.1	19.6	14.3

1-11 续表2

指标	Item	总量指标 Total quantity index			
		1995	2000	2005	2010
交通运输	**Transportation**				
货运量(万吨)	Freight Traffic(10 000 tons)	9590	6999	12051	34323
铁 路	Railways	3317	3101	540	706
公 路	Highways	6268	3890	11505	33610
民用航空	Civil Aviation	5	8	6	7
客运量(万人次)	Passenger Traffic(10 000 persons-times)	9069	8068	10479	30294
铁 路	Railways	2678	2130	1796	2781
公 路	Highways	6128	5578	8294	26536
民用航空	Civil Aviation	263	360	389	977
邮电通信业	**Post and Telecommunication Services**				
邮电业务总量(亿元)	Total Business Revenue(100 mil. yuan)	7.65	46.16	132.04	323.11
函 件(万件)	Number of Letters Delivered(10 000 pieces)	14647	8230	9526	8176
本地电话局用交换机容量 (万门)	Capacity of Local Office Telephone Exchanges (10 000 line)	58.3	204.8	457.3	449.0
本地电话年末用户(万户)	Local fixed telephone end users (million)	29.95	124.26	321.48	261.77
城市电话用户	Urban Telephone Subscribers	29.11	107.24	271.40	228.26
乡村电话用户	Rural Telephone Subscribers	0.84	17.02	50.08	33.50
移动电话用户(万户)	Number of Mobile Telephone Subscribers (10 000 subscribers)		73.10	419.96	1423.08
互联网年末宽带用户(万户)	Number of Subscribers of Intemet Services (10 000 subscribers)			33.93	146.18
国内贸易	**Domestic Trade**				
社会消费品零售总额 (亿元)	Total Retail Sales of Consumer Goods (100 mil. yuan)	186.60	360.42	670.56	1678.01
对外经济贸易	**Foreign Trade**				
进出口总值(万美元)	Total Value of Exports and Imports(USD 10 000)	137510	173696	390146	1039273
出口总值	Exports	110163	106062	263441	531729
进口总值	Imports	27347	67634	126705	507544
旅游	**Tourism**				
旅游者人数(万人次)	Number of Tourists(10 000 persons)	791.35	1567.00	2423.60	5285.18
旅游总收入(亿元)	Earnings from Tourism (10 000yuan)	44.00	105.00	178.50	405.18
金融业	**Financial Intermediation**				
金融机构（不含外资）人民币存款余额(亿元)	Balance of Deposits in Domestic Funded Financial Institutions (100 mil. yuan)	359.51	1335.63	3599.70	8863.36
金融机构（不含外资）人民币贷款余额 (亿元)	Balance of Loans in Domestic Funded Financial Institutions (100 mil. yuan)	334.50	972.52	2158.10	6420.72
保险公司保费收入(亿元)	Insurance premium income (100 million Yuan)	4.70	13.58	44.94	129.38
保险公司赔款及付给金额(亿元)	Indemnity Insurance and Amount Paid(100 million yuan)	1.70	1.39	9.50	26.39

注：2006年铁路数据按新口径统计；
2006年国际互联网络用户改为互联网宽带用户。
2009—2013年社会消费品零售总额为全国第三次经济普查修订数据。
2014年起，海关不发布美元口径数据，为了数据可持续性，使用年均汇率折算为美元口径。

continued 2

2012	2013	2014	2015	2016	速度指标 （%）				Indices and Growth Rates（%）		
					指数（2016比以下各年） (2016 as percentage of the following years)				平均增长速度 Average Annual Growth Rate		
					2000	2005	2010	2015	2001-2005	2006-2010	2011-2015
44924	50119	42039	46270	23888					11.5	23.3	
825	858	900	848	854					-29.5	5.5	
44082	49243	41120	45401	23011					24.2	23.9	
17	18	19	21	23					-5.6	3.1	
36154	38289	25719	26904	23671					5.4	23.7	
2919	3071	3511	3982	4199					-3.4	9.1	
30893	32614	19282	19625	15773					8.3	26.2	
2342	2604	2926	3297	3699					1.6	20.2	
216.21	247.94	292.20	331.53	383.11	830.2	290.3	118.6	115.6	23.4	19.6	0.5
2769	2856	2112	1707	1367	16.6	14.3	16.7	80.1	3.0	-3.0	-26.9
420.4	378.0	230.0	145.1	75.92	37.0	16.6	16.9	52.3	17.4	-0.4	-20.2
311.02	319.11	306.66	292.08	284.33	228.8	88.4	108.6	97.3	20.9	-4.0	2.2
277.43	286.05	269.38	261.44	252.88	235.8	93.1	110.7	96.7	20.4	-3.4	2.8
33.59	33.06	37.28	30.63	31.45	184.9	62.9	93.9	102.7	24.1	-7.7	-1.8
1803.54	2160.67	2025.32	1767.00	1739.50	2378.5	414.1	122.2	98.4	41.9	27.6	4.4
202.31	267.05	277.95	289.97	335.83		989.6	229.7	115.8		33.9	14.7
2400.67	2742.89	3093.89	3405.38	3730.7	1035.5	556.5	222.4	109.6	13.2	19.5	15.2
1301446	1798534	2494223	2828479	2754991	1586.1	706.2	265.1	97.4	17.6	21.6	39.6
729878	847819	1196005	1316350	1426175	1344.1	541.2	268.2	108.3	20.0	15.1	35.3
571568	950715	1298218	1512129	1328816	1965.3	1049.0	261.9	87.9	13.4	32.0	43.9
7978.35	10130.00	12000.00	13600.80	15012.6	958.3	619.6	284.1	110.4	17.6	21.6	37.0
654.39	811.44	950.00	1073.69	1213.81	1156.6	680.3	299.7	113.1	20.0	15.1	38.4
12044.68	13665.89	15064.10	17682.94	18957.55	1419.2	526.6	213.9	107.2	21.9	19.7	14.8
8559.27	9930.04	11576.30	13604.89	15159.40	1558.4	702.3	236.1	111.4	17.3	24.4	16.2
173.21	202.41	219.49	263.02	345.85	2546.9	769.7	267.3	131.5	27.0	23.6	15.2
47.55	66.49	80.77	87.62	115.91	8339.5	1220.2	439.2	132.3	46.9	24.8	27.1

1-11 续表3

指 标	Item	总量指标 Total quantity index			
		1995	2000	2005	2010
教育、科技、文化	**Education, Science and Technology and Culture**				
教育	**Education**				
专任教师数(人)	Full-time Teachers(person)				
#普通高等学校	Institutions of Higher Education	15914	15679	29498	42098
普通中等专业学校	Regular Specialized Secondary Schools	2533	3172	2130	1845
普通中学	Regular Middle Schools	21984	26230	31094	31506
小 学	Primary Schools	30270	30215	29647	29944
在校学生数(万人)	Students Enrollment(10 000 person)				
#普通高等学校	Institutions of Higher Education	11.67	19.41	53.06	73.30
普通中等专业学校	Regular Specialized Secondary Schools	3.74	6.02	6.16	6.75
普通中学	Regular Schools	32.32	48.31	55.74	48.89
小 学	Primary Schools	79.36	77.81	60.47	51.56
科技	**Science and Technology**				
高新技术企业(个)	Hi-tech Enterprises (unit)				827
企事业单位累计授权专利数（件）	Accumulated patents awarded(unit)	3164	6139	11670	31999
文化	**Accumulated patents awarded(unit)**				
图书馆总藏量(千册件)	Total Collections in Library (1000 Volume-time)	2830	3214	3671	4465
文化馆、站（个）	Cultural Centers or Stations (unit)	201	251	192	197
电视节目制作时间(小时)	Time for TV Programs Production(hour)	5738	11871	27377	29626
家庭、生活、环境	**Family, People's Livelihood and Environment**				
家庭	**Family**				
家庭总户数户籍人口 (万户)	Total Number of Households(10 000 household)	171.25	187.08	203.04	226.71
城镇常住居民平均每户家庭人口(人)	Average Household Size in Urban Areas(person)	3.88	2.99	2.93	2.81
农村常住居民平均每户家庭人口(人)	Average Household Size in Rural Areas(person)	4.60	4.30	4.22	3.94
婚姻	**Marriages and Divorces**				
结婚(对)	Number of Marriages(couple)	47236	46415	49962	83645
离婚(对)	Number of Divorces(couple)	4296	5161	12747	19060
居住	**Housing**				
城镇居民人均现住房建筑面积 (平方米)	Per Capita Building Area of Urban Residents (sq.m)	13.05	14.82	16.38	28.70
农村居民人均现住房建筑面积(平方米)	Per Capita Building Area of Rural Residents(sq.m)	21.77	28.31	36.73	66.73

注：2008年及以前图书馆总藏量为图书馆藏书量。

2005年以前城镇居民人均现住房总建筑面积为城镇人均住房使用面积。

2014年城乡居民人均住房面积为城乡住户调查一体化改革后新口径数据，与往年不可比。

continued 3

2012	2013	2014	2015	2016	速度指标 （%） Indices and Growth Rates（%） 指数（2016比以下各年） (2016 as percentage of the following years) 2000	2005	2010	2015	平均增长速度 Average Annual Growth Rate 2001-2005	2006-2010	2011-2015
44487	46436	46766	47768	47158	300.7	159.8	112.0	98.7	13.5	7.4	2.6
1595	1474	1346	1228	1210	38.1	56.8	65.6	98.5	-7.7	-2.8	-7.8
31526	31419	32615	33014	33962	129.6	109.3	107.8	102.9	3.5	0.3	0.9
29651	29421	28395	28748	30941	101.1	103.1	102.0	107.6	-0.4	0.2	-1.1
80.70	83.83	85.42	84.83	83.1	428.3	156.7	113.4	98.0	22.3	6.7	3.0
5.43	4.66	4.07	3.47	3.11	51.6	50.4	46.1	89.6	0.7	1.9	-12.5
45.33	43.73	42.57	41.37	40.7	84.2	73.0	83.2	98.4	2.9	-2.6	-3.3
50.85	51.95	53.79	56.62	59.79	76.9	98.8	115.9	105.6	-4.9	-3.1	1.9
917	1026	1253	1316	1506			182.0	114.4			9.7
53118	69368	86639	103910	150021	2444.1	1285.7	468.9	144.4	13.7	22.4	26.6
6123	6647	6285	6522	6957	216.5	189.6	155.9	106.7	2.7	4.0	7.9
197	198	199	199	190	75.7	98.9	96.5	95.5	-5.4	0.6	0.2
30091	46614	35182	43563	54200	456.5	197.9	182.9	124.4	18.2	1.6	8.0
239.54	245.53	250.26	253.13	256.65	137.2	126.4	113.3	101.4	1.7	2.2	2.2
2.76	2.73	2.7	2.8	2.8	93.6	95.6	99.6	100.0	-0.4	-0.8	-0.1
4.09	4.09	3.5	3.6	3.6	83.7	85.3	91.4	100.0	-0.4	-1.6	-1.8
89877	89136	91123	80790	77371	166.8	154.9	92.5	95.8	1.5	10.9	-0.7
18579	20304	21887	22748	25448	493.3	199.7	133.5	111.9	19.8	8.4	3.6
32.98	33.43	32.06	32.1	33.4					2.0	11.9	
78	81	48.83	50.7	51.7					5.3	12.7	

1-11 续表4

指 标	Item	总量指标 Total quantity index			
		1995	2000	2005	2010
生活	**People's Livelihood**				
城镇居民人均可支配收入(元)	Per Capita Annual Disposable Income of Urban Households (yuan)	4153	6364	9628	22244
农村居民人均纯收入(元)	Per Capita Net Income of Rural Residents(yuan)	1353	2344	3460	7750
住户存款	Household deposits	230.63	675.83	1716.76	3641.09
工资	**Wages**				
在岗职工工资总额(亿元)	The Gross Salary of Workers (100 mil. yuan)	67.23	101.68	211.14	501.76
城镇非私营单位从业人员年平均工资(元)	Aunual Average Wage of Stuff and Workers in Urban Non-privite Enterprises(yuan)	4763	9179	17728	37870
卫生	**Health Care**				
医院、卫生院(个)	Number of Hospitals(unit)	368	426	479	412
执业（助理）医师（人）	Licensed (Assistant) Doctors (person)	18846	18750	17730	18763
医院、卫生院床位数(张)	Number of Hospital Beds(unit)	28265	28697	30087	36796
市政建设	**City Construction**				
自来水供应量(万立方米)	Volume of Tap Water Supply(10 000 cu.m)	35885	30273	35776	41089
自来水供水管道长度(公里)	Length of Water Supply Pipelines(km)	1066	2237	2315	2416
城市天然气供气总量 (万立方米)	Volume of Natural Gas Supply in Urban Areas (10 000 cu.m)	8419	11513	53202	109052
城市公共运营车辆(辆)	Total Number of Public Buses and Trolley Buses(unit)	977	2573	4762	7107
道路长度(公里)	Length of Paved Roads(km)	835	975	1382	2662
绿地面积(公顷)	Areas of Green Land(hectare)	5603	4116	4867	12140
环境、灾害	**Environment and Disaster**				
工业废水排放量(万吨)	Volume of Waste Water up to the Standard for Discharge(10 000 tons)	12479	9145	16969	13840
火灾发生数(起)	Number of Fire Disasters(case)	426	1040	2664	1825
火灾事故损失额（万元）	Fire Loss(10 000 yuan)	742.1	472.4	1565.5	2224.2
交通事故发生数（起）	Number of Traffic Accidents(case)	3065	4099	4903	2323
交通事故损失额（万元）	Loss of Traffic Accidents(10 000 yuan)	1103.2	1116.1	2024.4	736.6

注：1、城镇非私营单位从业人员年平均工资2012年前为城镇非私营单位在岗职工年平均工资。
2、2014年及以后城乡居民人均收入为新口径数据，“农村居民人均纯收入”改为“农村居民人均可支配收入”

continued 4

2012	2013	2014	2015	2016	速度指标 （%） Indices and Growth Rates（%） 指数（2016比以下各年） (2016 as percentage of the following years) 2000	2005	2010	2015	平均增长速度 Average Annual Growth Rate 2001-2005	2006-2010	2011-2015
29982	33100	30715	33188	35630	658.3	435.1	188.4	107.4	8.6	18.2	15.1
11442	12930	12898	14072	15191	726.9	492.5	219.9	108.0	8.1	17.5	15.3
4787.03	5357.05	5698.15	6571.18	7035.81	1041.3	410.0	193.3	107.1	16.5	13.3	12.5
742.16	987.80	1094.02	1202.01	1309.69	1288.6	620.5	261.2	109.0	15.7	18.9	19.1
44533	49350	54573	60557	67205	732.3	379.2	177.5	111.0	14.1	16.4	9.8
376	381	381	395	392	92.0	81.8	95.1	99.2	2.4	-3.0	-0.8
23051	23885	24820	26626	27864	148.5	157.1	148.4	104.6	-1.1	1.1	7.3
40585	44190	47075	51345	53008	184.6	176.2	144.0	103.2	1.0	4.1	6.9
45792	51372	53799	56055	59953	198.2	167.7	145.9	107.0	3.4	2.8	6.4
3208	3385	3500	4371	4522	202.2	195.4	187.2	103.5	0.7	0.9	12.6
142263	153489	186259	196826	206068	1790.0	387.4	189.0	104.7	35.8	15.4	12.5
7695	8128	7769	7781	7829	304.2	164.4	110.2	100.6	13.1	8.3	1.8
3119	3387	3461	3571	3683	377.7	266.4	138.3	103.1	7.2	14.0	6.1
15196	17751	18914	20582	22503	546.5	462.2	185.3	109.3	3.4	20.1	11.1
10224	8973	6340	5204	4030	44.0	23.8	29.1	77.4	13.2	-4.0	-17.8
2568	4062	3199	2590	3434	330.2	128.9	188.2	132.6	20.7	-7.3	7.3
2793.7	3011.9	4381.1	2401.5	1901.1	402.7	121.5	85.5	79.2	27.1	7.3	1.5
2446	2252	1970	2392	2943	71.8	60.0	126.7	123.0	3.6	-13.9	0.6
1011.1	1143.9	1264	1470.2	1653.7	148.2	81.7	224.6	112.5	12.6	-18.3	14.8

1-12 主要年份国民经济和社会发展结构指标

单位: %

指　　标	Item	1995	2000	2005
人口与就业	**Population and Employment**			
人 口	**Population**			
城乡结构	Structure			
城镇人口	Urban Population	39.45	41.54	44.91
乡村人口	Rural Population	60.55	58.46	55.09
性别结构	Sexual Structure			
男	Male	51.64	51.62	51.50
女	Female	48.36	48.38	48.50
就 业	**Employment**			
全社会从业人员产业结构	Industrial Structure of the Whole Society			
第一产业	Primary Industry	41.17	37.78	32.78
第二产业	Secondary Industry	29.43	27.57	27.46
第三产业	Tertiary Industry	29.40	34.65	39.76
宏观经济	**Macro Economy**			
国民经济核算	**National Accounting**			
生产总值产业结构	Industrial Structure			
第一产业	Primary Industry	12.53	6.91	5.02
第二产业	Secondary Industry	40.97	42.89	41.14
第三产业	Tertiary Industry	46.50	50.20	53.84
生产总值支出结构	Structure of Gross Domestic by Expenditures			
最终消费	Total Consumption	72.54	63.99	58.35
资本形成总额	Total Investment	45.88	44.55	63.85
货物和服务净出口	Net Export of Goods and Services	-18.42	-8.54	-22.20
投 资	**Investment**			
全社会固定资产投资结构	Structure of Total Investment in Fixed Assets			
报表种类结构	By classification			
固定资产投资（不含农户）	Investment in Fixed Assets (excluding farmers)	85.57	87.36	92.96
#房地产开发投资	Real Estate Investment	20.93	22.31	27.00
农户投资	Farmer Investment	14.43	12.64	7.04
经济成分结构	Registion Status Composition			
国有经济	State-owned Enterprises Investment	66.79	68.68	44.75
集体经济	Collective-owned Enterprises Investment	9.46	6.30	7.09
个体经济	Self-employed Individual	10.76	10.50	9.46
其他经济	Other	12.99	14.51	38.69

注：2015年，市公安局提供户籍人口分类为“城镇人口”和“乡村人口”，2015年之前，分类为“非农业人口”和“农业人口”。

Structural Indicators of National Economic and Social Development in Representative Years

(%)

2008	2009	2010	2011	2012	2013	2014	2015	2016
47.12	47.42	47.86	49.42	50.05	50.79	51.29	66.93	66.94
52.88	52.58	52.14	50.58	49.95	49.21	48.71	33.07	33.06
51.22	51.08	50.95	50.83	50.75	50.66	50.59	50.54	50.49
48.78	48.92	49.05	49.17	49.25	49.34	49.41	49.46	49.51
28.50	26.40	25.65	24.41	22.33	20.81	19.71	20.39	19.5
29.10	28.45	29.65	30.51	31.55	28.55	28.49	24.53	23.72
42.40	45.15	44.70	45.08	46.12	50.64	51.80	55.08	56.78
4.46	4.05	4.32	4.47	4.45	4.07	3.91	3.80	3.69
42.34	42.01	41.86	40.91	40.53	40.59	39.96	36.65	35.02
53.20	53.94	53.82	54.62	55.02	55.34	56.13	59.55	61.29
51.02	51.51	49.31	48.07	47.93				
79.28	83.77	87.47	84.52	86.65				
-30.30	-35.28	-36.78	-32.60	-34.58				
93.72	94.70	95.52	95.87	96.80	97.03	96.25	98.47	98.18
28.34	27.85	25.91	29.79	30.21	31.08	29.84	35.46	37.67
6.28	5.30	4.48	4.13	3.20	2.97	3.75	1.53	1.52
36.45	37.31	41.49	36.00	39.15	34.49	32.46	35.36	44.92
12.95	11.60	10.04	7.71	4.59	4.28	3.44	3.06	2.93
2.65	3.91	1.68	2.23	1.95	1.64	1.41	1.56	1.57
47.95	47.18	46.78	54.05	54.31	59.58	62.69	60.02	50.58

1–12 续表1

单位: %

指　　标	Item	1995	2000	2005
财 政	**Government Finance**			
财政收入结构	Structure of Government Revenue			
中　央	Central Government		31.94	58.30
地　方	Local Governments		68.06	41.70
产　业	**Industry**			
农　业	**Agriculture**			
农林牧渔及服务业总产值结构	Structure of Gross Output Value of Farming,Forestry,Animal Husbandry, Fishery and Service			
农　业	Farming	68.03	69.23	61.69
林　业	Forestry	0.96	1.14	1.23
牧　业	Animal Husbandry	30.29	28.58	30.96
渔　业	Fishery	0.72	1.05	0.69
农林牧渔服务业	Farming,Forestry,Animal Husbandry, Fishery and Service			5.43
工 业	**Industry**			
工业总产值经济类型结构	Structure of Gross Output Value of Industry by Registion Status			
国有经济	State-owned Enterprises	51.04	43.00	45.21
集体经济	Collective-owned Enterprises	40.98	32.76	5.16
其他经济类型	Others	7.98	24.24	49.63
工业总产值轻重结构	Structure of Gross Output Value of Industry by Light Industry and Heavy Industry			
轻工业	Light Industry	40.31	48.81	31.17
重工业	Heavy Industry	59.69	51.19	68.83
工业总产值规模结构	Structure of Gross Output Value of Industry by Size of Enterprises			
大型企业	Large Enterprises	38.80	36.29	35.46
中型企业	Medium-sized Enterprises	9.14	5.14	24.67
小型企业	Small Enterprises	52.06	58.57	39.87

注：本表2008年以后财政收入结构中地方指地方财政一般公共预算收入。

continued 1

(%)

2008	2009	2010	2011	2012	2013	2014	2015	2016
39.49	39.68	37.28	35.78	32.37	30.80	29.61	28.94	31.68
44.87	45.32	47.36	49.02	52.71	55.60	57.25	58.39	56.45
56.85	59.42	63.36	63.42	62.69	63.38	64.37	64.19	63.79
1.13	1.27	1.18	1.27	2.02	2.34	2.37	2.57	2.52
33.52	30.56	27.72	27.68	26.61	25.19	23.95	23.30	23.2
0.66	0.66	0.56	0.55	0.65	0.66	0.65	0.51	0.48
7.84	8.09	7.18	7.09	8.04	8.42	8.66	9.43	10.01
52.26	51.07	51.52	50.46	52.20	50.29	48.32	48.47	44.85
1.85	1.38	1.22	0.92	0.81	0.64	0.59	0.31	0.25
45.89	47.55	47.26	48.62	46.99	49.07	51.09	51.22	54.9
25.17	23.47	22.01	21.97	21.95	18.44	18.32	19.55	17.89
74.83	76.53	77.99	78.03	78.05	81.56	81.68	80.45	82.11
43.85	43.54	42.11	41.15	48.46	34.49	43.95	51.33	52.36
20.96	21.88	23.96	15.17	13.41	14.42	15.47	16.34	14.78
35.19	34.58	33.93	43.68	38.13	51.09	40.58	32.33	32.86

1-12 续表2

单位: %

指　　标	Item	1995	2000	2005
建筑业	**Construction**			
建筑业总产值结构	Structure of Gross Output Value of Construction Industry			
房屋建筑业	Building Construction	12.84	9.28	34.05
土木工程建筑业	Civil Engineering Construction	86.27	88.50	56.59
建筑安装业	Installation of Construction			
建筑装饰和其他建筑业	Decoration and others	0.89	2.22	9.36
交通运输业	**Transportation**			
客运量结构	Structure of Passenger Traffic			
铁　路	Railways	29.53	26.40	17.14
公　路	Highways	67.57	69.14	79.15
民　航	Civil Aviation	2.90	4.46	3.71
货运量结构	Structure of Freight Traffic			
铁　路	Railways	34.59	44.30	26.92
公　路	Highways	65.36	55.58	73.04
民　航	Civil Aviation	0.05	0.12	0.04
国内贸易	**Domestic Trade**			
社会消费品零售总额结构	Composition of Retail Sales of Consumer Goods			
城　镇	Urban Area	88.95	87.99	90.17
农　村	Rural Area	11.05	12.01	9.83
国际旅游	**International Tourism**			
国际旅游人数结构	Structure of Tourists			
外国人	Foreigners	89.76	84.03	84.91
华侨及港澳台同胞	Overseas Chinese and Compatriots form Hong Kong, Macao and Taiwan	10.24	15.97	15.09
教育文化、卫生、人民生活	**Education and Culture，Health Care，People's Livelihood**			
教　育	**Education**			
在校学生结构	Structure of Student Enrollment			
#普通高等学校	Institutions of Higher Education	8.81	12.44	28.48
普通中等专业学校	Regular Specialized Secondary Schools	2.84	3.84	3.33
普通中学	Regular Schools	24.55	30.93	29.89
小　学	Primary Schools	59.91	49.89	32.45

continued 2

(%)

2008	2009	2010	2011	2012	2013	2014	2015	2016
29.80	25.50	24.63	36.81	43.03	43.03	41.58	38.41	36.69
59.14	67.14	68.61	53.75	47.57	47.86	49.43	51.84	53.63
		4.39	6.70	6.49	5.86	5.32	5.91	6.61
11.06	7.36	2.37	2.74	2.91	3.25	3.67	3.84	3.07
10.11	9.01	9.18	8.57	8.07	8.02	13.65	14.80	17.74
87.45	88.07	87.59	87.96	85.45	85.18	74.97	72.95	66.63
2.44	2.92	3.23	3.46	6.48	6.80	11.38	12.25	15.63
2.20	2.01	2.06	2.10	1.84	1.71	2.14	1.83	3.58
97.78	97.97	97.92	97.88	98.13	98.25	97.81	98.12	96.32
0.02	0.02	0.02	0.02	0.04	0.04	0.05	0.05	0.10
90.43	95.57	96.00	96.53	96.92	96.89	96.85	96.69	96.46
9.57	4.43	4.00	3.47	3.08	3.11	3.15	3.31	3.54
84.78	87.81	86.97	88.43	87.91	88.26			
15.22	12.19	13.03	11.58	12.08	11.74			
30.53	31.54	32.60	29.74	31.00	33.09	33.16	32.78	31.38
3.71	3.32	3.02	2.37	2.08	1.84	1.58	1.34	1.17
24.17	22.70	21.74	18.32	17.40	17.26	16.53	16.00	15.37
25.03	23.56	22.95	19.95	19.52	20.51	20.88	21.88	22.58

1-12 续表3

单位: %

指　　标	Item	1995	2000	2005
专任教师结构	Structure of Full-time Teachers			
#普通高等学校	Institutions of Higher Education	21.25	19.89	29.93
普通中等专业学校	Regular Specialized Secondary Schools	3.38	4.02	2.16
普通中学	Regular Middle Schools	29.37	33.21	31.55
小 学	Primary Schools	40.41	38.34	30.08
人民生活	**People's Livelihood**			
城镇居民消费结构	Consumption Structure of Urban Residents			
食品烟酒	Food,Tobacco and Alcohol	44.68	36.46	37.04
衣 着	Clothing	12.67	8.13	9.03
居 住	Residence	6.49	11.23	9.10
生活用品及服务	Living Articles and Services	13.75	11.33	4.73
交通和通信	Transport and Communication Services	5.58	6.93	9.67
教育文化娱乐	Recreation, Education and Culture Services	9.05	13.74	17.18
医疗保健	Medical and Health Care Services	3.27	7.23	9.45
其他用品和服务	Other Commodities and Services	4.51	4.95	3.80
农村居民消费结构	Consumption Structure of Rural Residents			
食品烟酒	Food,Tobacco and Alcohol	50.31	36.63	36.34
衣 着	Clothing	8.39	6.65	6.11
居 住	Residence	5.92	21.41	17.76
生活用品及服务	Living Articles and Services	5.17	5.47	5.11
交通和通信	Transport and Communication Services	8.09	4.21	8.19
教育文化娱乐	Recreation, Education and Culture Services	18.53	14.49	16.15
医疗保健	Medical and Health Care Services	1.78	6.93	8.19
其他用品和服务	Other Commodities and Services	1.81	4.21	2.15
卫 生	**Health Care**			
卫生技术人员结构	Medical Technical Personnel by Types			
执业（助理）医师	Licensed（Assistant） Doctors	45.42	44.82	41.96
注册护士	Registered Nurses	32.68	34.29	33.14
药 师	Junior Paramedics	8.78	8.31	7.30
技 师	Technicians	5.21	5.21	5.33
其 他	Others	7.91	7.37	12.27

注：2014年及以后为城乡住户调查一体化改革后数据，居民消费结构与2014年之前不可比。

continued 3

(%)

2008	2009	2010	2011	2012	2013	2014	2015	2016
31.63	31.90	32.47	31.97	32.96	33.91	33.87	34.52	32.63
1.55	1.35	1.42	1.29	1.18	1.08	0.97	0.89	0.84
25.53	24.68	24.30	23.70	23.36	22.95	23.62	23.86	23.5
24.68	23.83	23.10	22.37	21.97	21.49	20.57	20.52	21.41
36.40	32.43	31.29	31.29	32.48	32.44	29.21	29.59	29.26
10.25	10.98	11.11	12.27	12.17	12.02	9.09	8.78	8.22
8.81	8.86	9.33	8.26	8.47	7.82	17.89	17.78	17.87
6.33	7.28	7.56	8.11	7.87	7.80	7.21	7.42	7.59
10.37	11.33	12.06	12.81	14.26	14.01	14.16	13.31	13.67
14.35	14.34	14.66	14.27	14.33	14.17	12.60	12.48	12.29
9.67	9.65	9.50	9.00	8.52	7.99	7.32	7.92	8.14
3.82	5.13	4.49	4.00	1.91	3.76	2.53	2.72	2.96
36.95	35.81	32.54	31.89	33.83	32.96	29.93	28.18	26.86
6.52	6.40	6.55	7.20	7.42	7.87	7.44	7.12	6.65
19.39	19.47	24.41	23.92	21.91	19.82	21.99	23.28	23.38
7.02	6.97	6.53	7.10	7.46	7.76	6.97	6.60	7.59
7.84	9.83	8.45	9.01	10.19	9.86	10.66	10.70	10.76
12.43	11.13	11.20	10.43	10.20	10.56	10.26	11.68	11.86
8.05	8.50	8.54	8.65	8.85	8.41	11.07	10.68	11.17
1.80	1.89	1.78	1.80	0.14	2.77	1.68	1.76	1.73
38.09	37.34	33.16	35.17	34.46	33.58	32.66	32.69	32.3
36.23	39.05	40.01	40.87	41.61	42.13	42.28	42.74	43.5
5.74	5.45	5.36	5.10	5.05	4.99	4.88	4.86	4.72
6.68	6.49	8.11	5.91	5.91	5.75	5.63	5.76	5.86
13.26	11.67	13.36	12.95	12.97	13.55	14.56	13.97	13.62

1-13 主要年份国民经济和社会发展比例和效益指标

指　　标	Item	1995
人口与就业	Population and Employment	
人口	Population	
出生率(‰)	Birth Rate(‰)	11.95
死亡率(‰)	Death Rate(‰)	4.98
自然增长率(‰)	Natural Growth Rate(‰)	6.79
就业	Employment	
就业者负担人口	Dependency Ratio	1.7
三次产业就业者比例	Employment Ratio by Type of Industry	
(以第一产业为100)	(Employment in primary industry=100)	
第一产业	Primary Industry	100
第二产业	Secondary Industry	71.5
第三产业	Tertiary Industry	71.4
城镇登记失业率(%)	Unemployment Rate in Urban Areas(%)	3.1
宏观经济	Macro Economy	
国民经济核算	National Accounting	
三次产业增加值比例	Ratio of Value-added by Type of Industry	
(以第一产业为100)	(Employment in primary industry=100)	
第一产业	Primary Industry	100
第二产业	Secondary Industry	326.9
第三产业	Tertiary Industry	371.1
全社会劳动生产率(元／人)	Overall Labor Productivity(yuan/person)	8963
第一产业	Primary Industry	2698
第二产业	Secondary Industry	12404
第三产业	Tertiary Industry	14488
人均生产总值(元)	Per Capita GDP(yuan)	5131
固定资产投资	Investment in Fixed Assets	
全社会固定资产投资相当于生产总值比例(%)	Proportion of Investment in fixed Assets to GDP(%)	31.3
房屋建筑面积竣工率(%)	Rate of Floor Space of Buildings Completed in Construction(%)	33.4
固定资产交付使用率(%)	Rate of Fixed Assets Completed in Capital Construction and Put into Use(%)	70.7
建设项目建成投产率(%)	Rate of Projects Completed in Capital Construction and Put into Use(%)	43.7
财政	Finance	
财政总收入相当于生产总值比例(%)	Proportion of Government Revenue to GDP(%)	5.5
一般公共预算支出相当于生产总值比例(%)	Proportion of Government General Public Budgeary Expenditures to GDP(%)	5.6
利用外资	Utilization of Foreign Capital	
外商实际直接投资额相当于利用外资协议金额比例(%)	Proportion of Foreign Capital Actually Used to Total Amount of Foreign Capital for Utilization by Signed Contracts or Agreements (%)	64.4

注：本表财政收入数据2009年及以前为一般预算财政收入和基金收入之和。

Proportions of National Economic and Social Development and Benefit Index in Representative Years

2000	2005	2007	2008	2009	2010	2011	2012	2013	2014	2015	2016
13.07	9.58	10.00	10.15	10.08	9.73	9.71	10.13	9.57	10.11	10.15	11.54
5.96	5.16	5.48	5.57	5.63	5.34	5.38	5.57	5.37	5.47	5.51	5.40
7.11	4.42	4.52	4.58	4.45	4.39	4.33	4.56	4.20	4.64	4.64	6.14
1.8	1.8	1.9	1.9	1.9	1.8	1.7	1.7	1.6	1.6	1.6	1.6
100	100	100	100	100	100	100	100	100	100	100	100
73.0	83.8	93.8	101.9	107.7	124.0	125.0	141.3	137.2	144.6	120.3	121.7
91.7	121.3	133.5	148.6	171.0	183.3	184.7	206.5	243.3	262.9	270.1	291.3
3.4	4.3	4.3	4.2	4.3	4.2	3.9	3.5	3.4	3.4	3.4	3.3
100	100	100	100	100	100	100	100	100	100	100	100
620.7	818.8	947.7	948.8	1037.1	969.3	914.4	910.6	997.2	1023.0	965.6	948.4
726.4	1071.7	1202.5	1192.0	1331.50	1246.1	1220.7	1236.2	1359.8	1437.1	1568.9	1659.5
16367	31837	43252	52422	59850	68990	79498	86971	94233	103281	109356	117736
2960	4747	6148	7921	8830	11701	14530	16578	17789	19915	20705	21805
25443	47853	64851	76899	87452	98027	106710	113561	127374	144703	151144	170975
24024	44024	56870	67031	73714	82377	96392	104914	107722	113188	121876	128977
9484	16406	22463	27794	32420	38357	45561	51499	57464	63794	66938	71647
36.0	65.8	81.4	82.2	91.8	100.2	86.5	96.6	104.3	107.5	89.1	82.6
42.0	28.1	29.0	16.9	16.0	6.9	10.0	8.7	13.2	11.4	6.8	9.9
74.0	52.8	49.8	40.5	42.8	38.4	40.4	42.4	37.1	42.5	40.3	38.3
44.2	54.2	40.6	53.3	72.5	53.9	54.9	56.1	56.1	62.5	61.0	64.6
7.3	6.6	7.1	10.9	14.7	15.7	16.8	17.1	18.3	18.6	19.2	18.1
8.0	8.1	9.9	14.5	10.2	11.5	12.8	13.6	14.8	14.9	15.8	15.0
28.9	47.0	77.5	97.1	203.0	130.9	167.0	68.8	124.3	145.0	207.0	441.2

1-13 续表1

指　　标	Item	1995
能　　源	**Energy**	
单位生产总值能耗降低率(%)	Decreasing Rate of Energy Consumption per Unit GDP(%)	
规模以上工业单位工业增加值能耗降低率(%)	Decreasing Rate of Energy Consumption per Unit Industrial value-added of Industry Above Designated Size(%)	
单位生产总值电耗降低率(%)	Decreasing Rate of Electricity Consumption per Unit GDP(%)	
产　　业	**Industries**	
农业	**Agriculture**	
农业从业者人均耕地面积(公顷)	Cultivated Land per Agricultural Laborer(hectare)	0.20
每公顷耕地农业机械总动力(千瓦)	Total Power of Agricultural Machinery per Hectare of Cultivated Land(kw)	5.23
每公顷耕地化肥施用量(公斤)	Chemical Fertilizer Consumption per Hectare of Cultivated Land(kg)	536
每公顷耕地生产的农业总产值(元)	Agricultural Output Value per Hectare of Cultivated Land(yuan)	24396
每个农林牧渔及服务业劳动力农产品生产量(公斤)	Output of Farm Products per Farming,Forestry,Animal Husbandry,Fishery and Service Husbandry and Fishery Laborer (kg)	
粮食	Grain	1150
蔬菜	Vegetables	877
禽蛋	Poultry Eggs	93
肉类	Meat	84
水产品	Aquatic Products	6
每公顷播种面积农产品产量(公斤)	Output of Farm Crops per Hectare of Sown Area(kg)	
粮食	Grain	3806
油料	Oil-bearing Crops	1753
蔬菜	Vegetables	34800
工业	**Industrial**	
规模以上工业企业经济效益	**Economic Benefit of Industrial Enterprises above Designated Size**	
总资产贡献率(%)	Ratio of Total Assets to Industrial Output Value (%)	
资产负债率(%)	Assets-Liability Ratio (%)	
流动资产周转次数（次/年）	Rate of Annual Turnover Working Capitals(times/year)	
成本费用利润率(%)	Ratio of Profits to Cost (%)	
产品销售率(%)	Proportion of Industrial Products Sold(%)	
全员劳动生产率（元/人）	Overall Labor Productivity (yuan/person)	
建筑业	**Construction**	
机械装备率(元／人)	Value of Machinery per Laborer(yuan/person)	5990
产值利润率(%)	Ratio of Per-tax Profits to Gross Output Value (%)	3.5
全员劳动生产率(元／人)(按总产值计算)	Overall Labor Productivity(yuan/person) (in terms of gross output value per employee)	37689
邮电通信业	**Post and Communication Services**	
电话普及率(含移动电话）(部/百人)	Access to Telephones, National(include mobilphone) (set/100 persons)	7.9
移动电话普及率(部/百人)	Access to Mobilphones (set/100 persons)	0.48

continued 1

2000	2005	2007	2008	2009	2010	2011	2012	2013	2014	2015	2016
		5.75	6.65	5.56	2.06	3.56	3.51	3.57	5.89	3.20	3.83
		12.56	13.43	10.48	12.18	15.44	10.56	17.69	15.21	19.48	
		6.94	6.93	5.33	1.00	4.43	2.92	2.26			
0.20	0.22	0.25	0.21	0.21	0.22	0.22	0.22	0.23	0.22	0.23	0.22
6.78	8.39	8.99	10.41	10.12	10.48	11.50	12.10	12.73	13.32	13.68	11.31
664	794	843	867	891	922	953	987	982	1045	1035	1050
25161	39937	51361	64593	69106	88869	108457	125041	140441	152695	160033	175446
1382	1493	1433	1695	1792	1901	1567	1700	1688	1592	1721	1668
1110	1421	1549	1752	1990	2171	2253	2452	2748	2867	3166	3203
95	86	74	86	96	106	108	115	125	123	133	134
101	132	77	91	104	117	124	134	145	147	153	149
8	7	9	10	11	10	10	12	13	13	14	13
4342	4796	4452	5102	5206	5349	4764	5045	4837	4777	5045	4983
1526	1821	1934	2008	1956	2004	1988	1987	1956	2097	2086	2087
37797	35231	33677	35723	38344	39667	40475	42607	44767	46713	48235	49037
	8.4	10.2	8.6	11.3	12.2	8.6	7.7	8.5	7.4	5.7	6.4
65	65.0	64.6	62.6	61.1	57.6	57.7	59.4	59.5	59.7	57.3	55.7
1.0	1.3	1.6	1.5	1.7	1.7	1.5	1.5	1.5	1.4	1.3	1.3
4.2	3.1	7.3	4.6	8.1	8.8	5.2	4.5	5.2	5.2	4.8	6.0
97.1	97.5	96.8	96.1	97.6	97.1	97.4	96.7	95.7	94.9	94.5	96.0
29496	82815	129706	150641	161289	188483	194105	230032	264324	275288	268182	277240
6805	13332	9079	12026	11928	9461	28669	12216	10339		12712	14193
3.4	4.8	5.2	6.0	6.3	4.4	4.4	2.8	2.6	2.3	2.3	3.1
74347	206337	203994	226669	285854	321340	334172	479232	354419	347000	406962	422421
31.2	100.0	117.9	124.7	167.1	199.0	221.3	247.2	288.7	270.3	236.5	229.1
10.62	56.62	80.02	88.09	132.79	168.00	189.58	210.87	251.59	234.75	203.0	197.0

1-13 续表2

指　　标	Item	1995
国内贸易	**Domestic Trade**	
人均批发零售和住宿餐饮业消费品零售额(元)	Per Capita Retail Sales of Wholesale,Retail Trade and Accommodation Catering Trade (yuan)	1979
对外经济贸易	**Foreign Trade**	
进出口总值相当于地区生产总值比例(%)	Proportion of Total Imports & Exports to GDP(%)	34.76
旅游	**International Tourism**	
每一游客花费(元)	Expenditure per Tourist (yuan)	556
金融业	**Finance and Insurance**	
金融机构存款相当于生产总值比例(%)	Bank Deposits as Percentage of GDP(%)	108.83
金融机构贷款相当于生产总值比例(%)	Bank Loans as Percentage of GDP(%)	101.26
教育、科技、文化	**Education, Science and Technology and Culture**	
教育	**Education**	
毕业率(%)	Graduation Rate(%)	
小学	Primary Schools	
初中	Junior Schools	
学校教师负担系数	Student-teacher Ratio(in percentage)	
高等学校	Colleges and Universities	6.83
中等学校	Secondary Schools	14.42
小学	Primary Schools	26.22
文化	**Culture (unit)**	
每百万人有艺术表演团体	Number of Troupes per Million Persons	3.39
每百万人有公共图书馆	Number of Public Libraries per Million Persons	2.31
家庭、生活、环境	**Family, People's Livelihood and Environment**	
家庭	**Family**	
城市居民家庭	Urban Households	
平均每户就业面(%)	Percentage of Employees Per Household (%)	55.9
平均每一劳动力负担人口（人）	Persons supported by Each Laborer (person)	1.8
农村居民家庭	Rural Households	
平均每一劳动力负担人口（人）	Persons supported by Each Laborer (person)	1.6
卫生	**Health Care**	
每万人医院数（个）	Number of Hospitals per 10 000 Persons(unit)	0.60
每万人医生数(人)	Number of Doctors per 10 000 Persons(person)	29.10
每万人医院床位数(张)	Number of Hospital Beds per 10 000 Persons(unit)	43.60
市政建设	**City Construction**	
城市自来水普及率(%)	Percentage of Households with Access to Tap Water(%)	
城市用气普及率(%)	Percentage of Households with Access to Tap Gas (%)	
人均公园绿地面积(平方米)	Public Green Areas per 10 000 Persons(hectare)	3.80

continued 2

2000	2005	2007	2008	2009	2010	2011	2012	2013	2014	2015	2016
4027	8795	10932	13840	16638	19848	24007	28132	32004	35943	39293	42545
22.25	24.79	22.21	21.97	18.16	21.22	20.52	18.61	22.27	27.89	30.37	29.13
645	737	761	753	757	767	797	820	801	792	789	809
206.71	283.41	259.80	264.31	273.69	273.32	267.47	274.09	277.48	274.26	304.82	301.74
150.51	169.91	152.16	149.22	162.81	198.00	193.71	194.77	201.63	210.76	234.52	241.29
					100.4	100.2	100.2	99.8	99.6	99.6	99.8
					99.7	100.6	98.7	99.3	99.9	98.3	98.7
12.38	17.99	16.97	17.13	17.32	17.41	17.92	18.15	18.05	18.27	17.76	17.62
17.84	18.47	19.99	18.97	18.27	17.78	16.91	16.43	15.07	14.01	13.88	25.7
25.75	20.38	18.61	17.99	17.32	17.22	18.06	17.15	17.66	18.94	19.94	11.98
3.20	2.56	2.16	2.15	2.13	1.53	3.52	2.22	2.10	2.09	2.07	2.04
2.18	2.02	1.81	1.79	1.78	1.77	1.76	1.75	1.75	1.74	1.49	1.47
45.7	47.4	47.8	47.9	53.2	53.7	54.8	54.0	54.6	54.5	50.4	48.7
2.2	2.1	2.1	2.1	1.9	1.9	1.8	1.9	1.8	1.3	1.3	1.3
1.6	1.6	1.6	1.5	1.5	1.5	1.5	1.5	1.5	1.4	1.4	1.4
0.57	0.59	0.55	0.52	0.49	0.49	0.43	0.44	0.44	0.44	0.45	0.44
25.30	21.98	20.79	21.57	22.86	22.14	25.31	26.95	27.81	28.77	30.58	31.55
38.72	37.29	37.11	39.40	41.38	43.42	43.77	47.45	51.45	54.56	58.98	60.02
98.95	99.00	100	111.22	100	98.77	99.95	100	100	100	100	100
81.51	91.30	98.60	97.66	98.15	97.02	97.46	98.19	98.68	98.71	98.79	98.89
5.12	5.63	7.61	7.80	7.90	9.11	9.89	10.22	10.70	11.22	11.47	11.61

1-14 主要年份平均每天主要社会经济活动

指　　标	Item	1995	2000
一、每天创造的财富	**Daily Production**		
生产总值(万元)	Gross Domestic Product(10 000 yuan)	9050.7	17702.2
第一产业	Primary Industry	1134.3	1223.3
第二产业	Secondary Industry	3707.7	7592.6
第三产业	Tertiary Industry	4208.8	8886.3
工业	Industry	3082.2	5984.7
建筑业	Construction	625.5	1608.0
批发和零售业	Wholesale and Retail Trade	909.6	1804.7
交通运输、仓储和邮政业	Transport, Storage, Post & Telecommunication Services	674.0	1178.4
住宿和餐饮业	Hotels and Catering Services		505.8
财政总收入(万元)	Total Government Revenue(10 000 yuan)	498.8	1304.0
财政一般公共预算支出(万元)	Government General Public Budgetary Expenditures(10 000 yuan)	504.7	1274.1
粮食(吨)	Grain(ton)	4801.0	5532.0
奶类(吨)	Milk(ton)	364	674
蔬菜(吨)	Vegetables(ton)	3660	4442
肉类(吨)	Meat(ton)	350	404
水产品(吨)	Aquatic Products(ton)	23	31
布(万米)	Cloth(10 000 m)	83	77
发电量(万千瓦小时)	Electricity(10 000 kwh)	610	534
钢材(吨)	Steel(ton)	861	274
汽车(辆)	Motor Vehicle(unit)	8	25
二、每天消费量	**Daily National Consumption**		
最终消费(万元)	Final Consumption Expenditure(10 000 yuan)	6565.5	11326.9
社会消费品零售总额(万元)	Total Retail Sales of Consumer Goods (10 000 yuan)	5112.3	9874.5
三、每天其他经济活动	**Other Daily Economic Activities**		
资本形成总额(万元)	Gross Capital Formation(10 000 yuan)	4152.1	7885.5
固定资本形成	Fixed Capital Formation		
存货增加	Changes in Stock		
竣工住宅面积(平方米)	Floor Space of Buildings Completed (sq.m)	6927	14930
货运量(万吨)	Freight Traffic(10 000 tons)	26.3	19.2
客运量(万人次)	Passenger Traffic(10 000 person-times)	24.8	22.1
邮电业务总量(万元)	Business Volume of Postal and Telecommunications Services(10 000 yuan)	209.6	1264.7
进出口总值(万美元)	Total Value of Imports and Exports (USD 10 000)	110.2	475.9
出口值	Exports	82.5	290.6
进口值	Imports	27.7	185.3
外商实际直接投资额(万美元)	Foreign Capital Actually Used(USD 10 000)	51.1	42.8
旅游者人数（人次）	Number of Tourists (person-time)	21681	42932
四、每天人口变动和婚姻	**Daily Population Changes and Marriages**		
出 生(人)	Births(person)	211	247
死 亡(人)	Deaths(person)	88	113
结 婚(对)	Marriages(couple)	129	129
离 婚(对)	Divorces(couple)	12	14

注：本表财政收入数据2009年及以前为一般预算财政收入和基金收入之和。

Major Social and Economic Activities Per Day in Representative Years

2005	2008	2009	2010	2011	2012	2013	2014	2015	2016
35998.1	63510.7	74654.2	88845.5	106023.0	120396.4	134930.7	150483.3	158937.0	172127.4
1808.5	2834.3	3024.1	3837.3	4743.6	5358.6	5491.8	5878.1	6032.9	6356.4
14808.2	26892.6	31363.0	37192.6	43375.6	48797.0	54762.2	60131.0	58254.5	60283.8
19381.4	33783.8	40267.1	47815.6	57903.8	66240.8	74676.7	84474.2	94649.6	105487.1
11506.9	19764.4	22381.6	26147.7	30095.9	33644.9	37718.9	40767.7	37718.4	38280.8
3301.4	7128.2	8981.6	11045.2	13279.5	15151.8	17596.2	19965.5	21103.8	22433.4
4032.9	6655.1	8172.3	9654.0	12047.9	14053.7	15773.2	17360.3	18301.1	19241.1
1816.4	2716.7	3069.0	3717.8	4525.5	5272.9	5893.4	6454.2	7132.3	8178.6
1381.9	2346.6	2570.4	2816.4	3233.4	3550.1	3714.5	3949.3	4360.0	4675.9
2300.6	6417.8	9080.0	13991.5	17805.0	20632.1	24733.3	27936.7	30547.4	31114.5
2819.6	8679.2	11509.0	10181.4	13550.0	16369.6	19994.8	22453.2	25129.9	25822.5
5631	5874	5978	6074	4987	5275	5017	4811	4955	4804
1157	1616	1694	1736	1775	1826	1802	1803	1746	1540
5362	6069	6641	6934	7169	7611	8168	8665	9118	9226
499	316	346	374	396	416	431	444	442	430
26	34	36	33	32	38	39	39	39	37
74.0	62.3	60.8	65.2	44.8	39.1	38.0	33.0	28.5	33.4
1316.3	1964.1	2279.7	2655.9	2603.0	2725.5	5055	4920	4347	4411
658	1312	3028	3035	506	857	1488	1175	1015	1203
112	734	1389	1787	1525	1484	1156	1027	935	1048
21003.3	32400.3	38441.1	43794.8	50874.2	57341.6				
18371.5	32235.1	37838.9	44850.4	53862.5	62023.6	75147.7	84764.1	93298.1	102211.0
22986.6	50352.3	62518.1	77682.7	89447.4	103646.6				
20918.4	45315.3	58878.9	72237.8	83395.6	97509.0				
2068.2	5037.0	3639.2	5444.9	6051.8	6137.5				
16400	18998	22537	12287	23601	24762	23014	40078	22632	36472
33.0	75.5	83.9	94.0	107.5	123.1	137.3	115.2	126.8	65.4
28.7	72.6	78.6	83.0	91.4	99.1	104.9	70.5	73.7	64.9
3617.7	7256.4	8189.6	8852.3	5494.8	5923.6	6793.0	8016.4	9083.1	10496.2
1068.9	1928.9	1985.3	2847.3	3452.5	3565.6	4927.5	6833.5	7749.3	7547.9
721.8	1225.0	912.6	1456.8	1596.3	1999.7	2322.8	3276.7	3606.4	3907.3
347.1	703.9	1072.6	1390.5	1856.2	1565.9	2604.7	3556.8	4142.8	3640.6
156.5	314.4	333.9	429.2	549.4	678.9	857.5	1014.5	1098.2	1234.2
66400	88553	107652	144799	182280	218585	277534	328767	372625	411303
210	232	232	225	226	237	225	238	241	277
63	127	130	124	125	130	126	129	131	130
137	213	241	229	259	246	244	250	221	212
35	43	43	52	53	51	56	60	62	70

1-15 各区县国民经济和社会发展主要指标（2016年）

指 标	Item	新城区 Xincheng	碑林区 Beilin
一、年底总人口（常住人口）（万人）	Population at the Year-end Permanent population(10 000 persons)	60.91	63.87
二、生产总值（亿元）	Gross Domestic Product(100 mil. yuan)	540.66	741.68
第一产业	Primary Industry		
第二产业	Secondary Industry	192.05	151.36
第三产业	Tertiary Industry	348.61	590.32
三、全社会固定资产投资总额（亿元）	Total Investment in Fixed Assets(100 mil. yuan)	253.71	207.57
固定资产投资（不含农户）	Investment in Fixed Assets (excluding farmers)	253.71	207.57
#房地产开发投资	Real Estate	87.46	132.81
四、财政一般公共预算收入（亿元）	General Public Budgetary Revenue(100 mil. yuan)	36.48	45.01
财政一般公共预算支出（亿元）	General Public Budgetary Expenditure(100 mil. yuan)	37.70	35.86
五、农林牧渔及服务业总产值（万元）	Gross Output Value of Farming Forestry Animal Husbandry and Fishery(10 000 yuan)		
主要农产品产量（万吨）	Output of Major Farm Products(10 000 tons)		
粮食	Grain		
蔬菜	Vegetables		
瓜果	Melon and Fruit		
肉类(吨)	Meat (Ton)		
奶类(吨)	Milk (Ton)		
六、规模以上工业总产值（亿元）	Gross industrial Output Value(100 mil. yuan)	401.62	31.91
七、建筑业	Construction		
房屋建筑施工面积（万平方米）	Floor Space of Buildings under Construction (10 000 sq.m)	1221.74	3621.7
房屋建筑竣工面积（万平方米）	Total Retail Sales of Consumer Goods (100 mil. yuan)	293.76	660.97
八、社会消费品零售总额（亿元）	Floor Space of Buildings Completed(100 mil. yuan)	607.98	610.53
九、城镇居民人均可支配收入（元）	Per Capita Annual Disposable Income of Urban Households (yuan)	37212	37539
农村居民人均可支配收入（元）	Per Capita Disposable Income of Rural Households (yuan)		
十、医疗机构数（个）	Number of Health Care Institutions(unit)	268	383
卫生技术人员（人）	Number of Medical Technical Personnel (person)	11343	12261
床位数（张）	Number of Beds(unit)	7065	8119

Major Indicators of National Economy and Social Development by Region（2016）

莲湖区 Lianhu	灞桥区 Baqiao	未央区 Weiyang	雁塔区 Yanta	阎良区 Yanliang	临潼区 Lintong	长安区 Chang'an	高陵区 Gaoling	蓝田县 Lantian	周至县 Zhouzhi	户　县 Huxian
72.23	62.73	85.08	123.11	29.08	68.18	114.11	35.11	52.86	58.5	57.44
621.91	329.78	772.88	1235.43	193.94	183.11	608.02	300.24	122.44	114.99	162.81
	19.73	1.06		22.56	30.59	38.47	30.23	27.59	33.17	28.59
194.55	117.98	379.68	338.05	102.39	59.25	332.60	205.14	34.87	26.08	63.80
427.36	192.07	392.14	897.38	68.99	93.27	236.95	64.87	59.98	55.74	70.42
225.14	581.06	983.64	892.79	158.35	141.75	738.02	459.53	264.37	159.99	125.44
225.14	574.87	979.67	892.79	154.68	129.01	724.18	456.42	251.78	132.33	114.85
159.7	247.61	503.68	566.26	18.49	29.93	156.44	25.79	5.63	9.77	12.25
48.18	46.51	21.99	32.63	12.76	14.91	35.50	12.02	4.29	3.65	9.41
43.71	35.11	27.22	31.80	23.07	38.42	61.26	23.23	35.62	38.04	40.29
	327061	20405		381618	569391	621269	555928	492519	572627	515503
	5.26	0.08		8.68	31.69	33.24	18.78	25.57	22.26	29.77
	30.03	1.93		80.34	45.03	58.99	50.32	18.26	21.87	29.98
	1.34	0.08		24.6	7.36	8.45	3.46	4.07	0.50	5.35
	7327	3060		7441	43252	20416	11198	19322	26482	18331
	30802	3021		102581	269013	34977	48887	41429	13564	17764
405.48	181.17	959.84	648.80	342.53	204.22	956.32	835.74	55.47	53.84	189.31
1588.44	96.15	2140.66	2676.52	54.46	51.43	150.62	109.24	47.66	73.52	113.59
337.07	30.74	230.3	387.3	9.48	18.18	51.75	67.68	29.2	45.52	71.25
491.72	200.82	566.17	714.37	41.22	84.66	202.49	36.04	62.08	42.64	69.98
37425	36784	37085	37631	36931	30753	34627	29464	26321	26899	27970
	20431	21294		20262	16389	16741	16431	12082	12207	14638
350	448	406	491	172	541	814	210	624	549	613
11071	4056	8267	15300	2133	2816	7195	2676	2291	2672	4177
7213	2825	4948	8885	1438	2524	5592	1702	1525	1470	3026

主要统计指标解释

行政区划 指国家对行政区域的划分。根据有关法规规定，我国的行政区域划分如下：（1）全国分为省、自治区、直辖市；（2）省、自治区分为自治州、县、自治县、市；（3）自治州分为县、自治县、市；（4）县、自治县分为乡、民族乡、镇；（5）直辖市和较大的市分为区、县；（6）国家在必要时设立的特别行政区。

气候 指地球与大气之间长期能量交换与质量交换所形成的一种自然环境状态，它是多种因素综合作用的结果。气候既是人类生活和生产的环境要素之一，又是供给人类生活和生产的重要资源。气温、降水、湿度等气象要素的多年平均值是用来描述一个地区气候状况的主要参数，而各种气象要素某年、某月的平均值（或总量）则可以反映出该时期天气气候状况的重要特征。

自然资源 指人类可以直接从自然界获得，并用于生产和生活的物质资源。自然资源一般可以分成可再生资源和非再生资源两大类。可再生资源指在较短时间内可以再生、可以循环利用的资源，包括土地资源、水资源、气候资源、生物资源和海洋资源等。非再生资源指在使用后不能再生的资源，包括矿产资源和地热能源。

土地资源 土地指陆地的表层部分，它主要由岩石、岩石的风化物和土壤构成。土地资源按利用类型可以分为农用地、建筑用地和未利用地。农用地包括耕地、园地、林地、牧草地和水面。建筑用地包括居民点及工矿用地、交通用地和水利设施用地。未利用地指农用地和建筑用地以外的土地，包括滩涂、荒漠、戈壁、冰川和石山等。

耕地面积 指经过开垦用以种植农作物并经常进行耕耘的土地面积。包括种有作物的土地面积、休闲地、新开荒地和抛荒未满三年的土地面积。

森林面积 指由乔木树种构成，郁闭度0.2以上（含0.2）的林地或冠幅宽度10米以上的林带的面积，即有林地面积。森林面积包括天然起源和人工起源的针叶林面积、阔叶林面积、针阔混交林面积和竹林面积，不包括灌木林地面积和疏林地面积。

林业用地面积 指生长乔木、竹类、灌木、沿海红树林等林木的土地面积，包括有林地、灌木林、疏林地、未成林造林地、迹地、苗圃等。

水资源总量 指评价区内降水形成的地表和地下产水总量，即地表产流量与降水入渗补给地下水量之和，不包括过境水量。

地表水资源量 指评价区内河流、湖泊、冰川等地表水体中可以逐年更新的动态水量，即当地天然河川径流量。

地下水资源量 指评价区内降水和地表水对饱水岩土层的补给量，包括降水入渗补给量和河道、湖库、渠系、渠灌田间等地表水体的入渗补给量。

气温 指空气的温度，我国一般以摄氏度（℃）为单位表示。气象观测的温度表是放在离地面约1.5米处通风良好的百叶箱里测量的，因此，通常说的气温指的是离地面1.5米处百叶箱中的温度。其统计计算方法为：

月平均气温是将全月各日的平均气温相加，除以该月的天数而得。

年平均气温是将12个月的月平均气温累加后除以12而得。

降水量 指从天空降落到地面的液态或固态（经融化后）水，未经蒸发、渗透、流失而在地面上积聚的深度。其统计计算方法为：

月降水量是将全月各日的降水量累加而得。

年降水量是将12个月的月降水量累加而得。

日照时数 指太阳实际照射地面的时间。其统计方法与降水量相同。

平均增长速度 平均增长速度表明社会经济现象在一个较长的时期内逐期平均增长变化的程度，它不能根据各个环比增长速度直接求得，但与平均发展速度之间存在着一定的数量关系：平均增长速度 = 平均发展速度 - 1。

平均发展速度 是一种根据环比发展速度计算的序时平均数,由于各时期对比的基础不同，所以计算平均发展速度不能采用一般的序时平均数的计算方法，计算方法分为水平法和累计法。水平法，又称几何平均法，即将环比发展速度按连乘法用几何平均数公式计算。累计法，也称方程法，根据一段时期内各年发展水平总和与基期水平的关系，列出方程式计算平均发展速度。水平法着重考虑最后一年所达到的发展水平；累计法着重考虑整个时期累计发展水平的总量。

本《年鉴》内所列的平均增长速度，均用“水平法”计算。从某年到某年平均增长速度的年份，均不包括基期年在内。如建国六十年以来的平均增长速度是以1949年为基期计算的，则写为1950-2009年平均增长速度，其余类推。

Explanatory Notes on Main Statistical Indicators

Divisions of Administrative Areas refers to the division of administrative areas by the State. The relative laws stipulate that (1)the whole country is divided into provinces, autonomous regions and municipalities directly under the Central Government;(2)provinces and autonomous regions are further divided into autonomous prefectures, counties, autonomous counties and cities; (3)autonomous prefectures are further divided into counties, autonomous counties and cities; (4)counties and autonomous counties are further divided into townships, ethnic townships and towns; (5)municipalities directly under the Central Government and large cities are divided into districts and counties, (6)the State shall, when necessary, establish special administrative regions.

Climate refers to the natural environmental status formed by the long-term exchange of energy and mass between the earth and the atmosphere, and is the result of interaction of many factors. Climate is both one of the environment factors and also the important resources for living and production activities of the human being. The average values across several years of meteorological factors such as temperature, rainfall and humidity are used as important parameters to describe the climate of a region, while the average values (or total values)of a given year or month of meteorological factors reflect the key characteristics of climate for that period of time.

Natural Resources refer to material resources that could be obtained from the nature by human being and used for production and living. Natural resources in general can be classified as renewable resources and non-renewable resources. Renewable resources refer to resources that could be renewed and recycled during a relatively short period of time, including land resource, water resource, climate resource, biology resource and marine resource. Non-renewable resources include resources that could not be renewed, such as minerals and geothermal resource.

Land Resource Land refers to the surface of the earth, consisting of mainly rocks and its whethering and earth. Land resource can be classified, by its utilization, as land for agriculture, land for construction and unused land. Land for agriculture includes cultivated land, plantation land, forestland, grassland and waters. Land for construction includes land for residential purpose, for manufacturing and mining, for transportation and for water-conservancy projects. Unused land refers to land other than land for agriculture and.construction, including beaches, deserts, Gobi, glaciers and rock mountains.

Area of Cultivated Land refers to area of land reclaimed for the regular cultivation of various farm crops, including crop-cover land, fallow, newly reclaimed land and land laid idle for less than 3 years.

Forest Area refers to the area of trees and bamboo grow with canopy density above 0.2, the area of shrubby tree according to regulations of the government, the area of forest land inside farm land and the area of trees planted by the side of villages, farm houses and along roads and rivers.

Area of Afforested Land refers to area for land for trees bamboo, bushes and mangrove, including forest-covered land, bush-covered land, sparse forest land, land planned for afforestation and nurseries of young trees.

Total Water Resources refers to total volume of water resources measured as run-off for surface water from rainfall and recharge for groundwater in a given area, excluding transit water.

Surface Water Resources refers to total renewable resources which exist in rivers, lakes, glaciers and other collectors from rainfall and are measured as run-off of rivers.

Groundwater Resources refers to replenishment of aquifers with rainfall and surface water.

Temperature refers to the air temperature. China uses centigrade as the unit. The thermometry used for weather observation is put in a breezy shutter, which is 1.5 meters high from the ground. Therefore, the commonly used temperature refers to the temperature in the breezy shutter 1.5 meters away from the ground. The calculation method is as follows:

Monthly average temperature is the summation of average daily temperature of one month divided by the actual days of that particular month.

Annual average temperature is the summation of monthly average of a year divided by 12 months.

Volume of Precipitation refers to the deepness of liquid state or solid state (thawed)water falling from the sky to the ground that has not been evaporated, infiltrated or run off. The calculation method is as follows:

Monthly precipitation is the summation of daily precipitation of a month.

Annual precipitation is the summation of 12 months precipitation of a year.

Sunshine Hours refer to the actual hours of sun irradiating the earth. The calculation method is the same as that of the precipitation.

Average Annual Growth Rate shows the average growth rate of social and economic development during a longer period. It can not be directly calculated by chain based growth rate. The relation is:

Average Annual Growth Rate=Average Speed of Development 1

Average speed of development is the time series average of speed which calculated by chain based.Because the reference bases during the different periods are not same, average speed of development can not be calculated by the general method. Level approach and accumulative approach for calculating average speed of development rate are applied. The "level approach" , or the method of calculating the geometric average, is derived by the formula of geometric average of the chain-based speeds of development, or comparing the level of the last year of the interval with that of the beginning year; the other is called the "accumulative approach" or the "algebraic average" , "equation" method, which is derived by the summation of the actual figure of each year in the interval divided by the figure in the base year. The level approach focuses on the level of the last year, while the accumulative approach emphasizes the aggregate development in the duration.

The average annual growth rates listed in the Yearbook are calculated by the level approach except for the growth rate of investment in fixed assets. The base year is not listed in the duration for which average annual growth rates are computed. For instance, the average annual growth rate of the 60 years since 1949 is shown as the average annual growth rate of 1950-2009 without showing the base year 1949.

2 基本单位

BASIC UNIT

资料整理：张　奇　张　斌
Data management：Zhang Qi　Zhang Bin
数据审核：张利民
Data audit：Zhang Limin

第二部分 基本单位

一、简要说明

本章资料主要包括法人单位、产业活动单位和企业一套表调查单位数等资料，由西安市统计局普查中心提供。本年统计年鉴一套表单位数为年报数，使用时请注意。

二、主要指标

法人单位数（个）	130291	比上年增长	6.2%
产业活动单位数（个）	142442	比上年增长	5.3%
规模以上工业企业数（个）	1186	比上年增长	6.2%
限额以上批发零售住宿餐饮业企业数（个）	1582	比上年增长	15.2%
资质内建筑业企业数（个）	893	比上年增长	26.5%
房地产开发经营企业数（个）	923	比上年增长	7.5%
规模以上服务业企业数（个）	1229	比上年增长	16.4%

2 BASIC UNIT

Ⅰ.Brief Introduction

This chapter consists of unified data of enterprises and industrial active unites and investigation unit in “Enterprises Data in One sheet”, provided by census center of Xi’an Municipal Bureau of statistics . Data of “Enterprises Data in One Sheet” in this Yearbook is the number of annual reports, please note that when used.

Ⅱ.Major Indicators

		Increase over Preceding Year
Number of Enterprises (unit)	130291	6.2%
Number of Industrial Active Units (unit)	142442	5.3%
Number of Industrial Enterprises above Designed Size (unit)	1186	6.2%
Number of Enterprises about Wholesale、Retail、Accommodation and Catering above Designed Size (unit)	1582	15.2%
Number of Qualified Construction Enterprises (unit)	893	26.5%
Number of Real Estate Development Enterprises (unit)	923	7.5%
Number of service Enterprises above Designed Size (unit)	1229	16.4%

2-1 按登记注册类型分法人单位数（2016年）

Impersonal Entities by Status of Registion（2016）

单位：个 (unit)

分 组	Classify	法人单位数 Number of Enterprises	企业 Enterprises
总 计	**Total**	**130291**	**113335**
#非公有制企业法人	Non-public corporate	107449	107449
按登记注册类型分	**Grouped by Status of Registion**		
（一）内资	Domestic Funded Enterprises	129387	112439
国有	State-owned Enterprises	7075	1654
集体	Collective-owned Enterprises	2658	1513
股份合作	Cooperative Enterprises	329	310
联营	Joint Ownership Enterprises	231	194
国有联营	State Joint Ownership Enterprises	30	23
集体联营	Collective Joint Ownership Enterprises	119	113
国有与集体联营	Joint State-collective Ownership Enterprises	16	10
其他联营	Other Joint Ownership Enterprises	66	48
有限责任公司	Limited Liability Corporations	45839	45720
国有独资公司	State Sole Funded Corporations	313	312
其他有限责任公司	Other Limited Liability Corporations	45526	45408
股份有限公司	Share-holding Corporations Limited	1142	1134
私营	Private Enterprises	57492	57217
私营独资企业	Private-funded Enterprises	12450	12263
私营合伙	Private Partnership Enterprises	1543	1501
私营有限责任公司	Private Limited Liability Corporations	42205	42161
私营股份有限公司	Private Share-holding Corporations Ltd.	1294	1292
其他	Other Domestic Funded Enterprises	14621	4697
（二）港、澳、台商投资企业	Enterprises with Funds from Hong Kong, Macao and Taiwan	292	291
与港、澳、台商合资经营	Joint-venture with Funds from Hong Kong,Macao and Taiwan	110	110
与港、澳、台商合作经营	Cooperative Enterprises with Funds from Hong Kong Macau and Taiwan	12	11
港澳台商独资经营	Enterprises with Sole Investment from Hong Kong Macau and Taiwan	150	150
港澳台商投资股份有限公司	Share-holding Corporations Ltd. with funds from Hong Kong, Macao & Taiwan	18	18
其他港澳台商投资	Other Enterprises with Funds from Hong Kong, Macao and Taiwan	2	2
（三）外商投资	Foreign Funded Enterprises	612	605
中外合资经营	Sino-foreign Joint Ventures	225	224
中外合作经营	Sino-Foreign Cooperation Enterprises	12	11
外资企业	Foreign Owned Enterprises	317	313
外商投资股份有限公司	Limited Company Funded by Foreign Investment	32	32
其他外商投资	Other Foreign Funded Enterprises	26	25

2-2 按国民经济行业分法人单位数（2016年）

Impersonal Entities by Industry of the National Economy（2016）

单位：个 (unit)

分 组	Classify	法人单位数 Number of Enterprises	企业 Enterprises
总 计	**Total**	**130291**	**113335**
（一）农、林、牧、渔业	Agriculture,Forestry,Animal Husbandry and Fishery	4416	2854
农业	Farming	2218	1307
林业	Forestry	552	424
畜牧业	Animal Husbandry	1227	861
渔业	Fishery	75	59
农、林、牧、渔服务业	Services in Support of Agriculture	344	203
（二）采矿业	Mining	259	259
煤炭开采和洗选业	Mining and Washing of Coal	7	7
石油和天然气开采业	Extraction of Petroleum and Natural Gas	25	25
黑色金属矿采选业	Mining of Ferrous Metal Ores	12	12
有色金属矿采选业	Mining of Non-ferrous Metal Ores	23	23
非金属矿采选业	Mining and Processing of Nonmetal Ores	79	79
开采辅助活动	Mining of Other Ores	89	89
其他采矿业	Manufacturing	24	24
（三）制造业	Processing of Food from Agricultural Products	14932	14919
农副食品加工业	Manufacture of Foods	480	476
食品制造业	Manufacture of Beverages	474	473
酒、饮料和精制茶制造业	Manufacture of Tobacco	146	146
烟草制品业	Manufacture of Textile	2	2
纺织业	Manufacture of Textile Wearing Apparel, Footware and Caps	158	158
纺织服装、服饰业	Manufacture of Leather, Fur, Feather and Related Products	141	140
皮革、毛皮、羽毛及其制品和制鞋业	Processing of Timber,Manufacture of Wood, Bamboo,Rattan, its Froducts and Footwear	35	34
木材加工和木、竹、藤、棕、草制品业	Plam and Straw Products and Straw Products	212	212
家具制造业	Manufacture of Furniture	435	435
造纸及纸制品业	Manufacture of Paper and Paper Products	337	337
印刷和记录媒介复制业	Printing,Reproduction of Recording Media	561	561
文教、工美、体育和娱乐用品制造业	Manufacture of Articles For Culture, Education and Sport Activities	215	215

2-2 续表1 continued 1

单位：个 (unit)

分　组	Classify	法人单位数 Number of Enterprises	企业 Enterprises
石油加工、炼焦和核燃料加工业	Processing of Petroleum, Coking, Processing of Nuclear Fuel	53	53
化学原料和化学制品制造业	Manufacture of Raw Chemical Materials and Chemical Products	734	734
医药制造业	Manufacture of Medicines	364	364
化学纤维制造业	Manufacture of Chemical Fibers	27	27
橡胶和塑料制品业	Manufacture of Rubber and Manufacture of Plastics	491	491
非金属矿物制品业	Manufacture of Non-metallic Mineral Products	1366	1366
黑色金属冶炼和压延加工业	Smelting and Pressing of Ferrous Metals	245	245
有色金属冶炼和压延加工业	Smelting and Pressing of Non-ferrous Metals	196	196
金属制品业	Manufacture of Metal Products	1044	1044
通用设备制造业	Manufacture of General Purpose Machinery	1928	1928
专用设备制造业	Manufacture of Special Equipment	1533	1528
汽车制造业	Manufacture of Motor Vehicle	186	186
铁路、船舶、航空航天和其他运输设备制造业	Railways,Shipbuilding,Aerospace and Other Transportation Equipment Manufacturing Industry	330	330
电气机械和器材制造业	Manufacture of Electric Equipment and Machinery	1433	1433
计算机、通信和其他电子设备制造业	Manufacture of Communication Equipment, Computers and other Electronic Equipment	838	838
仪器仪表制造业	Manufacture of Measuring Instruments and Machinery	583	583
其他制造业	Other Manufacturing	150	150
废弃资源综合利用	Recycling and Disposal of Waste	54	54
金属制品、机械和设备修理业	Metal Products,Machinery and Equipment Repair Industry	181	180
（四）电力、燃气及水的生产供应业	Production and Distribution of Electricity,Gas and Water	344	343
电力、热力生产和供应业	Production and Supply of Electric Power and Heat Power	204	204
燃气生产和供应业	Gas mining and supplying industry	45	45
水的生产和供应业	Production and Supply of Water	95	94
（五）建筑业	Construction	10112	10112
房屋建筑业	Construction of Building	1885	1885
土木工程建筑业	Civil Engineering	2004	2004
建筑安装业	Architectural Installation	1780	1780
建筑装饰和其他建筑业	Architectural Decoration and Other Construction	4443	4443
（六）批发和零售业	Wholesale and Retail Trades	42307	42235

2-2 续表2 continued 2

单位：个 (unit)

分 组	Classify	法人单位数 Number of Enterprises	企业 Enterprises
批发业	Wholesale Trade	23520	23481
零售业	Retail Trade	18787	18754
（七）交通运输、仓储和邮政业	Traffic, Transport, Storage and Post	2368	2315
铁路运输业	Transport Via Railway	30	26
道路运输业	Transport Via Road	1288	1258
水上运输业	Water Transport	3	3
航空运输业	Air Transport	65	64
管道运输业	Transport Via Pipeline	8	8
装卸搬运和运输代理服务业	Loading, Unloading, Portage and Other Transport Services	539	537
仓储业	Storage	327	314
邮政业	Post	108	105
（八）住宿和餐饮业	Hotels and Catering Services	3613	3605
住宿业	Hotels	1382	1378
餐饮业	Catering Services	2231	2227
（九）信息传输、软件和信息技术服务业	Information Transmission, Computer Services and Software	5615	5591
电信、广播电视和卫星传输服务	Telecom & Other Information Transmission Services	238	234
互联网和相关服务	internet and relevant services	783	779
软件和信息技术服务	Software Industry	4594	4578
（十）金融业	Financial Intermediation	785	772
货币金融服务	Monetary and Financial Services	190	186
资本市场服务	Capital Market Services	333	331
保险业	Insurance	162	159
其他金融业	Other Financial Intermediation	100	96
（十一）房地产业	Real Estate	6801	6781
房地产业	Real Estate	6801	6781
（十二） 租赁和商务服务业	Leasing and Business Services	12578	12270
租赁业	Leasing	964	961
商务服务业	Business Services	11614	11309
（十三）科学研究和技术服务业	Scientific Research, Technical Sevice	5368	4769
研究与试验发展	Research and Experimental Development	559	471
专业技术服务业	Professional Technical Services	3589	3290

2-2 续表3 continued 3

单位：个 (unit)

分 组	Classify	法人单位数 Number of Enterprises	企业 Enterprises
科技推广和应用服务业	Services of Science and Technology Exchanges and Promotion	1220	1008
（十四）水利、环境和公共设施管理业	Management of Water Conservancy, Environment and Public Facilities	1065	863
水利管理业	Management of Water Conservancy	167	80
生态保护和环境治理业	Environmental Management	126	99
公共设施管理业	Management of Public Facilities	772	684
（十五）居民服务、修理和其他服务业	Services to Households and Other Services	2883	2820
居民服务业	Services to Households	975	920
机动车、电子产品和日用产品修理业	The repair service industry for motor vehicle、electronic	1188	1185
其他服务业	Other Services	720	715
（十六）教育	Education	3736	464
教育	Education	3736	464
（十七）卫生和社会工作	Health, Social Security	3295	283
卫生	Health	3078	260
社会工作	Social	217	23
（十八）文化、体育和娱乐业	Culture, Sports and Entertainment	2390	2074
新闻和出版业	Journalism and Publishing Activities	178	130
广播、电视、电影和影视录音制作业	Broadcasting, Movies, Television and Audiovisual Activities	398	382
文化艺术业	Cultural and Art Activities	727	523
体育	Sports Activities	189	154
娱乐业	Entertainment	898	885
（十九）公共管理、社会保障和社会组织	Public Management and Social Organizaion	7424	6
中国共产党机关	Organs of Communist Party of China	158	
国家机构	Government Agencies	2097	
人民政协、民主党派	People's Pc~litical Consultative Conference and Democratic Parties	32	
社会保障	Social Security	67	6
群众团体、社会团体和其他成员组织	Mass organizations、social groups and other members of the organization	1351	
基层群众自治组织	Grass-roots Mass Self-Government Organizations	3719	
（二十）国际组织	International Organizations		
国际组织	International Organizations		

2–3 按行政区划分法人单位数（2016年）

Impersonal Entities by Region（2016）

单位：个 (unit)

区 县	Region	法人单位数 Number of Enterprises	企业 Enterprises
总 计	**Total**	**130291**	**113335**
新城区	Xincheng	8686	7779
碑林区	Beilin	14273	13257
莲湖区	Lianhu	12896	11950
灞桥区	Baqiao	5035	4072
未央区	Weiyang	22100	21108
雁塔区	Yanta	33373	32319
阎良区	Yanliang	3053	2457
临潼区	Lintong	4686	2952
长安区	Chang'an	9017	6796
高陵区	Gaoling	3689	2794
蓝田县	Lantian	4376	2558
周至县	Zhouzhi	3660	1946
户 县	Huxian	5447	3347

2-4 按登记注册类型分产业活动单位数（2016年）

Industrial Active Units by Status of Registion（2016）

单位：个 (unit)

分 组	Classify	产业活动单位数 Number of Industrial Active Units	企业 Enterprises
总计	**Total**	**142442**	**122682**
按登记注册类型分	Grouped by Status of Registion		
（一）内资	Domestic Funded Enterprises	140810	121058
国有	State-owned Enterprises	10327	2780
集体	Collective-owned Enterprises	3333	1886
股份合作	Cooperative Enterprises	556	535
联营	Joint Ownership Enterprises	324	280
国有联营	State Joint Ownership Enterprises	51	44
集体联营	Collective Joint Ownership Enterprises	152	142
国有与集体联营	Joint State-collective Ownership Enterprises	26	18
其他联营	Other Joint Ownership Enterprises	95	76
有限责任公司	Limited Liability Corporations	49174	49049
国有独资公司	State Sole Funded Corporations	336	335
其他有限责任公司	Other Limited Liability Corporations	48838	48714
股份有限公司	Share-holding Corporations Limited	2319	2311
私营	Private Enterprises	59582	59295
私营独资企业	Private-funded Enterprises	12894	12700
私营合伙	Private Partnership Enterprises	1632	1588
私营有限责任公司	Private Limited Liability Corporations	43671	43624
私营股份有限公司	Private Share-holding Corporations Ltd.	1385	1383
其他	Other Enterprises	15195	4922

2-4 续表 continued

单位：个 (unit)

分 组	Classify	产业活动单位数 Number of Industrial Active Units	企业 Enterprises
（二）港、澳、台商投资企业	Enterprises with Funds from Hong Kong,Macao and Taiwan	498	497
与港、澳、台商合资经营	Joint-venture with Funds from Hong Kong,Macao and Taiwan	137	137
与港、澳、台商合作经营	Cooperative Enterprises with Funds from Hong Kong Macau and Taiwan	23	22
港澳台商独资经营	Enterprises with Sole Investment from Hong Kong Macau and Taiwan	306	306
港澳台商投资股份有限公司	Share-holding Corporations Ltd. with funds from Hong Kong, Macao & Taiwan	24	24
其他港澳台商投资	Other Enterprises with Funds from Hong Kong,Macao and Taiwan	8	8
（三）外商投资	Foreign Funded Enterprises	1134	1127
中外合资经营	Sino-foreign Joint Ventures	332	331
中外合作经营	Sino-Foreign Cooperation Enterprises	23	22
外资企业	Foreign Owned Enterprises	589	585
外商投资股份有限公司	Limited Company Funded by Foreign Investment	123	123
其他外商投资	Other Foreign Funded Enterprises	67	66

2-5 按国民经济行业分产业活动单位数（2016年）

Industrial Active Units by Industry of the National Economy（2016）

单位：个 (unit)

分 组	Classify	产业活动单位数 Number of Industrial Active Units	企业 Enterprises
总 计	**Total**	**142442**	**122682**
（一）农、林、牧、渔业	Agriculture,Forestry,Animal Husbandry and Fishery	4436	2868
农业	Farming	2225	1313
林业	Forestry	558	426
畜牧业	Animal Husbandry	1231	865
渔业	Fishery	75	59
农、林、牧、渔服务业	Services in Support of Agriculture	347	205
（二）采矿业	Mining	272	270
煤炭开采和洗选业	Mining and Washing of Coal	8	8
石油和天然气开采业	Extraction of Petroleum and Natural Gas	28	26
黑色金属矿采选业	Mining of Ferrous Metal Ores	12	12
有色金属矿采选业	Mining of Non-ferrous Metal Ores	23	23
非金属矿采选业	Mining and Processing of Nonmetal Ores	79	79
开采辅助活动	Mining of Other Ores	98	98
其他采矿业	Manufacturing	24	24
（三）制造业	Processing of Food from Agricultural Products	15264	15187
农副食品加工业	Manufacture of Foods	490	482
食品制造业	Manufacture of Beverages	486	482
酒、饮料和精制茶制造业	Manufacture of Tobacco	155	154
烟草制品业	Manufacture of Textile	2	2
纺织业	Manufacture of Textile Wearing Apparel, Footware and Caps	160	160
纺织服装、服饰业	Manufacture of Leather, Fur, Feather and Related Products	145	144
皮革、毛皮、羽毛及其制品和制鞋业	Processing of Timber,Manufacture of Wood, Bamboo,Rattan its Froducts and Footwear	35	34
木材加工和木、竹、藤、棕、草制品业	Plam and Straw Products and Straw Products	219	218
家具制造业	Manufacture of Furniture	442	441
造纸及纸制品业	Manufacture of Paper and Paper Products	339	339
印刷和记录媒介复制业	Printing,Reproduction of Recording Media	579	577
文教、工美、体育和娱乐用品制造业	Manufacture of Articles For Culture, Education and Sport Activities	219	218

2-5 续表1 continued 1

单位：个 (unit)

分 组	Classify	产业活动单位数 Number of Industrial Active Units	企业 Enterprises
石油加工、炼焦和核燃料加工业	Processing of Petroleum, Coking, Processing of Nuclear Fuel	53	53
化学原料和化学制品制造业	Manufacture of Raw Chemical Materials and Chemical Products	750	748
医药制造业	Manufacture of Medicines	373	369
化学纤维制造业	Manufacture of Chemical Fibers	27	27
橡胶和塑料制品业	Manufacture of Rubber and Manufacture of Plastics	500	499
非金属矿物制品业	Manufacture of Non-metallic Mineral Products	1398	1390
黑色金属冶炼和压延加工业	Smelting and Pressing of Ferrous Metals	249	248
有色金属冶炼和压延加工业	Smelting and Pressing of Non-ferrous Metals	197	197
金属制品业	Manufacture of Metal Products	1067	1061
通用设备制造业	Manufacture of General Purpose Machinery	1967	1960
专用设备制造业	Manufacture of Special Equipment	1560	1551
汽车制造业	Manufacture of Motor Vehicle	197	196
铁路、船舶、航空航天和其他运输设备制造业	Railways,Shipbuilding,Aerospace and Other Transportation Equipment Manufacturing Industry	335	335
电气机械和器材制造业	Manufacture of Electric Equipment and Machinery	1462	1455
计算机、通信和其他电子设备制造业	Manufacture of Communication Equipment, Computers and other Electronic Equipment	858	856
仪器仪表制造业	Manufacture of Measuring Instruments and Machinery	603	600
其他制造业	Other Manufacturing	155	154
废弃资源综合利用	Recycling and Disposal of Waste	57	55
金属制品、机械和设备修理业	Metal Products,Machinery and Equipment Repair Industry	185	182
（四）电力、燃气及水的生产供应业	Production and Distribution of Electricity,Gas and Water	430	408
电力、热力生产和供应业	Production and Supply of Electric Power and Heat Power	277	256
燃气生产和供应业	Gas mining and supplying industry	50	50
水的生产和供应业	Production and Supply of Water	103	102
（五）建筑业	Construction	10699	10602
房屋建筑业	Construction of Building	2187	2137
土木工程建筑业	Civil Engineering	2093	2077
建筑安装业	Architectural Installation	1849	1842
建筑装饰和其他建筑业	Architectural Decoration and Other Construction	4570	4546
（六）批发和零售业	Wholesale and Retail Trades	45796	45106

2–5 续表2 continued 2

单位：个 (unit)

分　组	Classify	产业活动单位数 Number of Industrial Active Units	企业 Enterprises
批发业	Wholesale Trade	24144	24013
零售业	Retail Trade	21652	21093
（七）交通运输、仓储和邮政业	Traffic, Transport, Storage and Post	2918	2750
铁路运输业	Transport Via Railway	66	53
道路运输业	Transport Via Road	1434	1377
水上运输业	Water Transport	4	4
航空运输业	Air Transport	69	67
管道运输业	Transport Via Pipeline	12	11
装卸搬运和运输代理服务业	Loading, Unloading, Portage and Other Transport Services	610	595
仓储业	Storage	343	326
邮政业	Post	380	317
（八）住宿和餐饮业	Hotels and Catering Services	4309	4179
住宿业	Hotels	1545	1509
餐饮业	Catering Services	2764	2670
（九）信息传输、软件和信息技术服务业	Information Transmission, Computer Services and Software	6039	5934
电信、广播电视和卫星传输服务	Telecom & Other Information Transmission Services	445	386
互联网和相关服务	internet and relevant services	828	819
软件和信息技术服务	Software Industry	4766	4729
（十）金融业	Financial Intermediation	2291	1884
货币金融服务	Monetary and Financial Services	1331	1016
资本市场服务	Capital Market Services	376	372
保险业	Insurance	472	389
其他金融业	Other Financial Intermediation	112	107
（十一）房地产业	Real Estate	7161	7075
房地产业	Real Estate	7161	7075
（十二） 租赁和商务服务业	Leasing and Business Services	13275	12860
租赁业	Leasing	997	990
商务服务业	Business Services	12278	11870
（十三）科学研究和技术服务业	Scientific Research, Technical Sevice	5667	5011
研究与试验发展	Research and Experimental Development	577	487
专业技术服务业	Professional Technical Services	3790	3460

2-5 续表3 continued 3

单位：个 (unit)

分 组	Classify	产业活动单位数 Number of Industrial Active Units	企业 Enterprises
科技推广和应用服务业	Services of Science and Technology Exchanges and Promotion	1300	1064
（十四）水利、环境和公共设施管理业	Management of Water Conservancy, Environment and Public Facilities	1158	928
水利管理业	Management of Water Conservancy	202	101
生态保护和环境治理业	Environmental Management	133	102
公共设施管理业	Management of Public Facilities	823	725
（十五）居民服务、修理和其他服务业	Services to Households and Other Services	3184	3054
居民服务业	Services to Households	1167	1058
机动车、电子产品和日用产品修理业	The repair service industry for motor vehicle、electronic	1263	1252
其他服务业	Other Services	754	744
（十六）教育	Education	4336	872
教育	Education	4336	872
（十七）卫生和社会工作	Health, Social Security	3620	466
卫生	Health	3392	434
社会工作	Social	228	32
（十八）文化、体育和娱乐业	Culture, Sports and Entertainment	2550	2193
新闻和出版业	Journalism and Publishing Activities	192	140
广播、电视、电影和影视录音制作业	Broadcasting, Movies, Television and Audiovisual Activities	408	392
文化艺术业	Cultural and Art Activities	820	582
体育	Sports Activities	207	171
娱乐业	Entertainment	923	908
（十九）公共管理、社会保障和社会组织	Public Management and Social Organizaion	9037	1035
中国共产党机关	Organs of Communist Party of China	173	13
国家机构	Government Agencies	3528	902
人民政协、民主党派	People's Pc~litical Consultative Conference and Democratic Parties	42	7
社会保障	Social Security	98	27
群众团体、社会团体和其他成员组织	Mass organizations、social groups and other members of the organization	1470	80
基层群众自治组织	Grass-roots Mass Self-Government Organizations	3726	6
（二十）国际组织	International Organizations		
国际组织	International Organizations		

2-6 按行政区划分产业活动单位数（2016年）

Industrial Active Units by Region（2016）

单位：个 (unit)

区 县	Region	产业活动单位数 Number of Industrial Active Units	企业 Enterprises
总 计	**Total**	**142442**	**122682**
新城区	Xincheng	9628	8556
碑林区	Beilin	16374	15218
莲湖区	Lianhu	14318	13221
灞桥区	Baqiao	5823	4579
未央区	Weiyang	23243	22126
雁塔区	Yanta	34949	33751
阎良区	Yanliang	3377	2695
临潼区	Lintong	5614	3427
长安区	Chang'an	9652	7334
高陵区	Gaoling	3981	3044
蓝田县	Lantian	5177	2830
周至县	Zhouzhi	4249	2155
户 县	Huxian	6057	3746

2-7 按统计机构分企业一套表调查单位数（2016年）

Number of Survey Units by Statistical Agencies of "One Sheet"（2016）

单位：个 (unit)

区县、开发区	Region	合计 Total	规模以上工业 Industrial Enterprises above Designed Size	限额以上批发零售住宿餐饮业 Above wholesale and Retail Accommodation and Catering Industry	资质内建筑业 Qualified Construction Enterprises	房地产开发经营企业 Real Estate Development Enterprises	规模以上服务业 Service Enterprises above Designed Size
全　市	**Total**	**5813**	**1186**	**1582**	**893**	**923**	**1229**
新城区	Xincheng	324	10	153	54	33	74
碑林区	Beilin	643	13	253	141	88	148
莲湖区	Lianhu	455	28	149	72	82	124
灞桥区	Baqiao	220	65	54	34	38	29
未央区	Weiyang	266	26	78	48	54	60
雁塔区	Yanta	515	41	129	153	63	129
阎良区	Yanliang	158	63	30	23	28	14
临潼区	Lintong	147	56	32	26	11	22
长安区	Chang'an	230	45	80	32	45	28
高陵区	Gaoling	178	72	41	10	34	21
蓝田县	Lantian	91	33	20	12	14	12
周至县	Zhouzhi	129	45	40	13	17	14
户　县	Huxian	152	62	39	7	33	11
高新技术开发区	GaoXin	919	289	169	147	76	238
经济技术开发区	JingKai	746	227	193	90	80	156
曲江新区	Qujiang	197		30	11	75	81
阎良国家航空技术产业基地	Aviation Industry Base	49	33	3		8	5
国家民用航天产业基地	Aerospace Base	94	31	17	5	30	11
浐灞生态区	Chanba Eco-District	107		21	1	65	20
国际港务区	International Trade &Logistic Park	70	16	15	3	12	24
沣东新城	FengDongXinCheng	123	31	36	11	37	8
其他	other						

注：由于统计口径不同，一套表调查单位数与各专业有差异。

2-8 按行政区划分企业一套表调查单位数（2016年）

Number of Survey Units of "One Sheet" by Region (2016)

单位：个 (unit)

区 县	Region	合计 Total	规模以上工业 Industrial Enterprises above Designed Size	限额以上批发零售住宿餐饮业 Above wholesale and Retail Accommodation and Catering Industry	资质内建筑业 Qualified Construction Enterprises	房地产开发经营企业 Real Estate Development Enterprises	规模以上服务业 Service Enterprises above Designed Size
全 市	**Total**	**5813**	**1186**	**1582**	**893**	**923**	**1229**
新城区	Xincheng	327	10	154	54	35	74
碑林区	Beilin	647	14	253	141	91	148
莲湖区	Lianhu	461	30	148	74	84	125
灞桥区	Baqiao	361	85	83	38	87	68
未央区	Weiyang	1081	206	308	150	194	223
雁塔区	Yanta	1462	227	307	296	192	440
阎良区	Yanliang	207	96	33	23	36	19
临潼区	Lintong	154	58	33	26	15	22
长安区	Chang'an	448	149	117	49	87	46
高陵区	Gaoling	263	144	46	10	36	27
蓝田县	Lantian	91	33	20	12	14	12
周至县	Zhouzhi	131	47	40	13	17	14
户 县	Huxian	180	87	40	7	35	11

2-9 按行政区划和国民经济行业分法人单位数（2016年）

单位：个

区 县	Region	合计 Total	农、林、牧、渔业 Agriculture Forestry Animal Husbandry and Fishery	采矿业 Mining	制造业 Manufacturing	电力、燃气及水的生产和供应业 Production and Distribution of Electricity Gas and Water
全 市	**Total**	**130291**	**4416**	**259**	**14932**	**344**
新城区	Xincheng	8686	5	1	318	3
碑林区	Beilin	14273		6	267	10
莲湖区	Lianhu	12896	8	2	379	3
灞桥区	Baqiao	5035	117		1054	16
未央区	Weiyang	22100	78	43	2784	43
雁塔区	Yanta	33373	133	98	3389	116
阎良区	Yanliang	3053	257		751	18
临潼区	Lintong	4686	805		672	20
长安区	Chang'an	9017	629	19	2074	26
高陵区	Gaoling	3689	432	12	733	24
蓝田县	Lantian	4376	779	28	558	13
周至县	Zhouzhi	3660	509	23	281	28
户 县	Huxian	5447	664	27	1672	24

Impersonal Entities by Administrative Districts and Industry of the National Economy (2016)

(unit)

建筑业 Construction	批发和零售业 Wholesale and Retail Trades	交通运输、仓储和邮政业 Traffic Transport Storage and Post	住宿和餐饮业 Hotels and Catering Services	信息传输、软件和信息技术服务业 Information Transmission Software and Information Technology Services	金融业 Financial Intermediation
10112	**42307**	**2368**	**3613**	**5615**	**785**
438	4220	255	458	183	41
928	6199	116	698	523	101
968	5968	304	508	330	109
396	1194	208	109	61	7
2022	10143	580	418	435	78
3420	9550	245	740	3531	333
175	644	86	72	55	19
364	628	113	91	70	10
612	1355	106	243	324	50
251	671	105	76	33	10
264	553	53	93	28	13
93	713	109	48	10	3
181	469	88	59	32	11

2-9 续表

单位：个

区 县	Region	房地产业 Real Estate	租赁和商务服务业 Leasing and Business Services	科学研究和技术服务业 Scientific Research Technical Services	水利、环境和公共设施管理业 Management of Water Conservancy, Environment and Public Facilities
全 市	**Total**	**6801**	**12578**	**5368**	**1065**
新城区	Xincheng	500	684	266	47
碑林区	Beilin	831	2101	828	77
莲湖区	Lianhu	794	1504	468	110
灞桥区	Baqiao	352	282	176	53
未央区	Weiyang	1148	1727	867	173
雁塔区	Yanta	2069	4861	1973	200
阎良区	Yanliang	111	184	59	33
临潼区	Lintong	91	281	181	58
长安区	Chang'an	422	459	278	97
高陵区	Gaoling	192	177	55	33
蓝田县	Lantian	74	114	39	48
周至县	Zhouzhi	82	47	74	61
户 县	Huxian	135	157	104	75

continued

(unit)

居民服务、修理和其他服务业 Services to Households Repairs and Other Services	教育 Education	卫生和社会工作 Health and Social Work	文化、体育和娱乐业 Culture Sports and Entertainment	公共管理、社会保障和社会组织 Public Administration Social Security and Social Organizations	国际组织 International Orgnizations
2883	**3736**	**3295**	**2390**	**7424**	
257	200	74	154	582	
356	337	109	316	470	
349	269	123	218	482	
119	268	68	80	475	
450	276	92	169	574	
826	480	157	787	465	
53	99	105	62	270	
78	254	354	99	517	
164	459	451	179	1070	
79	198	207	78	323	
53	238	563	89	776	
34	383	466	75	621	
65	275	526	84	799	

2-10 按行政区划和机构类型分法人单位数（2016年）

Impersonal Entities by Agencies Types and Adminstration Districts（2016）

单位：个 (unit)

区 县	Region	法人单位数 Number of Enterprises	企业法人 Business Entity	事业法人 Institution Entity	机关法人 Government Entity	社会团体 Social Organization	其他 other
全 市	**Total**	**130291**	**113335**	**4670**	**1218**	**1245**	**9823**
新城区	Xincheng	8686	7779	284	158	219	246
碑林区	Beilin	14273	13257	338	93	218	367
莲湖区	Lianhu	12896	11950	330	96	142	378
灞桥区	Baqiao	5035	4072	243	74	77	569
未央区	Weiyang	22100	21108	316	151	65	460
雁塔区	Yanta	33373	32319	332	96	70	556
阎良区	Yanliang	3053	2457	145	62	54	335
临潼区	Lintong	4686	2952	578	77	62	1017
长安区	Chang'an	9017	6796	802	79	48	1292
高陵区	Gaoling	3689	2794	311	78	28	478
蓝田县	Lantian	4376	2558	223	107	72	1416
周至县	Zhouzhi	3660	1946	386	71	106	1151
户 县	Huxian	5447	3347	382	76	84	1558

2-11 按行政区划和登记注册类型分企业法人单位数（2016年）

The Corporate Units by Types of Corporate Registration and Adminstration Districts（2016）

单位：个 (unit)

区 县	Region	企业单位数 Number of Enterprises	内资企业 Domestic Investment Enterprises	国有企业 State-owned Enterprises	集体企业 Collective-owned Enterprises	股份合作企业 Share-holding Corperative Enterprises	联营企业 Joint Ownership Enterprises
全 市	**Total**	**113335**	**112439**	**1654**	**1513**	**310**	**194**
新城区	Xincheng	7779	7752	259	286	45	19
碑林区	Beilin	13257	13173	289	154	46	40
莲湖区	Lianhu	11950	11891	264	240	19	29
灞桥区	Baqiao	4072	4031	76	117	16	7
未央区	Weiyang	21108	20947	135	165	44	24
雁塔区	Yanta	32319	31957	174	83	38	15
阎良区	Yanliang	2457	2437	43	45	17	4
临潼区	Lintong	2952	2941	88	75	18	12
长安区	Chang'an	6796	6709	86	97	25	18
高陵区	Gaoling	2794	2773	53	33	16	7
蓝田县	Lantian	2558	2548	48	79	11	11
周至县	Zhouzhi	1946	1945	49	30	2	3
户 县	Huxian	3347	3335	90	109	13	5

2-11 续表 continued

区 县	Region	有限责任公司 Limited Liability Corporations	股份有限公司 Share-holding Corperation Ltd.	私营企业 Private Enterprises	港、澳、台商投资企业 Enterprises with Funds from Hong Kong, Macao and Taiwan	外商投资企业 Enterprises with Foreign Investment
全 市	**Total**	**45720**	**1134**	**57217**	**291**	**605**
新城区	Xincheng	4103	94	2893	11	16
碑林区	Beilin	8133	159	4103	35	49
莲湖区	Lianhu	1306	90	9159	24	35
灞桥区	Baqiao	1756	35	1870	16	25
未央区	Weiyang	8844	155	11450	70	91
雁塔区	Yanta	16227	306	15015	92	270
阎良区	Yanliang	809	33	1014	10	10
临潼区	Lintong	843	41	1523	3	8
长安区	Chang'an	2001	94	3843	23	64
高陵区	Gaoling	897	51	1446	3	18
蓝田县	Lantian	303	22	1512		10
周至县	Zhouzhi	125	9	937		1
户 县	Huxian	373	45	2452	4	8

主要统计指标解释

企业（单位）登记注册类型 是以在工商行政管理机关登记注册的各类企业为划分对象，以工商行政管理部门对企业登记注册的类型为依据，将企业登记注册类型分为内资企业、港澳台商投资企业和外商投资企业三大类。内资企业包括国有企业、集体企业、股份合作企业、联营企业、有限责任公司、股份有限公司、私营公司和其他企业；港澳台商投资企业和外商投资企业分别包括合资经营企业、合作经营企业、独资经营企业和股份有限公司。对不在工商行政管理部门进行登记注册的行政机关、事业单位和社会团体，主要按其经费来源和管理方式进行划分。

国有企业 指企业全部资产归国家所有，并按《中华人民共和国企业法人登记管理条例》规定登记注册的非公司制的经济组织。不包括有限责任公司中的国有独资公司。

集体企业 指企业资产归集体所有，并按《中华人民共和国企业法人登记管理条例》规定登记注册的经济组织。

股份合作企业 指以合作制为基础，由企业职工共同出资入股，吸收一定比例的社会资产投资组建，实行自主经营，自负盈亏，共同劳动，民主管理，按劳分配与按股分红相结合的一种集体经济组织。

联营企业 指两个及两个以上相同或不同所有制性质的企业法人或事业单位法人，按自愿、平等、互利的原则，共同投资组成的经济组织。联营企业包括国有联营企业、集体联营企业、国有与集体联营企业和其他联营企业。

有限责任公司 指根据《中华人民共和国公司登记管理条例》规定登记注册，由两个以上、五十个以下的股东共同出资，每个股东以其所认缴的出资额对公司承担有限责任，公司以其全部资产对其债务承担责任的经济组织。有限责任公司包括国有独资公司以及其他有限责任公司。

股份有限公司 指根据《中华人民共和国公司登记管理条例》规定登记注册，其全部注册资本由等额股份构成并通过发行股票筹集资本，股东以其认购的股份对公司承担有限责任，公司以其全部资产对其债务承担责任的经济组织。

私营企业 指由自然人投资设立或由自然人控股，以雇佣劳动为基础的营利性经济组织。包括按照《公司法》、《合伙企业法》、《私营企业暂行条例》规定登记注册的私营有限责任公司、私营股份有限公司、私营合伙企业和私营独资企业。

其他企业 指上述企业之外的其他内资经济组织。

与港澳台商合资经营企业 指港澳台地区投资者与内地企业依照《中华人民共和国中外合资经营企业法》及有关法律的规定，按合同规定的比例投资设立、分享利润和分担风险的企业。

与港澳台商合作经营企业 指港澳台地区投资者与内地企业依照《中华人民共和国中外合作经营企业法》及有关法律的规定，依照合作合同的约定进行投资或提供条件设立、分配利润和分担风险的企业。

港澳台商独资经营企业 指依照《中华人民共和国外资企业法》及有关法律的规定，在内地由港澳台地区投资者全额投资设立的企业。

港澳台商投资股份有限公司 指根据国家有关规定，经原外经贸部依法批准设立，其中港、澳、台商的股本占公司注册资本的比例达25%以上的股份有限公司。凡其中港、澳、台商的股本占公司注册资本的比例小于25%的，属于内资企业中的股份有限公司。

中外合资经营企业 指外国企业或外国人与中国内地企业依照《中华人民共和国中外合资经营企业法》及有关法律的规定，按合同规定的比例投资设立、分享利润和分担风险的企业。

中外合作经营企业 指外国企业或外国人与中国内地企业依照《中华人民共和国中外合作经营企业法》及有关法律的规定，依照合作合同的约定进行投资或提供条件设立、分配利润和分担风险的企业。

外资企业 指依照《中华人民共和国外资企业法》及有关法律的规定，在中国内地由外国投资者全额投资设立的企业。

外商投资股份有限公司 指根据国家有关规定，经原外经贸部依法批准设立，其中外资的股本占公司注册资本的比例达25%以上的股份有限公司。凡其中外资股本占公司注册资本的比例小于25%的，属于内资企业中的股份有限公司。

行政机关、事业单位和社会团体 参照企业登记注册类型，主要按其经费来源和管理方式划分。具体规定如下：

（1）行政机关：包括国家机关和政党机关，原则上均列为“国有”。但有特殊规定的，如供销社等，则列为“集体”。

（2）事业单位：包括经国家机构编制部门和有关业务主管部门批准成立的各类事业单位，不包括实行企业化管理的事业单位。事业单位的划分办法如下：

①由国家财政预算拨款或列入财政预算外资金管理以及经费主要来源于国有主管部门或国有上级单位的事业单位，列为“国有”。

②经费主要来源于集体单位的事业单位，列为“集体”。

③公民个人（或个人合伙）开办的事业单位，列为“私营”。

④上述以外的其他事业单位，如果其经费来源不明确，按管理方式进行归类。

（3）社会团体：包括经民政部门批准成立以及未纳入社会团体管理条例范围的工会、妇联等各类社会团体。社会团体的划分办法如下：

①未纳入民政部社会团体管理条例范围的工会、妇联、共青团、青联、工商联、科协、侨联等社会团体，国家拨款设立的基金会或基金管理组织以及经费主要来源于国有业务主管部门或国有上级单位的社会团体，列为“国有”。

②经费主要来源于集体单位的社会团体，列为“集体”。

③公民个人（或个人合伙）开办的社会团体，划为“私营”。

④上述以外的其他社会团体，如果其经费来源不明确，改按管理方式进行归类。

Explanatory Notes on Main Statistical Indicators

Registration Status of Enterprises Enterprises are classified into 3 categories, namely domestic-funded enterprises, enterprises with investment from Hong Kong, Macau and Taiwan, and enterprises with foreign investment, according to the registration status of an enterprise in industrial and commercial administration agencies. Domestic-funded enterprises include State- owned enterprises, collective-owned enterprises, cooperative enterprises, joint ownership enterprises, limited liability corporations, share-holding corporations Ltd., private enterprises and other enterprises. Included in the enterprises with investment from Hong Kong, Macau and Taiwan and enterprises with foreign investment are joint-venture enterprises, cooperative enterprises, sole investment enterprises and share-holding corporations Ltd. For government agencies, institutions and social organizations which are not registered in industrial and commercial administration agencies, they are classified mainly by their sources of funding and manner of management.

State–owned Enterprises refer to non-corporation economic units where the entire assets are owned by the State and which have been registered in accordance with the Regulation of the People's Republic of China on the Management of Registration of Corporate Enterprises. Not included from this category are solely State-funded corporations in the limited liability corporations.

Collective–owned Enterprises refer to economic units where the assets are owned collectively and which have been registered in accordance with the Regulation of the People's Republic of China on the Management of Registration of Corporate Enterprises.

Cooperative Enterprises refer to a form of collective economic units (enterprises)where capitals come mainly from employees as their shares, with certain proportion of capital from the outside, where production is organized on the basis of independent operation, independent accounting for profits and losses, joint work, democratic management, and a distribution system that integrates remuneration according to work with dividend according to capital share.

Joint Ownership Enterprises refer to economic units established by two or more corporate enterprises or corporate institutions of the same or different ownership, through joint investment on the basis of voluntary participation, equality, and mutual benefits. They include State joint ownership enterprises; collective joint ownership enterprises; joint State-collective enterprises; and other joint ownership enterprises.

Limited Liability Corporations refer to economic units established with investment from 2-50 investors and registered in accordance with the Regulation of the People's Republic of China on the Management of Registration of Corporations, each investor bearing limited liability to the corporation depending on its share of investment, and the corporation bearing liability to its debt to the maximum of its total assets. Limited liability corporations include solely State-funded limited liability corporations and other limited liability corporations.

Share–holding Corporations Ltd. refer to economic units registered in accordance with the Regulation of the People's Republic of China on the Management of Registration of Corporations, with total registered capital divided into equal shares and raised through issuing stocks. Each investor bears limited liability to the corporation depending on the holding of shares, and the corporation bears liability to its debt to the maximum of its total assets.

Private Enterprises refer to profit-making economic units invested and established by natural persons, or controlled by natural persons using employed labour~ Included in this category are private limited liability corporations, private share-holding corporations Ltd., private partnership enterprises and private-funded enterprises registered in accordance with the Company Law, the Law on Partnership Business and Interim Regulations on Private Enterprises.

Other Domestic–funded Enterprises refer to domestic-funded economic units other than those mentioned above.

Joint Venture Enterprises with Funds from Hong Kong, Macau and Taiwan are enterprises established by investors from Hong Kong, Macau and Taiwan with enterprises in the mainland of China in accordance with the Law of the People's Republic of China on Sino-foreign Equity Joint Ventures and other relevant laws, where the establishment of the investment and the sharing of profits and risks are stipulated under joint venture contracts.

Cooperative Enterprises with Funds from Hong Kong, Macan and Taiwan established by investors from Hong Kong, Macau and Taiwan with enterprises in the mainland of China in accordance with the Law of the People's Republic of China on Sino-foreign Contractual Joint Venture and other relevant laws, where the investment or provision of facilities and the sharing of profits and risks are stipulated under cooperative contracts.

Enterprises with Sole (exclusive)Investment from

Hong Kong, Macau and Taiwan refer to enterprises established in the mainland of China with exclusive investment from investors from Hong Kong, Macau and Taiwan in accordance with the Law of the People's Republic of China on Wholly Foreign-owned Enterprises and other relevant laws.

Share–holding Corporations Ltd. with Investment from Hong Kong, Macau and Taiwan refer to share- holding corporations Ltd. established with the approval from the former Ministry of Foreign Trade and Economic Relations in line with relevant State regulations, where the share of investment from Hong Kong, Macau or Taiwan businessmen exceeds 25% of the total registered capital of the corporation. In case the share of investmentfrom Hong Kong, Macau or Taiwan is less than 25% of thetotal registered capital, the enterprise is to be classified as domestic-funded share-holding corporation Ltd.

Joint Venture Enterprises with Foreign Investment refer to enterprises jointly established byforeign enterprises or foreigners with enterprises in themainland of China in accordance with the Law of thePeople's Republic of China on Sino-foreign Equity JointVentures and other relevant laws, where the sharing ofinvestment, profits and risks is stipulated under contract.

Cooperative Enterprises with Foreign Investment refer to enterprises jointly established by foreign enterprises or foreigners with enterprises in the mainland of China in accordance with the Law of the People's Republic of China on Sino-foreign Contractual Joint Venture and other relevant laws, where the investment or provision of facilities and the sharing of profits and risks are stipulated under cooperative contracts.

Enterprises with Sole (exclusive)Foreign Investment refer to enterprises established in the mainland of China with exclusive investment from foreign investors in accordance with the Law of the People's Republic of China on Wholly Foreign-owned Enterprises and other relevant laws.

Share–holding Corporations Ltd. with Foreign Investment refer to share-holding corporations Ltd. established with the approval from the former Ministry of Foreign Trade and Economic Relations in line with relevant State regulations, where the share of investment from foreign investors exceeds 25% of the total registered capital of the corporation. In case the share of foreign investment is less than 25% ofthe total registered capital, the enterprise is to be classified as domestic-funded share-holding corporation Ltd.

Government Agencies, Institutions and Social Organizations are classified into the following categories by source of funds and manner of management taking reference of thc registration status of enterprises:

(1)Government agencies: include State and party agencies, classified in principle as State-owned. There are exceptions, such as supply and marketing cooperatives which are classified as collective-owned.

(2)Institutions: include institutions of various types established with the approval by organization and staffing departments of the government, but exclude institutions where enterprise management system is introduced. Institutions are further classified as follows:

(a)Institutions for which their main budgets are from government budget appropriations or extra-budget funds, or allocated from the budget of their competent government agencies. Such institutions are classified as state-owned.

(b)Institutions for which their budget mainly come from collective units. Such institutions are classified as collective-owned.

(c)Social institutions established by individual or a group of citizens, which are classified as private.

(d)Institutions other than those mentioned above for which their sources of budget are not clear. Such institutions are classified by the manner of management.

(3)Social organizations: include social organizations established with the approval from the Ministry of Civil Affairs, and organizations that are not covered by social organization management regulations such as trade unions, women's federations etc.. Social organizations are further classified as follows:

(a)Social organizations that are not covered by social organization management regulations of the Ministry of Civil Affairs such as trade unions, women federations, communist youth leagues, youth associations, industrial and commerce associations, scientist associations, overseas Chinese associations, etc., foundations and fund management organizations established with funds from the state, and social organizations whose funds mainly come from the budget of their competent government agencies. Such institutions are classified as State-owned.

(b)Social organizations for which their budget mainly come from collective units. Such institutions are classified as collective-owned.

(c)Social organizations established by individual or a group of citizens, which are classified as private.

(d)Social organizations other than those mentioned above for which their sources of budget are not clear. Such organizations are classified by the manner of management.

3 国民经济核算

NATIONAL ECONOMIC ACCOUNTS

资料整理：刘晓敏　段　斐　张　洁
Data management：Li xiaomin　Duan Fei　Zhang Jie
数据审核：连　鹏
Data audit：Lian Peng

第三部分　国民经济核算

一、简要说明

本章资料包括西安市生产总值、构成和指数，分区县生产总值和指数，非公有制经济增加值及占比等。根据国家统计局的统一要求，2009年—2012年数据为第三次经济普查修订结果，2013年数据为第三次经济普查结果，2014年、2015年、2016年数据为年报最终核实数据；区县2016年数据为初步核算数；2013年（含）之后三次产业分类依据国家统计局2012年制定的新《三次产业划分规定》；2004年（含）之前人均GDP按户籍人口计算，2005年（含）之后按常住人口计算。资料由西安市统计局国民经济核算处提供。

二、主要指标

生产总值（亿元）	6282.65	比上年增长	8.6%
第一产业	232.01	比上年增长	3.8%
第二产业	2200.36	比上年增长	8.5%
第三产业	3850.28	比上年增长	9.0%
人均生产总值（元/人）	71647	比上年增长	7.4%

3　NATIONAL ECONOMIC ACCOUNTS

Ⅰ.Brief Introduction

The data in this chapter consists of Xi'an GDP, composition, index, and sub-county gross production, index the added value of non-public-owned economics According to the uniform requirements of National Bureau of Statistics date between 2009 to 2012 were amended by the Third Economic Census, of 2013 data was revised by the Third Economic Census, data of 2014 and 2015 and 2016 was the Annual Report final verification data. The data of the districts and counties in Xi'an in 2016 are preliminary accounting data.Three industrial classification after 2013（included）based on the new "three industrial division rule" for mulated according to National Bureau of Statistics in 2012.per capita GDP was calculated on permanent population after 2005（included）, had been calculated on register population before 2005.Data in this chapter is provided by National Economics Accounting Division of the Xi'an Bureau of Statistics.

Ⅱ.Major Indicators

		Increase over Preceding Year
Gross Domestic Product(100 mil. yuan)	6282.65	8.6%
Primary Industry	232.01	3.8%
Secondary Industry	2200.36	8.5%
Tertiary Industry	3850.28	9.0%
Per Capita Gross Domestic Product (yuan/person)	71647	7.4%

3-1 主要年份生产总值

Gross Domestic Product in Representative Years

(本表按当年价格计算)　　　　(Data in the table are calculated at current prices)
单位：亿元　　　　(100 million yuan)

年份 Year	生产总值 Gross Domestic Product	第一产业 Primary Industry	第二产业 Secondary Industry	第三产业 Tertiary Industry	人均生产总值 (元/人) Per Capita GDP (yuan/person)
1952	3.37	1.59	0.88	0.90	135
1965	12.76	2.62	7.22	2.92	323
1970	17.76	3.13	10.96	3.67	412
1975	21.33	4.14	12.63	4.56	448
1978	25.35	4.83	14.59	5.93	513
1980	31.66	4.73	18.69	8.24	623
1983	35.89	5.22	20.14	10.53	674
1984	44.14	7.45	24.17	12.52	817
1985	57.58	8.76	30.83	17.99	1049
1986	65.78	9.59	33.86	22.33	1178
1987	80.16	10.73	37.69	31.74	1409
1988	99.22	11.47	46.58	41.17	1711
1989	109.38	12.78	48.91	47.69	1861
1990	116.51	13.94	50.15	52.42	1932
1991	136.14	17.17	57.06	61.91	2224
1992	164.85	18.78	69.22	76.85	2662
1993	229.56	22.58	110.88	96.10	3661
1994	289.82	31.68	128.27	129.87	4563
1995	330.35	41.40	135.33	153.62	5131
1996	406.95	46.94	161.63	198.38	6246
1997	488.82	51.33	197.97	239.52	7424
1998	525.85	51.91	216.32	257.62	7906
1999	577.29	45.53	243.35	288.41	8599
2000	646.13	44.65	277.13	324.35	9484
2001	734.86	45.87	312.90	376.09	10628
2002	826.68	47.77	353.58	425.33	11831
2003	946.66	50.72	407.38	488.56	13341
2004	1102.39	60.21	476.92	565.26	15294
2005	1313.93	66.01	540.50	707.42	16406
2006	1538.94	70.44	645.65	822.85	18890
2007	1856.63	82.51	781.94	992.18	22463
2008	2318.14	103.45	981.58	1233.11	27794
2009	2724.88	110.38	1144.75	1469.75	32420
2010	3242.86	140.06	1357.53	1745.27	38357
2011	3869.84	173.14	1583.21	2113.49	45561
2012	4394.47	195.59	1781.09	2417.79	51499
2013	4924.97	200.45	1998.82	2725.70	57464
2014	5492.64	214.55	2194.78	3083.31	63794
2015	5801.20	220.20	2126.29	3454.71	66938
2016	6282.65	232.01	2200.36	3850.28	71647

注：1.2004年（含）之前人均GDP按户籍人口计算，2005年（含）之后按常住人口计算。
2.全市2009年—2012年数据为第三次经济普查修订结果，2013年数据为第三次经济普查结果。
3.2013年（含）之后三次产业分类依据国家统计局2012年制定的新《三次产业划分规定》。
4.全市2014年、2015年、2016年数据为年报最终核实数据。（下同）

3-2 主要年份生产总值指数（上年 = 100）

Indices of Gross Domestic Product in Representative Years(preceding year = 100)

(本表按可比价格计算) (Data in the table are calculated at constant prices)

年 份	Year	生产总值 Gross Domestic Product	第一产业 Primary Industry	第二产业 Secondary Industry	第三产业 Tertiary Industry	人均生产总值 Per Capita GDP
1952		103.6	92.2	137.5	123.7	
1965		126.1	134.1	133.0	106.7	
1970		122.0	109.4	140.0	100.1	
1975		103.8	92.6	107.1	107.5	
1978		101.7	101.6	99.4	108.2	
1980		111.5	83.3	119.7	116.5	
1985		112.6	107.5	111.8	116.9	
1986		111.4	107.7	108.4	118.8	
1987		113.6	100.8	109.1	126.6	
1988		111.4	81.2	115.5	114.7	
1989		106.7	103.0	104.5	110.8	
1990		105.2	103.0	102.5	109.6	
1991		109.8	118.6	108.6	108.6	108.2
1992		115.6	109.4	118.1	115.0	114.3
1993		123.9	112.5	142.7	108.4	122.3
1994		110.3	98.4	110.6	113.2	108.8
1995		110.0	104.5	112.1	108.6	108.5
1996		114.9	106.8	118.8	111.7	113.5
1997		114.4	109.1	116.7	112.4	113.2
1998		113.3	106.5	117.5	108.8	112.1
1999		112.2	97.4	115.7	110.1	111.2
2000		113.0	103.5	115.1	111.5	111.4
2001		113.1	102.5	115.3	112.6	111.4
2002		113.3	103.1	115.0	113.0	112.1
2003		113.5	101.8	117.5	111.2	111.7
2004		113.5	106.7	115.9	112.0	111.7
2005		114.0	107.5	112.3	116.3	112.2
2006		114.0	107.1	113.7	114.9	112.9
2007		115.6	104.5	115.7	116.4	113.9
2008		116.3	107.6	116.4	116.9	115.3
2009		114.5	106.3	112.8	116.3	113.7
2010		114.5	106.9	115.2	114.5	113.8
2011		113.5	106.7	112.5	114.9	113.0
2012		112.2	106.0	112.0	112.9	111.7
2013		111.1	104.7	113.6	109.7	110.6
2014		109.9	105.1	109.3	110.7	109.4
2015		108.2	105.0	105.6	110.4	107.5
2016		108.6	103.8	108.5	109.0	107.4
平均每年增长	**Yearly Average Growth Rates**					
“一五”时期	**The First Five-Year Plan Period**	**15.8**	**5.9**	**37.7**	**16.9**	
“二五”时期	**The Second Five-Year Plan Period**	**2.0**	**-3.7**	**2.5**	**8.4**	
1963--1965年	**Readjust Period**	**14.2**	**16.1**	**23.4**	**0.3**	
“三五”时期	**The Third Five-Year Plan Period**	**7.1**	**0.1**	**11.7**	**5.4**	
“四五”时期	**The Fourth Five-Year Plan Period**	**5.0**	**4.0**	**5.3**	**5.0**	
“五五”时期	**The Fifth Five-Year Plan Period**	**6.0**	**-0.7**	**6.5**	**10.1**	
“六五”时期	**The Sixth Five-Year Plan Period**	**10.7**	**7.9**	**10.4**	**12.9**	
“七五”时期	**The Seventh Five-Year Plan Period**	**9.6**	**-1.3**	**7.9**	**15.9**	
“八五”时期	**The Eighth Five-Year Plan Period**	**13.8**	**8.5**	**17.8**	**10.7**	**12.3**
“九五”时期	**The Ninth Five-Year Plan Period**	**13.6**	**4.6**	**16.8**	**10.9**	**12.3**
“十五”时期	**The Tenth Five-Year Plan Period**	**13.5**	**4.3**	**15.2**	**13.0**	**11.8**
“十一五”时期	**The Eleventh Five-Year Plan Period**	**15.0**	**6.5**	**14.8**	**15.8**	**13.9**
“十二五”时期	**The Twelve Five-Year Plan Period**	**11.0**	**5.5**	**10.6**	**11.7**	**10.4**

3-3 主要年份生产总值指数（1952年=100）

Indices of Gross Domestic Product in Representative Years(1952= 100)

(本表按可比价格计算)　　(Data in the table are calculated at constant prices)

年份 Year	生产总值 Gross Domestic Product	第一产业 Primary Industry	第二产业 Secondary Industry	第三产业 Tertiary Industry
1952	100.0	100.0	100.0	100.0
1965	341.6	173.3	1048.3	329.2
1970	481.6	174.3	1821.0	428.6
1975	614.2	211.9	2362.5	547.9
1978	678.7	231.3	2560.8	643.8
1980	821.4	204.2	3237.2	885.2
1983	988.4	222.5	3846.2	1154.4
1984	1213.6	278.2	4748.8	1388.7
1985	1366.8	299.1	5310.6	1632.4
1986	1523.1	322.3	5756.7	1928.9
1987	1730.0	324.9	6280.6	2441.6
1988	1926.3	263.7	7256.6	2801.2
1989	2054.8	271.6	7583.1	3104.6
1990	2162.5	279.7	7772.7	3403.6
1991	2374.4	331.7	8441.2	3696.3
1992	2744.8	362.9	9969.1	4250.7
1993	3400.8	408.2	14225.9	4607.8
1994	3751.1	401.8	15733.8	5216.0
1995	4126.2	419.9	17637.6	5664.6
1996	4741.0	448.5	20953.5	6327.4
1997	5423.7	489.3	24452.7	7112.0
1998	6145.1	521.1	28731.9	7737.9
1999	6894.8	507.6	33242.8	8519.4
2000	7791.1	525.4	38262.5	9499.1
2001	8811.7	538.5	44116.7	10696.0
2002	9983.7	555.2	50734.2	12086.5
2003	11331.5	265.2	59612.7	13440.2
2004	12861.3	603.1	69091.1	15053.0
2005	14661.9	648.3	77589.3	17506.6
2006	16714.6	694.3	88219.0	20115.1
2007	19322.1	725.5	102069.4	23414.0
2008	22471.6	780.6	118808.8	27371.0
2009	25730.0	829.8	134016.3	31832.5
2010	29460.8	887.0	154386.8	36448.2
2011	33438.0	946.5	173685.2	41879.0
2012	37517.5	1003.3	194527.4	47281.3
2013	41681.9	1050.4	220983.1	51867.6
2014	45808.4	1104.0	241534.5	57417.5
2015	49580.4	1158.8	255076.2	63393.7
2016	53863.1	1202.3	276727.1	69125.3

3-4 主要年份生产总值构成

Composition of Gross Domestic Product in Representative Years

(本表按当年价格计算) (Data in the table are calculated at current prices)

单位:% (%)

年 份	Year	生产总值 Gross Domestic Product	第一产业 Primary Industry	第二产业 Secondary Industry	第三产业 Tertiary Industry
1952		100	47.18	26.11	26.71
1965		100	20.53	56.58	22.89
1970		100	17.62	61.71	20.67
1975		100	19.41	59.21	21.38
1978		100	19.05	57.55	23.40
1980		100	14.94	59.03	26.03
1985		100	15.21	53.54	31.25
1986		100	14.58	51.47	33.95
1987		100	13.39	47.02	39.59
1988		100	11.56	46.95	41.49
1989		100	11.68	44.72	43.60
1990		100	11.96	43.04	45.00
1991		100	12.61	41.91	45.48
1992		100	11.39	41.99	46.62
1993		100	9.84	48.30	41.86
1994		100	10.93	44.26	44.81
1995		100	12.53	40.97	46.50
1996		100	11.53	39.72	48.75
1997		100	10.50	40.50	49.00
1998		100	9.87	41.14	48.99
1999		100	7.89	42.15	49.96
2000		100	6.91	42.89	50.20
2001		100	6.24	42.58	51.18
2002		100	5.78	42.77	51.45
2003		100	5.36	43.03	51.61
2004		100	5.46	43.26	51.28
2005		100	5.02	41.14	53.84
2006		100	4.58	41.95	53.47
2007		100	4.44	42.12	53.44
2008		100	4.46	42.34	53.20
2009		100	4.05	42.01	53.94
2010		100	4.32	41.86	53.82
2011		100	4.47	40.91	54.62
2012		100	4.45	40.53	55.02
2013		100	4.07	40.59	55.34
2014		100	3.91	39.96	56.13
2015		100	3.80	36.65	59.55
2016		100	3.69	35.02	61.29
“一五”时期	**The First Five-Year Plan Period**	**100**	**32.88**	**43.92**	**23.20**
“二五”时期	**The Second Five-Year Period**	**100**	**18.08**	**58.63**	**23.29**
1963--1965年	**Readjust Period**	**100**	**19.36**	**55.38**	**25.26**
“三五”时期	**The Third Five-Year Plan Period**	**100**	**18.60**	**57.33**	**24.07**
“四五”时期	**The Fourth Five-Year Plan Period**	**100**	**20.46**	**59.59**	**19.95**
“五五”时期	**The Fifth Five-Year Plan Period**	**100**	**18.41**	**57.69**	**23.90**
“六五”时期	**The Sixth Five-Year Plan Period**	**100**	**16.03**	**55.01**	**28.96**
“七五”时期	**The Seventh Five-Year Plan Period**	**100**	**12.42**	**46.11**	**41.47**
“八五”时期	**The Eighth Five-Year Plan Period**	**100**	**11.44**	**43.52**	**45.04**
“九五”时期	**The Ninth Five-Year Plan Period**	**100**	**9.09**	**41.45**	**49.46**
“十五”时期	**The Tenth Five-Year Plan Period**	**100**	**5.49**	**42.47**	**52.04**
“十一五”时期	**The Eleventh Five-Year Plan Period**	**100**	**4.34**	**42.04**	**53.62**
“十二五”时期	**The Twelve Five-Year Plan Period**	**100**	**4.10**	**39.55**	**56.35**

3-5 主要年份分行业增加值

The Value added by Industry in Representative Years

单位：亿元　　　　　　　　　　　　　　　　　　　　　　　　　　　　　　　　（100 million yuan）

年　份 Year	地区生产总值 Gross Domestic Product	农、林、牧、渔业 Farming Forestry Animal Husbandry Fishery	工业 Industry	建筑业 Construction	批发和零售业 Wholesale and Retail Trades
1992	164.85	18.78	61.33	7.89	18.16
1993	229.56	22.58	98.88	12.00	22.63
1994	289.82	31.68	110.52	17.75	27.83
1995	330.35	41.40	112.50	22.83	33.20
1996	406.95	46.94	132.52	29.11	44.51
1997	488.82	51.33	161.97	36.00	59.31
1998	525.85	51.91	175.00	41.32	64.93
1999	577.29	45.53	194.00	49.35	70.27
2000	646.13	44.65	218.44	58.69	65.87
2001	734.86	45.87	246.90	66.00	78.38
2002	826.68	47.77	280.20	73.38	91.57
2003	946.66	50.72	324.88	82.50	106.82
2004	1102.39	60.21	383.46	93.46	125.12
2005	1313.93	66.01	420.00	120.50	147.20
2006	1538.94	70.44	494.22	151.43	166.72
2007	1856.63	82.51	594.95	186.99	195.51
2008	2318.14	103.45	721.40	260.18	242.91
2009	2724.88	110.38	816.92	327.83	298.29
2010	3242.86	140.06	954.38	403.15	352.37
2011	3869.84	173.14	1098.51	484.70	439.75
2012	4394.47	195.59	1228.05	553.04	512.96
2013	4924.97	217.76	1376.74	642.26	575.72
2014	5492.64	233.61	1488.02	728.74	633.65
2015	5801.20	241.69	1376.72	770.29	667.99
2016	6282.65	256.38	1397.25	818.82	702.30

注：1999年（含）之前，批发和零售业与住宿和餐饮业无法分类，故1999年（含）之前批发和零售业数据为批发和零售业与住宿和餐饮业合计数。

3-5 续表 continued

单位：亿元 （100 million yuan）

年 份 Year	交通运输、仓储和邮政业 Transportation Storage Post and Telecommunications	住宿和餐饮业 Accommodation and Catering Trade	金融业 Financial Intermediation	房地产业 Real Estate	其他服务业 Others Services
1992	15.21		16.28	1.58	25.62
1993	18.01		20.59	1.97	32.90
1994	22.02		31.19	3.76	45.07
1995	24.60		35.20	4.90	55.72
1996	32.73		40.15	7.42	73.57
1997	43.02		37.50	8.74	90.95
1998	48.64		32.95	11.95	99.15
1999	55.35		30.37	14.42	118.00
2000	43.01	18.46	33.00	16.96	147.05
2001	45.50	21.97	36.21	21.38	172.65
2002	48.25	25.27	43.48	26.90	189.86
2003	51.37	29.41	50.76	32.42	217.78
2004	55.10	35.89	61.49	39.05	248.61
2005	66.30	50.44	75.00	52.48	316.00
2006	74.08	52.23	96.50	62.32	371.00
2007	84.21	70.09	128.50	75.26	438.61
2008	99.16	85.65	160.84	92.97	551.58
2009	112.02	93.82	197.87	128.18	639.57
2010	135.70	102.80	236.36	186.42	731.62
2011	165.18	118.02	294.44	235.20	860.90
2012	192.46	129.58	359.63	260.53	962.63
2013	215.11	135.58	429.51	292.41	1039.88
2014	235.58	144.15	534.00	326.10	1168.79
2015	260.33	159.14	658.90	398.34	1267.80
2016	298.52	170.67	724.35	459.20	1455.16

3-6 主要年份分行业增加值指数（上年=100）

Indices of the Value added by Industry in Representative Years（preceding year = 100）

(本表按可比价格计算) (Data in the table are calculated at constant prices)

年份 Year	地区生产总值 Gross Domestic Product	农、林、牧、渔业 Farming Forestry Animal Husbandry Fishery	工业 Industry	建筑业 Construction	批发和零售业 Wholesale and Retail Trades
1992	115.6	109.4	118.1	118.2	130.7
1993	123.9	112.5	143.7	135.6	108.0
1994	110.3	98.4	106.8	141.3	103.1
1995	110.0	104.5	108.1	136.6	109.6
1996	114.9	106.8	117.1	126.8	116.0
1997	114.4	109.1	116.4	117.8	124.0
1998	113.3	106.5	116.1	123.4	110.7
1999	112.2	97.4	114.0	122.8	106.4
2000	113.0	103.5	113.8	120.1	111.4
2001	113.1	102.5	116.3	111.8	110.5
2002	113.3	103.1	116.4	109.3	115.3
2003	113.5	101.8	115.7	125.0	110.8
2004	113.5	106.7	115.5	117.3	109.1
2005	114.0	107.5	110.3	120.0	112.7
2006	114.0	107.1	112.3	118.7	112.5
2007	115.6	104.5	114.9	118.4	112.9
2008	116.3	107.6	115.7	118.9	115.0
2009	114.5	106.3	110.1	121.2	121.8
2010	114.5	106.9	114.3	117.6	115.0
2011	113.5	106.7	112.8	111.7	119.5
2012	112.2	106.0	112.7	110.3	114.0
2013	111.1	104.8	114.0	113.9	110.4
2014	109.9	105.1	108.4	110.9	109.3
2015	108.2	105.1	104.8	107.4	105.6
2016	108.6	104.0	109.2	106.5	104.8

注：1999年（含）之前，批发和零售业与住宿和餐饮业无法分类，故1999年（含）之前批发和零售业数据为批发和零售业与住宿和餐饮业合计数。

3-6 续表 continued

(本表按可比价格计算) (Data in the table are calculated at constant prices)

年份 Year	交通运输、仓储和邮政业 Transportation Storage Post and Telecommunications	住宿和餐饮业 Accommodation and Catering Trade	金融业 Financial Intermediation	房地产业 Real Estate	其他服务业 Others Services
1992	111.3		107.6	119.5	112.2
1993	102.7		109.7	107.4	111.4
1994	102.5		126.9	160.7	114.8
1995	102.6		103.7	119.7	113.6
1996	115.1		98.7	130.8	114.2
1997	122.4		87.0	109.6	115.1
1998	114.4		88.8	138.3	110.3
1999	111.9		90.6	118.6	117.0
2000	111.7	111.7	107.7	116.6	111.7
2001	111.6	114.2	103.6	123.5	114.2
2002	106.1	116.5	104.6	106.0	116.5
2003	113.6	111.6	107.4	108.8	111.6
2004	115.6	112.9	107.1	110.3	112.9
2005	113.2	136.1	109.3	112.9	117.7
2006	112.3	116.6	107.3	117.5	117.7
2007	110.3	117.3	126.7	119.7	116.3
2008	108.4	111.6	113.6	107.6	122.5
2009	111.0	106.6	123.7	130.8	112.5
2010	119.4	106.6	116.1	128.1	111.9
2011	115.7	108.5	117.9	113.5	112.9
2012	112.6	105.4	124.8	108.8	110.4
2013	108.2	100.7	119.0	111.9	106.1
2014	106.2	102.0	121.1	107.7	110.2
2015	111.3	109.2	119.3	107.9	109.7
2016	109.5	105.7	109.3	113.1	110.7

3-7 主要年份三次产业贡献率

Three Industries Contribution Rate in Representative Years

(本表按可比价格计算) (Data in the table are calculated at constant prices)

年 份 Year	生产总值 Gross Domestic Product	第一产业 Primary Industry	第二产业 Secondary Industry	第三产业 Tertiary Industry
2000	100	1.8	66.9	31.3
2001	100	1.3	50.4	48.3
2002	100	1.5	49.4	49.1
2003	100	0.8	57.7	41.5
2004	100	2.5	54.1	43.4
2005	100	2.6	41.3	56.1
2006	100	2.5	40.2	57.3
2007	100	1.4	41.4	57.2
2008	100	2.0	41.4	56.6
2009	100	1.7	36.5	61.8
2010	100	1.7	42.5	55.8
2011	100	2.1	38.5	59.4
2012	100	2.0	40.7	57.3
2013	100	1.5	50.3	48.2
2014	100	1.7	39.3	59.0
2015	100	1.9	28.4	69.7
2016	100	1.7	36.0	62.3

3-8 主要年份三次产业拉动率

Three Industries Pulling Rate in Representative Years

(本表按可比价格计算) (Data in the table are calculated at constant prices)

年 份 Year	生产总值 Gross Domestic Product	第一产业 Primary Industry	第二产业 Secondary Industry	第三产业 Tertiary Industry
2000	13.0	0.2	8.7	4.1
2001	13.1	0.2	6.6	6.3
2002	13.3	0.2	6.6	6.5
2003	13.5	0.1	7.8	5.6
2004	13.5	0.3	7.3	5.9
2005	14.0	0.4	5.8	7.8
2006	14.0	0.4	5.7	7.9
2007	15.6	0.2	6.4	9.0
2008	16.3	0.3	6.8	9.2
2009	14.5	0.2	5.3	9.0
2010	14.5	0.3	6.2	8.0
2011	13.5	0.3	5.2	8.0
2012	12.2	0.2	5.0	7.0
2013	11.1	0.2	5.6	5.3
2014	9.9	0.2	3.9	5.8
2015	8.2	0.2	2.3	5.7
2016	8.6	0.1	3.1	5.4

3-9 分行业增加值

Value added by Industry

单位：亿元　　(100 million yuan)

指 标	Item	增加值 Value Added		指数（上年=100） Index	
		2015	2016	2015	2016
地区生产总值	**Gross Domestic Product**	**5801.20**	**6282.65**	**108.2**	**108.6**
农、林、牧、渔业	Farming Forestry Animal Husbandry Fishery	241.69	256.38	105.1	104.0
工业	Industry	1376.72	1397.25	104.8	109.2
建筑业	Construction	770.29	818.82	107.4	106.5
批发和零售业	Wholesale and Retail Trades	667.99	702.30	105.6	104.8
交通运输、仓储和邮政业	Transportation,Storage,Post and Telecommunications	260.33	298.52	111.3	109.5
住宿和餐饮业	Accommodation and Catering Trade	159.14	170.67	109.2	105.7
金融业	Financial Intermediation	658.90	724.35	119.3	109.3
房地产业	Real Estate	398.34	459.20	107.9	113.1
其他服务业	Others Services	1267.80	1455.16	109.7	110.7
第一产业	Primary Industry	220.20	232.01	105.0	103.8
第二产业	Secondary Industry	2126.29	2200.36	105.6	108.5
第三产业	Tertiary Industry	3454.71	3850.28	110.4	109.0

3-10 各区县生产总值（2016年）

Gross Domestic Product by Region（2016）

单位：亿元　　　　（100 million yuan）

指　标	Item	生产总值 Gross Domestic Product	第一产业 Primary Industry	第二产业 Secondary Industry	第三产业 Tertiary Industry	人均生产总值（元） Per Capita GDP（yuan）
全　市	**Total**	**6282.65**	**232.01**	**2200.36**	**3850.28**	**71647**
新城区	Xincheng	540.66		192.05	348.61	89188
碑林区	Beilin	741.68		151.36	590.32	117021
莲湖区	Lianhu	621.91		194.55	427.36	86702
灞桥区	Baqiao	329.78	19.73	117.98	192.07	53139
未央区	Weiyang	772.88	1.06	379.68	392.14	91938
雁塔区	Yanta	1235.43		338.05	897.38	101236
阎良区	Yanliang	193.94	22.56	102.39	68.99	66968
临潼区	Lintong	183.11	30.59	59.25	93.27	26968
长安区	Chang'an	608.02	38.47	332.60	236.95	53821
高陵区	Gaoling	300.24	30.23	205.14	64.87	85930
蓝田县	Lantian	122.44	27.59	34.87	59.98	23236
周至县	Zhouzhi	114.99	33.17	26.08	55.74	19726
户　县	Huxian	162.81	28.59	63.80	70.42	28446

注：本表区县数据为初步核算数。

3-11 各区县生产总值指数（2016年）（上年=100）

Indices of Gross Domestic Product by Region（2016）（preceding year = 100）

(本表按可比价格计算) (Data in the table are calculated at constant prices)

指 标	Item	生产总值 Gross Domestic Product	第一产业 Primary Industry	第二产业 Secondary Industry	第三产业 Tertiary Industry	人均生产总值 Per Capita GDP
全 市	**Total**	**108.6**	**103.8**	**108.5**	**109.0**	**107.4**
新城区	Xincheng	108.2		106.7	109.1	107.3
碑林区	Beilin	108.3		114.3	106.9	107.1
莲湖区	Lianhu	108.0		107.5	108.2	106.8
灞桥区	Baqiao	109.6	103.8	108.3	111.1	107.9
未央区	Weiyang	108.7	95.2	110.8	106.7	106.9
雁塔区	Yanta	108.0		103.8	109.9	106.5
阎良区	Yanliang	102.3	104.0	99.3	106.4	101.3
临潼区	Lintong	104.2	103.1	96.3	112.4	103.4
长安区	Chang'an	112.0	103.8	116.9	107.3	110.2
高陵区	Gaoling	107.3	102.9	106.8	111.1	105.9
蓝田县	Lantian	108.2	104.4	106.9	110.8	107.6
周至县	Zhouzhi	108.2	105.2	109.3	109.5	107.4
户 县	Huxian	108.5	104.1	109.5	109.5	107.7

注：本表区县数据为初步核算数。

3-12 主要年份非公有制经济增加值

The Added Value of Non-public-owned Economic in Representative Years

年 份 Year	非公有制经济增加值（亿元） the Added Value of Non-public-owned Economic (100 million yuan)	第一产业 Primary Industry	第二产业 Secondary Industry	第三产业 Tertiary Industry
2005	568.45	20.86	232.66	314.93
2006	684.66	26.27	279.06	379.33
2007	854.26	25.25	365.24	463.77
2008	1103.96	36.42	468.58	598.96
2009	1327.87	36.32	535.02	756.53
2010	1611.71	42.66	636.73	932.32
2011	1956.41	52.93	761.31	1142.17
2012	2258.95	59.79	831.93	1367.23
2013	2569.20	53.72	970.24	1545.24
2014	2892.90	57.40	1079.59	1755.91
2015	3060.38	58.09	1060.92	1941.37
2016	3314.20	61.42	1071.54	2181.24

3-12 续表 continued

年 份 Year	非公有制经济增加值占GDP比重(%) the Added Value of Non-public-owned Economic Percentage to GDP(%)	第一产业 Primary Industry	第二产业 Secondary Industry	第三产业 Tertiary Industry
2005	43.3	31.6	43.1	44.5
2006	44.5	37.3	43.2	46.0
2007	46.0	30.6	46.7	46.7
2008	47.6	35.2	47.7	48.6
2009	48.7	32.9	46.7	51.5
2010	49.7	30.5	46.9	53.4
2011	50.6	30.6	48.1	54.0
2012	51.4	30.6	46.7	56.6
2013	52.2	26.8	48.5	56.7
2014	52.7	26.8	49.2	56.9
2015	52.8	26.4	49.9	56.2
2016	52.8	26.5	48.7	56.7

注：1、2009年—2012年数据根据第三次经济普查GDP修订结果相应进行了调整。
2、2013年—2016年数据为年报最终核实数据。

主要统计指标解释

生产总值（GDP） 是按市场价格计算的一个地区（或国家）所有常住单位在一定时期内生产活动的最终成果。生产总值有三种表现形态，即价值形态、收入形态和产品形态。从价值形态看，它是所有常住单位在一定时期内生产的全部货物和服务价值超过同期中间投入的全部非固定资产货物和服务价值的差额，即所有常住单位的增加值之和；从收入形态看，它是所有常住单位在一定时期内创造并分配给常住单位和非常住单位的初次收入分配之和；从产品形态看，它是所有常住单位在一定时期内最终使用的货物和服务价值与货物和服务净出口价值之和。在实际核算中，生产总值有三种计算方法，即生产法、收入法和支出法。三种方法分别从不同的方面反映生产总值及其构成。

人均生产总值 即“人均GDP”，常作为发展经济学中衡量经济发展状况的指标，是最重要的宏观经济指标之一，它是人们了解和把握一个国家或地区的宏观经济运行状况的有效工具。将一个国家核算期内（通常是一年）实现的国内生产总值与这个国家的常住人口（或户籍人口）相比进行计算，得到人均生产总值。

三次产业 指根据社会生产活动历史发展的顺序对产业结构的划分。目前我国的三次产业划分是：

第一产业是指农、林、牧、渔业（不含农、林、牧、渔服务业）。

第二产业是指采矿业（不含开采辅助活动），制造业（不含金属制品、机械和设备修理业），电力、热力、燃气及水生产和供应业，建筑业。

第三产业即服务业，是指除第一产业、第二产业以外的其他行业。

劳动者报酬 指劳动者因从事生产活动所获得的全部报酬。包括劳动者获得的各种形式的工资、奖金和津贴，既包括货币形式的，也包括实物形式的，还包括劳动者所享受的公费医疗和医药卫生费、上下班交通补贴、单位支付的社会保险费、住房公积金等。

生产税净额 指生产税减生产补贴后的余额。生产税指政府对生产单位从事生产、销售和经营活动以及因从事生产活动使用某些生产要素（如固定资产、土地、劳动力）所征收的各种税、附加费和规费。生产补贴与生产税相反，指政府对生产单位的单方面转移支出，因此视为负生产税，包括政策亏损补贴、价格补贴等。

固定资产折旧 指一定时期内为弥补固定资产损耗按照规定的固定资产折旧率提取的固定资产折旧，或按国民经济核算统一规定的折旧率虚拟计算的固定资产折旧。它反映了固定资产年当期生产中的转移价值。各类企业和企业化管理的事业单位的固定资产折旧是指实际计提的折旧费；不计提折旧的政府机关、非企业化管理的事业单位和居民住房的固定资产折旧是按照统一规定的折旧率和固定资产原值计算的虚拟折旧。原则上，固定资产折旧应按固定资产当期的重置价值计算，但是目前我国尚不具备对全社会固定资产进行重估价的基础，所以暂时只能采用上述办法。

营业盈余 指常住单位创造的增加值扣除劳动者报酬、生产税净额和固定资产折旧后的余额。它相当于企业的营业利润加上生产补贴，但要扣除从利润中开支的工资和福利等。

三次产业贡献率 各产业不变价增加值增量与不变价GDP增量之比。

三次产业拉动率 GDP增长速度与各产业贡献率之乘积。

非公有制经济 非公有制经济是指国民经济中除国有经济和集体经济以外的部分，对其中的混合制经济要依据实收资本之间的比例，按经济成分对各主要经济总量进行划分。

Explanatory Notes on Main Statistical Indicators

Gross Domestic Product (GDP) refers to the final products at market prices produced by all resident units in a country (or a region) during a certain period of time. Gross domestic product is expressed in three different perspectives, namely value, income, and products respectively. GDP in its value perspective refers to the total value of all goods and services produced by all resident units during a certain period of time, minus the total value of input of goods and services of the nature of non-fixed assets; in other words, it is the sum of the value-added of all resident units. GDP from the perspective of income includes the primary income created by all resident units and distributed to resident and non-resident units. GDP from the perspective of products refers to the value of all goods and services for final demand by all resident units plus the net exports of goods and services during a given period of time. In the practice of national accounting, gross domestic product is calculated from three approaches, namely production approach, income approach and expenditure approach, which reflect gross domestic product and its composition from different angles.For a region, it is called as Gross Regional Product (GRP) or regional GDP.

Per capita gross domestic product: "per capita GDP", often used as a measure of economic development in development economics, it is one of the most important macroeconomic indicators, and people's understanding and grasp of a country or a region effective tool of macroeconomic performance. The gross domestic product (GDP) of a country's accounting period (usually one year) is divided by the country's resident population (or household population), resulting in per capita GDP.

Three Strata of Industry Classification of economic activities into three strata of industry is a common practice in the world, although the grouping varies to some extent from country to country. In China economic activities are categorized into the following three strata of industry:

Primary industry refers to agriculture, forestry, animal husbandry and fishery and services in support of these industries.

Secondary industry refers to mining and quarrying, manufacturing, production and supply of electricity, water and gas, and construction.

Tertiary industry refers to all other economic activities not included in the primary or secondary industries.

Compensation of Employees refers to the total payment of various forms to employees for the productive activities they are engaged in. It includes wages, bonuses and allowances, which the employees earn in cash or in kind. It also includes the free medical services provided to the employees and the medicine expenses, transport subsidies and social insurance, and housing fund paid by the employers.

Net Taxes on Production refers to taxes on production less subsidies on production. The taxes on production refers to the various taxes, extra charges and fees levied on the production units on their production, sale and business activities as well as on the use of some factors of production, such as fixed assets, land and labour in the production activities they are engaged in. In contrast to taxes on production, subsidies on production refer to the unilateral government transfer to the production units and are therefore regarded as negative taxes on production. They include subsidies on the loss due to implementation of government policies, price subsidies, etc.

Depreciation of Fixed Assets refers to the depreciation of fixed assets in a given period, drawn in accordance with the stipulated depreciation rate for the purpose of compensating the wear-and-tear loss of the fixed assets or the depreciation of fixed assets imputed in accordance with the stipulated unified depreciation rate in the national economic accounting system. It reflects the value of transfer of the fixed assets in the production of the current period. The depreciation of fixed assets in various enterprises and institutions managed as enterprises refers to the depreciation expenses actually drawn. In government agencies and institutions not managed as enterprises which do not draw the depreciation expenses, as well as for the houses of residents, the depreciation of fixed assets is the imputed depreciation, which is calculated in accordance with the stipulated unified depreciation rate. In principle, the depreciation of fixed assets should be calculated on the basis of the re-purchased value of the fixed assets. However, currently the conditions in China do not facilitate the revaluation of all the fixed assets. Therefore, only the above-mentioned methods can be adopted at present.

Operating Surplus refers to the balance of the value added created by the resident units after deducting the labourers remuneration, net taxes on production and the depreciation of fixed assets. It is equivalent to the business profit of the enterprises plus subsidies to production, but the wages and welfare expenses paid from the profits should be deducted.

Three Industry Contribution Rate The ratio of all industries incremental value added to GDP increment at constant prices.

Three Industries Pulling Rate The product of GDP growth rate and the contribution rate of each industry.

Non–public Economy It refers to the part of in addition to state-owned economy and collective economy in the national economy,On which the mixed-economy should be divided according to the major economic components of total economic output based on the proportion in paid-in capital.

4 人口、从业人员与职工工资

POPULATION,EMPLOYMENT AND WAGES

资料整理：王义龙　安海军　严孟飞

Data management：Wang Yilong An Haijun Yan Mengfei

数据审核：冯军魁

Data audit：Feng Junkui

第四部分　人口、从业人员与职工工资

一、简要说明

本章资料包括主要年份人口、分区县户籍和常住人口及变动、从业人员及劳动报酬等。户籍人口数为公安年报数，1991年以前年份市区数未包括临潼、长安。主要数据由西安市统计局人口就业处提供。

二、主要指标

年末户籍人口（万人）	824.93	比上年增长	1.1%
人口自然增长率（‰）	6.14	比上年上升	1.5个千分点
常住人口（万人）	883.21	比上年增长	1.5%
男女性别比（以女性为100）	105.50	比上年上升	0.01个百分点
户籍人口密度（人/平方公里）	817	比上年增加	9人/平方公里
城镇非私营单位在岗职工年平均工资（元）	69611	比上年增长	10.1%

4　POPULATION,EMPLOYMENT AND WAGES

Ⅰ.Brief Introduction

This chapter consists of the data about registered population and permanent resident population in representative years population of all the districts and counties and the correspondent changes, the employed and their wages. The registered population data are from the annual report of the Xi'an Bureau of Public Security, with Lintong, Chang'an not included before 1991. The population data is provided primarily by Population & Employment Office of the Xi'an Bureau of Statistics.

Ⅱ.Major Indicators

		Increase over Preceding Year
Total registered Population of Year-end(10 000 persons)	824.93	1.1%
Natural Growth Rate(‰)	6.14	1.5per thousand
Permanent Population(10 000 persons)	883.21	1.5%
Sex Ratio (Female=100)	105.50	0.01 percentage points
Density of Population (person/sq.km)	817	9 persons per square kilometeks
Aunual Average Wage of Staff and Workers in Urban Non-privite Enterprises(yuan)	69611	10.1%

4-1 主要年份人口数、人口密度和人口发展情况

Population, Population Density and Population Development in Representative Years

单位：万人 (10 000 persons)

年份 Year	总人口 Total population	市区 Urban Area	女性人口 Number of Female	城填人口 Urban Population	人口密度 (人 / 平方公里) Density of Population (person/sq.km)	总人口指数（上年为100）Total Population Index (100 for preceding year) 全市 Whole City	市区 Urban Area
1952	252.92	92.42	118.81	57.61	254	102.6	103.1
1965	400.05	179.88	190.72	136.39	401	102.5	103.4
1970	435.12	188.12	210.47	139.12	436	101.9	101.4
1978	498.10	210.15	241.82	159.98	499	101.7	102.7
1980	511.91	221.19	249.26	172.85	513	101.4	102.6
1985	553.11	245.76	268.40	201.90	554	101.6	102.2
1986	563.97	251.80	273.30	205.92	565	102.0	102.5
1987	574.46	257.69	278.12	210.25	575	101.9	102.3
1988	585.85	264.94	283.68	216.99	587	102.0	102.8
1989	597.36	270.80	289.44	222.54	598	102.0	102.2
1990	608.89	275.69	295.29	226.98	610	101.9	101.8
1991	615.48	419.29	298.13	230.85	617	101.1	152.1
1992	623.20	429.54	301.92	236.45	624	101.3	102.4
1993	630.91	435.41	305.30	240.85	632	101.2	101.4
1994	639.45	442.30	309.17	248.35	641	101.4	101.6
1995	648.21	448.65	313.46	255.71	645	101.4	101.4
1996	654.87	454.68	316.60	261.28	653	101.0	101.3
1997	662.06	461.17	320.18	267.52	663	101.1	101.4
1998	668.22	466.31	323.20	271.75	669	100.9	101.1
1999	674.50	463.56	326.12	276.14	676	100.9	99.4
2000	688.01	483.10	332.83	285.79	689	102.0	104.2
2001	694.84	489.88	336.04	292.62	696	101.0	101.4
2002	702.59	497.38	339.51	300.05	704	101.1	101.5
2003	716.58	510.26	346.26	312.88	718	102.0	102.6
2004	725.01	516.30	350.85	318.50	717	101.2	101.2
2005	741.73	533.21	359.71	333.14	734	102.3	103.3
2006	753.11	540.97	365.74	343.78	745	101.5	101.5
2007	764.25	549.19	371.84	353.85	756	101.5	101.5
2008	772.30	554.73	376.76	363.87	764	101.1	101.0
2009	781.67	561.58	382.39	370.66	773	101.2	101.2
2010	782.73	562.65	383.93	374.64	774	100.1	100.2
2011	791.83	568.77	389.31	391.31	783	101.2	101.1
2012	795.98	572.76	392.04	398.40	788	100.5	100.7
2013	806.93	580.60	398.15	409.82	799	101.4	101.4
2014	815.29	587.16	402.83	418.16	807	101.0	101.1
2015	815.66	588.43	403.43	545.95	808	100.0	100.2
2016	824.93	629.24	408.39	552.21	817	101.1	106.9

注：本表为公安年报数据,系户籍人口。2016年起公安年报调整至11月30日，市区数1991年增加临潼、长安，2016年增加高陵，行政区划面积自2012年发生变更，调整了2012年和2013年户籍人口密度。2015年公安局户籍改革，按统计上城乡划分标准统计城镇与乡村人口。

4-2 主要年份人口自然变动情况

Natural Population Movements in Representative Years

单位：万人 (10 000 persons)

年份 Year	出生 Birth 人数 Population	出生率 (‰) Birth Rate (‰)	死亡 Death 人数 Population	死亡率 (‰) Death Rate (‰)	自然增长率 (‰) Natural Growth Rate (‰)	迁入人口 Immigrant population	迁出人口 Emigrant population
1985	8.95	16.30	3.01	5.48	10.82	11.60	8.74
1986	10.14	18.15	2.78	4.97	13.18	11.79	8.39
1987	9.76	17.14	2.83	4.97	12.17	12.58	9.26
1988	9.42	16.24	2.89	4.98	11.26	13.54	8.97
1989	11.78	19.92	3.04	5.13	14.79	12.73	10.15
1990	12.40	20.55	3.45	5.72	14.83	11.82	9.86
1991	8.73	14.25	3.26	5.33	8.92	8.98	6.09
1992	8.98	14.49	3.39	5.48	9.01	13.94	9.54
1993	9.25	14.75	3.37	5.38	9.37	11.50	8.33
1994	8.08	12.71	3.16	4.97	7.74	13.40	8.59
1995	7.69	11.95	3.21	4.98	6.97	14.41	8.85
1996	7.26	11.15	3.41	5.24	5.91	11.94	8.88
1997	6.84	10.38	3.12	4.75	5.63	12.58	8.62
1998	6.40	9.62	3.10	4.66	4.96	10.89	8.36
1999	6.19	9.22	3.88	5.78	3.44	12.58	9.23
2000	8.90	13.07	4.06	5.96	7.11	17.12	9.23
2001	5.11	7.39	2.89	4.19	3.20	15.16	10.83
2002	5.34	7.64	3.08	4.41	3.23	13.90	9.41
2003	6.02	8.48	3.32	4.68	3.80	20.60	9.15
2004	6.63	9.19	4.23	5.87	3.32	15.56	10.19
2005	7.67	9.58	4.13	5.16	4.42	22.61	9.46
2006	8.13	9.98	4.45	5.46	4.52	17.23	11.75
2007	8.27	10.00	4.53	5.48	4.52	19.90	14.01
2008	8.47	10.15	4.65	5.57	4.58	18.49	15.04
2009	8.47	10.08	4.73	5.63	4.45	16.84	13.14
2010	8.23	9.73	4.51	5.34	4.39	14.09	13.50
2011	8.25	9.71	4.57	5.38	4.33	14.21	11.74
2012	8.64	10.13	4.75	5.57	4.56	12.55	13.10
2013	8.20	9.57	4.60	5.37	4.20	10.83	8.60
2014	8.70	10.11	4.71	5.47	4.64	9.10	7.61
2015	8.80	10.15	4.78	5.51	4.64	8.08	11.61
2016	10.12	11.54	4.74	5.40	6.14	6.21	4.68

注：2004年以前为公安年报数据。迁入人口和迁出人口为公安年报数据。2010年出生、死亡、自然增长率根据第六次人口普查数据推算得出。2005-2009、2011-2016年出生、死亡、自然增长率为人口变动抽样调查推算数据。

4-3 人口年龄构成和抚养比

Population Age Composition and Dependency Ratio

单位：%　　(%)

年 份 Year	各年龄段人口比重 Proportion of Population of All Ages			总抚养比 Total dependency ratio		
	0-14岁 0-14 year old	15-64岁 15-64 year old	65岁及以上 65 year old and above		少年儿童 children	老年人口 Elderly population
1990	25.71	69.08	5.21	44.76	37.21	7.55
2000	22.27	71.26	6.47	40.33	31.25	9.08
2010	12.89	78.65	8.46	27.15	16.39	10.76
2011	12.57	78.33	9.10	27.66	16.04	11.62
2012	12.54	78.02	9.44	28.17	16.07	12.10
2013	12.46	77.88	9.66	28.40	16.00	12.40
2014	12.52	77.46	10.02	29.10	16.16	12.94
2015	12.56	76.94	10.50	29.98	16.33	13.65
2016	12.76	76.35	10.89	30.97	16.71	14.26

注：1990、2000、2010年数据根据人口普查数据加工整理，2011-2016年数据根据人口变动抽样调查数据推算。
抚养比指0-14岁、65岁及以上人口占15-64岁人口的比重。

4-4 全市及各区县人口数和户数（2016年）

Population and Households by Region（2016）

单位：万人　　(10 000 persons)

区 县	Region	总户数（万户） Number of Households (10 000 households)	总人口 Total Population	城填人口 Urban Population	按性别划分Grouped by Sex 男 Male	女 Female	迁入人口(人) Immigrant population (person)	迁出人口(人) Emigrant population (person)
全 市	**Total**	**256.65**	**824.93**	**552.21**	**416.54**	**408.39**	**62126**	**46762**
新城区	Xincheng	17.30	50.43	50.43	25.51	24.92	2571	1986
碑林区	Beilin	21.60	69.35	69.35	35.05	34.30	8774	10077
莲湖区	Lianhu	23.37	66.49	66.49	33.37	33.12	4834	2078
灞桥区	Baqiao	18.13	54.68	54.42	26.88	27.80	3793	1538
未央区	Weiyang	20.30	61.78	61.78	30.68	31.10	7450	3939
雁塔区	Yanta	28.85	86.95	86.95	43.36	43.59	14230	12041
阎良区	Yanliang	8.08	26.49	12.31	13.29	13.20	1223	734
临潼区	Lintong	20.92	71.55	24.15	36.20	35.35	2285	1548
长安区	Chang'an	32.47	108.30	46.62	53.91	54.39	7295	3714
高陵区	Gaoling	10.29	33.22	21.96	16.51	16.71	2150	2408
蓝田县	Lantian	19.20	65.53	18.61	33.98	31.55	2209	2416
周至县	Zhouzhi	17.87	68.94	16.81	36.32	32.62	2507	2345
户 县	Huxian	18.26	61.22	22.33	31.48	29.74	2805	1938

注：本表均为公安年报数据。总户数未机械配平。

4-5 全市及各区县常住人口数和人口变动情况（2016年）

Permanent Population and Population Changes by Region（2016）

区 县	Region	常住人口（万人） Permanent Population (10 000 persons)	城镇 Urban	出生率（‰） Birth Rate（‰）	死亡率（‰） Death Rate（‰）	自然增长率（‰） Natural Growth Rate（‰）
全 市	**Total**	**883.21**	**648.54**	**11.54**	**5.40**	**6.14**
新城区	Xincheng	60.91	60.91	8.14	3.36	4.78
碑林区	Beilin	63.87	63.87	9.81	3.88	5.93
莲湖区	Lianhu	72.23	72.23	9.41	3.74	5.67
灞桥区	Baqiao	62.73	59.38	12.07	5.48	6.59
未央区	Weiyang	85.08	82.41	11.39	5.33	6.06
雁塔区	Yanta	123.11	123.11	11.15	4.50	6.65
阎良区	Yanliang	29.08	16.59	11.18	5.48	5.70
临潼区	Lintong	68.18	23.66	11.72	5.66	6.06
长安区	Chang'an	114.11	66.34	13.02	6.97	6.05
高陵区	Gaoling	35.11	22.54	12.70	5.80	6.90
蓝田县	Lantian	52.86	15.63	13.40	7.12	6.28
周至县	Zhouzhi	58.50	18.22	13.72	7.27	6.45
户 县	Huxian	57.44	23.65	12.61	6.13	6.48

注：本表数据均为人口变动抽样调查推算数据。

4-6 主要年份常住人口数

Permanent Population in Representative Years

单位：万人 (10 000 persons)

年 份 Year	年末常住人口 Permanent population (year-end)	城镇 Urban	乡村 Rural
2000	741.14	450.36	290.78
2005	806.81	510.55	296.26
2006	822.52	530.94	291.58
2007	830.54	548.99	281.55
2008	837.52	565.16	272.36
2009	843.46	581.4	262.06
2010	847.41	584.71	262.70
2011	851.34	596.79	254.55
2012	855.29	611.62	243.67
2013	858.81	618.77	240.04
2014	862.75	626.44	236.31
2015	870.56	635.68	234.88
2016	883.21	648.54	234.67

注：2000年常住人口为普查数据。2010年常住人口为年末常住人口数，根据第六次人口普查数据推算得出。2005-2009、2011-2016年常住人口为人口变动抽样调查推算数据。

4-7 主要年份社会从业人数

Number of Social Laborers in Representative Years

单位：万人 (10 000 persons)

年份 Year	合计 Total	一、按城乡分 Grouped by Urban area and Rural area					二、按三次产业分 Grouped by Industry		
		1.城镇 Urban	国有经济 State-owned Enterprises	集体经济 Collective Enterprises	其他经济 Others	2.乡村 Village	第一产业 Primary Industry	第二产业 Secondary Industry	第三产业 Tertiary Industry
1985	**296.80**	129.07	96.80	29.07	3.20	167.73	135.89	98.61	62.30
1986	**299.45**	132.82	101.28	28.43	3.11	166.63	127.46	100.61	71.38
1987	**312.16**	138.56	104.58	30.72	3.26	173.60	130.36	107.75	74.05
1988	**327.76**	142.24	106.46	30.73	5.05	185.52	138.87	108.12	80.77
1989	**332.65**	145.65	108.80	30.44	6.41	187.00	142.21	106.40	84.04
1990	**343.06**	147.93	110.95	29.78	7.20	195.13	149.64	106.74	86.68
1991	**347.65**	149.48	111.87	29.80	7.81	198.17	152.24	108.19	87.22
1992	**357.51**	151.67	113.19	29.97	8.51	205.84	154.75	110.22	92.54
1993	**363.70**	155.72	112.98	29.77	12.97	207.98	154.02	114.02	95.66
1994	**364.56**	154.88	113.39	27.97	13.52	209.68	153.51	108.53	102.52
1995	**372.60**	158.80	113.79	25.58	19.43	213.80	153.39	109.67	109.54
1996	**379.29**	164.54	113.29	24.82	26.43	214.75	153.43	109.17	116.69
1997	**385.14**	169.52	112.44	23.52	33.56	215.62	153.23	109.46	122.45
1998	**393.95**	177.20	106.06	21.50	49.64	216.75	153.00	110.45	130.50
1999	**400.43**	180.27	105.08	20.50	54.69	220.16	154.64	110.58	135.21
2000	**389.10**	176.45	103.46	18.40	54.59	212.65	147.03	107.26	134.81
2001	**389.30**	177.94	100.47	17.10	60.37	211.36	145.09	108.96	135.25
2002	**397.16**	181.85	100.54	16.90	64.41	215.31	143.04	111.62	142.50
2003	**404.92**	183.23	94.51	16.78	71.94	221.69	146.67	109.09	149.16
2004	**409.57**	187.53	93.43	15.41	78.69	222.04	141.81	111.70	156.06
2005	**415.83**	192.53	93.27	14.47	84.79	223.30	136.31	114.20	165.32
2006	**422.15**	196.16	84.46	14.41	97.29	225.99	135.10	116.09	170.96
2007	**436.36**	214.27	90.58	11.88	111.81	222.09	133.33	125.06	177.97
2008	**448.05**	224.20	90.17	10.60	123.43	223.85	127.87	130.23	189.95
2009	**462.52**	239.39	90.83	7.63	140.93	223.13	122.13	131.57	208.82
2010	**477.58**	252.54	94.01	5.48	153.05	225.04	117.27	145.40	214.91
2011	**495.99**	265.43	91.62	5.33	168.48	230.56	121.05	151.33	223.61
2012	**514.57**	287.65	95.33	5.10	187.22	226.92	114.92	162.35	237.30
2013	**530.71**	308.04	86.06	7.29	214.69	222.67	110.45	151.50	268.76
2014	**532.92**	316.59	84.83	6.67	225.09	216.33	105.02	151.85	276.05
2015	**528.06**	327.68	84.52	5.29	237.87	200.38	107.68	129.51	290.87
2016	**539.18**	335.07	87.15	4.85	243.07	204.11	105.12	127.88	306.18

注：第一产业从业人员中包括城镇农林牧渔及服务业企业人员。

4-8 按国民经济行业分从业人数（2016年）

单位：万人

行 业	Sector	合计 Total
总计	**Total**	**539.18**
（一）农、林、牧、渔业	Agriculture ,Forestry,Animal Husbandry and Fishery	105.13
（二）采矿业	Mining	0.83
（三）制造业	Manufacturing	72.67
（四）电力、燃气及水的生产供应业	Production and Distribution of Electricity,Gas and Water	5.33
（五）建筑业	Construction	49.05
（六）批发和零售业	Wholesale and Retail Trades	89.43
（七）交通运输、仓储和邮政业	Traffic,Transport,Storage and Post	29.61
（八）住宿和餐饮业	Hotels and Catering Services	33.71
（九）信息传输、软件和信息技术服务业	Information Transmission,Software and Information Technology Services	16.31
（十）金融业	Financial Intermediation	10.03
（十一）房地产业	Real Estate	10.06
（十二）租赁和商务服务业	Leasing and Business Services	20.31
（十三）科学研究和技术服务业	Scientific Research and Technical Services	15.94
（十四）水利、环境和公共设施管理业	Management of Water Conservancy, Environment and Public Facilities	2.90
（十五）居民服务、修理和其他服务业	Services to Households, Repairs and Other Services	23.37
（十六）教育	Education	23.06
（十七）卫生和社会工作	Health and Social Work	15.31
（十八）文化、体育和娱乐业	Culture, Sports and Entertainment	3.32
（十九）公共管理、社会保障和社会组织	Public Administration, Social Security and Social Organizations	12.81
（二十）国际组织	International Organizations	

Number of Employed Persons Grouped by Industry of the National Economy (2016)

(10 000 persons)

国有经济 State-owned Enterprises	集体经济 Collective Enterprises	城镇其他经济 Urban Other Enterprises	城镇私营经济及个体劳动者 Urban Private Enterprises and Individual Labors	乡村从业人员 Rural Employed Persons
87.15	**4.85**	**107.19**	**135.88**	**204.11**
0.22		0.01	2.58	102.32
		0.52	0.31	
17.35	0.20	27.94	7.62	19.56
3.08	0.05	2.07	0.13	0.00
2.49	2.77	19.01	3.92	20.86
1.52	0.17	10.61	63.58	13.55
11.32	0.01	5.13	2.73	10.42
0.55	0.01	5.06	18.73	9.36
0.10		8.34	6.94	0.93
1.36	0.23	7.39	0.23	0.82
1.35	0.05	5.90	2.76	0.00
1.13	1.04	6.07	7.95	4.12
9.61	0.05	3.64	2.02	0.62
1.51	0.01	1.05	0.33	
0.43	0.07	0.54	13.78	8.55
15.45	0.05	1.82	0.49	5.25
6.65	0.14	0.93	0.62	6.97
1.05		1.12	1.15	
11.98		0.04	0.01	0.78

4-9 全部单位从业人员情况（2016年）

单位：人

分 组	Classify	单位从业人员 Employed Persons	女性 Female
总计	**Total**	**1991909**	**729948**
一、按机构类型分组	**Grouped by Organization Type**		
#企业	Enterprises	1584810	537842
事业	Public institutions	276320	146514
机关	Government units	110893	35481
二、按国民经济行业分组	**Grouped by Economic Sector**		
（一）农业	Agriculture ,Forestry,Animal Husbandry and Fishery	2256	580
（二）采矿业	Mining	5215	1422
（三）制造业	Manufacturing	454908	152887
（四）电力、燃气及水的生产供应业	Production and Distribution of Electricity,Gas and Water	52053	14461
（五）建筑业	Construction	242586	36013
（六）批发和零售业	Wholesale and Retail Trades	123055	63695
（七）交通运输、仓储和邮政业	Traffic,Transport,Storage and Post	164525	45430
（八）住宿和餐饮业	Hotels and Catering Services	56198	33553
（九）信息传输、软件和信息技术服务业	Information Transmission,Software and Information Technology Services	84393	32205
（十）金融业	Financial Intermediation	89838	51540
（十一）房地产业	Real Estate	73110	28616
（十二） 租赁和商务服务业	Leasing and Business Services	82308	16112
（十三）科学研究和技术服务业	Scientific Research and Technical Services	132961	42616
（十四）水利、环境和公共设施管理业	Management of Water Conservancy, Environment and Public Facilities	25761	10748
（十五）居民服务、修理和其他服务业	Services to Households, Repairs and Other Services	10456	4347
（十六）教育	Education	173200	94969
（十七）卫生和社会工作	Health and Social Work	77151	51812
（十八）文化、体育和娱乐业	Culture, Sports and Entertainment	21787	9805
（十九）公共管理、社会保障和社会组织	Public Administration, Social Security and Social Organizations	120148	39137
（二十）国际组织	International Organizations		

注：采矿业因企业行业代码发生变化，故从业人员与上年同比变化较大。

Basic Facts on All Employees (2016)

(person)

在岗职工合计 Total Fully Employed Staff and Workers	其他从业人员 Other Employed Persons	单位从业人员平均人数 Average Employment	在岗职工 Staff and Workers	其他从业人员 Other Employed Persons
1849293	**142616**	**2022100**	**1881425**	**140675**
1471929	112881	1602621	1491188	111433
260477	15843	285939	270603	15336
97365	13528	113779	100270	13509
2051	205	2260	2055	205
4587	628	5215	4576	639
445951	8957	470302	460433	9869
51412	641	49007	48386	621
194429	48157	238204	192471	45733
119919	3136	122186	119005	3181
158329	6196	167213	160876	6337
51778	4420	56379	52490	3889
84093	300	79257	78940	317
63681	26157	89731	63103	26628
71472	1638	72928	71293	1635
79127	3181	86679	83942	2737
127154	5807	142778	136893	5885
23165	2596	25576	23051	2525
10146	310	10564	10200	364
162294	10906	181948	171127	10821
73327	3824	77101	73302	3799
20470	1317	21848	20564	1284
105908	14240	122924	108718	14206

4-10 国有单位从业人员情况（2016年）

单位：人

分　组	Classify	单位从业人员 Employed Persons	女性 Female
总计	**Total**	**871454**	**344776**
一、按机构类型分组	**Grouped by Organization Type**		
#企业	Enterprises	487397	164680
事业	Public institutions	272262	144130
机关	Government units	110563	35387
二、按国民经济行业分组	**Grouped by Economic Sector**		
（一）农业	Agriculture ,Forestry,Animal Husbandry and Fishery	2183	551
（二）采矿业	Mining		
（三）制造业	Manufacturing	173536	62270
（四）电力、燃气及水的生产供应业	Production and Distribution of Electricity,Gas and Water	30836	8570
（五）建筑业	Construction	24858	5221
（六）批发和零售业	Wholesale and Retail Trades	15220	7820
（七）交通运输、仓储和邮政业	Traffic,Transport,Storage and Post	113113	28949
（八）住宿和餐饮业	Hotels and Catering Services	5502	2927
（九）信息传输、软件和信息技术服务业	Information Transmission,Software and Information Technology Services	995	291
（十）金融业	Financial Intermediation	13610	7238
（十一）房地产业	Real Estate	13549	5196
（十二）租赁和商务服务业	Leasing and Business Services	11254	5020
（十三）科学研究和技术服务业	Scientific Research and Technical Services	96063	32608
（十四）水利、环境和公共设施管理业	Management of Water Conservancy, Environment and Public Facilities	15110	6058
（十五）居民服务、修理和其他服务业	Services to Households, Repairs and Other Services	4262	1058
（十六）教育	Education	154523	83569
（十七）卫生和社会工作	Health and Social Work	66503	44167
（十八）文化、体育和娱乐业	Culture, Sports and Entertainment	10540	4270
（十九）公共管理、社会保障和社会组织	Public Administration, Social Security and Social Organizations	119797	38993
（二十）国际组织	International Organizations		

Basic Facts on Employees in State-owned Units（2016）

(person)

		单位从业人员		
在岗职工合计 Total Fully Employed Staff and Workers	其他从业人员 Other Employed Persons	平均人数 Average Employment	在岗职工 Staff and Workers	其他从业人员 Other Employed Persons
826427	**45027**	**913550**	**868900**	**44650**
471413	15984	516953	500808	16145
256860	15402	281882	266987	14895
97035	13528	113482	99973	13509
1978	205	2187	1982	205
169384	4152	189355	185047	4308
30707	129	27975	27860	115
23521	1337	28803	27495	1308
14649	571	14930	14374	556
109145	3968	116819	112919	3900
4935	567	5507	4971	536
976	19	988	969	19
13265	345	13662	13304	358
12863	686	13543	12952	591
10827	427	11266	10823	443
93288	2775	105576	102772	2804
12950	2160	14980	12920	2060
4173	89	4165	4065	100
145383	9140	163894	154949	8945
62862	3641	66727	63106	3621
9963	577	10611	10035	576
105558	14239	122562	108357	14205

4-11 城镇集体单位从业人员情况（2016年）

单位：人

分　组	Classify	单位从业人员 Employed Persons	女性 Female
总计	**Total**	**48536**	**8136**
一、按机构类型分组	**Grouped by Organization Type**		
#企业	Enterprises	47657	7611
事业	Public institutions	846	509
机关	Government units		
二、按国民经济行业分组	**Grouped by Economic Sector**		
（一）农业	Agriculture ,Forestry,Animal Husbandry and Fishery		
（二）采矿业	Mining		
（三）制造业	Manufacturing	1995	677
（四）电力、燃气及水的生产供应业	Production and Distribution of Electricity,Gas and Water	548	55
（五）建筑业	Construction	27662	2627
（六）批发和零售业	Wholesale and Retail Trades	1694	595
（七）交通运输、仓储和邮政业	Traffic,Transport,Storage and Post	57	23
（八）住宿和餐饮业	Hotels and Catering Services	63	40
（九）信息传输、软件和信息技术服务业	Information Transmission,Software and Information Technology Services	20	9
（十）金融业	Financial Intermediation	2329	1147
（十一）房地产业	Real Estate	548	184
（十二）租赁和商务服务业	Leasing and Business Services	10386	1223
（十三）科学研究和技术服务业	Scientific Research and Technical Services	547	188
（十四）水利、环境和公共设施管理业	Management of Water Conservancy, Environment and Public Facilities	131	55
（十五）居民服务、修理和其他服务业	Services to Households, Repairs and Other Services	745	298
（十六）教育	Education	458	201
（十七）卫生和社会工作	Health and Social Work	1351	814
（十八）文化、体育和娱乐业	Culture, Sports and Entertainment	2	
（十九）公共管理、社会保障和社会组织	Public Administration, Social Security and Social Organizations		
（二十）国际组织	International Organizations		

Basic Facts on Employees in Urban Collective-owned Units（2016）

(persons)

在岗职工合计 Total Fully Employed Staff and Workers	其他从业人员 Other Employed Persons	单位从业人员 平均人数 Average Employment	在岗职工 Staff and Workers	其他从业人员 Other Employed Persons
45427	**3109**	**47705**	**45018**	**2687**
44564	3093	46827	44156	2671
830	16	843	827	16
1861	134	2030	1897	133
548		550	514	36
26990	672	27309	26676	633
1402	292	1692	1396	296
57		55	55	
63		59	59	
20		22	22	
2200	129	2270	2140	130
514	34	533	506	27
8729	1657	9999	8754	1245
525	22	546	526	20
131		137	137	
592	153	751	600	151
452	6	452	446	6
1341	10	1298	1288	10
2		2	2	

4-12 其他经济类型单位从业人员情况（2016年）

单位：人

分　组	Classify	单位从业人员 Employed Persons	女性 Female
总计	**Total**	**1071919**	**377035**
一、按机构类型分组	**Grouped by Organization Type**		
#企业	Enterprises	1049756	365551
事业	Public institutions	3212	1875
机关	Government units	330	94
二、按国民经济行业分组	**Grouped by Economic Sector**		
（一）农业	Agriculture ,Forestry,Animal Husbandry and Fishery	73	29
（二）采矿业	Mining	5215	1422
（三）制造业	Manufacturing	279377	89940
（四）电力、燃气及水的生产供应业	Production and Distribution of Electricity,Gas and Water	20669	5836
（五）建筑业	Construction	190066	28165
（六）批发和零售业	Wholesale and Retail Trades	106141	55280
（七）交通运输、仓储和邮政业	Traffic,Transport,Storage and Post	51355	16457
（八）住宿和餐饮业	Hotels and Catering Services	50633	30586
（九）信息传输、软件和信息技术服务业	Information Transmission,Software and Information Technology Services	83378	31905
（十）金融业	Financial Intermediation	73899	43155
（十一）房地产业	Real Estate	59013	23236
（十二）租赁和商务服务业	Leasing and Business Services	60668	9869
（十三）科学研究和技术服务业	Scientific Research and Technical Services	36351	9820
（十四）水利、环境和公共设施管理业	Management of Water Conservancy, Environment and Public Facilities	10520	4635
（十五）居民服务、修理和其他服务业	Services to Households, Repairs and Other Services	5449	2991
（十六）教育	Education	18219	11199
（十七）卫生和社会工作	Health and Social Work	9297	6831
（十八）文化、体育和娱乐业	Culture, Sports and Entertainment	11245	5535
（十九）公共管理、社会保障和社会组织	Public Administration, Social Security and Social Organizations	351	144
（二十）国际组织	International Organizations		

Basic Facts on Employees in Other Units (2016)

(persons)

在岗职工合计 Total Fully Employed Staff and Workers	其他从业人员 Other Employed Persons	单位从业人员 平均人数 Average Employment	在岗职工 Staff and Workers	其他从业人员 Other Employed Persons
977439	**94480**	**1060845**	**967507**	**93338**
955952	93804	1038841	946224	92617
2787	425	3214	2789	425
330		297	297	
73		73	73	
4587	628	5215	4576	639
274706	4671	278917	273489	5428
20157	512	20482	20012	470
143918	46148	182092	138300	43792
103868	2273	105564	103235	2329
49127	2228	50339	47902	2437
46780	3853	50813	47460	3353
83097	281	78247	77949	298
48216	25683	73799	47659	26140
58095	918	58852	57835	1017
59571	1097	65414	64365	1049
33341	3010	36656	33595	3061
10084	436	10459	9994	465
5381	68	5648	5535	113
16459	1760	17602	15732	1870
9124	173	9076	8908	168
10505	740	11235	10527	708
350	1	362	361	1

4-13 城镇非私营单位分行业从业人员年平均工资

单位：元

分　组	Classify	2010
总计	**Grouped by Economic Sector**	**37870**
（一）农业	Agriculture ,Forestry,Animal Husbandry and Fishery	21436
（二）采矿业	Mining	32154
（三）制造业	Manufacturing	26663
（四）电力、燃气及水的生产供应业	Production and Distribution of Electricity,Gas and Water	39508
（五）建筑业	Construction	26875
（六）批发和零售业	Wholesale and Retail Trades	25103
（七）交通运输、仓储和邮政业	Traffic,Transport,Storage and Post	41737
（八）住宿和餐饮业	Hotels and Catering Services	19647
（九）信息传输、软件和信息技术服务业	Information Transmission,Software and Information Technology Services	45904
（十）金融业	Financial Intermediation	63952
（十一）房地产业	Real Estate	45273
（十二）租赁和商务服务业	Leasing and Business Services	30267
（十三）科学研究和技术服务业	Scientific Research and Technical Services	55456
（十四）水利、环境和公共设施管理业	Management of Water Conservancy, Environment and Public Facilities	25322
（十五）居民服务、修理和其他服务业	Services to Households, Repairs and Other Services	26443
（十六）教育	Education	53084
（十七）卫生和社会工作	Health and Social Work	44035
（十八）文化、体育和娱乐业	Culture, Sports and Entertainment	31925
（十九）公共管理、社会保障和社会组织	Public Administration, Social Security and Social Organizations	39964
（二十）国际组织	International Organizations	

Average Wages of Urban Non-private Employees by Industry

(yuan)

2011	2012	2013	2014	2015	2016
41679	**44533**	**49350**	**54573**	**60557**	**67205**
23567	31846	36658	42881	43426	48626
38551	33489	40605	42116	46645	108827
34698	38957	44321	49482	56686	61434
47705	55409	59955	61252	65887	69092
29773	35828	39507	48275	52783	60475
27996	34382	37362	40915	46203	48210
48231	48760	54147	59189	62816	63583
22925	26637	29497	30914	33746	37507
51135	63328	67495	100550	109448	137210
72195	75652	97140	104433	106807	108569
34626	37567	44832	48120	52423	56979
31549	34291	42109	46828	52637	54395
64448	68274	69951	69958	72731	79539
26009	29938	38429	43033	45356	44062
23993	25103	32066	32478	37019	35721
54442	54581	59143	58451	63761	71635
48836	56764	61602	59892	61623	74797
34717	40833	50201	57239	61561	65974
42163	47691	49893	47000	51681	59437

4–14 主要年份单位从业人员数及工资总额

Number of Employees and Remuneration in Representative Years

年 份 year	单位从业人员（万人） Number of Employed Persons (10 000 persons)	从业人员工资总额（亿元） Remuneration of Employed Persons (100mil. yuan)	城镇非私营单位从业人员年平均工资（元） Aunual Average Wage of Employees in Urban Non-privite Units(yuan)	国有单位从业人员年平均工资（元） Aunual Average Wage of Employees in State Owned units(yuan)	城镇集体单位从业人员年平均工资（元） Aunual Average Wage of Employees in Urban Collective units(yuan)	其他经济类型单位从业人员年平均工资（元） Aunual Average Wage of Employees in Other units (yuan)
1978	67.19	4.71	713	705	609	
1980	91.76	7.31	859	849	699	
1985	127.04	14.17	1148	1215	923	1409
1986	132.78	16.87	1311	1388	1048	1659
1987	135.48	19.13	1446	1544	1107	1583
1988	137.56	22.81	1702	1842	1216	2065
1989	139.86	25.64	1873	2010	1385	2188
1990	141.55	29.48	2133	2290	1545	2044
1991	142.86	26.88	2276	2435	1657	2966
1992	144.51	30.80	2545	2758	1709	3504
1993	146.03	43.25	2999	3274	1910	3551
1994	142.37	58.87	4172	4588	2337	5243
1995	141.17	67.23	4763	5168	2837	5863
1996	140.60	75.64	5407	5858	3216	6225
1997	138.89	80.83	5785	6204	3437	7487
1998	138.78	82.85	6900	7445	3964	6942
1999	115.88	90.13	7764	8238	4374	8217
2000	112.45	103.80	9179	9742	5178	9451
2001	113.93	123.12	10786	11570	5431	10781
2002	115.77	138.88	12138	12877	6230	12543
2003	116.68	155.95	13504	14217	6892	14215
2004	118.15	184.63	15473	15994	7428	17030
2005	123.66	215.67	17728	18420	7612	19066
2006	125.10	250.87	20475	21392	8494	21859
2007	129.40	319.23	25012	25696	9768	27400
2008	130.85	379.29	29749	30246	10834	33344
2009	135.64	450.48	34032	34611	11940	37307
2010	140.38	520.88	37870	38122	12505	40721
2011	154.33	658.73	41679	45217	23241	37643
2012	165.59	770.86	44533	47493	29988	41218
2013	198.42	1031.46	49350	52782	34591	47462
2014	199.41	1151.53	54573	54138	41006	55766
2015	198.46	1255.75	60557	60301	43291	61590
2016	199.19	1358.95	67205	66295	48098	68847

4-15 全部单位从业人员工资总额（2016年）

Total Wages of All Employees of All Units（2016）

单位：万元 （10 000yuan）

分组	Classify	单位从业人员工资总额 Total Wages of Employment	在岗职工工资总额 Total Wages of Employed Staff and Workers
总计	**Total**	**13589501**	**13096850**
一、按机构类型分组	**Grouped by Organization Type**		
#企业	Enterprises	10745044	10343107
事业	Public institutions	2059113	1998232
机关	Government units	672397	643603
二、按国民经济行业分组	**Grouped by Economic Sector**		
（一）农业	Agriculture ,Forestry,Animal Husbandry and Fishery	10989	10784
（二）采矿业	Mining	56753	49408
（三）制造业	Manufacturing	2889272	2855923
（四）电力、燃气及水的生产供应业	Production and Distribution of Electricity, Gas and Water	338601	336011
（五）建筑业	Construction	1440550	1225088
（六）批发和零售业	Wholesale and Retail Trades	589060	580261
（七）交通运输、仓储和邮政业	Traffic,Transport,Storage and Post	1063196	1041166
（八）住宿和餐饮业	Hotels and Catering Services	211461	201805
（九）信息传输、软件和信息技术服务业	Information Transmission,Software and Information Technology Services	1087484	1085347
（十）金融业	Financial Intermediation	974196	928904
（十一）房地产业	Real Estate	415535	410060
（十二）租赁和商务服务业	Leasing and Business Services	471493	463328
（十三）科学研究和技术服务业	Scientific Research and Technical Services	1135644	1108714
（十四）水利、环境和公共设施管理业	Management of Water Conservancy, Environment and Public Facilities	112692	106229
（十五）居民服务、修理和其他服务业	Services to Households, Repairs and Other Services	37735	36847
（十六）教育	Education	1303388	1271474
（十七）卫生和社会工作	Health and Social Work	576688	545905
（十八）文化、体育和娱乐业	Culture, Sports and Entertainment	144139	139191
（十九）公共管理、社会保障和社会组织	Public Administration, Social Security and Social Organizations	730625	700405
（二十）国际组织	International Organizations		

注：采矿业因企业行业代码发生变化，故从业人员与上年同比变化较大。

4-15 续表 continued

单位：万元 (10 000 yuan)

分组	Classify	其他从业人员劳动报酬 Remuneration of Other Employed Persons	城镇非私营单位从业人员平均工资（元） Aunual Average Wage of Employees in UrbanNon-privite Units(yuan)
总计	**Total**	**492651**	**67205**
一、按机构类型分组	**Grouped by Organization Type**		
#企业	Enterprises	401938	67047
事业	Public institutions	60881	72012
机关	Government units	28794	59097
二、按国民经济行业分组	**Grouped by Economic Sector**		
（一）农业	Agriculture ,Forestry,Animal Husbandry and Fishery	205	48626
（二）采矿业	Mining	7345	108826
（三）制造业	Manufacturing	33349	61434
（四）电力、燃气及水的生产供应业	Production and Distribution of Electricity, Gas and Water	2590	69092
（五）建筑业	Construction	215462	60475
（六）批发和零售业	Wholesale and Retail Trades	8799	48210
（七）交通运输、仓储和邮政业	Traffic,Transport,Storage and Post	22030	63583
（八）住宿和餐饮业	Hotels and Catering Services	9656	37507
（九）信息传输、软件和信息技术服务业	Information Transmission,Software and Information Technology Services	2137	137210
（十）金融业	Financial Intermediation	45292	108569
（十一）房地产业	Real Estate	5475	56979
（十二）租赁和商务服务业	Leasing and Business Services	8165	54395
（十三）科学研究和技术服务业	Scientific Research and Technical Services	26930	79539
（十四）水利、环境和公共设施管理业	Management of Water Conservancy, Environment and Public Facilities	6463	44062
（十五）居民服务、修理和其他服务业	Services to Households, Repairs and Other Services	888	35721
（十六）教育	Education	31914	71635
（十七）卫生和社会工作	Health and Social Work	30783	74797
（十八）文化、体育和娱乐业	Culture, Sports and Entertainment	4948	65974
（十九）公共管理、社会保障和社会组织	Public Administration, Social Security and Social Organizations	30220	59437
（二十）国际组织	International Organizations		

4-16 国有单位从业人员工资总额（2016年）

Total Wages of State-owned Units Employees（2016）

单位：万元 (10 000yuan)

分 组	Classify	单位从业人员工资总额 Total Wages of Employment	在岗职工工资总额 Total Wages of Employed Staff and Workers
总计	**Total**	**6056431**	**5908190**
一、按机构类型分组	**Grouped by Organization Type**		
#企业	Enterprises	3344318	3284595
事业	Public institutions	2031673	1972158
机关	Government units	671438	642644
二、按国民经济行业分组	**Grouped by Economic Sector**		
（一）农业	Agriculture ,Forestry,Animal Husbandry and Fishery	10716	10511
（二）采矿业	Mining		
（三）制造业	Manufacturing	1144543	1131670
（四）电力、燃气及水的生产供应业	Production and Distribution of Electricity, Gas and Water	205119	204629
（五）建筑业	Construction	129887	120786
（六）批发和零售业	Wholesale and Retail Trades	75894	74810
（七）交通运输、仓储和邮政业	Traffic,Transport,Storage and Post	763031	749155
（八）住宿和餐饮业	Hotels and Catering Services	20356	18951
（九）信息传输、软件和信息技术服务业	Information Transmission,Software and Information Technology Services	5492	5318
（十）金融业	Financial Intermediation	192199	190543
（十一）房地产业	Real Estate	86678	85344
（十二）租赁和商务服务业	Leasing and Business Services	55120	54094
（十三）科学研究和技术服务业	Scientific Research and Technical Services	756904	745643
（十四）水利、环境和公共设施管理业	Management of Water Conservancy, Environment	63946	59123
	and Public Facilities	16058	15752
（十五）居民服务、修理和其他服务业	Services to Households, Repairs and Other Services		
（十六）教育	Education	1212090	1185778
（十七）卫生和社会工作	Health and Social Work	515532	485566
（十八）文化、体育和娱乐业	Culture, Sports and Entertainment	75332	73203
（十九）公共管理、社会保障和社会组织	Public Administration, Social Security and Social Organizations	727534	697314
（二十）国际组织	International Organizations		

4-16 续表 continued

单位：万元 (10 000yuan)

分 组	Classify	其他从业人员工资总额 Remuneration of Other Employed Persons	城镇非私营单位从业人员平均工资（元） Aunual Average Wage of Employees in UrbanNon-privite Units(yuan)
总计	**Total**	**148241**	**66295**
一、按机构类型分组	**Grouped by Organization Type**		
#企业	Enterprises	59723	64693
事业	Public institutions	59515	72075
机关	Government units	28794	59167
二、按国民经济行业分组	**Grouped by Economic Sector**		
（一）农业	Agriculture ,Forestry,Animal Husbandry and Fishery	205	48998
（二）采矿业	Mining		
（三）制造业	Manufacturing	12873	60444
（四）电力、燃气及水的生产供应业	Production and Distribution of Electricity, Gas and Water	490	62203
（五）建筑业	Construction	9101	54568
（六）批发和零售业	Wholesale and Retail Trades	1084	50833
（七）交通运输、仓储和邮政业	Traffic,Transport,Storage and Post	13876	65317
（八）住宿和餐饮业	Hotels and Catering Services	1405	36963
（九）信息传输、软件和信息技术服务业	Information Transmission,Software and Information Technology Services	174	55587
（十）金融业	Financial Intermediation	1656	140681
（十一）房地产业	Real Estate	1334	64002
（十二） 租赁和商务服务业	Leasing and Business Services	1026	48926
（十三）科学研究和技术服务业	Scientific Research and Technical Services	11261	71693
（十四）水利、环境和公共设施管理业	Management of Water Conservancy, Environment	4823	42688
	and Public Facilities	306	38556
（十五）居民服务、修理和其他服务业	Services to Households, Repairs and Other Services		
（十六）教育	Education	26312	73956
（十七）卫生和社会工作	Health and Social Work	29966	77260
（十八）文化、体育和娱乐业	Culture, Sports and Entertainment	2129	70993
（十九）公共管理、社会保障和社会组织	Public Administration, Social Security and Social Organizations	30220	59360
（二十）国际组织	International Organizations		

4-17 城镇集体单位从业人员工资总额（2016年）

Total Wages of Urban Collective-owned Units Employees (2016)

单位：万元 (10 000yuan)

分 组	Classify	单 位 从业人员 工资总额 Total Wages of Employment	在岗职工 工资总额 Total Wages of Employed Staff and Workers
总计	**Total**	**229451**	**219207**
一、按机构类型分组	**Grouped by Organization Type**		
#企业	Enterprises	224731	214521
事业	Public institutions	4593	4559
机关	Government units		
二、按国民经济行业分组	**Grouped by Economic Sector**		
（一）农、林、牧、渔业	Agriculture ,Forestry,Animal Husbandry and Fishery		
（二）采矿业	Mining		
（三）制造业	Manufacturing	5654	5231
（四）电力、燃气及水的生产供应业	Production and Distribution of Electricity, Gas and Water	6081	5745
（五）建筑业	Construction	138264	135238
（六）批发和零售业	Wholesale and Retail Trades	5102	4273
（七）交通运输、仓储和邮政业	Traffic,Transport,Storage and Post	209	209
（八）住宿和餐饮业	Hotels and Catering Services	246	246
（九）信息传输、软件和信息技术服务业	Information Transmission,Software and Information Technology Services	85	85
（十）金融业	Financial Intermediation	21803	20967
（十一）房地产业	Real Estate	2102	2035
（十二）租赁和商务服务业	Leasing and Business Services	33809	29656
（十三）科学研究和技术服务业	Scientific Research and Technical Services	3899	3668
（十四）水利、环境和公共设施管理业	Management of Water Conservancy, Environment and Public Facilities	436	436
（十五）居民服务、修理和其他服务业	Services to Households, Repairs and Other Services	3473	3164
（十六）教育	Education	3038	3022
（十七）卫生和社会工作	Health and Social Work	5237	5219
（十八）文化、体育和娱乐业	Culture, Sports and Entertainment	13	13
（十九）公共管理、社会保障和社会组织	Public Administration, Social Security and Social Organizations		
（二十）国际组织	International Organizations		

4-17 续表 continued

单位：万元 (10 000 yuan)

分 组	Classify	其他从业人员工资总额 Remuneration of Other Employed Persons	城镇非私营单位从业人员平均工资（元） Aunual Average Wage of Employees in UrbanNon-privite Units(yuan)
总计	**Total**	**10244**	**48098**
一、按机构类型分组	**Grouped by Organization Type**		
#企业	Enterprises	10210	47992
事业	Public institutions	34	54485
机关	Government units		
二、按国民经济行业分组	**Grouped by Economic Sector**		
（一）农、林、牧、渔业	Agriculture ,Forestry,Animal Husbandry and Fishery		
（二）采矿业	Mining		
（三）制造业	Manufacturing	423	27848
（四）电力、燃气及水的生产供应业	Production and Distribution of Electricity, Gas and Water	336	110562
（五）建筑业	Construction	3026	50631
（六）批发和零售业	Wholesale and Retail Trades	829	30152
（七）交通运输、仓储和邮政业	Traffic,Transport,Storage and Post		38018
（八）住宿和餐饮业	Hotels and Catering Services		41644
（九）信息传输、软件和信息技术服务业	Information Transmission,Software and Information Technology Services		38455
（十）金融业	Financial Intermediation	836	96045
（十一）房地产业	Real Estate	67	39439
（十二）租赁和商务服务业	Leasing and Business Services	4153	33812
（十三）科学研究和技术服务业	Scientific Research and Technical Services	231	71401
（十四）水利、环境和公共设施管理业	Management of Water Conservancy, Environment and Public Facilities		31788
（十五）居民服务、修理和其他服务业	Services to Households, Repairs and Other Services	309	46237
（十六）教育	Education	16	67219
（十七）卫生和社会工作	Health and Social Work	18	40346
（十八）文化、体育和娱乐业	Culture, Sports and Entertainment		65000
（十九）公共管理、社会保障和社会组织	Public Administration, Social Security and Social Organizations		
（二十）国际组织	International Organizations		

4-18 其他经济类型单位从业人员工资总额（2016年）

Total Wages of Other Units Employees（2016）

单位：万元 （10 000yuan）

分 组	Classify	单 位 从业人员 工资总额 Total Wages of Employment	在岗职工 工资总额 Total Wages of Employed Staff and Workers
总计	**Total**	**7303619**	**6969464**
一、按机构类型分组	**Grouped by Organization Type**		
#企业	Enterprises	7175995	6843990
事业	Public institutions	22847	21515
机关	Government units	959	959
二、按国民经济行业分组	**Grouped by Economic Sector**		
（一）农、林、牧、渔业	Agriculture ,Forestry,Animal Husbandry and Fishery	274	274
（二）采矿业	Mining	56754	49409
（三）制造业	Manufacturing	1739076	1719023
（四）电力、燃气及水的生产供应业	Production and Distribution of Electricity, Gas and Water	127402	125638
（五）建筑业	Construction	1172378	969060
（六）批发和零售业	Wholesale and Retail Trades	508065	501179
（七）交通运输、仓储和邮政业	Traffic,Transport,Storage and Post	299956	291802
（八）住宿和餐饮业	Hotels and Catering Services	190861	182609
（九）信息传输、软件和信息技术服务业	Information Transmission,Software and Information Technology Services	1081908	1079944
（十）金融业	Financial Intermediation	760196	717395
（十一）房地产业	Real Estate	326756	322682
（十二）租赁和商务服务业	Leasing and Business Services	382566	379579
（十三）科学研究和技术服务业	Scientific Research and Technical Services	374841	359403
（十四）水利、环境和公共设施管理业	Management of Water Conservancy, Environment and Public Facilities	48311	46671
（十五）居民服务、修理和其他服务业	Services to Households, Repairs and Other Services	18205	17932
（十六）教育	Education	88261	82675
（十七）卫生和社会工作	Health and Social Work	55921	55122
（十八）文化、体育和娱乐业	Culture, Sports and Entertainment	68796	65976
（十九）公共管理、社会保障和社会组织	Public Administration, Social Security and Social Organizations	3092	3091
（二十）国际组织	International Organizations		

4-18 续表 continued

单位：万元 (10 000 yuan)

分组	Classify	其他从业人员工资总额 Remuneration of Other Employed Persons	城镇非私营单位从业人员平均工资（元） Aunual Average Wage of Employees in UrbanNon-privite Units(yuan)
总计	**Total**	**334155**	**68847**
一、按机构类型分组	**Grouped by Organization Type**		
#企业	Enterprises	332005	69077
事业	Public institutions	1332	71086
机关	Government units		32293
二、按国民经济行业分组	**Grouped by Economic Sector**		
（一）农、林、牧、渔业	Agriculture ,Forestry,Animal Husbandry and Fishery		37479
（二）采矿业	Mining	7345	108827
（三）制造业	Manufacturing	20053	62351
（四）电力、燃气及水的生产供应业	Production and Distribution of Electricity, Gas and Water	1764	62202
（五）建筑业	Construction	203318	64385
（六）批发和零售业	Wholesale and Retail Trades	6886	48129
（七）交通运输、仓储和邮政业	Traffic,Transport,Storage and Post	8154	59587
（八）住宿和餐饮业	Hotels and Catering Services	8252	37561
（九）信息传输、软件和信息技术服务业	Information Transmission,Software and Information Technology Services	1964	138268
（十）金融业	Financial Intermediation	42801	103009
（十一）房地产业	Real Estate	4074	55522
（十二）租赁和商务服务业	Leasing and Business Services	2987	58484
（十三）科学研究和技术服务业	Scientific Research and Technical Services	15438	102259
（十四）水利、环境和公共设施管理业	Management of Water Conservancy, Environment and Public Facilities	1640	46191
（十五）居民服务、修理和其他服务业	Services to Households, Repairs and Other Services	273	32232
（十六）教育	Education	5586	50142
（十七）卫生和社会工作	Health and Social Work	799	61614
（十八）文化、体育和娱乐业	Culture, Sports and Entertainment	2820	61234
（十九）公共管理、社会保障和社会组织	Public Administration, Social Security and Social Organizations	1	85436
（二十）国际组织	International Organizations		

4-19 主要年份城镇登记失业人数及失业率

Registered Unemployed Persons and Unemployment Rate in Urban Area in Representative Years

年 份 year	城镇登记失业人员数（万人） Real Number of Registered Unemployed Persons (10 000 persons)	城镇登记失业率（%） Registered Unemployment in Urban Area (%)
2002		3.7
2003		4.5
2004	8.29	4.3
2005	8.45	4.3
2006	8.74	4.3
2007	8.77	4.3
2008	9.40	4.2
2009	10.02	4.3
2010	10.46	4.2
2011	10.37	3.9
2012	9.60	3.5
2013	10.13	3.4
2014	10.84	3.4
2015	10.74	3.4
2016	11.29	3.3

主要统计指标解释

人口数 指一定时点、一定地区范围内的有生命的个人的总和。年度统计的年末人口数，指每年12月31日24时的人口数。

常住人口 指实际经常居住在某地区一定时间（半年以上，含半年）的人口。常住人口包括户口在本辖区人也在本辖区居住的人，户口在本辖区之外但在户口登记地半年以上的人，户口待定（无户口和口袋户口）的人，户口在本辖区但离开本辖区半年以下的人。

城镇人口和乡村人口 城镇人口是指居住在城镇范围内的全部常住人口；乡村人口是除上述人口以外的全部人口。

出生率（又称粗出生率） 指在一定时期内（通常为一年）平均每千人所出生的人数的比率，一般用千分率表示。其计算公式为：

出生率＝年出生人数／年平均人数×1000‰

式中：出生人数指活产婴儿，即胎儿脱离母体时（不管怀孕月数），有过呼吸或其他生命现象。年平均人数指年初、年底人口数的平均数，也可用年中人口数代替。

死亡率（又称粗死亡率） 指在一定时期内（通常为一年）一定地区的死亡人数与同期内平均人数（或期中人数）之比，一般用千分率表示。本资料中的死亡率指年死亡率，其计算公式为：

死亡率＝年死亡人数／年平均人数×1000‰

人口自然增长率 指在一定时期内（通常为一年）人口自然增加数（出生人数减死亡人数）与该时期内平均人数（或期中人数）之比，一般用千分率表示。计算公式为：

人口自然增长率＝（本年出生人数—本年死亡人数）／年平均人数×1000‰。

从业人员 指在16周岁及以上，从事一定社会劳动并取得劳动报酬或经营收入的人员。这一指标反映了一定时期内全部劳动力资源的实际利用情况，是研究我国基本国情国力的重要指标。

单位从业人员 指在各级国家机关、政党机关、社会团体及企业、事业单位中工作，取得工资或其他形式的劳动报酬的全部人员。包括在岗职工、再就业的离退休人员、民办教师以及在各单位中工作的外方人员和港澳台方人员、兼职人员、借用的外单位人员和第二职业者。不包括离开本单位仍保留劳动关系的职工。各单位的就业人员反映了各单位实际参加生产或工作的全部劳动力。

城镇私营和个体就业人员 城镇私营就业人员指在工商管理部门注册登记，其经营地址设在县城关镇（含城关镇）以上的私营企业就业人员；包括私营企业投资者和雇工。城镇个体就业人员指在工商管理部门注册登记，并持有城镇户口或在城镇长期居住，经批准从事个体工商经营的就业人员；包括个体经营者和在个体工商户劳动的家庭帮工和雇工。

国有单位 指资产归国家所有的经济组织。包括按《中华人民共和国企业法人登记管理条例》规定登记注册的非公司制的经济组织，以及中央、地方各级国家机关、事业单位和社会团体。

集体单位 指生产资料归集体所有，并按《中华人民共和国企业法人登记管理条例》规定登记注册的经济组织。

其他单位 包括股份合作单位、联营单位、有限责任公司、股份有限公司、港澳台商投资单位以及外商投资单位等其他登记注册类型单位。

在岗职工 指在本单位工作并由单位支付工资的人员，以及有工作岗位，但由于学习、病伤产假等原因暂未工作，仍由单位支付工资的人员。

职工工资总额 指各单位在一定时期内直接支付给本单位全部职工的劳动报酬总额。工资总额的计算原则应以直接支付给职工的全部劳动报酬为根据。各单位支付给职工的劳动报酬以及其他根据有关规定支付的工资，不论是计入成本的还是不计入成本的，不论是按国家规定列入计征奖金税项目的，还是未列入计征奖金税项目的，不论是以货币形式支付的还是以实物形式支付的，均包括在工资总额内。

职工平均工资 指企业、事业、机关单位的职工在一定时期内平均每人所得的货币工资额。它表明一定时期职工工资收入的高低程度，是反映职工工资水平的主要指标。计算公式为：

职工平均工资＝报告期实际支付的全部职工工资总额/报告期全部职工平均人数

城镇登记失业人员 指有非农业户口，在一定的劳动年龄内，有劳动能力，无业而要求就业，并在当地就业服务机构进行求职登记的人员。

城镇登记失业率 指城镇登记失业人数同城镇从业人数与城镇从业人数与城镇登记失业人数之和的比。计算公式为：

$$\text{城镇登记失业率}=\frac{\text{城镇登记失业人数}}{\text{（城镇单位就业人员-使用的农村劳动力-聘用的离退休人员-聘用的港澳台及外方人员）+不在岗职工+城镇私营业主+城镇个体户主+城镇私营企业及个体就业人员+城镇登记失业人数}}\times 100\%$$

Explanatory Notes on Main Statistical Indicators

The annual statistics on total population is taken at midnight, the 31st of December, not including residents in Taiwan province, Hong Kong SAR and Macao SAR and Chinese national residing abroad.

Permanent population refers to the population of actual habitual residence in a certain area six months or over six months. Permanent popul ation include the accounts in this area which are also living in this area, accounts outside this area but with more than half a year of household registration, accounts to be determined including people without accounts or pockets of accounts, and accounts in the area but leaving this area less than six months.

Urban Population and Rural Population Urban population refers to all people residing in cities and towns, while rural population refers to population other than urban population.

Birth Rate (or Crude Birth Rate) refers to the ratio of the number of births to the average population (or mid-period population) during a certain period of time (usually one year), expressed in ‰. Birth rate in the chapter refers to annual birth rate. The following formula is used:

$$\text{Birth Rate}=\frac{\text{Number of Births}}{\text{Annual Average Population}}\times 1000‰$$

Number of births in the formula refers to live births, i.e. when a baby has breathed or showed any vital phenomena regardless of the length of pregnancy.

Annual average population is the average of the number of population at the beginning of the year and that at the end of the year. Sometimes it is substituted by the mid-year population.

Death Rate (or Crude Death Rate) refers to the ratio of the number of deaths to the average population (or mid-period population) during a certain period of time (usually one year), expressed in ‰. Death rate in the chapter refers to annual death rate. The following formula is used:

$$\text{DeathRate}=\frac{\text{Number of Deaths}}{\text{Annual Average Population}}\times 1000‰$$

Natural Growth Rate of Population refers to the ratio of natural increase in population (number of births minus number of deaths) in a certain period of time (usually one year) to the average population (or mid-period population) of the same period, expressed in ‰. The following formula is applied:

Natural Growth Rate of Population =(Number of Births-Number of Deaths)/Annual Average Population× 1000‰

Employed Persons refer to the ones aged 16 and over who are engaged in gainful employment and thus receive remuneration payment or earn business income. This indicator reflects the actual utilization of total labour force during a certain period of time and is often used for the research on China's economic situation and national power.

Persons Employed in Various Units refer to all the persons working in government agencies of various levels, political and party organizations, social organizations, enterprises and institutions, and receiving wages or other forms of payment. They include fully-employed staff and workers, re-employed retirees, teachers in the schools run by the local people, foreigners and Chinese compatriots from Hong Kong, Macao, and Taiwan working in various units, part-time employees, employees of other units working temporarily at current posts, and employees holding the second job, but do not include persons who have left their working units while keeping their labour contract (employment relation) unchanged. This indicator reflects the total number of laborers actually engaged in production or other operations in various units.

Persons Employed in Private Enterprises and Self- Employed Individuals in Urban Areas Persons employed in private enterprises refer to the persons employed in the private enterprises which have been registered at the departments of industrial and commercial administration for which the business operation are situated at a county town (i.e. a town where the county government is located), or at urban areas with administrative hierarchy higher than a county town. The self-employed individuals in urban areas refer to persons who hold the certificates of residence in urban areas or have resided in the urban areas for a long time and have been registered at the departments of industrial and commercial administration and approved to be engaged in individual industrial or commercial business, including self-employed persons as well as helpers and hired labourers who work in individual households.

State-owned Units refer to economic units whose assets are owned by the state, including non-corporation units registered according to Regulation of the People's Republic of China on the Registration of Enterprises and

Corporations, state organs, institutions and social organizations at the central-level and local levels.

Collective-owned Units refer to economic units registered according to Regulation of the People's Republic of China on the Registration of Enterprises and Corporations where the means of production are collectively owned.

Units of Other Types of Ownership refer to units registered with other types of ownership, including cooperative units, joint ownership units, limited liability corporations, share holding corporations, units funded by entrepreneurs from Hong Kong, Macao, and Taiwan, and foreign- funded units.

Employed Staff and Workers refer to persons who work in, and receive wages from their working units, including persons who have their work posts but are temporarily absent from work for reasons of study or on sick, injury or maternal leave and still receive wages from their working units.

Total Wage Bill refers to the total remuneration payment to employed persons in various units during a certain period of time. The calculation of total wage bill is based on the total remuneration payment to employed persons . Therefore, all the wages and salaries and other payments to employed persons are included in the total wage bill regardless of sources, reckoning the cost of production or not, category, listing as items of premium taxation or not, and forms, paying in cash or in kind.

Average Wage refers to the average wage in money terms per person during a certain period of time for employed persons in enterprises, institutions, and government agencies, which reflects the general level of wage income during a certain period of time and is calculated as follows:

$$\text{AverageWage} = \frac{\text{TotalWage Billof Employed Personsat Reference Time}}{\text{Average Number of Persons Employedat Reference Time}}$$

Registered Unemployed Persons in Urban Areas refer to the persons with non-agricultural household registration at certain working ages (16 years old to retirement age), who are capable of working, unemployed and willing to work, and have been registered at the local employment service agencies to apply for a job.

Registered Unemployment Rate in Urban Areas refers to the ratio of the number of the registered unemployed persons to the sum of the number of persons employed in various units (minus the employed rural labour force, re-employed retirees, and Hong Kong, Macao, Taiwan or foreign employees), laid-off staff and workers in urban units, owners of private enterprises in urban areas, owners of self-employed individuals in urban areas, employees of private enterprises in urban areas, employee of self-employed individuals in urban areas, and the registered unemployed persons in urban areas. The formula is as follows:

$$\text{Registered Unemployment rate in urban areas} = \frac{\text{numberof registered urban unemployed persons}}{\begin{array}{c}\text{number of persons employed in}\\ \text{urbanunits-employed rurallabour force}\\ \text{re-employed retirees - HongKong,}\\ \text{Macao,Taiwan or foreign employees}\\ \text{+ laid-off staff and workers+owners of}\\ \text{urban private Enterprises+ owners of}\\ \text{urbanself-employed Individuals + employees}\\ \text{ofurbanprivate Enterprises+employees of}\\ \text{urbanself- employed Individuals+ registered}\\ \text{unemployed persons in urbanareas}\end{array}} \times 100\%$$

5 固定资产投资

INVESTMENT IN FIXED ASSETS

资料整理：席锋旭　康　敏　王　峰
Data management：Xi Fengxu　Kang Min　Wang Feng
数据审核：黄小丹
Data audit：Huang Xiaodan

第五部分　固定资产投资

一、简要说明

本章资料主要包括全社会固定资产投资、项目投资、房地产开发投资和农户投资以及分区县情况，由西安市统计局固定资产投资处提供。

二、主要指标

全社会固定资产投资（亿元）	5191.36	比上年增长	2.0%
#国有经济单位	2332.08	比上年增长	15.9%
集体经济单位	152.05	比上年下降	17.5%
#固定资产投资	5097.00	比上年增长	3.4%
#房地产开发	1955.82	比上年增长	6.8%
全市新增固定资产（亿元）	1952.92	比上年下降	4.7%
全市竣工住宅面积（万平方米）	1331.24	比上年增长	61.2%

5　INVESTMENT IN FIXED ASSETS

Ⅰ.Brief Introduction

This chapter consists of primarily the data on fixed asset investment, Project investment real estate development investment, and farmer Investment provided by Fixed Asset Investment Division of the Xi'an Bureau of Statistics.

Ⅱ.Major Indicators

		Increase over Preceding Year
Total Investment In Fixed Assets(100 mil. Yuan)	5191.36	2.0%
State-owned Enterprises	2332.08	15.9%
Collective-owned Enterprises	152.05	-17.5%
Project Investment	5097.00	3.4%
Real Estate Development	1955.82	6.8%
Investment Newly Increased Fixed Assets(100 mil. yuan)	1952.92	-4.7%
Total Floor Space of Building Completed(10 000 sq.m)	1331.24	61.2%

5-1 主要年份按类别分全社会固定资产投资

Total Investment in Fixed Assets in the Whole Country by Classifications in Representative Years

单位：亿元 (100 million yuan)

年份 Year	全社会固定资产投资合计 Total Investment in Fixed Assets in the Whole Country	固定资产投资 Fixed Assets Investment	房地产开发投资 Real Estate Investment	农户投资 Farmer Investment
1979	4.08	3.01		1.07
1980	6.12	4.48		1.64
1981	5.59	4.56		1.03
1982	9.49	8.02		1.47
1983	10.46	9.17		1.29
1984	12.89	10.69		2.20
1985	18.44	14.44		4.00
1986	22.15	18.54		3.61
1987	27.05	23.15		3.90
1988	29.14	24.43		4.71
1989	28.30	23.85		4.45
1990	26.39	23.10	0.91	3.29
1991	30.76	25.55	2.01	5.21
1992	38.48	32.85	3.32	5.63
1993	75.06	66.65	7.39	8.41
1994	85.57	73.47	12.02	12.10
1995	103.42	88.50	21.65	14.92
1996	114.38	96.98	24.66	17.40
1997	116.90	95.17	24.68	21.73
1998	154.80	138.68	38.21	16.12
1999	197.31	172.64	44.30	24.67
2000	232.37	203.01	51.85	29.36
2001	287.72	256.95	67.42	30.77
2002	338.15	307.24	79.37	30.91
2003	478.10	445.74	124.82	32.36
2004	646.69	612.03	169.67	34.66
2005	835.10	776.33	225.23	58.77
2006	1066.62	971.84	285.76	94.78
2007	1435.33	1340.59	387.33	94.74
2008	1906.36	1786.60	540.26	119.76
2009	2500.13	2367.58	696.34	132.55
2010	3250.56	3104.92	842.34	145.64
2011	3346.26	3207.97	996.81	138.29
2012	4243.43	4107.54	1281.90	135.89
2013	5134.56	4982.25	1595.64	152.31
2014	5903.98	5682.42	1761.88	221.56
2015	5165.98	5086.93	1831.67	79.05
2016	5191.36	5097.00	1955.82	78.65

注：2015年国家取消了城乡投资分组，表中“农户投资”2014年以前为原先的农村投资。
2016年全社会固定资产投资不含跨省项目，固定资产投资不含跨省和跨市项目。

5-2 主要年份按经济类型分全社会固定资产投资

Total Investment in Fixed Assets in the Whole Country by Registion Stares in Representative Years

单位：亿元 (100 million yuan)

年 份 Year	合计 Total	国有经济 State-owned	集体经济 Collective-owned	个体经济 Self-employed Individual	其他经济 Others
1985	18.44	13.96	1.36	3.12	
1986	22.15	18.05	0.97	3.13	
1987	27.05	22.18	1.50	3.37	
1988	29.14	23.72	1.86	3.56	
1989	28.30	23.22	1.46	3.62	
1990	26.39	22.21	1.44	2.74	
1991	30.76	24.42	2.26	4.08	
1992	38.48	32.04	1.45	4.99	
1993	75.06	59.66	3.03	6.55	5.82
1994	85.57	64.71	4.14	10.09	6.63
1995	103.42	69.08	9.78	11.13	13.43
1996	114.38	80.66	8.73	12.50	12.49
1997	116.90	77.46	10.21	15.11	14.12
1998	154.80	113.07	7.89	10.59	23.25
1999	197.31	136.50	13.62	16.22	30.97
2000	232.37	159.60	14.65	24.40	33.72
2001	287.72	175.58	14.67	38.57	58.90
2002	338.15	200.06	13.70	44.68	79.71
2003	478.10	264.83	22.33	73.43	117.51
2004	646.69	329.14	40.06	48.95	228.54
2005	835.10	373.70	59.23	79.04	323.13
2006	1066.62	401.14	110.68	107.33	447.47
2007	1435.33	476.78	207.08	183.09	568.38
2008	1906.36	694.89	246.89	50.43	914.15
2009	2500.13	932.91	289.91	97.86	1179.45
2010	3250.56	1348.76	326.44	54.73	1520.63
2011	3346.26	1204.80	258.15	74.64	1808.67
2012	4243.43	1661.22	194.71	82.72	2304.78
2013	5134.56	1770.84	219.88	84.43	3059.41
2014	5903.98	1916.31	203.35	83.28	3701.04
2015	5165.98	1826.62	158.14	80.47	3100.75
2016	5191.36	2332.08	152.05	81.68	2625.55

注：集体经济：包括城镇集体和农村集体。
个体经济：包括私营个体投资及城镇工矿区私人建房和农村私人建房。

5-3 主要年份按产业分全市固定资产投资

Total Investment in Fixed Assets in the Whole City by Three Strata of Industry in Representative Years

单位：亿元 (100 million yuan)

年份 Year	全市固定资产投资合计 Total Investment in Fixed Assets in The Whole City	第一产业 Primary Industry	第二产业 Secondary Industry	工业 Industry	第三产业 Tertisry Industry
1979	3.01	0.06	1.24	1.20	1.71
1980	4.48	0.06	2.09	1.99	2.33
1981	4.56	0.11	2.10	1.83	2.35
1982	8.02	0.04	4.07	3.63	3.91
1983	9.17	0.11	4.97	4.41	4.09
1984	10.69	0.19	4.56	3.99	5.94
1985	14.44	0.18	7.22	6.45	7.04
1986	18.54	0.16	8.98	8.37	9.40
1987	23.15	0.19	11.81	11.26	11.15
1988	24.43	0.15	11.95	11.20	12.33
1989	23.85	0.13	11.94	11.50	11.78
1990	23.10	0.25	11.03	10.59	11.82
1991	25.55	0.27	12.48	11.95	12.80
1992	32.85	0.10	15.60	14.73	17.15
1993	66.65	0.07	24.50	22.44	42.08
1994	73.47	0.03	27.04	25.85	46.40
1995	88.50	0.14	28.80	27.71	59.56
1996	96.98	0.13	25.96	24.24	70.89
1997	95.17	0.24	23.65	21.66	71.28
1998	138.68	0.48	35.33	29.86	102.87
1999	172.64	0.94	39.88	36.40	131.82
2000	203.01	0.76	57.21	54.37	145.04
2001	256.95	0.86	63.31	61.28	192.78
2002	307.24	4.29	74.34	68.45	228.61
2003	445.74	3.34	83.25	78.41	359.15
2004	612.03	3.38	97.69	95.67	510.96
2005	776.33	5.26	144.25	140.44	626.82
2006	971.84	10.04	213.43	206.48	748.37
2007	1340.59	10.20	297.53	286.61	1032.86
2008	1786.60	23.75	369.74	356.12	1393.11
2009	2367.58	24.46	458.44	442.70	1884.68
2010	3104.92	39.83	556.10	498.62	2508.99
2011	3207.97	43.10	474.73	390.30	2690.14
2012	4165.99	99.34	671.92	578.17	3394.73
2013	5055.23	73.15	983.09	868.57	3998.99
2014	5824.53	75.15	1261.70	1205.53	4487.68
2015	5086.93	99.78	1158.30	1135.87	3828.85
2016	5097.00	89.70	963.80	949.27	4043.50

5-4 主要年份按资金来源及建设性质分全市固定资产投资

单位：万元

指标	Item	1995	2000	2001	2002	2003	2004
一. 投资总额(万元)	**Total Investment (10 000 yuan)**	**884994**	**2030122**	**2569496**	**3072442**	**4457381**	**6120324**
（一）按资金来源分	Grouped by Funds Source						
1. 国家预算内投资	State Budgetary Funds	69185	160982	256403	355960	365263	436496
2. 国内贷款	Domestic Loans	216565	432282	672379	666146	1219234	1565246
3. 债券	Bonds	873	32460	6753	766	3278	
4. 利用外资	Utilization of Foreign Funds	80792	31622	54907	15192	47509	47401
5. 自筹资金	Self-raising Funds	385047	875352	1121502	1392915	1733132	2629720
6. 其他资金	Others	132532	497424	457552	641463	1088965	1441461
（二）按构成分	Grouped by Composition of Funds						
1. 建筑安装工程	Construction and Installation Projects	527220	1404184	1698777	2119151	3067309	4127677
2. 设备、工器具购置	Purchasing of Equipment and Instruments	233730	382495	452602	552251	577240	708988
3. 其它费用	Others	124044	243443	418117	401040	812832	1283659
（三）按建设性质分	Grouped by Type of Construction						
#新建	New Construction	210926	533058	723957	874392	1294032	1874116
扩建	Expansion	180210	542510	581138	868603	1102914	1169537
改建	Reconstruction	157457	263657	344879	343184	447944	670229
二. 房屋施工面积（万平方米）	**Floor Space Under Construction (10 000sq.m)**	**1070.58**	**1702.58**	**1767.13**	**2396.89**	**2716.18**	**3177.36**

Total Investment in Fixed Assets in the Whole City

by Sources of Funds and Type of Construction in Representative Years

(10 000 yuan)

2005	2006	2007	2008	2009	2010	2011	2012	2013	2014	2015	2016
7763283	**9718418**	**13405920**	**17865977**	**23675759**	**31049184**	**32079666**	**41659924**	**50552171**	**58245332**	**50869319**	**50970036**
728885	677145	670592	1555809	2562756	1649563	1480412	1851860	1439721	1622413	2250911	2528528
1257175	1631689	1619218	2162957	3301919	4288663	3546561	4023452	4146647	5592450	4510474	5018722
								11356			
40583	165390	183422	261325	144124	126802	89047	135147	182153	789982	2067810	957646
4001700	5538393	8565573	12771844	15776565	18279153	19400468	28680236	36446760	41430249	33936574	30562975
1734940	1705801	2367115	1114042	1890395	6705003	7563178	6969229	8325534	8810238	8103551	11902165
5086664	6486233	9165668	12864657	16337466	21690205	25553161	34268466	41672647	44701184	41024301	39843259
1021079	1409589	1858720	2024631	2619783	3094336	1911180	3311375	4861642	8847403	4990590	5682434
1655540	1822596	2381532	2976689	4718510	6264643	4615325	4080083	4017882	4696745	4854428	5444343
2907551	3511432	5123975	6356716	8567540	14292899	16077747	21651399	26063028	29798357	26685245	26057561
1208430	1101740	994841	2118013	3054929	2649749	1956527	1685922	1232264	1102377	1017226	1714627
782953	1099304	1548130	1921664	2738799	2620997	2155112	2810903	3183300	2605272	1439734	1622434
4030.38	**4589.39**	**5759.28**	**6570.94**	**9571.25**	**11166.19**	**12353.11**	**14093.91**	**14749.84**	**16249.30**	**16325.63**	**18977.88**

5-5 主要年份全市新增固定资产投资及房屋竣工面积

Newly Added Fixed Assets and Floor Spaces Completed of Municipal Units in Representative Years

年 份 Year	新增固定资产（亿元） Newly Increased Fixed Assets (10 000 mil.yuan)	房屋竣工面积（万平方米） Floor Space of Buildings Completed (10 000sq.m)	住宅 Residential Buildings
1978	4.96	99.10	40.76
1980	4.64	164.87	100.15
1985	8.62	222.42	129.07
1986	13.40	272.95	155.91
1987	16.72	241.48	119.21
1988	16.82	211.83	102.43
1989	16.58	178.45	87.77
1990	20.30	211.88	111.05
1991	17.86	185.34	95.84
1992	22.33	204.75	112.66
1993	41.70	257.90	144.88
1994	55.37	282.91	184.49
1995	62.58	357.67	252.84
1996	60.04	332.18	249.52
1997	62.88	374.46	286.54
1998	80.23	382.80	275.63
1999	118.92	681.04	550.83
2000	150.16	714.83	544.95
2001	167.77	692.56	502.26
2002	198.97	773.28	486.13
2003	279.44	917.96	578.06
2005	261.95	776.59	498.33
2004	409.72	1131.41	598.61
2006	453.01	1199.45	583.10
2007	667.97	1672.16	929.50
2008	725.17	1113.31	693.42
2009	1013.44	1529.13	822.62
2010	1193.05	775.16	521.08
2011	1297.35	1231.91	861.44
2012	1765.05	1626.25	1189.04
2013	1875.00	1118.69	840.02
2014	2476.12	1856.70	1462.86
2015	2049.71	1109.00	826.05
2016	1952.92	1884.05	1331.24

5-6 全市固定资产投资（2016年）

Total Investment in Fixed Assets in the Whole City（2016）

单位：万元 (10 000 yuan)

指　标	Item	合计 Total	房地产开发投资 Real Estate Investment
一、本年完成投资（万元）	**Investment Completed This Year(10 000 yuan)**	**50970036**	**19558202**
#住宅	Residential Buildings	14100510	13420504
（一）按登记注册类型分	**Grouped by Registion Status**		
内资	Domestic Funded Enterprises	46840664	18654377
国有	State-owned Enterprises	13597705	903376
集体	Collective-owned Enterprises	902050	137648
股份合作	Cooperative Enterprises	183544	170941
联营	Joint Ownership Enterprises	2680	
国有联营	State Joint Ownership Enterprises		
集体联营	Collective Joint Ownership Enterprises	180	
国有与集体联营	Joint State-collective Ownership Enterprises		
其他联营	Other Joint Ownership Enterprises	2500	
有限责任公司	Limited Liability Corporations	20718871	12027763
国有独资公司	State-funded Corporations	2815975	661355
其他有限责任公司	Other Limited Liability Corporations	17902896	11366408
股份有限公司	Stock Limited Corporation	1570555	176834
私营	Private Enterprises	9355757	5226699
私营独资	Private -funded Enterprises	832323	155096
私营合伙	Private Limited Liability Corporations	35081	
私营有限责任公司	Private Limited Liability Corporations	8209032	4941225
私营股份有限公司	Private Share Holding Corporations	279321	130378
其他	Other	509502	11116
港澳台商投资	Enterprises Funded by Hong Kong, Macao and Taiwan	1069183	470970
与港澳台合资经营	Joint-venture Enterprises	222869	49669
与港澳台合作经营	Cooperative Enterprises	33119	33119
港澳台独资	Wholly Funded from Hong Kong,Macao and Taiwan	764215	388182
港澳台投资股份有限公司	Share-holding Corporations Ltd.	48980	
其他港澳台投资	Investment From Hongkong,Macao,Taiwan		

5-6 续表1 continued 1

单位：万元 (10 000 yuan)

指　标	Item	合计 Total	房地产开发投资 Real Estate Investment
外商投资	Foreign Owned Enterprises	3029989	432855
中外合资经营	Joint-venture Enterprises	1084841	197661
中外合作经营	Cooperation Enterprises		
外资企业	Foreign Funded Enterprises	1890144	193110
外商投资股份有限公司	Share-holding Corporations Ltd. With Foreign Funds	47004	42084
其他外商投资	Foreign Investment	8000	
（二）按隶属关系分	**Grouped by Jurisdiction of Management**		
中央	Central	3102564	549902
省属	Provincial	3035153	535599
市属	Municipal	44832319	18472701
（三）按建设性质分	**Grouped by Type of Construction**		
#新建	New Construction	26057561	
扩建	Expansion	1714627	
改建和技术改造	Reconstruction	1622434	
（四）按构成分	**Grouped by Composition**		
1. 建筑工程	Construction Projects	35519851	14132688
2. 安装工程	Installment Projects	4323408	2475881
3. 设备、工器具购置	Purchasing of Equipment and Instruments	5682434	277199
4. 其他费用	Others	5444343	2672434

5-6 续表2 continued 2

单位：万元 (10 000 yuan)

指 标	Item	合计 Total	房地产开发投资 Real Estate Investment
二、构成(%)	**Proportion (%)**		
（一）按登记注册类型分组	**Grouped by Status**		
#国有经济	State-owned	44.9	8.2
集体经济	Collective-owned	2.9	1.1
（二）按隶属关系分组	**Grouped by Jurisdiction of Management**		
中央	Central	6.0	2.8
省属	Provincial	6.0	2.7
市属	Municipal	88.0	94.5
（三）按建设性质分	**Grouped by Type of Construction**		
#新建	New Construction	51.1	
扩建	Expansion	3.4	
改建和技术改造	Reconstruction	3.2	
（四）按构成分	**Grouped by Composition of Funds**		
1. 建筑工程	Construction Projects	69.7	72.2
2. 安装工程	Installation Projects	8.5	12.7
3. 设备、工器具购置	Purchasing of the Equipment and Instruments	11.1	1.4
4. 其他	Others	10.7	13.7
三、本年新增固定资产（万元）	**Newly Increase in Fixed Assets This Year(10 000 yuan)**	**19529150**	**5745448**
四、房屋面积（万平方米）	**Floor Space (10 000 sq.m)**		
房屋施工面积	Floor Space of Buildings Under Construction	18977.88	14727.10
#住宅	Residential Buildings	10976.22	10468.80
房屋竣工面积	Floor Space of Buildings Completed	1884.05	1560.18
#住宅	Residential Buildings	1331.24	1259.24
五、本年房屋竣工价值（万元）	**Value of the Building Completed This Year (10 000 yuan)**	**4564777**	**4564777**
#住宅	Residential Buildings	3514585	3514585

5-7 按国民经济行业分全市固定资产投资（2016年）

Investment in Fixed Assets in the Whole City by Industry（2016）

单位：万元 (10 000 yuan)

行 业	Sector	固定资产投资 Grouped by Sector	工业改建和技术改造 Industrial Reconstruction and Technical Transformation
本年完成固定资产投资（万元）	**Grouped by Sector (10 000 yuan)**	**50970036**	**1573832**
（一）农、林、牧、渔业	Agriculture,Forestry,Animal Husbandry and Fishery	1011539	
（二）采矿业	Mining	6994	
（三）制造业	Manufacturing	7804464	1316823
农副食品加工业	Processing of Food from Agricultural Products	112866	30440
食品制造业	Manufacture of Foods	350380	125312
酒、饮料和精制茶制造业	Wine, soft drinks and refined tea industry	147043	27585
烟草制品业	Tobacco Processing	10000	10000
纺织业	Textile Industry	20977	
纺织服装、服饰业	Textile, apparel industry	47099	500
皮革、毛皮、羽毛及其制品和制鞋业	Leather, Fur, Feather (eiderdown) and Their Products Industry		
木材加工和木、竹、藤、棕、草制品业	Timber Processing,Bamboo,Cane, Palm Fiber and Straw Products	74918	34871
家具制造业	Furniture Manufacturing	50725	25078
造纸及纸制品业	Papermaking and Paper products	28802	10112
印刷和记录媒介复制业	Printing,Record Medium Reproduction	98576	15317
文教、工美、体育和娱乐用品制造业	Culture, education, Craft art, sports and entertainment goods manufacturing industry	26926	4310
石油加工、炼焦和核燃料加工业	Petroleum Refining, Ccoke Making and Nuclear Fuel Processing Industry	6048	284
化学原料和化学制品制造业	Raw Chemical Materials and Chemical Products	100023	16000
医药制造业	Medical and Pharmaceutical Products	367551	28738
化学纤维制造业	Chemical Fiber		
橡胶和塑料制品业	Rubber and plastic products industry	33774	15834
非金属矿物制品业	Nonmetal Mineral Products	215319	19229
黑色金属冶炼和压延加工业	Smelting and Pressing of Ferrous Metals	48964	20500
有色金属冶炼和压延加工业	Smelting and Pressing of Nonferrou Metals	482646	85761
金属制品业	Metal Products	87235	21693

5-7 续表 continued

单位：万元 (10 000 yuan)

行业	Sector	固定资产投资 Grouped by Sector	工业改建和技术改造 Industrial Reconstruction and Technical Transformation
通用设备制造业	General Equipment Manufacturing Industry	410932	82653
专用设备制造业	Special Purpose Equipment	811238	314050
汽车制造业	Automotive Manufacturing	541439	28877
铁路、船舶、航空航天和其他运输设备制造业	Railroad, Marine, Aerospace and other Transportation Equipment Manufacturing	873234	61936
电气机械和器材制造业	Electric Equipment and Machinery	854850	186553
计算机、通信和其他电子设备制造业	Communication Equipment, Computer and Other Electronic Equipment Manufacturing Industry	1735987	68049
仪器仪表制造业	Instrument Manufacturing Industry	139419	69167
其他制造业	Other Manufacturing	119417	8498
废弃资源综合利用	Comprehensive Utilization of waste Resources	2600	
金属制品、机械和设备修理业	Metal Products, Machinery and Equipment Repair Industry	5476	5476
（四）电力、燃气及水的生产供应业	Production & Supply of Electricity,Gas & Water	1681286	257009
（五）建筑业	Construction	155745	
（六）批发和零售业	Wholesale and Retail Trades	1015828	
（七）交通运输、仓储和邮政业	Transport, Storage and Post	3223718	
（八）住宿和餐饮业	Hotels and Catering Services	318411	
（九）信息传输、软件和信息技术服务业	Information Transmission,Computer Service and Software	850622	
（十）金融业	Financial Intermediation	69789	
（十一）房地产业	Real Estate	24680525	
（十二） 租赁和商务服务业	Leasing and Business Services	920517	
（十三）科学研究和技术服务业	Scientific Research,Technical Service and Geologic Prospecting	511076	
（十四）水利、环境和公共设施管理业	Management of Water Conservancy, Environment and Public Facilities	6274271	
（十五）居民服务、修理和其他服务业	Services to Households, repairs and other services	57865	
（十六）教育	Education	758138	
（十七）卫生和社会工作	Health and social work	574206	
（十八）文化、体育和娱乐业	Culture, Sports and Entertainment	400889	
（十九）公共管理、社会保障和社会组织	Public administration, social security and social organizations	654153	
（二十）国际组织	International Organizations		

5-8 按国民经济行业分民间投资（2016年）

Private Investment of Municipal Units by Industry（2016）

行 业	Sector	投资额（万元）Investment (10000 yuan)	占民间投资比重（%）Rate(%)
民间投资总计	**Total**	**24273555**	**100.0**
（一）农、林、牧、渔业	Agriculture, Forestry, Animal Husbandry and Fishery	691232	2.8
（二）采矿业	Mining	6994	
（三）制造业	Manufacturing	4124719	17.0
（四）电力、燃气及水的生产供应业	Generation and Supply of Electricity, Production and Supply of Gas and Water	237101	1.0
（五）建筑业	Construction	4400	
（六）批发和零售业	Wholesale and Retail Trades	692749	2.9
（七）交通运输、仓储和邮政业	Transportation, Storage and Post	390285	1.6
（八）住宿和餐饮业	Hotels and Catering Services	214490	0.9
（九）信息传输、软件和信息技术服务业	Information Transmission, Computer Service and Software	35105	0.1
（十）金融业	Financial Intermediation		
（十一）房地产业	Real Estate	15609700	64.3
（十二） 租赁和商务服务业	Leasing and Business Services	714690	2.9
（十三）科学研究和技术服务业	Scientific Research and Technical Service	145578	0.6
（十四）水利、环境和公共设施管理业	Management of Water Conservancy, Environment and Public Facilities	873627	3.6
（十五）居民服务、修理和其他服务业	Services to Households, repairs and other services	12763	0.1
（十六）教育	Education	64426	0.3
（十七）卫生和社会工作	Health and social work	311748	1.3
（十八）文化、体育和娱乐业	Culture, Sports and Entertainment	140413	0.6
（十九）公共管理、社会保障和社会组织	Public administration, social security and social organizations	3535	
（二十）国际组织	International Organizations		

5-9 按国民经济行业分基础设施投资（2016年）

Investment for Basic Infrastructure of Municipal Units by Industry（2016）

指　标	Item	投资额（万元）Investment (10000 yuan)	占基础设施投资比重（%）Rate(%)
基础设施投资总计	**Total Investment of Infrastructure**	**10644390**	**100.0**
一、交通运输、仓储和邮政业	**Traffic, Transport, Storage and Post**	**3223718**	**30.3**
铁路运输业	Railway transport industry	204080	1.9
道路运输业	The road transport industry	2052920	19.3
水上运输业	Water transportation		
航空运输业	The air transport industry	6871	0.1
管道运输业	Pipeline transportation	4666	
装卸搬运和运输代理服务业	Handling and transport industry	45950	0.4
仓储业	Warehousing industry	902012	8.5
邮政业	The postal service	7219	0.1
二、信息传输、软件和信息技术服务业	**Information Transmission,Software and Information Technology Services**	**850622**	**8.0**
三、电网建设	**Grid Construction**	**295779**	**2.8**
四、水利、环境和公共设施管理业	**Management of Water Conservancy, Environment and Public Facilities**	**6274271**	**58.9**
水利管理业	Water resources management industry	348038	3.2
生态保护和环境治理业	Ecological protection and environmental control industries	71052	0.7
公共设施管理业	Public facilities management industry	5855181	55.0

5-10 全市固定资产投资资金来源（2016年）

Source of Funds for Total Fixed Assets Investment of Whole City（2016）

单位：万元　　(10 000 yuan)

指　标	Item	固定资产投资 Fixed Assets Investment	房地产开发 Real Estate
一、本年资金来源合计	**Total of Sources of Funds This Year**	**62677997**	**29329918**
1. 上年末结余资金	Balance of Last Year	10797308	6084461
2. 本年实际到位资金	Fully Funded Capital this Year	51880689	23245457
(1) 国家预算资金	State Budgetary Funds	3328838	
(2) 国内贷款	Domestic Loans	4264306	2795272
(3) 债券	Bonds		
(4) 利用外资	Utilization of Foreign Funds	1260752	
(5) 自筹资金	Self-raising Funds	33173155	11628282
(6) 其他资金来源	Others	9853638	8821903
二、各项应付款合计	**Total Sums of Money to be Paid This Year**	**7488504**	**5079651**

5-11 全市按行业分施工项目（2016年）

Construction Project Grouped by Industry in the Whole City（2016）

行 业	Sector	本年新增固定资产（万元）Increased Fixed Assets This Year (10 000 yuan)	施工项目个数（个）Number of Constructing Projects (unit)
总计	**Total**	**19529150**	**2610**
（一）农、林、牧、渔业	Agriculture, Forestry, Animal Husbandry and Fishery	726111	242
（二）采矿业	Mining	397	2
（三）制造业	Manufacturing	3895403	561
（四）电力、燃气及水的生产供应业	Generation and Supply of Electricity,Production and Supply of Gas and Water	846594	145
（五）建筑业	Construction	110476	3
（六）批发和零售业	Wholesale and Retail Trades	409718	142
（七）交通运输、仓储和邮政业	Transportation, Storage and Post	788681	165
（八）住宿和餐饮业	Hotels and Catering Services	186877	55
（九）信息传输、软件和信息技术服务业	Information Transmission, Computer Service and Software	704524	29
（十）金融业	Financial Intermediation	21750	3
（十一）房地产业	Real Estate	7271162	224
（十二） 租赁和商务服务业	Leasing and Business Services	672590	34
（十三）科学研究和技术服务业	Scientific Research and Technical Service	190677	43
（十四）水利、环境和公共设施管理业	Management of Water Conservancy, Environment and Public Facilities	2350183	628
（十五）居民服务、修理和其他服务业	Services to Households, repairs and other services	44077	14
（十六）教育	Education	316697	163
（十七）卫生和社会工作	Health and social work	361033	60
（十八）文化、体育和娱乐业	Culture, Sports and Entertainment	129771	47
（十九）公共管理、社会保障和社会组织	Public administration, social security and social organizations	502429	50
（二十）国际组织	International Organizations		

5-11 续表 continued

行 业	Sector	本年新开工 Newly Started This Year	本年投产项目个数（个） Projects put into Use (unit)
总计	**Total**	**1794**	**1687**
（一）农、林、牧、渔业	Agriculture, Forestry, Animal Husbandry and Fishery	220	202
（二）采矿业	Mining		
（三）制造业	Manufacturing	358	308
（四）电力、燃气及水的生产供应业	Generation and Supply of Electricity,Production and Supply of Gas and Water	95	79
（五）建筑业	Construction	2	21
（六）批发和零售业	Wholesale and Retail Trades	113	105
（七）交通运输、仓储和邮政业	Transportation, Storage and Post	108	95
（八）住宿和餐饮业	Hotels and Catering Services	46	39
（九）信息传输、软件和信息技术服务业	Information Transmission, Computer Service and Software	18	20
（十）金融业	Financial Intermediation	2	4
（十一）房地产业	Real Estate	125	89
（十二） 租赁和商务服务业	Leasing and Business Services	18	58
（十三）科学研究和技术服务业	Scientific Research and Technical Service	18	18
（十四）水利、环境和公共设施管理业	Management of Water Conservancy, Environment and Public Facilities	450	398
（十五）居民服务、修理和其他服务业	Services to Households, repairs and other services	7	12
（十六）教育	Education	101	101
（十七）卫生和社会工作	Health and social work	38	61
（十八）文化、体育和娱乐业	Culture, Sports and Entertainment	36	31
（十九）公共管理、社会保障和社会组织	Public administration, social security and social organizations	39	46
（二十）国际组织	International Organizations		

5-12 全市固定资产投资效果（2016年）

Achievements of Total Assets Investment of Whole City（2016）

指 标	Item	固定资产投资 Fixed Assets Investment	房地产开发投资 Real Estate Investment
一、建设项目投产率（%）	**Rate of Projects Put Into use(%)**	**64.6**	
施工项目个数（个）	Number of Constructing Projects (unit)	2610	
本年投产项目个数（个）	Number of Projects Put into Use (unit)	1687	
二、固定资产交付使用率（%）	**Rate of Fixed Assets Put into Use(%)**	**38.3**	**29.4**
本年新增固定资产（亿元）	Newly Increased Fixed Assets This Year(100 million yuan)	1952.92	574.54
本年完成投资（亿元）	Investment Completed This Year (100 million yuan)	5097.00	1955.82
三、建设周期（年）	**Construction Period (year)**	**4.3**	**6.5**
计划总投资（亿元）	Total Planned Investment(100 million yuan)	21987.31	12789.94
本年完成投资（亿元）	Investment Completed This Year (100 million yuan)	5097.00	1955.82
四、房屋建筑面积竣工率（%）	**Completion Rate of Buildings (%)**	**9.9**	**10.6**
本年房屋施工面积（万平方米）	Floor Space of the Constructing Buildings This Year (10 000 sq.m)	18977.90	14727.10
本年房屋竣工面积（万平方米）	Floor Space of the Buildings Completed This Year (10 000 sq.m)	1884.00	1560.20

5-13 固定资产投资新增生产能力或效益（2016年）

Newly Increased Production Capacity or Project Efficiency through Investment（2016）

能源名称	Name	累计新增生产能力或效益 Cumulative Newly Increased Production Capacity or Project Efficiency
粗钢（万吨/年）	Crude Steel (10 000 tons/year)	
太阳能发电（万千瓦）	Solar Energy (10 000 kw)	6.8
其他发电（万千瓦）	Others (10 000 kw)	0.63
输电线路长度（11万伏及以上）（公里）	Length of Transmission Lines (above 110 000 VA) (km)	72.8
水泥（万吨/年）	Cement (10 000 tons/year)	
平板玻璃（万重量箱/年）	Plate Glass (10 000 Weight-boxs/year)	65
氮肥（吨/年）	Nitrogen Fertilizers (ton/year)	
磷肥（吨/年）	Phosphate Fertilizer (ton/year)	8100
钾肥（吨/年）	Potash Fertilizer (ton/year)	
塑料树脂及共聚物（吨/年）	Plastic Resin and Copolymer (ton/year)	1720
合成橡胶（吨/年）	Synthetic Rubber (ton/year)	120
轿车制造（辆/年）	Car Manufacturing (car/year)	
化学纤维（吨/年）	Chemical Fiber (ton/year)	
棉纺锭（锭）	Cotton Spirit（Spindle）	
啤酒（万吨/年）	Beer (10 000 tons/year)	
白酒（万吨/年）	White Spirit (10 000 tons/year)	
其他酒（万吨/年）	Other Alcohols (10 000 tons/year)	
新建铁路里程（公里）	Newly Railway (km)	
复线里程（公里）	Double-Tracking Length (km)	
新建高速铁路里程（公里）	Length of Newly highways(km)	
新建公路（公里）	Newly Highways (km)	70.8
#高速公路（公里）	Expressway (km)	4.7
一级公路（公里）	First Class (km)	2
二级公路（公里）	Second Class (km)	64.1
改建公路（公里）	Reconstructed Highways (km)	
新建独立公路桥梁（延长米）	New-built Separate Highway Bridge (extended meters)	3407.4
新建独立公路隧道（延长米）	New-built Separate Highway Tunnel (extended meters)	
新（扩）建客、货运站（个）	New (expanded) Passenger and Freight Stations （unit）	
新（扩）建客、货运站（平方米）	New (expanded) Passenger and Freight Stations（sq.m）	
城市自来水供水能力（万吨/日）	Tap Water Supply Capacity in City(10 000 tons/day)	
城市污水处理能力（万吨/日）	Waste Water Treated Capacity in City(10 000 tons/day)	14

5-14 全市按国民经济行业分房屋建筑面积（2016年）

单位：平方米

行 业	Sector	本年施工房屋面积 Floor Space of Buildings Under Construction This Year	住宅 Residential Residence
总 计	**Total**	**189778754**	**109762152**
（一）农、林、牧、渔业	Agriculture, Forestry, Animal Husbandry and Fishery	50020	2416
（二）采矿业	Mining	23160	
（三）制造业	Manufacturing	7712509	58430
（四）电力、燃气及水的生产供应业	Generation and Supply of Electricity, Production and Supply of Gas and Water	49636	760
（五）建筑业	Construction	221936	
（六）批发和零售业	Wholesale and Retail Trades	856651	50600
（七）交通运输、仓储和邮政业	Transportation, Storage and Post	10893479	2100
（八）住宿和餐饮业	Hotels and Catering Services	249065	
（九）信息传输、软件和信息技术服务业	Information Transmission, Computer Service and Software	113280	
（十）金融业	Financial Intermediation	151593	
（十一）房地产业	Real Estate	161720323	108923947
（十二） 租赁和商务服务业	Leasing and Business Services	1036936	31430
（十三）科学研究和技术服务业	Scientific Research and Technical Service	937141	
（十四）水利、环境和公共设施管理业	Management of Water Conservancy, Environment and Public Facilities	877359	800
（十五）居民服务、修理和其他服务业	Services to Households, repairs and other services	14028	2400
（十六）教育	Education	2368888	614609
（十七）卫生和社会工作	Health and social work	1502907	11660
（十八）文化、体育和娱乐业	Culture, Sports and Entertainment	396297	2000
（十九）公共管理、社会保障和社会组织	Public administration, social security and social organizations	603546	61000
（二十）国际组织	International Organizations		

Floors Space of Buildings Construction of Municipal Units by Industry（2016）

(sq.m)

本年竣工房屋面积 Floor Space of Buildings Completed This Year	住宅 Residential Residence	本年竣工房屋价值（万元） Value of Buildings Completed this Year (10 000 yuan)	住宅 Residential Residence
18840468	**13312414**	**4564777**	**3514585**
3970	1710		
354921	6000		
4391			
219836			
69976			
144041			
33000			
17034822	13298004	4564777	3514585
294488	4700		
62726			
39205			
104969			
360000			
38710	2000		
75413			

5-15 主要年份市属固定资产投资

Investment In Fixed Assets of Municipal Units in Representative Years

单位：万元 (10 000 yuan)

指　标	Item	1995	2000	2001	2002	2003	2004	2005	2006	2007
一、投资总额	**Total Investment**	**432451**	**1263023**	**1539717**	**1848833**	**2978747**	**4355271**	**5788693**	**7835681**	**10555849**
#房地产开发	Real Estate	171291	473787	566557	702233	1114809	1492693	2062940	2641871	3515719
按经济类型分	Grouped by Type of Enterprises									
国有经济	State-owned Enterprises	258545	890546	894700	1006245	1586057	1884624	2198836	2591184	2972840
集体经济	Collective-owned Enterprises	5720	52893	62895	63877	142849	257226	258327	363909	1366567
其他经济	Others	168186	319584	582122	778711	1249841	2213421	3331530	4880588	6216442
二、本年新增固定资产	**Newly Increased Fixed Assets this Year**	**273324**	**953173**	**1159980**	**1295389**	**1812099**	**1962795**	**3011104**	**3495179**	**5279938**
三、本年房屋竣工面积（万平方米）	**Floor Space of the Building this Year Completed(10 000sq.m)**	**202.52**	**509.48**	**535.98**	**537.44**	**631.89**	**606.23**	**767.70**	**914.80**	**1343.88**
#住宅	Residential Buildings	143.30	373.51	396.01	331.45	387.82	388.79	436.43	432.43	734.05

5-15 续表1 continued 1

单位：万元 (10 000 yuan)

指　标	Item	2008	2009	2010	2011	2012	2013	2014	2015	2016
一、投资总额	**Total Investment**	**14648360**	**19063075**	**25474854**	**26820029**	**35875223**	**44187825**	**50533650**	**45066446**	**44832319**
#房地产开发投资	Real Estate Investment	4938202	6575526	8020893	9001953	11655613	14410956	16107323	17238478	18472701
按经济类型分	Grouped by Type of Enterprises									
国有经济	State-owned Enterprises	4480627	6527566	9306901	8750285	12264895	12847731	12835067	13496036	17842932
集体经济	Collective-owned Enterprises	1646111	1614290	2253851	1897980	1932578	2148977	1927394	1493122	1318545
其他经济	Others	8521622	10921219	13914102	16171764	21677750	29191117	35771189	30077288	25670842
二、本年新增固定资产	**Newly Increased Fixed Assets this Year**	**6488364**	**8380033**	**10423906**	**10663882**	**15376910**	**16019776**	**21603094**	**17837619**	**17090770**
三、本年房屋竣工面积（万平方米）	**Floor Space of the Building this Year Completed(10 000sq.m)**	**987.05**	**1359.46**	**668.49**	**1002.82**	**1450.29**	**975.03**	**1591.28**	**902.22**	**1725.49**
#住宅	Residential Buildings	602.69	727.41	448.46	531.38	1069.61	760.87	1262.20	640.60	1245.54

5-16 市属固定资产投资（2016年）

Investment in Fixed Assets of Municipal Units（2016）

单位：万元 （10 000 yuan）

指 标	Item	固定资产投资 Fixed Assets Investment	房地产开发 Real Estate
一、本年完成投资	**Investment Completed This Year**	**44832319**	**18472701**
#住宅	Residential Buildings	13130686	12733030
（一）按登记注册类型分	**Grouped by Registion Status**		
内资	Domestic Funded Enterprises	40910856	17568876
国有	State-owned Enterprises	10981130	829283
集体	Collective-owned Enterprises	882075	137648
股份合作	Cooperative Enterprises	157383	144780
联营	Joint Ownership Enterprises	2500	
国有联营	State Joint Ownership Enterprises		
集体联营	Collective Joint Ownership Enterprises		
国有与集体联营	Joint State-collective Ownership Enterprises		
其他联营	Other Joint Ownership Enterprises	2500	
有限责任公司	Limited Liability Corporations	18204212	11054166
国有独资公司	State-funded Corporations	2017374	415455
其他有限责任公司	Other Limited Liability Corporations	16186838	10638711
股份有限公司	Stock Limited Corporation	836309	176834
私营	Private Enterprises	9344107	5215049
私营独资	Private -funded Enterprises	832323	155096
私营合伙	Private Limited Liability Corporations	35081	
私营有限责任公司	Private Limited Liability Corporations	8197382	4929575
私营股份有限公司	Private Share Holding Corporations	279321	130378
其他	Other	503140	11116
港澳台商投资	Enterprises Funded by Hong Kong, Macao and Taiwan	957908	470970
与港澳台合资经营	Joint-venture Enterprises	220827	49669
与港澳台合作经营	Cooperative Enterprises	33119	33119
港澳台独资	Wholly Funded from Hong Kong,Macao and Taiwan	654982	388182
港澳台投资股份有限公司	Share-holding Corporations Ltd.	48980	
其他港澳台投资	Investment From Hongkong,Macao,Taiwan		
外商投资	Foreign Owned Enterprises	2933355	432855
中外合资经营	Joint-venture Enterprises	1009909	197661
中外合作经营	Cooperation Enterprises		
外资企业	Foreign Funded Enterprises	1868442	193110

5-16 续表 continued

单位：万元 (10 000 yuan)

指　标	Item	固定资产投资 Fixed Assets Investment	房地产开发 Real Estate
外商投资股份有限公司	Share-holding Corporations Ltd. With Foreign Funds	47004	42084
其他外商投资	Foreign Investment	8000	
（二）按建设性质分	**Grouped by Type of Construction**		
#新建	New Construction	22550437	
扩建	Expansion	1415789	
改建和技术改造	Reconstruction	713812	
（三）按构成分	**Grouped by Composition**		
建筑工程	Construction Projects	31762515	13314988
安装工程	Installment Projects	3774499	2325680
设备、工器具购置	Purchasing of Equipment and Instruments	4380347	275499
其他费用	Others	4914958	2556534
二、本年完成投资额构成(%)	**the Constitution of Compeleted Investment this year (%)**		
（一）按登记注册类型分组	**Grouped by Status**		
# 国有经济	State-owned	39.8	7.8
集体经济	Collective-owned	2.9	0.9
（二）按建设性质分	**Grouped by Type of Construction**		
# 新建	New Construction	50.3	
扩建	Expansion	3.2	
改建和技术改造	Reconstruction	1.6	
（三）按构成分	**Grouped by Composition of Funds**		
建筑工程	Construction Projects	70.8	72.1
安装工程	Installation Projects	8.4	12.6
设备、工器具购置	Purchasing of the Equipment and Instruments	9.8	1.5
其他	Others	11	13.8
三、本年新增固定资产	**Newly Increase in Fixed Assets this Year**	**17090770**	**5400988**
四、房屋面积（万平方米）	**Floor Space (10 000 sq.m)**		
本年房屋施工面积	Floor Space of Buildings Under Construction This Year	17477.69	13827.85
#住宅	Residential Buildings	10133.31	9824.22
本年房屋竣工面积	Floor Space of Buildings Completed this Year	1725.49	1440.04
#住宅	Residential Buildings	1245.54	1173.54
五、本年竣工房屋价值	**Value of the Building Completed this Year**	**4238010**	**4238010**
#住宅	Residential Buildings	3277017	3277017

5-17 按国民经济行业分市属固定资产投资（2016年）

Investment in Fixed Assets of Municipal Units by Industry（2016）

单位：万元　　　　(10 000 yuan)

行 业	Sector	2016
本年完成固定资产投资	**Grouped by Sector**	**44832319**
（一）农、林、牧、渔业	Agriculture,Forestry,Animal Husbandry and Fishery	958212
（二）采矿业	Mining	6994
（三）制造业	Manufacturing	6765185
农副食品加工业	Processing of Food from Agricultural Products	112866
食品制造业	Manufacture of Foods	350380
酒、饮料和精制茶制造业	Wine, soft drinks and refined tea industry	147043
烟草制品业	Tobacco Processing	
纺织业	Textile Industry	20977
纺织服装、服饰业	Textile, apparel industry	47099
皮革、毛皮、羽毛及其制品和制鞋业	Leather, Fur, Feather (eiderdown) and Their Products Industry	
木材加工和木、竹、藤、棕、草制品业	Timber Processing,Bamboo,Cane,Palm Fiber and Straw Products	74918
家具制造业	Furniture Manufacturing	50725
造纸及纸制品业	Papermaking and Paper products	28802
印刷和记录媒介复制业	Printing,Record Medium Reproduction	89194
文教、工美、体育和娱乐用品制造业	Culture, education, Craft art, sports and entertainment goods manufacturing industry	25546
石油加工、炼焦和核燃料加工业	Petroleum Refining, Ccoke Making and Nuclear Fuel Processing Industry	6048
化学原料和化学制品制造业	Raw Chemical Materials and Chemical Products	95652
医药制造业	Medical and Pharmaceutical Products	292619
化学纤维制造业	Chemical Fiber	
橡胶和塑料制品业	Rubber and plastic products industry	33774
非金属矿物制品业	Nonmetal Mineral Products	214763
黑色金属冶炼和压延加工业	Smelting and Pressing of Ferrous Metals	46685
有色金属冶炼和压延加工业	Smelting and Pressing of Nonferrou Metals	482646
金属制品业	Metal Products	76836

5-17 续表 continued

单位：万元 (10 000 yuan)

行 业	Sector	2016
通用设备制造业	General Equipment Manufacturing Industry	342592
专用设备制造业	Special Purpose Equipment	744957
汽车制造业	Automotive Manufacturing	493710
铁路、船舶、航空航天和其他运输设备制造业	Railroad, Marine, Aerospace and other Transportation Equipment Manufacturing	617595
电气机械和器材制造业	Electric Equipment and Machinery	733166
计算机、通信和其他电子设备制造业	Communication Equipment, Computer and Other Electronic Equipment Manufacturing Industry	1546390
仪器仪表制造业	Instrument Manufacturing Industry	81608
其他制造业	Other Manufacturing	1618
废弃资源综合利用	Comprehensive Utilization of waste Resources	1500
金属制品、机械和设备修理业	Metal Products, Machinery and Equipment Repair Industry	5476
（四）电力、燃气及水的生产供应业	Production & Supply of Electricity,Gas & Water	1176169
（五）建筑业	Construction	54790
（六）批发和零售业	Wholesale and Retail Trades	887662
（七）交通运输、仓储和邮政业	Transport, Storage and Post	2790507
（八）住宿和餐饮业	Hotels and Catering Services	304969
（九）信息传输、软件和信息技术服务业	Information Transmission,Computer Service and Software	83369
（十）金融业	Financial Intermediation	2100
（十一）房地产业	Real Estate	23085249
（十二） 租赁和商务服务业	Leasing and Business Services	846703
（十三）科学研究和技术服务业	Scientific Research,Technical Service and Geologic Prospecting	336484
（十四）水利、环境和公共设施管理业	Management of Water Conservancy, Environment and Public Facilities	5884945
（十五）居民服务、修理和其他服务业	Services to Households, repairs and other services	57865
（十六）教育	Education	462101
（十七）卫生和社会工作	Health and social work	502739
（十八）文化、体育和娱乐业	Culture, Sports and Entertainment	367669
（十九）公共管理、社会保障和社会组织	Public administration, social security and social organizations	258607
（二十）国际组织	International Organizations	

5-18 按资金来源及建设性质分市属固定资产投资（2016年）

Investment in Fixed Assets of Municipal Units by Sources of Funds and Type of Construction (2016)

单位：万元　　　　(10 000 yuan)

指　标	Item	2016
投资总额	**Total Investment**	**44832319**
一、按资金来源分	**Grouped by Funds Sources**	
1. 国家预算内资金	State Budgetary Funds	1913062
2. 国内贷款	Domestic Loans	4603917
3. 债券	Bonds	
4. 利用外资	Utilization of Foreign Funds	911451
5. 自筹资金	Self-raising Funds	26542102
6. 其他资金	Others	10861787
二、按建设性质分	**Grouped by Type of Construction**	
#新建	New Construction	22550437
扩建	Expansion	1415789
改建	Reconstruction	713812
三、按构成分	**Grouped by Composition of Funds**	
1. 建筑工程	Construction Project	31762515
2. 安装工程	Installation Projects	3774499
3. 设备、工器具购置	Purchasing of Equipment and Instruments	4380347
4. 其他费用	Others	4914958
四、房屋施工面积（万平方米）	**Floor Space of Buildings Under Construction (10 000 sq.m)**	**17477.69**

5-19 分区县、开发区全社会固定资产投资额（2016年）

Total Investment in Fixed Assets by Region and Development Zone（2016）

单位：亿元 （100 million yuan）

区县、开发区	Region	全社会固定资产投资 Fixed Assets Investment	固定资产投资 Urban Area	房地产 Real Estate	农户投资 Farmer Investment
全市	**Total**	**5191.36**	**5097.00**	**1955.82**	**78.66**
新城区	Xincheng	253.71	253.71	87.46	
碑林区	Beilin	207.57	207.57	132.81	
莲湖区	Lianhu	225.14	225.14	159.70	
灞桥区	Baqiao	581.06	574.87	247.61	6.20
未央区	Weiyang	983.64	979.67	503.68	2.67
雁塔区	Yanta	892.79	892.79	566.26	
阎良区	Yanliang	158.35	154.68	18.49	3.67
临潼区	Lintong	141.75	129.01	29.93	12.74
长安区	Chang'an	738.02	724.18	156.44	13.83
高陵区	Gaoling	459.53	456.42	25.79	3.12
蓝田县	Lantian	264.37	251.78	5.63	12.59
周至县	Zhouzhi	159.99	132.33	9.77	13.25
户　县	Huxian	125.44	114.85	12.25	10.59
#开发区	**Development Zones**	**3056.54**	**3056.54**	**1225.45**	
高新区	GaoXin	783.14	783.14	294.36	
经开区	JingKai	664.85	664.85	243.87	
曲江新区	Qujiang	386.55	386.55	243.98	
浐灞生态区	Chanba Eco-District	475.90	475.90	230.37	
航空基地	Aviation Industry Base	114.61	114.61	11.08	
航天基地	Aerospace Base	131.81	131.81	58.93	
国际港务区	International Trade&Logistic Park	173.42	173.42	29.41	
沣东新城	FengDongXinCheng	326.26	326.26	113.45	

5-20 分区县工业投资（2016年）

Industrial Investment by Region（2016）

单位：万元 (10 000 yuan)

区县	Region	投资额 Investment	工业企业技术改造 Technological Transformation of Industrial Enterprises
全　市	**Total**	**9492744**	**1573832**
新城区	Xincheng	151176	65404
碑林区	Beilin	99290	
莲湖区	Lianhu	126358	43766
灞桥区	Baqiao	244286	27367
未央区	Weiyang	1343097	35424
雁塔区	Yanta	728074	357212
阎良区	Yanliang	772358	112649
临潼区	Lintong	303298	33907
长安区	Chang'an	2480382	410127
高陵区	Gaoling	1953285	156381
蓝田县	Lantian	402334	227478
周至县	Zhouzhi	310666	65895
户　县	Huxian	578140	38222

5-21 分区县、开发区新增固定资产及房屋施工、竣工面积（2016年）

区县、开发区	Region	本年新增固定资产（亿元）Increased Fixed Assets this Year (100 million yuan)	房屋施工面积（万平方米）Floor Space of Buildings Under Construction (10 000sq.m)	住宅 Residencial Buildings
区县	**Region**	**1883.94**	**18977.68**	**10976.21**
新城区	Xincheng	61.48	803.76	531.60
碑林区	Beilin	120.68	1266.62	892.67
莲湖区	Lianhu	81.06	1626.19	1294.91
灞桥区	Baqiao	199.49	1832.70	1233.47
未央区	Weiyang	224.21	4091.21	2499.69
雁塔区	Yanta	272.86	3873.22	2315.92
阎良区	Yanliang	34.09	266.24	125.67
临潼区	Lintong	103.27	324.81	137.08
长安区	Chang'an	311.67	2150.62	1193.28
高陵区	Gaoling	178.32	2186.36	440.30
蓝田县	Lantian	208.06	107.34	76.27
周至县	Zhouzhi	56.90	170.58	91.44
户　县	Huxian	31.85	278.03	143.91
开发区	**Development Zones**	**907.67**	**7937.86**	**4443.88**
高新区	GaoXin	345.87	1466.73	548.27
经开区	JingKai	163.59	1540.85	843.60
曲江新区	Qujiang	104.22	1655.31	1055.34
浐灞生态区	Chanba Eco-District	82.33	1481.98	1020.83
航空基地	Aviation Industry Base	13.26	81.21	44.25
航天基地	Aerospace Base	26.30	840.83	395.73
国际港务区	International Trade&Logistic Park	98.66	248.41	73.61
沣东新城	FengDong Xincheng	73.44	622.54	462.25

Newly Added Fixed Assets and Floor Space of Constructing and Completed Buildings by Region and Development Zone（2016）

本年房屋竣工面积（万平方米）Floor Space of Buildings this Year Completed(10 000 sq.m)	住宅 Residenctial Buildings	本年房屋竣工价值（亿元）Value of Buildings Completed this Year (100 million yuan)	住宅 Residenctial Buildings	本年商品房销售面积（万平方米）Floor Space of Houses Sales this year (sq.m) Houses(10 000sq.m)	本年商品房销售额（亿元）Sales Income of Commercial Houses this year(100 million yuan)
1884.05	**1331.25**	**456.49**	**351.47**	**2047.66**	**1347.07**
28.71	13.05	6.26	2.27	107.12	37.12
331.76	251.87	89.16	71.77	109.27	73.25
216.22	170.69	62.63	48.04	138.89	82.87
285.50	153.20	88.35	43.84	261.02	163.94
294.48	204.64	55.02	42.40	521.88	340.73
304.65	279.79	85.73	79.12	607.88	501.41
7.39	5.40	2.14	1.55	30.85	12.52
153.73	46.71	2.84	2.84	17.77	8.22
89.75	66.90	32.18	29.87	136.62	82.07
100.91	92.68	20.91	19.18	68.96	27.17
29.91	22.89	3.80	3.63	11.97	3.69
0.66				6.02	1.78
40.38	23.43	7.47	6.96	29.41	12.30
596.91	**394.95**	**189.40**	**133.01**	**1099.31**	**806.04**
66.05	55.76	27.89	24.92	159.41	150.32
102.98	87.84	31.77	26.90	234.57	146.86
116.21	100.40	32.11	28.42	299.00	247.71
128.70	78.72	28.12	26.46	266.77	188.75
0.50				8.38	3.34
41.15	27.75	9.30	6.80	64.71	33.65
92.72	10.17	41.83	2.80	23.38	13.23
48.60	34.31	18.38	16.71	43.09	22.18

5-22 主要年份房地产开发投资主要指标

单位：万平方米

指 标	Item	1997	1998	1999	2000	2001	2002
本年完成投资额（亿元）	Investment Completed This Year(100 million yuan)	24.68	38.21	44.30	51.85	67.42	79.37
本年房屋施工面积	Floor Space of Buildings Under Construction This Year	451.47	678.87	793.46	763.18	743.78	1172.58
#住宅	Residential Buildings	331.16	552.37	649.53	619.85	580.43	964.68
本年房屋竣工面积	Floor Space of Buildings Completed This Year	135.62	156.17	377.79	321.10	316.24	329.71
#住宅	Residential Buildings	120.33	133.33	352.28	295.55	269.61	290.30
本年房屋竣工价值（亿元）	Value of Floor Space of Buildings Completed this Year(100million yuan)	11.96	14.36	38.22	26.94	37.20	36.93
#住宅	Residential Buildings	9.63	11.00	33.02	22.97	28.62	30.46
本年商品房销售面积	Floor Space of Commercialized Buildings sold	78.45	117.11	296.97	212.92	225.35	252.90
#住宅	Residential Buildings	72.69	108.61	284.95	200.77	192.20	237.04
本年商品房销售额（亿元）	Total Sales of Commercialized Buildings(100 million yuan)	12.81	17.74	35.19	32.52	47.22	51.35
#住宅	Residential Buildings	11.39	15.46	32.35	29.46	35.53	45.46
本年批准预售面积	Approved Pre-sale Area of This Year	26.35	252.02	30.25	253.03	67.44	61.02
#住宅	Residential Buildings	23.27	246.77	27.34	253.03	65.20	55.73
待售面积	Area for Sale	58.71	32.52	62.38	36.41	50.82	57.14
#住宅	Residential Buildings	50.26	22.81	52.32	24.02	34.18	44.70
房屋出租面积	Rental Housing Area	25.69	1.04	1.88	1.17	9.19	15.75
#住宅	Residential Buildings	22.87	0.01	0.15	0.02	0.10	1.13
本年新增固定资产（亿元）	Newly Increased Fixed Assets This Year(100 million yuan)	14.36	19.93	43.10	38.38	50.77	48.43

Main Indicators of Investment in Real Estate Development in Representative Years

(10 000 sq.m)

2003	2004	2005	2006	2007	2008	2009	2010	2011	2012	2013	2014	2015	2016
124.82	169.67	225.23	285.76	387.33	540.26	696.34	842.34	996.81	1281.90	1595.64	1761.88	1831.67	1955.82
1343.12	1633.68	2174.29	2383.56	2915.95	3632.87	5708.63	6697.39	8247.69	9947.89	10454.27	12422.10	13392.94	14727.10
943.61	1204.01	1783.36	1890.27	2376.82	3079.13	4901.59	5777.71	7108.27	8294.92	8461.71	9727.60	9777.23	10468.80
339.67	380.84	361.62	399.64	483.30	443.96	542.81	463.65	631.03	1063.70	795.35	1533.70	976.64	1560.18
289.56	308.06	316.52	342.15	422.47	412.46	453.49	412.44	564.59	903.82	663.20	1307.64	766.58	1259.24
54.73	73.75	80.58	82.02	101.13	106.50	168.08	145.62	213.29	310.57	279.63	442.74	301.86	456.48
44.01	55.58	68.11	65.80	77.13	96.02	137.42	128.69	185.31	260.04	222.64	368.25	236.66	351.46
252.74	305.47	497.34	621.50	833.92	760.72	1256.02	1587.81	1778.02	1538.91	1662.75	1707.71	1763.68	2047.67
230.28	279.90	476.39	584.06	782.91	715.76	1202.12	1523.24	1674.85	1383.84	1522.50	1525.95	1584.08	1877.78
54.29	81.35	171.29	206.15	281.79	296.44	488.55	707.00	1091.31	1017.74	1112.87	1100.71	1146.79	1347.08
44.25	71.27	158.03	179.47	251.74	268.92	450.71	661.27	973.71	858.53	976.19	928.74	985.35	1194.41
52.35	176.40	300.07	428.20	491.07	569.22	1125.44	1510.20	3105.76	2627.73	1787.89	842.98	751.15	717.54
49.12	159.10	287.13	408.11	457.54	541.20	1095.17	1452.20	2826.79	2340.69	1597.82	727.31	583.55	508.17
63.85	108.52	123.59	112.49	45.42	55.40	40.68	34.32	59.76	102.58	74.59	187.13	296.50	378.24
52.34	72.76	99.17	85.89	38.62	35.40	28.73	26.23	45.41	83.78	61.24	143.21	185.96	215.40
10.56	11.18	17.32	8.53	10.84	34.94	38.23	28.60	8.01	15.16	15.57	7.15	19.64	48.67
5.43	5.78	4.09	3.74	5.36	4.53	6.55	0.70	3.25	4.03	0.73	0.07	1.47	1.47
62.13	83.36	92.78	100.22	143.17	124.02	195.71	168.20	25.53	358.03	334.41	531.44	335.91	574.54

5-23 分区县、开发区房地产开发主要指标（2016年）

单位：万元

区县、开发区	Region	企业（单位）个数（个） Number of Enterprises (Unit)	本年完成投资 Investment Completed This Year	本年新增固定资产 Increased Fixed Assets This Year
全市	**Total**	923	19558202	5745448
新城区	Xincheng	35	874568	137614
碑林区	Beilin	92	1328098	1006164
莲湖区	Lianhu	84	1597007	637825
灞桥区	Baqiao	88	2476070	935253
未央区	Weiyang	194	5036795	851962
雁塔区	Yanta	191	5658658	1387562
阎良区	Yanliang	36	184881	27404
临潼区	Lintong	15	299294	28400
长安区	Chang'an	88	1564516	398449
高陵区	Gaoling	35	257935	217444
蓝田县	Lantian	14	60208	37971
周至县	Zhouzhi	17	97675	
户　县	Huxian	34	122497	79400
#开发区	**Development Zones**	383	12254673	2751726
高新区	GaoXin	76	2943635	283065
经开区	JingKai	80	2438680	532005
曲江新区	Qujiang	75	2439799	825922
浐灞生态区	Chanba Eco-District	65	2303726	332526
航空基地	Aviation Industry Base	8	110848	6000
航天基地	Aerospace Base	30	589304	130412
国际港务区	International Trade&Logistic Park	12	294140	418259
沣东新城	FengDongXinCheng	37	1134541	223537

Main Indicators of Real Estate Development by Region and Development Zone（2016）

(10 000 yuan)

房屋施工面积（平方米）Floor Space of Buildings Under Constmction(sq.m)	住宅 Residenctial Buildings	本年房屋竣工面积（平方米）Floor Space of Buildings Completed this Year(sq.m)	住宅 Residenctial Buildings	本年房屋竣工价值 Value of Buildings Completed this Year	住宅 Residenctial Buildings
147271009	104688020	15601797	12592426	4564777	3514585
6687502	4875093	287086	130496	62568	22668
10995010	8307323	3157558	2518718	891595	717666
15785745	12764161	2113606	1706891	626306	480392
16540997	12071611	2428517	1466963	883539	438364
37015488	23901353	2129706	1701658	550191	423982
34972516	22987362	3027093	2797885	857283	791201
1845955	1236731	68875	53975	21404	15529
1146447	988315	162825	162825	28400	28400
13928509	10879294	757923	667516	321771	298730
5129982	4197518	984277	926829	209062	191769
835415	781826	232983	224356	37971	36331
1083295	758530				
1304148	938903	251348	234314	74687	69553
67284958	43185608	5354611	3887814	1893993	1330142
12187538	5482668	629766	557589	278900	249174
14905666	8326779	1013609	878441	317709	269033
14153804	10514763	1152642	1004038	321137	284187
12675331	10132525	807341	726894	281156	264632
782094	422466				
5693460	3944299	381299	277473	92995	68033
2333860	736135	900072	101744	418259	27991
4553205	3625973	469882	341635	183837	167092

5-24 房地产开发投资主要指标（2016年）

Main Indicators of Investment in Real Estate Development（2016）

单位：万元 (10 000 yuan)

指标	Item	全市合计 Total	国有 State-owned	市区 Urban	市属 Municipal
一、企业（单位）个数（个）	**Number of Enterprises(unit)**	**923**	**125**	**859**	**863**
二、本年完成投资	**Investment Completed This Year**	**19558202**	**1564731**	**18472701**	**19277822**
按工程用途分	Grouped by Function				
住宅	Residential Buildings	13420504	1215255	12733030	13222646
#别墅、高档公寓	Villas and Top-Grade Apartments	429635	69770	403474	402726
办公楼	Office Buildings	1721890	81496	1597145	1720925
商业营业用房	Houses for Business Use	2902846	172385	2769584	2831142
其他	Others	1512962	95595	1372942	1503109
三、本年新增固定资产	**Increased Fixed Assets This Year**	**5745448**	**672563**	**5400988**	**5628077**
四、房屋施工面积（平方米）	**Floor Space of Buildings Under Construction (sq.m)**	**147271009**	**12485070**	**144048151**	**138278545**
#住宅	Residential Buildings	104688020	9506455	102208761	98242189
五、本年房屋竣工面积（平方米）	**Floor Space of Buildings this Year Completed (sq.m)**	**15601797**	**1680806**	**15117466**	**14400429**
#住宅	Residential Buildings	12592426	1606514	12133756	11735414
六、本年房屋竣工价值	**Value of Buildings Completed this Year**	**4564777**	**468236**	**4452119**	**4238010**
#住宅	Residential Buildings	3514585	442927	3408701	3277017
七、本年商品房屋销售面积（平方米）	**Floor Space of Commercialized Buildings Sold this Year(sq.m)**	**20476744**	**1069868**	**19992461**	**19105835**
本年商品房销售额	Sales Income of Commercialized Buildings	13470804	780053	13288056	12573832

5-25 商品房销售情况（2016年）

Sales of Commercial Houses（2016）

指 标	Item	全市合计 Total	国有 State-owned	市区 Urban	市属 Municipal
本年商品房销售面积（平方米）	**Floor Space of Commercialized Buildings Sold(sq.m)**	**20476744**	**1069868**	**19992461**	**19105835**
现房销售面积（平方米）	**Floor Space of Completed Apartment Sales**	**2998984**	**110265**	**2842698**	**2878894**
期房销售面积（平方米）	**Floor Space of Forward Delivery Housing Sales**	**17477760**	**959603**	**17149763**	**16226941**
住宅	Residential Buildings	18777848	1038098	18315138	17470022
#别墅、高档公寓	Villas and High-grade Apartments	375370	95468	369908	369972
办公楼	Office Buildings	640426	9187	640426	620619
商业营业用房	Houses for Business Use	726181	21722	704608	704346
其他	Others	332289	861	332289	310848
本年商品房销售额（万元）	**Real estate sales this year(Wan Yuan)**	**13470804**	**780053**	**13288056**	**12573832**
现房销售额（万元）	**Floor Space of Completed Apartment Sales**	**1487879**	**64391**	**1429321**	**1416670**
期房销售额（万元）	**Floor Space of Forward Delivery Housing Sales**	**11982925**	**715662**	**11858735**	**11157162**
住宅	Residential Buildings	11944103	739257	11778241	11113171
#别墅高档公寓	Villas and High-grade Apartments	391022	65683	384135	386905
办公楼	Office Buildings	549855	14153	549855	524089
商业营业用房	Houses for Business Use	785463	26130	768577	754530
其他	Others	191383	513	191383	182042
待售面积（平方米）	**Area for Sale(Sqm)**	**3782352**	**205449**	**3411569**	**3563310**
#待售一年以上（一到三年）	Being Idle for One Year	1406791	99863	1255385	1330449
待售三年以上（含三年）	Being Idle for Three Years	60542	1016	46880	59526
住宅	Residence	2153978	168930	1855355	2041827
#别墅高档公寓	Villas and High-grade Apartments				
办公楼	Office Buildings	72304		72304	72304
商业营业用房	Houses for Business Use	1104902	31971	1042490	1067592
其他	Others	451168	4548	441420	381587
房屋出租面积（平方米）	**Rental area(Sqm)**	**486662**		**486662**	**393437**
住宅	Residential Buildings	14652		14652	14652
办公楼	Office Buildings	67390		67390	67390
商业营业用房	Houses for Business Use	389620		389620	296395
其他	Others	15000		15000	15000

5-26 房地产开发投资资金来源（2016年）

Source of Funds for Investment in Real Estate Development（2016）

单位：万元　　　　　　　　　　　　　　　　　　　　　　　　　(10 000 yuan)

指　标	Item	全市合计 Total	国有 State-owned	市区 Urban	市属 Municipal
一. 本年资金来源合计	**Total**	**29329918**	**2324913**	**27458737**	**28845544**
1. 上年末结余资金	Balance of Last Year	6084461	418859	5636396	6000003
2. 本年实际到位资金	Fully Funded Capital this Year	23245457	1906054	21822341	22845541
(1) 国内贷款	Domestic Loans	2795272	22863	2612654	2767841
#银行贷款	Bank Loan	2423048	22863	2240430	2395722
非银行金融机构贷款	Loans from financial Institutions except Bank	372224		372224	372119
(2) 自筹资金	Self-raising Funds	11628282	1359230	11108956	11398283
(3) 其他资金	Others	8821903	523961	8100731	8679417
#定金及预收款	Earnest Money and Advance payment	4352240	216221	4057134	4289273
个人按揭贷款	Personal Mortgage loan	3416263	113499	3128793	3368299
二. 本年各项应付款合计	**Total Sums of Money to be Paid This Year**	**5079651**	**373437**	**4603628**	**4985619**
#工程款	Project Fund	3078568	175667	2860536	3009014

5-27 房地产开发经营情况（2016年）

Running of Real Estate Development（2016）

单位：万元 （10 000 yuan）

指 标	Item	全市合计 Total	国有 State-owned	市区 Urban	市属 Municipal
一、资产负债情况	**Assets and Liabilities**				
1. 资产总计	Total Assets	78137823	6833489	76906765	73113284
2. 负债合计	Total Liabilities	66151866	5261328	65071562	61713065
3. 所有者权益合计	Total Creditor's Equity	11985957	1572162	11835203	11400219
#实收资本	Held Capital	8996426	736024	8843924	8549715
二、损益及分配情况	**Profit or Loss and the Distribution**				
1. 主营业务收入	Revenue from Principal Business	13382411	1048624	13079683	12286453
土地转让收入	Revenue of Land Transferred	22003	7295	21999	22003
商品房屋销售收入	Revenue of Commercial Houses Sold	12979895	915161	12678022	11906228
房屋出租收入	Revenue of Houses Leased	93148	11501	92997	83063
其他收入	Other Revenue	287365	114667	286665	275159
2. 主营业务成本	Cost of Principal Business	10931847	837921	10691004	10063185
3. 主营业务税金及附加	Taxes and Other Charges on Principal Business	759325	44867	750036	690918
4. 其他业务利润	Other Business Profit	15534	2310	15499	14896
5. 销售费用	Sales Expenditures	421993	22003	413687	384007
6. 管理费用	Management Cost	453211	43137	443548	418308
#税金	Tax	27881	1219	27245	25075
7. 财务费用	Fiscal Expenditure	242641	17984	238974	233641
#利息支出	Interest Exchange	153988	13184	149313	147771
8. 营业利润	Operating Profit	684015	106576	689990	601851
投资收益	Investment Revenue	49131	26674	49087	39558
营业外收入	Non-business Revenue	71999	4242	71880	70955
营业外支出	Non-business Expenditures	34008	2660	34681	32649
9. 利润总额	Total Profit	721952	108158	727134	640103
10. 应付职工薪酬	Salary Payable	396919	85683	387810	363618
11. 应交增值税	Value-added Tax Payable	163064	22141	161638	153368
三、全部从业人员年平均人数	**Average Number of Employed Persons**	**72928**	**13543**	**68552**	**60528**
四、本年应付工资总额	**Total Wages This Year**	**415535**	**83107**	**390602**	**344894**

主要统计指标解释

全社会固定资产投资 是以货币形式表现的在一定时期内全社会建造和购置固定资产的工作量以及与此有关的费用的总称。该指标是反映固定资产投资规模、结构和发展速度的综合性指标，又是观察工程进度和考核投资效果的重要依据。全社会固定资产投资按登记注册类型可分为国有、集体、联营、股份制、私营和个体、港澳台商、外商、其他等。

城镇固定资产投资 指城镇各种登记注册类型的企业、事业、行政单位及个体户进行的计划总投资500万元及500万元以上的建设项目投资和房地产开发投资。县城及以上区域内发生的投资，县及县以上各级政府及主管部门直接领导、管理的建设项目和企业事业单位的投资均为城镇固定资产投资。

房地产开发投资 指各种登记注册类型的房地产开发公司、商品房建设公司及其他房地产开发法人单位和附属于其他法人单位实际从事房地产开发或经营活动的单位统一开发的包括统代建、拆迁还建的住宅、厂房、仓库、饭店、宾馆、度假村、写字楼、办公楼等房屋建筑物和配套的服务设施，土地开发工程（如道路、给水、排水、供电、供热、通讯、平整场地等基础设施工程）的投资；不包括单纯的土地交易活动。

农村投资 包括在农村区域范围内进行固定资产投资活动的企业、事业、行政单位及农户投资。

固定资产投资的资金来源 根据固定资产投资的资金来源不同，分为国家预算资金、国内贷款、利用外资、自筹资金和其他资金。

（1）国家预算资金：包括一般预算、政府性基金预算、国有资本经营预算和社保基金预算等资金。

（2）国内贷款：指报告期固定资产投资单位向银行及非银行金融机构借入的用于固定资产投资的各种国内借款，包括银行利用自有资金及吸收的存款发放的贷款、上级主管部门拨入的国内贷款、国家专项贷款、地方财政专项资金安排的贷款、国内储备贷款、周转贷款等。

（3）利用外资：指报告期收到的用于固定资产建造和购置的境外资金（包括设备、材料、技术在内）。包括对外借款（外国政府、国际金融组织贷款、出口信贷、外国银行商业贷款、对外发行债券和股票）、外商直接投资及外商其他投资。不包括我国自有外汇资金（国家外汇、地方外汇、留成外汇、调剂外汇和中国银行自有资金发行的外汇贷款等）。计算利用外资时，需要折算成人民币，折算中所使用的外汇汇率按现汇计算，即按使用外汇时的汇率计算。

（4）自筹资金：指固定资产投资单位报告期收到的，由各地区、各部门及企、事业单位筹集用于固定资产投资的预算外资金，包括中央各部门、各级地方和企、事业单位的自筹资金。

（5）其他资金：指在报告期收到的除以上各种资金之外其他用于固定资产投资的资金，包括企业或金融机构通过发行各种债券筹集到的资金、社会集资、个人资金、无偿捐赠的资金及其他单位拨人的资金等。

固定资产投资按国民经济行业分 根据现有企业、事业、行政单位和建设项目建成投产后的主要产品种类或主要用途及社会经济活动性质来确定国民经济行业。一般情况下，一个建设项目或一个企业、事业单位只能属于一种国民经济行业。

固定资产投资按隶属关系分 是按建设单位或企业、事业、行政单位的主管上级机关确定的。

（1）中央：是指中共中央、人大常委会和国务院各部、委、局、总公司以及直属机构直接领导的建设项目和企业、事业、行政单位。这些单位的固定资产投资计划由国务院各部门直接编制和下达，建设中所需物资、主要设备以及建设中的问题都由中央有关部门安排和解决。

（2）地方：是由省（自治区、直辖市）、地区（州、盟、省辖市）、县（旗、县级市）三级政府及业务主管部门直接领导和管理的建设项目、企业、事业、行政单位。地方项目还包括不隶属以上各级政府及主管部门的建设项目和企业、事业单位，如外商投资企业和无主管部门的企业等。

固定资产投资按建设性质分 根据整个建设项目情况来确定。建设项目的性质一般分为新建、扩建、改建和技术改造、单纯建造生活设施、迁建、恢复、单纯购置。房地产开发单位、农户投资不划分建设性质。

（1）新建：一般指从无到有开始建设的企业、事业和行政单位或建设项目。有的单位原有基础很小，经过建设后新增的固定资产价值超过该企、事业、行政单位原有固定资产价值（原值）三倍以上的也应作为新建。

（2）扩建：指在厂内或其他地点，为扩大原有产品的生产能力（或效益）或增加新的产品生产能力，而增建主要的生产车间（或主要工程）、分厂、独立的生产线。行政、事业单位在原单位增建业务用房（如学校增建教学用房、医院增建门诊部、病房等）也作为扩建。

现有企、事业单位为扩大原有主要产品生产能力或增加新的产品生产能力，增建一个或几个主要生产车间（或主要工程）、分厂，同时进行一些更新改造工程的，也应作为扩建。

（3）改建和技术改造：指现有企业、事业单位，对原有设施进行技术改造或更新（包括相应配套的辅助性生产、生活福利设施）的建设项目。现有企业、事业单位为适应市场变化的需要，而改变企业的主要产品种类（如军工企业转产民用品等）的建设项目，应作为改建。原有产品生产作业线由于各工序（车间）之间能力不平衡，为填平补齐充分发挥原有生产能力而增建不增加本企业主要产品设计能力的车间，也应作为改建。技术改造是指企业、事业单位在现有基础上，用先进的技术代替落后的技术，用先进的工艺和装备代替落后的工艺和装备，以改变企业落后的技术经济面貌，实现以内涵为主的扩大再生产，达到提高产品质量、促进产品更新换代、节约能源、降低消耗、扩大生产规模、全面提高社会经济效益的目的。技术改造具体包括以下内容：机器设备和工具的更新改造；生产工艺改革、节约能源和原材料的改造；厂房建筑和公共设施的改造；劳动条件和生产环境的改造等。

固定资产投资按构成分 固定资产投资活动按其工作内容和实现方式分为建筑安装工程，设备工具器具购置和其他费用三个部分。

（1）建筑安装工程（建筑安装工作量）：指各种房屋、建筑物的建造工程和各种设备、装置的安装工程。包括各种房屋建造工程；各种用途设备基础和各种工业窑炉的砌筑工程及金属结构工程；为施工而进行的各种准备工作和临时工程以及完工后的清理工作等；铁路、道路的铺设，矿井的开凿及石油管道的架设等；水利工程；防空地下建筑等特殊工程；列入房屋丁程预算内的暖气、卫生、通风、照明、煤气等设备的价值及装设油饰工程；列入建筑工程预算内的各种管道（蒸汽、压缩空气、石油、给排水等管道）、电力、电讯电缆导线等的敷设工程；以及各种机械设备的安装下程；为测定安装工程质量，对设备进行的试运工作；房地产开发单位进行的商品房屋开发建设工程、土地开发工程。

在建筑安装工程中，不包括被安装设备本身的价值。

（2）设备工具器具购置：指建设单位或企、事业单位购置或自制的，达到固定资产标准的设备、工具、器具的价值。新建单位及扩建单位的新建车间，按照设计或计划要求购置或自制的全部设备、工具、器具，不论是否达到固定资产标准均计入“设备工具器具购置”中。

（3）其他费用：指在固定资产建造和购置过程中发生的，除上述几项内容以外的各种应分摊计入固定资产的费用。

施工项目 指报告期内所有施工的建设项目个数，包括本年新开工的项目和以前年度开工在本年继续施工的建设项目。凡是报告期内施过工的建设项目，不论施工时间长短，均作为施工项目统计。施工项目个数可以反映一定时期固定资产投资的实际规模，与同期全部建成投产项目个数相比，可以从建设速度的角度反映固定资产投资的效果。

全部建成投产项目 指报告期内按设计文件规定的全部生产能力（或效益）建成投产，经验收合格交付使用的建设项目。

新增生产能力（或工程效益） 指通过固定资产投资活动而增加的设计能力（或工程效益）。主要指标包括建设规模、本年施工规模、自开始建设累计新增生产能力（或工程效益）、本年新增生产能力（或工程效益）等。

建设规模 指建设项目或工程设计文件中规定的全部设计能力（或工程效益）。包括已经建成投产和尚未建成投产的工程的生产能力（或工程效益）。

本年施工规模 指报告期内施工的单项工程的设计能力（或工程效益），即全部建设规模中在本年正式施工的部分。

自开始建设累计新增生产能力（或工程效益） 指自开始建设至本年底止建成投产的全部单项工程累计的新增生产能力（或工程效益）。

本年新增生产能力（或工程效益） 指在本年度内按照新增生产能力（或工程效益）的计算条件和标准，实际建成投人生产或交付使用的生产能力（或工程效益）。

施工房屋面积 指报告期内施工的全部房屋（包括地下室、半地下室以及配套房屋）建筑面积。包括本期新开工的面积和上期开工跨入本期继续施工的房屋面积，以及上期已停建在本期恢复施工的房屋面积。本期竣工和本期施工后又停缓建的房屋，其建筑面积仍计入本期房屋施工面积中。

竣工房屋面积 指在报告期内房屋建筑按照设计要求已经全部完工，达到住人和使用条件，经验收鉴定合格（或达到竣工验收标准），可正式移交使用单位的各栋房屋建筑面积的总和。

新增固定资产 指报告期内交付使用的固定资产价值。包括本年内建成投入生产或交付使用的工程投资和达到固定资产标准的设备、工具、器具的投资及有关应摊入的费用。该指标是表示固定资产投资成果的价值指标，也是反映建设进度，计算固定资产投资效果的重要指标。

项目建成投产率 指一定时期内全部建成投产项目个数与同期施工项目个数的比率。该指标是从建设单位建设速度的角度反映投资效果的指标。

固定资产交付使用率 指一定时期新增固定资产与同期完成投资额的比率。该指标是反映固定资产动用速度，衡量建设过程中宏观投资效果的综合指标。由于新增固定资产是较长时期内形成的结果，而投资额则是当年完成的，因此，该指标一般适宜于反映较长时期内固定资产的动用情况。

商品房销售面积 指报告期内出售商品房屋的合同总面积（即双方签署的正式买卖合同中所确定的建筑面积）。由现房销售建筑面积和期房销售建筑面积两部分组成。

商品房销售额 指报告期内出售商品房屋的合同总价款（即双方签署的正式买卖合同中所确定的合同总价）。该指标与商品房销售面积同口径，由现房销售额和期房销售额两部分组成。

经济适用房 指根据经济适用房计划安排建设的政策性住宅。经济是指房屋建筑造价和销售价格低于一般商品住宅；适用是指适合中低收入家庭购买使用。经济适用房主要是由地方政府统一下达投资计划，房地产公司开发，对外销售；用地一般采用行政划拨或招标投标方式，免收土地出让金；对各种经批准的收费减半征收，开发利润不超过3%；销售价格实行政府指导价。该指标可以分析房地产投资结构，反映中低收入家庭商品住宅的供求平衡情况。

Explanatory Notes on Main Statistical Indicators

Total Investment in Fixed Assets in the Whole Country refers to the volume of activities in construction and purchases of fixed assets of the whole country and related fees, expressed in monetary terms during the reference period. It is a comprehensive indicator which shows the size, structure and growth of the investment in fixed assets, providing a basis for observing the progress of construction projects and evaluating results of investment. Total investment in fixed assets in the whole country includes, by type of ownership, the investment by State-owned units, collective-owned units, joint ownership units, share-holding units, private units individuals as well as investments by entrepreneurs from Hong Kong, Macao and Taiwan, foreign investors and others.

Urban Investment in Fixed Assets refers to construction projects involving a total planned investment of 5000 000 yuan and over by enterprises of various types of ownership, institutions, administrative units and individuals in urban areas, investment in real estate development. In other words, all investments that take place in county towns and urban areas, investment in construction projects under the direct leadership and management of government agencies at and above county levels and investments by enterprises and institutions at and above county levels are covered in urban investment in fixed assets.

Investment in Real Estate Development refers to investment by real estate development companies, commercialized buildings construction companies and other real estate development units of various types of ownership in the construction of buildings, such as residential buildings, factory buildings, warehouses, hotels, guesthouses, holiday villages, office buildings, and the complementary service facilities and land development projects, such as roads, water supply, water drainage, power supply, heating supply, telecommunications, land leveling and other infrastructural projects. It does not include activities in pure land transactions.

Investment in Rural Areas refers to investment in fixed assets by enterprises, institutions, administrative units and households in rural areas.

Sources of Funds for Investment in Fixed Assets are categorized as funds from the State budget, domestic loans, foreign investment, self-raised funds, and others, depending on the sources of investment.

(1) Fund from the State budget consists of budgetary appropriation and loans from the State budget. More specifically, it includes, from the budget of the central government, capital construction fund (operation fund and non-operational fund), special expenses, loans from repayment, discount fund, expenses on innovation and trial production of new products, expenses on urban construction, expenses on temporary construction from business departments, development fund for less developed areas, as well as local budgetary fund transferred from the central budget.

(2) Domestic loans refer to loans of various forms borrowed by investing units from banks and non-bank financial institutions during the reference period for the purpose of investment in fixed assets, including loans issued by banks from their self-owned funds and deposit, loans appropriated by higher authorities, special loans by government, loans arranged by local government from special funds, domestic reserve loan, and working loan.

(3) Foreign investment refers to overseas funds received during the reference period for the construction and purchase of investment in fixed assets (covering equipment, materials and technology), including foreign borrowings (loans from foreign governments and international financial institutions, export credit, commercial loans from foreign banks, issue of bonds and stocks overseas), foreign direct investment and other foreign investments. Excluded from this category is capital in foreign exchanges owned by China (foreign exchanges owned by the central and local governments, foreign exchanges retained by enterprises, foreign exchanges by enterprises through the regulating mechanism, loans in foreign exchanges issued by the Bank of China with its own fund, etc). In calculating the utilization of foreign capital, foreign currencies are converted into Chinese Renminbi applying the current exchange rate when the foreign capitals are actually used.

(4) Self-raised funds refer to extra-budgetary funds for investment in fixed assets received during the reference period by investing units from central government ministries, local governments, enterprises and institutions, including their self-raised funds.

(5) Others refer to funds for investment in fixed assets received from sources other than those listed above, including capital raised through issuing bonds by

enterprises or financial institutions, funds raised from individuals and through donations, and funds transferred from other units.

Investment in Fixed Assets by Sector The classification of construction projects by sector is determined by enterprises, institutions, administrative units and the major products or the purpose of the projects of existing enterprises, institutional and administrative units when they are put into production or use, and by the nature of their social economic activities. In general, one project or one enterprise or institution can only be classified into one sector.

Investment in Fixed Assets by Jurisdiction of Management refers to the classification of investment by the competent authorities under which investment is made by construction units, enterprises, institutions or administrative units.

(1) Central investment refers to the investment in projects or by enterprises, institutions or administrative units which are under the direct leadership and management of the State Council and of the national commissions, ministries, agencies and State-owned large corporations. Various ministries and departments of the State Council prepare and implement plans for investment in fixed assets by those departments, and arrange and ensure the supply of materials and key equipment required for the projects.

(2) Local investment refers to the investment in projects or by enterprises, institutions or administrative units which are under the direct leadership and management of departments under the provincial, prefecture and county governments. Also included are projects by foreign-invested enterprises and enterprises without competent managing authorities.

Investment in Fixed Assets by Type of Construction Construction projects in general can be classified, by the type of construction, into new construction, expansion, reconstruction and technical transformation, purely construction of living facilities, moving, restoration and purely purchasing. However, investment by type of construction is not applied to investment by real-estate development units and investment by rural households.

(1) New construction in general refers to construction projects, which start from scratch, of enterprises, institutions, administrative agencies. In case the size of the existing unit is quite small, and the value of newly added fixed assets is more than three times of the original value, the expansion will be considered as new construction.

(2) Expansion refers to construction of new major production workshop, branch factory or independent production line within a factory or in other locations, for the purpose of increasing the production capacity (or improving efficiency) or adding new production capacity. Newly constructed accommodation for the operation of institutions and administrative organizations (such as newly constructed buildings for teaching in schools, buildings for clinics or wards in hospitals, etc.) are also classified as expansion.

Also included in expansion are investments by existing enterprises or institutions in building major production line(s) or branch factory(ies) along with some work on innovation, for the purpose of expanding the production capacity of original products or producing new products.

(3) Reconstruction and technical transformation refers to construction projects by existing enterprises or institutions in innovation or technical transformation of the old facilities (including auxiliary production equipment and welfare facilities). Also considered as reconstruction is the construction of new workshops by the existing enterprises or institutions to change the variety of products to meet the market demand (such as the production of civil products by defence industries), or to bring the designed production capacity into full play through a more balanced production process on production lines. Technical transformation refers to replacement of old technology or equipment by new technology or equipment, in order to expand the reproduction through improvement of technology contents in production, to improve product quality, to promote new products to save energy,to reduce consumption, to expand the production scale and to improve overall social-economic efficiency. Contents of technical transformation include: updating of machinery, equipment and tools; reforming production process by using energy or materials saving technology; construction of factory workshops and transformation of public facilities; improvement of working conditions and environment, etc.

Investment in Fixed Assets by Structure By their

contents and the mode of implementation, investment activities are classified into 3 categories, i.e. construction and installation, purchase of equipment and instrument, and other expenses.

(1) Construction and installation (work volume of construction and installation) refers to the construction of houses and buildings and the installation of various kinds of equipment and instruments. They include construction of houses; equipment foundations, industrial kilns and stoves, and metal structure work; preparation works and temporary works for project construction, and clearing up works post project construction; pavement of railways and roads, drilling of mines and putting up of oil pipes; construction of water conservancy; construction of underground air-raid shelters and construction of other special projects; value of equipment for heating, sanitation, ventilation, lighting, gas, painting, etc. that are covered by the budget of housing projects; laying out of various pipelines (for steam, compressed air, petroleum, tap water and sewage) and wiring and cabling for electric power and for communications; installation of various machinery and equipment; testing operation for pre- testing the quality of installation projects, and land and other development work conducted by real estate developers for commercialized housing.

The value of equipment installed is itself not included in the value of construction and installation projects.

(2) Purchase of equipment and instruments refers to the total value of equipment, tools, and instruments purchased or self-produced which come up to the cut-off point for fixed assets by the construction units or investing enterprises or institutions. Equipment, tools and instruments purchased or self-produced for new workshops by newly established or expanded units are categorized as "purchase of equipment and instruments" no matter whether they come up to the cut-off point for fixed assets.

(3) Other expenses refer to expenses arising during the construction or purchase of fixed assets other than those mentioned above.

Projects under Construction refer to number of all projects with construction activities newly started in current year or left-over from the previous year in the reference period. All projects that have construction activities undertaken during the reference period are reported as projects under construction irrespective of the length of construction work. The number of projects under construction can reflect the actual size of investment in fixed assets during a given period, and when compared with the number of projects completed and put into use during the same period, it demonstrates the results of investment in fixed assets from the angle of the speed of the construction.

Projects Completed and Put into Use refer to projects have been completed in accordance with the design documents, resulting in forming production capacity (efficiency) and have been checked and accepted after relevant tests, and have been formally delivered for use.

Newly Increased Production Capacity (or Project Efficiency) refers to the increase in design capacity (or project efficiency) through investment in fixed assets. The main indicators include: construction scale, scale of projects under construction in current year, the accumulated newly increased production capacity (project efficiency) since the start of the projects and the newly increased production capacity (project efficiency) of current year.

Construction Scale refers to the total designed production capacity (project efficiency) of the construction projects in accordance with the design document, including those have been put into operation and those that have not been completed.

Scale of Projects under Construction in Current Year refers to the designed production capacity (project efficiency) of a single project under construction in the reference period, i.e. the part of the total scale of project which is officially under construction in current year.

The Accumulated Newly Increased Production Capacity (project efficiency) since the Start of the Projects refers to the accumulated newly increased production capacity of all the single projects which have been put into use from the beginning of the projects till the end of current year.

The Newly Increased Production Capacity (project efficiency) of Current Year refers to the production capacity (project efficiency) that has been completed and put into operation in current year according to the calculation conditions and standards on newly increased production capacity (project efficiency).

Floor Space of Buildings under Construction refers to the total floor space of all the buildings (including basement, semi-basement and auxiliary buildings), including the effective area and the area occupied by the structure. This indicator is one of the important indicators in physical terms to reflect the scale and accomplishment of the construction industry and also an important basis for monitoring the progress, Calculating the cost, analyzing the efficiency and studying the supply of building materials in relation to the construction projects.

Floor Space Completed refers to the floor space of all buildings completed in the reference period, which have been appraised and accepted (or come up to the designed standards) and have been transferred to owner units.

Newly Increased Fixed Assets refer to the value of fixed that has been put into use, including investment in projects that have been completed and put into operation in current year and the investment in equipment, tools and appliance that meet the standard of fixed assets and fees that should be apportioned. This is an indicator that demonstrates the results of investment in fixed assets in monetary terms, and an important indicator to reflect the speed of construction and to calculate the efficiency of investment.

Rate of Construction Projects Completed and Put into Use refers to the ratio of the number of construction projects completed and put into use in a certain period of time to the number of projects under construction in the same period. This reflects the investment efficiency from the perspective of the speed of projects construction.

Rate of Projects of Fixed Assets Completed and Put into Operation refers to the ratio of the newly increased fixed assets to the total investment made in the same period. This is a comprehensive indicator reflecting the speed of the employment of fixed assets and the investment efficiency at the macro-level. As the newly increase fixed assets is the result of a long period while the investment is completed in the current year, this indicator is expected to be used to reflect the employment of fixed assets over a long period of time.

6 财　政

GOVERNMENT FINANCE

资料整理：罗延庆
Data management:Luo yanqing
数据审核：陈　英
Data audit:Chen Ying

第六部分　财政

一、简要说明

本章资料主要包括地方财政收入、支出总额构成及分区县情况，由西安市统计局综合处根据西安市财政局提供资料整理。

二、主要指标

财政总收入（亿元）	1135.68	比上年增长	8.5%
一般公共预算收入（亿元）	641.07	比上年增长	11.1%
一般公共预算支出（亿元）	942.52	比上年增长	2.8%

6　GOVERNMENT FINANCE

Ⅰ.Brief Introduction

This chapter consists of primarily data on regional revenue, expenditure of the municipal government, regional revenue and expenditure of the districts and the counties. The data are provided by the Xi'an Bureau of Finance and are compiled by Integration division of the Xi'an Bureau of Statistics.

Ⅱ.Major Indicators

		Increase over Preceding Year
Total Government Revenue(100 mil. Yuan)	1135.68	8.5%
General Pubilc Budgetary Revenue(100 mil. Yuan)	641.07	11.1%
General Pubilc Budgetary Expenditures(100 mil. Yuan)	942.52	2.8%

6-1 主要年份地方财政一般公共预算收入及支出

General Public Budgetary Revenue and Expenditure of Local Finance in Representative Years

单位：亿元 （100 million yuan）

年 份 Year	财政总收入 Fiscal Revenue	一般公共预算收入 General Public Budgetary Revenue	一般公共预算支出 General Public Budgetary Expenditure	收支差额 Balance of Payments	财政总收入比上年增长（%） Fiscal Revenue Increased over the Previous Year（%）	一般公共预算收入比上年增长（%） General Public Budget Revenue Growth over the Previous Year（%）	一般公共预算支出比上年增长（%） General Public Budget Expenditures Growth over the Previous Year（%）
2000	61.57	46.80	52.00	-5.20		14.4	
2001	75.79	51.45	57.30	-5.85	23.1	9.9	10.2
2002	99.84	54.50	63.80	-9.30	31.7	16.9	11.3
2003	120.64	72.90	76.60	-3.70	20.8	33.8	20.1
2004	133.52	75.30	87.30	-12.00	10.7	3.3	14.0
2005	163.87	72.92	97.61	-24.69	22.7	15.8	11.8
2006	195.96	85.89	119.22	-33.33	19.6	18.6	21.9
2007	260.70	112.92	161.25	-48.33	33.0	31.5	35.3
2008	324.49	145.61	226.99	-81.38	24.5	28.9	40.8
2009	400.29	181.40	276.85	-95.45	23.4	24.6	22.0
2010	510.69	241.86	371.62	-129.76	27.6	33.3	34.2
2011	649.88	318.55	494.58	-176.03	27.3	31.7	33.1
2012	753.07	396.96	597.49	-200.53	15.9	24.6	20.8
2013	902.76	501.98	729.81	-227.83	19.9	26.5	22.1
2014	1019.69	583.79	819.54	-235.75	13.0	16.3	12.3
2015	1114.98	650.99	917.24	-266.25	9.3	16.3	12.9
2016	1135.68	641.07	942.52	-301.45	8.5	11.1	2.8

注：本表数据来源于市财政局。

6-2 财政收入（2016年）

Government Revenue（2016）

单位：万元 （10 000 yuan）

指　标	Item	2016
财政总收入	**Total Government Revenue**	**11356793**
#一般公共预算收入	**General Public Budgetary Revenue**	**6410655**
一、税收收入	**Total Tax Revenue**	**3705560**
1. 国内增值税	Value-added Tax	508583
2. 改征增值税	Levying VAT	445351
3. 营业税	Business Tax	548123
4. 企业所得税	Corporate Income Tax	397460
5. 个人所得税	Individual Income Tax	197448
6. 城建税	City Maintenance and Construction Tax	309809
7. 房产税	House Property Tax	176617
8. 城镇土地使用税	Urban Land Use Tax	79012
9. 印花税	Stamp Tax	96871
10. 车船税	Tax on the Use of Vehicles and Ships	85437
11. 土地增值税	Land Appreciation Tax	270661
12. 资源税	Resource Tax	381
13. 耕地占用税	Farm Land Occupatian Tax	291751
14. 契税	Deed Tax	298056
二、非税收入	**Total Non-tax Revenue**	2705095
1. 行政性收费收入	Charge of Adminnistrative and Institutional Units	385792
2. 罚没收入	Penalty Receipts	162422
3. 专项收入	Special Program Receipts	398090
4. 国有资本经营收入	State-owned Assets Profit	711023
5. 国有资源（资产）有偿使用收入	Revenue for the use of State-owned Assets (Resources)	933474
6. 捐赠收入	Donation Income	1175
7. 政府住房基金收入	Governmental Housing Fund Income	100930
8. 其他收入	Other Revenue	12189
政府性基金预算收入	**Governmental Fund Budgetary Revenue**	**2624324**

注：本表数据来源于市财政局。

6-3 财政支出（2016年）

Government Expenditures (2016)

单位：万元 （10 000 yuan）

指 标	Item	2016
一、政府性基金预算支出	**Governmental Fund Budgetary Expenditure**	**2680223**
二、一般公共预算支出	**General Public Budgetary Expenditure**	**9425238**
1.一般公共服务支出	Expenditure for General Public Services	601382
2.国防支出	Expenditure for National Defense	7982
3.公共安全支出	Expenditure for Public Security	520903
4.教育支出	Expenditure for Education	1196292
5.科学技术支出	Expenditure for Science and Technology	274783
6.文化体育与传媒支出	Expenditure for Cultural, Sports and Media	287592
7.社会保障和就业支出	Expenditure for Social Safety Net and Employment Effort	1052390
8.医疗卫生与计划生育支出	Expenditure for Medical 、 Health Care and Brith Control Planning	734202
9.节能环保支出	Expenditure for Energy Saving	185671
10.城乡社区支出	Expenditure for Urban and Rural Community Aaffairs	2621003
11.农林水支出	Expenditure for Agriculture, Forestry and Water Conservancy	565856
12.交通运输支出	Expenditure for Transportation	204042
13.资源勘探信息等支出	Expenditure for Exploration of the Power of Information	356812
14.商业服务业等支出	Expenditure for Business Services	221431
15.金融支出	Expenditure for Finance	36700
16.国土海洋气象等支出	Expenditure for Land and Marine Meteorology	34441
17.住房保障支出	Expenditure for Housing Secnrity	438584
18.粮油物资储备支出	Expenditure for Grain and Oil Stockpiles	16397
19.债务付息支出	Debt Service Expenditure	57933
20.其它支出	Other Expenditure	10842

注：本表数据来源于市财政局。

6-4 各区县、开发区财政收入（2016年）

单位：万元

区县、开发区	Region	一般公共预算收入 General Public Budgetary Revenue	税收收入 Tax Revenue	增值税 Value Added Tax	营业税 Business Revenue	企业所得税 Corporate Income Tax
合计	**Total**	**6410655**	**3705560**	**953934**	**548123**	**397460**
市本级合计	**Sum of city level**	**970613**	**349446**	**69811**	**8463**	**68846**
区、县合计	**Region**	**3233391**	**2036745**	**534062**	**360938**	**204634**
新城区	Xincheng	364816	171684	42280	27497	42540
碑林区	Beilin	450089	293862	100787	43697	47145
莲湖区	Lianhu	481780	268033	94000	39500	28538
雁塔区	Yanta	465070	351876	96441	67196	32720
灞桥区	Baqiao	219910	156464	26324	35014	9637
未央区	Weiyang	326330	224663	56765	52252	18959
阎良区	Yanliang	127552	82066	13715	5702	2603
临潼区	Lintong	149128	109108	17105	13715	4462
长安区	Chang'an	354999	202453	36361	41982	11423
高陵区	Gaoling	120185	80737	23527	12727	2776
蓝田县	Lantian	42872	26404	4423	4867	561
周至县	Zhouzhi	36522	17020	4507	6065	382
户　县	Huxian	94138	52375	17827	10724	2888
开发区合计	**Sum of Development Zones**	**2206651**	**1319369**	**350061**	**178722**	**123980**
高新区	GaoXin	1066609	640696	204656	55139	75486
经开区	JingKai	453264	239110	77488	38486	22036
曲江新区	Qujiang	409275	262333	35925	54721	15098
浐灞生态区	Chanba Eco-District	165713	97725	12508	20703	4235
航天基地	Aerospace Base	49924	33410	7509	5223	3134
航空基地	Aviation Industry Base	11661	9255	2781	1215	697
国际港务区	International Trade&Logistic Park	50205	36840	9194	3235	3294

注：本表数据来源于市财政局。

Goverment Revenue by Region and Development Zone（2016）

（10 000 yuan）

一般公共预算收入 General Public Budgetary Revenue					
税收收入 Tax Revenue					
个人所得税 Individual Income Tax	资源税 Resource Tax	城市维护建设税 City Maintenance and Construction Tax	耕地占用税 Farm Land Occupation Tax	契税 Deed Tax	其他各项税收收入 Other Tax Revenue
197448	**381**	**309809**	**291751**	**298056**	**708598**
45068		**51553**		**-67**	**105772**
87827	**379**	**150876**	**246782**	**147972**	**303275**
8826	1	14491		7480	28569
22890		24246		16643	38454
11803	1	24471		24108	45612
19463		27442	25047	28409	55158
2653	1	10907	33275	9978	28675
7625		19563	4720	19819	44960
5040		3255	33062	10834	7855
2044	3	5094	56506	2904	7275
4319	10	9362	59553	16590	22853
1535		6014	15371	6232	12555
301	87	1115	11861	873	2316
417	102	977	2132	502	1936
911	174	3939	5255	3600	7057
64553	**2**	**107380**	**44969**	**150151**	**299551**
50791		61815	38000	40711	114098
7216	2	22240		30127	41515
3063		12134		43464	97928
1017		5005		22518	31739
1546		2807		7126	6065
359		1101		987	2115
561		2278	6969	5218	6091

6-4 续表1

单位：万元

区县、开发区	Region	一般公共预算收入 General Public Budgetary Revenue		
		非税收入 Non-tax Revenue	专项收入 Special Program Receipts	行政事业性收费收入 Charge of Adiministrative and Institutional Units
合计	**Total**	**2705095**	**398090**	**385792**
市本级合计	**Sum of city level**	**621167**	**188590**	**128377**
区、县合计	**Region**	**1196646**	**117189**	**234639**
新城区	Xincheng	193132	8194	5197
碑林区	Beilin	156227	13708	7571
莲湖区	Lianhu	213747	15209	13332
雁塔区	Yanta	113194	14537	17492
灞桥区	Baqiao	63446	16726	4235
未央区	Weiyang	101667	10760	11095
阎良区	Yanliang	45486	10055	33409
临潼区	Lintong	40020	2941	1933
长安区	Chang'an	152546	5132	94708
高陵区	Gaoling	39448	5902	14229
蓝田县	Lantian	16468	2147	7305
周至县	Zhouzhi	19502	2620	9437
户　县	Huxian	41763	9258	14696
开发区合计	**Sum of Development Zones**	**887282**	**92311**	**22776**
高新区	GaoXin	425913	35475	10226
经开区	JingKai	214154	13215	2504
曲江新区	Qujiang	146942	11518	7452
浐灞生态区	Chanba Eco-District	67988	17306	1064
航天基地	Aerospace Base	16514	12156	109
航空基地	Aviation Industry Base	2406	693	1421
国际港务区	International Trade&Logistic Park	13365	1948	

continued 1

(10 000 yuan)

罚没收入 Penalty Receipts	国有资本经营收入 State-owned Assets Profit	国有资源(资产)有偿使用收入 The Revenues of the Compensation for the Use of State-owned Resoures(Assants)	其他收入 Other Income	政府性基金预算收入 Governmental Funds Budgetary Revenue
162422	**711023**	**933474**	**12189**	**100930**
103409	**598**	**100543**	**3376**	**96274**
52311		**789537**	**1765**	**30**
4411		175330		
2054		131523	1371	
1977		183229		
2881		78284		
1229		41083		
3062		76750		
878		943	201	
2787		32261	98	
11948		40728		30
4748		14569		
2724		4197	95	
4048		2395		
9564		8245		
6702	**710425**	**43394**	**7048**	**4626**
3268	357300	15018		4626
1078	196000	1357		
1405	113767	12800		
601	32000	14104	2913	
71		54	4124	
277		4	11	
2	11358	57		

6-5 各区县、开发区财政支出（2016年）

单位：万元

区县、开发区	Region	一般公共预算支出 General Public Budgetary Expenditures	一般公共服务支出 General Public Services Expenditure	国防支出 Expenditure for National Defense	公共安全支出 Expenditure for Public Safety
合计	**Total**	**9425238**	**601382**	**7982**	**520903**
市本级合计	**Sum of city level**	**2467602**	**172915**	**5270**	**249773**
区、县合计	**Region**	**4713271**	**297286**	**2680**	**250278**
新城区	Xincheng	377029	16602	256	27472
碑林区	Beilin	358550	24571	290	22811
莲湖区	Lianhu	437088	24946	298	26066
雁塔区	Yanta	351053	23256	235	31245
灞桥区	Baqiao	272233	17356	204	17765
未央区	Weiyang	318025	18789	232	21110
阎良区	Yanliang	230682	14333		11313
临潼区	Lintong	384236	22096		16849
长安区	Chang'an	612604	49138	418	26356
高陵区	Gaoling	232310	25506	197	11103
蓝田县	Lantian	356183	19486	261	11801
周至县	Zhouzhi	380428	17682	156	11509
户　县	Huxian	402850	23525	133	14878
开发区合计	**Sum of Development Zones**	**2244365**	**131181**	**32**	**20852**
高新区	GaoXin	1060577	31986	32	8421
经开区	JingKai	458923	18681		4791
曲江新区	Qujiang	391697	27251		1590
浐灞生态区	Chanba Eco-District	160852	31628		4759
航天基地	Aerospace Base	59138	8715		1291
航空基地	Aviation Industry Base	16023	2045		
国际港务区	International Trade&Logistic Park	97155	10875		

注：本表数据来源于市财政局。

Government Expenditure by Region and Development Zone（2016）

（10 000 yuan）

教育支出 Expenditure for Education	科学技术支出 Expenditure for Science and Technology	文化体育与传媒支出 Expenditure for Culture,Sport and Media	社会保障和就业支出 Expenditure for Social Safety Net and Employment Effort	医疗卫生与计划生育支出 Medical 、 Health and Family Planning Expenditure	节能环保支出 Expenditure for Energy Saving and Environment Protection
1196292	**274783**	**287592**	**1052390**	**734202**	**185671**
116514	**47816**	**58313**	**353005**	**234758**	**57259**
977137	**27161**	**43716**	**696160**	**497220**	**54320**
59681	1643	748	58440	15439	29
55481	4030	1888	64154	20236	1048
75856	1765	774	64222	26044	364
67548	1934	1464	44122	27032	978
63059	1668	2842	51878	25592	9256
74046	2046	3530	38608	24861	1984
39507	2441	1401	31745	24651	227
83800	381	3807	67722	48438	4572
148580	3094	7431	76654	101117	1972
46247	2641	3455	32671	35956	667
72694	413	3382	60379	50001	4870
105983	715	7694	55112	53877	7344
84655	4390	5300	50453	43976	21009
102641	**199806**	**185563**	**3225**	**2224**	**74092**
15354	189654	4165	1557	174	13803
13024	6587		739		50471
48686		179542	135	50	2673
8622		42			2528
8693	3501	464	731	2000	3306
2000	64	30			24
6262		1320	63		1287

6–5 续表1

单位：万元

区县、开发区	Region	一般公共预算支出 General Public Budgetary Expenditures			
		城乡社区支出 Expenditure for Urban and Rural Community Affairs	农林水支出 Expenditure for Agriculture, Foresty and Water Conservancy	交通运输支出 Expenditure for Industry,Commerce and Banking	资源勘探电力信息等支出 Expenditure for Exploration of the Power of Information
合计	**Total**	**2621003**	**565856**	**204042**	**356812**
市本级合计	**Sum of city level**	**353754**	**116884**	**161068**	**114723**
区、县合计	**Region**	**1147772**	**440707**	**42674**	**29292**
新城区	Xincheng	182439	1245	1400	623
碑林区	Beilin	156628	72	501	885
莲湖区	Lianhu	194395	1334	531	2054
雁塔区	Yanta	143510	3748	1125	675
灞桥区	Baqiao	36045	16812	2166	881
未央区	Weiyang	112597	6075	2002	430
阎良区	Yanliang	59646	27443	2207	3525
临潼区	Lintong	70894	41395	2245	3421
长安区	Chang'an	94810	52658	9459	439
高陵区	Gaoling	22467	27086	5596	2683
蓝田县	Lantian	30324	76620	3856	7166
周至县	Zhouzhi	22932	80159	3721	1184
户　县	Huxian	21085	106060	7865	5326
开发区合计	**Sum of Development Zones**	**1119477**	**8265**	**300**	**212797**
高新区	GaoXin	544957	794		179376
经开区	JingKai	336298	155		25267
曲江新区	Qujiang	105196	5790	300	1040
浐灞生态区	Chanba Eco-District	96404	1010		162
航天基地	Aerospace Base	20213			3961
航空基地	Aviation Industry Base	7721	504		2001
国际港务区	International Trade&Logistic Park	8688	12		990

continued 1

(10 000 yuan)

商业服务业等支出 Expenditure for Business Services:	金融支出 Expenditure for Finance	国土海洋气象等支出 Land and Marine Meteorological and Other Expenses	住房保障支出 Expenditure for Housing Support	粮油物资储备支出 Expenditure for Grain and Oil Stockpiles
221431	**36700**	**34441**	**438584**	**16397**
100275	**30882**	**5587**	**228303**	**12943**
25976	**4518**	**27036**	**132229**	**3454**
1274	2003	592	6712	11
2784	1363	737	258	5
2871	419	825	13235	6
1938		1751	172	6
733		1035	23176	186
605	100	1835	5897	3
696	221	6670	3022	579
3375		1725	11825	356
2692	1	3787	33208	383
1103	11	2006	12239	448
3235		1582	8224	375
3174	330	1992	5408	372
1496	70	2499	8853	724
95180	**1300**	**1818**	**78052**	
42667	10	608	21341	
1552		55	843	
1532	114		17743	
6701	1100	933	6610	
176		222	5862	
80	76		1136	
42472			24517	

6-5 续表2 continued 2

单位：万元 （10 000 yuan）

区县、开发区	Region	一般公共预算支出 General Public Budgetary Expenditures 债务付息支出 Debt Service Expenditure	其他支出 Other Expenditure	政府性基金预算支出 Governmental Fund Budgetary Expenditure
合计	**Total**	**57933**	**10842**	**2680223**
市本级合计	**Sum of city level**	**40648**	**6912**	**763047**
区、县合计	**Region**	**11734**	**1921**	**579648**
新城区	Xincheng	420		6005
碑林区	Beilin	558	250	37992
莲湖区	Lianhu	507	576	166094
雁塔区	Yanta	314		17904
灞桥区	Baqiao	1500	79	68256
未央区	Weiyang	3270	5	43142
阎良区	Yanliang	807	248	8035
临潼区	Lintong	1290	45	49431
长安区	Chang'an	397	10	62069
高陵区	Gaoling	228		28462
蓝田县	Lantian	1054	460	13679
周至县	Zhouzhi	846	238	14290
户　县	Huxian	543	10	64289
开发区合计	**Sum of Development Zones**	**5551**	**2009**	**1337528**
高新区	GaoXin	4928	750	257180
经开区	JingKai	201	259	407260
曲江新区	Qujiang	55		267497
浐灞生态区	Chanba Eco-District	3	350	164697
航天基地	Aerospace Base	3		174434
航空基地	Aviation Industry Base	342		31673
国际港务区	International Trade&Logistic Park	19	650	34787

主要统计指标解释

财政收入 指国家财政参与社会产品分配所取得的收入，是实现国家职能的财力保证。主要包括：

（1）税收收入：包括增值税、消费税、营业税、企业所得税、企业所得税退税、个人所得税、资源税、城市维护建设税、房产税、印花税、城镇土地使用税、土地增值税、车船税、船舶吨税、车辆购置税、关税、耕地占用税、契税、烟叶税等。

（2）非税收入：包括专项收入、行政事业性收费、罚没收入、国有资本经营收入、国有资源（资产）有偿使用收入和其他收入。

财政支出 指国家财政将筹集起来的资金进行分配使用，以满足经济建设和各项事业的需要。主要包括：

（1）一般公共服务支出：指政府提供基本公共管理与服务的支出，包括人大事务、政协事务、政府办公厅（室）及相关机构事务、发展与改革事务、统计信息事务、财政事务、税收事务、审计事务、海关事务、人力资源事务、纪检监察事务、商贸事务、知识产权事务、工商行政管理事务、质量技术监督与检验检疫事务、民族事务、宗教事务、港澳台侨事务、档案事务、民主党派及工商联事务、群众团体事务、共产党事务等。

（2）外交支出：指政府外交事务支出，包括外交管理事务、驻外机构、对外援助、国际组织、对外合作与交流、对外宣传、边界勘界联检等方面的支出。

（3）国防支出：指政府用于国防方面的支出，包括用于现役部队、国防科研事业、专项工程、国防动员等方面的支出。

（4）公共安全支出：指政府维护社会公共安全方面的支出，包括武装警察、公安、国家安全、检察、法院、司法、监狱、劳教、国家保密、缉私警察等。

（5）教育支出：指政府教育事务支出，包括教育管理、学前教育、普通教育、职业教育、成人教育、广播电视教育、留学教育、特殊教育、进修及培训、教育费附加安排的支出等。

（6）科学技术支出：指用于科学技术方面的支出，包括科学技术管理事务、基础研究、应用研究、技术研究与开发、科技条件与服务、社会科学、科学技术普及、科技交流与合作、科技重大专项等。

（7）文化体育与传媒支出：指政府在文化、文物、体育、广播影视、新闻出版等方面的支出。

（8）社会保障和就业支出：指政府在社会保障与就业方面的支出，包括人力资源和社会保障管理事务、民政管理事务、财政对社会保险基金的补助、补充全国社会保障基金、行政事业单位离退休、企业改革补助、就业补助、抚恤、退役安置、社会福利、残疾人事业、城市居民最低生活保障、其他城市生活救助、自然灾害生活救助、红十字事业、农村最低生活保障、其他农村生活救助、补充道路交通事故社会救助基金等。

（9）医疗卫生和计划生育支出：指政府医疗卫生方面的支出，包括医疗卫生管理事务、公立医院、基层医疗卫生机构、公共卫生、医疗保障、中医药、食品和药品监督管理、人口与计划生育事务等。

（10）节能环保支出：指政府节能环保支出，包括环境保护管理事务、环境监测与监察、污染治理、自然生态保护、天然林保护工程、退耕还林、风沙荒漠治理、退牧还草、已垦草原退耕、能源节约利用、污染减排、可再生能源和资源综合利用等支出。

（11）城乡社区支出：指政府城乡社区事务支出，包括城乡社区管理事务、城乡社区规划与管理、城乡社区公共设施、城乡社区环境卫生、建设市场管理与监督等。

（12）农林水支出：指政府用于农林水事务支出，包括农业、林业、水利、南水北调、扶贫、农业综合开发、农业综合改革、促进金融支农等。

（13）交通运输支出：指政府交通运输和邮政业方面的支出，包括公路水路运输、铁路运输、民用航空运输、石油价格改革对交通运输的补贴、邮政业、车辆购置税等。

（14）资源勘探电力信息支出：指政府用于资源勘探、制造业、建筑业、电力信息等方面的支出，包括资源勘探开发、制造业、建筑业、电力监管、工业和信息产业监管、安全生产监管、国有资产监管、支持中小企业发展和管理等。

（15）商业服务业支出：指政府用于商业服务业方面的支出，包括商业流通事务、旅游业管理与服务、涉外发展服务等。

（16）金融支出：指政府用于金融方面的支出，包括金融部门行政、金融部门监管、金融发展、金融调控等。

（17）援助其他地区支出：指用于援助方政府安排并管理的对其他地区各类援助、捐赠等资金支出。

（18）国土海洋气象支出：指政府用于国土资源、海洋、测绘、地震、气象等公益服务事业方面的支出。

（19）住房保障支出：指政府用于住房方面的支出，包括保障性安居工程、住房改革、城乡社区住宅等。

（20）粮油物资储备支出：指政府用于粮油物资储备方面的支出，包括粮油事务、物资事务、能源储备、粮油储备、重要商品储备等。

（21）国债还本付息支出：指国债还本、付息、发行等方面的支出。

（22）其他支出：指不能划分到上述功能科目的其它政府支出。

中央财政收入和地方财政收入　指按现行分税制财政体制划分的中央本级收入和地方本级收入。属于中央财政的收入包括关税，进口货物增值税和消费税，出口货物退增值税和消费税，消费税，铁道部门、各银行总行、各保险公司总公司等集中交纳的营业税和城市维护建设税，增值税75%部分，纳入共享范围的企业所得税60%部分，未纳入共享范围的中央企业所得税、中央企业上交的利润，个人所得税60%部分，车辆购置税，船舶吨税，证券交易印花税97%部分，海洋石油资源税，中央非税收入等。属于地方财政的收入包括营业税（不含铁道部门、各银行总行、各保险公司总公司集中交纳的营业税），地方企业上交利润，城市维护建设税（不含铁道部门、各银行总行、各保险公司总公司集中交纳的部分），房产税，城镇土地使用税，土地增值税，车船税，耕地占用税，契税，烟叶税，印花税，增值税25%部分，纳入共享范围的企业所得税40%部分，个人所得税40%部分，证券交易印花税3%部分，海洋石油资源税以外的其他资源税，地方非税收入等。

中央财政支出和地方财政支出　指根据政府在经济和社会活动中的不同职责，划分中央和地方政府的责权，按照政府的责权划分确定的支出。中央财政支出包括一般公共服务，外交支出，国防支出，公共安全支出，以及中央政府调整国民经济结构、协调地区发展、实施宏观调控的支出等。地方财政支出包括一般公共服务，公共安全支出，地方统筹的各项社会事业支出等。

Explanatory Notes on Main Statistical Indicators

Government Revenue refers to income for the government finance through participating in the distribution of social products. It is the financial guarantee to ensure government functioning. The contents of government revenue include the following main items:

(1)Tax revenue, including business tax, corporate income tax, corporate income tax refund ,individual income tax, resource tax, city maintenance and construct tax, house property tax, stamp tax, urban land use tax, land appreciation tax, tax on vehicles and boat operation, ship tonnage tax, vehicle purchase tax, tariffs, farm land occupation tax, deed tax, and tobacco leaf tax, etc.

(2) Non-tax revenue, including special program receipts, charge of administrative and institutional units, penalty receipts ,state-owned capital operating income,State-owned resources (assets) compensation for the use of incomeand others non-tax receipts.

Government Expenditure refers to the distribution and use of the funds which the government finance has raised, so as to meet the needs of economic construction and various causes. It includes the following main items:

(1) Expenditure for general public services: It refers to the spending on the basic public management and services which provided by governments, including the expense on affairs of People' s Congress, affairs of People' s Political Consultative Conference, affairs of government general office and relative institutions, affairs of development and reform, affairs of statistics, affairs of finance, affairs of taxation, affairs of audit, affairs of customs, affairs of human resources and social security, affairs of discipline inspection and supervision, affairs of population and family planning, affairs of commerce and trade, affairs of intellectual property, affairs of administration for industry and commerce, affairs of land and resources, affairs of oceanic administration, affairs of surveying and mapping, affairs of earthquake, ethnic affairs, religious affairs, affairs of Hong Kong, Macao, Taiwan, and Overseas Chinese, affairs of archives administration, affairs of Chinese Communist Party, affairs of democratic parties and federation of industry and commerce, affairs of mass organization, and affairs of lottery, etc.

(2) Expenditure for foreign affairs: It refers to the spending of government on foreign affairs, including the expense on administration of foreign affairs, missions overseas, external assistance, international organizations, foreign cooperation and communication, surveying and joint inspection on borderline, etc.

(3) Expenditure for national defense: It refers to the spending of government on national defense, including the expense on active force, scientific research on national defense, special projects, mobilization of national defense, etc.

(4) Expenditure for public security: It refers to the spending of government on maintaining social and public security, including the expense on armed police force, public security, state security, prosecution, courts, justice, prison, labor education and rehabilitation, protection of state secrecy, anti-smuggling police, etc.

(5) Expenditure for education: It refers to the spending of government on education, including the expense on the administration of education, pre-primary education, regular vocational school education, adult education,radio and television education, student abroad education, special education, education and training,education surtax arrangementsspending, etc.

(6) Expenditure for science and technology: It refers to the spending of government on science and technology (S&T), including the expense on the administration of S&T, basic research, applied research, research and development, conditions and services of S&T, popularization of social science, science and technology, exchanges and cooperation of S&T, etc.

(7) Expenditure for culture, sport and media: It refers to the spending of government on culture, cultural heritage, sports, radio, film, television, press and publication, etc.

(8) Expenditure for social safety net and employment effort: It refers to the spending of government on social safety net and employment, including the expense on administration of social safety net and employment, civil affairs, budgetary subsidy on the social insurance funds, subsidy on National Social Security Fund, retirees of administrative units and institutions, subsidy on enterprise reform, subsidy on

employment effort, pension, placement of ex-serviceman, social welfare, the handicapped undertakings, the system of cost of living allowances for urban residents, other urban social relief, rural social relief, living relief of natural disasters, affairs of Red Cross Society, etc.

(9) Expenditure for medical health care and birth control planning: It refers to gov ernment spending on health care, including health management services, public hospitals, primary health care institutions, public health, health care, the pharmaceutical, food and drug supervision and manangement, population and family planning affairs.

(10) Expenditure for energy saving: It refers to the government energy-saving and environmental protection expenditures, including environmental management services, environmental monitoring and surveillance, pollution control, ecological protection, natural forest protection project, forest, desert sand control, pasture, grassland of cultivated farmland, energy conservation and utilization expenditure pollution reduction, renewable energy and comprehensive utilization of resources, etc.

(11) Expenditure for urban and rural community affairs: It refers to the spending of government on urban and rural community affairs, including the expense on administration of urban and rural community, planning and management of urban and rural community, public facilities of urban and rural community, housing of urban and rural community, sanitation of urban and rural community, management and supervision on the construction market, etc.

(12) Expenditure for agriculture, forestry and water conservancy: It refers to the spending of government on agriculture, forestry and water conservancy, including the expense on agriculture, forestry, water conservancy, South-to-North Water Diversion Project, poverty alleviation, agricultural comprehensive development, comprehensive agricultural reform, promoting financial support for agriculture, etc.

(13) Expenditure for transportation: It refers to the spending of government on transportation and postal services, including the expense on road transport, sea transport, rail transport, civil aviation transportation, oil price reform subsidies for transportation, postal services, vehicle purchase tax, etc.

(14) Expenditure for exploration of the power of information: It refers to the spending on exploration, manufacturing, construction, electricity and other aspects of information, including resource exploration and development, manufacturing, construction, electricity regulation, industry and information industry regulation, safety supervision, the state-owned assets supervision and support of small and medium enterprise development and management, etc.

(15) Expenditure for business services: It refers to government spending on commercial aspects of services, including commercial distribution business, tourism management and services, foreign development services, etc.

(16) Expenditure for financial: It refers to government spending on financial aspects, including administrative of financial sector, financial sector supervision, financial development, financial control, etc.

(17) Expenditure for assistance to other parts: It refers to the various types of assistance to other regions, financial donations, donors, government expenditure and management arrangements, etc.

(18) Expenditure for Land and Marine Meteorology: It refers to government spending on land resources, marine, mapping, seismic, weather and other aspects of public service undertakings, etc.

(19) Expenditure for housing security: It refers to government spending on housing, including affordable housing projects, housing reform, urban and rural communities housing, etc.

(20) Expenditure for Grain and Oil stockpiles: It refers to government spending on supplies of grain and oil reserves, including grain and oil services, supplies services, energy reserves, grain and oil reserves, reserves of other important commodities, etc.

(21) Expenditure for Treasury debt service: It refers to the national debt principal, interest expenses, and other aspects of the issue, etc.

(22) Other expenditure:It refers to other government spending cannot be divided into the above functions subjects.

Revenue of the Central Government and Revenue of the Local Governments refers to the revenue collected by the Central Government and that by the local governments as defined by the decentralized taxation system. In accordance with this system, the revenue of the Central Government includes tariff, VAT and consumption tax from imports, VAT and consumption tax rebate for exports, consumption tax, business tax and city maintenance and construct tax from the Ministry of Railways, head offices of banks, head offices of insurance company, which are handed over to the government in a centralized way, 75% of the value added tax, 60% the share part of the corporate income tax, unshared part of corporate income tax of the central enterprises, profit handed in by the central enterprises, 60% of individual income tax, vehicle purchase tax, ship tonnage tax, 97% of stamp tax on securities transactions, resource tax on the offshore petroleum resources. The revenue of the local governments includes business tax (excluding the part of the Ministry of Railways, head offices of banks, head offices of insurance company, which are handed over to the government in a centralized way), profit handed in by the local enterprises, city maintenance and construct tax (excluding the part of the Ministry of Railways, head offices of banks, head offices of insurance company, which are handed over to the government in a centralized way), house property tax, urban land use tax, land appreciation tax, tax on vehicles and boat operation, farm land occupation tax, deed tax, and tobacco leaf tax, stamp tax, 25% of the value added tax, 40% the share part of the corporate income tax, 40% of individual income tax, 3% of stamp tax on securities transactions, resource tax other than the tax on offshore petroleum resources, local non-tax revenue, etc.

Expenditure of the Central Government and Expenditure of the Local Governments according to the different functions of the Central Government and local governments in economic and social activities, the rights of affairs administration are demarcated between those of the Central Government and those of local governments; and the classification of the expenditure between the Central Government and local governments are made on the basis of the classification of the rights of affairs administration between them. The expenditure of the Central Government includes the expenditure for general public services, expenditure for foreign affairs, expenditure for public security, and the expenditure of the Central Government for adjusting the national economic structure; coordinating the development among different regions; and exercising macroeconomic regulation. The expenditure of the local governments includes mainly the expenditure for general public services, expenditure for public security, and expenditures for social development which are planned by local governments, etc.

7 物价指数

PRICE INDICES

资料整理：周　文　王　晶　王　茹
Data management:Zhou Wen Wang Jing Wang Ru
数据审核：刘　青　祝立新　党　军　雷麦鸽
Data audit：Liu Qing Zhu Lixin Dang Jun Lei Maige

第七部分　物价指数

一、简要说明

本章资料主要包括居民消费、商品零售、工业生产者出厂、工业生产者购进、房地产销售以及固定资产投资等价格指数，由国家统计局西安调查队提供。

二、主要指标

商品零售价格总指数（上年=100）	100.1	比上年上升	0.4个百分点
居民消费价格总指数（上年=100）	100.9	比上年上升	0.2个百分点

7　PRICE INDICES

Ⅰ.Brief Introduction

This chapter consists of primarily data on consumer price indices, retail price indices, producer price indices for industrial products,purchasing price indices for industrial products,real estate selling, fixed asset investment,provided by Fixed Asset NBS Survey Office in Xi'an.

Ⅱ.Major Indicators

		Increase over Preceding Year
Retail Price Index(the price of preceding year=100)	100.1	0.4 percentage points
Consumer Price Index(the price of preceding year=100)	100.9	0.2 percentage points

7-1 主要年份各种价格指数

Price Indices in Representative Years

(以上年价格为100) (the price of preceding year= 100)

年 份 Year	居民消费价格指数 Consumer Price Index	商品零售价格指数 Retail Price Index	工业生产者出厂价格指数 Producer Price Indiees (PPI) for Industrial Producers	工业生产者购进价格指数 Industrial Purchasing Indices （IPI） for Industrial Producers	固定资产投资价格指数 Price Index for Investment in Fixed Assets
1980	108.7	109.3			
1981	102.4	102.7			
1982	100.9	101.0			
1983	102.6	102.0			
1984	104.7	104.8			
1985	109.7	109.3			
1986	108.5	107.4			
1987	110.6	111.4			
1988	122.8	123.2			
1989	118.3	117.8			
1990	102.5	100.9			
1991	109.4	108.3			
1992	112.2	112.4			
1993	117.2	112.8	102.5	104.3	
1994	128.5	126.2	132.2	115.0	
1995	117.0	114.6	110.8	113.1	
1996	110.9	107.9	100.7	103.8	
1997	106.0	101.5	98.6	102.5	
1998	97.9	95.5	94.4	97.5	
1999	96.8	97.4	97.5	96.9	100.8
2000	100.2	98.7	99.4	102.4	102.1
2001	99.9	98.9	99.3	101.0	101.3
2002	98.6	98.5	98.2	98.4	101.2
2003	100.5	100.0	101.5	105.3	102.4
2004	102.3	101.9	102.7	110.4	103.3
2005	100.3	99.7	103.9	109.6	102.4
2006	101.6	101.5	103.2	106.1	102.0
2007	104.7	103.7	101.9	106.2	103.5
2008	106.0	105.4	103.7	108.5	110.5
2009	99.7	99.5	99.9	100.7	97.9
2010	103.5	102.7	102.3	106.3	103.8
2011	105.6	104.4	102.5	108.8	105.4
2012	102.8	102.3	100.5	97.2	101.9
2013	102.7	101.7	99.5	97.2	100.8
2014	101.4	100.7	99.5	99.5	100.8
2015	100.7	99.7	98.5	94.5	97.9
2016	100.9	100.1	97.8	97.6	100.0

注：本表数据来源国家统计局西安调查队。

7-2 居民消费价格指数（2016年）

Residents Consumer Price Indices（2016）

(以上年价格为100) (the price of preceding year=100)

指 标	Item	2016
居民价格消费指数	**Consumer Price Index**	**100.9**
非食品烟酒价格指数	Non-Food，Tobaccol and Liquor Price Index	100.1
服务价格指数	Price Index of Service	100.3
工业品价格指数	Industrial Price Index	100.0
鲜活食品价格指数	Price Index of Fresh Food	106.7
消费品价格指数	Price Index of Consumer Goods	101.2
能源价格指数	Energy Price Index	99.1
非食品价格指数	Non-foodstuff Price Index	100.3
扣除食品和能源价格指数	Price Index with Food And Energy Excluded	100.4
扣除鲜菜鲜果价格指数	Price Index with Fresh Vegetables Fruits and Excluded	100.5
扣除自有住房价格指数	Price Index with Self-owned Housing Excluded	100.9
居住（扣自有住房）价格指数	Housing (Self-owned Housing Excluded) Price Index	100.7
一、食品和烟酒	**Food，Tobaccol and Liquor**	**102.8**
1. 食品	Food	103.5
（1）粮食	Grain	99.3
（2）薯类	Potato	118.2
（3）豆类	Beans	99.9
（4）食用油	Cooking Oil	102.2
（5）菜	Vegetables	116.5
（6）畜肉类	Livestock Meat	106.7
（7）禽肉类	Poultry Meat	98.9
（8）水产品	Aquatic Products	104.8
（9）蛋类	Eggs	93.8
（10）奶类	Milk	93.9
（11）干鲜瓜果类	Dried and Fresh Melons and Fruits	100.8
（12）糖果糕点类	Sweets and Cakes	100.2
（13）调味品	Flavouring	101.4
（14）其他食品类	Other Food	100.7
2. 茶及饮料	Tea and Drinks	99.0
3. 烟酒	Tobaccol and Liquor	102.1
（1）烟草	Tobacco	103.1
（2）酒类	Liquor	100.3
4. 在外用餐	Dining Out	101.7
二、衣着	**Clothing**	**102.1**
1. 服装	Garments	102.9
2. 服装材料	Clothing Material	100.0
3. 其他衣着及配件	Other Clothing And Accessories	102.3
4. 衣着加工服务费	Clothing Manufacturing Services	100.3
5. 鞋类	Footgear	99.9
三、居住	**Residence**	**100.6**
1. 租赁房房租	Rental Housing	100.0
2. 住房保养维修及管理	Housing Maintenance And Management	99.1
3. 水电燃料	Water,Electricity, Fuels	101.8
4. 自有住房	Private Housing	100.4

注：本表数据来源国家统计局西安调查队。

7-2 续表 continued

(以上年价格为100) (the price of preceding year= 100)

指　标	Item	2016
四、生活用品及服务	**Daily Necessities and Services**	**99.1**
1. 家具及室内装饰品	Furniture and Interior Decorations	97.9
2. 家用器具	Household Appliances	96.7
3. 家用纺织品	Home Textiles	94.4
4. 家庭日用杂品	Daily Use Household Articles	101.9
5. 个人护理用品	Personal Care Articles	102.0
6. 家庭服务	Home Services	100.4
五、交通和通信	**Transportation And Communication**	**97.3**
1. 交通	Transportation	97.7
（1）交通工具	Transportation Facility	96.6
（2）交通工具用燃料	Fuels For Vehicles	95.2
（3）交通工具使用和维修	Vehicles Use And Maintenance	102.6
（4）交通费	Traffic Fare	99.5
2. 通信	Communications	96.4
（1）通信工具	Telecommunication facility	88.9
（2）通信服务	Telecommunication Service	100.0
（3）邮递服务	Postal Service	100.0
六、教育文化和娱乐	**Education, Culture And Recreation**	**99.2**
1. 教育	Education	100.4
（1）教育用品	Educational Articles	101.3
（2）教育服务	Education Service	100.3
2. 文化娱乐	Culture And Recreation	98.1
（1）文娱耐用消费品	Durable Consumer Goods for Cultural and Recreational Use and Service	88.6
（2）其他文娱用品	Other Recreational Articles	100.4
（3）文化娱乐服务	Cultural And Recreational Services	100.5
（4）旅游	Touring	100.6
七、医疗保健	**Health Care**	**102.3**
1. 药品及医疗器具	Medical Instrument Articles	105.2
（1）中药	Traditional Chinese Medicine	106.4
（2）西药	Western Medicine	105.8
（3）滋补保健品	Health Care Articles	103.3
（4）医疗卫生器具	Medical Apparatus	101.2
（5）保健器具	Health Care Appliances	104.2
2. 医疗服务	Medical Service	100.0
八、其他用品和服务	**Other Supplies And Services**	**102.4**
1. 其他用品类	Other Supplies	104.0
（1）首饰手表	Jewelry and Watches	107.8
（2）其他杂项用品	Other Miscellaneous Articles	99.2
2. 其他服务类	Other Service	100.6

7-3 商品零售价格指数（2016年）

Retail Price Indices（2016）

(以上年价格为100)　　(the price of preceding year= 100)

指　标	Item	2016
商品零售价格指数	**Retail Price Indices**	**100.1**
一、食品	**Food**	**103.0**
1. 粮食	Grain	99.3
2. 薯类	Potato	118.2
3. 豆类	Beans	99.9
4. 食用油	Cooking Oil	102.1
5. 菜	Vegetables	116.5
6. 畜肉类	Livestock Meat	107.8
7. 禽肉类	Poultry Meat	98.9
8. 水产品	Aquatic Products	105.3
9. 蛋类	Eggs	93.8
10. 奶类	Milk	93.9
11. 干鲜瓜果类	Dried and Fresh Melons and Fruits	100.8
12. 糖果糕点类	Sweets and Cakes	100.2
13. 调味品	Flavouring	101.4
14. 其他食品类	Other Food	100.7
15. 在外餐饮	Dining Out	101.7
二、饮料、烟酒	**Drinks, Tobaccol and Liquor**	**101.2**
1. 茶及饮料	Tea and Drinks	99.0
2. 烟草	Tobacco	103.1
3. 酒类	Liquor	100.3
三、服装、鞋帽	**Garments, Shoes And Hats**	**102.1**
1. 服装	Garments	102.9
2. 鞋帽袜	Footgear and Hats	100.3
3. 其他衣着配件	Other Clothing Accessories	97.8
四、纺织品	**Textiles**	**96.3**
1. 服装材料	Cotton Cloth	100.0
2. 床上用品	Blend Cloth	95.9
五、家用电器及音像器材	**Household Appliances，Music and Video Equipment**	**92.7**
1. 家庭设备	Household Facility	96.8
2. 文娱用耐用消费品	Durable Consumer Goods for Cultural and Recreational Use	85.7
3. 专业音响器材	Music and Video Equipment	100.7

注：本表数据来源国家统计局西安调查队。

7-3 续表 continued

(以上年价格为100)　　(the price of preceding year= 100)

指　标	Item	2016
六、文化办公用品	**Cultural and Office Appliances**	**95.7**
七、日用品	**Articles for Daily Use**	**100.5**
1. 日用百货	General Merchandise for Daily Use	98.8
2. 厨具餐具茶具	Kitchenware, Tableware, Tea Set	104.4
3. 清洗用品	Daily Use Articles For Washing	101.2
4. 其他日用品	Other Daily Articles	98.1
八、体育娱乐用品	**Sports And Recreation Articles**	**100.2**
1. 体育户外用品	Sports Outdoor Articles	99.5
2. 娱乐用品	Recreation Articles	100.7
九、交通、通信用品	**Transportation And Communication Goods**	**97.2**
1. 交通运输机械	Transportation Machinery	98.9
2. 通信器材	Communication Equipment	88.9
十、家具	**Furniture**	**97.4**
十一、化妆品	**Cosmetics**	**102.3**
十二、金银饰品	**Gold , Silver and Jewelry**	**109.2**
十三、中西药品及医疗保健用品	**Traditional Chinese And Western Medicines And Health Care Articles**	**105.1**
1. 医疗卫生器具	Medical Apparatus	101.2
2. 中药	Traditional Chinese Medicine	106.4
3. 西药	Western Medicine	105.8
4. 保健器具及用品	Health Care Apparatus and Article	103.7
十四、书报杂志及电子出版物	**Books, Newspapers,Magazines And Electronic Publications**	**101.0**
1. 教材及参考书	Teaching Materials and Reference Books	101.3
2. 书报杂志	Books, Newspapers,Magazines	101.0
3. 计算机办公软件	Computer Office Software	100.0
十五、燃料	**Fuel**	**97.2**
1. 煤炭及制品	Coal and Its Products	96.4
2. 石油及制品	Oil and Its Products	97.4
十六、建筑材料及五金电料	**Building Materials And Hardware**	**99.4**
1. 建筑装潢材料	Building Decoration Materials	99.6
2. 五金水暖	Hardware Plumbing	98.4

7-4 主要年份工业生产者出厂价格指数

(上年价格=100)

类别	Classify	1997	1998	1999	2000	2001	2002
工业生产者出厂价格指数	**Producer Price Index**	**98.6**	**94.4**	**97.5**	**99.4**	**99.3**	**98.2**
按轻重工业分	Grouped by Light Industry and Heavy Industry						
轻工业	Light Industry	98.2	91.1	95.9	97.8	99.6	98.4
以农产品为原料	Using Farm Products as Raw Materials	99.2	89.5	95.2	99.2	99.0	98.4
以非农产品为原料	Using Non-farm Products as Raw Materials	96.8	93.4	97.0	95.5	100.6	98.6
重工业	Heavy Industry	99.0	97.3	98.9	100.8	99.2	98.2
采掘	Mining & Quarrying		104.1	101.5	97.5	94.8	101.3
原料	Raw Materials	101.0	100.7	102.3	107.7	101.1	101.3
加工	Processing	97.9	95.6	98.0	98.4	98.5	97.7
按生产生活资料分	by means of production and livelihood						
生产资料	Means of Production	99.6	96.6	98.3	100.5	99.1	98.0
采掘	Mining & Quarrying		104.1	101.5	97.5	94.8	101.3
原料	Raw Materials	100.9	100.6	100.2	106.4	101.1	101.0
加工	Processing	98.9	94.7	97.6	98.7	98.5	97.4
生活资料	Consumer Goods	97.0	91.4	96.5	97.3	99.9	99.1
（1）食品	Food	108.2	97.8	95.8	94.4	99.6	101.2
（2）衣着	Clothing	93.0	83.9	95.2	101.6	99.4	100.8
（3）一般日用品	Articles for Daily Use	91.6	95.1	97.6	96.9	101.9	97.9
（4）耐用消费品	Durable Consumer Goods	99.7	95.4	98.0	95.9	97.0	98.1
按工业部门分	Grouped by Industrial Sector						
1. 冶金工业	Metallurgical Industry	99.2	97.5	91.2	98.2	97.2	98.7
2. 电力工业	Power Industry	111.3	111.2	109.3	109.6	102.4	100.0
3. 煤炭及炼焦工业	Coal and Coking Industry	98.9	98.5	96.3	100.5	110.3	106.7
4. 石油工业	Petroleum Industry			107.1	134.2	96.6	100.7
5. 化学工业	Chemical Industry	91.8	92.9	96.6	96.7	100.5	99.2
6. 机械工业	Machine Manufacturing Industry	98.8	94.6	98.1	98.0	98.3	97.6
7. 建筑材料工业	Building Materials Industry	98.2	99.3	96.7	98.5	100.6	99.6
8. 森林工业	Timber Industry	107.6	104.5	97.9	98.9	98.1	98.9
9. 食品工业	Food Industry	106.8	95.3	95.5	94.3	99.8	101.1
10. 纺织工业	Textiles Industry	94.3	82.6	93.7	103.4	97.5	94.9
11. 缝纫工业	Tailoring Industry	100.1	97.3	99.1	103.5	100.0	101.1
12. 皮革工业	Leather Industry	91.2	96.8	98.0	99.2	101.0	101.8
13. 造纸工业	Paper Industry			95.3	96.7	102.3	95.0
14. 文教艺术用品工业	Cultural,Educational & Handicrafts Articles			96.7	96.4	101.1	103.4
15. 其它工业	Other Industry	109.5	109.2	98.9	104.8	107.1	99.4

注：本表数据来源国家统计局西安调查队。

Producer Price Indices (PPI) for Industrial Producers in Representative Years

(the price of preceding year= 100)

2003	2004	2005	2006	2007	2008	2009	2010	2011	2012	2013	2014	2015	2016
101.5	**102.7**	**103.9**	**103.2**	**101.9**	**103.7**	**99.9**	**102.3**	**102.5**	**100.5**	**99.5**	**99.5**	**98.5**	**97.8**
101.3	103.4	99.9	100.2	101.8	103.7	100.6	102.5	107.0	100.4	100.7	100.9	100.3	98.5
104.5	108.7	97.3	100.1	103.3	106.0	98.9	104.0	109.3	100.3	101.0	100.8	99.1	97.8
99.9	100.8	101.2	100.2	100.8	102.1	101.8	101.4	100.9	100.5	99.9	101.3	103.3	100.1
101.6	101.9	107.9	105.5	101.9	103.8	99.3	102.2	101.6	100.5	99.2	99.2	98.2	97.6
103.4	140.5	107.9	100.6	111.6	122.3	90.0	150.2	102.6	101.8	100.6	100.6	99.8	99.8
111.2	109.0	114.2	111.8	104.9	110.8	99.5	108.9	111.2	108.6	95.1	97.6	90.4	91.4
100.1	100.6	106.7	104.2	101.2	101.9	99.4	100.8	100.1	99.2	99.9	99.5	99.3	98.3
101.8	102.7	105.3	104.2	101.3	103.4	99.3	102.2	101.9	100.3	99.2	99.5	98.3	97.4
103.4	140.5	107.9	100.6	111.6	122.3	90.0	150.2	102.6	101.8	100.6	100.6	99.8	99.8
108.1	106.6	111.3	111.6	104.8	110.2	99.7	109.0	111.3	108.7	95.2	97.7	90.5	91.2
100.9	102.0	104.3	103.0	100.6	102.0	99.3	101.0	100.3	98.9	99.9	99.7	99.6	98.3
100.5	102.5	100.4	100.4	103.5	104.7	101.4	102.5	104.5	100.8	100.4	99.7	99.4	98.6
101.0	103.6	100.3	100.4	105.3	106.6	100.3	103.3	109.5	101.6	100.9	101.2	100.1	97.7
99.4	102.7	102.0	103.3	104.6	105.1	102.7	101.2	111.9	99.4	100.4	99.1	96.0	100.2
101.2	101.2	101.3	100.8	100.1	102.7	102.6	101.2	101.5	101.5	99.1	101.3	102.1	98.9
97.2	98.3	99.1	99.4	100.7	100.7	103.9	101.9	99.5	99.0	100.9	95.9	95.6	99.5
103.8	107.1	103.9	106.5	103.2	104.8	92.0	105.8	116.3	100.7	97.5	97.5	96.5	95.2
103.2	104.1	110.6	107.9	105.5	110.0	109.0	101.2	104.7	111.2	100.6	99.4	98.9	92.3
136.8	131.4	97.1	95.4	106.8	104.8	101.7	110.6	109.3	101.5	100.0	100.0	100.0	
118.6	110.5	121.7	117.6	104.8	115.6	96.7	114.2	108.4	108.2	89.7	97.2	81.0	95.4
100.2	100.8	103.2	100.8	101.1	104.1	102.6	100.8	104.2	100.3	99.6	100.9	100.6	96.8
99.8	100.6	104.9	103.4	101.0	101.7	99.9	100.9	99.5	99.0	100.0	99.4	99.5	98.6
99.7	100.0	98.6	98.9	98.9	101.8	101.9	99.9	100.6	99.6	99.3	99.1	99.5	98.0
100.1	100.2	101.6	101.6	101.1	101.1	101.1	101.7	105.2	103.2	103.4	101.6	91.7	99.9
102.8	107.5	98.3	99.0	106.1	109.3	98.3	104.3	110.1	101.7	101.0	101.3	99.8	97.0
117.3	119.1	89.9	102.4	98.4	99.7	97.5	108.9	107.2	88.7	103.9	99.3	96.0	93.7
100.2	103.6	100.8	103.5	104.6	105.1	102.6	101.3	113.4	99.4	100.4	99.0	93.4	100.5
98.7	99.6	101.2	100.0	99.0	99.6	99.7	99.6	98.0	99.9	99.9	100.0	118.9	99.8
96.9	100.2	101.2	100.0	100.1	104.5	98.4	100.4	103.4	99.2	98.4	98.1	98.1	100.9
97.5	96.5	98.1	100.1	99.1	99.2	102.2	99.9	100.7	106.0	97.5	100.0	102.6	98.0
103.3	105.0	103.4	105.7	111.4	104.3	99.7	100.5	104.3	101.2	99.6	100.0	100.0	99.7

7-5 主要年份工业生产者购进价格指数

Industrial Purchasing Indices (IPI) for Industrial Producers in Representative Years

(上年价格=100) (the price of preceding year= 100)

指　标	Item	2000	2001	2002	2003	2004	2005	2006	2007
工业生产者购进价格指数	**Industrial Producer Price Index**	**102.4**	**101.0**	**98.4**	**105.3**	**110.4**	**109.6**	**106.1**	**106.2**
(一)燃料、动力类	Fuel and Power	105.0	101.8	100.9	105.7	109.4	123.5	112.6	107.0
(二)黑色金属材料类	Ferrous Metals	102.7	102.1	98.5	107.4	117.4	107.6	99.2	104.8
#钢材	Steel	103.4	102.4	97.9	106.0	114.8	107.5	98.5	104.9
(三)有色金属材料和电线类	Non-ferrous Metals and Electric Wires	105.2	95.5	96.8	105.8	114.1	107.8	116.5	110.7
(四)化工原料类	Raw Chemical Materials	104.6	102.5	97.9	102.4	106.3	106.1	101.6	105.6
(五)木材及纸浆类	Timber and Paper Pulp	101.2	102.8	99.4	101.2	100.3	108.2	111.7	105.9
(六)建筑材料及非金属矿类	Building Materials and Non-metal ores	100.3	99.7	98.6	99.6	110.4	99.3	100.7	104.0
(七)其它工业原材料及半成品类	Other Industrial Raw Materials and Semi-Products	98.8	100.8	98.9	102.5	111.2	106.1	104.3	108.8
(八)农副产品类	Agricultural Products	100.4	102.8	98.2	113.7	112.7	100.9	107.2	107.2
(九)纺织原料类	Textile Materials	98.0	96.8	90.6	103.4	103.9	97.6	101.5	100.5

注：本表数据来源国家统计局西安调查队。

7-5 续表 continued

(上年价格=100) (the price of preceding year= 100)

指　标	Item	2008	2009	2010	2011	2012	2013	2014	2015	2016
工业生产者购进价格指数	**Industrial Producer Price Index**	**108.5**	**100.7**	**106.3**	**108.8**	**97.2**	**97.2**	**99.5**	**94.5**	**97.6**
(一)燃料、动力类	Fuel and Power	109.8	105.1	108.6	113.5	102.3	96.8	98.2	95.3	98.3
(二)黑色金属材料类	Ferrous Metals	111.3	99.2	103.1	102.9	93.4	98.0	97.9	91.6	96.0
#钢材	Steel	111.7	98.7	103.5	102.9	93.3	98.0	97.9	91.5	96.0
(三)有色金属材料和电线类	Non-ferrous Metals and Electric Wires	99.1	93.9	113.6	118.9	93.0	94.5	96.6	96.3	99.3
(四)化工原料类	Raw Chemical Materials	111.4	95.0	103.9	108.1	87.7	90.8	104.6	91.3	94.1
(五)木材及纸浆类	Timber and Paper Pulp	106.5	102.6	101.1	105.4	100.9	99.2	100.7	101.0	98.7
(六)建筑材料及非金属矿类	Building Materials and Non-metal ores	104.8	106.8	102.1	102.9	97.4	102.2	101.1	98.1	97.1
(七)其它工业原材料及半成品类	Other Industrial Raw Materials and Semi-Products	110.6	101.4	108.1	109.4	100.3	98.9	100.9	99.1	98.9
(八)农副产品类	Agricultural Products	108.9	99.6	106.5	107.4	103.4	100.5	98.8	92.8	100.4
(九)纺织原料类	Textile Materials	99.8	97.6	104.6	107.0	89.1	97.6	99.3	89.7	94.1

7-6 住宅销售价格指数（2016年）

Selling Price Indices of Residential Buildings（2016）

(上年价格=100) (the price of preceding year= 100)

指 标	Item	2016
新建住宅	**Newly built residential buildings**	**102.9**
一、保障性住房	guaranteed house	
二、新建商品住宅	New commodity residential house	103.2
（一）90平方米及以下	90 square meters and less	104.2
（二）90-144平方米	90-144 square metre	102.7
（三）144平方米以上	144 square meters and more	103.1
二手住宅	**used/second hand residential buildings**	**97.0**
一、90平方米及以下	90 square meters and the following	97.1
二、90-144平方米	90-144 square metre	97.0
三、144平方米以上	144 square meters and more	96.8

注：本表数据来源国家统计局西安调查队。

7-7 主要年份固定资产投资价格指数

Price Indices for Investment in Fixed Assets in Representative Years

(上年价格=100) (the price of preceding year= 100)

指 标	Item	2000	2005	2006	2007	2008	2009	2010	2011	2012	2013	2014	2015	2016
固定资产投资价格指数	**Price Indices for Investment in Fixed Assets**	**102.1**	**102.4**	**102.0**	**103.5**	**110.5**	**97.9**	**103.8**	**105.4**	**101.9**	**100.8**	**100.8**	**97.9**	**100.0**
一、建筑安装工程	**Construction and Installation Engineering**	**103.9**	**102.3**	**102.6**	**104.9**	**114.9**	**97.1**	**105.5**	**107.2**	**102.6**	**101.0**	**100.8**	**97.0**	**100.5**
1. 材料费	Material Costs	104.4	101.4	101.1	104.3	117.6	94.1	105.2	106.3	99.0	97.5	98.1	93.3	99.8
钢材	Steel	109.0	101.4	97.0	104.5	127.2	86.7	106.4	107.9	94.7	92.9	93.7	84.6	100.0
木材	Wood	103.6	101.9	101.9	102.5	106.9	101.8	105.0	104.5	104.9	104.5	105.2	107.6	101.4
水泥	Cement	101.5	100.1	101.1	102.7	107.8	109.4	103.8	100.9	100.3	101.4	100.4	97.3	98.1
地方材料	Local Materials	101.6	101.4	102.6	103.5	108.5	103.8	104.7	105.8	102.0	102.4	102.0	100.4	100.0
化工材料	Chemical Materials	107.1	104.6	113.6	113.0	110.0	95.5	104.5	105.4	104.2	102.5	100.9	95.6	95.3
电料	Electrical Materials and Sppliances	100.6	100.9	107.5	110.4	110.1	102.6	104.1	104.1	101.5	100.9	99.9	97.8	99.1
其他材料	Other Materials	103.4	101.7	103.2	107.4	108.5	101.6	102.7	104.5	102.7	101.6	100.7	100.4	100.7
2. 人工费	Labor Costs	103.6	106.9	108.3	109.1	114.5	110.6	111.9	114.0	112.9	109.7	108.8	105.7	102.9
3. 机械使用费	Mechanical Service Costs	103.9	102.5	104.5	104.5	106.5	99.3	103.3	106.7	104.8	104.0	102.2	100.8	100.7
二、设备、工器具购置	**Purchase of Equipment and Instruments**	**97.9**	**104.5**	**100.8**	**100.7**	**101.0**	**98.6**	**100.0**	**100.6**	**99.1**	**99.5**	**99.9**	**99.1**	**99.1**
三、其他费用	**Others**	**100.0**	**100.5**	**100.5**	**100.6**	**101.9**	**100.9**	**100.8**	**102.8**	**102.7**	**101.9**	**101.8**	**100.4**	**99.0**

注：本表数据来源国家统计局西安调查队。

主要统计指标解释

居民消费价格指数 是反映一定时期内城乡居民所购买的生活消费品和服务项目价格变动趋势和程度的相对数，是对城市居民消费价格指数和农村居民消费价格指数进行综合汇总计算的结果。通过该指数可以观察和分析消费品的零售价格和服务项目价格变动对城乡居民实际生活费支出的影响程度。

商品零售价格指数 是反映一定时期内城乡商品零售价格变动趋势和程度的相对数。商品零售价格的变动与国家的财政收入、市场供需的平衡、消费与积累的比例关系有关。因此，该指数可以从一个侧面对上述经济活动进行观察和分析。

工业生产者价格指数 是反映工业产品价格变化趋势和变动幅度的统计指标，是工业企业的产品价格在不同的时间和空间条件下平均变动的相对数。工业生产者价格包括工业品第一次出售时的出厂价格和企业作为中间投入的原材料、燃料、动力购进价格，简称工业生产者出厂价格和工业生产者购进价格。工业生产者价格指数是进行国民经济核算和经济管理的主要依据。

固定资产投资价格指数 是反映一定时期内固定资产投资品和取费项目价格的变动趋势和变动幅度的相对数。固定资产投资额是由建筑安装工程投资完成额、设备工器具购置投资完成额和其他费用投资完成额三部分组成的。编制固定资产投资价格指数应首先分别编制上述三部分投资的价格指数，然后采用加权算术平均法求出固定资产投资价格总指数。

该指数可以准确地反映固定资产投资中涉及的各类投资品和取费项目价格变动趋势和变动幅度，消除按现价计算的固定资产投资指标中的价格变动因素，真实地反映固定资产投资的规模、速度、结构和效益，为国家科学地制定、检查固定资产投资计划和进行国民经济核算提供科学的、可靠的依据。

Explanatory Notes on Main Statistical Indicators

Consumer Price Indices reflect the trend and degree of changes in prices of consumer goods and services purchased by urban and rural households during a given period. They are obtained by combining Consumer Price Indices of Urban Household and Consumer Price Indices of Rural Household. The Indices enable the observation and analysis of the degree of impact of the changes in the prices of retailed goods and services on the actual living expenses of urban and rural residents.

Retail Price Indices reflect the trend and degree of change in retail prices of commodities during a given period. The change in retail prices of commodities is related to government revenue, the equilibrium of market supply and demand, and the ratio of consumption to accumulation. Therefore, the retail price indices are useful from an oblique perspective for observing and analyzing the changes of the above economic activities.

Industrial Producer Price Index refelct the trend and degree of changes of industrial product price, which is the relative number of average change prices of industrial enterprises products under different condition of time and space. Including the first time of sale prices of industrial products and the price of raw materials, fuel and power as intermediate inputs, be called for short of PPI and IPI.

Industrial producer price Index is an important basis for national accounts and economic manegement.

Price Indices for Investment in Fixed Assets reflect the trend and degree of changes in prices of investment goods and projects in fixed assets during a given period. The investment in fixed assets consists of three components, namely the investment in construction and installation, the investment in purchases of equipment and instrument, and the investment in other items. Price indices for investment in fixed assets are calculated as the weighted arithmetic mean of the price indices for the three components of investment in fixed assets.

Removing the factor of price change in the aggregates of investment at current prices, this indicator shows the changes in the prices of commodities and fees involved in the investment of fixed assets, and can be used to observe the actual size, growth, structure, and efficiency of investment in fixed assets and provides reliable and scientific data for government planning and further improving the current national accounting .

8 人民生活

PEOPLE´S LIVELIHOOD

资料整理：王红梅 陈燮函
Data management：Wang Hongmei ChenXiehan
数据审核：高小琴
Data audit：Gao Xiaoqin

第八部分　人民生活

一、简要说明

本章资料反映我市城乡常住居民生活现状及变化情况，2014年以后数据为实施城乡住户调查一体化改革后的全市居民生活主要数据，由国家统计局西安调查队住户专项处提供。

二、主要指标

全体居民人均可支配收入（元）	30032	比上年增长	7.9%
城镇常住居民人均可支配收入（元）	35630	比上年增长	7.4%
城镇常住居民人均消费支出（元）	23799	比上年增长	6.2%
农村常住居民人均可支配收入（元）	15191	比上年增长	8.0%
农村常住居民人均消费支出（元）	10199	比上年增长	7.2%

8　PEOPLE'S LIVELIHOOD

Ⅰ.Brief Introduction

The data in this chapter reflected the city's urban and rural residents living situation and changes in circumstances,Data reflected the implementation of the city's residents in 2014 integrated household survey reformed life.The data is provided by Resident Special Investigation offices of the Survey Office of National of Statistics Xi'an .

Ⅱ.Major Indicators

		Increase over Preceding Year
Per capita disposable income of all residents(yuan)	30032	7.9%
Per capita disposable income of Urban residents (yuan)	35630	7.4%
Per capita consumption expenditure of Urban residents (yuan)	23799	6.2%
Per capita disposable income of Rural residents (yuan)	15191	8.0%
Per capita consumption expenditure of Rural residents(yuan)	10199	7.2%

8-1 主要年份城乡居民人均收入及恩格尔系数

Per Capita Annual Income and Engel's Coefficient of Urban and Rural Households in Representative Years

年 份 Year	城镇居民家庭人均可支配收入 Per Capita Annual Disposable Income of Urban Households		农村居民家庭人均纯收入 Per Capita Annual Net Income of Rural Households		城镇居民家庭恩格尔系数（%） Engel's Coefficient of Urban Households（%）	农村居民家庭恩格尔系数（%） Engel's Coefficient of Rural Households（%）
	绝对数(元) Absoulte number (yuan)	指数 1980年=100 Index year of 1980=100	绝对数(元) Absoulte number (yuan)	指数 1978年=100 Index year of 1978=100		
1978			140			
1979						
1980	414	100.0	190	135.7	53.3	53.3
1981	446	107.7	207	147.9	52.9	53.7
1982	479	115.6	254	181.4	55.1	56.7
1983	509	122.9	245	175.0	55.1	58.4
1984	540	130.3	299	213.6	54.9	51.7
1985	719	173.5	351	250.7	49.5	48.5
1986	911	219.8	390	278.6	49.9	47.9
1987	1034	249.7	434	310.0	50.6	50.3
1988	1142	275.6	482	344.3	44.9	47.5
1989	1344	324.3	530	378.6	51.7	48.2
1990	1518	366.5	610	435.7	53.1	49.5
1991	1619	390.9	707	505.0	51.6	46.7
1992	1992	481.0	783	559.3	52.5	50.9
1993	2661	642.5	870	621.4	46.4	46.0
1994	3517	849.1	1078	770.0	45.2	50.1
1995	4153	1002.5	1353	966.4	44.7	50.3
1996	5023	1212.6	1586	1132.9	42.6	49.9
1997	5344	1290.1	1846	1318.6	40.7	49.2
1998	5670	1368.7	2052	1465.7	39.8	42.4
1999	5999	1448.3	2203	1573.6	36.3	39.1
2000	6364	1536.5	2344	1674.3	36.5	36.6
2001	6705	1618.8	2490	1778.6	34.8	33.9
2002	7184	1734.3	2641	1886.4	34.4	31.1
2003	7748	1870.7	2838	2027.1	34.8	37.6
2004	8544	2062.8	3143	2245.0	36.1	35.7
2005	9628	2324.5	3460	2471.4	37.0	36.3
2006	10905	2632.9	3808	2720.0	34.4	36.8
2007	12662	3057.0	4399	3142.1	36.6	38.2
2008	15207	3671.4	5212	3722.9	36.4	37.0
2009	18963	4578.2	6275	4482.3	32.4	35.8
2010	22244	5370.4	7750	5535.7	31.3	32.5
2011	25981	6272.6	9788	6991.4	31.3	31.9
2012	29982	7238.5	11442	8172.9	32.5	33.8
2013	33100	7991.3	12930	9235.7	32.5	33.0
2014	30715	8718.5	12898	10334.7	29.2	29.9
2015	33188	9422.0	14072	11270.0	29.6	28.2
2016	35630	10119.2	15191	12171.6	29.3	26.9

注：2014年实施城乡住户一体化调查后，统计口径发生变化，新老口径存在差异。本表2014年开始为新口径数据，“农村居民家庭人均纯收入”改为“农村居民家庭人均可支配收入”。

8-2 主要年份城乡居民人民币储蓄存款

Savings Deposit of Urban and Rural Households in Representative Years

单位：亿元 (100 million yuan)

年 份 Year	年末余额 Balance at Ycar-end	指数（上年＝100） Index(preccding year=100)
1978	3.72	
1979	4.85	130.4
1980	5.48	113.0
1981	6.36	116.1
1982	7.76	122.0
1983	10.02	129.1
1984	14.70	146.7
1985	16.70	113.6
1986	23.10	138.3
1987	32.13	139.1
1988	32.51	101.2
1989	45.78	140.8
1990	62.23	135.9
1991	78.64	126.4
1992	96.09	122.2
1993	124.61	129.7
1994	174.19	139.8
1995	230.63	132.4
1996	394.02	170.8
1997	358.78	91.1
1998	499.68	139.3
1999	586.40	117.4
2000	675.83	115.3
2001	800.86	118.5
2002	988.04	123.4
2003	1210.56	122.5
2004	1432.86	118.4
2005	1716.76	119.8
2006	1950.53	113.6
2007	2002.38	102.7
2008	2513.70	125.5
2009	3084.20	122.7
2010	3641.09	118.1
2011	4155.65	114.1
2012	4787.03	115.2
2013	5357.05	111.9
2014	5698.15	106.4
2015	6571.18	105.8
2016	7035.81	107.1

注：本表数据来源于人民银行西安营管部。

8-3 各区县城乡居民人均可支配收入

Per Capita Income of Urban and Rural Households by Region

区 县	Region	城镇居民人均可支配收入 Per Capita Disposable Income of Urban Households			农村居民人均可支配收入 Per Capita Disposable Income of Rural Households		
		绝对数（元） Absoulte number(yuan)		2016年比2015年增长% Growth of 2016 than 2015 (%)	绝对数（元） Absoulte number(yuan)		2016 年比2015年增长% Growth of 2016 than 2015 (%)
		2015	2016		2015	2016	
全 市	**Total**	**33188**	**35630**	**7.40**	**14072**	**15191**	**8.00**
新城区	Xincheng	34622	37212	7.48			
碑林区	Beilin	34924	37539	7.49			
莲湖区	Lianhu	34820	37425	7.48			
灞桥区	Baqiao	34236	36784	7.44	18891	20431	8.15
未央区	Weiyang	34525	37085	7.41	19824	21294	7.42
雁塔区	Yanta	35071	37631	7.30			
阎良区	Yanliang	34382	36931	7.41	18850	20262	7.49
临潼区	Lintong	28628	30753	7.42	15164	16389	8.08
长安区	Chang'an	32204	34627	7.52	15486	16741	8.10
高陵区	Gaoling	27423	29464	7.44	15191	16431	8.16
蓝田县	Lantian	24509	26321	7.39	11084	12082	9.00
周至县	Zhouzhi	25070	26899	7.30	11148	12207	9.50
户 县	Huxian	26043	27970	7.40	13616	14638	7.51

8-4 全市居民家庭基本情况

Basic Conditions of All Households

指标名称	Item	2015	2016
调查户数（户）	Number of Households Surveyed (household)	2382	2369
调查户人口（人）	Residents Surveyed(person)		
平均每户常住人口	Average Household Size	3.1	3.0
平均每户劳动力人数	Average Number of Employed Persons	2.3	2.2
平均每劳动力负担人口	Average Number of Persons Supported by a Laborer	1.3	1.4
人均可支配收入（元）	Annual Per Capita Disposable Income(yuan)	27844.9	30032.5
工资性收入	Wages Income	17210.8	18588.9
经营净收入	Household Business Income	2667.8	2787.4
财产净收入	Property Income	2220.1	2304.0
转移净收入	Transfer Income	5746.2	6352.3
人均消费支出（元）	Annual Per Capita Consumption Expenditure (yuan)	18810.2	20074.2
食品烟酒	Food,Tobacco and Alcohol	5528.3	5806.5
衣着	Clothing	1607.8	1605.7
居住	Residence	3491.1	3740.9
生活用品及服务	Living Articles and Services	1373.8	1523.5
交通通信	Transport and Communication Services	2434.7	2663.4
教育文化娱乐	Recreation, Education and Culture Services	2325.8	2455.7
医疗保健	Medical and Health Care Services	1562.3	1718.8
其他用品和服务	Other Commodities and Services	486.4	559.6

8-5 全市居民家庭人均可支配收入

Per Capita Annual Disposable Income of All Households

单位：元 (yuan)

指标名称	Item	2015	2016
可支配收入	Disposable income	27844.9	30032.5
一、工资性收入	Wage income	17210.8	18588.9
（一）工资	Wage	16147.8	17051.4
（二）实物福利	Benefits in kind	81.8	77.2
（三）其他	Others	981.2	1460.3
二、经营净收入	Net Income from Business	2667.8	2787.4
（一）第一产业经营净收入	Net Income from Primary Industry Business	528.8	494.9
（二）第二产业经营净收入	Net Income from Secondary Industry Business	156.1	119.0
（三）第三产业经营净收入	Net Income from Tertiary Industry Business	1982.9	2173.4
三、财产净收入	Net Income from Properties	2220.1	2304.0
#利息净收入	Net interest	40.4	32.4
红利收入	Bonus	182.9	154.0
转让承包土地经营权租金净收入	Net Rental from Transfer of Contracted Land Management Rights	49.3	64.5
出租房屋财产性收入	The Property Income by Renting House	986.5	1125.1
出租机械、专利、版权等资产的收入	The Income by Renting Assets like Mechanical, Patents, Copyright ect.	19.6	82.7
四、转移净收入	Net Income from Transfer	5746.2	6352.3
（一）转移性收入	Net Income from Transfer	7016.7	7837.8
（二）转移性支出	Transfer Expenditure	1270.5	1485.6

8-6 全市居民家庭年人均消费支出

Per Capita Living Expenditure of All Households

单位：元　　　　(yuan)

指标名称	Item	2015	2016
消费支出	**Total Living Expenditure**	**18810.2**	**20074.2**
一、食品烟酒	**Food,Tobacco and Alcohol**	**5528.3**	**5806.5**
1.食品	food	3390.0	3413.5
2.烟酒	Alcohol and tobacco	541.7	639.9
3.饮料	Drink	153.4	158.7
4.饮食服务	Catering Services	1443.2	1594.4
二、衣着	**Clothing**	**1607.8**	**1605.7**
衣类	Garments	1203.4	1220.2
鞋类	Footwear	404.4	385.5
三、居住	**Residence**	**3491.1**	**3740.9**
#租赁房房租	Rental Housing Rent	332.8	303.1
住房维修及管理	Housing Repair and Management	386.5	652.2
水电燃料及其他	Water,Electric Power Fuel and Others	886.2	912.2
四、生活用品及服务	**Living Articles and Services**	**1373.8**	**1523.5**
家具及室内装饰品	Furniture and External Decorations	279.9	272.0
家用器具	Household Appliances	285.3	405.0
家用纺织品	Household textile	114.4	127.1
家庭日用杂品	Household Articles of Daily Use	352.5	352.8
个人用品	Personal Items	283.3	326.3
家庭服务	Household Services	58.4	40.2
五、交通通信	**Transportation and Communications**	**2434.7**	**2663.4**
交通	Transportation	1596.8	1812.4
通信	Communications	837.9	851.0
六、教育文化娱乐	**Recreation, Education and Culture Services**	**2325.8**	**2455.7**
教育	Education	1091.7	1187.1
文化娱乐	Recreation	1234.1	1268.5
七、医疗保健	**Medicine and Medical Services**	**1562.3**	**1718.8**
医疗器具及药品	Medical Instruments and Medicines	635.5	739.9
医疗服务	Medical Services	926.8	978.9
八、其他用品和服务	**Others**	**486.4**	**559.6**

8-7 全市居民家庭人均购买主要商品数量

Per Capita Annual Purchases of Major Commodities of All Households

单位：千克 (kg)

指标名称	Item	2015	2016
面粉	Flour	20.5	22.2
大米	Rice	18.1	18.0
薯类	Potato	13.3	13.1
豆类	Beans	9.7	9.8
食用植物油	Edible vegetable oil	11.4	11.2
鲜菜	Fresh vegetables	87.3	89.2
猪肉	Pork	10.4	10.0
牛肉	Beef	1.5	1.4
羊肉	Lamb	0.7	0.8
鸡	Chicken	2.4	2.7
鱼类	Fish	3.2	3.2
虾类	Shrimp	0.6	0.7
鲜蛋	Eggs	9.8	9.4
鲜奶	Milk	14.9	14.0
酸奶	Yogurt	4.8	5.5
奶粉	Milk	0.9	0.6
鲜瓜果	Fresh fruit	55.6	54.4
糕点	Cake	5.2	4.7
茶叶	Tea	0.5	0.4
卷烟（盒）	Cigarettes (box)	28.2	31.7
啤酒	Beer	4.4	4.4
白酒	Liquor	1.1	1.0
果酒	Wine	0.4	0.6
鞋(双)	Footwear (pair)	3.0	3.1
水（吨）	Water (tons)	25.0	24.5
电（度）	Electricity （kwh）	665.9	746.0
煤炭	Coal	51.6	50.8
管道天燃气（立方米）	Gas pipeline (cu.m)	65.0	55.4
罐装液化石油气	Bottled liquefied petroleum gas	3.4	3.7

8-8 全市居民家庭每百户年末耐用品拥有情况

Ownership of Major Durable Consumer Goods Every 100 Households

指标名称	Item	2015	2016
家用汽车（辆）	Automobile (unit)	28.8	31.0
摩托车（辆）	Motorcycles (unit)	18.9	17.5
助力车（台）	Strength-aid Cycle (unit)	38.1	44.6
洗衣机（台）	washing machine (unit)	97.6	99.3
电冰箱（柜）	Refrigerator (unit)	91.7	94.6
微波炉（台）	Microwave Oven (unit)	49.2	45.4
彩色电视机（台）	Color TV Set (unit)	115.0	115.6
#接入有线电视（台）	Cable TV Set(unit)	76.1	66.3
空调（台）	Air conditioning(unit)	126.4	129.2
热水器（台）	Water heaters(unit)	81.5	83.8
#太阳能热水器（台）	Solar water heaters (unit)	37.1	41.0
消毒碗柜（台）	Sterilizing Cupboard (unit)	5.1	3.9
洗碗机（台）	Dishwasher (unit)	1.3	1.3
排油烟机（台）	Exhauster (unit)	69.1	66.9
固定电话（线）	Ordinary Telephone (unit)	45.9	39.2
移动电话（部）	Mobile phones (unit)	234.2	242.2
#接入互联网（部）	Access to the Internet(unit)	99.0	115.1
计算机（台）	Computer (a)	68.8	66.4
#接入互联网（台）	Access to the Internet(unit)	54.9	54.2
摄像机（台）	Pickup Camera (unit)	7.6	5.4
照相机（台）	Camera (unit)	39.5	33.8
中高档乐器（架）	High-end Instruments (unit)	3.3	3.5
健身器材（台）	Setting-up Apparatus (unit)	4.8	4.2
组合音响（套）	Music Center (unit)	6.5	5.3

8-9 城镇常住居民家庭基本情况

Basic Conditions of Urban Households

指标名称	Item	2015	2016
调查户数（户）	Number of Households Surveyed (household)	1696	1670
调查户人口（人）	Residents Surveyed(person)		
平均每户常住人口	Average Household Size	2.8	2.8
平均每户劳动力人数	Average Number of Employed Persons	2.2	2.1
平均每劳动力负担人口	Average Number of Persons Supported by a Laborer	1.3	1.3
人均可支配收入（元）	Annual Per Capita Disposable Income(yuan)	33187.6	35630.1
工资性收入	Wages Income	21095.9	22607.6
经营净收入	Household Business Income	2200.8	2329.0
财产净收入	Property Income	2915.1	3011.8
转移净收入	Transfer Income	6975.8	7681.7
人均消费支出（元）	Annual Per Capita Consumption Expenditure (yuan)	22414.8	23798.9
食品烟酒	Food,Tobacco and Alcohol	6632.5	6963.3
衣着	Clothing	1968.6	1955.6
居住	Residence	3985.8	4252.3
生活用品及服务	Living Articles and Services	1663.0	1806.5
交通通信	Transport and Communication Services	2983.8	3254.3
教育文化娱乐	Recreation, Education and Culture Services	2796.8	2925.5
医疗保健	Medical and Health Care Services	1774.2	1937.4
其他用品和服务	Other Commodities and Services	610.1	703.9

8-10 按收入五等份分组的城镇常住居民人均可支配收入（2016年）

Per capita Annual Disposable Income of Urban Households by Income Percentile (2016)

单位：元 (yuan)

指标名称	Item	总平均 Total	低收入户 Low income households	中低收入户 Lower Middle income households
可支配收入	Disposable income	35630.1	10137.6	25264.5
一、工资性收入	Wage income	22607.6	7244.4	17872.8
（一）工资	Wage	20726.5	7183.6	17032.9
（二）实物福利	Benefits in kind	95.8	14.1	162.7
（三）其他	Others	1785.3	46.7	677.2
二、经营净收入	Net Income from Business	2329.0	689.2	1325.3
（一）第一产业经营净收入	Net Income from Primary Industry Business	52.0	141.4	26.1
（二）第二产业经营净收入	Net Income from Secondary Industry Business	100.6	0.5	13.4
（三）第三产业经营净收入	Net Income from Tertiary Industry Business	2176.4	547.3	1285.8
三、财产净收入	Net Income from Properties	3011.8	1039.0	2489.4
#利息净收入	Net interest	33.4	-0.8	-408.2
红利收入	Bonus	182.0	30.5	224.1
出租房屋财产性收入	The Property Income by Renting House	1474.9	561.6	1828.6
出租机械、专利、版权等资产的收入	The Income by Renting Assets like Mechanical, Patents, Copyright ect.Patents, Copyright ect.	110.3	6.7	37.2
四、转移净收入	Net Income from Transfer	7681.7	1165.0	3577.0
（一）转移性收入	Net Income from Transfer	9571.8	1881.5	5123.4
（二）转移性支出	Transfer Expenditure	1890.1	716.5	1546.4

8-10 续表 continued

单位：元 (yuan)

指标名称	Item	中等收入户 Middle income households	中高收入户 Upper Middle income households	高收入户 High income households
可支配收入	Disposable income	34457.5	44807.5	82010.0
一、工资性收入	Wage income	21388.2	23437.1	54139.0
（一）工资	Wage	20143.5	21880.9	46902.2
（二）实物福利	Benefits in kind	83.8	92.2	158.0
（三）其他	Others	1160.9	1464.0	7078.8
二、经营净收入	Net Income from Business	1943.7	2496.0	6544.7
（一）第一产业经营净收入	Net Income from Primary Industry Business	39.1	2.5	8.2
（二）第二产业经营净收入	Net Income from Secondary Industry Business	284.3	0.7	281.2
（三）第三产业经营净收入	Net Income from Tertiary Industry Business	1620.3	2492.8	6255.3
三、财产净收入	Net Income from Properties	4003.8	2844.3	5976.7
#利息净收入	Net interest	-1.9	117.9	616.1
红利收入	Bonus	280.3	153.1	294.6
出租房屋财产性收入	The Property Income by Renting House	2551.8	666.8	2165.1
出租机械、专利、版权等资产的收入	The Income by Renting Assets like Mechanical, Patents, Copyright ect.Patents, Copyright ect.	3.4	1.9	606.5
四、转移净收入	Net Income from Transfer	7121.8	16030.1	15349.6
（一）转移性收入	Net Income from Transfer	8665.5	18255.4	19614.3
（二）转移性支出	Transfer Expenditure	1543.7	2225.3	4264.7

8-11 城镇常住居民人均消费支出

Per Capita Living Expenditure of Urban Households

单位：元 (yuan)

指标名称	Item	2015	2016
消费支出	**Total Living Expenditure**	**22414.8**	**23798.9**
一、食品烟酒	**Food,Tobacco and Alcohol**	**6632.5**	**6963.3**
1.食品	food	3973.0	3960.4
2.烟酒	Alcohol and tobacco	606.9	772.3
3.饮料	Drink	189.9	196.1
4.饮食服务	Catering Services	1862.7	2034.5
二、衣着	**Clothing**	1968.6	1955.6
衣类	Garments	1472.1	1487.6
鞋类	Footwear	496.5	467.9
三、居住	**Residence**	**3985.8**	**4252.3**
#租赁房房租	Rental Housing Rent	418.2	402.1
住房维修及管理	Housing Repair and Management	414.9	819.4
水电燃料及其他	Water,Electric Power Fuel and Others	1060.4	1066.6
四、生活用品及服务	**Living Articles and Services**	**1663.0**	**1806.5**
家具及室内装饰品	Furniture and External Decorations	341.3	333.7
家用器具	Household Appliances	337.5	460.7
家用纺织品	Household textile	132.3	147.9
家庭日用杂品	Household Articles of Daily Use	416.4	406.8
个人用品	Personal Items	361.5	412.7
家庭服务	Household Services	74.0	44.7
五、交通通信	**Transportation and Communications**	**2983.8**	**3254.3**
交通	Transportation	1981.0	2241.0
通信	Communications	1002.8	1013.4
六、教育文化娱乐	**Recreation, Education and Culture Services**	**2796.8**	**2925.5**
教育	Education	1216.5	1283.0
文化娱乐	Recreation	1580.3	1642.6
#健身器材	Fitness Equipment	12.9	20.3
体育及户外用品	Sports and outdoor products	16.5	26.6
体育健身活动	Sports fitness activity	32.2	26.8
七、医疗保健	**Medicine and Medical Services**	**1774.2**	**1937.4**
医疗器具及药品	Medical Instruments and Medicines	749.8	889.5
医疗服务	Medical Services	1024.4	1047.9
八、其他用品和服务	**Others**	**610.1**	**703.9**

8-12 城镇常住居民家庭人均购买主要商品数量

Per Capita Annual Purchases of Major Commodities of Urban Households

单位：千克 (kg)

指标名称	Item	2015	2016
面粉	Flour	22.9	21.6
大米	Rice	20.0	20.5
薯类	Potato	15.0	14.5
豆类	Beans	10.7	10.8
食用植物油	Edible vegetable oil	11.5	11.5
鲜菜	Fresh vegetables	96.1	100.2
猪肉	Pork	11.3	11.2
牛肉	Beef	1.9	1.8
羊肉	Lamb	0.9	0.9
鸡	Chicken	3.0	3.3
鱼类	Fish	4.1	4.2
虾类	Shrimp	0.8	0.9
鲜蛋	Eggs	10.7	10.7
鲜奶	Milk	17.5	16.7
酸奶	Yogurt	5.8	6.6
奶粉	Milk	0.9	0.6
鲜瓜果	Fresh fruit	63.6	60.9
糕点	Cake	5.9	5.4
茶叶	Tea	0.5	0.5
卷烟（盒）	Cigarettes (box)	27.3	33.9
啤酒	Beer	4.7	4.7
白酒	Liquor	1.2	1.2
果酒	Wine	0.5	0.7
鞋(双)	Footwear (pair)	3.2	3.3
水（吨）	Water (tons)	31.6	29.6
电（度）	Electricity （kwh）	748.6	846.8
煤炭	Coal	41.2	48.1
管道天燃气（立方米）	Gas pipeline (cu.m)	88.9	70.5
罐装液化石油气	Bottled liquefied petroleum gas	3.3	3.6

8-13 城镇常住居民家庭每百户耐用品拥有情况

Ownership of Major Durable Consumer Goods Every 100 Urban Households

指标名称	Item	2015	2016
家用汽车（辆）	Automobile (unit)	31.5	32.5
摩托车（辆）	Motorcycles (unit)	9.4	7.3
助力车（台）	Strength-aid Cycle (unit)	29.4	32.7
洗衣机（台）	washing machine (unit)	97.8	98.6
电冰箱（柜）	Refrigerator (unit)	95.7	95.7
微波炉（台）	Microwave Oven (unit)	58.9	56.6
彩色电视机（台）	Color TV Set (unit)	113.3	111.2
空调（台）	Air conditioning(unit)	143.8	145.0
热水器（台）	Water heaters(unit)	87.0	88.0
#太阳能热水器（台）	Solar water heaters (unit)	32.2	33.6
消毒碗柜（台）	Sterilizing Cupboard (unit)	6.6	5.2
洗碗机（台）	Dishwasher (unit)	1.4	1.4
排油烟机（台）	Exhauster (unit)	82.1	80.6
固定电话（线）	Ordinary Telephone (unit)	51.8	44.7
移动电话（部）	Mobile phones (unit)	225.8	226.7
计算机（台）	Computer (a)	79.3	78.1
摄像机（台）	Pickup Camera (unit)	9.8	7.2
照相机（台）	Camera (unit)	49.2	43.4
中高档乐器（架）	High-end Instruments (unit)	4.2	4.5
健身器材（台）	Setting-up Apparatus (unit)	5.7	5.2
组合音响（套）	Music Center (unit)	6.4	5.8

8-14 城镇常住居民家庭居住情况

Housing Conditions of Urban Households

指标名称	Item	2015	2016
调查户数（户）	**Number of Households Surveyed (household)**	**1696**	**1670**
平均每户居住人口（人）	**Average Number of Resident Population (person)**	**2.8**	**2.8**
人均现住房建筑面积（平方米/人）	**The Average Floor Area Per Person (sq.m / person)**	**32.1**	**33.4**
一、按居住空间样式分（%）	**by Living space style（%）**	**100.0**	**100.0**
单栋楼房	Single building Room	4.1	6.1
单栋平房	Single-storey House	1.5	2.2
单元房	Apartment	87.5	84.9
筒子楼或连片平房	Tube-shaped Apartment or Lace Single-storey Houses	6.8	6.7
其他	Other	0.1	0.1
二、按主要建筑材料分（%）	**by main construction materials（%）**	**100.0**	**100.0**
钢筋混凝土	Reinforced concrete soil	29.1	29.9
砖混材料	Brick and concrete material	70.4	69.8
砖瓦砖土	Tile and brick earth	0.3	0.1
其他	Others	0.2	0.2
三、按房屋来源分（%）	**by Source of Housing（%）**	**100.0**	**100.0**
租赁住房	Rental housing	12.1	10.8
自建住房	Self-establish Housing	5.7	8.3
购买商品房	Commercial Residential Housing	34.9	35.0
购买房改住房	Private Housing through Housing Reform	37.3	35.2
购买保障性住房	Indemnificatory Housing	2.9	3.8
拆迁安置房	Resettlement Housing	4.0	3.8
继承或获赠住房	Inheriting and Donation Housing	0.9	0.9
其他	Others	2.2	2.2
四、住房外道路为硬化路面的户比重（%）	**proportion of households which outer road is Hardened road（%）**	**99.8**	**99.5**
五、按住宅有管道供水情况分（%）	**By Piped Water Supply Condition （%）**	**100.0**	**100.0**
管道供水入户	Pipe water into People's Homes	98.6	99.0
管道供水至公共取水点	Pipe water to Public Watering Points	1.1	0.9
没有管道设施	No Pipeline Facilities	0.3	0.1
六、按住户主要饮水来源情况分（%）	**By Source of main Drinking Water （%）**	**100.0**	**100.0**
经过净化处理的自来水	Purified Tap Water	91.9	91.2
受保护的井水和泉水	Protected Wells and Springs	5.3	6.7
不受保护的井水和泉水	Unprotected Wells and Springs	1.2	0.6
江河湖泊水	Rivers and Lakes Water	0.3	0.2
其他饮用水来源	Others	1.3	1.3
七、按住宅内厕所类型分（%）	**By Household Lavatory Type (%)**	**100.0**	**100.0**
水冲式卫生厕所	Sanitary Water Closet	98.3	96.1
水冲式非卫生厕所	Insanitary Water Closet	0.7	1.1
卫生旱厕	Sanitary Latrine	0.2	1.1
普通旱厕	Latrine	0.6	1.6
无厕所	No Lavatory	0.2	0.1
八、按主要炊用能源状况分（%）	**By Cooking Fuel Condition （%）**	**100.0**	**100.0**
天然气、煤气、液化石油气	Pipeline Natural Gas，Pipeline Gas，Pipeline Liquified Petroleum Gas	78.0	73.5
煤炭	Coal	1.0	0.6
电	Electricity	20.2	25.1
沼气	Methane		
其他	Others	0.8	0.8

8-15 农村常住居民家庭基本情况

Basic Conditions of Rural Households

指标名称	Item	2015	2016
调查户数（户）	Number of Households Surveyed (household)	686	699
调查户人口（人）	Residents Surveyed(person)		
平均每户常住人口	Average Household Size	3.6	3.6
平均每户劳动力人数	Average Number of Employed Persons	2.6	2.6
平均每劳动力负担人口	Average Number of Persons Supported by a Laborer	1.4	1.4
人均可支配收入（元）	Annual Per Capita Disposable Income(yuan)	14071.7	15191.2
工资性收入	Wages Income	7195.2	7933.9
经营净收入	Household Business Income	3871.5	4002.5
财产净收入	Property Income	428.6	427.3
转移净收入	Transfer Income	2576.4	2827.6
人均消费支出（元）	Annual Per Capita Consumption Expenditure (yuan)	9517.6	10198.7
食品烟酒	Food,Tobacco and Alcohol	2681.7	2739.3
衣着	Clothing	677.6	678.2
居住	Residence	2215.6	2384.8
生活用品及服务	Living Articles and Services	628.4	773.4
交通通信	Transport and Communication Services	1019.3	1096.7
教育文化娱乐	Recreation, Education and Culture Services	1111.4	1209.9
医疗保健	Medical and Health Care Services	1016.1	1139.4
其他用品和服务	Other Commodities and Services	167.5	177.0

8-16 按收入五等份分组的农村常住居民家庭人均可支配收入（2016年）

Per capita Annual Disposable Income of Rural Households by Income Percentile (2016)

单位：元 (yuan)

指标名称	Item	总平均 Total	低收入户 Low income households	中低收入户 Lower Middle income households
可支配收入	Disposable income	15191.2	3158.6	9053.9
一、工资性收入	Wage income	7933.9	1516.4	5688.1
（一）工资	Wage	7307.3	1269.3	4886.7
（二）实物福利	Benefits in kind	27.8	0.3	20.0
（三）其他	Others	598.8	246.8	781.4
二、经营净收入	Net Income from Business	4002.5	394.0	1984.8
（一）第一产业经营净收入	Net Income from Primary Industry Business	1669.2	355.6	1397.9
（二）第二产业经营净收入	Net Income from Secondary Industry Business	167.9	30.6	44.4
（三）第三产业经营净收入	Net Income from Tertiary Industry Business	2165.4	7.8	542.5
三、财产净收入	Net Income from Properties	427.2	55.1	160.3
#利息净收入	Net interest	29.7	-2.3	4.4
红利收入	Bonus	79.8	0.3	4.3
转让承包土地经营权租金净收入	Net Rental from Transfer of Contracted Land Management Rights	94.5	44.1	106.1
出租房屋财产性收入	The Property Income by Renting House	197.7		45.3
出租机械、专利、版权等资产的收入	The Income by Renting Assets like Mechanical, Patents, Copyright ect.Patents, Copyright ect.	9.4		0.4
四、转移净收入	Net Income from Transfer	2827.6	1193.1	1220.7
（一）转移性收入	Net Income from Transfer	3240.6	1456.6	1522.5
（二）转移性支出	Transfer Expenditure	413.0	263.5	301.8

8-16 续表 continued

指标名称	Item	中等收入户 Middle income households	中高收入户 Upper Middle income households	高收入户 High income households
可支配收入	Disposable income	13933.6	19047.3	35404.1
一、工资性收入	Wage income	6762.6	11482.9	16212.0
（一）工资	Wage	6184.8	10694.8	15470.7
（二）实物福利	Benefits in kind	24.6	48.8	52.2
（三）其他	Others	553.2	739.3	689.1
二、经营净收入	Net Income from Business	2729.6	3789.5	12924.1
（一）第一产业经营净收入	Net Income from Primary Industry Business	1773.9	2075.5	3084.0
（二）第二产业经营净收入	Net Income from Secondary Industry Business	60.8	96.4	710.9
（三）第三产业经营净收入	Net Income from Tertiary Industry Business	894.9	1617.6	9129.2
三、财产净收入	Net Income from Properties	487.5	514.9	1075.8
#利息净收入	Net interest	1.7	67.3	92.5
红利收入	Bonus	121.5	76.2	235.2
转让承包土地经营权租金净收入	Net Rental from Transfer of Contracted Land Management Rights	63.5	117.3	152.0
出租房屋财产性收入	The Property Income by Renting House	280.5	209.2	537.4
出租机械、专利、版权等资产的收入	The Income by Renting Assets like Mechanical, Patents, Copyright ect.Patents, Copyright ect.	15.7	32.0	
四、转移净收入	Net Income from Transfer	3953.9	3260.0	5192.2
（一）转移性收入	Net Income from Transfer	4371.4	3716.6	5883.9
（二）转移性支出	Transfer Expenditure	417.5	456.6	691.7

8-17 农村常住居民家庭人均消费支出

Per Capita Living Expenditure of Rural Households

单位：元 (yuan)

指标名称	Item	2015	2016
消费支出	**Total Living Expenditure**	**9517.7**	**10198.7**
一、食品烟酒	**Food,Tobacco and Alcohol**	**2681.7**	**2739.3**
1.食品	food	1887	1963.6
2.烟酒	Alcohol and tobacco	373.7	288.9
3.饮料	Drink	59.5	59.3
4.饮食服务	Catering Services	361.5	427.5
二、衣着	**Clothing**	**677.6**	**678.2**
衣类	Garments	510.7	511.2
鞋类	Footwear	166.9	167.1
三、居住	**Residence**	**2215.7**	**2384.8**
#租赁房房租	Rental Housing Rent	112.6	40.7
住房维修及管理	Housing Repair and Management	313.6	208.8
水电燃料及其他	Water,Electric Power Fuel and Others	436.9	502.9
四、生活用品及服务	**Living Articles and Services**	**628.4**	**773.4**
家具及室内装饰品	Furniture and External Decorations	121.6	108.7
家用器具	Household Appliances	150.8	257.3
家用纺织品	Household textile	68.2	72.1
家庭日用杂品	Household Articles of Daily Use	187.8	209.8
个人用品	Personal Items	81.7	97.3
家庭服务	Household Services	18.3	28.2
五、交通通信	**Transportation and Communications**	**1019.3**	**1096.7**
交通	Transportation	606.4	676.3
通信	Communications	412.9	420.4
六、教育文化娱乐	**Recreation, Education and Culture Services**	**1111.4**	**1209.9**
教育	Education	769.9	933.0
文化娱乐	Recreation	341.5	276.8
七、医疗保健	**Medicine and Medical Services**	**1016.1**	**1139.4**
医疗器具及药品	Medical Instruments and Medicines	340.7	343.3
医疗服务	Medical Services	675.4	796.0
八、其他用品和服务	**Others**	**167.5**	**177.0**

8-18 农村常住居民家庭人均购买主要商品数量

Per Capita Annual Purchases of Major Commodities of Rural Households

单位：千克 (kg)

指标名称	Item	2015	2016
面粉	Flour	14.5	23.8
大米	Rice	13.3	11.4
薯类	Potato	8.8	9.4
豆类	Beans	7.2	7.0
食用植物油	Edible vegetable oil	11.2	10.4
鲜菜	Fresh vegetables	64.6	60.2
猪肉	Pork	8.1	7.0
牛肉	Beef	0.4	0.3
羊肉	Lamb	0.3	0.4
鸡	Chicken	0.7	1.0
鱼类	Fish	0.8	0.8
虾类	Shrimp	0.1	0.1
鲜蛋	Eggs	7.5	5.8
鲜奶	Milk	8.2	7.1
酸奶	Yogurt	2.3	2.8
奶粉	Milk	0.8	0.8
鲜瓜果	Fresh fruit	35.1	37.1
糕点	Cake	3.1	2.7
茶叶	Tea	0.6	0.2
卷烟（盒）	Cigarettes (box)	30.7	25.7
啤酒	Beer	3.8	3.7
白酒	Liquor	0.8	0.5
果酒	Wine	0.3	0.3
鞋(双)	Footwear (pair)	2.5	2.5
水（吨）	Water (tons)	8.0	10.9
电（度）	Electricity （kwh）	452.9	478.9
煤炭	Coal	78.5	57.7
管道天燃气（立方米）	Gas pipeline (cu.m)	3.3	15.3
罐装液化石油气	Bottled liquefied petroleum gas	3.8	3.9

8-19 农村常住居民家庭平均每百户耐用品拥有情况

Ownership of Major Durable Consumer Goods Every 100 Rural Households

指标名称	Item	2015	2016
家用汽车（辆）	Automobile (unit)	21.3	27.3
摩托车（辆）	Motorcycles (unit)	45.7	41.8
助力车（台）	Strength-aid Cycle (unit)	62.5	73.2
洗衣机（台）	washing machine (unit)	97.0	100.9
电冰箱（柜）	Refrigerator (unit)	80.6	92.0
微波炉（台）	Microwave Oven (unit)	21.9	18.6
彩色电视机（台）	Color TV Set (unit)	119.8	126.0
空调（台）	Air conditioning(unit)	77.4	91.3
热水器（台）	Water heaters(unit)	66.0	73.7
#太阳能热水器（台）	Solar water heaters (unit)	50.8	58.7
消毒碗柜（台）	Sterilizing Cupboard (unit)	1.0	0.9
洗碗机（台）	Dishwasher (unit)	0.9	0.9
排油烟机（台）	Exhauster (unit)	32.4	34.2
固定电话（线）	Ordinary Telephone (unit)	29.2	26.2
移动电话（部）	Mobile phones (unit)	257.7	279.1
计算机（台）	Computer (a)	39.1	38.4
#接入互联网（台）	Access to the Internet(unit)	30.8	31.2
摄像机（台）	Pickup Camera (unit)	1.3	1.1
照相机（台）	Camera (unit)	12.0	10.7
中高档乐器（架）	High-end Instruments (unit)	0.9	1.1
健身器材（台）	Setting-up Apparatus (unit)	2.1	1.9
组合音响（套）	Music Center (unit)	6.8	4.3

8-20 农村常住居民家庭居住情况

Housing Conditions of Rural Households

指标名称	Item	2015	2016
调查户数（户）	**Number of Households Surveyed (household)**	**686**	**699**
平均每户居住人口（人）	**Average Number of Resident Population (person)**	**3.6**	**3.6**
人均现住房建筑面积（平方米/人）	**The Average Floor Area Per Person (sq.m / person)**	**50.7**	**51.7**
一、按居住空间样式分（%）	**by Living space style（%）**	100.0	100.0
单栋楼房	Single building Room	43.0	45.2
单栋平房	Single-storey House	41.4	38.7
单元房	Apartment	11.4	12.4
筒子楼或连片平房	Tube-shaped Apartment or Lace Single-storey Houses	2.8	2.4
其他	Other	1.4	1.3
二、按主要建筑材料分（%）	**by main construction materials（%）**	**100.0**	**100.0**
钢筋混凝土	Reinforced concrete soil	19.0	20.4
砖混材料	Brick and concrete material	73.9	74.9
砖瓦砖土	Tile and brick earth	5.9	4.0
竹草土坯	Bamboo grass mud	0.9	0.6
其他	Others	0.3	0.1
三、按房屋来源分（%）	**by Source of Housing（%）**	**100.0**	**100.0**
租赁住房	Rental housing	2.3	1.6
自建住房	Self-establish Housing	86.5	85.3
购买商品房	Commercial Residential Housing	4.0	4.1
购买房改住房	Private Housing through Housing Reform	0.9	1.4
购买保障性住房	Indemnificatory Housing	1.1	1.3
拆迁安置房	Resettlement Housing	5.0	6.0
继承或获赠住房	Inheriting and Donation Housing	0.1	0.1
其他	Others	0.1	0.1
四、住房外道路为硬化路面的户比重（%）	**proportion of households which outer road is Hardened road（%）**	**94.4**	**97.6**
五、按住宅有管道供水情况分（%）	**By Piped Water Supply Condition （%）**	**100.0**	**100.0**
管道供水入户	Pipe water into People's Homes	92.0	94.4
管道供水至公共取水点	Pipe water to Public Watering Points	0.8	1.0
没有管道设施	No Pipeline Facilities	7.2	4.6
六、按住户主要饮水来源情况分（%）	**By Source of main Drinking Water （%）**	**100.0**	**100.0**
经过净化处理的自来水	Purified Tap Water	63.3	66.1
受保护的井水和泉水	Protected Wells and Springs	26.6	29.0
不受保护的井水和泉水	Unprotected Wells and Springs	8.1	4.6
江河湖泊水	Rivers and Lakes Water	0.8	0.1
其他饮用水来源	Others	1.2	0.1
七、按住宅内厕所类型分（%）	**By Household Lavatory Type (%)**	**100.0**	**100.0**
水冲式卫生厕所	Sanitary Water Closet	38.8	44.3
水冲式非卫生厕所	Insanitary Water Closet	4.5	7.3
卫生旱厕	Sanitary Latrine	19.4	18.3
普通旱厕	Latrine	36.3	29.2
无厕所	No Lavatory	1.0	1.0
八、按主要炊用能源状况分（%）	**By Cooking Fuel Condition （%）**	**100.0**	**100.0**
天然气、煤气、液化石油气	Pipeline Natural Gas，Pipeline Gas，Pipeline Liquified Petroleum Gas	31.3	32.6
煤炭	Coal	7.5	7.4
电	Electricity	35.0	37.2
沼气	Methane	0.4	0.3
其他	Others	25.8	22.5

主要统计指标解释

住户　指居住在一个住宅内，共同分享生活开支或收入的一群人。居住在同一房间内、不共同分享生活开支的人群，每个人都视为一个住户。住家保姆、住家家庭帮工视为单独的住户。

常住居民　指住户成员中，经常在家居住、或者调查期内居住时间超过一半的人员，以及本住户供养的学生。常住居民是住户收支的调查对象。

整、半劳动力　整劳动力是指男子18周岁到50周岁，女子18周岁到45周岁；半劳动力是指男子16周岁到17周岁，51周岁到60周岁；女子16周岁到17周岁，46周岁到55周岁，同时具有劳动能力的人。虽然在劳动年龄之内，但已丧失劳动能力的人，不应算为劳动力；超过劳动年龄，但能经常参加劳动，计入半劳动力数内。常住人口中的职工，若这些职工为劳动力，就包括在本户的整半劳动力中。

居民人均可支配收入　指调查期内居民家庭成员人均获得的、可用于最终消费支出和储蓄的总和，即居民可以用来自由支配的收入，既包括现金收入，也包括实物收入。全体居民可支配收入可以体现各地区城乡一体的居民收入及生活水平变化情况。按照收入的来源，可支配收入包含四项，分别为：工资性收入、经营净收入、财产净收入、转移净收入。

工资性收入　指就业人员通过各种途径得到的全部劳动报酬和各种福利，包括受雇于单位或个人、从事各种自由职业、兼职和零星劳动得到的全部劳动报酬和福利。

经营净收入　指住户或住户成员从事生产经营活动所获得的净收入，是全部经营收入中扣除经营费用、生产性固定资产折旧和生产税净额（生产税减去生产补贴）之后得到的净收入。计算公式为：

经营净收入 = 经营收入 – 经营费用 – 生产性固定资产折旧 – 生产税净额（生产税–生产补贴）

财产净收入　指住户或住户成员将其所拥有的金融资产和自然资源交由其他机构单位、住户或个人支配而获得的回报并扣除相关的费用之后得到的净收入。计算公式为：

财产净收入 = 财产性收入 – 财产性支出

转移净收入　指国家、单位、社会团体对住户的各种经常性转移支付和住户之间的经常性收入转移。包括政府、非行政事业单位、社会团体对居民转移的养老金或退休金、社会救济和补助、政策性生活补贴、救灾款、经常性捐赠和赔偿以及报销医疗费等；住户之间的赡养收入、经常性捐赠和赔偿以及农村地区（村委会）在外（含国外）工作的本住户非常住成员寄回带回的收入等。计算公式为：

转移净收入=转移性收入–转移性支出

居民收入五等份分组　指将所有调查户按人均收入水平从低到高顺序排列，平均分为五个等份，处于最高20%的收入群体为高收入组，依此类推依次为中高收入组、中等收入组、中低收入组、低收入组。

居民人均生活消费支出　指住户用于满足家庭日常生活消费需要的全部支出，包括用于消费品的支出和用于服务性消费的支出。根据用途不同，消费支出可划分为食品烟酒、衣着、居住、生活用品及服务、交通通信、教育文化娱乐、医疗保健、其他用品及服务八大类。

城镇居民人均可支配收入（老口径）　指城镇家庭总收入扣除交纳的个人所得税和个人交纳的各项社会保障支出之后，按照城镇居民家庭人口平均的收入水平。其中家庭总收入是指该家庭中生活在一起的所有家庭人员从各种渠道得到的所有收入之和。计算公式为：

可支配收入= 家庭总收入– 交纳个人所得税–个人交纳的社会保障支出–记账补贴

农村居民人均纯收入（老口径）　指农村住户当年从各个来源得到的家庭总收入扣除有关费用性支出后，最终归农村居民所有的收入总和，按照农村住户人口平均的纯收入水平。计算公式为：

纯收入 = 总收入–家庭经营费用支出–税费支出–生产性固定资产折旧–赠送农村内部亲友

Explanatory Notes on Main Statistical Indicators

Households refer to persons living and sharing economically together in one house. When people don't share living expenses, every single person are deemed to be one household. Live-in Nanny and family helpers are deemed to be one household.

Usual Resident Population refers to persons staying at home regularly or for over half of time in survey period and students provided by the household. Usual resident population is the respondent of household living expenses.

Full/Semi Labour Force Full labour force refers to persons capable of work, aged 18-50 for males and 18-45 for females. Semi labour force refers to persons capable of work, aged 16-17 and 51-60 for males and 16-17 and 46-55 for females. Persons at their working ages but not capable of work are not to be included as labour force. Persons not at working ages but participating regularly in work are included in semi labour force. For staff and workers who are usual residents, are included as full or semi labour force of the household if they are in the labour force.

Disposable Income of Residents refers to the actual income at the disposal of members of the households which can be used for final consumption and savings in survey period, residents can use that at their disposal. It includes cash income and physical income. This income demonstrates the situation about incomes of both rural and urban residents and living standard in various regions. According to the source of income, disposable income include wage income, net business income, net property income and net transferability income.

Wages Income refers to the work reward and all benefits received in various ways by the members of rural households,include the work reward and all benefits received from employed by other units or individuals,liberal professions, part-time job and sporadic labor.

Net Business Income refers to the net income received by households engaged in manufacturing & managing activities.This equals to total business income minus operating costs, depreciation for productive plant assets and net product tax(production taxes minus production subsidies).The following formula is used:

Net business income=business income-operating costs-depreciation for productive plant assets- net product tax(production taxes-production subsidies)

Net Property Income refers to the income received as returns by owners of financial assets or nature sources by providing nature sources to other institutional units,households and individuals. The following formula is used:

Net property income = property income - property expenditure

Net Transferability Income refers to various current transfers of nation, units and social organizations pay to households and recurring revenue transfer between households. This income includes pension transferred from government, the non administrative institutions and social organizations to households, social assistance, policy living allowance, disaster relief funds, regular donation and compensation, recoverable medical cost; alimony income, regular donation and compensation, income from the ones who are not resident in rural areas between the households.The following formula is used:

Net transferability income = transfer income - transfer expenditure

Five Equal Groups of Resident Income According to income per head, all investigative households are arranged from low to high. Divided five groups equally, the maximum 20% of the income groups is high-income groups, and so on, there are middle and upper-income groups, middle-income groups, medium-low-income groups and low-income groups.

Consumption Expenditure of Households refers to total expenditure of households for consumption in daily life, including expenditure on the eight categories of food; clothing; housing; household appliances and services; health care and medical services; transport and communications; recreation, education and cultural services; and miscellaneous goods and services.

The per capita disposable income(the old range) This equals to total income minus income tax, personal contribution to social security and subsidy for keeping diaries in being a sample household. The following formula is used:

Disposable income = total household income - income tax - personal contribution to social security - subsidy for keeping diaries for a sampled household

The Average Per Capita Net Income of Rural Residents(the old range) refers to the total income of rural households from all sources minus all corresponding expenses. The formula for calculation is as follows:

Net income = total income - household operation expenses - taxes and fees paid - taxes and fees depreciation of fixed assets for production - gifts to non-rural relatives.

9 城市公用事业

URBAN PUBLIC UTILITIES

资料整理：郝　静
Data management：Hao Jing
数据审核：王金桂
Data audit：Wang Jingui

第九部分　城市公用事业

一、简要说明

本章资料主要包括城市供水、供燃气、供热、公共交通、市政设施、市政设施水平、城市规模及用地状况、园林绿地、环境卫生等情况，由西安市统计局服务业和社会科技处根据西安市建委、市交通局及地铁办提供的数据整理。

二、主要指标

人均公园绿地面积（平方米）	11.61	比上年增加	0.14
人均城市道路面积（平方米）	18.15	比上年减少	0.11
用水普及率（%）	100	与上年	持平
燃气普及率（%）	98.89	比上年提高	0.10个百分点

9　URBAN PUBLIC UTILITIES

Ⅰ.Brief Introduction

Data in this chapter reflects basic condition of urban public utilities of Xi'an City. Data on public utilities primarily consists of urban water supply, gas sales, urban heating, public transportation, municipal facilities, level of municipal construction, scale of the city, condition of land utilization, parks, greenbelt and environmental sanitation. Data in this chapter is compiled by Tertiary Industry and Social Science & Technology Division of Xi'an Bureau of Statistics according to the data provided by Committee of Urban Construction of Xi'an, Xi'an Burean of Transportation and Xi'an Metro Office.

Ⅱ.Major Indicators

		Increase over Preceding Year
Per Capita Public Green Areas (sq.m)	11.61	0.14
Per Captia Area of Roads (sq.m)	18.15	-0.11
Water-Consuming Popularization (%)	100	essentially on a par with last year's
Gas-Consuming Popularization (%)	98.89	0.10 percenage points

9-1 城市供水

Urban Water Supply

指　标	Item	2011	2012	2013	2014	2015	2016
年末水厂个数（个）	Number of Water Factory at Year-end (units)	15	15	15	16	22	22
供水综合生产能力（万立方米/日）	Total Volume of Water Supply (10 000 cu.m/day)	197.40	200.33	195.52	196.50	211.50	219.38
# 地下水	Groundwater	54.80	57.04	51.35	51.33	62.86	64.61
年末供水管道总长度（公里）	Length of Water Supply Pipelines at Year-end (kms)	2721	3207.73	3385.33	3499.97	4371.05	4522.46
全年供水总量（万立方米）	Total Annual Volume of Water Supply (10 000 cu.m)	38934	45791.77	51372.07	53798.99	56055.25	59953.03
#全年售水量	Annual Volume of Water Sales	33139	39734.86	44701.26	46755.71	49499.10	51922.87
#生产运营用水	For Productive Use	5484	5334.28	6272.62	15680.53	16146.29	16567.21
居民家庭用水	For Residential Use	19945	24703.73	26138.73	28497.40	30742.79	32182.87
用水人口（万人）	Population with Access to Tap Water (10 000 persons)	394.10	406.32	444.35	452.57	463.05	475.00

注：本表数据来源于市建委和市水务局。

9-2 城市供燃气

Gas Supply in Urban Area

指　标	Item	2011	2012	2013	2014	2015	2016
一、天然气	**Natural Gas**						
管道长度（公里）	Total Length of Gas Pipelines (km)	4500	5075.19	6163.39	6892.25	7465.73	8199.80
供气总量（万立方米）	Total Gas Supply(10 000 cu.m)	120330	142262.84	153488.90	186259.15	196826.38	206068.05
#销售气量	Volume of Gas Sales	114955	136530.93	147592.97	179536.78	189066.21	201078.36
#家庭用量	Residential Households	22868	27760.63	36671.17	59057.38	65952.81	67024.75
用气人口（万人）	Population with Access to Gas (10 000 persons)	356	371.54	410.56	425.72	437.96	452.11
二、液化石油气	**Liquefied Petroleum Gas**						
供气总量（吨）	Total Gas Supply (tons)	5920	4529.70	6047.90	5299.70	5030.30	4955.50
#销售气量	Volume of Gas Sales	5891	4482.00	5986.20	5244.00	4950.00	4875.20
#家庭用量	Residential Households	4352	4254.00	4945.00	4281.00	4064.00	4056.00
用气人口（万人）	Population with Access to Gas (10 000 persons)	28.60	27.44	27.92	21.00	19.50	17.60

注：本表数据来源于市建委。

9-3 城市供热

Heating in Urban Area

指　标	Item	2011	2012	2013	2014	2015	2016
供热能力	Heating Capacity						
蒸气（吨/小时）	Steam (tons/hour)	2075	3073	4283	2893	3013	3013
热水（兆瓦）	Hot Water (megawatts)	4570.00	5401.90	12691.10	13967.00	17191.90	17765.90
供热总量(万吉焦）	Volume Supplied (10 000 gigajoules)						
蒸气	Steam	1421	1616.98	1667.88	1743.87	1671.14	1789.13
热水	Hot Water	2901	2443.57	2990.38	3726.89	4241.30	5032.84
管道长度（公里）	Length of Pipelines (km)						
蒸气	Steam	167	187.07	204.33	231.04	235.24	239.69
热水	Hot Water	500	516.18	608.12	663.20	819.17	901.55
供热面积（万平方米）	Heated Area (10 000sq.m)	6524	8512.84	10980.27	13492.55	16690.65	19566.81
#住宅	Residential Buildings	5226	7328.16	9874.54	11828.59	14730.49	17282.39

注：本表数据来源于市建委。

9-4 城市公共交通

Urban Public Traffic

指　标	Item	2011	2012	2013	2014	2015	2016
运营车辆（辆）	Operating Vehicles (units)	7462	7695	8128	7769	7781	7829
标准运营车辆（标台）	Standard Vehicles (units)	8598	8926	9371	9050	9061	9140
公交客运总量（万人次）	Total of Bus Passenger(10 000 person-times)	175234	175241	174051	170960	161032	147089
公交客运收入（万元）	Bus Passenger Transport Income (10 000 yuan)	141505	135505	146417	140914	137492	129132
出租汽车数（辆）	Number of Taxis (units)	13839	14139	14139	14159	14459	14459
地铁运营线路长度（公里）	Length of Subway Lines in Operation(km)		19.87	44.68	50.94	50.94	88.97
地铁客运量（万人次）	Total of Subway Passenger(10 000 person-times)		5911.64	12189.61	29953.07	34209.35	40815.75

注：本表数据来源于市交通局和地铁办。

9-5 市政设施

Municipal Facilities

指　标	Item	2011	2012	2013	2014	2015	2016
一、道路长度（公里）	**Length of Roads (km)**	**2755**	**3119.30**	**3387.43**	**3461.18**	**3570.58**	**3683.14**
二、道路面积（万平方米）	**Area of Roads (10 000 sq.m)**	**6259**	**7126.56**	**7931.80**	**8144.22**	**8457.14**	**8618.93**
三、人行道面积（万平方米）	**Area of Sidewalks (10 000 sq.m)**	**1867**	**2105.31**	**2259.29**	**2310.46**	**2381.20**	**2423.70**
四、桥梁数（座）	**Number of Bridges (units)**	**402**	**422**	**432**	**437**	**448**	**449**
#立交桥	Overpasses	91	97	97	105	106	107
五、路灯盏数（盏）	**Number of Street Lights (units)**	**311991**	**329881**	**333393**	**337991**	**343465**	**349808**
六、排水管道长度（公里）	**Length of Drainage Pipelines (km)**	**4043**	**4435.92**	**4629.70**	**4839.49**	**4984.94**	**5161.83**
七、污水年排放量（万立方米）	**Annual Discharge Volume of Sewage (10 000 cu.m)**	**36673**	**40302.7**	**46186**	**51673**	**62092**	**56578**
八、污水处理厂处理能力（万立方米/日）	**Daily Disposal Capacity of Sewage (10 000 cu.m/day)**	**111.6**	**128.1**	**153.1**	**153.1**	**200.6**	**212.1**
九、污水年处理量（万立方米）	**Yearly Disposal Capacity of Sewage Disposal Plant (10 000 cu.m)**	**31512**	**35463**	**41898**	**47907**	**57034**	**52011**

注：本表数据来源于市建委。

9-6 城市设施水平

Urban Municipal Facilities

指　标	Item	2011	2012	2013	2014	2015	2016
一、人均日生活用水量（升）	**Per Capita Daily Consumption of Tap Water For Residential Use (liters)**	**185.20**	**220.96**	**225.78**	**178.45**	**187.79**	**191.35**
二、用水普及率(%)	**Water-Consuming Popularization (%)**	**100**	**100**	**100**	**100**	**100**	**100**
三、每万人拥有公共交通车辆（标台）	**Number of Public Transport Vehicles Per 10 000 Population (units)**	**14.4**	**14.6**	**15.1**	**14.4**	**14.3**	**13.9**
四、燃气普及率(%)	**Gas-Consuming Popularization (%)**	**98**	**98.19**	**98.68**	**98.71**	**98.79**	**98.89**
五、人均城市道路面积（平方米）	**Per Captia Area of Roads (sq.m)**	**15.9**	**17.54**	**17.85**	**18.00**	**18.26**	**18.15**
六、建成区排水管道密度（公里/平方公里）	**Density of Drainage Pipelines in Developed Areas (km/sq.km)**	**9.7**	**9.83**	**9.17**	**9.27**	**9.09**	**9.12**
七、污水处理率(%)	**Rate of Sewerage Disposal (%)**	**85.90**	**89.51**	**90.72**	**92.71**	**91.85**	**91.93**
八、园林绿化	**Afforestation and Parks and Gardens**						
人均公园绿地面积（平方米）	Per Capita Public Green Areas (sq.m)	9.9	10.22	10.70	11.22	11.47	11.61
建城区绿地率（%）	Rate of Green Areas in Developed Areas (%)	30.9	31.20	32.32	32.60	34.03	34.95
九、生活垃圾无害化处理率(%)	**Rate of No Harm Disposal of Garbage (%)**	**93.7**	**94.93**	**93.95**	**93.48**	**98.09**	**96.70**

注：本表数据来源于市建委。
每万人拥有公共交通车辆计算数据口径调整，故与2009年前数据不可比。

9-7　城市规模及用地情况

City Scale and Land Use

单位：平方公里　　(sq.km)

指　标	Item	2011	2012	2013	2014	2015	2016
建成区面积	Area of the Constructed Regions	415	451.38	504.68	521.91	548.60	565.75
城市建设用地	Land use for Construction	349	376.39	489.03	507.66	536.10	553.29

注：本表数据来源于市建委。

9-8　城市园林绿化

Urban Parks,Gardens and Green Areas in Cities

指　标	Item	2011	2012	2013	2014	2015	2016
一、公园个数（个）	**Number of Parks (units)**	**66**	**72**	**81**	**85**	**91**	**95**
二、公园面积（公顷）	**Area of Parks (hectares)**	**1478**	**1529.00**	**2406.00**	**2483.83**	**2599.83**	**2647.40**
三、绿地面积（公顷）	**Total Area of Parks,Gardens and Green Areas (hectares)**	**13680**	**15196.00**	**17751.00**	**18914.05**	**20582.44**	**22502.87**
#公园绿地面积	Public Green Areas	3898	4154.00	4756.00	5075.85	5310.58	5517.08
四、年末绿化覆盖面积（公顷）	**Coverage Space of Green Areas at year-end (hectares)**	**17325**	**19017.00**	**21865.00**	**23216.65**	**25639.88**	**27617.83**
五、建成区绿化覆盖率（%）	**Coverage of Green Areas in Developed Areas (%)**	**38.96**	**39.53**	**40.29**	**40.76**	**42.04**	**42.57**

注：本表数据来源于市建委。

9-9 城市环境卫生

Urban Environment Sanitation

指　标	Item	2011	2012	2013	2014	2015	2016
清扫面积（万平方米）	Area Under Cleaning Program (10 000 sq.m)	6411	6952	8725	10110	9842	9137
清运生活垃圾（万吨）	Volume of Residential Garbage Disposal (10 000 tons)	265	287.32	290.76	359.37	359.16	371.51
清运粪便（万吨）	Volume of Excrement and Urine Disposal (10 000 tons)	4	2.99	2.96	2.90	3.15	3.18
公共厕所（座）	Number of Public Lavatories (units)	1493	1594	1770	2151	2239	2314
市容环卫专用车辆设备总数（辆）	Special Vehicles of Environmental Sanitation (units)	1200	1279	1639	1990	2050	2000

注：本表数据来源于市建委。

9-10 市区及县供水（2016年）

Urban and County Water Supply (2016)

指　标	Item	西安 Xi'an	市区 City	蓝田 Lantian	周至 ZhouZhi	户县 Huxian
年末水厂个数（个）	Number of Water Factory at Year-end (units)	22	18	1	1	2
供水综合生产能力（万立方米/日）	Total Volume of Water Supply (10 000 cu.m/day)	219.38	209.33	2.70	1.80	5.55
#地下水	Groundwater	64.61	59.26	1.90	1.20	2.25
年末供水管道总长度（公里）	Length of Water Supply Pipelines at Year-end (km)	4522.46	4245.86	124.92	56.00	95.68
全年供水总量（万立方米）	Total Annual Volume of Water Supply (10 000 cu.m)	59953.03	57396.50	607.87	537.99	1410.67
#销售水量	Volume of Water Sales	51922.87	49522.34	581.87	482.99	1335.67
#生产运营用水	For Productive Use	16567.21	16119.67	125.91	12.00	309.63
居民家庭用水	For Residential Use	32182.87	30646.81	395.10	399.00	741.96
用水人口（万人）	Population with Access to Tap Water (10 000 persons)	475.00	436.03	15.10	7.20	16.67

注：本表数据来源于市建委及市水务局。

9-11 市区及县供燃气（2016年）

Urban and County Gas Supply (2016)

指　标	Item	西安 Xi'an	市区 Urban	蓝田 Lantian	周至 ZhouZhi	户县 Huxian
一、天然气	**Natural Gas**					
管道长度（公里）	Total Length of Gas Pipelines (km)	8199.80	7981.78	79.02	42.00	97.00
供气总量（万立方米）	Total Gas Supply(10 000 cu.m)	206068.05	201925.05	1523.00	652.00	1968.00
#销售气量	Volume of Gas Sales	201078.36	197000.36	1520.00	650.00	1908.00
#家庭用量	Residential Households	67024.75	65734.75	760.00	130.00	400.00
用气人口（万人）	Population with Access to Gas (10 000 persons)	452.11	434.03	6.87	1.51	9.70
二、液化石油气	**Liquefied Petroleum Gas**					
供气总量（吨）	Total Gas Supply (tons)	4955.50	1957.60	687.40	1130.50	1180.00
#销售气量	Volume of Gas Sales	4875.20	1928.00	687.20	1130.00	1130.00
#家庭用量	Residential Households	4056.00	1125.00	671.00	1130.00	1130.00
用气人口（万人）	Population with Access to Gas (10 000 persons)	17.60	2.00	3.41	5.30	6.89

注：本表数据来源于市建委。

9-12 市区及县供热（2016年）

Urban and County Heating (2016)

指　标	Item	西安 Xi'an	市区 Urban	蓝田 Lantian	周至 ZhouZhi	户县 Huxian
供热能力	Heating Capacity					
蒸气（吨/小时）	Steam (tons/hour)	3013.00	2583.00			430.00
热水（兆瓦）	Hot Water (megawatts)	17765.90	17765.90			
供热总量(万吉焦)	Volume Supplied(10 000 gigajoules)					
蒸气	Steam	1789.13	1689.13			100.00
热水	Hot Water	5032.84	5032.84			
管道长度（公里）	Length of Pipelines (km)					
蒸气	Steam	239.69	213.39			26.30
热水	Hot Water	901.55	901.55			
供热面积（万平方米）	Heated Area (10 000sq.m)	19566.81	19418.81			148.00
#住宅	Residential Buildings	17282.39	17134.39			148.00

注：本表数据来源于市建委。

9-13 市区及县市政设施（2016年）

Urban and County Municipal Facilities (2016)

指　标	Item	西安 Xi'an	市区 Urban	蓝田 Lantian	周至 ZhouZhi	户县 Huxian
一、道路长度（公里）	**Length of Roads (km)**	**3683.14**	**3434.75**	**75.60**	**43.63**	**129.16**
二、道路面积（万平方米）	**Area of Roads (10 000 sq.m)**	**8618.93**	**7990.36**	**136.18**	**85.10**	**407.29**
三、人行道面积（万平方米）	**Area of Sidewalks (10 000 sq.m)**	**2423.70**	**2244.84**	**58.96**	**34.00**	**85.90**
四、桥梁数（座）	**Number of Bridges (units)**	**449**	**431**	**11**		**7**
#立交桥	Crossroads	107	104			3
五、路灯盏数（盏）	**Number of Street Lights (units)**	**349808**	**333109**	**1936**	**5164**	**9599**
六、排水管道长度（公里）	**Length of Drainage Pipelines (km)**	**5161.83**	**4859.74**	**88.53**	**47.46**	**166.10**
七、污水年排放量（万立方米）	**Annual Discharge Volume of Sewage (10 000 cu.m)**	**56578**	**54500**	**578**	**402**	**1098**
八、污水处理厂处理能力（万立方米/日）	**Daily Disposal Capacity of Sewage (10 000 cu.m/day)**	**212.1**	**206.5**	**1.5**	**1.1**	**3.0**
九、污水年处理量（万立方米）	**Yearly Disposal Capacity of Sewage Disposal Plant (10 000 cu.m)**	**52011**	**50358**	**458**	**318**	**877**

注：本表数据来源于市建委。

9-14 市区及县市政设施水平（2016年）

Urban and County Municipal Facilities Level(2016)

指　标	Item	西安 Xi'an	市区 City	蓝田 Lantian	周至 ZhouZhi	户县 Huxian
一、人均日生活用水量（升）	**Per Capita Daily Consumption of Tap Water For Residential Use (liters)**	**191.35**	**196.91**	**82.15**	**178.67**	**150.36**
二、用水普及率(%)	**Water-Consuming Popularization (%)**	**100**	**100**	**100**	**100**	**100**
三、每万人拥有公共交通车辆（标台）	**Number of Public Transport Vehicles Per 10 000 Population (units)**	**13.9**				
四、燃气普及率（%）	**Gas-Consuming Popularization (%)**	**98.89**	**100**	**68.08**	**94.58**	**99.52**
五、人均城市道路面积（平方米）	**Per Captia Area of Roads (sq.m)**	**18.15**	**18.33**	**9.02**	**11.82**	**24.43**
六、建成区排水管道密度（公里/平方公里）	**Density of Drainage Pipelines (km/sq.km)**	**9.12**	**9.39**	**7.37**	**4.75**	**6.39**
七、污水处理率(%)	**Rate of Sewerage Disposal (%)**	**91.93**	**92.40**	**79.24**	**79.10**	**79.87**
八、园林绿化	**Afforestation and Parks and Gardens**					
人均公园绿地面积（平方米）	Per Capita Public Green Areas (sq.m)	11.61	11.87	4.72	15.00	9.73
建城区绿地率（%）	Rate of Green Areas in Developed Areas(%)	34.95	35.24	30.81	21.40	36.28
九、生活垃圾无害化处理率(%)	**Rate of No Harm Disposal of Garbage (%)**	**96.7**	**99.7**		**95.7**	**97.4**

注：本表数据来源于市建委。

主要统计指标解释

建成区面积 城市行政区内实际已成片开发建设、市政公用设施和公共设施基本具备的区域。对核心城市，它包括集中连片的部分以及分散的若干个已经成片建设起来，市政公用设施和公共设施基本具备的地区；对一城多镇来说，它包括由几个连片开发建设起来的，市政公用设施和公共设施基本具备的地区组成。因此建成区范围，一般是指建成区外轮廓线所能包括的地区，也就是这个城市实际建设用地所达到的范围。

供水综合生产能力 指按供水设施取水、净化、送水、出厂输水干管等环节设计能力计算的综合生产能力。包括在原设计能力的基础上，经挖、革、改增加的生产能力。计算时，以四个环节中最薄弱的环节为主确定能力。

供水管道长度 指从送水泵至用户水表之间所有管道的长度。不包括新安装尚未使用、水厂内以及用户建筑物内的管道。在同一条街道埋设两条或两条以上管道时，应按每条管道的长度计算。

供水总量 指报告期供水企业（单位）供出的全部水量。包括有效供水量和漏损水量。

用水普及率 指报告期末城区内用水人口与总人口的比率。计算公式:

$$用水普及率=\frac{用水人口（含暂住人口）}{人口+暂住人口}\times100\%$$

供气管道长度 指报告期末从气源厂压缩机的出口或门站出口至各类用户引入管之间的全部已经通气投入使用的管道长度。不包括煤气生产厂、输配站、液化气储存站、灌瓶站、储配站、气化站、混气站、供应站等厂（站）内的管道。

供气总量 指报告期燃气企业（单位）向用户供应的燃气数量。包括销售量和损失量。

燃气普及率 指报告期末城区内使用燃气的人口与总人口的比率。计算公式：

$$燃气普及率=\frac{用气人口（含暂住人口）}{人口+暂住人口}\times100\%$$

供热能力 指供热企业（单位）向城市热用户输送热能的设计能力。不是热电厂的生产能力。

供热总量 指在报告期供热企业（单位）向城市热用户输送全部蒸汽和热水的总热量。

供热管道长度 指从各类热源到热用户建筑物接入口之间的全部蒸汽和热水的管道长度。不包括各类热源厂内部的管道长度。

供热面积 指供热企业（单位）向城市各类房屋建筑物、构筑物及其附属设施供热的全部建筑面积。

道路长度 指道路长度和与道路相通的桥梁、隧道的长度，按车行道中心线计算。

道路面积 指道路实际铺装面积和与道路相通的广场、桥梁、隧道的铺装面积（统计时，将人行道面积单独统计）。

人行道面积按道路两侧面积相加计算，包括步行街和广场，不含人车混行的道路。

排水管道长度 指所有排水总管、干管、支管、检查井及连接井进出口等长度之和。计算时按单管计算，即在同一条街道上如有两条或两条以上并排的排水管道时，应按每条排水管道的长度相加计算。

绿化覆盖面积 指城市中的乔木、灌木、草坪等所有植被的垂直投影面积。包括公园绿地、防护绿地、生产绿地、附属绿地、其他绿地的绿化种植覆盖面积、屋顶绿化覆盖面积以及零散树木的覆盖面积，不含各类绿地中的水域面积以及没有被植被覆盖的面积（硬化道路、无屋顶绿化的建筑物等）。乔木树冠下重迭的灌木和草本植物不重复计算。

人均城市道路面积 指报告期末城区内平均每人拥有的城市道路面积。计算公式：

$$人均城市道路面积=\frac{城区道路面积}{城区人口+城区暂住人口}$$

建成区排水管道密度 指报告期末建成区排水管道分布的疏密程度，计算公式：

$$排水管道密度=\frac{排水管道长度}{建成区面积}$$

污水处理率 指报告期内污水处理总量与污水排放总量的比率。计算公式：

$$污水处理率=\frac{污水处理总量}{污水排放总量}\times100\%$$

人均公园绿地面积 指报告期末城区内平均每人拥有的公园绿地面积。计算公式：

$$人均公园绿地面积=\frac{城区公园绿地面积}{城区人口+城区暂住人口}$$

建成区绿地率 指报告期末建成区内绿地面积与建成区面积的比率。计算公式：

$$建成区绿地率\frac{建成区绿地面积}{建成区面积}\times100\%$$

Explanatory Notes on Main Statistical Indicators

Area of the Constructed Regions refers to developed and built city administrative area where basic municipal utilities and public facilities complete constructed. To core city, it includes part of contiguous centralized and a number of decentralized part where basic municipal utilities and public facilities complete constructed. To a multi-city town, it consists of several contiguous developed and build area where municipal utilities and public facilities with basic composition. Therefore, the range of built-up area, generally refers to the built-up areas in the contour line, which is the actual construction site of the city achieved range.

Production Capacity of Water Supply refers to the designed overall production capacity of water facilities, covering the four segments of water collection, purification, conveyance, and out flow through trunk pipelines. Increased capacity through transformation and innovation projects is included as well. The capacity is determined mainly on the weakest of the above-mentioned four segments.

Length of Water Supply Pipelines at Year–end refers to the total length of all the pipelines between the water pumps and the user water meters, excluding pipelines newly installed but not used yet, pipeline in the water factory, and pipeline in the user's buildings.

Volume of Water Supply refers to the total volume of water supplied by water-works(units) during the reference period, including both the effective water supply and loss during the water supply.

Coverage Rate of Urban Population with Access to Tap Water refers to the ratio of the urban population with access to tap water to the total urban population . The formula is :

$$\text{Coverage of urban population with access to tap water} = \frac{\text{population with access to tap water}}{\text{population}} \times 100\%$$

Length of Gas Pipeline refers to the total length of pipelines in use between the outlet of the compressor of gas-work of outlet gas stations and the leading pipe of users , excluding pipelines within gasworks , delivery stations ,LPG storage stations ,refilling stations, gas-mixing stations and supply stations.

Volume of Gas Supply refers to the total volume of gas provided to users by gas-producing enterprises (units) in a year ,including the volume sold and the volume lost .

Coverage Rate of Urban Population with Access to Gas refers to the ratio of the urban population with access to gas to the total urban population at the end of the reference period. The formula is :

$$\text{Coverage rate of urban population with access to gas} = \frac{\text{population with access to gas}}{\text{population}} \times 100\%$$

City Heating capacity in Urban Areas refers to the designed capacity of heating enterprises (units) in supplying heating energy to urban users during the reference period .

City Quantity of Heat Supplied in Urban Areas refers to the total quantity of heat from steam and hot water urban users by heating enterprises (units) during the reference period .

City Length of Urban Heating Pipelines refers to the total length of steam or hot water pipelines for sources of heat to the leading pipelines of the building of the users ,excluding internal pipelines in heat generating enterprises

Heated Area refers to the total structure area of heat supplied to urban constructions, structures and ancillary facilities by heating enterprises (units) during the reference period .

Length of Paved Roads refers to the length of roads with paved surface including bridges and tunnels connected with roads. Length of the roads is measured by the central lines .

Area of Paved Roads refers to the actual pavement area of roads and the actual pavement area of squares, bridges and tunnels connecting to the roads (the area of sidewalk pavements is calculated separately).

The area of sidewalk pavements is the sum of area of roads on sides of road, including pedestrian streets and squares, excluding roads for both pedestrians and vehicles .

Length of exhaust pipelines refers to the total length of all main drain piles ,trunk pipes ,branch pipes

,access manholes ,and connector well entrances and exits ,and so on . The whole length is calculated as of single pipes. Namely ,if there are two or more drain pipes parallel on a street ,the length of every pipe shall be summed .

Total area of green land refers to vertical projection area of all vegetation including trees, shrubs, lawns. Including parks, protective green space, production green space, green subsidiaries, green plants covering area, covering an area other green spaces, green roofs and covering area of scattered trees, excluding kinds of water area in kinds of green area and the area not covered by vegetation(hardened road, building of no green roof). shrubs and herbaceous plants overlap under the canopy of trees do not double counting.

Per Capita Area of Paved Roads refers to the area of urban roads per capita at the end of the reporting period. The formula is :

$$\text{Per capita area of paved roads} = \frac{\text{Area of urban roads}}{\text{Urban population+temporary resident population}}$$

Density of Drainage Pipelines refers to density of drainage pipelines in developed areas at the end of the reporting period .The formula is :

$$\text{Density of drainage pipelines} = \frac{\text{Length of drainage pipelines}}{\text{Ares of developed areas}}$$

Rate of Sewerage Disposal refers to the ratio of waste water disposed with the total discharge of waste water in the reporting period .The formula is:

$$\text{Rate of Sewerage Disposal} = \frac{\text{Waste Water Disposed}}{\text{Total Discharge of Waste Water}} \times 100\%$$

Per Capita Area of Public Green refers to the area of public green areas per capita at end of the reporting period .The formula is :

$$\text{Per capita area of public green} = \frac{\text{Area of public green areas}}{\text{Urban population+temporary resident population}}$$

Coverage of Green Areas in Developed Areas refers to the ratio of green areas in built-up areas with the area of developed areas at the end of reporting period . The formula is:

$$\text{Coverage of green land in developed areas} = \frac{\text{Area of green land in developed aresa}}{\text{Area of developed areas}} \times 100\%$$

10 环境保护

ENVIRONMENT PROTECTION

资料整理：李　炜
Data management：Li Wei
数据审核：陈　英
Data audit：Chen Ying

第十部分　环境保护

一、简要说明

本章资料反映环境保护、工业污染排放及处理利用情况、危险废物集中处置情况、生活及其他污染情况和工业污染治理项目建设情况，由西安市统计局综合处根据西安市环保局提供的数据资料整理。

二、主要指标

工业固体废物综合利用率（%）	85.31	比上年下降	5.51个百分点
全年环境空气达到二级以上天数（天）	192	比上年减少	59天

10 ENVIRONMENT PROTECTION

Ⅰ.Brief Introduction

This chapter contains information that reflect environment protection, discharge and treatment of industrial pollutant, centralized treatment of dangerous wastes, domestic pollution and other pollution, construction of projects of industrial pollution treatment. Data in this chapter is compiled by General Division of the Xi'an Bureau of Statistics according to the reported data from Xi'an Environment Protection Bureau.

Ⅱ.Major Indicators

		Increase over Preceding Year
Percentage of Industrial Solid Waste Utilized (%)	85.31	-5.51percentage points
Days of Air Quality up to the Second Levels（day）	192	-59 days

10-1 城市环境保护（2016年）

Urban Environmental Protection（2016）

指 标	Item	2016
一、饮用水环境	**Potable Water Environment**	
全市饮用水水质达标率(%)	Compliance Rate of the City's Potable Water Quality (%)	99.72
二、大气环境	**Atmospheric Environment**	
颗粒物（PM10）年平均浓度（微克/立方米）	Particulate matter (PM10) Annual average concentration (μg / m^3)	137
颗粒物（PM2.5）年平均浓度（微克/立方米）	Particulate matter (PM2.5) Annual average concentration (μg / m^3)	71
二氧化硫浓度年平均值（微克/立方米）	Annual Average Concentration of Sulphur Dioxide (μg / m^3)	20
二氧化氮浓度年平均值（微克/立方米）	Annual Average Concentration of Nitrogen Dioxide (μg / m^3)	53
一氧化碳第95百分位数（微克/立方米）	The 95th percentile of carbon monoxide (μg / m^3)	3.1
臭氧八小时第90百分位数（微克/立方米）	Ozone eight hours 90th percentile (μg / m^3)	162
全年环境空气质量达标天数(天)	Days of Air Quality up to the Standards(days)	192
全年环境空气质量达标率(%)	Annual compliance rate of Ambient Air Quality(%)	52.60
三、声环境	**Voice**	
1、功能区噪声平均值(dB(A))	Average Noise Value of Functional Districts(dB(A))	
0类区	Class 0	55.0
1类区	Class 1	56.0
2类区	Class 2	58.0
3类区	Class 3	61.0
4类区	Class 4	70.0
2、道路交通噪声平均值(dB(A))	Average Noise Value of Road Traffic(dB(A))	55.7
3、区域噪声平均值(dB(A))	Average Noise Value of Region(dB(A))	71.2
四、环境污染治理	**Environmental pollution treatment**	
当年完成环保验收项目环境保护投资（亿元）	Year Completed Investment in Environmental Protection Projects of Environmental acceptance(100 million yuan)	53.69

注：本表数据来源于市环保局。

10-2 主要年份工业“三废”排放及处理利用情况

指 标	Item	2000	2006
一、工业废水排放量（万吨）	**Volume of Waste Water Discharge (10 000 tons)**	**9145**	**16389**
工业废水处理量（万吨）	Volume of Industrial Wastewater Disposal (10 000 tons)		
废水治理设施数（套）	Number of Facilities for Treatment of Waste Water (sets)		
二、工业废气排放量（亿立方米）	**Total Volume of Industrial Waste Gas Emission (100 million cu.m)**	**275.97**	**642.51**
废气治理设施数（套）	Number of Facilities for Treatment of Waste Gas(sets)		466
三、工业固体废物产生量（万吨）	**Volume of Industrial Solid Wastes Produced (10 000 tons)**	**107**	**161**
工业固体废物处置量（万吨）	Volume of Industrial Solid Wastes Treated (10 000 tons)	20	5
工业固体废物综合利用量（万吨）	Volume of Industrial Solid Waste Utilized (10 000 tons) in a Comprehensive Way	63	143
工业固体废物综合利用率（%）	Percentage of Volume of Industrial Solid Waste Utilized in a Comprehensive Way(%)	58.88	89.07
四、工业锅炉（台/蒸吨）	**Industrial Boilers (units/tons)**		

注：本表数据来源于市环保局。

2010年全国统一进行了污染源普查动态更新调查工作，“十二五”的环境统计体系与污染源普查体系相衔接，与“十一五”环境统计口径不同。

Discharge and Treatrment of Waste Gas, Water & Solid Wastes in Repersentative Years

2010	2011	2012	2013	2014	2015	2016
13840	**13148**	**10223.73**	**8972.97**	**6339.85**	**5203.56**	**4029.83**
10673.52	12632.38	9089.04	6798.71	5818.27	4783.60	4264.99
267	314	312	295	305	315	266
791.56	**1018.46**	**1043.31**	**844.11**	**901.23**	**1108.48**	**1034.46**
816	745	649	661	740	801	834
267.29	**279**	**259.14**	**255.78**	**252.66**	**238.53**	**195.99**
3.56	6	9.24	9.68	17.54	20.95	28.66
262	271	248.58	244.08	233.52	216.64	167.20
98.05	97.3	95.92	95.43	92.43	90.82	85.31
		503/8785	**576/13466**	**520/14177**	**501/18278**	**480/12791.8**

10-3 工业污染排放及处理利用情况（2016年）

Discharge and Treatment of Industrial Pollution（2016）

指 标	Item	2016
一、被调查企业基本情况	**Basic condition of Enterprises investigated**	
1. 企业数（个）	Number of Enterprises (units)	442
2. 工业总产值（亿元）	Gross Industry Output Value (100 millian yuan)	2463.01
3. 工业锅炉数（台/蒸吨）	Industrial Boilers (units/tons)	480/12791.8
4. 工业炉窑数（座）	Number of Industrial Grates (items)	134
二、工业废水	**Industrial Waste Water**	
1. 工业取水量（万吨）	Industrial water intake (10000 tons)	9444.08
#新鲜水量	Volume of Fresh Water	
重复用水量	Volume of Water Recycled	
2. 工业用水重复利用率（%）	Percentage of Industrial Water Recycled (%)	
3. 废水治理设施数（套）	Number of Facilities for Treatment of Waste Water (sets)	266
4. 废水治理设施处理能力（万吨/日）	Disposal Capacity of Facilities for Treatment of Waste Water (10 000 tons/day)	24.4
5. 废水治理设施运行费用（万元）	Operating Expense of Facilities for Treatment of Waste Water (10 000 yuan)	24273.1
6. 工业废水排放量（万吨）	Volume of Industrial Waste Water Discharged (10 000 tons)	4029.83
三、工业废气	**Industrial Waste Gas**	
1. 煤炭消费量（万吨）	Total Coal Consumption (10 000 tons)	740.95
2. 燃料油消费量（不含车船用）（万吨）	Fuel Oil Consumption (10 000 tons)	0.15
3. 天然气消费量（亿立方米）	Natural Gas Consumption (100 millian cu.m)	3.23
4. 工业废气排放总量（亿立方米）	Total Volume of Industrial Waste Gas Emission (100 millian cu.m)	1034.46
5. 废气治理设施数（套）	Number of Facilities for Treatment of Waste Gas (sets)	834
6. 废气治理设施处理能力（万立方米/时）	Disposal Capacity of Facilities for Treatment of Waste Gas (10 000 cu.m./h)	4708.53
7. 废气治理设施设备运行费用（万元）	Operating Expense of Facilities for Treatment of Waste gas(10 000 yuan)	62195.10
8. 二氧化硫产生量（吨）	Sulfur dioxide production (tons)	74753.51
9. 二氧化硫排放量（吨）	Volume of Sulphur Dioxide Emission (tons)	4913.89
10. 氮氧化物产生量（吨）	Production of nitrogen oxides(tons)	33831.73
11. 氮氧化物排放量（吨）	Nitrogen oxide emissions(tons)	6168.56
12. 烟（粉）尘产生量（吨）	Tobacco (powder) dust production(tons)	1093460.11
13. 烟（粉）尘排放量（吨）	The smoke (powder) dust emissions(tons)	2853.13
四、工业固体废物	**Industrial Solid Waste**	
1. 工业固体废物产生量（万吨）	Volume of Industrial Solid Waste Produced (10 000tons)	195.99
2. 工业固体废物综合利用量（万吨）	Volume of Industrial Solid Waste Utilized (10 000tons)	167.2
3. 工业固体废物综合利用率（%）	Percentage of Industrial Solid Waste Utilized (%)	85.31
4. 工业固体废物贮存量（万吨）	Volume of Industrial Solid Waste Accumulated (10 000tons)	
5. 工业固体废物处置量（万吨）	Volume of Industrial Solid Waste Treated (10 000tons)	28.66
6. 工业固体废物倾倒丢弃量（吨）	Volume of Industrial Solid Waste Discharged (tons)	

注：本表数据来源于市环保局。

10-4 城市污水处理情况（2016年）

Urban Sewage Treatment（2016）

指　标	Item	2016
一、污水处理厂数（座）	**Number of Sewage Treatment Works(units)**	**38**
污水处理厂处理能力（万吨/日）	Daily Disposal Capacity of Sewage(10 000 tons/day)	232.70
二、污水处理	**Sewgae Disposal**	
污水实际处理量（万吨）	Volume of Sewgae Disposal(10 000 tons)	70351.65
生活污水处理量	Volume of Domestic Sewgae Disposal	65857.98
工业污水处理量	Volume of Industrial Sewage Disposal	4493.67
三、再生水（万吨）	**Recycled water (10 000 tons)**	
生产量	Production	1066.20
利用量	Utilization	935.33
四、化学需氧量去除量（吨）	**Volume of COD Removed (tons)**	**304252.86**
五、氨氮去除量（吨）	**Volume of Ammonia and Nitrogen Removed(tons)**	**25619.76**
六、总磷去除量（吨）	**Volume of Total Phosphorus Removed(tons)**	**4097.61**
七、污泥产生量（吨）	**Volume of Sludge Produced(tons)**	**217270**
八、污泥处置量（吨）	**Volume of Sludge Disposal(tons)**	**216602**
九、污泥倾倒丢弃量（吨）	**Dumping sludge discards (tons)**	**668**
十、本年运行费用（万元）	**Operating Expense(10 000 yuan)**	**70432.92**

注：本表数据来源于市环保局。

10–5 危险废物（医疗废物）集中处理情况（2016年）

Condition of Concentrated Disposal of Dangerous Wastes（Medical Wastes）（2016）

指　标	Item	2016
一、危险废物集中处理（置）厂数（个）	**Number of Colleted Dangerous Wastes Treated Plants(items)**	**1**
二、医疗废物集中处理（置）厂数（个）	**The number of Manufacturing Plants of Medical waste treatment (units)**	**1**
三、危险废物设计处置能力（吨/日）	**Design hazardous waste disposal capacity (tons / day)**	**350.20**
四、实际处置危险废物量（吨）	**The actual amount of hazardous waste disposal (tons)**	**30007.52**
五、危险废物综合利用量（吨）	**Volume of Dangerous Wastes Utilized in a Comprehensive Way (tons)**	
六、焚烧残渣流向（千克）	**Flow Direction of Residuum after Burning (kg)**	
1. 焚烧残渣量	Volume of Residuum after Burning	429075.00
2. 焚烧残渣安全填埋处置量	Secure landfill disposal incineration residues	429075.00
3. 焚烧飞灰产生量	Fly ash production	74373.00
4. 焚烧飞灰安全填埋处置量	Fly ash landfill disposal safety	74373.00
七、当年运行费用（万元）	**Operating Expenses in Current year(10 000 yuan)**	**5032.40**

注：本表数据来源于市环保局。

10–6 生活及其他污染情况（2016年）

Domestic Pollution and Other Conditions（2016）

指　标	Item	2016
一、基本情况	**Basic Condition**	
1. 生活天然气消费量（万立方米）	Volume of Living natural gas consumption (10 000 cu.m)	206068.05
2. 生活用水总量（万吨）	Volume of Living water (10 000 tons)	78642.41
二、污染排放情况	**Discharge of Pollutant**	
1. 城镇生活污水排放量（万吨）	Volume of Urban Domestic Sewage Discharged(10 000 tons)	66846.05
2. 生活污水处理量（万吨）	Volume of Domestic Sewgae Disposal(10 000 tons)	63503.75
3. 生活CDD产生量（吨）	Volume of Life CDD production (tons)	144398.10
4. 生活CDD排放量（吨）	Volume of Life CDD emissions (tons)	25452.17
5. 生活氨氮产生量（吨）	Volume of Ammonia and Nitrogen in Urban Domestic Sewage Produced (tons)	18700.74
6. 生活氨氮排放量（吨）	Volume of Ammonia and Nitrogen in Urban Domestic Sewage Discharged (tons)	2886.24
7. 二氧化硫排放量（吨）	Volume of Domestic and Other Sulphur Dioxide Emission (tons)	42635.73
8. 氨氮化物排放量（吨）	Volume of Ammonia and Nitrogen in Urban Domestic Sewage Discharged (tons)	7918.50
9. 烟尘排放量（吨）	Volume of Soot Emission (tons)	28214.82

注：本表数据来源于市环保局。

10-7 工业污染治理项目建设情况（2016年）

Condition of Anti-Industrial-Pollution Projects（2016）

指　标	Item	2016
一、工业企业数（个）	**Number of Industrial Enterprises (units)**	**27**
二、老工业污染源项目治理本年施工总数（个）	**The total number of construction projects of Old industrial pollution sources control this year(units)**	**25**
#工业废水治理项目	Treatment of Waste Water	3
工业废气治理项目	Treatment of Waste Gas	18
工业固体废物治理项目	Treatmen of Solid Wastes	2
三、老工业污染源项目治理本年竣工总数（个）	**The Total Number of Old Industrial Pollution Control Projects Completed this year(units)**	**20**
#工业废水治理项目	Treatment of Waste Water	1
工业废气治理项目	Treatment of Waste Gas	15
工业固体废物治理项目	Treatmen of Solid Wastes	2
四、老工业污染源治理项目本年完成投资（万元）	**Investment completed in Old industrial pollution control projects this Year(10 000 yuan)**	**18040.58**
#废水治理项目	Treatment of Waste Water	395.78
废气治理项目	Treatment of Waste Gas	17511.05
固体废物治理项目	Treatmen of Solid Wastes	65
五、老工业污染源治理项目本年投资来源（万元）	**Source of Investment in Old industrial pollution control projects this Year(10 000 yuan)**	18040.58
#排污费补助	Pollution Charges Subsidies	
政府其他补助	Other Government Subsidies	831.06
企业自筹	Self-raising Funds	17209.52
#银行贷款	Lonans	7569.00
六、“三同时”项目竣工验收数（个）	**number of "Three simultaneous"project completion and acceptance (a)**	**12**
七、“三同时”竣工验收项目实际环保投资（万元）	**"Three simultaneous" actual environmental investment completed and accepted (10 000 yuan)**	**8201.05**
八、“三同时”项目废水治理新增处理能力（万吨/日）	**"Three simultaneous"Add processing capacity of wastewater treatment (10 000 tons / day)**	**0.418**
九、“三同时”项目废气治理新增处理能力（万立方米/时）	**"Three simultaneous"Add processing capacity of Exhaust treatment (10 000 cu.m/h)**	**82.38**

注：本表数据来源于市环保局。

“三同时”指建设项目中防治污染的措施，必须与主体工程同时设计，同时施工，同时投产使用。

10-8 各区县、开发区环境保护基本情况（2016年）

区县、开发区	Region	本年完成环保验收项目环保投资额（万元）Investment Completed in accepted Environmental projects this year (10 000 yuan)	工业二氧化硫排放量（吨）Volume of Industrial Sulphur Dioxide Discharged (tons)
全　市	**Total**	**536894.96**	**4913.89**
新城区	Xincheng	3625.80	3.41
碑林区	Beilin	12563.00	86.61
莲湖区	Lianhu	1144.30	35.78
灞桥区	Baqiao	14191.80	510.98
未央区	Weiyang	84382.66	142.49
雁塔区	Yanta	2321.10	501.16
阎良区	Yanliang	2374.80	392.50
临潼区	Lintong	7725.32	244.30
长安区	Chang'an	5431.70	704.22
高陵区	Gaoling	8342.10	171.66
蓝田县	Lantian	822.00	189.96
周至县	Zhouzhi	2666.57	141.17
户　县	Huxian	3522.50	315.05
高新开发区	Gaoxinkaifaqu	39236.90	772.46
经济开发区	Jingjikaifaqu	28912.70	269.22
航天基地	Hangtianjidi	4569.80	215.15
沣东新城	Fendongxincheng	7827.43	217.78

注：本表数据来源于市环保局。
环境统计中污水处理厂个数包含部分大学园区及部分大型小区的污水处理厂。
区县、开发区环保验收项目环保投资额未包括市本级完成数。

Condition of Environment Protection by Regions （2016）

工业化学需氧量排放量 （吨） Volume of COD Removed (tons)	垃圾处理站数 （座） Number of Rubbish Disposal Works (units)	污水处理厂数 （个） Number of Sewage Treatment Works (units)
1415.53	**3**	**38**
69.17		
19.60		
93.91		2
80.09	1	4
57.45		6
56.74		3
100.20	1	1
50.89		3
85.57		8
94.47	1	1
10.16		3
25.42		1
336.20		3
162.32		1
78.98		1
43.70		1
50.66		

主要统计指标解释

工业用水 指工矿企业在生产过程中用于制造、加工、冷却、空调、净化、洗涤等方面的用水，按新水取用量计，不包括企业内部的重复利用水量。

工业废水排放量 指经过企业厂区所有排放口排到企业外部的工业废水量。包括生产废水、外排的直接冷却水、超标排放的矿井地下水和与工业废水混排的厂区生活污水，不包括外排的间接冷却水（清污不分流的间接冷却水应计算在内）。

直接排入海的 指经企业位于海边的排放口，直接排入海的废水量。直接排放指废水经过工厂的排污口直接排入海，而未经过城市下水道或其他中间体，也不受其他水体的影响。

工业废水排放达标量 指报告期内废水中各项污染物指标都达到国家或地方排放标准的外排工业废水量，包括未经处理外排达标的，经废水处理设施处理后达标排放的，以及经污水处理厂处理后达标排放的。

生活污水排放量 指城镇居民每年排放的生活污水。用人均系数法测算。测算公式为：

$$\frac{\text{生活污水}}{\text{排放量}} = \frac{\text{城镇生活污水}}{\text{排放系数}} \times \frac{\text{市镇非}}{\text{农业人口}} \times 365$$

生活污水中化学需氧量（COD）排放量 指城镇居民每年排放的生活污水中的COD的量。用人均系数法测算。测算公式为：

$$\frac{\text{城镇生活污水中}}{\text{COD产生系数}} = \frac{\text{城镇牛活污水}}{\text{中COD排放量}} \times \frac{\text{市镇非}}{\text{农业人口}} \times 365$$

化学需氧量（COD） 指用化学氧化剂氧化水中有机污染物时所需的氧量。COD值越高，表示水中有机污染物污染越重。

工业废气排放量 指报告期内企业厂区内燃料燃烧和生产工艺过程中产生的各种排入大气的含有污染物的气体的总量，以标准状态（273K，101325Pa）计算。测算公式为：

$$\frac{\text{工业废气}}{\text{排放量}} = \frac{\text{燃料燃烧过程}}{\text{中废气排放量}} + \frac{\text{生产工艺过程}}{\text{中废气排放量}}$$

生活及其他SO_2排放量 以生活及其他煤炭消费量和其含硫量为基础，根据以下公式计算：

$$\frac{\text{生活及其他}}{SO_2\text{排放量}} = \frac{\text{生活及其他}}{\text{煤炭消费量}} \times \text{含硫量} \times 0.8 \times 2$$

工业SO_2排放量 指报告期内企业在燃料燃烧和生产工艺过程中排入大气的SO_2总量，计算公式为：

$$\frac{\text{工业}SO_2}{\text{排放量}} = \frac{\text{燃料燃烧过程}}{\text{中}SO_2\text{排放量}} + \frac{\text{生产工艺过程}}{\text{中}SO_2\text{排放量}}$$

工业烟尘排放量 指企业厂区内燃料燃烧过程中产生的烟气中夹带的颗粒物排放量。

生活及其他烟尘排放量 指除工业生产活动以外的所有社会、经济活动及公共设施的经营活动中燃烧所排放的烟尘纯重量。以生活及其他煤炭消费量为基础进行测算。

工业粉尘排放量 指企业在生产工艺过程中排放的能在空气中悬浮一定时间的固体颗粒物排放量。如钢铁企业的耐火材料粉尘、焦化企业的筛焦系统粉尘、烧结机的粉尘、石灰窑的粉尘、建材企业的水泥粉尘等。不包括电厂排入大气的烟尘。

工业固体废物产生量 指报告期内企业在生产过程中产生的固体状、半固体状和高浓度液体状废弃物的总量，包括危险废物、冶炼废渣、粉煤灰、炉渣、煤矸石、尾矿、放射性废物和其他废物等；不包括矿山开采的剥离废石和掘进废石（煤矸石和呈酸性或碱性的废石除外）。酸性或碱性废石指采掘的废石其流经水、雨淋水的pH值小于4或pH值大于10.5者。

危险废物 指列入国家危险废物名录或根据国家规定的危险废物鉴别标准和鉴别方法认定的，具有爆炸性、易燃性、易氧化性、毒性、腐蚀性、易传染疾病等危险特性之一的废物。

工业固体废物综合利用量 指报告期内企业通过回收、加工、循环、交换等方式，从固体废物中提取或者使其转化为可以利用的资源、能源和其他原材料的固体废物量（包括当年利用往年的工业固体废物贮存量），如用作农业肥料、生产建筑材料、筑路等。综合利用量由原产生固体废物的单位统计。

工业固体废物综合利用率 指工业固体废物综合利用量占丁业固体废物产生量（包括综合利用往年贮存量）的百分率。计算公式为：

$$\text{工业固体废物综合利用率}=\frac{\text{工业固体废物综合利用量}}{\text{工业固体废物产生量}+\text{综合利用往年贮存量}}\times 100\%$$

工业固体废物贮存量 指报告期内企业以综合利用或处置为目的，将固体废物暂时贮存或堆存在专设的贮存设施或专设的集中堆存场所内的数量。专设的固体废物贮存场所或贮存设施必须有防扩散、防流失、防渗漏、防止污染大气、水体的措施。

工业固体废物处置量 指报告期内企业将固体废物焚烧或者最终置于符合环境保护规定要求的场所，并不再回取的工业固体废物量（包括当年处置往年的工业固体废物贮存量）。处置方式有填埋（其中危险废物应安全填埋）、焚烧、专业贮存场（库）封场处理、深层灌注、回填矿井及海洋处置（经海洋管理部门同意投海处置）等。

工业固体废物排放量 指报告期内企业将所产生的固体废物排到固体废物污染防治设施、场所以外的数量，不包括矿山开采的剥离废石和掘进废石（煤矸石和呈酸性或碱性的废石除外）。

“三废”综合利用产品产值 指报告期内利用“三废”作为主要原料生产的产品价值（现行价）；已经销售或准备销售的应计算产品价值，留作生产自用的不应计算产品价值。

生活垃圾清运量 指报告期内收集和运送到各生活垃圾处理厂（场）和生活垃圾最终消纳点的生活垃圾数量。生活垃圾指城市日常生活或为城市日常生活提供服务的活动中产生的固体废物以及法律行政规定的视为城市生活垃圾的固体废物。包括：居民生活垃圾、商业垃圾、集市贸易市场垃圾、街道清扫垃圾、公共场所垃圾和机关、学校、厂矿等单位的生活垃圾。

生活垃圾无害化处理率 指报告期生活垃圾无害化处理量与生活垃圾产生量的比率。在统计上，由于生活垃圾产生量不易取得，可用清运量代替。计算公式为：

$$\text{生活垃圾无害化处理率}=\frac{\text{生活垃圾无害化处理量}}{\text{生活垃圾产生量}}\times 100\%$$

Explanatory Notes on Main Statistical Indicators

Water Use by Industry refers to new withdrawals of water, excluding reuse of water within enterprises.

Waste Water Discharged by Industry refers to the volume of waste water discharged by industrial enterprises through all their outlets, including waste water from production process, directly cooled water, groundwater from mining wells which does not meet discharge standards and sewage from households mixed with waste water produced by industrial activities, but excluding indirectly cooled water discharged (It should be included if the discharge is not separated from waste water).

Waste Water Directly Discharged into Sea refers to the volume of waste water directly discharged into sea through outlets of enterprises situated by sea without going through municipal sewerage networks or any other intermediates or being affected by any other water bodies.

Industrial Waste Water Meeting Discharge Standards refers to volume of industrial waste water discharge which, with or without treatment, reaches national or local standards with regard to all pollutants.

Urban Non-industrial Waste Water Discharge refers to annual discharge of non-industrial waste water by urban households. It is estimated by per capita coefficient using the formula:

$$\text{Urban non-industrial waste water discharge} = \text{urban non-industrial waste water discharge coefficient} \times \text{urban non-alagricultur population} \times 365$$

Volume of Chemical Oxygen Demand (COD) Generated by Urban Non-industrial Waster Water refers to chemical oxygen demand generated through the annual discharge of non-industrial waste water by urban households. It is estimated as:

$$\text{Volume of chemical oxygen demand (cod) generated by urban non-industrial waster water} = \text{Coefficient of COD generated through urban non-industrial waste water} \times \text{urban non-agricultural population} \times 365$$

Chemical Oxygen Demand (COD) refers to the amount of oxygen required when chemical oxidants are used to oxidize organic pollutants in water. A higher value of COD corresponds to more serious pollution by organic pollutants.

Industrial Waste Air Emission refers to the discharge into atmosphere of waste air containing pollutants generated from fuel burning and production processes in enterprises within a given period of time. It is calculated at standard status (273K, 101325Pa) as:

$$\text{Industrial waste air emission} = \text{tnoissimehrough fuel burning} + \text{tnoissimehrough production process}$$

SO_2 Emission through Non-industrial and Other Activities is calculated on the basis of consumption of coal by households and other activities and the sulphur content of coal with the following formula:

$$SO_2\ \text{emission through non-industrial and other activities} = \text{of coalby households andother activities} \times \text{sulphur content} \times 0.8 \times 2$$

SO_2 Emission through Industrial Activities refers to volume of sulphur dioxide emission from fuel burning and production process by enterprises during a given period of time. It is calculated as:

$$SO_2\ \text{emission through industrial activities} = SO_2\text{emIssIon from fuel burning} + SO_2\ \text{emission from production process}$$

Industrial Soot Emission refers to the volume of soot in smoke emitted in the process of fuel burning in the premises of enterprises.

Soot Emission by Consumption and Others refers to the net volume of soot emitted by fuel burning from all social and economic activities and operations of public facilities other than industrial activities. It is calculated on the basis of coal consumption by households and others.

Industrial Dust Emission refers to volume of dust emitted by production process of enterprises and suspended in the air for a given period of time, including dust from refractory material of iron and steel works, dust from coke-screening systems and sintering machines of coke plants, dust from lime kilns and dust from cement production in building material enterprises, but excluding soot and dust emitted from power plants.

Industrial Solid Wastes Produced refers to total volume of solid, semi-solid and high concentration liquid residues produced by industrial enterprises from production process in a given period of time, including hazardous wastes, slag, coal ash, gangue, tailings, radioactive residues and other wastes, but excluding stones stripped or dug out in mining - gangue and acid or alkaline stones not included (a stone is acid or alkaline according to the pH value of the water being below 4 or above 10.5 when the stone is in, or soaked by water).

Hazardous Wastes refers to those included in the national hazardous wastes catalogue or specified as any one of the following properties in the national hazardous wastes identification standards: explosive, ignitable, oxidizable, toxic, corrosive or liable to cause infectious diseases or lead to other dangers.

Industrial Solid Wastes Utilized refers to volume of solid wastes from which useful materials can be extracted or which can be converted into usable resources, energy or other materials by means of reclamation, processing, recycling and exchange (including utilizing in the year the stocks of industrial solid wastes of the previous year). Examples of such utilizations include fertilizers, building materials and road materials. The information shall be collected by the producing units of the wastes.

Rate of Utilization of Industrial Solid Wastes refers to the percentage of industrial solid wastes utilized over industrial solid wastes produced (including stocks of the previous years). It is calculated as:

$$\text{Rate of utilization of industrial solid wastes} = \frac{\text{volume of industrial solid wastes utilized}}{\text{industrial solid wastes produced} + \text{stock of previous years}} \times 100\%$$

Stock of Industrial Solid Wastes refers to the volume of solid wastes placed in special facilities or special sites for purposes of utilization or disposal. The sites or facilities should take measures against dispersion, loss, seepage, and air and water contamination.

Industrial Solid Wastes Disposed refers to the quantity of industrial solid wastes which are burnt or placed ultimately in the sites meeting the requirements for environmental protection and not salvaged or recycled (including disposition in the year of those wastes of previous years). The disposition includes landfill (Safe landfills should be conducted for hazardous wastes), incineration, containment spaces, deep underground disposal, backfill in mining pits and disposal at sea.

Industrial Solid Wastes Discharged refers to the volume of industrial solid wastes discharged by producing enterprises to disposal facilities or to other sites. The wastes exclude stones stripped or dug from mining (gangue and acid or alkaline waste stones not included).

Output Value of Products Made from Waste Gas, Waste Water and Solid Wastes refers to the current value of products with waste gas, waste water and solid wastes as main materials of production. Products sold and ready to sell shall be included while those produced for own use shall not be included.

Consumption Wastes Transported refers to volume of consumption wastes collected and transported to disposal factories or sites. Consumption wastes are solid wastes produced from urban households or from service activities for urban households, and solid wastes regarded by laws and regulations as urban consumption wastes, including those from households, commercial activities, markets, cleaning of streets, public sites, offices, schools, factories, mining units and other sources.

Ratio of Consumption Wastes Treated refers to consumption wastes treated over that produced. In practical statistics, as it is difficult to estimate, the volume of consumption wastes produced is replaced with that transported. It is calculated as:

$$\text{Ratio of consumption wastes treated} = \frac{\text{consumption wastes treated}}{\text{consumption wastes produced}} \times 100\%$$

11 农 业

AGRICULTURE

资料整理：张喜兰　马秋娟　薛　丰
Data management：Zhang Xilan　Ma Qiujuan　Xue Feng
数据审核：王明珠
Data audit：Wang Mingzhu

第十一部分　农业

一、简要说明

本章资料主要包括农村基本情况、农业生产条件与生产情况、耕地、农林牧渔及服务业产值、主要农产品产量以及各区县农业生产和农村经济效益主要指标，由西安市统计局农村处提供。

二、主要指标

年末常用耕地面积（万亩）	346.80	比上年下降	2.8%
农林牧渔及服务业总产值（亿元）	405.63	比上年增长	4.2%
农作物播种面积（万亩）	659.04	比上年下降	2.4%
粮食产量（万吨）	175.33	比上年下降	3.1%

11 AGRICULTURE

Ⅰ.Brief Introduction

Data in this chapter reflects basic condition of agriculture production of Xi'an city. It is primarily consist of basic condition of rural area, condition of agriculture production, plow land, production value of farming, forestry, animal husbandry and fishery, gross yield of primary produce and primary indicators of agriculture production and rural area economic performance. The data are provided and compiled by Rural Area Division of the Xi'an Bureau of Statistics.

Ⅱ.Major Indicators

		Increase over Preceding Year
Cultivated Area Year-end(10 000 mu)	346.80	–2.8%
Gross Output Value of Farming, Forestry, Animal Husbandry, Fishery and Service(100 mil. Yuan)	405.63	4.2%
Sown Area of Crops(10 000 mu)	659.04	–2.4%
Grain Output(10 000 tons)	175.33	–3.1%

11-1 主要年份农村基层组织、乡村户数、人口及劳动力情况

Grassroots Organizations in Rural Areas, Rural Households, Population and Labor Force in Representative Years

指　标	Item	2005	2006	2007	2008	2009	2010
一、乡村户数（万户）	**Rural Households(10000 households)**	**101.50**	**102.35**	**100.85**	**101.02**	**101.00**	**101.43**
二、农村人口和从业人员情况	**Condition of Rural Population and Employment**						
1.乡村劳动力资源总数（万人）	Total Rural Labor Force (10000 persons)	255.93	257.66	254.06	256.17	255.00	256.36
2.乡村从业人员数（万人）	Number of Rural Workers (10000 persons)	223.30	225.99	222.09	223.85	223.13	225.04
#女性	Female	103.22	103.87	101.83	103.11	102.76	103.25
#农业	Agricultural	137.69	135.64	131.96	126.46	121.78	116.58
三、自来水受益村数（个）	**The Number of Tap Water Villages (unit)**	**1756**	**1794**	**1881**	**1934**	**2058**	**2184**
四、通汽车村数（个）	**The Number of Villages with Bus Service (unit)**	**2952**	**2923**	**2973**	**2996**	**2989**	**2989**
五、通电话村数（个）	**The Number of Villages with Telephone Service (unit)**	**3101**	**3113**	**3129**	**3086**	**3071**	**3052**

11-1 续表 continued

指　标	Item	2011	2012	2013	2014	2015	2016
一、乡村户数（万户）	**Rural Households(10000 households)**	**102.59**	**101.92**	**101.37**	**99.26**	**92.77**	**92.63**
二、农村人口和从业人员情况	**Condition of Rural Population and Employment**						
1.乡村劳动力资源总数（万人）	Total Rural Labor Force (10000 persons)	260.97	259.06	257.96	252.40	230.21	230.62
2.乡村从业人员数（万人）	Number of Rural Workers (10000 persons)	230.56	226.92	222.67	216.33	200.38	204.11
#女性	Female	109.61	107.63	106.70	104.03	96.46	98.10
#农业	Agricultural	116.15	113.29	108.48	110.30	105.10	102.32
三、自来水受益村数（个）	**The Number of Tap Water Villages (unit)**	**2400**	**2545**	**2650**	**2765**	**2718**	**2507**
四、通汽车村数（个）	**The Number of Villages with Bus Service (unit)**	**2978**	**2936**	**2927**	**2186**	**2209**	
五、通电话村数（个）	**The Number of Villages with Telephone Service (unit)**	**3033**	**2974**	**2966**	**2536**	**2593**	

11-2 各区县乡村从业人员数（2016年）

Number of Rural Employees by Region（2016）

单位：万人 （10 000 persons）

区 县	Region	乡村劳动力资源总数 Total rural labor force	乡村从业人员数合计 Total number of employees in rural areas	女性从业人员 Female employees	农林牧渔业 Forestry Animal Husbandry and Fishery
合 计	**Total**	**230.62**	**204.11**	**98.10**	**102.32**
新城区	Xingcheng				
碑林区	Beilin				
莲湖区	Lianhu				
灞桥区	Baqiao	18.34	14.44	6.05	4.83
未央区	Weiyang	6.71	2.55	1.24	0.51
雁塔区	Yanta				
阎良区	Yanliang	11.06	9.99	4.77	5.90
临潼区	Lintong	36.56	32.14	15.29	19.14
长安区	Chang'an	40.08	43.35	19.11	21.51
高陵区	Gaoling	9.80	8.19	3.88	2.82
蓝田县	Lantian	34.42	32.56	20.77	13.68
周至县	Zhouzhi	40.21	32.35	13.65	18.13
户 县	Huxian	33.44	28.54	13.34	15.80

11-3 主要年份耕地面积

Area of Cultivated Land in Representative Years

单位：万亩 (10 000 mu)

年 份 Year	年末常用耕地面积 Cultivated Area Year-end	水田 Paddy Field	水浇地 Irrigable Land
1970	554.09	18.20	297.05
1975	538.35	20.34	349.13
1978	530.96	16.70	370.46
1980	526.29	17.45	372.96
1985	508.88	17.63	328.10
1990	495.32	17.97	311.91
1991	492.09	17.03	309.17
1992	485.30	16.44	298.19
1993	479.04	14.36	304.49
1994	471.44	13.98	299.58
1995	463.97	17.04	278.01
1996	451.50	14.21	283.76
1997	456.62	11.90	290.49
1998	455.15	11.18	282.23
1999	450.74	11.31	281.96
2000	443.37	10.26	284.04
2001	431.69	9.00	274.73
2002	424.46	7.98	275.96
2003	413.84	6.65	263.75
2004	404.87	6.59	254.04
2005	400.17	5.55	254.04
2006	395.79	5.33	263.75
2007	391.77	4.80	255.95
2008	390.77	4.64	255.36
2009	387.89	4.39	260.71
2010	383.32	4.03	257.43
2011	377.10	3.80	253.46
2012	369.91	3.32	248.97
2013	366.23	5.33	263.75
2014	360.73	2.42	237.26
2015	356.89	2.37	228.14
2016	346.80	0.96	223.91

11-4 各区县耕地面积（2016年）

单位：亩

区 县	Region	年末常用耕地面积 Cultivated Area Year-end	水田 Paddy Field	旱地 Dry Land	水浇地 Irrigable Land
合 计	**Total**	**3467987**	**9555**	**3458432**	**2239138**
新城区	Xincheng				
碑林区	Beilin				
莲湖区	Lianhu				
灞桥区	Baqiao	78628		78628	57316
未央区	Weiyang	6067		6067	2475
雁塔区	Yanta				
阎良区	Yanliang	231857		231857	222643
临潼区	Lintong	688893		688893	526928
长安区	Chang'an	590323	7715	582608	297220
高陵区	Gaoling	224893		224893	224893
蓝田县	Lantian	592100	400	591700	46050
周至县	Zhouzhi	493216	830	492386	361463
户 县	Huxian	562010	610	561400	500150

Area of Cultivated Land by Region（2016）

(mu)

当年增加的耕地面积 Area of Newly Increased Cultivated Land	新开荒地面积 Area of Newly Reclamation of Wasteland	当年减少的耕地面积 Decrease in Cultivated Area in the Year	国家基建占地 Capital Construction	退耕改果、茶、桑面积 Area for Change into Fruit, Tea and Mulberry	退耕造林面积 Area for Change into Woods
13270	**5390**	**107647**	**31573**		**3191**
5224		57224	11375		7
130	130	6562	6141		
		315	290		
		4908	4256		
4444	4344	21700	6828		1348
		1250	1056		
		3000			1600
3427	916	11834	1443		236
45		854	184		

11-5 主要年份农业机械拥有量（年末数）

指标	Item	2006	2007	2008
农用机械总动力（千瓦）	Total Power of Agricultural Machinery(kw)	2277584	2348856	2712616
大中型拖拉机（台）	Large and Medium Tractors(unit)	8963	10431	11092
小型拖拉机（台）	Mini-tractors(unit)	23437	21555	19036
大中型拖拉机配套农具（台）	Number of Large and Medium Tractor Towing Farm Machinery(unit)	18724	23487	25125
小型拖拉机配套农具（台）	Mini-Tractor Towing Farm Machinery (unit)	30439	28780	26984
农用排灌柴油机（台）	Agricultural Diesel Engines(unit)	3547	2709	2670
农用排灌电动机（台）	Agricultural Motors(unit)	76614	84416	85349
农用水泵（台）	Agricultural Water Pump(unit)	73039	80722	80462
节水灌溉类机械（套）	Equipment in Water-saving Irrigation(set)	2656	1991	1728
联合收割机（台）	Combine Harvesters(unit)	5026	5294	5390
自走式机动割晒机（台）	Self-propelled Motorized Swather(unit)	1342	4918	2174
机动脱粒机（台）	Motorized Huller (unit)	5806	11585	23781
农用运输车（辆）	Agricultual Transporter(unit)	50395	49576	54860

注：本表数据来源于市农林委。

Possession of Agricultural Machinery

in Representative Years（Number of year-end）

2009	2010	2011	2012	2013	2014	2015	2016
2616053	2677334	2890247	2983979	3108354	3203302	3253733	2615435
11479	14675	12585	12987	12927	9946	9652	10177
18406	14194	13008	11471	8971	7538	8447	9175
26575	29215	36209	32166	32662	31451	32602	38833
29039	24393	29624	27869	25853	21806	21518	20972
2691	3309	2639	2891	2509	2409	2409	1772
83243	79462	87461	87056	86216	85244	84975	84734
80174	77367	75426	80982	80575	79849	79695	79681
1799	1710	1733	2106	2218	2562	2517	2476
6155	6718	7854	8502	9114	7815	8144	8458
1220	208	187					
11960	13231	13407	14493	14700	14749	14504	14272
50671	51665	51838	51850	51710	51410	51365	

11-6 各区县农业机械拥有量（2016年）

指标	Item	西安市 Xi' an	灞桥区 Baqiao	未央区 Weiyang
农用机械总动力（千瓦）	Total Power of Agricultural Machinery(kw)	2615435	150471	47552
大中型拖拉机（台）	Large and Medium Tractors(unit)	10177	120	19
小型拖拉机（台）	Mini-tractors(unit)	9175	108	
大中型拖拉机配套农具（台）	Number of Large and Medium Tractor Towing Farm Machinery(unit)	38833	318	57
小型拖拉机配套农具（台）	Mini-Tractor Towing Farm Machinery (unit)	20972	132	57
农用排灌柴油机（台）	Agricultural Diesel Engines(unit)	1772		
农用排灌电动机（台）	Agricultural Motors(unit)	84734	3057	934
农用水泵（台）	Agricultural Water Pump(unit)	79681	2927	757
节水灌溉类机械（套）	Equipment in Water-saving Irrigation(set)	2476	55	90
联合收割机（台）	Combine Harvesters(unit)	8458	86	6
自走式机动割晒机（台）	Self-propelled Motorized Swather(unit)			
机动脱粒机（台）	Motorized Huller (unit)	14272	50	6

注：本表数据来源于市农林委。

Possession of Agricultural Machinery by Region (2016)

	雁塔区 Yanta	阎良区 Yanliang	临潼区 Lintong	长安区 Chang'an	高陵区 Gaoling	蓝田县 Lantian	周至县 Zhouzhi	户 县 Huxian
	62016	165476	466695	444945	208893	248644	337537	483206
	35	852	1677	1628	1448	1146	1483	1769
	7	238	212	1097	163	861	4712	1777
	70	2129	8159	7723	5680	6519	2101	6077
	26	522	3783	2754	670	2421	7161	3446
			73	714		652	277	56
	520	5952	16974	22406	3760	3147	15249	12735
	500	5796	16460	16823	3760	2486	17437	12735
		483	142	1267		63	227	149
	16	656	2286	1410	630	384	353	2631
		1121	4948	982	545	1815	2431	2374

11-7 主要年份农业机械化、化肥、水利、水电情况

指标	Item	2000	2005	2006
一、农业机械化水平（万亩）	**Statistics on Agricultural Machinery (10 000 mu)**			
当年机械耕地面积（实际）	Area Ploughed by Tractors	366.81	360.68	354.05
当年机械播种面积（作业）	Seeded Area by Tractors	482.74	485.62	519
当年机械收获面积（作业）	Harvest Area by Tractors	272.83	271.77	280.88
二、农用化肥施用量（吨）	**Use of Agricultural Fertilizers and Insecticides(ton)**			
1. 按实物量计算合计	Practicality Consumption	697243	749802	759882
氮肥	Nitrogenous Fertilizer	392366	411161	413514
磷肥	Phosphate Fertilizer	155480	161444	164781
钾肥	Potash Fertilizer	31841	34114	31414
复合肥	Compound Fertilizer	78620	115458	121124
2. 按折纯法计算合计	Standard Consumption	196343	211790	216093
氮肥	Nitrogenous Fertilizer	102982	107645	110137
磷肥	Phosphate Fertilizer	18658	19368	19772
钾肥	Potash Fertilizer	15921	17055	15709
复合肥	Compound Fertilizer	39313	57009	59731
三、农用塑料薄膜使用量（公斤）	**Plastic Sheet for Agricultural Use(kg)**	**1622198**	**1855383**	**1931527**
四、农用柴油使用量（吨）	**Diesel Oil for Agricultural Use (ton)**	**52706**	**50832**	**49686**
五、农药使用量（公斤）	**Pesticide (kg)**	**1559333**	**1427879**	**1471672**
六、农村水利化情况（万亩）	**Irrigation and Water Conservancy (10 000 mu)**			
有效灌溉面积	Effective Irrigation Area	335.97	280.1	276.58
旱涝保收面积	Stable-Harvesting Arable Land	294.06	255.37	253.66
机电排灌面积	Electrical Irrigation Area	249.11	223.74	214.03
七、农村电气化情况	**Rural electrization**			
乡村及村以下办水电站（个）	Hydropower Station in Rural Areas(unit)	67	79	79
装机容量（千瓦）	Installed Power Generation Capacity(kw)	7236	13775	14252
发电量（万千瓦小时）	Generating Capacity (10 000 kwh)	1137.95	2239	2253
已配套机电井（眼）	Electricity Powered Well(unit)	50289	46505	46112

注：本表部分数据来源于市农林委。

Agricultural Machinery,Chemical Fertilizers,Water Conservancy, Hydropower in Representative Years

2007	2008	2009	2010	2011	2012	2013	2014	2015	2016
361.62	404.42	413.7	367.32	427.03	425.4	425.21	549.07	533.21	518.07
521.36	539.81	544.86	548.28	507.55	529.99	523.15	509.58	492.9	499.36
296.06	313.11	342.82	403.5	413.93	428.28	443.57	466.21	474.1	488.85
762401	767980	776319	781072	785885	807900	794361	820315	810849	771144
408847	413397	414481	397975	398395	414339	401140	412544	408396	374476
160932	157145	153825	152943	151005	151967	152565	156662	157601	152278
34284	34149	33069	37715	38195	43356	39630	42504	46284	46388
124784	132481	142137	158062	163797	198238	201026	208605	198568	198002
220251	225949	230299	235532	239497	243281	239701	251217	246284	242871
109484	112000	112275	108868	110412	113662	109497	116055	108833	111150
19311	18855	18457	18315	18026	18061	18023	18505	18584	18033
17141	17077	16534	17997	18095	21267	18973	20110	21986	21779
62398	66247	71042	78811	81764	90291	93208	96547	96881	91909
2096169	**2122310**	**2141969**	**2450496**	**2533372**	**2683201**	**2678745**	**2657870**	**2770750**	**2880480**
50137	**51097**	**51346**	**61917**	**61637**	**57451**	**62563**	**74935**	**59360**	**55982**
1444867	**1465819**	**1325459**	**1243105**	**1242773**	**1252490**	**1210060**	**1220638**	**1174883**	**1126305**
276.28	274.48	273.17	281.28	262.32	267.84	240.22	248.34	244.72	259.78
247.99	249.31	247.6	234.15	214.62	211.31	196.96	189.69	188.5	201.7
210.51	211.01	213.42	224.6	200.36	198.66	229.29	230.58	239.63	
76	76	75	44	44	46	46	48	48	
24827	24827	25047	22325	22325	78848	80433	80633	80423	
10085	10477	10678	7268	7268	26447	19613	25526.08		
45783	47032	46790	44310	40345	33959				

11-8 各区县农业机械化、化肥、水利、水电情况（2016年）

指标	Item	西安市 Xi'an	灞桥区 Baqiao	未央区 Weiyang
一、农业机械化水平（万亩）	**Statistics on Agricultural Machinery (10 000 mu)**			
当年机械耕地面积（实际）	Area Ploughed by Tractors	518.07	18.10	
当年机械播种面积（作业）	Seeded Area by Tractors	499.36	13.20	
当年机械收获面积（作业）	Harvest Area by Tractors	488.85	18.00	
二、农用化肥施用量（吨）	**Use of Agricultural Fertilizers and Insecticides(ton)**			
1. 按实物量计算合计	Practicality Consumption	771144	18999	1283
氮肥	Nitrogenous Fertilizer	374476	6824	470
磷肥	Phosphate Fertilizer	152278	1158	304
钾肥	Potash Fertilizer	46388	1820	133
复合肥	Compound Fertilizer	198002	9197	376
2.按折纯法计算合计	Standard Consumption	242871	7645	281
氮肥	Nitrogenous Fertilizer	111150	3142	85
磷肥	Phosphate Fertilizer	18033	141	28
钾肥	Potash Fertilizer	21779	911	64
复合肥	Compound Fertilizer	91909	3451	104
三、农用塑料薄膜使用量（公斤）	**Plastic Sheet for Agricultural Use(kg)**	**2880480**	**166740**	**57400**
四、农用柴油使用量（吨）	**Diesel Oil for Agricultural Use (ton)**	**55982**	**529**	**700**
五、农药使用量（公斤）	**Pesticide (kg)**	**1126305**	**24755**	**2215**
六、农村水利化情况（万亩）	**Irrigation and Water Conservancy (10 000 mu)**			
有效灌溉面积	Effective Irrigation Area	259.78	11.76	1.50
旱涝保收面积	Stable-Harvesting Arable Land	201.70	0.65	2.10
机电排灌面积	Electrical Irrigation Area			

注：本表部分数据来源于市农林委、水务局。

Agricultural Machinery,Chemical Fertilizers,Water Conservancy, Hydropower by Region（2016）

雁塔区 Yanta	阎良区 Yanliang	临潼区 Lintong	长安区 Chang'an	高陵区 Gaoling	蓝田县 Lantian	周至县 Zhouzhi	户　县 Huxian
	28.68	88.67	105.75	38.80	53.63	97.95	86.04
	23.71	98.50	103.35	40.08	63.00	71.40	86.04
	23.07	95.90	100.42	39.89	62.24	63.21	86.04
	71421	152032	80305	60932	122558	149564	114050
	32207	80826	36097	25429	64965	62560	65098
	14527	44723	15015	17154	25853	16024	17520
	6127	2868	8375	2849	8352	9152	6712
	18560	23615	20818	15500	23388	61828	24720
	25766	39949	21888	14005	46235	52778	34324
	12285	21339	8890	4322	28337	15365	17385
	1662	5367	1872	2058	2897	1923	2085
	2988	1434	3729	1425	3638	4576	3014
	8831	11809	7397	6200	11363	30914	11840
	1280000	**227810**	**101170**	**38450**	**305000**	**98910**	**605000**
	3106	**15323**	**9371**	**2546**	**9987**	**3350**	**11070**
	204145	**303129**	**109996**	**178543**	**74896**	**165536**	**63090**
	23.84	56.18	31.77	21.31	13.89	51.26	48.27
	24.56	48.76	20.76	21.55	1.87	31.21	50.24

11-9 主要年份农林牧渔及服务业总产值及指数

Gross Output Value of Farming,Forestry,Animal Husbandry,Fishery, Service and Related Indices in Representative Years

单位：万元　　　　(10 000 yuan)

年 份 Year	农林牧渔及服务总产值（现价） Gross Output Value (At current prices)	农业 Farming	林业 Forestry	牧业 Animal Husbandry	渔业 Fishery	农林牧渔服务业 Service of Farming, Forestry, Animal Husbandry and Fishery	指数（上年=100）（可比价） Indices(preceding year= 100) (At cinstant prices)
1970	40617	35965	713	3896	43		111.2
1975	55322	47378	1509	6403	32		93.9
1978	65423	56519	1444	7427	33		104.7
1980	65322	54004	1177	10106	35		85
1985	134933	105888	2559	26186	300		106.4
1990	262073	191088	3134	65840	2011		102.5
1991	295620	208324	3362	81070	2864		108.6
1992	321155	219160	4225	94045	3725		108.6
1993	387068	261959	5031	115810	4268		112.8
1994	565056	359609	7819	192140	5488		102.4
1995	754597	513348	7185	228598	5466		106.8
1996	786003	552726	7573	219214	6490		102.1
1997	836201	585973	9226	233623	7379		110.3
1998	853279	625465	8146	212045	7623		107.5
1999	739905	530029	8883	194552	6441		100.7
2000	743712	514845	8482	212612	7773		104.3
2001	767511	527160	8427	223861	8063		102.8
2002	797444	539978	11378	238761	7327		103
2003	837857	551398	10550	269610	6299		101.5
2004	967946	580798	12773	314517	6728	53130	108.4
2005	1065437	657262	13086	329856	7340	57893	107.7
2006	1141484	686748	15188	346626	7017	85905	107.2
2007	1341450	798163	15845	410213	9051	108178	105.3
2008	1682725	956549	19031	564095	11084	131966	107.8
2009	1787032	1061756	22663	546191	11830	144592	106.5
2010	2270994	1438934	26787	629376	12830	163067	107.4
2011	2726608	1729295	34453	754593	14856	193411	106.6
2012	3083562	1933149	62291	820392	19877	247853	106
2013	3428905	2173363	80199	863902	22773	288668	104.9
2014	3672101	2363649	86889	879515	24030	318018	105.1
2015	3807573	2444234	97776	887325	19519	358719	105.1
2016	4056321	2587519	102222	940934	19640	406006	104.2

11-10 主要年份农林牧渔及服务业总产值指数

Related Indices of Gross Output Value of Farming,Forestry,Animal Husbandry,Fishery and Service in Representative Years

年 份 Year	农林牧渔及服务业总产值指数（上年=100）（可比价） Indices(preceding year= 100) (At constant prices)	农业 Farming	林业 Forestry	牧业 Animal Husbandry	渔业 Fishery	农林牧渔服务业 Service of Farming, Forestry, Animal Husbandry and Fishery
2005	107.7	108.0	98.7	107.3	112.6	107.9
2006	107.2	106.0	102.5	109.3	104.5	109.4
2007	105.3	106.4	101.3	102.4	106.3	108.7
2008	107.8	107.9	112.2	106.0	100.5	113.7
2009	106.5	105.4	121.3	106.8	107.4	110.2
2010	107.4	108.7	115.2	104.3	92.7	108.9
2011	106.6	108.2	105.7	102.9	102.1	107.7
2012	106.0	105.6	143.0	104.8	113.4	108.5
2013	104.9	104.3	131.3	104.0	110.1	105.9
2014	105.1	105.8	105.7	103.2	106.0	105.9
2015	105.1	106.7	113.8	100.2	71.2	106.2
2016	104.2	104.8	114.7	100.6	100.1	106.6

11-11 主要年份农林牧渔及服务业总产值构成

Gross Output Value and Its Composition of Farming, Forestry, Animal Husbandry,Fishery and Service at Current Price in Representative Years

年 份 Year	农林牧渔及服务业总产值(%) Service of Farming, Forestry, Animal Husbandry and Fishery(%)	农业 Farming	林业 Forestry	牧业 Animal Husbandry	渔业 Fishery	农林牧渔服务业 Service of Farming, Forestry, Animal Husbandry and Fishery
2005	100	61.7	1.2	31.0	0.7	5.4
2006	100	60.9	1.3	31.5	0.6	5.7
2007	100	59.5	1.2	30.6	0.7	8.0
2008	100	56.9	1.1	33.5	0.7	7.8
2009	100	59.4	1.3	30.5	0.7	8.1
2010	100	63.3	1.2	27.7	0.6	7.2
2011	100	63.4	1.3	27.7	0.5	7.1
2012	100	62.7	2.0	26.6	0.7	8.0
2013	100	63.4	2.3	25.2	0.7	8.4
2014	100	64.4	2.4	24.0	0.7	8.5
2015	100	64.2	2.6	23.3	0.5	9.4
2016	100	63.8	2.5	23.2	0.5	10.0

11-12 各区县农林牧渔及服务业总产值（2016年）

Gross Output Value of Farming, Forestry, Animal Husbandry, Fishery and Service by Region (2016)

单位：万元 (10 000 yuan)

区县	Region	农林牧渔及服务业总产值 Gross Output Value	农业 Farming	林业 Forestry	牧业 Animal Husbandry	渔业 Fishery	农林牧渔服务业 Service of Farming, Forestry, Animal Husbandry and Fishery
合计	**Total**	**4056321**	**2587519**	**102222**	**940934**	**19640**	**406006**
新城区	Xincheng						
碑林区	Beilin						
莲湖区	Lianhu						
灞桥区	Baqiao	327061	254764	672	36352	847	34426
未央区	Weiyang	20405	8241	523	9649	274	1718
雁塔区	Yanta						
阎良区	Yanliang	381618	274488	639	68008	213	38270
临潼区	Lintong	569391	295636	2687	204479	6296	60293
长安区	Chang'an	621269	414912	12560	130891	8036	54870
高陵区	Gaoling	555928	311250	1378	182098	242	60960
蓝田县	Lantian	492519	302346	12790	131231	1463	44689
周至县	Zhouzhi	572627	393145	56023	77989	598	44872
户县	Huxian	515503	332737	14950	100237	1671	65908

11-13 各区县农林牧渔及服务业总产值指数和构成（2016年）

Gross Output Value and Its Composition of Farming, Forestry, Animal Husbandry,Fishery and Service at Current Price by Region (2016)

单位：%　　　　(%)

区　县	Region	农林牧渔及服务业总产值 Gross Output Value	农业 Farming	林业 Forestry	牧业 Animal Husbandry	渔业 Fishery	农林牧渔服务业 Service of Farming, Forestry, Animal Husbandry and Fishery
全市指数	**Total**	**104.2**	**104.8**	**114.7**	**100.6**	**100.1**	**106.6**
新城区	Xincheng						
碑林区	Beilin						
莲湖区	Lianhu						
灞桥区	Baqiao	104.0	106.2	57.7	93.2	58.3	104.9
未央区	Weiyang	91.8	92.0	232.8	95.0	69.3	65.3
雁塔区	Yanta						
阎良区	Yanliang	104.3	103.2	81.4	108.8	67.1	106.0
临潼区	Lintong	103.7	104.7	68.6	102.3	99.5	106.7
长安区	Chang'an	104.1	103.8	111.4	103.3	113.0	105.2
高陵区	Gaoling	104.9	104.3	76.2	102.1	71.2	119.6
蓝田县	Lantian	104.5	108.1	62.5	104.4	75.2	105.7
周至县	Zhouzhi	105.3	103.9	147.7	90.9	92.0	103.4
户　县	Huxian	104.4	105.0	127.8	97.6	152.8	106.1
全市构成	**Total**	**100.0**	**63.8**	**2.5**	**23.2**	**0.5**	**10.0**
新城区	Xincheng						
碑林区	Beilin						
莲湖区	Lianhu						
灞桥区	Baqiao	100.0	77.9	0.2	11.1	0.3	10.5
未央区	Weiyang	100.0	40.4	2.6	47.3	1.3	8.4
雁塔区	Yanta						
阎良区	Yanliang	100.0	71.9	0.2	17.8	0.1	10.0
临潼区	Lintong	100.0	51.9	0.5	35.9	1.1	10.6
长安区	Chang'an	100.0	66.8	2.0	21.1	1.3	8.8
高陵区	Gaoling	100.0	56.0	0.2	32.8		11.0
蓝田县	Lantian	100.0	61.4	2.6	26.6	0.3	9.1
周至县	Zhouzhi	100.0	68.7	9.8	13.6	0.1	7.8
户　县	Huxian	100.0	64.5	2.9	19.4	0.3	12.9

11-14 主要年份农林牧渔及服务业增加值

Value-Added of Farming, Forestry, Animal Husbandry, Fishery and Service in Representative Years

单位：万元 (10 000 yuan)

年 份 Year	农林牧渔及服务业增加值 Farming,Forestry, Animal Husbandry, Fishery and Service	农业 Farming	林业 Forestry	牧业 Animal Husbandry	渔业 Fishery	农林牧渔服务业 Service of Farming, Forestry, Animal Husbandry and Fishery
1995	413981	329662	4413	76746	3160	
1996						
1997						
1998						
1999						
2000	446481	336777	4323	101353	4028	
2001	458720	342427	4258	108096	3939	
2002	477691	351358	6419	116591	3323	
2003	458378	312849	5473	137236	2820	
2004	582009	393349	6811	164572	2919	14358
2005	660148	444320	6888	169701	3373	35866
2006	704427	465823	8556	177431	3227	49390
2007	825053	538794	8420	210930	4467	62442
2008	1034471	639071	10592	301305	5598	77905
2009	1103793	698043	11958	303594	5913	84285
2010	1400575	935489	14362	349204	6503	95017
2011	1731398	1161249	18807	428169	7679	115494
2012	1955931	1297824	33973	465476	10115	148543
2013	2177588	1459093	43740	490162	11589	173004
2014	2336074	1586842	47388	499021	12229	190594
2015	2416880	1632882	53533	505551	9986	214928
2016	2563772	1718635	56239	535111	10061	243726

11-15 主要年份农林牧渔及服务业增加值指数

Indices of Value-Added of Farming, Forestry, Animal Husbandry, Fishery and Service in Representative Years

年份 Year	农林牧渔及服务业增加值指数（上年=100）（可比价） Farming,Forestry,Animal Husbandry,Fishery and Service	农业 Farming	林业 Forestry	牧业 Animal Husbandry	渔业 Fishery	农林牧渔服务业 Service of Farming, Forestry, Animal Husbandry and Fishery
2008	107.6	107.6	112.0	105.8	100.0	114.0
2009	106.3	103.6	114.6	111.2	106.3	108.8
2010	106.9	107.9	108.7	104.3	94.0	108.9
2011	106.7	108.1	106.1	102.8	102.7	108.1
2012	106.0	105.6	142.8	104.8	113.4	108.5
2013	104.8	104.3	131.3	104.0	110.1	105.9
2014	105.2	105.8	104.1	103.2	106.0	105.9
2015	105.1	106.5	114.0	100.5	71.3	106.2
2016	104.1	104.5	112.6	100.5	100.3	106.9

11-16 各区县农林牧渔及服务业增加值（2016年）

Value-Added of Farming, Forestry, Animal Husbandry, Fishery and Service by Region（2016）

单位：万元 (10 000 yuan)

年份 Year	Region	农林牧渔及服务业增加值 Farming,Forestry, Animal Husbandry, Fishery and Service	农业 Farming	林业 Forestry	牧业 Animal Husbandry	渔业 Fishery	农林牧渔服务业 Service of Farming, Forestry, Animal Husbandry and Fishery
合　计	**Total**	**2563772**	**1718635**	**56239**	**535111**	**10061**	**243726**
新城区	Xincheng						
碑林区	Beilin						
莲湖区	Lianhu						
灞桥区	Baqiao	216618	172389	390	24285	304	19250
未央区	Weiyang	11677	5351	287	4939	42	1058
雁塔区	Yanta						
阎良区	Yanliang	249255	185295	362	39778	105	23715
临潼区	Lintong	344135	193396	1579	108320	2616	38224
长安区	Chang'an	417614	308759	7401	63541	5012	32901
高陵区	Gaoling	344501	196566	788	104881	67	42199
蓝田县	Lantian	302043	188361	7578	79216	745	26143
周至县	Zhouzhi	357199	255556	29378	46489	308	25468
户　县	Huxian	320730	212962	8476	63662	862	34768

11-17 各区县农林牧渔及服务业增加值指数（2016年）

Indices of Value-Added of Farming, Forestry, Animal Husbandry, Fishery and Service by Region（2016）

（上年=100）（可比价） (preceding year = 100) (At constant prices)

区 县 Region	农林牧渔及服务业增加值指数 Farming,Forestry,Animal Husbandry,Fishery and Service	农业 Farming	林业 Forestry	牧业 Animal Husbandry	渔业 Fishery	农林牧渔服务业 Service of Farming, Forestry, Animal Husbandry and Fishery
合 计 Total	**104.1**	**104.5**	**112.6**	**100.5**	**100.3**	**106.9**
新城区 Xincheng						
碑林区 Beilin						
莲湖区 Lianhu						
灞桥区 Baqiao	103.8	106.0	55.5	92.4	58.3	104.0
未央区 Weiyang	91.0	90.6	236.4	98.3	31.3	59.9
雁塔区 Yanta						
阎良区 Yanliang	104.3	103.4	91.1	106.8	75.5	107.7
临潼区 Lintong	103.6	104.2	73.0	102.9	76.3	107.6
长安区 Chang'an	103.9	102.3	115.5	108.6	122.3	104.8
高陵区 Gaoling	104.8	105.9	78.4	97.9	73.6	121.4
蓝田县 Lantian	104.3	107.5	62.5	104.6	98.1	103.5
周至县 Zhouzhi	105.0	104.5	147.5	89.7	100.3	102.1
户 县 Huxian	104.2	104.9	128.4	98.2	145.7	105.1

11-18 主要年份农作物播种面积

Sown Areas of Farm Crops In Representative Years

单位：万亩 （10 000mu）

年 份 Year	总播种面积 Total Sown Area	粮食 Grain Crops	小麦 Wheat	玉米 Corn	油料 Oil-bearing Crops	蔬菜 Vegetables
1980	835.43	706.35	324.17	273.14	10.01	24.02
1985	795.41	704.36	378.20	271.14	8.01	45.03
1990	816.41	731.42	387.20	282.14	12.00	51.03
1991	820.41	731.37	389.19	283.14	13.01	47.03
1992	820.65	715.50	384.60	273.60	16.20	54.60
1993	821.63	713.49	380.40	273.69	14.84	63.90
1994	821.10	719.00	375.90	272.40	13.80	59.90
1995	784.74	690.63	370.41	259.55	18.57	57.59
1996	797.40	709.00	366.30	286.80	18.80	55.50
1997	755.78	670.83	367.71	248.79	15.53	59.36
1998	789.99	705.03	370.17	285.45	14.69	60.95
1999	793.08	709.95	371.94	294.00	12.74	60.68
2000	784.94	697.55	369.89	283.70	13.46	64.35
2001	763.16	678.05	359.19	278.57	11.87	61.77
2002	751.10	655.59	350.64	271.95	11.40	67.71
2003	737.06	632.55	336.05	261.89	11.04	69.44
2004	753.83	630.63	311.52	286.50	9.74	77.55
2005	757.91	642.75	325.10	287.87	9.51	83.33
2006	769.49	648.00	313.23	307.89	8.58	87.03
2007	762.38	637.05	306.98	304.13	7.41	91.07
2008	756.06	630.31	319.39	286.69	8.59	93.02
2009	757.11	628.69	318.36	285.20	8.59	94.83
2010	751.74	621.71	317.18	279.93	8.98	95.71
2011	704.17	573.13	306.39	243.06	8.83	96.97
2012	701.33	572.50	305.34	242.20	7.70	97.82
2013	695.53	567.87	298.93	245.64	7.67	99.89
2014	684.28	551.46	290.53	238.65	7.01	101.56
2015	675.59	537.69	280.73	235.83	6.83	103.49
2016	659.04	527.74	275.66	231.96	6.18	103.01

注：2011年农作物播种面积为陕西省统计局依据(国统字办[2011]68号)文件调整数。

11-19 各区县主要农作物播种面积（2016年）

Sown Areas of Major Farm Crops by Region（2016）

单位：万亩 (10 000 mu)

区 县 Region	总播种面积 Total Sown Area	粮食 Grain Crops	小麦 Wheat	玉米 Corn	油料 Oil-bearing Crops	蔬菜 Vegetables	瓜果类 Fruits Class
合 计 Total	**659.04**	**527.74**	**275.66**	**231.96**	**6.18**	**103.01**	**16.75**
新城区 Xincheng							
碑林区 Beilin							
莲湖区 Lianhu							
灞桥区 Baqiao	24.35	16.03	9.56	6.17	0.29	7.37	0.58
未央区 Weiyang	0.99	0.24	0.17	0.07		0.73	0.02
雁塔区 Yanta							
阎良区 Yanliang	45.43	20.95	11.14	9.79	0.08	17.62	6.76
临潼区 Lintong	116.04	98.20	53.76	40.61	1.02	14.41	1.59
长安区 Chang'an	127.23	98.27	49.65	47.59	1.27	23.08	3.72
高陵区 Gaoling	52.01	39.95	20.35	19.30		11.59	0.47
蓝田县 Lantian	108.85	94.33	49.58	32.67	2.14	9.56	1.63
周至县 Zhouzhi	85.42	72.99	36.83	34.53	1.01	9.14	0.13
户 县 Huxian	98.72	86.78	44.62	41.23	0.36	9.51	1.85

11-20 主要年份农作物产品产量

Yield of Major Farm Crops in Representative Years

单位：万吨 (10 000 ton)

年份 Year	粮食作物 Grain Crops	夏粮 Summer Grain	小麦 Wheat	秋粮 Autumn Grain	稻谷 Rice	玉米 Corn	油料 Oil-bearing Crops	油菜籽 Rapeseeds	蔬菜 Vegetables
1978	132.80	64.20	58.20	68.70	5.10	55.80	0.09	0.07	45.66
1979	145.70	81.80	74.20	63.90	4.50	53.40	0.33	0.29	49.11
1980	114.40	56.60	52.20	57.80	4.70	47.70	0.54	0.50	40.13
1981	116.10	78.70	74.30	37.40	3.40	31.50	0.76	0.75	34.06
1982	148.90	85.60	82.20	63.30	4.90	55.50	0.51	0.49	53.71
1983	148.10	81.80	79.60	66.30	4.80	58.50	0.36	0.34	46.99
1984	157.60	82.40	81.00	75.20	5.00	66.50	0.46	0.29	75.47
1985	150.10	76.10	74.80	74.00	5.10	65.10	0.75	0.39	86.44
1986	162.40	91.70	90.10	70.70	4.80	61.80	1.25	0.82	85.84
1987	171.20	87.00	85.20	84.20	5.00	74.30	1.57	1.22	95.16
1988	158.00	86.80	84.60	71.10	3.80	61.40	0.89	0.51	113.50
1989	173.60	93.50	91.20	80.20	4.70	70.40	1.33	0.94	129.32
1990	172.40	91.70	89.70	80.80	5.50	70.40	1.35	0.94	119.32
1991	178.80	91.10	89.20	87.70	5.00	77.50	1.20	0.74	117.41
1992	183.40	101.70	99.60	81.70	4.70	72.30	1.49	0.87	128.12
1993	190.00	101.10	99.00	88.90	4.90	78.60	1.40	1.00	145.80
1994	157.40	86.90	84.90	70.50	4.50	61.40	1.08	0.78	135.26
1995	175.30	99.80	97.40	75.50	3.40	67.80	2.17	1.90	133.60
1996	187.50	80.10	78.40	107.40	3.40	95.60	1.83	1.55	138.01
1997	190.50	114.30	112.30	76.30	3.50	69.40	1.86	1.65	142.11
1998	212.70	104.40	104.00	108.30	3.20	99.10	1.67	1.36	148.87
1999	204.40	95.50	94.40	108.90	2.90	99.70	1.30	1.00	153.24
2000	201.90	92.60	91.60	109.30	3.10	100.50	1.34	0.95	162.14
2001	197.10	98.10	97.20	98.90	2.70	91.30	1.23	0.90	152.80
2002	192.40	94.50	93.50	97.90	2.10	91.60	1.22	0.84	169.74
2003	176.30	98.20	96.70	78.20	1.60	72.30	1.13	0.70	169.67
2004	195.80	97.80	96.00	98.00	1.70	91.60	1.14	0.84	180.96
2005	205.50	100.00	99.10	105.50	1.60	99.30	1.16	0.89	195.70
2006	193.50	86.00	85.40	107.40	1.40	101.20	1.08	0.87	189.30
2007	189.10	77.30	76.70	111.80	1.50	105.60	0.96	0.77	204.30
2008	214.40	105.90	105.60	108.50	0.90	103.00	1.15	0.95	221.53
2009	218.20	103.00	102.10	115.20	0.90	109.50	1.12	0.93	242.41
2010	221.70	106.60	105.80	115.10	0.80	108.90	1.20	1.00	253.10
2011	182.04	90.54	89.68	91.49	0.67	85.30	1.17	0.95	261.66
2012	192.55	95.73	94.92	96.82	0.57	89.29	1.02	0.88	277.80
2013	183.12	83.59	82.77	99.52	0.39	91.83	1.00	0.87	298.12
2014	175.61	88.05	87.35	87.56	0.25	83.30	0.98	0.80	316.28
2015	180.86	93.12	92.40	87.74	0.00	84.04	0.95	0.80	332.79
2016	175.33	89.90	89.24	85.43	0.08	81.91	0.86	0.77	336.75

注：2011年农作物产品产量为陕西省统计局依据(国统字办[2011]70号)文件调整数。

11–21 各区县主要农作物产品产量（2016年）

Yield of Major Farm Crops by Region（2016）

单位：万吨 (10 000 tons)

区县	Region	粮食作物 Grain Crops	夏粮 Summer Grain	小麦 Wheat	秋粮 Autumn Grain	稻谷 Rice	玉米 Corn
合计	Total	**175.33**	**89.90**	**89.24**	**85.43**	**0.08**	**81.91**
新城区	Xincheng						
碑林区	Beilin						
莲湖区	Lianhu						
灞桥区	Baqiao	5.26	3.35	3.35	1.91		1.85
未央区	Weiyang	0.08	0.05	0.05	0.03		0.03
雁塔区	Yanta						
阎良区	Yanliang	8.68	4.57	4.57	4.11		4.10
临潼区	Lintong	31.69	17.15	17.15	14.54		13.32
长安区	Chang'an	33.24	15.74	15.74	17.50	0.08	17.27
高陵区	Gaoling	18.78	8.79	8.79	9.99		9.92
蓝田县	Lantian	25.57	13.71	13.39	11.86		10.13
周至县	Zhouzhi	22.26	11.34	11.16	10.92		10.77
户县	Huxian	29.77	15.20	15.04	14.57		14.52

11–21 续表 continued

单位：万吨 (10 000 tons)

区县	Region	油料 Oil-bearing Crops	油菜籽 Rapeseeds	蔬菜 Vegetables	瓜果类 Fruits Class
合计	Total	**0.86**	**0.77**	**336.75**	**55.21**
新城区	Xincheng				
碑林区	Beilin				
莲湖区	Lianhu				
灞桥区	Baqiao	0.04	0.03	30.03	1.34
未央区	Weiyang			1.93	0.08
雁塔区	Yanta				
阎良区	Yanliang	0.01	0.01	80.34	24.60
临潼区	Lintong	0.13	0.11	45.03	7.36
长安区	Chang'an	0.22	0.22	58.99	8.45
高陵区	Gaoling			50.32	3.46
蓝田县	Lantian	0.24	0.24	18.26	4.07
周至县	Zhouzhi	0.15	0.11	21.87	0.50
户县	Huxian	0.07	0.05	29.98	5.35

11-22 主要年份农作物单位面积产量

Yield of Farm Crops Per Unit Area in Representative Years

单位：公斤/亩 (kg/mu)

年份 Year	粮食作物 Grain Crops	夏粮 Summer Grain	小麦 Wheat	秋粮 Autumn Grain	玉米 Corn	油料 Oil-bearing Crops	油菜籽 Rapeseeds	蔬菜 Vegetables
1990	236	232	232	241	249	103	101	2349
1991	245	229	229	264	274	94	89	2332
1992	256	259	259	253	264	92	101	2344
1993	266	260	260	274	287	94	107	2282
1994	219	226	226	211	225	79	84	2260
1995	254	263	263	243	261	117	128	2320
1996	265	214	214	321	333	86	100	2489
1997	284	305	306	257	279	76	129	2395
1998	302	278	279	328	347	114	121	2443
1999	288	253	254	327	339	102	106	2526
2000	289	247	248	338	354	102	112	2520
2001	291	270	271	314	328	104	113	2474
2002	293	266	267	326	337	107	115	2507
2003	279	287	288	269	276	102	110	2444
2004	310	308	308	313	320	117	129	2333
2005	320	304	305	336	345	121	132	2349
2006	299	273	273	323	329	125	135	2175
2007	297	250	250	341	347	129	132	2245
2008	340	330	331	350	359	134	137	2382
2009	347	320	321	375	384	131	131	2556
2010	357	333	334	381	389	130	131	2644
2011	318	293	293	347	351	133	134	2698
2012	336	310	311	367	369	132	130	2840
2013	322	277	277	374	374	130	125	2985
2014	318	301	301	339	349	140	130	3114
2015	336	329	329	345	356	139	133	3216
2016	332	323	324	342	353	140	132	3269

注：2011年农作物单产为陕西省统计局依据(国统字办[2011]72号)文件调整数。

11-23 各区县主要农作物单位面积产量（2016年）

The Output of Main Crops Per Unit Area by Region（2016）

单位：公斤/亩 (kg/mu)

区 县	Region	粮食作物 Grain Crops	夏粮 Summer Grain	小麦 Wheat	秋粮 Autumn Grain	玉米 Corn
合 计	**Total**	**332**	**323**	**324**	**342**	**353**
新城区	Xincheng					
碑林区	Beilin					
莲湖区	Lianhu					
灞桥区	Baqiao	328	350	350	295	299
未央区	Weiyang	339	322	322	378	378
雁塔区	Yanta					
阎良区	Yanliang	414	410	410	419	419
临潼区	Lintong	323	319	319	327	328
长安区	Chang'an	338	317	317	360	363
高陵区	Gaoling	470	432	432	509	514
蓝田县	Lantian	271	271	270	271	310
周至县	Zhouzhi	305	301	303	309	312
户 县	Huxian	343	335	337	352	352

11-23 续表 continued

单位：公斤/亩 (kg/mu)

区 县	Region	油料 Oil-bearing Crops	油菜籽 Rapeseeds	蔬菜 Vegetables	瓜果类 Fruits Class
合 计	**Total**	**140**	**132**	**3269**	**3296**
新城区	Xincheng				
碑林区	Beilin				
莲湖区	Lianhu				
灞桥区	Baqiao	128	132	4075	2310
未央区	Weiyang			2619	4059
雁塔区	Yanta				
阎良区	Yanliang	128	127	4559	3637
临潼区	Lintong	133	115	3126	4629
长安区	Chang'an	175	175	2556	2273
高陵区	Gaoling			4343	7407
蓝田县	Lantian	113	113	1910	2505
周至县	Zhouzhi	148	106	2392	3798
户 县	Huxian	188	190	3153	2884

11-24 设施农业生产情况（2016年）

Agricultural Production Facilities（2016）

指　标	Item	种植面积（亩） planting area (mu)	产量（吨） output(ton)
一、蔬菜	**Vegetables**	**245732**	**1333525**
其中：芹菜	Celery	82154	378217
油菜	Rape	5029	11869
菠菜	Spinach	17103	40554
黄瓜	Cucumber	24602	156680
西红柿	Tomato	26541	113309
辣椒	Chilli	14976	62156
二、瓜果类	**Fruits class**	**98755**	**359969**
其中：草莓	Strawberry	7557	18141
三、花卉苗木	**Flower seedling wood**	**4386**	
四、食用菌	**Edible Fungi**	**1321**	**14335**
五、其他	**Others**	**945**	
补充资料：　设施数量（个）	Number of Facilities (unit)		129435
设施占地面积（亩）	Area of Facilities(mu)	229425	

11-25 主要年份林业生产情况

Statistics on Forestry in Representative Years

指　标	Item	2000	2010	2011	2012	2013	2014	2015	2016
一、营林情况	**Afforestation**								
当年造林面积合计（万亩）	Build Forestry Areas(10 000 mu)	27.47	16.10	10.42	9.08	12.29	14.70	8.28	4.51
迹地更新面积（万亩）	Reforestation Area (10000 mu)	1.08							
封山育林面积（万亩）	Hill-closeure for Afforestation Areas (10 000 mu)	18.78	55.10	41.30	41.90	44.40	42.99	44.00	43.80
零星四旁植树（万株）	Planting(10 000 plants)	731.0	509.2	536.7	579.2	588.3	621.0	516.0	462.0
育苗面积（万亩）	Raise Seedlings Areas(10 000 mu)	2.05	11.95	9.93	11.64	17.37	17.73	19.84	22.78
#本年新育	New Seedling of Current Year	1.69	1.75	1.93	1.98	6.10	2.70	1.00	1.72
二、主要林产品产量（吨）	**Main Forestry Product(ton)**								
生漆	Lacquer	11	10	4					
核桃	Walnuts	997	7875	13235	15253	18033	16531	24344	19240
板栗	Chinese Chestnut	744	7736	8229	7654	4379	6922	8225	6694
花椒	Pepper	140	1420	889	879	319	371	204	402
三、村及村以下采伐木材（万立方米）	**Timber Harvested at or below** Village Level (10 000 cu.m)	1.62	3.30	1.39	1.04	0.88		0.07	0.28

注：本表数据来源于市农林委。

11-26 各区县林业生产情况（2016年）

Statistics On Forestry by Region（2016）

区 县 Region	当年造林面积（亩）Build Forestry Areasin in The Year(mu)	零星植树（万株）Planting (10 000 plants)	育苗面积（亩）Raise Seedlings Areas(mu)	核桃产量（吨）Output of Walnuts (ton)	板栗产量（吨）Output of Chinese Chestnut (ton)
合 计 Total	**45105**	**462**	**227805**	**19240**	**6694**
新城区 Xincheng					
碑林区 Beilin					
莲湖区 Lianhu					
灞桥区 Baqiao	495	20	5175		
未央区 Weiyang		30			
雁塔区 Yanta		1		200	
阎良区 Yanliang	2145	31	510		
临潼区 Lintong	6870	72	2745		
长安区 Chang'an	3720	110	1710	700	500
高陵区 Gaoling	4005	30	4605		
蓝田县 Lantian	11385		52005	10000	5000
周至县 Zhouzhi	12840	80	134025	8010	1170
户 县 Huxian	3375	88	24765	330	24

注：本表数据来源于市农林委。

11-27 主要年份果业生产情况

Statistics on Fruits in Representative Years

指标	Item	2000	2005	2012	2013	2014	2015	2016
果园面积合计（万亩）	**Areas of Orchards (10 000 mu)**	**47.86**	**55.55**	**76.83**	**78.06**	**81.23**	**79.21**	**79.76**
苹果园	Apple Orchards	12.15	5.96	1.44	1.28	1.22	1.24	1.19
梨园	Pears Orchards	5.79	3.01	1.65	1.68	1.61	1.55	1.43
葡萄园	Grapes Orchards	1.89	3.02	5.46	6.70	9.39	9.50	10.20
桃园	Peach Orchards	3.47	8.66	6.78	6.49	6.14	6.09	6.05
猕猴桃园	Chinese Goosebeery Orchards	16.83	4.33	41.36	41.99	42.16	39.62	39.67
杏园	Apricot Orchards	0.62	2.50	3.59	3.52	3.99	3.96	3.86
柿子园	Presimmons Orchards	1.96	2.69	2.91	2.78	2.59	3.05	3.13
石榴园	Pomegranate Orchards			3.61	3.57	3.59	3.59	3.59
水果产量（吨）	**Output of Fruits (ton)**	**343551**	**512869**	**932054**	**951851**	**996570**	**1052000**	**1077442**
苹果	Apple	89416	53387	28675	25212	26047	31970	30522
梨	Pears	65459	57059	47463	47618	48757	50729	49888
葡萄	Grapes	16647	30951	75516	92380	99889	126625	133627
桃	Peach	27010	89755	125857	122186	125147	131228	132329
猕猴桃	Chinese Goosebeery	96640	137853	386336	395847	410614	425250	441735
杏	Apricot			57772	55330	61145	63726	60877
柿子	Persimmon			41211	41712	43705	39560	38445
石榴	Pomegranate			32329	30642	32793	29840	29859

11-28 各区县果业生产情况（2016年）

Area and Output of Fruits by Region（2016）

区 县	Region	果园面积（万亩） Area of Orchards(10 000 mu)	水果产量（吨） Output of Fruits(ton)
合 计	**Total**	**79.76**	**1077442**
新城区	Xincheng		
碑林区	Beilin		
莲湖区	Lianhu		
灞桥区	Baqiao	7.39	125467
未央区	Weiyang	0.05	419
雁塔区	Yanta		
阎良区	Yanliang	2.76	68745
临潼区	Lintong	5.32	60160
长安区	Chang'an	5.35	76558
高陵区	Gaoling	3.14	72539
蓝田县	Lantian	7.58	127695
周至县	Zhouzhi	40.44	445984
户 县	Huxian	7.73	99875

11-29 主要年份畜牧业生产情况

Statistics on Livestock Husbandry in Representative Years

指标	Item	2000	2005	2010	2012	2013	2014	2015	2016
一、大牲畜年末总头数（头）	**Large Animals In Stock at Year-end (head)**	**260742**	**322521**	**216043**	**211852**	**211791**	**217257**	**199438**	**169273**
# 役畜	Draught Animals	98130	90717	42243	31866	31510	26760	24412	19161
1. 牛	Cattle	256073	320773	215072	210819	210743	216326	199386	169242
# 能繁殖母畜	Female Animals of Reprductive Ability	136626	176445	144012					
# 当年生仔畜	Newborn Livestock in the Year	69015	72163	40052					
#肉牛	Farm Cattle			65447	60233	60165	64478	65863	72567
#奶牛	Dairy Cattle	48164	96498	118747	119888	120836	126174	109520	77453
2. 马（匹）	Horses	736	559	456	533	549	513	52	31
3. 驴	Donkeys	476	175	67	46	52	59		
4. 骡	Mules	3457	1014	448	454	447	359		
二、猪年末头数（头）	**Hogs in Stock Year-end (head)**	**1284592**	**1472869**	**943183**	**966018**	**965683**	**950124**	**924870**	**895272**
# 能繁殖的母猪	Female Hogs of Reprductive Ability	93775	123543	106610	103926	103967	99989	94000	85637
三、羊年末只数（只）	**Sheeps and Goats in Stock at Year-end(head)**	**421103**	**532471**	**294539**	**284596**	**273747**	**279207**	**283334**	**265668**
1. 山羊	Goats	397121	520354	288738	278738	267382	271722	273941	258354
# 奶山羊	Milch Goats	266525	358733	246442	234643	222546	224901	208909	185249
2. 绵羊	Sheeps	23982	12117	5801	5858	6365	7485	9393	7314
四、家禽年末存栏（万只）	**Poultry in Stock at Year-end (10 000 heads)**	**1623.81**	**1372.56**	**1034.2**	**1176.73**	**1172.61**	**1161.16**	**1183.23**	**1125.25**
五、年末养蜂箱数(箱)	**Honey (box)**	**20408**	**24287**	**22984**	**17161**	**17415**	**20663**	**19536**	**15031**

11-30 各区县畜牧业生产情况（2016年）

Statistics On Livestock, Animal Husbandry by Region（2016）

区 县	Region	大牲畜年末头数（头）Large Animals In Stock at Year-end (head)	役畜 Draught Animals	牛（头）Cattle (head)	奶牛 Dairy Cattle	马（匹）Horses (head)	驴（头）Donkeys (head)	骡（头）Mutes (head)
合 计	**Total**	**169273**	**19161**	**169242**	**77453**	**31**		
新城区	Xincheng							
碑林区	Beilin							
莲湖区	Lianhu							
灞桥区	Baqiao	5883		5862	5812	21		
未央区	Weiyang	1511		1511	1092			
雁塔区	Yanta							
阎良区	Yanliang	18420		18420	17710			
临潼区	Lintong	37756	6525	37756	31231			
长安区	Chang'an	11487	28	11477	4634	10		
高陵区	Gaoling	18132		18132	8138			
蓝田县	Lantian	38358	7503	38358	2960			
周至县	Zhouzhi	30410	5105	30410	2856			
户 县	Huxian	7316		7316	3020			

11-30 续表 continued

区 县	Region	猪（头）Swine (head)	能繁殖的母猪 breeding sows	羊（只）Sheep and Goats (head)	山羊 Goats	奶山羊 Milch Goats	家禽（万只）Poultry (10 000 head)	蜂（箱）Honey (box)
合 计	**Total**	**895272**	**85637**	**265668**	**258354**	**185249**	**1125.25**	**15031**
新城区	Xincheng							
碑林区	Beilin							
莲湖区	Lianhu							
灞桥区	Baqiao	41975	5139	9917	9917	9917	35.63	330
未央区	Weiyang	10728	428	685	515		1	
雁塔区	Yanta							
阎良区	Yanliang	37665	4188	53365	53365	53365	61.65	660
临潼区	Lintong	226525	20128	69865	69865	69865	241.3	1592
长安区	Chang'an	133156	10241	18176	14766	3893	292.42	4350
高陵区	Gaoling	49065	3308	21026	18399		151.75	
蓝田县	Lantian	79453	8195	72954	71979	45996	118	3167
周至县	Zhouzhi	179905	19780	13120	12988	2213	97.5	4932
户 县	Huxian	136800	14230	6560	6560		126	

11-31 主要年份畜产品和水产品产量

单位：吨

年 份 Year	肉类总产量 Output of Meat	猪 肉 Pork	牛 肉 Beef	羊 肉 Mutton	禽 肉 Poultry
1990	63273	50646	4667	1931	5885
1991	72268	55086	5623	2162	9062
1992	88994	68134	6468	2460	11290
1993	93420	71274	7249	2220	12174
1994	106691	79433	8298	2350	15681
1995	127815	86513	11251	3731	23948
1996	91468	63750	5402	2578	19324
1997	106597	75381	6672	3468	20596
1998	134152	98974	8788	4710	21424
1999	130124	93859	9827	4147	21963
2000	147571	106137	12066	4766	23760
2001	157277	113353	11900	5153	20540
2002	161092	118634	11516	5394	20515
2003	165860	122759	13241	5180	19682
2004	171545	126404	13641	5874	18493
2005	182046	136503	14031	6106	18803
2006	108634	81199	8267	2841	13417
2007	102191	73254	8589	3111	14075
2008	115352	84654	9840	3335	16060
2009	126182	94490	10142	3677	17190
2010	136501	102296	10854	3875	18338
2011	144631	104816	11860	3645	19390
2012	151711	110506	12079	3697	20046
2013	157449	114288	12143	4036	20817
2014	161886	118627	12288	4198	20887
2015	161254	115953	12361	4287	21441
2016	156829	112629	12541	4340	20652

注：2010年起，根据统计制度要求，水产品产量及养殖面积统计数据取自市水务局。

Output of Livestock Products and Aquatic Products in Representative Years

(ton)

奶类产量 Output of Milk	牛 奶 Cow Milk	禽 蛋 Poultry Eggs	蜂蜜（公斤） Honey(kg)	水产品 Output of Aquatic Products	养殖面积（万亩） Water Raise Areas (10 000 mu)
82017	50528	55938	1035392	4259	2.55
91006	57700	90558	1022797	4949	2.63
100080	63586	104970	739275	6015	2.8
111070	73897	125244	662049	7132	2.97
145412	99025	146503	547808	7900	3.1
132909	85753	141227	535891	8517	3.21
133372	86103	138044	613290	8910	3.51
150964	98078	156066	713918	10054	3.46
174099	119719	142519	537304	10480	3.4
209144	145191	135981	541613	11061	3.38
245913	176155	138305	460598	11384	3.35
255437	179977	132303	479839	12480	3.17
288009	202826	134336	497530	12017	3.31
336296	245407	128833	537805	9967	2.48
384319	289564	117597	449765	9721	2.46
422229	327961	118115	421052	9370	2.38
471438	374813	97816	414271	11937	1.6
528037	428462	98140	401761	12402	1.38
589697	475681	108515	503031	12487	1.4
618186	498394	116685	528731	13044	1.52
633663	509178	123793	436759	11850	2.24
647978	509777	125639	217632	11800	2.2
666439	513337	129970	213174	14010	2.95
657748	512796	135382	219344	14200	2.19
658016	514587	135191	250464	14218	2.31
637340	485640	145470	243198	14190	2.26
562038	420765	140357	219646	13449	1.96

11-32 各区县主要畜产品和水产品产量（2016年）

Output of Major Livestock Products and Aquatic Products by Region（2016）

单位：吨 (ton)

区 县	Region	肉类总产量 Output of Meat	猪 肉 Pork	牛 肉 Beef	羊 肉 Mutton	禽 肉 Poultry
合 计	**Total**	**156829**	**112629**	**12541**	**4340**	**20652**
新城区	Xincheng					
碑林区	Beilin					
莲湖区	Lianhu					
灞桥区	Baqiao	7327	5302	1026	158	819
未央区	Weiyang	3060	2162	750	25	109
雁塔区	Yanta					
阎良区	Yanliang	7441	4893	693	693	1058
临潼区	Lintong	43252	29485	3854	1653	4286
长安区	Chang'an	20416	14218	590	272	5178
高陵区	Gaoling	11198	7932	505	256	2047
蓝田县	Lantian	19322	10571	2754	1040	3232
周至县	Zhouzhi	26482	22676	1792	171	1664
户 县	Huxian	18331	15390	577	72	2259

11-32 续表 continued

单位：吨 (ton)

区 县	Region	奶类产量 Output of Milk	牛 奶 Cow Milk	禽 蛋 Poultry Eggs	蜂 蜜（公斤） Honey(kg)	水产品 Output of Aquatic Products	养殖面积（亩） Water Raise Areas (mu)
合 计	**Total**	**562038**	**420765**	**140357**	**219646**	**13449**	**19575**
新城区	Xincheng						
碑林区	Beilin						
莲湖区	Lianhu						
灞桥区	Baqiao	30802	25114	5005	8330	700	1245
未央区	Weiyang	3021	3018	10		750	585
雁塔区	Yanta					50	15
阎良区	Yanliang	102581	76444	6688	18090	225	180
临潼区	Lintong	269013	224261	35442	41256	3300	4965
长安区	Chang'an	34977	21515	42127	75680	5145	5640
高陵区	Gaoling	48887	37882	17171		235	180
蓝田县	Lantian	41429	8640	10280	25458	1305	3660
周至县	Zhouzhi	13564	9951	10241	50832	500	2310
户 县	Huxian	17764	13940	13393		1239	795

注：2010年起，根据统计制度要求，水产品产量及养殖面积统计数据取自市水务局。

11-33 农业科技、教育情况（2016年）

Agricultural Science and Technology Education (2016)

指标	Item	2016
农业研究开发机构（个）	Agricultural research and development institutions (unit)	368
农业科技人员（人）	Agricultural scientific and technical personnel(persons)	3535
农业科研成果（个）	Agricultural scientific research achievements (unit)	12
农民技能培训人数（万人）	The number of peasants skills training(10000 persons)	16.2
良种推广面积（万亩）	Thoroughbred promotion area (10000 mu)	511.91
农业信息站（个）	information station of Agricultural (unit)	3104

注：本表数据来源于市农林委。

11-34 主要年份农产品人均占有量

Per Capita Output of Major Farm Products in Representative Years

单位：公斤/人 (kg/ person)

年份 Year	粮食 Grain	油料 Oil-bearing Crops	猪牛羊肉 Pork Beef and Mutton	禽蛋 Poultry Eggs	奶类 Milk	水果 Fruits	蔬菜 Vegetables
1978	266.7	0.2	5.4	0.9	3.3	6.8	91.7
1979	288.6	0.6	6.7	1.0	4.0	5.1	97.3
1980	223.5	1.1	5.9	1.2	4.1	6.9	78.4
1981	222.9	1.5	6.6	1.7	4.7	5.8	65.4
1982	281.5	1.0	4.9	2.7	5.6	5.9	101.6
1983	276.6	0.7	4.9	3.2	6.5	5.0	87.8
1984	289.4	0.8	4.8	6.2	8.7	4.8	138.6
1985	271.4	1.4	6.8	5.7	10.2	7.6	156.3
1986	288.0	2.2	7.8	6.4	12.1	9.6	152.2
1987	298.0	2.7	7.3	6.8	13.8	10.6	165.6
1988	269.7	1.5	8.0	8.9	15.6	11.1	193.7
1989	290.7	2.2	8.4	7.6	13.1	10.2	216.5
1990	298.7	2.1	9.4	9.2	14.2	11.5	196.0
1991	290.6	2.0	10.2	14.7	14.8	11.7	190.8
1992	294.3	2.4	12.4	16.8	16.2	17.3	205.6
1993	301.2	2.2	12.8	19.9	17.6	25.9	231.1
1994	246.1	1.7	14.1	22.9	22.7	28.0	211.5
1995	270.4	3.4	15.7	21.8	20.5	37.5	206.1
1996	286.3	3.2	11.0	21.1	20.4	43.9	210.8
1997	287.8	2.8	12.9	23.6	22.8	43.3	214.7
1998	318.3	2.5	16.8	21.3	26.1	50.0	222.8
1999	303.0	1.9	16.0	20.2	31.0	52.7	227.2
2000	293.5	1.9	17.9	20.1	35.7	49.9	235.7
2001	283.7	1.8	18.8	19.0	36.8	48.8	219.9
2002	273.8	1.7	19.3	19.1	41.0	53.5	241.6
2003	246.0	1.6	19.7	18.0	46.9	53.6	236.8
2004	270.1	1.6	20.1	16.2	53.0	63.9	249.6
2005	277.1	1.6	21.1	15.9	56.9	69.1	263.8
2006	256.9	1.4	12.3	13.0	62.6	73.5	251.4
2007	247.4	1.3	11.1	12.8	69.1	79.2	267.3
2008	256.0	1.4	11.7	13.0	70.4	85.6	264.5
2009	258.7	1.3	12.8	13.8	73.3	93.6	287.4
2010	261.8	1.4	13.8	14.6	74.8	100.1	298.9
2011	213.8	1.4	14.1	14.8	76.1	107.1	318.9
2012	225.6	1.2	14.8	15.2	78.1	109.2	325.6
2013	213.2	1.2	15.2	15.8	76.6	110.8	347.1
2014	204.0	1.1	15.7	15.7	76.3	115.8	367.5
2015	208.7	1.1	15.3	16.8	73.5	121.4	384.0
2016	200.0	1.0	14.8	16.0	64.1	122.9	384.0

11-35 主要年份农村经济效益指标

Main Indicators of Rural Economic Benefit in Representative Years

年份 Year	每一劳动力创造的 Average Labor Force Production 农林牧渔及服务业总产值（元） Gross Output Value of Farming,Forestry, Animal Husbandry, Fishery and Service (yuan)	粮食（公斤） Grain Crops(kg)	油料（公斤） Oil-bearing Crops(kg)	每亩耕地种植业总产值（元） Output of Each Unit of Area Planting(yuan)	每百元物耗生产的总产值（元） Output per 100-Yuan of Material Consumed(yuan)
1978	504.7	1024.6	0.7	104.3	
1979	549.0	1096.5	2.3	116.0	
1980	483.1	846.1	4.0	99.2	
1981	502.8	840.5	5.5	105.4	
1982	631.5	1058.9	3.6	139.3	
1983	606.5	1053.2	2.6	124.1	
1984	850.7	1154.2	3.4	163.6	
1985	1020.1	1134.6	5.6	183.1	
1986	1132.2	1236.4	9.5	204.6	
1987	1280.3	1277.2	11.7	231.5	
1988	1558.4	1148.0	6.5	273.2	
1989	1605.3	1231.9	9.5	295.0	
1990	1766.3	1279.1	10.0	343.4	233.3
1991	1958.8	1326.6	8.9	380.4	238.4
1992	2093.7	1360.7	11.1	451.6	241.8
1993	2528.9	1409.7	10.4	546.8	240.1
1994	3705.0	1167.8	8.0	762.8	227.6
1995	4953.0	1300.6	16.1	1106.5	225.9
1996	5154.8	1391.2	13.6	1224.2	234.5
1997	5493.0	1413.4	13.8	1283.3	239.2
1998	5615.9	1578.1	12.4	1374.3	247.0
1999	4826.5	1516.6	9.7	1175.9	251.7
2000	5091.5	1498.0	9.9	1161.1	250.2
2001	5328.5	1462.4	9.1	1221.1	248.6
2002	5617.4	1427.5	9.1	1272.0	265.9
2003	5761.2	1308.1	8.4	1332.4	254.3
2004	6885.4	1452.7	8.5	1434.6	261.7
2005	7737.9	1524.7	8.6	1642.3	262.9
2006	8415.5	1435.7	8.0	1756.9	263.1
2007	10165.6	1403.0	7.1	2037.3	259.8
2008	13306.4	1695.4	9.1	2447.9	259.6
2009	14674.3	1791.7	9.2	2737.9	261.6
2010	19480.7	1901.3	10.0	3753.4	260.9
2011	23474.6	1567.2	10.1	4585.8	274.0
2012	27219.4	1699.6	10.1	5175.7	273.5
2013	31608.7	1688.0	9.2	5934.5	274.0
2014	33292.2	1605.0	8.9	6552.4	274.9
2015	36228.8	1720.9	9.0	7069.8	273.8
2016	39643.3	1713.6	8.5	7461.2	271.8

主要统计指标解释

农林牧渔业总产值 指以货币表现的农、林、牧、渔业全部产品和对农林牧渔业生产活动进行的各种支持性服务活动的价值总量，它反映一定时期内农林牧渔业生产总规模和总成果。1957年以前的农林牧渔业总产值中包括了厩肥和农民自给性手工业（如农民自制衣服、鞋、袜，自己从事粮食初步加工等）。1958年及以后，林业中增加了村及村以下竹木采伐产值；牧业中取消了厩肥产值；副业中取消了农民自给性手工业产值，增加了村及村以下办的工业产值；渔业中增加了海洋捕捞水产品产值。1980年及以后，在副业中增加了农民家庭兼营工业商品部分的产值。从1984年起村及村以下工业产值划归工业。从1993年起取消副业，将野生动物的捕猎划入牧业，野生植物采集和农民家庭兼营商品性工业划归农业。从2003年起，执行新的国民经济行业分类标准，农林牧渔业总产值中包括了农林牧渔服务业产值。林业中增加了森林采运业产值。农业中取消了家庭兼营商品性工业产值，将野生林产品的采集划归林业。第一次农业普查以后，由于畜牧业产品年报数据与普查数据之间存在一定的差距，根据农业普查结果对畜牧业年报数据进行了修正，对畜牧业产值进行了相应修正。

农林牧渔业总产值的计算方法通常是按农、林、牧、渔业产品及其副产品的产量分别乘以各自单位产品价格求得；少数生产周期较长，当年没有产品或产品产量不易统计的，则采用间接方法匡算其产值；然后将四业产品产值及农林牧渔服务业产值相加即为农林牧渔业总产值。

粮食产量 指全社会的产量。包括国有经济经营的、集体统一经营的和农民家庭经营的粮食产量，还包括工矿企业办的农场和其他生产单位的产量。粮食除包括稻谷、小麦、玉米、高粱、谷子及其他杂粮外，还包括薯类和豆类。其产量计算方法，豆类按去豆荚后的干豆计算；薯类（包括甘薯和马铃薯，不包括芋头和木薯）1963年以前按每4公斤鲜薯折1公斤粮食计算，从 1964年开始改为按5公斤鲜薯折1公斤粮食计算。城市郊区作为蔬菜的薯类（如马铃薯等）按鲜品计算，并且不作粮食统计。其他粮食一律按脱粒后的原粮计算。1989年以前全国粮食产量数据主要靠全面报表取得，1989年开始使用抽样调查数据。

棉花产量 指全社会的产量。包括春播棉和夏播棉。产量按皮棉计算。不包括木棉。

油料产量 指全部油料作物的生产量。包括花生、油菜籽、芝麻、向日葵籽、胡麻籽（亚麻籽）和其他油料。不包括大豆、木本油料和野生油料。花生以带壳干花生计算。

水产品产量 指人工养殖的水产品和天然生长的水产品的捕捞量。包括海水的鱼类、虾蟹类、贝类和藻类以及内陆水域的鱼类、虾蟹类和贝类，不包括淡水生植物。水产品产量是通过各级水产和统计部门逐级上报取得数据。1995年及以前，贝类中牡蛎按鲜肉计算；蚶、蛤、蛙按5斤鲜品折1斤计算。1996年以后则统一按鲜品计算。

猪、牛、羊肉产量 指当年出栏并已屠宰、除去头蹄下水后带骨肉（即胴体重）的重量。包括全社会范围内的产量。1996年前为各级逐级上报数据。1996年第一次农业普查以后，由于畜牧业产品年报数据与普查数据之间存在一定的差距，根据普查结果对畜牧业年报数据进行了修正。1999年以后，国家统计局在部分地区开展了猪、牛、羊、禽等主要畜禽品种的抽样调查，并用抽样数据作为国家定案数据使用。未开展抽样调查的地区和品种，仍使用各级统计部门逐级上报数据。2007年，根据第二次农业普查结果，对2000-2006年畜牧业年报数据进行了修正。2008年，建立了主要畜禽监测调查制度，猪、牛、羊、禽等主要畜牧业数据均以抽样调查数为法定数据。

期初（末）畜禽存栏头（只）数 指报告期初（末）农村各种合作经济组织和国营农场、农民个人、机关、团体、学校、工矿企业、部队等单位以及城镇居民饲养的大牲畜、猪、羊、家禽等畜禽的存栏数。

常用耕地 是指耕地总资源中专门种植农作物并经常进行耕种、能够正常收获的土地。包括当年实际耕种的熟地；弃耕、休闲不满三年，随时可以复耕的地；开荒利用三年以上的地。不包括临时种植农作物的坡度在 25度以上的陡坡地；在河套、湖畔、库区临时开发的成片或零星土地；也不包括已列为国家和省（区、市）退耕计划但临时耕种的土地。

农作物播种面积 指实际播种或移植有农作物的面积。凡是实际种植有农作物的面积，不论种植在耕地上还是种植在非耕地上，均包括在农作物播种面积中。在播种季节基本结束后，因遭灾而重新改种和补种的农作物面积，也包括在内。它是反映我国耕地面积利用情况的一个重要指标。目前，农作物播种面积主要包括粮食、棉花、油料、糖料、麻类、烟叶、蔬菜和瓜类、药材和其他农作物九大类。

有效灌溉面积 指具有一定的水源，地块比较平整，灌溉工程或设备已经配套，在一般年景下，当年能够进行正常灌溉的耕地面积。在一般情况下，有效灌溉面积应等于灌溉工程或设备已经配备，能够进行正常灌溉的水田和水浇地面积之和。它是反映我国耕地抗旱能力的一个重要指标。

农用化肥施用量 指本年内实际用于农业生产的化肥数量，包括氮肥、磷肥、钾肥和复合肥。化肥施用量要求按折纯量计算数量。折纯量是指把氮肥、磷肥、钾肥分别按含氮、含五氧化二磷、含氧化钾的百分之百成份进行折算后的数量。复合肥按其所含主要成分折算。公式为：

折纯量=实物量×某种化肥有效成份含量的百分比

农业机械总动力 指主要用于农、林、牧、渔业的各种动力机械的动力总和。包括耕作机械、排灌机械、收获机械、农用运输机械、植物保护机械、牧业机械、林业机械、渔业机械和其他农业机械【内燃机按引擎马力折成瓦（特）计算、电动机按功率折成瓦（特）计算】。不包括专门用于乡、镇、村、组办工业、基本建设、非农业运输、科学试验和教学等非农业生产方面用的动力机械与作业机械。这个指标的统计数据主要来源于农机部门。

Explanatory Notes on Main Statistical Indicators

Gross Output Value of Agriculture, Forestry, Animal Husbandry and Fishery refers to the total value of products of agriculture, forestry, animal husbandry and fishery, and total value of services in support of agriculture, forestry, animal husbandry and fishery activities. It reflects the total scale and results of agricultural production during a given period. Prior to 1957, China's gross agricultural output value included barnyard manure and handicraft products for self- consumption (clothes, shoes, stockings, and initial grain processing undertaken by peasants). Since 1958, cutting and felling of bamboo and trees by villages and other cooperative organizations under villages have been included in forestry; value of barnyard manure has been excluded from animal husbandry; self consumed handicrafts have not been included from sideline occupations, while the output value of industries run by villages and cooperative organizations under village has been included in sideline occupations; and the output value of fish catches by motor fishing boats has been added to fishery. Since 1980, the value of handicraft products made for sale by individuals in households has been added to sideline occupations. Since 1984, industries run by villages and under villages have been included in the sector of industry. Since 1993, the subdivision of sideline occupations has been cancelled, and the hunting of wild animals has been classified into animal husbandry, and the gathering of wild plants and commodity industry run by rural household have been included in farming. A new industrial classification of economic activities was introduced in 2003. Under the new classification, value of services to agriculture, forestry, animal husbandry and fishery is included in the gross output value of agriculture, value of wood felling and transport is included in forestry, value of industrial output by rural households is not included in agriculture, and the collection of wild forest products is taken from agriculture and included in forestry. The First Agriculture Census of China revealed some discrepancy between the production of animal products from the annual reports and that from the census. According to the result of the First Agriculture census, efforts were made to adjust the output value of animal husbandry to make the figures from the annual reports consistent with the census data.

Gross output value of agrieulture is obtained by multiplying the output of each product or by-product by its price, resulting in the output value of each single item. For a small number of products, annual output of which is not available or difficult to get due to the long production (growing) process involved, the output value is estimated through an indirect approach. The sum of output values of all products of agriculture, forestry, animal husbandry and fishery and services in support to those industries is then equal to the gross output value of agriculture.

Grain Output refers to the total output in the whole country including grains produced by State farms, collective units, rural households, as well as by farms affiliated to industrial and mining enterprises and other production units. Grain includes rice, wheat, corn, sorghum, millet and other miscellaneous grains as well as tubers and beans. Output of beans refers to dry beans without pods. The output of tubers (sweet potatoes and potatoes, not including taros and cassava) are converted into that of grain at the ratio 4:1, i.e. 4 kilograms of fresh tubers were equivalent to 1 kilogram of grain up to 1963. Since 1964 the ratio for conversion has been 5:1. Tubers supplied as vegetables (such as potatoes) in cities and suburbs are calculated as fresh vegetables and their output is not included in the output of grain. Output of all other grains refers to husked grain. Data on grain production before 1989 were obtained through the Comprehensive Statistical Reporting System. Since 1989, data from sample surveys are used.

Cotton Output refers to cotton production in the whole country including cotton planted in spring and in autumn. Output is measured as the weight of ginned cotton. Ceiba is not included.

Output of Oil-bearing Crops refers to the total production of oil-bearing crops of various kinds, including peanuts (dry, in shell), rapeseeds, sesame, sunflower seeds, flax seeds, and other oil-bearing crops. Soybeans, oil-bearing woody plants, and wild oil-bearing crops are not included.

Output of Aquatic Products refers to catches of both artificially cultured and naturally grown aquatic products, including fish, shrimps, crabs and shellfish in sea and inland water as well as seaweed. Freshwater plants are not included. Data on output of aquatic products are reported by aquatic product and statistical agencies level by level. Before 1995, among the shellfish, oyster was counted as fresh meat; 5 kilograms of ark shell, clams and frogs are equivalent to 1 kilogram of fresh aquatic products; they have all been counted as flesh aquatic products since 1996.

Output of Pork, Beef, and Mutton refers to the meat of slaughtered hogs, cattle, sheep and goats with head, feet, and offal taken away. Data refers to the production of the whole country. The First Agricultural Census of China in 1996 revealed some discrepancy between the production of animal products from the annual reports and that from the census. Efforts were made to adjust the output value of animal husbandry to make the figures from the annual reports consistent with the census data. Since 1999, the NBS conducted sample surveys for the major animal husbandry products, such as hogs, cattle, sheep and goats and fowls, and the data from sample surveys are used as national finalized data. Those products, which are not covered by the sample survey, are still reported by statistical agencies level by level. In 2007. the data on animal husbandry from 2000 to 2006 were revised according to the results of the Second Agriculture Census of China. In 2008, A Monitoring and Survey Program was set up on main livestock, the data on the main livestock such as hog, cattle, sheep and poultry became the official data based on the sampling survey.

Number of Livestock or Poultry in Stock at Beginning (or End) of Period refers to the total number of large animals, pigs, sheep, fowls, etc. raised by rural cooperative organizations, State farms, rural individuals, government agencies, schools, industrial and mining enterprises, army, and urban residents at the beginning (or end) of the reference period.

Regularly Cultivated Land refers to farmland among the total land resources which is exclusively used for farming and is under regular cultivation with harvest in normal years. Included are currently cultivated land, land that has been abandoned or put in idle for less than 3 years and could be re-used for cultivation at any time, and new-claimed land that has been put into cultivation for more than 3 years. Excluded under this category are steep slope land over 25 degrees under temporary cultivation, land (large or small plots) that is claimed along river bends, lake sides or banks of reservoirs, as well as land that has been designated under the "Green for Grain" programmes of the state and provincial governments but is still temporarily under cultivation.

Sown Area of Crops refers to area of transplanted with crops regardless of being land sown or in cultivated area or non-cultivated area. Area of land re-sown due to lso included. This is an important indicator that can reflect the utilization condition of the cultivated land in China. At present, the sown area of crops mainly include the following 9 categories of crops: grain, cotton, oil-bearing crops, sugar crops, flax crops, tobacco, vegetables and melons, medicinal materials and other farm crops.natural disasters is also included. This is an important indicator that can reflect the utilization condition of the cultivated land in China. At present, the sown area of crops mainly include the following 9 categories of crops: grain, cotton, oil-bearing crops, sugar crops, flax crops, tobacco, vegetables and melons, medicinal materials and other farm crops.

Irrigated Area refers to area of land that are effectively irrigated, i.e. relatively level land, where there are water sources or complete sets of irrigation facilities to lift and move adequate water for irrigation purpose under normal conditions. Under normal situations, irrigated area is the sum of watered fields and irrigated fields where irrigation systems or equipment have been installed for regular irrigation purpose. This important indicator reflects drought resistance capacity of the cultivated land in China.

Consumption of Chemical Fertilizers in Agriculture refers to the quantity of chemical fertilizers applied in agriculture in the year, including nitrogenous fertilizer, phosphate fertilizer, potash fertilizer, and compound fertilizer. The consumption of chemical fertilizers is calculated in terms of volume of effective components by means of converting the gross weight of the respective fertilizers into weight containing effective component (e.g. nitrogen content in nitrogenous fertilizer, phosphorous pentoxide contents in phosphate fertilizer, and potassium oxide contents in potash fertilizer). Compound fertilizer is converted in regard to its major components. The formula is:

Volume of effective component= physical quantity × effective component of certain chemical fertilizer (%)

Total Power of Agricultural Machinery refers to total mechanical power of machinery used in agriculture, forestry, animal husbandry and fishery, including machinery for ploughing, irrigation and drainage, harvesting, transport, plant protection, animal husbandry, forestry and fishery and other agricultural machineries. (For the power of internal combustion engines, it is converted from its horsepower into watts while for electric motors the output power is converted into watts.) Machinery employed for non-agricultural purposes, such as the machines used in township-run and village-run industry, construction, non-agricultural transport, scientific experiments and teaching, are not included. Data are mainly from agricultural machinery agencies.

12 工 业

INDUSTRY

资料整理：赵　晖　王凤玲　赵　博　陈小兵　李　玫　王　玥　沈佳慧
Data management：Zhao Hui Wang Fengling Zhao Bo Chen Xiaobing Li Mei Wang Yue Shen Jiahui
数据审核：马　琰
Data audit：Ma Yan

第十二部分　工业

一、简要说明

本章资料包括规模以上工业企业单位数、总产值、主要经济指标等，由西安市统计局工业处提供。

二、主要指标

规模以上工业企业单位数（个）	1220	比上年增长	6.1%
规模以上工业增加值（亿元）	1320.61	比上年增长	9.6%

12　INDUSTRY

Ⅰ.Brief Introduction

Data in this chapter includes number of industrial enterprises above designated size and gross product, primary economic. Data in this chapter are provided and compiled by Industry Division of the Xi'an Bureau of Statistics.

Ⅱ.Major Indicators

		Increase over Preceding Year
Number of Industrial Enterprises Above Designated Size(item)	1220	6.1%
Value Added of Industry Above Designated Size(100 million yuan)	1320.61	9.6%

12-1 主要年份全部工业总产值

Gross Output Value of Industry in Representative Years

单位：万元 (10 000 yuan)

年份 Year	全部工业总产值 Gross Industrial Output Value	工业总产值指数（上年=100） Index of Gross Industry Output Value (Preceding Year=100)	国有经济 State-owned Enterprises	集体经济 Collective-owned Enterprises	其他经济类型 Enterprises of Other Ownership
1952	23512	139.6	9917	464	13131
1962	120833	86.8	102103	17599	1131
1965	200416	132.1	183164	17252	
1970	333386	143.5	305303	28083	
1975	385509	106.1	332982	52527	
1978	483262	116.9	405376	77886	
1979	517483	106.6	438850	78633	
1980	531755	101.8	440139	91577	39
1981	524587	98.6	433740	90675	172
1982	549200	107.1	450308	98516	456
1983	603507	112.2	493773	108923	811
1984	674963	112.8	520593	153056	1314
1985	853196	120.4	632702	218893	1601
1986	976326	112.1	706380	267282	2664
1987	1142220	114.2	809186	328701	4341
1988	1429811	116.0	1012268	416217	1326
1989	1653472	106.1	1160877	486754	5814
1990	1771310	107.4	1196777	548605	25928
1991	2002727	110.0	1325242	604495	72990
1992	2300472	112.5	1488541	561369	250562
1993	3045988	121.7	1748145	1071122	226721
1994	3891584	120.6	1960533	1581321	349730
1995	4058952	108.7	2071755	1663536	323661
1996	5338510	133.4	2132140	2836176	370194
1997	5794532	121.8	1915536	2005610	1873386
1998	6738224	117.3	2593405	2077273	2067546
1999	7151528	117.1	2128243	2174220	2849065
2000	6394812	115.3	2749778	2094680	1550354
2001	7361510	116.4	3098431	2380910	1882169
2002	8379363	115.8	3472067	2312923	2594373
2003	9750800	115.1	4149015	1501372	4100413
2004	11853224	118.4	5414952	875412	5562860
2005	13085580	106.3	5916553	674900	6494127
2006	15573516	119.0	7527607	514810	7531099
2007	19798593	122.1	10179303	365329	9253961
2008	23881446	120.6	12479652	441987	10959807
2009	28270652	118.3	14440321	388777	13441554
2010	35628753	126.0	18353877	435206	16839669
2011	40933178	114.9	20654524	377199	19901455
2012	46560824	113.8	24303736	376427	21880661
2013	50426416	108.3	25358096	325004	24743316
2014	56606272	112.3	27352693	332712	28920867
2015	51599121	91.2	25008248	161009	26429864
2016	54624261	105.9	24498532	139018	29986711

注：2013年数据为全国第三次经济普查数据。

12-1 续表 continued

单位：万元 (10 000 yuan)

年份 Year	轻工业 Light Industry	重工业 Heavy Industry	大型工业 Large-size Industry Enterprises	中型工业 Medium-size Industry Enterprises	小型工业 Small-size Industry Enterprises
1952	20800	2712			
1962	68221	52618			
1965	98631	101785			
1970	124467	208919			
1975	167285	218224	145262	130592	109655
1978	220480	262782	168397	121813	193052
1979	243043	274440	189877	133759	193847
1980	283475	248280	193092	130053	208610
1981	309199	215388	178130	140810	205639
1982	303249	246031	213015	128597	207668
1983	315785	287722	245053	127164	231290
1984	321678	353285	241842	143165	289956
1985	401748	451448	333820	147488	371888
1986	458270	518056	401037	150644	424609
1987	516776	625452	472958	171698	497572
1988	699593	730210	615946	210089	603776
1989	712743	940729	696368	258414	698690
1990	787857	983453	716421	279098	775791
1991	897676	1105051	888052	303151	844524
1992	967104	1333368			
1993	1121957	1924031	1258137	384255	1403596
1994	1578875	2312709	1479613	390233	2021738
1995	1636219	2432733	1575030	371156	2112766
1996	2347887	2990623	1693985	358913	3285612
1997	2700085	3094447	1675521	274888	3844123
1998	3232681	3505543	1821556	308424	4608244
1999	3488547	3662981	1744637	337795	5069096
2000	3121419	3273393	2320973	328494	3745345
2001	3518054	3843456	2656010	368497	4337003
2002	3935764	4443599	3038828	398834	4941701
2003	4028859	5721941	2662073	2027256	5061471
2004	4211592	7641632	3595150	3237701	5020373
2005	4078417	9007163	4640325	3228553	5216702
2006	4510970	11062546	5970535	3414468	6188513
2007	7331719	12466874	8351303	4171131	7276159
2008	6010865	17870581	10472686	5005676	8403084
2009	6636464	21634188	12309192	6186395	9775065
2010	7841869	27786884	15002737	8537140	12088876
2011	8992547	31940631	16844272	6207660	17881246
2012	10218288	36342536	22563292	6243799	17753733
2013	9297919	41128497	17390620	7271086	25764710
2014	10369659	46236614	24880136	8754767	22971370
2015	10089660	41509461	26485412	8432031	16681678
2016	9774967	44849294	28603440	8074967	17945853

12-2 主要年份各区县规模以上工业总产值

Gross Output Value of Industry in Representative Years

单位：亿元 (100 million yuan)

区 县	Region	1998	1999	2000	2001	2002	2003	2004	2005	2006	2007
合 计	**Total**	**350.38**	**366.59**	**417.97**	**482.61**	**544.78**	**638.66**	**830.06**	**981.02**	**1187.74**	**1577.05**
新城区	Xincheng	67.19	71.36	78.25	89.87	105.92	137.46	145.61	196.00	135.14	157.18
碑林区	Beilin	20.57	19.48	21.50	23.15	30.32	22.22	15.92	20.13	18.31	19.10
莲湖区	Lianhu	63.24	65.92	75.68	93.78	106.33	124.24	157.67	185.86	200.75	281.57
灞桥区	Baqiao	19.55	19.95	21.35	20.56	22.99	28.80	37.25	42.29	57.11	80.01
未央区	Weiyang	53.31	52.84	61.41	73.63	80.14	93.23	145.63	170.16	220.08	265.93
雁塔区	Yanta	65.00	75.88	94.38	102.58	107.75	113.99	151.61	144.51	167.58	204.70
阎良区	Yanliang	26.54	26.06	27.56	36.22	40.04	40.98	55.86	68.10	75.84	95.29
临潼区	Lintong	8.90	7.55	7.64	9.36	14.14	34.67	53.49	66.91	85.96	114.09
长安区	Chang'an	7.92	7.70	8.70	8.42	9.96	10.81	19.40	26.43	67.19	101.61
高陵区	Gaoling	1.60	1.83	2.58	3.28	3.97	7.09	14.89	16.50	97.94	177.65
蓝田县	Lantian	2.58	2.37	3.81	4.76	5.12	5.00	5.34	5.69	8.35	13.13
周至县	Zhouzhi	1.24	2.41	2.05	1.73	1.51	1.45	2.92	3.16	3.94	5.52
户 县	Huxian	12.75	13.24	13.07	15.27	16.58	18.74	24.48	35.28	49.55	61.28

12-2 续表 continued

单位：亿元 (100 million yuan)

区 县	Region	2008	2009	2010	2011	2012	2013	2014	2015	2016
合 计	**Total**	**2007.85**	**2468.27**	**3130.15**	**3552.21**	**4066.31**	**4436.58**	**4961.12**	**4924.57**	**5266.25**
新城区	Xincheng	147.54	195.45	272.13	323.64	307.67	344.30	372.75	398.68	401.62
碑林区	Beilin	48.99	58.60	108.14	138.72	18.46	23.48	27.66	29.59	31.91
莲湖区	Lianhu	356.90	399.83	458.30	457.96	459.41	419.81	407.16	402.62	405.48
灞桥区	Baqiao	123.34	178.82	242.15	280.52	278.37	308.04	300.73	175.89	181.17
未央区	Weiyang	327.65	393.22	499.88	510.39	684.55	733.75	858.40	839.29	959.84
雁塔区	Yanta	262.32	249.69	286.19	367.97	587.65	624.55	694.34	677.00	648.80
阎良区	Yanliang	109.43	128.99	163.55	176.67	219.31	276.71	300.25	321.23	342.53
临潼区	Lintong	130.93	165.77	222.01	277.75	341.01	404.45	418.75	263.29	204.22
长安区	Chang'an	154.74	277.98	334.89	350.68	354.65	383.41	546.35	720.87	956.32
高陵区	Gaoling	256.55	305.94	402.98	516.33	662.99	741.34	854.73	869.60	835.74
蓝田县	Lantian	17.62	23.40	31.93	35.87	41.60	49.33	46.22	49.32	55.47
周至县	Zhouzhi	6.76	9.03	11.11	15.29	17.08	26.01	29.10	41.25	53.84
户 县	Huxian	65.09	81.54	96.89	100.42	93.55	101.40	104.68	135.94	189.31

12-3 各区县规模以上工业企业工业总产值（2016年）

单位：亿元

区县	Regin	单位数（个）Number of Enterprises (unit)	工业总产值 Gross Industrial Output Value	国有经济 State-owned Enterprises	集体经济 Collective-owned Enterprises	其他经济类型 Enterprises of Other Ownership
新城区	Xincheng	13	401.62	268.23		133.39
碑林区	Beilin	14	31.91			31.91
莲湖区	Lianhu	33	405.48	209.49		195.99
灞桥区	Baqiao	87	181.17	33.70	4.50	142.97
未央区	Weiyang	210	959.84	3.24	0.56	956.04
雁塔区	Yanta	241	648.80	73.67		575.13
阎良区	Yanliang	99	342.53	8.87	2.54	331.12
临潼区	Lintong	58	204.22	5.71		198.51
长安区	Chang'an	152	956.32	81.47		874.85
高陵区	Gaoling	144	835.74	3.15		832.59
蓝田县	Lantian	34	55.47	9.82	0.36	45.29
周至县	Zhouzhi	47	53.84		0.87	52.97
户　县	Huxian	88	189.31	10.30	0.55	178.46

Gross Output Value of Industrial Enterprises above Designated Size by Region (2016)

(100 million yuan)

轻工业 Light Industry	重工业 Heavy Industry	大型工业 Large-size Industry Enterprises	中型工业 Medium-size Industry Enterprises	小型工业 Small-size Industry Enterprises
78.49	323.13	381.05	18.08	2.48
15.46	16.45	8.53	14.95	8.43
43.15	362.33	373.67	22.79	9.02
48.17	133.00	69.85	23.29	88.03
292.24	667.60	183.34	166.07	610.43
83.06	565.74	274.97	193.64	180.19
54.26	288.27	169.85	20.90	151.78
103.99	100.23	83.58	62.74	57.90
50.91	905.41	771.38	90.97	93.97
60.10	775.64	408.42	173.29	254.03
23.91	31.56	9.82	5.45	40.20
32.38	21.46		0.82	53.02
55.86	133.45	125.87	14.52	48.92

12-4 主要年份规模以上工业企业主要经济指标

单位：亿元

年份 Year	企业单位数（个） Number of Enterprises (unit)	工业总产值（当年价格） Gross Industrial Output Value (At Current Prices)	工业增加值（现价） Industrial added value （at current prices）	从业人员年平均人数（万人） Annual Average Employers (10 000person)
1998	793	350.38	99.20	51.71
1999	770	366.59	106.56	45.64
2000	816	417.97	130.18	43.25
2001	785	482.61	149.06	40.12
2002	771	544.78	170.39	38.48
2003	735	638.66	202.74	36.55
2004	1066	830.06	254.17	38.08
2005	902	981.02	314.01	37.92
2006	904	1187.74	370.11	37.94
2007	937	1577.05	499.96	38.55
2008	1032	2007.85	605.25	40.17
2009	1131	2468.27	700.31	43.42
2010	1126	3130.15	824.09	47.11
2011	891	3552.21	951.58	50.42
2012	970	4066.31	1064.29	49.23
2013	1056	4436.57	1194.88	44.27
2014	1146	4961.12	1304.12	49.53
2015	1150	4924.57	1285.08	50.59
2016	1220	5266.25	1320.61	49.54

注：2013年数据为全国第三次经济普查数据，根据三经普对2009-2012年规模以上工业增加值数据进行了修订。

Major Economic Indicators of Industrial Enterprises above Designated Size in Representative Years

(100 million yuan)

资产总计 Total Assets	负债合计 Total Liabilites	所有者权益合计 Total Owners' Equities	主营业务收入 Cost of Principal Business	利润总额 Total Profits	利税总额 Total Pre-tax Profits
810.56	548.68	261.88	346.84	-1.26	14.82
853.90	577.94	275.96	346.26	8.26	27.30
958.05	622.46	323.72	420.42	16.11	36.29
1054.36	657.88	384.65	451.62	17.97	40.84
1065.76	643.78	412.27	541.64	25.43	51.31
1195.69	733.04	460.97	645.53	33.82	64.99
1333.91	869.30	464.60	812.46	38.57	74.23
1503.85	977.42	508.82	980.97	28.72	67.25
1651.67	1062.11	578.33	1183.51	61.46	110.23
1940.52	1254.01	686.51	1561.25	106.22	168.54
2426.13	1518.86	907.27	1928.05	84.89	168.63
2913.56	1779.38	1130.76	2384.52	177.20	280.68
3592.13	2069.29	1515.65	3011.19	245.37	373.56
3975.38	2295.49	1678.19	3381.27	172.94	312.78
4775.92	2835.55	1926.72	3758.56	167.77	320.57
5127.69	3049.36	2071.72	4171.21	211.26	392.14
6048.34	3607.62	2436.06	4566.20	226.17	401.20
6740.26	3860.55	2926.55	4374.11	206.88	341.40
7473.07	4158.75	3302.36	5028.28	290.96	438.59

12-5 各区县规模以上工业企业主要经济指标（2016年）

单位：亿元

区县	Region	企业单位数（个）Number of Enterprises (unit)	从业人员年平均人数（万人）Annual Average Employers (10 000 persons)	资产合计（亿元）Total Assets (100 mill yuan)
新城区	Xingcheng	13	4.08	556.30
碑林区	Beilin	14	0.52	87.59
莲湖区	Lianhu	33	5.87	909.76
灞桥区	Baqiao	87	2.76	246.02
未央区	Weiyang	210	6.60	789.37
雁塔区	Yanta	241	8.73	1478.80
阎良区	Yanliang	99	3.61	423.42
临潼区	Lintong	58	1.42	294.94
长安区	Chang'an	152	7.92	1477.40
高陵区	Gaoling	144	5.36	918.19
蓝田县	Lantian	34	0.50	67.62
周至县	Zhouzhi	47	0.39	26.03
户　县	Huxian	88	1.79	197.62

Major Economic Indicators of Industrial Enterprises above Designated Size by Region (2016)

(100 million yuan)

负债合计 Total Liabilites	所有者权益合计 Total Owners' Equities	主营业务收入 Revenue from Principal Business	利润总额 Total Profits	利税总额 Total Pre-tax Profits
325.85	230.45	369.90	15.47	36.84
60.38	27.20	43.75	6.73	9.71
391.48	517.91	399.60	30.11	49.53
150.86	94.61	159.49	12.53	18.24
428.32	361.05	893.41	36.29	60.29
815.82	663.05	674.03	39.01	63.25
283.62	139.80	331.20	10.79	13.16
156.18	138.77	178.88	8.50	13.06
757.02	719.50	1009.07	103.89	121.12
626.14	292.05	786.86	16.06	35.68
34.41	32.63	48.39	2.05	2.88
9.63	16.41	31.32	1.93	2.63
119.05	68.92	102.37	7.59	12.19

12-6 规模以上工业企业主要工业产品产量（2016年）

Major Output of Industrial Enterprises above Designated Size（2016）

产品名称	Name of Products	2016	比上年增长(%) Increase over Preceding Year (%)
自来水生产量(亿立方米)	Tap Water Production (100 million cu.m)	4.51	1.6
大米(万吨)	Rice (10 000 ton)	3.15	11.6
小麦粉(万吨)	Wheat Flour (10 000 ton)	87.63	-37.7
精制食用植物油(万吨)	Edible Vegetable Oil (10 000 ton)	18.32	7.0
鲜、冷藏肉（万吨）	Fresh/Frozen Meat(10 000 ton)	4.80	-0.8
饲料（万吨）	Mixed Feed(10 000 ton)	94.75	-9.3
配合饲料	Compound feed	6.68	-25.1
混合饲料	Mixed feed	87.26	-7.6
方便面(万吨)	instant Noodle(10 000 ton)	11.30	25.0
乳制品(万吨)	Dairy Products (10 000 ton)	88.42	-17.7
液体乳	Milk	78.50	-15.3
固体及半固体乳制品	Solid and semi-solid dairy products	9.92	-32.8
饮料酒(万千升)	Beverage Wine (10 000 kiloliter)	44.71	-2.5
白酒（折65度，商品量）	Liquor (as 65 degree, amount of goods)	0.02	-47.5
啤酒	Beer	44.69	-2.5
软饮料(万吨)	Soft Beverage (10 000 ton)	211.82	-19.5
碳酸饮料类（汽水）	Carbonated Beverage	42.12	-10.5
果汁和蔬菜汁饮料	Juice and Fruit Beverage	34.49	-50.8
包装饮用水类	Canned Drinking Water	63.85	-11.0
纱(万吨)	Yarn (10 000 ton)	4.21	19.8
1. 棉纱	Cotton Yarn	2.21	24.7
2. 棉混纺纱	Blend Fabric	0.53	31.5
3. 化学纤维纱	Pure Chemical-Fibre Yarn	1.46	9.7
布(亿米)	Cloth (100 million m)	1.22	15.7
1. 棉布	Cotton Cloth	0.39	23.0
2. 棉混纺布	Blend Fabric	0.24	22.5
3. 化学纤维布	Pure Chemical-Fibre Cloth	0.59	9.0
人造板（万立方米）	Artificial Board (10 000 cu.m)	45.79	11.4
纤维板	Fibre Board	45.79	11.4
家具（万件）	Furniture (10 000unit)	27.23	21.0

12-6 续表1 continued1

产品名称	Name of Products	2016	比上年增长(%) Increase over Preceding Year (%)
木质家具	Wooden Furniture	9.21	-12.8
金属家具	Metal furniture	4.05	18.0
软体家具	Soft Furniture (inc.: Sofa ,Mattress etc.)	6.93	-15.0
机制纸及纸板（外购原纸加工除外）（万吨）	Machine Made Paper(not including processing of procured base paper)(10 000 ton)	13.44	10.1
纸制品（万吨）	Paper-Made Products (10 000 ton)	13.13	5.3
瓦楞纸箱	Corrugated Paper	8.96	0.0
单色印刷（万令）	Monochrom Printed products(10 000 ream)	54.78	-6.1
多色印刷品（万对开色令）	Colored Printed products(10 000 ream)	705.65	-27.2
化学农药原药(折有效成分100%)(万吨)	Chemical Pesticide(100% effective content)(10 000 ton)	0.41	21.0
涂料（万吨）	Construction Paint(10 000 ton)	1.11	-4.6
合成洗涤剂（万吨）	Synthetic Detergents (10 000 ton)	6.53	-27.9
合成洗衣粉（万吨）	Washing Power	1.55	-16.8
液体洗涤剂	Liquid detergent	3.76	-33.1
化学原料药（万吨）	Chemical Medicine (10 000 ton)	0.02	-11.3
中成药（万吨）	Traditional Chinese Medicine (10 000 ton)	0.33	-10.5
化学纤维（万吨）	Chemical Fiber	2.03	-9.8
人造纤维（纤维素纤维）（万吨）	Man-made Fiber	2.03	-9.8
塑料制品（万吨）	Plastic Product (10 000 ton)	9.66	-29.9
水泥（万吨）	Cement (10 000 ton)	217.71	-28.8
硅酸盐水泥熟料（万吨）	Portland Cement Clinker (10 000 ton)	84.60	-23.2
水泥混凝土电杆（万根）	Cement Pole(10 000 unit)	2.37	12.1
商品混凝土(万立方米)	Ready-mixed Concrete (10 000 cu.m)	2106.30	4.4
沥青和改性沥青防水卷材（万平方米）	Asphalt and Modified Bitumen Membrane(10 000 sq.m)	2293.21	-11.0
钢化玻璃(万平方米)	Toughened Glass(10 000 sq.m)	339.79	22.6
日用玻璃制品（万吨）	Glassware(10 000 ton)	0.30	-41.3
钢材（万吨）	Rolled-steel Final Products (10 000 ton)	43.92	18.3
线材（盘条）	Wire Rod	13.20	-3.7
其他钢材	Other steel	30.52	30.8
铁合金（万吨）	Ferroalloy (10 000 ton)	0.28	-0.7
铝材(万吨)	Aluminum Material (10 000 ton)	3.97	-14.3
黄金（千克）	Gold (kg)	327.00	12.8

12-6 续表2 continued2

产品名称	Name of Products	2016	比上年增长(%) Increase over Preceding Year (%)
单晶硅（万千克）	Monocrystalline Silicon (10 000kg)	780.00	140.6
工业锅炉（蒸发量吨）	industrial Boiler steam(ton)	1237.40	-28.9
发动机（万千瓦）	Engine (10 000 kw)	379.25	77.5
汽车发动机（万千瓦）	Motor Engine(10 000 kw)	379.25	77.5
金属切削机床(万台)	Metal-cutting Machines (10 000 unit)	0.43	-14.6
泵(万台)	Pump (Liquid pump)(10 000 unit)	0.67	-9.6
风机（万台）	Fan(10 000 unit)	0.71	-27.8
气体压缩机（万台）	Gas Compressor(10 000 unit)	27.72	-5.0
阀门（万吨）	Valves (10 000 ton)	1.31	22.0
铸铁件（万吨）	iron Castings (10 000 ton)	1.11	18.2
铸钢件（万吨）	Steel Castings (10 000 ton)	1.23	2.3
锻件（万吨）	Forgings (10 000 ton)	0.24	-59.7
矿山专用设备（万吨）	Mining Equipment (10 000 ton)	2.87	-17.0
炼油、化工生产专用设备（万吨）	Oil Refining and Chemical industry Machine(10 000 ton)	0.39	6.1
金属冶炼设备（吨）	Metal Smelting Equipments(ton)	2429.60	-23.4
金属轧制设备（吨）	Metal-rolling Machine(ton)	2863.40	40.7
印刷专用设备（吨）	Printing Equipment(ton)	121.00	-16.6
环境污染防治设备(台/套)	Special Equipment for Environment Protection	151.00	13.5
大气污染防治设备	Equipment for Preventing Atmospheric Pollution	144.00	8.3
汽车（万辆）	Motor Vehicle(10 000unit)	38.25	12.0
基本型乘用车（轿车）	Basic Type Passenger Vehicles(car)	19.59	-18.4
轿车（排量≤1升）	Car0L-1.0L Gas Displacement(1.0L included)	2.12	1737.3
轿车（1升＜排量≤1.6升）	Car1.0L-1.6L Gas Displacement(1.6L included)	17.47	-26.4
运动型多用途乘用车（SUV）	Sports Utility Vehicle (SUV)	6.83	359.5
交叉型乘用车	Cross Passenger Car	0.61	145.5
客车	Passenger Vehicles	0.23	152.3
大型客车（车长>10米）	Large Buses （Length>10m）	0.10	57.0
中型客车（7米＜车长≤10米）	Medium Bus 7m-10m Length	0.05	3113.3
轻型客车（车长≤7米）	Light Buses（Length≤7m）	0.08	203.7
载货汽车	Trucks	10.99	32.3
新能源汽车	New Energy Vehicles (10000 unit)	4.81	46.9
改装汽车（万辆）	Refit Trucks (10 000 unit)	0.13	35.8
铁路货车（万辆）	Freight(10 000 unit)	0.13	77.5
电动机（万千瓦）	Electric motor(Ten thousand kilowatts)	346.08	-52.3

12-6 续表3 continued 3

产品名称	Name of Products	2016	比上年增长(%) Increase over Preceding Year (%)
直流电动机	DC motors	26.35	-50.6
交流电动机	Alternating Current Motor(10 000kw)	318.23	-52.6
变压器（万千伏安）	Transformer(10 000KVA)	13471.36	-0.8
高压开关板（万面）	High-voltage Switch Panel(10 000 unit)	0.80	-36.0
低压开关板（万面）	Low-voltage Switch Panel(10 000 unit)	1.01	-17.4
电力电缆(万千米)	Electric Power Cables(10 000 km)	3.32	10.6
通信及电子网络用电缆(万对千米)	Communication Cables(10 000 pair km)	4.57	50.5
光缆（万芯千米）	Cable (10 000 Core.km)	501.91	24.6
绝缘制品(吨)	Insulating Products(ton)	14925.00	60.3
电子元件（亿只）	Electronic Components(100 million unit)	3.58	18.0
工业自动化调节仪表与控制系统（万台、套）	Automatization meter and system (10 000 unit)	2.88	-43.9
电工仪器仪表（万台）	Electrical instrumentation (10 000 set)	84.85	-4.5
分析仪器及装置（万台、套）	Analysis instruments and Apparatus(10 000 set)	1.94	-36.8
化学试剂（万吨）	Chemicals Reagents(10000 ton)	24.47	-14.2
十种有色金属（万吨）	Ten kinds of nonferrous metals (10 000ton)	11.97	19.6
锌	Zinc	9.10	20.3
镍	Nickel	2.87	17.5
起重机（吨）	Crane (ton)	368.00	53.3
减速机（台）	Reducer (a)	4786.00	69.4
石油钻井设备（台/套）	Oil drilling equipment (unit / set)	578.00	-44.4
模具（万套）	Molds (10 000set)	1.72	-27.1
机械化农业及园艺机具（万台）	Mechanization of agriculture and horticulture machinery (10 000a)	1.61	-20.9
电动自行车（万辆）	Electric bicycle (10 000car)	69.50	10.7
电力电容器（万千乏）	Power capacitors (10 000kW)	3230.23	37.7
高压开关设备（11万伏以上）（万台）	High Voltage Switchgear (above 110,000 volt) (10 000a)	2.15	50.7
灯具及照明装置（万套/台/个）	Lamps and lighting equipment (10 000set /a)	2.89	-33.2
半导体分立器件（亿只）	Discrete semiconductor devices (100million unit)	49.41	77.2
光电子器件（亿只/片）	Optoelectronic devices (100million unit)	19.90	34.4
工业仪表（万台/个）	Industrial Instrumentation (10 000a)	4.18	27.3
发电量（亿千瓦小时）	Power generation(One hundred million kilowatt-hours)	161.00	2.1
火力发电量（亿千瓦小时）	Thermal power generation(One hundred million kilowatt-hours	143.80	6.1
水力发电量（亿千瓦小时）	Hydropower(One hundred million kilowatt-hours)	15.28	-24.1
风力发电量（亿千瓦小时）	Wind power generation(One hundred million kilowatt-hours)	1.92	-4.9

12-7 规模以上工业企业分行业工业增加值（2016年）

Added Value of Industrial Enterprises above Designated Size by Sector（2016）

单位:亿元 （100 million yuan)

行 业	Sector	2016
总计	**Total**	**1320.61**
按工业行业大类分	**Grouped by Sector**	
煤炭开采和洗选业	Mining and Washing of Coal	
石油和天然气开采业	Extraction of Petroleum and Natural Gas	
黑色金属矿采选业	Mining and Processing of Ferrous Metal Ores	
有色金属矿采选业	Mining and Processing of Non-ferrous Metal Ores	
非金属矿采选业	Mining and Processing of Nonmetal Ores	
开采辅助活动	Mining Auxiliary Activities	14.16
其他采矿业	Mining of Other Ores	
农副食品加工业	Processing of Food from Agricultural Porducts	27.36
食品制造业	Manufacture of Foods	36.58
酒、饮料和精制茶制造业	Manufacture of Alcohol,Beverages and Tea	28.63
烟草制品业	Manufacture of Tobacco	0.83
纺织业	Manufacture of Textile	7.61
纺织服装、服饰业	Textile, Garments industry	0.87
皮革、毛皮、羽毛及其制品和制鞋业	Manufacture of Leather, Fur, Feather and Related Products	1.13
木材加工和木、竹、藤、棕、草制品业	Processing of Timber, Manufacture of Wood,Plam and Straw Products	3.56
家具制造业	Manufacture of Furniture	2.33
造纸及纸制品业	Manufacture of Paper and Paper Products	2.87
印刷和记录媒介复制	Printing,Reproduction of Recording Media	20.76
文教、工美、体育和娱乐用品制造业	Manufacture of Articles For Cultural,Educational and Sports Activities	3.57
石油加工业、炼焦和核燃料加工业	Processing of Petroleum, Cokeing,Processing of Nuclear and Nuclear Fuel	5.09
化学原料及化学制品制造业	Manufacture of Raw Chemical Materials and Chemical Products	81.54
医药制造业	Manufacture of Medicines	59.94
化学纤维制造业	Manufacture of Chemical Fibers	3.32
橡胶和塑料制品业	Manufacture of Rubber and Plastics	14.03
非金属矿物制品业	Manufacture of Non-metallic Mineral Products	31.67
黑色金属冶炼和压延加工业	Smelting and Pressing of Ferrous Metals	6.42
有色金属冶炼和压延加工业	Smelting and Pressing of Non-ferrous Metals	39.34
金属制品业	Manufacture of Metal Products	31.17
通用设备制造业	Manufacture of General Purpose Machinery	34.96
专用设备制造业	Manufacture of Special Equipment	68.92
汽车制造业	Manufacture of Motor Vehicle	163.62
铁路、船舶、航空航天和其他运输设备制造业	Railways, Shipbuilding,Aerospace and Other Transportation Equipment Manufacturing Industry	137.30
电气机械和器材制造业	Manufacture of Electric Equipment and Machinery	133.29
计算机、通讯和其他电子设备制造业	Manufacture of Communication Equipment, Computers and other Electronic Equipment	220.42
仪器仪表制造业	Manufacture of Measuring Instruments and Machinery	37.16
其他制造业	Manufacture of Other Manufacturing	1.49
废弃资源综合利用业	Recycling and Disposal of Waste	0.11
金属制品、机械和设备修理业	Metal Products,Machinery and Equipment Repair Industry	0.79
电力、热力的生产和供应业	Production and Supply of Electric Power and Heat Power	78.03
燃气生产和供应业	Gas Mining and Supplying Industry	15.91
水的生产和供应业	Production and Supply of Water	5.82

12-8 主要年份规模以上工业企业经济效益指标

Indicators of Economic Performance of Industrial Enterprises above Designated Size in Representative Years

年 份 Year	总资产贡献率 (%) Ratio of Total Assets to Industrial Output Value (%)	资产负债率 (%) Assets-Liability Ratio (%)	流动资产周转次数 (次/年) Rate of Annual Turnover Working Capitals (times/year)	成本费用利润率 (%) Ratio of Profits to Cost (%)	全员劳动生产率 (元/人·年) Overall Labor Productivity (yuan/person·ear)	产品销售率 (%) Proportion of Industrial Products Sold (%)
1998		67.7	0.9	-266.1	19185	95.3
1999		67.7	0.9	2.5	22878	95.9
2000		65.0	1.0	4.2	29496	97.1
2001	5.8	62.4	0.9	4.1	38267	96.7
2002	6.2	60.4	1.1	5.1	46940	96.7
2003	7.0	61.3	1.1	5.7	58801	96.3
2004	6.9	65.2	1.2	5.0	66752	97.9
2005	8.4	65.0	1.3	3.1	82815	97.5
2006	7.8	64.3	1.4	5.5	97561	98.2
2007	10.2	64.6	1.6	7.3	129706	96.8
2008	8.6	62.6	1.5	4.6	150641	96.1
2009	11.3	61.1	1.7	8.1	161289	97.6
2010	12.2	57.6	1.7	8.8	188483	97.1
2011	8.6	57.7	1.5	5.2	194105	97.4
2012	7.7	59.4	1.5	4.5	230032	96.7
2013	8.5	59.5	1.5	5.2	264324	95.7
2014	7.4	59.7	1.4	5.2	266789	94.9
2015	5.7	57.3	1.3	4.8	268182	94.5
2016	6.4	55.7	1.3	6.0	277240	96.0

12-9 规模以上工业企业主要经济指标（2016年）

单位：万元

分 组	Classify	企业单位数（个）Number of Enterprises (unit)	亏损企业（个）Loss Making Enterprises	工业总产值（当年价格）Gross Industrial Output Value (At Current Prices)
总计	**Total**	**1220**	**219**	**52662497**
#市区	Urban	1051	193	49676248
#亏损企业	Deficit Enterprises	219	219	2994795
按隶属关系分	**Grouped by Jurisdiction of Management**			
中央企业	Central Enterprises	88	10	12239713
省属企业	Provincial Enterprises	71	13	7465602
市属企业	Municipal Enterprises	1061	196	32957182
按登记注册类型分组	**Grouped by Registion Status**			
内资企业	Domestic Investment Enterprises	1105	190	42800644
国有	State-owned Enterprises	34	2	7076483
集体	Collective-owned Enterprises	8		93897
股份合作	Share-holding Corperative	5		18206
联营	Joint Ownership Enterprises			
国有联营	State Joint Ownership Enterprises			
集体联营	Collective Joint Ownership Enterprises			
国有与集体联营	Joint State-collective Ownership Enterprises			
其他联营	Other Joint Ownership Enterprises			
有限责任公司	Limited Liability Corporations	605	118	23755202
国有独资公司	State Sole Funded Enterprises	39	7	3473675
其他有限责任公司	Other Limited Liability Corporation	566	111	20281527
股份有限公司	Share-holding Corperation Ltd.	105	12	4073700
私营	Private Enterprises	348	58	7783156
私营独资	Private-funded Enterprises	6		160103
私营合伙	Private Partnership Enterprises	1		2657
私营有限责任公司	Private Limited Liability Corporations	316	55	7365221
私营股份有限公司	Private Share Holding Corporations	25	3	255175
其他	Other Domestic Funded Enterprises			
港澳台商投资	Enterprises with Funds from Hong Kong,Macao and Taiwan	26	4	3026840
外商投资	Foreign Funded Enterprises	89	25	6835013
按轻重工业分	**Grouped by Light Industry and Heavy Industry**			
轻工业	Light Industry	324	61	9419611
重工业	Heavy Industry	896	158	43242886

Major Economic Indicators of Industrial Enterprises above Designated Size（2016）

(10 000yuan)

工业销售产值（当年价）Value of Industry Products Sales (At Current Prices)	出口交货值 Export Delivery Value	从业人员年平均人数（人）Annual Average Employers (person)	资产总计 Total Assets	流动资产合计 Total Working Capitals	固定资产合计 Total Fixed Assets	固定资产原价 Origing Value of Fixed Assets	累计折旧 Accumulative Total Depreciation
50563091	**5623736**	**495459**	**74730705**	**38229490**	**22002192**	**34997983**	**15854417**
47681230	5609248	468721	71818003	36858390	21196236	33700973	15209500
2934588	77963	52274	7817378	3545075	1969052	2614307	922715
11994217	537255	171934	25076681	11978514	8084184	12796163	6779209
7265932	260687	71317	12830613	7571504	2031020	3380941	1424336
31302942	4825794	252208	36823411	18679472	11886988	18820879	7650872
40952944	2402721	421482	61431949	33256272	15174672	24581183	12019897
6959707	230590	98117	13310185	7172398	4089018	7138666	3277155
91259		1302	78069	48435	23240	34217	16976
17702		482	32846	23867	5093	11101	6169
22938452	1259058	243435	34205418	19184948	8538595	12845203	6456678
3359604	356607	59639	11914666	4947821	4195781	5571086	3168647
19578848	902451	183796	22290752	14237127	4342814	7274117	3288031
3803244	438891	37135	8752631	4410122	1579814	2977964	1554237
7142580	474182	41011	5052800	2416502	938912	1574032	708682
157519		502	10761	7036	2917	5608	2693
2480		100	1220	940	281	962	697
6737935	473542	37810	3947222	2189439	892872	1445866	624788
244646	640	2599	1093597	219087	42842	121596	80504
3018555	208433	32953	2099065	813701	775060	1122649	414527
6591592	3012582	41024	11199691	4159517	6052460	9294151	3419993
9069846	658891	78931	8020736	4391593	2254367	3948495	1870520
41493245	4964845	416528	66709969	33837897	19747825	31049488	13983897

12-9 续表1

单位：万元

分 组	Classify	负债合计 Total Liabilites	流动负债合计 Total Working Liabilities	非流动负债 Non-Working Liabilities
总计	**Total**	**41587471**	**31918356**	**6687835**
#市区	Urban	39956622	30488496	6427598
#亏损企业	Deficit Enterprises	4975371	3811991	1043635
按隶属关系分	**Grouped by Jurisdiction of Management**			
中央企业	Central Enterprises	14355251	9573011	2268899
省属企业	Provincial Enterprises	7296993	6464640	730880
市属企业	Municipal Enterprises	19935227	15880705	3688056
按登记注册类型分组	**Grouped by Registion Status**			
内资企业	Domestic Investment Enterprises	34582491	26648889	5065082
国有	State-owned Enterprises	7365093	5641949	1708316
集体	Collective-owned Enterprises	47231	46063	833
股份合作	Share-holding Corperative	14143	12383	1760
联营	Joint Ownership Enterprises			
国有联营	State Joint Ownership Enterprises			
集体联营	Collective Joint Ownership Enterprises			
国有与集体联营	Joint State-collective Ownership Enterprises			
其他联营	Other Joint Ownership Enterprises			
有限责任公司	Limited Liability Corporations	21326547	16167488	2380428
国有独资公司	State Sole Funded Enterprises	7096106	3719910	826063
其他有限责任公司	Other Limited Liability Corporation	14230441	12447578	1554365
股份有限公司	Share-holding Corperation Ltd.	3370186	2726774	657786
私营	Private Enterprises	2459291	2054232	315959
私营独资	Private-funded Enterprises	2808	889	
私营合伙	Private Partnership Enterprises	720	700	20
私营有限责任公司	Private Limited Liability Corporations	2217230	1821612	310973
私营股份有限公司	Private Share Holding Corporations	238533	231031	4966
其他	Other Domestic Funded Enterprises			
港澳台商投资	Enterprises with Funds from Hong Kong,Macao and Taiwan	1232732	1066983	163837
外商投资	Foreign Funded Enterprises	5772248	4202484	1458916
按轻重工业分	**Grouped by Light Industry and Heavy Industry**			
轻工业	Light Industry	4644172	3570510	871189
重工业	Heavy Industry	36943299	28347846	5816646

continued1

(10 000yuan)

所有者权益合计 Total Owners' Equities	实收资本 Total Capital Hold	营业收入 Total Revenue	主营业务收入 Revenue from Principal Business	营业成本 Total Cost	主营业务成本 Cost of Principal Business	营业税金及附加 Taxs and Other Changes	主营业务税金及附加 Taxes and Other Charges on Principal Business
33023567	**13640672**	**51223577**	**50282752**	**43693923**	**42851616**	**263336**	**255125**
31844010	13169148	49395607	48461937	42258380	41420453	253703	245497
2841192	1870928	2760265	2670903	2437097	2359434	17976	16172
10626985	3842174	12496506	12310563	10746506	10523629	69787	67915
5533619	1813593	7858810	7540176	6720185	6436412	29393	29232
16862963	7984905	30868261	30432013	26227232	25891575	164156	157978
26729793	9774367	41267160	40501314	35509956	34813219	188546	180798
5945091	1284141	6863280	6680246	5710100	5575732	38262	37420
25029	9143	93642	78326	86380	77263	831	831
18703	9373	17034	16489	12740	12526	127	127
12778433	5914628	23698766	23229935	20616809	20128303	109835	104338
4723457	1545657	4250321	4181515	3552403	3492922	37686	33741
8054976	4368971	19448445	19048420	17064406	16635381	72149	70597
5383102	1554830	3669740	3627039	2932297	2895195	18586	17243
2579435	1002252	6924698	6869279	6151630	6124200	20905	20839
7952	2516	158856	157657	153175	151960	141	141
500	402	2506	2506	2054	2054	21	21
1715919	814592	6520764	6470004	5808736	5782621	18943	18883
855064	184742	242572	239112	187665	187565	1800	1794
866333	295461	3221005	3164034	2853313	2801016	51767	51767
5427441	3570844	6735412	6617404	5330654	5237381	23023	22560
3364269	1551143	8682395	8554656	6823483	6736310	46669	45375
29659298	12089529	42541182	41728096	36870440	36115306	216667	209750

12-9 续表2

单位：万元

分 组	Classify	销售费用 Expenses for Sales	管理费用 Expenses for Management	财务费用 Financial cost
总计	**Total**	**1826235**	**2872373**	**432956**
#市区	Urban	1710993	2735960	415690
#亏损企业	Deficit Enterprises	153956	284652	73721
按隶属关系分	**Grouped by Jurisdiction of Management**			
中央企业	Central Enterprises	241517	845325	162247
省属企业	Provincial Enterprises	429485	461264	35224
市属企业	Municipal Enterprises	1155233	1565784	235485
按登记注册类型分组	**Grouped by Registion Status**			
内资企业	Domestic Investment Enterprises	1321732	2295443	315505
国有	State-owned Enterprises	173649	547138	43127
集体	Collective-owned Enterprises	1800	1260	115
股份合作	Share-holding Corperative	685	2275	225
联营	Joint Ownership Enterprises			
国有联营	State Joint Ownership Enterprises			
集体联营	Collective Joint Ownership Enterprises			
国有与集体联营	Joint State-collective Ownership Enterprises			
其他联营	Other Joint Ownership Enterprises			
有限责任公司	Limited Liability Corporations	761262	1249755	210032
国有独资公司	State Sole Funded Enterprises	116111	330909	94903
其他有限责任公司	Other Limited Liability Corporation	645151	918846	115129
股份有限公司	Share-holding Corperation Ltd.	182189	255938	26017
私营	Private Enterprises	202147	239077	35989
私营独资	Private-funded Enterprises	1636	1222	243
私营合伙	Private Partnership Enterprises	146	167	1
私营有限责任公司	Private Limited Liability Corporations	190963	211569	33257
私营股份有限公司	Private Share Holding Corporations	9402	26119	2488
其他	Other Domestic Funded Enterprises			
港澳台商投资	Enterprises with Funds from Hong Kong,Macao and Taiwan	102293	84254	12096
外商投资	Foreign Funded Enterprises	402210	492676	105355
按轻重工业分	**Grouped by Light Industry and Heavy Industry**			
轻工业	Light Industry	839679	499741	75057
重工业	Heavy Industry	986556	2372632	357899

continued2

(10 000yuan)

营业利润 Operating Profit	利润总额 Total Profits	亏损企业亏损额 Total Loss of Deficit Enterprises	利税总额 Total Pre-tax Profits	应付职工薪酬 Salary Payable	本年应交增值税 Value Added Tax Payable
2111553	**2909622**	**181481**	**4385864**	**4347460**	**1212906**
2000035	2793923	170128	4208810	4197460	1161184
-223899	-181481	181481	-111412	336345	52093
546947	622448	16319	1048999	1945819	356764
113059	171594	12804	460459	618749	259471
1451547	2115580	152358	2876406	1782892	596671
1610767	1897194	115165	3099063	3620509	1013324
358071	408598	3616	689104	1012355	242244
3190	4345		7953	1948	2777
1156	1137		1920	1820	656
777200	937491	81725	1624467	2053834	577141
135003	199277	10805	416734	549646	179771
642197	738214	70920	1207733	1504188	397370
228329	277166	10287	391244	332434	95493
242821	268457	19537	384375	218118	95013
2440	2440		2910	1082	329
118	118		309	304	170
225249	247582	18902	357972	204189	91447
15014	18317	635	23184	12543	3067
120304	124719	949	190691	257539	14205
380482	887709	65367	1096110	469412	185377
361467	400991	53390	738826	586005	291166
1750086	2508631	128091	3647038	3761455	921740

12-9 续表3

单位：万元

分　组	Classify	企业单位数（个） Number of Enterprises (unit)	亏损企业（个） Loss Making Enterprises	工业总产值（当年价格） Gross Industrial Output Value (At Current Prices)
按企业规模分	**Grouped by Size of Enterprises**			
大型企业	Large-size	62	4	28603440
中型企业	Medium-size	158	27	8074967
小型企业	Small-size	1000	188	15984090
按经济组织类型分组	**Grouped by Economic Type of Orgnization**			
独资企业	Appropratorship	97	15	11922302
合作、合伙企业	Partnership	10	1	66677
股份有限公司	Corporaton	132	15	4499422
有限责任公司	Limited Liability Company	981	188	36174096
按控股情况分	**Grouped by Cast strand**			
国有控股	State owned shares	254	38	24221923
集体控股	Collective shares	28	4	1676419
私人控股	Private holdings	786	134	18583383
港澳台控股	Hong Kong and Macao Holdings	19	1	991938
外商投资	Foreign Investment	64	19	6069050
其他	Others	69	23	1119784
按工业行业大类分	**Grouped by Sector**			
煤炭开采和洗选业	Mining and Washing of Coal			
石油和天然气开采业	Extraction of Petroleum and Natural Gas			
黑色金属矿采选业	Mining and Processing of Ferrous Metal Ores			
有色金属矿采选业	Mining and Processing of Non-ferrous Metal Ores			
非金属矿采选业	Mining and Processing of Nonmetal Ores			
开采辅助活动	Mining Auxiliary Activities	5	3	379490
其他采矿业	Mining of other Ores			
农副食品加工业	Processing of Food from Agricultural Porducts	48	12	1719247
食品制造业	Manufacture of Foods	43	4	1368129
酒、饮料和精制茶制造业	Manufacture of Alcohol,Beverages and Tea	16	3	832035
烟草制品业	Manufacture of Tobacco	1		11355
纺织业	Manufacture of Textile	14	3	225221
纺织服装、服饰业	Textile, apparel industry	4	3	86375
皮革、毛皮、羽毛及其制品和制鞋业	Manufacture of Leather, Fur, Feather and Related Products, and Shoes	3		69254
木材加工和木、竹、藤、	Processing of Timber, Manufacture of Wood,Plam	5	2	131252

continued3

(10 000yuan)

工业销售产值（当年价）Value of Industry Products Sales (At Current Prices)	出口交货值 Export Delivery Value	从业人员年平均人数（人）Annual Average Employers (person)	资产总计 Total Assets	流动资产合计 Total Working Capitals	固定资产合计 Total Fixed Assets	固定资产原价 Origing Value of Fixed Assets	累计折旧 Accumulative Total Depreciation
28018778	3788510	304552	47351410	23189898	16439243	26355395	12125192
7488583	621255	89595	12544574	6593076	2597075	3817471	1534412
15055730	1213971	101312	14834721	8446516	2965874	4825117	2194813
11693278	3217315	121742	21445334	9606666	9328716	15205580	6193384
63961	346	846	48122	33607	9317	13974	8184
4192231	518593	41702	10392196	4945375	1842640	3425289	1740486
34613621	1887482	331169	42845053	23643842	10821519	16353140	7912363
23651834	1408437	296013	45409027	24332631	11975900	18866405	9190977
1621514	256696	8570	2020924	1034332	553941	1384485	867229
17386073	689689	138296	15029854	8010650	3132720	5093515	2244406
937452	177424	4784	350740	165089	128251	226051	104549
5872100	2952558	34147	10055859	3513006	5745271	8822100	3230763
1094118	138932	13649	1864301	1173782	466109	605427	216493
380075		5837	693730	443128	144431	344758	200327
1698435	2573	7506	936698	617771	212036	595969	389897
1293811	9343	12572	751617	343364	236499	403950	192762
946575	77700	6762	1083607	585481	386978	663093	276985
11992		178	23213	10133	3474	7188	3714
199697	10440	7818	379154	153592	180958	237182	66542
78181		1535	137045	99522	16533	19463	2930
64464		769	58030	35477	7784	7985	3849
121491		707	168491	54053	55657	69219	36538

12-9 续表4

单位：万元

分 组	Classify	负债合计 Total Liabilites	流动负债合计 Total Working Liabilities	非流动负债 Non-Working Liabilities
按企业规模分	**Grouped by Size of Enterprises**			
大型企业	Large-size	27371092	20470104	4309495
中型企业	Medium-size	6288018	4771703	1406623
小型企业	Small-size	7928361	6676549	971717
按经济组织类型分组	**Grouped by Economic Type of Orgnization**			
独资企业	Appropratorship	11432213	8481437	2894825
合作、合伙企业	Partnership	19423	15973	1820
股份有限公司	Corporaton	3961896	3189642	784091
有限责任公司	Limited Liability Company	26173939	20231304	3007099
按控股情况分	**Grouped by Cast strand**			
国有控股	State owned shares	26536713	20031310	3934831
集体控股	Collective shares	869461	727358	141743
私人控股	Private holdings	7899175	6604482	1016209
港澳台控股	Hong Kong and Macao Holdings	162479	136662	23906
外商投资	Foreign Investment	5163392	3624766	1427777
其他	Others	956251	793778	143369
按工业行业大类分	**Grouped by Sector**			
煤炭开采和洗选业	Mining and Washing of Coal			
石油和天然气开采业	Extraction of Petroleum and Natural Gas			
黑色金属矿采选业	Mining and Processing of Ferrous Metal Ores			
有色金属矿采选业	Mining and Processing of Non-ferrous Metal Ores			
非金属矿采选业	Mining and Processing of Nonmetal Ores			
开采辅助活动	Mining Auxiliary Activities	185912	185213	699
其他采矿业	Mining of other Ores			
农副食品加工业	Processing of Food from Agricultural Porducts	732615	644204	44200
食品制造业	Manufacture of Foods	347914	323712	20010
酒、饮料和精制茶制造业	Manufacture of Alcohol,Beverages and Tea	661049	532910	123785
烟草制品业	Manufacture of Tobacco	2120	2120	
纺织业	Manufacture of Textile	250824	145949	100798
纺织服装、服饰业	Textile, apparel industry	84590	53249	5170
皮革、毛皮、羽毛及其制品和制鞋业	Manufacture of Leather, Fur, Feather and Related Products, and Shoes	22299	15887	5531
木材加工和木、竹、藤、	Processing of Timber, Manufacture of Wood,Plam	90986	56529	31591

continued4

(10 000yuan)

所有者权益合计 Total Owners' Equities	实收资本 Total Capital Hold	营业收入 Total Revenue	主营业务收入 Revenue from Principal Business	营业成本 Total Cost	主营业务成本 Cost of Principal Business	营业税金及附加 Taxs and Other Changes	主营业务税金及附加 Taxes and Other Charges on Principal Business
19885873	7615871	28868950	28303969	24850992	24304140	160869	159093
6256555	2337689	7584485	7411456	6098149	5956478	44617	39588
6881139	3687112	14770142	14567327	12744782	12590998	57850	56444
10007309	4183106	11677671	11449367	9732360	9553576	49200	48213
28699	14272	62596	62041	54697	54482	185	185
6430960	1768150	4066714	4015650	3241386	3201547	21149	19800
16556599	7675144	35416596	34755694	30665480	30042011	192802	186927
18777867	6814496	24764383	24112982	21467687	20842156	129127	122764
1145653	305637	1448876	1420205	1191086	1169662	4669	4641
7111270	2651190	17032537	16841290	14576165	14444584	105994	104678
188262	121523	941677	935875	853270	849037	1314	1314
4892466	3201990	5950494	5904911	4692441	4645918	18028	17615
908049	545836	1085610	1067489	913274	900259	4204	4113
507817	274679	289777	285465	253356	251390	2503	2388
199544	113930	1511331	1480230	1367186	1357439	1185	1167
397333	200734	1266442	1234180	1013663	984896	4712	4712
422558	142438	906832	889657	658544	635028	14912	14824
21093	11515	13131	12866	8352	8220	117	117
128330	45593	198598	194542	172820	170170	692	692
52455	32300	50412	49861	41328	40982	874	53
35731	21680	67456	66803	60103	59546	315	315
77505	17286	94955	94155	92820	92125	279	269

12-9 续表5

单位：万元

分 组	Classify	销售费用 Expenses for Sales	管理费用 Expenses for Management	财务费用 Financial cost
按企业规模分	**Grouped by Size of Enterprises**			
大型企业	Large-size	881361	1615678	275894
中型企业	Medium-size	468479	534732	63908
小型企业	Small-size	476395	721963	93154
按经济组织类型分组	**Grouped by Economic Type of Orgnization**			
独资企业	Appropratorship	322632	864742	120131
合作、合伙企业	Partnership	2454	3363	264
股份有限公司	Corporaton	201413	299123	40385
有限责任公司	Limited Liability Company	1299736	1705145	272176
按控股情况分	**Grouped by Cast strand**			
国有控股	State owned shares	600825	1543909	218647
集体控股	Collective shares	70206	73863	6564
私人控股	Private holdings	704856	718655	98961
港澳台控股	Hong Kong and Macao Holdings	30544	14865	2120
外商投资	Foreign Investment	376635	435039	102048
其他	Others	43169	86042	4616
按工业行业大类分	**Grouped by Sector**			
煤炭开采和洗选业	Mining and Washing of Coal			
石油和天然气开采业	Extraction of Petroleum and Natural Gas			
黑色金属矿采选业	Mining and Processing of Ferrous Metal Ores			
有色金属矿采选业	Mining and Processing of Non-ferrous Metal Ores			
非金属矿采选业	Mining and Processing of Nonmetal Ores			
开采辅助活动	Mining Auxiliary Activities	2235	23710	-2768
其他采矿业	Mining of other Ores			
农副食品加工业	Processing of Food from Agricultural Porducts	43991	47407	12125
食品制造业	Manufacture of Foods	136386	47195	277
酒、饮料和精制茶制造业	Manufacture of Alcohol,Beverages and Tea	117389	50282	9660
烟草制品业	Manufacture of Tobacco	319	2414	-29
纺织业	Manufacture of Textile	3718	12111	789
纺织服装、服饰业	Textile, apparel industry	4064	5278	1423
皮革、毛皮、羽毛及其制品和制鞋业	Manufacture of Leather, Fur, Feather and Related Products, and Shoes	1485	2009	146
木材加工和木、竹、藤、	Processing of Timber, Manufacture of Wood,Plam	737	2829	2512

continued5

(10 000yuan)

营业利润 Operating Profit	利润总额 Total Profits	亏损企业亏损额 Total Loss of Deficit Enterprises	利税总额 Total Pre-tax Profits	应付职工薪酬 Salary Payable	本年应交增值税 Value Added Tax Payable
1118783	1764820	15985	2612925	3086579	687236
374224	465114	73072	760727	637237	250996
618546	679688	92424	1012212	623644	274674
595104	1136475	25639	1465842	1261004	280167
1806	1978	52	3347	3649	1183
237192	303575	10923	425043	372258	100320
1277451	1467594	144867	2491632	2710549	831236
864369	1070497	62325	1900889	2906675	701265
95552	113654	1043	150436	119750	32113
754800	813894	47893	1198625	782336	278737
42691	44311	424	56774	51926	11149
319624	823306	54501	1004216	390120	162883
34517	43960	15295	74924	96653	26759
10725	12170	1928	20972	98479	6298
19520	31105	4959	39616	39637	7325
61936	64940	1423	106140	72428	36488
56524	68774	5359	111605	82026	27919
1959	1932		3036	2564	986
7055	8576	916	16114	31425	6846
-2509	-4886	4896	-2826	4194	1186
3480	3650		4044	6021	80
-4283	-3341	3576	-1038	2692	2023

12-9 续表6

单位：万元

分组	Classify	企业单位数（个） Number of Enterprises (unit)	亏损企业（个） Loss Making Enterprises	工业总产值（当年价格） Gross Industrial Output Value (At Current Prices)
棕、草制品业	and Straw Products			
家具制造业	Manufacture of Furniture	14	1	85218
造纸及纸制品业	Manufacture of Paper and Paper Products	23	2	272196
印刷和记录媒介复制	Printing,Reproduction of Recording Media	23	3	650676
文教、工美、体育和娱乐用品制造业	Manufacture of Articles For Cultural,Educational and Sports Activities	7	1	697683
石油加工业、炼焦和核燃料加工业	Processing of Petroleum, Cokeing,Processing of Nuclear and Nuclear Fuel	7	3	146402
化学原料及化学制品制造业	Manufacture of Raw Chemical Materials and Chemical Products	75	13	2774114
医药制造业	Manufacture of Medicines	53	11	2061574
化学纤维制造业	Manufacture of Chemical Fibers	3	1	132624
橡胶和塑料制品业	Manufacture of Rubber and Plastics	30	4	645852
非金属矿物制品业	Manufacture of Non-metallic Mineral Products	112	30	1510881
黑色金属冶炼和压延加工业	Smelting and Pressing of Ferrous Metals	12	1	339791
有色金属冶炼和压延加工业	Smelting and Pressing of Non-ferrous Metals	38	7	2301736
金属制品业	Manufacture of Metal Products	64	6	1334733
通用设备制造业	Manufacture of General Purpose Machinery	75	14	1462884
专用设备制造业	Manufacture of Special Equipment	107	25	2467069
汽车制造业	Manufacture of Motor Vehicle	48	8	8228285
铁路、船舶、航空航天和其他运输设备制造业	Railways,Shipbuilding,Aerospace and Other Transportation Equipment Manufacturing Industry	70	4	5136475
电气机械和器材制造业	Manufacture of Electric Equipment and Machinery	128	24	6334127
计算机、通讯和其他电子设备制造业	Manufacture of Communication Equipment, Computers and other Electronic Equipment	85	8	6754296
仪器仪表制造业	Manufacture of Measuring Instruments and Machinery	57	7	1356767
其他制造业	Manufacture of Other Manufacturing	10	2	59459
废弃资源综合利用业	Recycling and Disposal of Waste	2	1	4230
金属制品、机械和设备修理业	Metal Products,Machinery and Equipment Repair Industry	5	2	17096
电力、热力的生产和供应业	Production and Supply of Electric Power and Heat Power	18	7	2422350
燃气生产和供应业	Gas Mining and Supplying Industry	11	2	531528
水的生产和供应业	Production and Supply of Water	4	2	112093

continued6

(10 000yuan)

工业销售产值（当年价） Value of Industry Products Sales (At Current Prices)	出口交货值 Export Delivery Value	从业人员年平均人数（人） Annual Average Employers (person)	资产总计 Total Assets	流动资产合计 Total Working Capitals	固定资产合计 Total Fixed Assets	固定资产原价 Origing Value of Fixed Assets	累计折旧 Accumulative Total Depreciation
80282		1576	90268	56655	29324	28663	6516
266970		2609	140776	80439	35708	45252	14648
632159	1362	6684	597995	302539	223600	484240	263437
675554	537758	644	188531	135088	52061	57827	5846
148740		4981	175307	47770	123742	125025	48305
2615776	454343	21314	3541893	1908497	948242	2084361	1162691
1904933	11869	16450	1881326	1091557	347091	547984	266294
110998	206	539	174019	83584	84567	143786	59219
625611	1359	15887	1206881	811710	254487	360969	139335
1460182	926	12071	1309272	768045	413491	812958	499376
328398	1292	1334	152810	104256	38930	79121	40692
2104837	123836	10635	2921216	1215950	555103	762579	265460
1296231	7894	23527	2893399	1220391	572596	946766	402483
1428036	37031	17092	3380851	2500880	384174	683600	334543
2327597	267227	27725	5696888	3098072	1110239	1520913	575334
8163711	238243	73987	8872242	5562984	1743176	2879831	1230307
4871589	651577	73804	9569573	5179709	1979962	2799656	1262532
5970120	205448	42306	7691627	5168089	1180855	2067642	899720
6272829	2916454	45539	9747200	3657427	5224821	8254236	2972605
1338503	65841	17026	2002022	1233120	412524	676100	274772
59373	1014	1266	90649	60909	6976	13656	6752
4176		58	3787	146	1054	1119	65
16886		404	48019	36298	6050	7871	2461
2422254		26559	6908354	1086292	4605864	6588319	3651480
530532		4627	927455	341457	280084	380634	115739
112093		3131	286760	135105	143121	296068	180261

12-9 续表7

单位：万元

分 组	Classify	负债合计 Total Liabilites	流动负债合计 Total Working Liabilities	非流动负债 Non-Working Liabilities
棕、草制品业	and Straw Products			
家具制造业	Manufacture of Furniture	45297	39351	5855
造纸及纸制品业	Manufacture of Paper and Paper Products	69530	66209	3047
印刷和记录媒介复制	Printing,Reproduction of Recording Media	166673	140933	23740
文教、工美、体育和娱乐用品制造业	Manufacture of Articles For Cultural,Educational and Sports Activities	182152	182150	2
石油加工业、炼焦和核燃料加工业	Processing of Petroleum, Cokeing,Processing of Nuclear and Nuclear Fuel	116388	116355	33
化学原料及化学制品制造业	Manufacture of Raw Chemical Materials and Chemical Products	1681352	1324750	442355
医药制造业	Manufacture of Medicines	946829	791279	56893
化学纤维制造业	Manufacture of Chemical Fibers	112944	68318	44626
橡胶和塑料制品业	Manufacture of Rubber and Plastics	909512	649454	237179
非金属矿物制品业	Manufacture of Non-metallic Mineral Products	793205	660738	80267
黑色金属冶炼和压延加工业	Smelting and Pressing of Ferrous Metals	82740	74779	90
有色金属冶炼和压延加工业	Smelting and Pressing of Non-ferrous Metals	896000	760325	120256
金属制品业	Manufacture of Metal Products	1425863	1138658	280899
通用设备制造业	Manufacture of General Purpose Machinery	1758467	1635919	116227
专用设备制造业	Manufacture of Special Equipment	2776413	2444835	315698
汽车制造业	Manufacture of Motor Vehicle	5612446	5099113	480218
铁路、船舶、航空航天和其他运输设备制造业	Railways,Shipbuilding,Aerospace and Other Transportation Equipment Manufacturing Industry	5382391	4255601	1120694
电气机械和器材制造业	Manufacture of Electric Equipment and Machinery	3752074	3158944	537559
计算机、通讯和其他电子设备制造业	Manufacture of Communication Equipment, Computers and other Electronic Equipment	5105715	3660226	1417093
仪器仪表制造业	Manufacture of Measuring Instruments and Machinery	940470	803354	111737
其他制造业	Manufacture of Other Manufacturing	46860	38302	8558
废弃资源综合利用业	Recycling and Disposal of Waste	1044	865	34
金属制品、机械和设备修理业	Metal Products,Machinery and Equipment Repair Industry	26127	25827	300
电力、热力的生产和供应业	Production and Supply of Electric Power and Heat Power	5606804	2150123	853000
燃气生产和供应业	Gas Mining and Supplying Industry	575439	548012	27427
水的生产和供应业	Production and Supply of Water	196427	124163	72264

continued7

(10 000yuan)

所有者权益合计 Total Owners' Equities	实收资本 Total Capital Hold	营业收入 Total Revenue	主营业务收入 Revenue from Principal Business	营业成本 Total Cost	主营业务成本 Cost of Principal Business	营业税金及附加 Taxs and Other Changes	主营业务税金及附加 Taxes and Other Charges on Principal Business
44970	17435	71344	70107	55636	54483	431	404
69864	35201	265757	261276	244596	243428	608	604
431322	227664	623823	609901	515009	504268	3901	3893
6379	4931	640464	640448	632379	632364	24	24
58919	51218	145141	142770	132798	131396	990	722
1765437	599704	2568199	2513207	2165766	2115795	8479	8287
934496	269537	1837378	1830017	1043810	1043559	13007	13006
61075	71800	110927	110905	94225	94225	254	254
297369	150157	661169	630528	564019	545827	3544	3543
516065	318156	1505812	1486715	1340487	1331788	5391	5205
64260	22936	285027	284778	257741	257530	2348	2348
2019709	619107	2243724	2181680	2063347	2008881	3107	3100
1467534	505429	1185531	1172401	1007284	995938	6725	6694
1623043	329916	1401743	1380715	1175017	1151491	8581	8278
2920473	1033611	2357430	2323247	1851899	1829244	12706	12452
3259796	1049190	8727740	8443580	7856704	7583063	68692	68690
4187181	1579915	5161317	5120069	4545723	4433755	14667	13908
3939551	1185480	5524141	5416752	4607280	4522481	28360	27501
4641484	3085717	6286162	6260387	5377077	5364667	11893	11875
1059952	377009	1296157	1283023	1023738	1003858	9021	8537
43789	22585	62950	62107	49865	49165	501	501
2742	405	4180	4050	4068	3655	13	11
21892	22023	32163	31620	24853	24336	159	159
1301550	914849	3110958	3083261	2805867	2790884	30148	26736
352015	243756	593439	520218	487357	441842	3444	3430
90334	42786	121967	111231	99206	93897	753	426

12-9 续表8

单位：万元

分 组	Classify	销售费用 Expenses for Sales	管理费用 Expenses for Management	财务费用 Financial cost
棕、草制品业	and Straw Products			
家具制造业	Manufacture of Furniture	3219	5391	536
造纸及纸制品业	Manufacture of Paper and Paper Products	4208	5947	1886
印刷和记录媒介复制	Printing,Reproduction of Recording Media	18527	56790	2191
文教、工美、体育和娱乐用品制造业	Manufacture of Articles For Cultural,Educational and Sports Activities	1080	1693	141
石油加工业、炼焦和核燃料加工业	Processing of Petroleum, Cokeing,Processing of Nuclear and Nuclear Fuel	5678	10872	1078
化学原料及化学制品制造业	Manufacture of Raw Chemical Materials and Chemical Products	70466	152303	21110
医药制造业	Manufacture of Medicines	439719	173973	23908
化学纤维制造业	Manufacture of Chemical Fibers	1030	4897	4292
橡胶和塑料制品业	Manufacture of Rubber and Plastics	25809	29342	10597
非金属矿物制品业	Manufacture of Non-metallic Mineral Products	30888	65548	9347
黑色金属冶炼和压延加工业	Smelting and Pressing of Ferrous Metals	1864	7206	1064
有色金属冶炼和压延加工业	Smelting and Pressing of Non-ferrous Metals	15232	65138	10205
金属制品业	Manufacture of Metal Products	23392	104997	18463
通用设备制造业	Manufacture of General Purpose Machinery	47576	131417	3522
专用设备制造业	Manufacture of Special Equipment	112256	220062	20313
汽车制造业	Manufacture of Motor Vehicle	257435	324682	9327
铁路、船舶、航空航天和其他运输设备制造业	Railways,Shipbuilding,Aerospace and Other Transportation Equipment Manufacturing Industry	77602	319216	50137
电气机械和器材制造业	Manufacture of Electric Equipment and Machinery	249800	364375	21236
计算机、通讯和其他电子设备制造业	Manufacture of Communication Equipment, Computers and other Electronic Equipment	43596	411708	77277
仪器仪表制造业	Manufacture of Measuring Instruments and Machinery	35781	139444	-2502
其他制造业	Manufacture of Other Manufacturing	2249	6531	1020
废弃资源综合利用业	Recycling and Disposal of Waste	4	59	2
金属制品、机械和设备修理业	Metal Products,Machinery and Equipment Repair Industry	1471	5360	-158
电力、热力的生产和供应业	Production and Supply of Electric Power and Heat Power	6516	32925	118190
燃气生产和供应业	Gas Mining and Supplying Industry	35777	26959	2872
水的生产和供应业	Production and Supply of Water	4736	12303	2767

continued8

(10 000yuan)

营业利润 Operating Profit	利润总额 Total Profits	亏损企业亏损额 Total Loss of Deficit Enterprises	利税总额 Total Pre-tax Profits	应付职工薪酬 Salary Payable	本年应交增值税 Value Added Tax Payable
6055	6112	24	7818	7116	1275
9470	11106	247	17152	8813	5439
26378	23356	723	47422	74817	20165
5147	5304	136	8333	3126	3005
-6317	-6322	9054	-18	14707	5314
150436	172170	5445	222436	226882	41788
135006	138255	4746	313733	163028	162471
6225	6335	4503	752	6567	-5837
25205	28066	1889	49609	47945	18000
43988	46354	6403	77655	52090	25911
14678	14812	122	24929	6246	7770
85064	98420	5727	135044	69261	33517
28173	38357	2079	62357	172090	17275
45305	74099	3122	120832	150981	38152
115819	189973	20859	272001	254888	69322
156706	184648	8461	393371	560024	140031
236749	245015	8108	362037	845907	102354
252259	278734	41649	476579	406806	169486
352039	858505	11544	930641	384063	60243
101665	128495	4067	167039	182005	29523
2571	3476	563	6547	7961	2569
35	30	1	54	178	10
196	315	1520	1961	12692	1486
117306	132528	15566	319925	281349	157249
44906	45615	891	62969	37940	13910
2082	2944	975	7023	30512	3327

12-10 规模以上国有及国有控股工业企业主要经济指标（2016年）

单位：万元

分组	Classify	企业单位数（个） Number of Enterprises (unit)	亏损企业 Loss Making Enterprises	工业总产值（当年价格） Gross Industrial Output Value (At Current Prices)
总计	**Total**	**254**	**38**	**24221923**
#市区	Urban	246	37	23733788
#亏损企业	Deficit Enterprises	38	38	961230
按隶属关系分	**Grouped by Jurisdiction of Management**			
中央企业	Central Enterprises	87	10	12235355
省属企业	Provincial Enterprises	50	10	6393487
市属企业	Municipal Enterprises	117	18	5593081
按轻重工业分	**Grouped by Light Industry and Heavy Industry**			
轻工业	Light Industry	37	10	969874
重工业	Heavy Industry	217	28	23252049
按企业规模分	Grouped by Size of Enterprises			
大型企业	Large-size	43	2	17522293
中型企业	Medium-size	68	10	3537887
小型企业	Small-size	143	26	3161743
按工业行业大类分	**Grouped by Sector**			
煤炭开采和洗选业	Mining and Washing of Coal			
石油和天然气开采业	Extraction of Petroleum and Natural Gas			
黑色金属矿采选业	Mining and Processing of Ferrous Metal Ores			
有色金属矿采选业	Mining and Processing of Non-ferrous Metal Ores			
非金属矿采选业	Mining and Processing of Nonmetal Ores			
开采辅助活动	Mining Auxiliary Activities	2		360471
其他采矿业	Mining of Other Ores			
农副食品加工业	Processing of Food from Agricultural Porducts	4	2	27949
食品制造业	Manufacture of Foods	5	1	122417
酒、饮料和精制茶制造业	Manufacture of Alcohol,Beverages and Tea	1		108155
烟草制品业	Manufacture of Tobacco	1		11355
纺织业	Manufacture of Textile	4	1	85777
纺织服装、服饰业	Textile, apparel industry			
皮革、毛皮、羽毛及其制品和制鞋业	Leather fur feathers and its products and footwear	1		59313
木材加工和木、竹、藤、棕、草制品业	Processing of Timber, Manufacture of Wood,Plato and Straw Products			

Major Economic Indicators of State-owned and State-holding Share Industrial Enterprises above Designated Size (2016)

(10 000yuan)

工业销售产值（当年价） Value of Industry Products Sales (At Current Prices)	出口交货值 Export Delivery Value	从业人员年平均人数（人） Annual Average Employers (person)	资产总计 Total Assets	流动资产合计 Total Working Capitals	固定资产合计 Total Fixed Assets	固定资产原价 Origing Value of Fixed Assets	累计折旧 Accumulative Total Depreciation
23651834	**1408437**	**296013**	**45409027**	**24332631**	**11975900**	**18866405**	**9190977**
23165641	1408437	287262	44614041	24027228	11619778	18147894	8774118
973736	24223	21876	3219233	1567603	958952	1242305	421587
11989859	537255	171867	25061845	11967151	8084011	12795583	6778801
6268752	258065	63691	11829809	6986198	1901908	3112697	1271472
5393223	613117	60455	8517373	5379282	1989981	2958125	1140704
1098069	13517	20836	1555319	790552	600631	1151445	592104
22553765	1394920	275177	43853708	23542079	11375269	17714960	8598873
17403453	764773	234098	34487076	18561991	9795375	15671907	7898966
3205619	360717	42225	7546869	3659192	1390890	2061448	872471
3042762	282947	19690	3375082	2111448	789635	1133050	419540
361059		5188	615098	392819	122447	302708	180254
27204	2573	1093	71502	48797	18582	38968	20387
120723		1731	58447	29505	18623	40954	22331
252266		1337	166325	101768	18793	51612	33578
11992		178	23213	10133	3474	7188	3714
87451	5393	6744	296496	101279	164368	210321	54656
56245		621	47311	24882	7719	7719	3642

12-10 续表1

单位：万元

分 组	Classify	负债合计 Total Liabilites	流动负债合计 Total Working Liabilities	非流动负债 Non-Working Liabilities
总计	**Total**	**26536713**	**20031310**	**3934831**
#市区	Urban	26182441	19749878	3783535
#亏损企业	Deficit Enterprises	2363989	1827820	518747
按隶属关系分	**Grouped by Jurisdiction of Management**			
中央企业	Central Enterprises	14347020	9564780	2268899
省属企业	Provincial Enterprises	6759380	6011815	721069
市属企业	Municipal Enterprises	5430313	4454715	944863
按轻重工业分	**Grouped by Light Industry and Heavy Industry**			
轻工业	Light Industry	842185	640960	201125
重工业	Heavy Industry	25694528	19390350	3733706
按企业规模分	Grouped by Size of Enterprises			
大型企业	Large-size	20877458	15556550	2797603
中型企业	Medium-size	3513749	2688015	776976
小型企业	Small-size	2145506	1786745	360252
按工业行业大类分	**Grouped by Sector**			
煤炭开采和洗选业	Mining and Washing of Coal			
石油和天然气开采业	Extraction of Petroleum and Natural Gas			
黑色金属矿采选业	Mining and Processing of Ferrous Metal Ores			
有色金属矿采选业	Mining and Processing of Non-ferrous Metal Ores			
非金属矿采选业	Mining and Processing of Nonmetal Ores			
开采辅助活动	Mining Auxiliary Activities	173399	172701	699
其他采矿业	Mining of Other Ores			
农副食品加工业	Processing of Food from Agricultural Porducts	92697	92697	
食品制造业	Manufacture of Foods	22868	22838	30
酒、饮料和精制茶制造业	Manufacture of Alcohol,Beverages and Tea	94922	93805	1117
烟草制品业	Manufacture of Tobacco	2120	2120	
纺织业	Manufacture of Textile	205227	106779	98448
纺织服装、服饰业	Textile, apparel industry			
皮革、毛皮、羽毛及其制品和制鞋业	Leather fur feathers and its products and footwear	19532	14001	5531
木材加工和木、竹、藤、棕、草制品业	Processing of Timber, Manufacture of Wood,Plato and Straw Products			

continued1

(10 000yuan)

所有者权益合计 Total Owners' Equities	实收资本 Total Capital Hold	营业收入 Total Revenue	主营业务收入 Revenue from Principal Business	营业成本 Total Cost	主营业务成本 Cost of Principal Business	营业税金及附加 Taxs and Other Changes	主营业务税金及附加 Taxes and Other Charges on Principal Business
18777867	**6814496**	**24764383**	**24112982**	**21467687**	**20842156**	**129127**	**122764**
18432256	6691887	24353091	23705128	21139364	20516086	127177	120816
855244	751080	943807	888669	825639	776430	5380	4797
10620380	3841874	12492148	12306226	10743783	10520906	69763	67891
5070429	1658904	6868104	6557313	6118460	5840014	23635	23474
3087058	1313718	5404131	5249443	4605444	4481236	35729	31399
713133	421265	1142107	1108789	903716	879369	15531	15194
18064734	6393231	23622276	23004193	20563971	19962787	113596	107570
13515174	4379796	18267792	17791170	15785565	15312887	98603	97099
4033119	1388581	3614856	3509774	3140006	3052297	18106	14096
1229574	1046119	2881735	2812038	2542116	2476972	12418	11569
441695	260495	266859	264218	232788	232102	2253	2165
-21194	11253	28704	28030	26233	25872	153	152
35579	24191	132892	119903	109150	96416	497	497
71403	28790	253771	253681	189009	188930	9829	9829
21093	11515	13131	12866	8352	8220	117	117
91269	17746	95128	91072	84601	81951	454	454
27779	15000	59313	58661	52534	51977	281	281

12-10 续表2

单位：万元

分组	Classify	销售费用 Expenses for Sales	管理费用 Expenses for Management	财务费用 Financial cost
总计	**Total**	**600825**	**1543909**	**218647**
#市区	Urban	596190	1501867	211555
#亏损企业	Deficit Enterprises	38631	123942	29044
按隶属关系分	**Grouped by Jurisdiction of Management**			
中央企业	Central Enterprises	241358	844561	162168
省属企业	Provincial Enterprises	206988	386375	19669
市属企业	Municipal Enterprises	152479	312973	36810
按轻重工业分	**Grouped by Light Industry and Heavy Industry**			
轻工业	Light Industry	49505	84537	4381
重工业	Heavy Industry	551320	1459372	214266
按企业规模分	Grouped by Size of Enterprises			
大型企业	Large-size	467278	1172237	170517
中型企业	Medium-size	86641	232114	26329
小型企业	Small-size	46906	139558	21801
按工业行业大类分	**Grouped by Sector**			
煤炭开采和洗选业	Mining and Washing of Coal			
石油和天然气开采业	Extraction of Petroleum and Natural Gas			
黑色金属矿采选业	Mining and Processing of Ferrous Metal Ores			
有色金属矿采选业	Mining and Processing of Non-ferrous Metal Ores			
非金属矿采选业	Mining and Processing of Nonmetal Ores			
开采辅助活动	Mining Auxiliary Activities	883	20870	-2934
其他采矿业	Mining of Other Ores			
农副食品加工业	Processing of Food from Agricultural Porducts	1817	2714	431
食品制造业	Manufacture of Foods	7934	5776	-12
酒、饮料和精制茶制造业	Manufacture of Alcohol,Beverages and Tea	18053	2636	-1391
烟草制品业	Manufacture of Tobacco	319	2414	-29
纺织业	Manufacture of Textile	1257	9816	436
纺织服装、服饰业	Textile, apparel industry			
皮革、毛皮、羽毛及其制品和制鞋业	Leather fur feathers and its products and footwear	1231	1766	138
木材加工和木、竹、藤、棕、草制品业	Processing of Timber, Manufacture of Wood,Plato and Straw Products			

continued2

(10 000yuan)

营业利润 Operating Profit	利润总额 Total Profits	亏损企业亏损额 Total Loss of Deficit Enterprises	利税总额 Total Pre-tax Profits	应付职工薪酬 Salary Payable	本年应交增值税 Value Added Tax Payable
864369	**1070497**	**62325**	**1900889**	**2906675**	**701265**
824302	1034221	62148	1848796	2834820	687398
-89956	-62325	62325	-32662	172245	24283
546517	622018	16319	1048327	1945180	356547
44859	103456	11509	277882	501263	150791
272993	345023	34497	574680	460232	193927
86070	91548	6942	150730	172771	43651
778299	978949	55383	1750159	2733904	657614
623480	755953	7056	1372636	2403598	518080
119421	170202	26192	299815	324600	111506
121468	144342	29077	228438	178477	71679
13049	14095	3	21624	92227	5274
-2653	-795	2977	308	7518	950
9532	9889	900	14051	9169	3665
36371	36329		57990	17228	11833
1959	1932		3036	2564	986
-565	948	785	2954	28279	1553
3446	3536		3885	5457	68

12-10 续表3

单位：万元

分 组	Classify	企业单位数（个） Number of Enterprises (unit)	亏损企业 Loss Making Enterprises	工业总产值（当年价格） Gross Industrial Output Value (At Current Prices)
家具制造业	Manufacture of Furniture			
造纸及纸制品业	Manufacture of Paper and Paper Products			
印刷和记录媒介复制	Printing,Reproduction of Recording Media	3	1	196664
文教、工美、体育和娱乐用品制造业	Manufacture of Articles For Cultural,Educational and Sports Activities			
石油加工业、炼焦和业核燃料加工	Processing of Petroleum, Cokeing,Processing of Nuclear and Nuclear Fuel			
化学原料及化学制品制造业	Manufacture of Raw Chemical Materials and Chemical Products	16	1	771233
医药制造业	Manufacture of Medicines	3		52013
化学纤维制造业	Manufacture of Chemical Fibers	2		86841
橡胶和塑料制品业	Manufacture of Rubber and Plastics	4		376925
非金属矿物制品业	Manufacture of Non-metallic Mineral Products	11	1	182433
黑色金属冶炼和压延加工业	Smelting and Pressing of Ferrous Metals	1		157959
有色金属冶炼和压延加工业	Smelting and Pressing of Non-ferrous Metals	16	3	882652
金属制品业	Manufacture of Metal Products	13		941267
通用设备制造业	Manufacture of General Purpose Machinery	14	1	954680
专用设备制造业	Manufacture of Special Equipment	27	6	1189375
汽车制造业	Manufacture of Motor Vehicle	17	3	5769229
铁路、船舶、航空航天和其他运输设备制造业	Railways,Shipbuilding,Aerospace and Other Transportation Equipment Manufacturing Industry	31	1	4370361
电气机械和器材制造业	Manufacture of Electric Equipment and Machinery	21	5	3014899
计算机、通讯和其他电子设备制造业	Manufacture of Communication Equipment, Computers and other Electronic Equipment	23	4	913182
仪器仪表制造业	Manufacture of Measuring Instruments and Machinery	13	1	772098
其他制造业	Manufacture of Other Manufacturing	2	1	25119
废弃资源综合利用业	Recycling and Disposal of Waste			
金属制品、机械和设备修理业	Metal Products,Machinery and Equipment Repair Industry	1		2334
电力、热力的生产和供应业	Production and Supply of Electric Power and Heat Power	10	4	2309378
燃气生产和供应业	Gas Mining and Supplying Industry	4		365751
水的生产和供应业	Production and Supply of Water	4	2	112093

continued3

(10 000yuan)

工业销售产值（当年价）Value of Industry Products Sales (At Current Prices)	出口交货值 Export Delivery Value	从业人员年平均人数（人）Annual Average Employers (person)	资产总计 Total Assets	流动资产合计 Total Working Capitals	固定资产合计 Total Fixed Assets	固定资产原价 Origing Value of Fixed Assets	累计折旧 Accumulative Total Depreciation
197781		2659	297811	160704	119439	298869	179431
693055	134869	13775	1060445	584748	282898	567595	280249
44780		992	86062	42693	37598	47003	9405
82956	206	344	62476	40361	19903	69996	50093
384818	1013	12913	986449	674025	197353	270620	93401
184236	926	1772	222598	154113	62316	65700	18276
153851		70	55790	47201	4474	9795	5321
784632	21568	4616	2037992	798035	277274	346589	128028
911239	4489	18840	1735724	1003458	465941	793091	355221
939944	16437	10002	2729186	2044176	279855	523128	255565
1101822	222215	15337	3487839	1877249	797662	1015946	365231
5670149	205961	41614	6688678	4598342	1017144	1845858	851791
4210222	605920	69777	8926773	4785145	1847852	2625729	1209660
2909615	122763	27871	5151743	3703623	848954	1562190	710637
891071	56552	15007	1967406	1229822	273057	655822	265955
762005	6538	11169	1330447	767282	280038	510827	229556
24775	1014	317	17194	13726	2499	4629	2130
2334		60	3650	3586	64	169	105
2307945		25149	6281985	701272	4423339	6382835	3596128
365571		3706	713627	258782	241113	314476	85971
112093		3131	286760	135105	143121	296068	180261

12-10 续表4

单位：万元

分 组	Classify	负债合计 Total Liabilites	流动负债合计 Total Working Liabilities	非流动负债 Non-Working Liabilities
家具制造业	Manufacture of Furniture			
造纸及纸制品业	Manufacture of Paper and Paper Products			
印刷和记录媒介复制	Printing,Reproduction of Recording Media	28756	28718	38
文教、工美、体育和娱乐用品制造业	Manufacture of Articles For Cultural,Educational and Sports Activities			
石油加工业、炼焦和业核燃料加工	Processing of Petroleum, Cokeing,Processing of Nuclear and Nuclear Fuel			
化学原料及化学制品制造业	Manufacture of Raw Chemical Materials and Chemical Products	506034	517882	77652
医药制造业	Manufacture of Medicines	48190	47962	127
化学纤维制造业	Manufacture of Chemical Fibers	13391	11890	1501
橡胶和塑料制品业	Manufacture of Rubber and Plastics	803448	571745	231703
非金属矿物制品业	Manufacture of Non-metallic Mineral Products	122212	110895	3483
黑色金属冶炼和压延加工业	Smelting and Pressing of Ferrous Metals	44144	44054	90
有色金属冶炼和压延加工业	Smelting and Pressing of Non-ferrous Metals	466059	391411	73467
金属制品业	Manufacture of Metal Products	1122478	853765	268712
通用设备制造业	Manufacture of General Purpose Machinery	1474876	1385269	89606
专用设备制造业	Manufacture of Special Equipment	1546379	1404774	141605
汽车制造业	Manufacture of Motor Vehicle	4331123	3994690	321266
铁路、船舶、航空航天和其他运输设备制造业	Railways,Shipbuilding,Aerospace and Other Transportation Equipment Manufacturing Industry	5099182	4005535	1088351
电气机械和器材制造业	Manufacture of Electric Equipment and Machinery	2410549	2118487	282275
计算机、通讯和其他电子设备制造业	Manufacture of Communication Equipment, Computers and other Electronic Equipment	1509838	1104115	388599
仪器仪表制造业	Manufacture of Measuring Instruments and Machinery	623261	529921	93340
其他制造业	Manufacture of Other Manufacturing	7152	6992	160
废弃资源综合利用业	Recycling and Disposal of Waste			
金属制品、机械和设备修理业	Metal Products,Machinery and Equipment Repair Industry	2654	2654	
电力、热力的生产和供应业	Production and Supply of Electric Power and Heat Power	5101523	1816840	681102
燃气生产和供应业	Gas Mining and Supplying Industry	468272	454607	13665
水的生产和供应业	Production and Supply of Water	196427	124163	72264

continued4

(10 000yuan)

所有者权益合计 Total Owners' Equities	实收资本 Total Capital Hold	营业收入 Total Revenue	主营业务收入 Revenue from Principal Business	营业成本 Total Cost	主营业务成本 Cost of Principal Business	营业税金及附加 Taxs and Other Changes	主营业务税金及附加 Taxes and Other Charges on Principal Business
269055	155362	201927	200499	154120	153374	2187	2178
459308	190791	755859	714387	612196	572974	4957	4937
37872	14377	44813	44779	25275	25272	367	367
49085	50800	82957	82957	68796	68796	254	254
183002	85414	421099	407461	364140	359612	2541	2540
100386	77764	183449	183260	168537	168404	456	456
11646	9500	135385	135385	131348	131348	203	203
1571933	488843	910222	851230	806066	754614	2163	2158
613245	299696	816393	805945	683311	674880	3867	3867
1254970	158492	895427	876052	748048	725115	6011	5716
1941460	683606	1151594	1137383	954360	945787	6917	6732
2357554	794423	6053588	5827437	5540100	5319668	16320	16320
3827590	1434856	4496429	4456604	3991003	3879096	12608	11849
2741194	493510	2499643	2410267	1933350	1868542	17926	17091
457568	246666	939410	930864	767263	763599	2762	2745
707186	188060	765900	755772	642832	627923	3287	2805
10042	4000	25022	24868	21502	21494	171	171
997	500	2334	2332	1307	1307	28	28
1180462	847615	2972602	2960244	2699639	2693772	28630	25304
245354	178445	438565	365594	352621	307214	3135	3122
90334	42786	121967	111231	99206	93897	753	426

12-10 续表5

单位：万元

分 组	Classify	销售费用 Expenses for Sales	管理费用 Expenses for Management	财务费用 Financial cost
家具制造业	Manufacture of Furniture			
造纸及纸制品业	Manufacture of Paper and Paper Products			
印刷和记录媒介复制	Printing,Reproduction of Recording Media	4698	29897	-1262
文教、工美、体育和娱乐用品制造业	Manufacture of Articles For Cultural,Educational and Sports Activities			
石油加工业、炼焦和业核燃料加工	Processing of Petroleum, Cokeing,Processing of Nuclear and Nuclear Fuel			
化学原料及化学制品制造业	Manufacture of Raw Chemical Materials and Chemical Products	21287	75335	8098
医药制造业	Manufacture of Medicines	3363	5457	398
化学纤维制造业	Manufacture of Chemical Fibers	458	2799	-118
橡胶和塑料制品业	Manufacture of Rubber and Plastics	12791	16317	7289
非金属矿物制品业	Manufacture of Non-metallic Mineral Products	1126	6378	2104
黑色金属冶炼和压延加工业	Smelting and Pressing of Ferrous Metals	442	748	850
有色金属冶炼和压延加工业	Smelting and Pressing of Non-ferrous Metals	6614	44953	1395
金属制品业	Manufacture of Metal Products	15694	80579	14564
通用设备制造业	Manufacture of General Purpose Machinery	30840	101725	-97
专用设备制造业	Manufacture of Special Equipment	45661	115147	8262
汽车制造业	Manufacture of Motor Vehicle	169501	228286	-2859
铁路、船舶、航空航天和其他运输设备制造业	Railways,Shipbuilding,Aerospace and Other Transportation Equipment Manufacturing Industry	63604	289203	47930
电气机械和器材制造业	Manufacture of Electric Equipment and Machinery	137551	237424	4429
计算机、通讯和其他电子设备制造业	Manufacture of Communication Equipment, Computers and other Electronic Equipment	17602	109357	18194
仪器仪表制造业	Manufacture of Measuring Instruments and Machinery	5218	93825	-2641
其他制造业	Manufacture of Other Manufacturing	376	862	107
废弃资源综合利用业	Recycling and Disposal of Waste			
金属制品、机械和设备修理业	Metal Products,Machinery and Equipment Repair Industry	144	464	24
电力、热力的生产和供应业	Production and Supply of Electric Power and Heat Power	675	25467	113041
燃气生产和供应业	Gas Mining and Supplying Industry	26950	21391	-467
水的生产和供应业	Production and Supply of Water	4736	12303	2767

continued5

(10 000yuan)

营业利润 Operating Profit	利润总额 Total Profits	亏损企业亏损额 Total Loss of Deficit Enterprises	利税总额 Total Pre-tax Profits	应付职工薪酬 Salary Payable	本年应交增值税 Value Added Tax Payable
13145	13269	647	28823	46791	13368
45280	62642	1998	92458	109754	24858
9835	9942		13043	7514	2735
10765	10838		13425	4376	2333
15424	17924		33950	35445	13485
4272	4476	178	8170	11661	3238
1667	1675		6664	1255	4786
48200	60749	853	89934	41932	27022
19789	26383		39340	148702	9091
19748	46411	609	81980	117253	29558
4482	57925	10911	98448	163166	33605
47488	72184	8010	212413	329199	123909
176019	182023	7681	266081	820487	71451
178321	192819	2007	330878	301690	120133
21657	28020	11181	46635	124940	15852
35635	56510	166	70087	137498	10289
1874	1910	341	2853	2906	772
366	366		631	667	237
105701	113739	12103	297568	275576	155199
41480	41814		56637	32909	11688
2082	2944	975	7023	30512	3327

12-11 规模以上外商及港澳台商投资工业企业主要经济指标（2016年）

单位：万元

分　组	Classify	企业单位数（个） Number of Enterprises (unit)	亏损企业 Loss Making Enterprises	工业总产值（当年价格） Gross Industrial Output Value (At Current Prices)
总计	**Total**	**115**	**29**	**9861852**
#市区	Urban Area	108	28	8874235
#亏损企业	Deficit Enterprises	29	29	586251
按隶属关系分	**Grouped by Jurisdiction of Management**			
中央企业	Central Enterprises	4	2	121444
省属企业	Provincial Enterprises	7	1	832513
市属企业	Municipal Enterprises	104	26	8907895
按登记注册类型分组	**Grouped by Type of Registration**			
港澳台商投资	Enterprises with Funds from Hong Kong, Macao &Taiwan	26	4	3026840
与港澳台商合资经营	Cooperative Enterprises	14	3	2626803
与港澳台商合作经营	Joint-venture Enterprises	1		2355
港澳台商独资	Enterprises with Sole Investment	10	1	345135
港澳台商投资股份有限公司	Share-holding Corporations Ltd. With their Investment	1		52547
其他港澳台投资	Other			
外商投资	Foreign Funded Enterprises	89	25	6835012
中外合资经营	Joint-venture Enterprises	46	12	2426870
中外合作经营	Cooperation Enterprises	2	1	8102
外资企业	Foreign Funded Enterprises	39	12	4246683
外商投资股份有限公司	Share-holding Corporations Ltd. With Foreign Funds	1		118000
其他外商投资	Other	1		35357
按轻重工业分	**Grouped by Light Industry and Heavy Industry**			
轻工业	Light Industry	34	10	2483880
重工业	Heavy Industry	81	19	7377972
按企业规模分	**Grouped by Size of Enterprises**			
大型企业	Large-size	12	1	6655890
中型企业	Medium-size	24	7	1234004
小型企业	Small-size	79	21	1971958
按工业行业大类分	**Grouped by Sector**			
煤炭开采和洗选业	Mining and Washing of Coal			
石油和天然气开采业	Extraction of Petroleum and Natural Gas			
黑色金属矿采选业	Mining and Processing of Ferrous Metal Ores			
有色金属矿采选业	Mining and Processing of Non-ferrous Metal Ores			
非金属矿采选业	Mining and Processing of Nonmetal Ores			
开采辅助活动	Mining Auxiliary Activities			
其他采矿业	Mining of Other Ores			

Major Economic Indicators of Foreign,Hong Kong,Macao and Taiwan Invested Industrial Enterprises above Designated Size (2016)

(10 000 yuan)

工业销售产值（当年价）Value of Industry Products Sales (At Current Prices)	出口交货值 Export Delivery Value	从业人员年平均人数（人）Annual Average Employers (person)	资产总计 Total Assets	流动资产合计 Total Working Capitals	固定资产合计 Total Fixed Assets	固定资产原价 Origing Value of Fixed Assets	累计折旧 Accumulative Total Depreciation
9610147	**3221016**	**73977**	**13298756**	**4973218**	**6827520**	**10416801**	**3834520**
8631441	3217084	72779	13119514	4898713	6728131	10260842	3735122
567502	58659	10506	1051179	376584	519109	665273	196776
117559	14363	878	136202	77649	28095	89339	62046
774093	1440	4920	681938	430196	61966	152400	96052
8718495	3205213	68179	12480616	4465373	6737459	10175062	3676422
3018555	208433	32953	2099065	813701	775060	1122649	414527
2615963	36495	28784	1859928	695628	673256	943839	337439
2971		75	3187	2941	246	909	663
348520	170576	3158	166857	81342	76073	136548	60556
51101	1362	936	69093	33790	25485	41353	15869
6591592	3012583	41024	11199691	4159517	6052460	9294152	3419993
2321270	118388	21140	2832484	1573826	716794	1118232	493456
7929	346	158	6487	4278	1002	1002	655
4136274	2816149	18663	7879463	2297455	5137469	7890542	2836005
93240	77700	1032	476876	282377	194499	284376	89877
32879		31	4381	1581	2696		
2345338	187070	17369	2520469	1286339	769691	1260997	528525
7264809	3033946	56608	10778287	3686879	6057829	9155804	3305995
6559822	2699704	51914	10224349	3234617	5808544	8933764	3256706
1228855	187551	13003	1439938	876830	408333	619180	238093
1821470	333761	9060	1634469	861771	610643	863857	339721

12-11 续表1

单位：万元

分 组	Classify	负债合计 Total Liabilites	流动负债合计 Total Working Liabilities	非流动负债 Non-Working Liabilities
总计	**Total**	**7004980**	**5269468**	**1622753**
#市区	Urban Area	6941044	5212444	1615841
#亏损企业	Deficit Enterprises	710896	460305	214336
按隶属关系分	**Grouped by Jurisdiction of Management**			
中央企业	Central Enterprises	27312	25062	2250
省属企业	Provincial Enterprises	377205	306297	4074
市属企业	Municipal Enterprises	6600463	4938109	1616429
按登记注册类型分组	**Grouped by Type of Registration**			
港澳台商投资	Enterprises with Funds from Hong Kong, Macao &Taiwan	1232732	1066983	163837
与港澳台商合资经营	Cooperative Enterprises	1121607	970176	151431
与港澳台商合作经营	Joint-venture Enterprises	497	497	
港澳台商独资	Enterprises with Sole Investment	93197	78882	12404
港澳台商投资股份有限公司	Share-holding Corporations Ltd. With their Investment	17431	17428	2
其他港澳台投资	Other			
外商投资	Foreign Funded Enterprises	5772248	4202485	1458916
中外合资经营	Joint-venture Enterprises	1508555	1272030	164267
中外合作经营	Cooperation Enterprises	2311	2311	
外资企业	Foreign Funded Enterprises	3923885	2713653	1173273
外商投资股份有限公司	Share-holding Corporations Ltd. With Foreign Funds	335746	214409	121336
其他外商投资	Other	1751	82	40
按轻重工业分	**Grouped by Light Industry and Heavy Industry**			
轻工业	Light Industry	1493669	1091688	330236
重工业	Heavy Industry	5511311	4177780	1292517
按企业规模分	**Grouped by Size of Enterprises**			
大型企业	Large-size	5439356	4068630	1302539
中型企业	Medium-size	698867	527258	142041
小型企业	Small-size	866757	673580	178173
按工业行业大类分	**Grouped by Sector**			
煤炭开采和洗选业	Mining and Washing of Coal			
石油和天然气开采业	Extraction of Petroleum and Natural Gas			
黑色金属矿采选业	Mining and Processing of Ferrous Metal Ores			
有色金属矿采选业	Mining and Processing of Non-ferrous Metal Ores			
非金属矿采选业	Mining and Processing of Nonmetal Ores			
开采辅助活动	Mining Auxiliary Activities			
其他采矿业	Mining of Other Ores			

continued 1

(10 000 yuan)

所有者权益合计 Total Owners' Equities	实收资本 Total Capital Hold	营业收入 Total Revenue	主营业务收入 Revenue from Principal Business	营业成本 Total Cost	主营业务收入 Cost of Principal Business	营业税金及附加 Taxs and Other Changes	主营业务税金及附加 Taxes and Other Charges on Principal Business
6293774	**3866305**	**9956417**	**9781438**	**8183967**	**8038397**	**74790**	**74328**
6178469	3812279	9825339	9650722	8074310	7928952	74110	73647
340282	506591	555575	548774	498377	490327	5254	4986
108890	93494	118075	118023	98159	98150	683	683
304733	71883	820357	814010	490054	485164	4677	4677
5880151	3700928	9017985	8849405	7595754	7455083	69430	68968
866333	295461	3221005	3164034	2853313	2801016	51767	51767
738321	225643	2838348	2786443	2537343	2488418	50664	50664
2690	714	2971	2960	2329	2327	24	24
73660	59104	340962	336147	283328	279958	885	885
51662	10000	38724	38484	30313	30313	194	194
5427441	3570844	6735412	6617404	5330654	5237381	23023	22561
1323927	720280	2358717	2269312	1702592	1642668	13358	13040
4177	1908	7594	7594	6436	6436	14	14
3955577	2828203	4220931	4196992	3499377	3468663	9081	8937
141130	18578	115678	111014	91110	88475	570	570
2630	1875	32492	32492	31139	31139		
1026799	461998	2336332	2300634	1716618	1680387	12219	12219
5266975	3404307	7620085	7480804	6467349	6358010	62571	62109
4784992	2820762	6825268	6675979	5548124	5431192	60964	60695
741071	492667	1158596	1150078	907797	899647	6014	6014
767711	552876	1972553	1955381	1728046	1707558	7812	7619

12-11 续表2

单位：万元

分 组	Classify	销售费用 Expenses for Sales	管理费用 Expenses for Management	财务费用 Financial cost
总计	**Total**	**504502**	**576930**	**117451**
#市区	Urban Area	503281	570266	115766
#亏损企业	Deficit Enterprises	35677	71524	13696
按隶属关系分	**Grouped by Jurisdiction of Management**			
中央企业	Central Enterprises	1364	9400	-671
省属企业	Provincial Enterprises	187227	61127	14471
市属企业	Municipal Enterprises	315911	506403	103651
按登记注册类型分组	**Grouped by Type of Registration**			
港澳台商投资	Enterprises with Funds from Hong Kong, Macao &Taiwan	102293	84254	12096
与港澳台商合资经营	Cooperative Enterprises	72669	71948	9984
与港澳台商合作经营	Joint-venture Enterprises	154	209	-24
港澳台商独资	Enterprises with Sole Investment	27107	9272	1493
港澳台商投资股份有限公司	Share-holding Corporations Ltd. With their Investment	2363	2825	643
其他港澳台投资	Other			
外商投资	Foreign Funded Enterprises	402209	492676	105355
中外合资经营	Joint-venture Enterprises	274841	171872	18902
中外合作经营	Cooperation Enterprises	467	559	1
外资企业	Foreign Funded Enterprises	118440	305850	75154
外商投资股份有限公司	Share-holding Corporations Ltd. With Foreign Funds	7459	14241	11236
其他外商投资	Other	1002	154	62
按轻重工业分	**Grouped by Light Industry and Heavy Industry**			
轻工业	Light Industry	347299	145035	33899
重工业	Heavy Industry	157203	431895	83552
按企业规模分	**Grouped by Size of Enterprises**			
大型企业	Large-size	399234	399798	90137
中型企业	Medium-size	59585	90674	8554
小型企业	Small-size	45683	86458	18760
按工业行业大类分	**Grouped by Sector**			
煤炭开采和洗选业	Mining and Washing of Coal			
石油和天然气开采业	Extraction of Petroleum and Natural Gas			
黑色金属矿采选业	Mining and Processing of Ferrous Metal Ores			
有色金属矿采选业	Mining and Processing of Non-ferrous Metal Ores			
非金属矿采选业	Mining and Processing of Nonmetal Ores			
开采辅助活动	Mining Auxiliary Activities			
其他采矿业	Mining of Other Ores			

continued 2

(10 000 yuan)

营业利润 Operating Profit	利润总额 Total Profits	亏损企业亏损额 Total Loss of Deficit Enterprises	利税总额 Total Pre-tax Profits	应付职工薪酬 Salary Payable	本年应交增值税 Value Added Tax Payable
500786	**1012428**	**66316**	**1286800**	**726951**	**199582**
489617	1000253	64133	1268749	718332	194386
-72461	-66316	66316	-56846	78527	4216
8247	8741	2437	12239	13371	2814
61637	60278	504	165507	105633	100552
430902	943409	63375	1109054	607947	96216
120304	124719	949	190691	257539	14205
96755	99989	525	156071	213746	5416
279	275		494	509	196
20484	21182	424	28900	35556	6834
2786	3273		5226	7728	1759
380482	887709	65367	1096109	469412	185377
178246	182531	43716	353122	238780	157233
118	91	52	267	865	161
210919	699912	21599	736975	210064	27983
-8937	4818		5388	19553	
136	357		357	150	
80486	99396	30516	242650	228264	131036
420300	913032	35800	1044150	498687	68546
327108	822277	6555	1021032	515343	137791
85306	92564	38997	137316	114989	38738
88372	97587	20764	128452	96619	23053

12-11 续表3

单位：万元

分组	Classify	企业单位数（个） Number of Enterprises (unit)	亏损企业 Loss Making Enterprises	工业总产值（当年价格） Gross Industrial Output Value (At Current Prices)
农副食品加工业	Processing of Food from Agricultural Porducts	2		13745
食品制造业	Manufacture of Foods	5	1	674988
酒、饮料和精制茶制造业	Manufacture of Alcohol,Beverages and Tea	7	3	604128
烟草制品业	Manufacture of Tobacco			
纺织业	Manufacture of Textile			
纺织服装、服饰业	Textile, apparel industry			
皮革、毛皮、羽毛及其制品和制鞋业	Leather fur feathers and its products and footwear			
木材加工和木、竹、藤、棕、草制品业	Processing of Timber,Manufacture of Wood,Plam and Straw Products			
家具制造业	Manufacture of Furniture			
造纸及纸制品业	Manufacture of Paper and Paper Products	2	1	78944
印刷和记录媒介复制	Printing,Reproduction of Recording Media	1		52547
文教、工美、体育和娱乐用品制造业	Manufacture of Articles For Cultural,Educational and Sports Activities	2		103321
石油加工业、炼焦和核燃料加工业	Processing of Petroleum, Cokeing,Processing of Nuclear and Nuclear Fuel	2	2	125063
化学原料及化学制品制造业	Manufacture of Raw Chemical Materials and Chemical Products	10	2	177105
医药制造业	Manufacture of Medicines	5	1	766810
化学纤维制造业	Manufacture of Chemical Fibers	2	1	122209
橡胶和塑料制品业	Manufacture of Rubber and Plastics	3	1	11417
非金属矿物制品业	Manufacture of Non-metallic Mineral Products	4	1	84836
黑色金属冶炼和压延加工业	Smelting and Pressing of Ferrous Metals	2		17946
有色金属冶炼和压延加工业	Smelting and Pressing of Non-ferrous Metals	4	1	132777
金属制品业	Manufacture of Metal Products	3	1	25537
通用设备制造业	Manufacture of General Purpose Machinery	5		103954
专用设备制造业	Manufacture of Special Equipment	9	1	393754
汽车制造业	Manufacture of Motor Vehicle	7	2	2161503
铁路、船舶、航空航天和其他运输设备制造业	Railways,Shipbuilding,Aerospace and Other Transportation Equipment Manufacturing Industry	7	1	188969
电气机械和器材制造业	Manufacture of Electric Equipment and Machinery	14	6	804070
计算机、通讯和其他电子设备制造业	Manufacture of Communication Equipment, Computers and other Electronic Equipment	11	2	2841122
仪器仪表制造业	Manufacture of Measuring Instruments and Machinery	2		78487
其他制造业	Manufacture of Other Manufacturing	2	1	5283
废弃资源综合利用业	Recycling and Disposal of Waste			
金属制品、机械和设备修理业	Metal Products,Machinery and Equipment Repair Industry	3	1	12262
电力、热力的生产和供应业	Production and Supply of Electric Power and Heat Power			
燃气生产和供应业	Gas Mining and Supplying Industry	1		281075
水的生产和供应业	Production and Supply of Water			

continued 3

(10 000 yuan)

工业销售产值（当年价）Value of Industry Products Sales (At Current Prices)	出口交货值 Export Delivery Value	从业人员年平均人数（人）Annual Average Employers (person)	资产总计 Total Assets	流动资产合计 Total Working Capitals	固定资产合计 Total Fixed Assets	固定资产原价 Origing Value of Fixed Assets	累计折旧 Accumulative Total Depreciation
13745		503	15452	10690	3191	6277	3086
644424		3753	334531	154247	99874	170254	76983
577594	77700	4598	866003	445263	361417	598337	236821
77006		283	32705	10776	10961	16139	5178
51101	1362	936	69093	33790	25485	41353	15869
103321	103321	184	8724	6341	1266	2342	1156
125063		4671	134309	16056	118002	117109	46100
172921	66608	465	245381	81130	145790	191037	48786
711762	3085	5418	699553	408151	85523	155919	98241
100583		397	156802	77769	75070	133193	58123
10391	346	389	29229	17284	8856	19699	12281
81032		647	152675	42477	106287	109505	54735
17088	615	166	10125	8368	1744	4454	2710
104984	87187	368	59113	29992	23227	26372	8708
24707	3342	632	56121	18644	33714	49498	15784
92628	12901	1098	135725	99691	26308	62227	39569
404392	57406	2455	317945	216993	72062	122278	51164
2201066	34834	29108	1911084	752996	694948	950201	319212
181016	30412	1286	273265	244311	28085	25530	14896
734341	10207	3532	645951	343305	159956	238317	80066
2804015	2689919	9399	6504817	1642400	4563264	7114472	2564020
78056	41771	676	84765	77889	6775	18311	12131
5574		212	8893	6250	2236	4672	2436
12262		288	40479	31406	3812	4682	1510
281075		2513	506016	196999	169667	234623	64955

12-11 续表4

单位：万元

分组	Classify	负债合计 Total Liabilites	流动负债合计 Total Working Liabilities	非流动负债 Non-Working Liabilities
农副食品加工业	Processing of Food from Agricultural Porducts	8568	8568	
食品制造业	Manufacture of Foods	184463	178911	4995
酒、饮料和精制茶制造业	Manufacture of Alcohol,Beverages and Tea	539637	412748	122535
烟草制品业	Manufacture of Tobacco			
纺织业	Manufacture of Textile			
纺织服装、服饰业	Textile, apparel industry			
皮革、毛皮、羽毛及其制品和制鞋业	Leather fur feathers and its products and footwear			
木材加工和木、竹、藤、棕、草制品业	Processing of Timber,Manufacture of Wood,Plam and Straw Products			
家具制造业	Manufacture of Furniture			
造纸及纸制品业	Manufacture of Paper and Paper Products	18746	18100	646
印刷和记录媒介复制	Printing,Reproduction of Recording Media	17431	17428	2
文教、工美、体育和娱乐用品制造业	Manufacture of Articles For Cultural,Educational and Sports Activities	7964	7962	2
石油加工业、炼焦和核燃料加工业	Processing of Petroleum, Cokeing,Processing of Nuclear and Nuclear Fuel	93196	93163	33
化学原料及化学制品制造业	Manufacture of Raw Chemical Materials and Chemical Products	149971	69564	78777
医药制造业	Manufacture of Medicines	401091	300226	34031
化学纤维制造业	Manufacture of Chemical Fibers	109509	66383	43125
橡胶和塑料制品业	Manufacture of Rubber and Plastics	13140	12620	520
非金属矿物制品业	Manufacture of Non-metallic Mineral Products	81261	67079	3808
黑色金属冶炼和压延加工业	Smelting and Pressing of Ferrous Metals	5424	5424	
有色金属冶炼和压延加工业	Smelting and Pressing of Non-ferrous Metals	34172	15234	18938
金属制品业	Manufacture of Metal Products	35410	35410	
通用设备制造业	Manufacture of General Purpose Machinery	32527	32206	321
专用设备制造业	Manufacture of Special Equipment	111136	95197	13513
汽车制造业	Manufacture of Motor Vehicle	1170362	1021543	148821
铁路、船舶、航空航天和其他运输设备制造业	Railways,Shipbuilding,Aerospace and Other Transportation Equipment Manufacturing Industry	112292	108012	4280
电气机械和器材制造业	Manufacture of Electric Equipment and Machinery	374266	212487	138899
计算机、通讯和其他电子设备制造业	Manufacture of Communication Equipment, Computers and other Electronic Equipment	3102697	2102483	996510
仪器仪表制造业	Manufacture of Measuring Instruments and Machinery	16966	16966	
其他制造业	Manufacture of Other Manufacturing	3846	3844	2
废弃资源综合利用业	Recycling and Disposal of Waste			
金属制品、机械和设备修理业	Metal Products,Machinery and Equipment Repair Industry	21493	21493	
电力、热力的生产和供应业	Production and Supply of Electric Power and Heat Power			
燃气生产和供应业	Gas Mining and Supplying Industry	359412	346417	12995
水的生产和供应业	Production and Supply of Water			

continued 4

(10 000 yuan)

所有者权益合计 Total Owners' Equities	实收资本 Total Capital Hold	营业收入 Total Revenue	主营业务收入 Revenue from Principal Business	营业成本 Total Cost	主营业务收入 Cost of Principal Business	营业税金及附加 Taxs and Other Changes	主营业务税金及附加 Taxes and Other Charges on Principal Business
6884	1892	16175	15620	12237	11984	155	155
150068	78908	629717	617025	520558	508374	2231	2231
326365	100307	548352	531347	413540	390144	4436	4436
13959	5540	76494	72078	73908	73792	86	86
51662	10000	38724	38484	30313	30313	194	194
760	845	104438	104438	103185	103185		
41113	39841	121534	120096	114688	113526	820	552
95410	92195	217730	217032	184225	183747	395	251
298461	79947	756358	755956	417726	417499	4630	4630
47294	45800	100512	100490	84589	84589	232	232
16089	11788	10222	10127	8553	8500	62	62
71414	26255	73632	73514	65874	65874	459	459
4701	3836	18989	18744	16948	16737	48	48
24941	20662	132685	132685	121248	121248	112	112
20711	19567	33194	33163	26811	26811	228	228
103198	52739	107447	106988	93897	93632	317	317
206809	65008	383095	381315	296519	295469	2141	2091
740721	239546	2408821	2351766	2099783	2046650	51249	51249
160973	44171	181113	181016	130317	130311	1308	1308
271685	308356	723943	722234	653894	649212	1497	1497
3402120	2486997	2810143	2805642	2354840	2352151	404	404
67799	10068	78777	78086	46346	46346	982	982
5047	2514	5718	5563	5004	5003	87	87
18986	19523	27609	27068	21797	21280	116	116
146604	100000	350995	280961	287167	242020	2601	2601

12-11 续表5

单位：万元

分　组	Classify	销售费用 Expenses for Sales	管理费用 Expenses for Management	财务费用 Financial cost
农副食品加工业	Processing of Food from Agricultural Porducts	185	1615	-98
食品制造业	Manufacture of Foods	73990	14047	-1768
酒、饮料和精制茶制造业	Manufacture of Alcohol,Beverages and Tea	69727	36215	10961
烟草制品业	Manufacture of Tobacco			
纺织业	Manufacture of Textile			
纺织服装、服饰业	Textile, apparel industry			
皮革、毛皮、羽毛及其制品和制鞋业	Leather fur feathers and its products and footwear			
木材加工和木、竹、藤、棕、草制品业	Processing of Timber,Manufacture of Wood,Plam and Straw Products			
家具制造业	Manufacture of Furniture			
造纸及纸制品业	Manufacture of Paper and Paper Products	860	1007	308
印刷和记录媒介复制	Printing,Reproduction of Recording Media	2363	2825	643
文教、工美、体育和娱乐用品制造业	Manufacture of Articles For Cultural,Educational and Sports Activities	539	617	4
石油加工业、炼焦和核燃料加工业	Processing of Petroleum, Cokeing,Processing of Nuclear and Nuclear Fuel	4943	9065	907
化学原料及化学制品制造业	Manufacture of Raw Chemical Materials and Chemical Products	7607	7212	7560
医药制造业	Manufacture of Medicines	193443	63856	17584
化学纤维制造业	Manufacture of Chemical Fibers	922	4242	4298
橡胶和塑料制品业	Manufacture of Rubber and Plastics	518	1260	-194
非金属矿物制品业	Manufacture of Non-metallic Mineral Products	358	4447	2445
黑色金属冶炼和压延加工业	Smelting and Pressing of Ferrous Metals	399	985	-35
有色金属冶炼和压延加工业	Smelting and Pressing of Non-ferrous Metals	1232	4335	1399
金属制品业	Manufacture of Metal Products	1475	3997	787
通用设备制造业	Manufacture of General Purpose Machinery	3729	5064	-201
专用设备制造业	Manufacture of Special Equipment	10093	25146	940
汽车制造业	Manufacture of Motor Vehicle	77647	83046	11178
铁路、船舶、航空航天和其他运输设备制造业	Railways,Shipbuilding,Aerospace and Other Transportation Equipment Manufacturing Industry	7155	13372	4924
电气机械和器材制造业	Manufacture of Electric Equipment and Machinery	20579	40352	3052
计算机、通讯和其他电子设备制造业	Manufacture of Communication Equipment, Computers and other Electronic Equipment	3921	228150	57628
仪器仪表制造业	Manufacture of Measuring Instruments and Machinery	5935	5129	-2577
其他制造业	Manufacture of Other Manufacturing	306	377	-25
废弃资源综合利用业	Recycling and Disposal of Waste			
金属制品、机械和设备修理业	Metal Products,Machinery and Equipment Repair Industry	1266	4309	-224
电力、热力的生产和供应业	Production and Supply of Electric Power and Heat Power			
燃气生产和供应业	Gas Mining and Supplying Industry	15310	16260	-2045
水的生产和供应业	Production and Supply of Water			

continued 5

(10 000 yuan)

营业利润 Operating Profit	利润总额 Total Profits	亏损企业亏损额 Total Loss of Deficit Enterprises	利税总额 Total Pre-tax Profits	应付职工薪酬 Salary Payable	本年应交增值税 Value Added Tax Payable
3664	3633		4831	4881	1043
21780	22061	88	42991	32569	18699
13219	25496	5359	43599	61756	13667
1284	2424	192	3243	1404	734
2786	3273		5226	7728	1759
93	210		1768	1009	1559
-8931	-8983	8983	-3455	12865	4707
10827	11193	298	12676	5051	1088
56566	54841	522	157762	103186	98292
6229	6244	4503	637	5282	-5839
22	15	202	630	2090	552
48	1519	1538	5430	3431	3452
644	675		1061	984	337
4317	5621	2183	6554	2991	821
-70	689	1268	1786	5611	869
3535	3813		5175	8817	1045
50179	51347	1015	69869	21713	16381
86040	88429	6717	147397	212977	7718
23574	23752	47	35761	13412	10702
2919	9247	31525	19606	43644	8862
160463	645208	166	646353	130929	741
22959	23086		26678	8716	2610
-62	-66	341	248	1080	227
46	100	1369	1341	11676	1125
38655	38601		49633	23149	8431

12-12 规模以上大中型工业企业主要经济指标（2016年）

单位：万元

分　组	Classify	企业单位数（个）Number of Enterprises (unit)	亏损企业 Loss Making Enterprises	工业总产值（当年价格）Gross Industrial Output Value (At Current Prices)
总计	**Total**	**220**	**31**	**36678407**
#市区	Urban	208	30	35962672
#亏损企业	Deficit Enterprises	31	31	1393200
按隶属关系分	**Grouped by Jurisdiction of Management**			
中央企业	Central Enterprises	45	5	11098272
省属企业	Provincial Enterprises	31	3	6863581
市属企业	Municipal Enterprises	144	23	18716554
按登记注册类型分组	**Grouped by Registion Status**			
内资企业	Domestic Investment Enterprises	184	23	28788512
国有	State-owned Enterprises	24	1	6969527
集体	Collective-owned Enterprises	1		45020
股份合作	Share-holding Corperative			
联营	Joint Ownership Enterprises			
国有联营	State Joint Ownership Enterprises			
集体联营	Collective Joint Ownership Enterprises			
国有与集体联营	Joint State-collective Ownership Enterprises			
其他联营	Other Joint Ownership Enterprises			
有限责任公司	Limited Liability Corporations	108	15	16191540
国有独资公司	State Sole Funded Enterprises	23	5	3222406
其他有限责任公司	Other Limited Liability Corporation	85	10	12969134
股份有限公司	Share-holding Corperation Ltd.	34	2	2922987
私营	Private Enterprises	17	5	2704458
私营独资	Private-funded Enterprises			
私营合伙	Private Partnership Enterprises			
私营有限责任公司	Private Limited Liability Corporations	17	5	2704458
私营股份有限公司	Private Share Holding Corporations			
其他	Other Domestic Funded Enterprises			
港澳台商投资	Enterprises with Funds from Hong Kong,Macao and Taiwan	7		2290576
外商投资	Foreign Funded Enterprises	29	8	5599319
按轻重工业分	**Grouped by Light Industry and Heavy Industry**			
轻工业	Light Industry	56	6	4548983
重工业	Heavy Industry	164	25	32129424
按企业规模分	**Grouped by Size of Enterprises**			
大型企业	Large-size	62	4	28603440

Major Economic Indicators of Large and Medium-sized Industrial Enterprises above Designated Size (2016)

(10 000 yuan)

工业销售产值（当年价）Value of Industry Products Sales (At Current Prices)	出口交货值 Export Delivery Value	从业人员年平均人数（人）Annual Average Employers (person)	资产总计 Total Assets	流动资产合计 Total Working Capitals	固定资产合计 Total Fixed Assets	固定资产原价 Origing Value of Fixed Assets	累计折旧 Accumulative Total Depreciation
35507361	**4409765**	**394147**	**59895984**	**29782974**	**19036318**	**30172866**	**13659604**
34795439	4409765	381569	58789082	29318830	18569585	29355662	13225094
1393811	27983	32634	4100838	1935911	1211565	1545584	544014
10867128	513734	166539	23846316	11225028	7834264	12386788	6596414
6704796	258108	65393	12185898	7137414	1912371	3208561	1344923
17935437	3637923	162215	23863770	11420532	9289683	14577517	5718267
27718684	1522511	329230	48231697	25671527	12819441	20619922	10164805
6859618	230023	96810	13150667	7073591	4059181	7089126	3260780
45020		536	43159	20954	17925	24865	12201
15748788	969764	192954	27779824	14990527	7224478	10552382	5326118
3105975	346302	57172	11532421	4784195	4153683	5465979	3099615
12642813	623462	135782	16247403	10206332	3070795	5086403	2226503
2744197	322663	27454	6289316	3090098	1247142	2556041	1425277
2366081	61	12012	1011890	517311	288640	422373	152630
2366081	61	12012	1011890	517311	288640	422373	152630
2338127	96495	31291	1882023	693977	724952	1034975	367753
5450551	2790759	33626	9782264	3417470	5491925	8517969	3127046
4508089	93348	49471	5159536	2883504	1363136	2372492	1108830
30999272	4316417	344676	54736448	26899470	17673182	27800374	12550774
28018778	3788510	304552	47351410	23189898	16439243	26355395	12125192

12-12 续表1

单位：万元

分组	Classify	负债合计 Total Liabilites	流动负债合计 Total Working Liabilities	非流动负债 Non-Working Liabilities
总计	**Total**	**33659110**	**25241806**	**5716119**
#市区	Urban	33115559	24779684	5555937
#亏损企业	Deficit Enterprises	2835571	2160116	636197
按隶属关系分	**Grouped by Jurisdiction of Management**			
中央企业	Central Enterprises	13694143	8959255	2194540
省属企业	Provincial Enterprises	6858271	6083278	692151
市属企业	Municipal Enterprises	13106696	10199273	2829428
按登记注册类型分组	**Grouped by Registion Status**			
内资企业	Domestic Investment Enterprises	27520886	20645919	4271538
国有	State-owned Enterprises	7296917	5607071	1674918
集体	Collective-owned Enterprises	37019	36919	
股份合作	Share-holding Corperative			
联营	Joint Ownership Enterprises			
国有联营	State Joint Ownership Enterprises			
集体联营	Collective Joint Ownership Enterprises			
国有与集体联营	Joint State-collective Ownership Enterprises			
其他联营	Other Joint Ownership Enterprises			
有限责任公司	Limited Liability Corporations	17274503	12813706	1903190
国有独资公司	State Sole Funded Enterprises	6904732	3562739	801645
其他有限责任公司	Other Limited Liability Corporation	10369771	9250967	1101545
股份有限公司	Share-holding Corperation Ltd.	2243940	1743303	499456
私营	Private Enterprises	705526	481839	193974
私营独资	Private-funded Enterprises			
私营合伙	Private Partnership Enterprises			
私营有限责任公司	Private Limited Liability Corporations	705526	481839	193974
私营股份有限公司	Private Share Holding Corporations			
其他	Other Domestic Funded Enterprises			
港澳台商投资	Enterprises with Funds from Hong Kong,Macao and Taiwan	1136739	988229	146598
外商投资	Foreign Funded Enterprises	5001485	3607658	1297982
按轻重工业分	**Grouped by Light Industry and Heavy Industry**			
轻工业	Light Industry	3060025	2287322	701958
重工业	Heavy Industry	30599085	22954484	5014161
按企业规模分	**Grouped by Size of Enterprises**			
大型企业	Large-size	27371092	20470104	4309495

continued 1

(10 000 yuan)

所有者权益合计 Total Owners' Equities	实收资本 Total Capital Hold	营业收入 Total Revenue	主营业务收入 Revenue from Principal Business	营业成本 Total Cost	主营业务成本 Cost of Principal Business	营业税金及附加 Taxs and Other Changes	主营业务税金及附加 Taxes and Other Charges on Principal Business
26142428	**9953560**	**36453436**	**35715425**	**30949141**	**30260618**	**205486**	**198682**
25674179	9820482	35748384	35014897	30413463	29727585	201925	195122
1265266	880924	1304561	1284035	1116936	1100666	7964	6458
10057729	3361627	11430465	11254139	9793301	9575306	65111	63800
5327626	1625875	7363115	7098009	6308573	6072139	26375	26253
10757073	4966058	17659856	17363277	14847267	14613173	114000	108629
20616365	6640132	28469572	27889368	24493220	23929778	138508	131972
5853749	1238034	6792024	6596326	5656451	5513763	37410	36568
6140	4861	45020	29704	43177	34061	669	669
10410216	4216337	16715948	16379234	14531021	14141479	84018	79392
4532585	1380199	4062653	3999937	3397721	3341398	36428	32518
5877631	2836138	12653295	12379297	11133300	10800081	47590	46874
4046036	1025183	2629104	2598573	2154232	2135381	11483	10415
306364	160578	2332496	2315235	2151516	2139155	5597	5597
306364	160578	2332496	2315235	2151516	2139155	5597	5597
745285	201426	2515939	2460312	2180989	2129705	51392	51392
4780779	3112002	5467925	5365746	4274931	4201135	15586	15318
2099511	833030	4287597	4214426	3062929	3004959	30796	29551
24042917	9120530	32165839	31500999	27886212	27255659	174690	169131
19885873	7615871	28868950	28303969	24850992	24304140	160869	159093

12-12 续表2

单位：万元

分 组	Classify	销售费用 Expenses for Sales	管理费用 Expenses for Management	财务费用 Financial cost
总计	**Total**	**1349840**	**2150409**	**339802**
#市区	Urban	1281129	2094284	331147
#亏损企业	Deficit Enterprises	75842	172756	43720
按隶属关系分	**Grouped by Jurisdiction of Management**			
中央企业	Central Enterprises	229688	802860	155163
省属企业	Provincial Enterprises	411022	422575	29221
市属企业	Municipal Enterprises	709130	924974	155418
按登记注册类型分组	**Grouped by Registion Status**			
内资企业	Domestic Investment Enterprises	891021	1659938	241112
国有	State-owned Enterprises	171311	534935	42582
集体	Collective-owned Enterprises			-173
股份合作	Share-holding Corperative			
联营	Joint Ownership Enterprises			
国有联营	State Joint Ownership Enterprises			
集体联营	Collective Joint Ownership Enterprises			
国有与集体联营	Joint State-collective Ownership Enterprises			
其他联营	Other Joint Ownership Enterprises			
有限责任公司	Limited Liability Corporations	550175	910447	164907
国有独资公司	State Sole Funded Enterprises	110447	310709	94578
其他有限责任公司	Other Limited Liability Corporation	439728	599738	70329
股份有限公司	Share-holding Corperation Ltd.	122415	166173	23076
私营	Private Enterprises	47120	48383	10547
私营独资	Private-funded Enterprises			
私营合伙	Private Partnership Enterprises			
私营有限责任公司	Private Limited Liability Corporations	47120	48383	10547
私营股份有限公司	Private Share Holding Corporations			
其他	Other Domestic Funded Enterprises			
港澳台商投资	Enterprises with Funds from Hong Kong,Macao and Taiwan	97462	75482	12024
外商投资	Foreign Funded Enterprises	361356	414990	86666
按轻重工业分	**Grouped by Light Industry and Heavy Industry**			
轻工业	Light Industry	639487	299697	46747
重工业	Heavy Industry	710353	1850712	293055
按企业规模分	**Grouped by Size of Enterprises**			
大型企业	Large-size	881361	1615678	275894

continued 2

(10 000 yuan)

营业利润 Operating Profit	利润总额 Total Profits	亏损企业亏损额 Total Loss of Deficit Enterprises	利税总额 Total Pre-tax Profits	应付职工薪酬 Salary Payable	本年应交增值税 Value Added Tax Payable
1493007	**2229935**	**89057**	**3373652**	**3723816**	**938232**
1447867	2186306	87314	3296614	3641277	908383
-122607	-89057	89057	-44971	214660	36123
498529	571368	13310	973709	1891549	337231
96997	150241	8443	421745	580982	245129
897481	1508326	67304	1978198	1251285	355872
1080593	1315094	43506	2215304	3093485	761703
356738	406846	2733	685659	998938	241403
1346	2013		4549	82	1866
522376	659274	32272	1171059	1746052	427768
124991	182552	10066	393619	527512	174640
397385	476722	22206	777441	1218540	253129
133143	166706	3024	241631	261884	63442
68336	82268	5477	116955	86611	29090
68336	82268	5477	116955	86611	29090
99158	101956		162433	243117	9085
313256	812886	45552	995915	387214	167443
201870	234197	25474	498229	434932	233235
1291137	1995738	63583	2875423	3288884	704997
1118783	1764820	15985	2612925	3086579	687236

12-12 续表3

单位：万元

分 组	Classify	企业单位数（个）Number of Enterprises (unit)	亏损企业 Loss Making Enterprises	工业总产值（当年价格）Gross Industrial Output Value (At Current Prices)
中型企业	Medium-size	158	27	8074967
按经济组织类型分组	**Grouped by Economic Type of Orgnization**			
独资企业	Appropratorship	42	4	10732861
合作、合伙企业	Partnership			
股份有限公司	Corporaton	36	2	3093535
有限责任公司	Limited Liability Company	142	25	22852011
按控股情况分	**Grouped by Cast strand**			
国有控股	State owned shares	111	12	21060180
集体控股	Collective shares	9	1	1486796
私人控股	Private holdings	60	9	8194331
港澳台控股	Hong Kong and Macao Holdings	5		277740
外商投资	Foreign Investment	24	6	5089922
其他	Others	11	3	569438
按工业行业大类分	**Grouped by Sector**			
煤炭开采和洗选业	Mining and Washing of Coal			
石油和天然气开采业	Extraction of Petroleum and Natural Gas			
黑色金属矿采选业	Mining and Processing of Ferrous Metal Ores			
有色金属矿采选业	Mining and Processing of Non-ferrous Metal Ores			
非金属矿采选业	Mining and Processing of Nonmetal Ores			
开采辅助活动	Mining Auxiliary Activities	2	1	366884
其他采矿业	Mining of other Ores			
农副食品加工业	Processing of Food from Agricultural Porducts	5		713480
食品制造业	Manufacture of Foods	11		865797
酒、饮料和精制茶制造业	Manufacture of Alcohol,Beverages and Tea	6	1	583881
烟草制品业	Manufacture of Tobacco			
纺织业	Manufacture of Textile	2	1	69337
纺织服装、服饰业	Textile, apparel industry	1	1	54306
皮革、毛皮、羽毛及其制品和制鞋业	Manufacture of Leather, Fur, Feather and Related Products, and Shoes	1		59313
木材加工和木、竹、藤、棕、草制品业	Processing of Timber, Manufacture of Wood,Plam and Straw Products	1	1	106647
家具制造业	Manufacture of Furniture	1		11723

continued 3

(10 000 yuan)

工业销售产值（当年价）Value of Industry Products Sales (At Current Prices)	出口交货值 Export Delivery Value	从业人员年平均人数（人）Annual Average Employers (person)	资产总计 Total Assets	流动资产合计 Total Working Capitals	固定资产合计 Total Fixed Assets	固定资产原价 Origing Value of Fixed Assets	累计折旧 Accumulative Total Depreciation
7488583	621255	89595	12544574	6593076	2597075	3817471	1534412
10582088	2940670	115184	20387091	9111616	8854831	14570894	5987035
2888538	401725	29422	6835284	3406264	1467125	2881770	1531022
22036735	1067370	249541	32673609	17265094	8714362	12720202	6141547
20609073	1125490	276323	42033945	22221183	11186265	17733355	8771437
1444249	256696	6384	1825508	902085	511204	1318076	840339
7637091	77986	70277	6009470	3042247	1719896	2450881	865437
279972	65562	3652	209802	95393	96746	169111	72364
4968584	2773027	29218	8973323	2985391	5263322	8195663	3020574
568392	111004	8293	843936	536675	258885	305780	89453
366737	1	5716	664231	428766	130649	323935	193290
711739	2573	3238	592503	458350	95853	183458	90305
834370		8981	488068	232204	157494	268749	117873
708952	77700	5692	956137	541127	319830	560856	241784
69568	4297	6271	270343	86219	162411	203791	50084
49501		1150	72399	59004	10245	11888	1643
56245		621	47311	24882	7719	7719	3642
98562		495	157254	46251	52654	65272	35278
12282		382	16957	9009	7579	9749	2170

12-12 续表4

单位：万元

分 组	Classify	负债合计 Total Liabilites	流动负债合计 Total Working Liabilities	非流动负债 Non-Working Liabilities
中型企业	Medium-size	6288018	4771703	1406623
按经济组织类型分组	**Grouped by Economic Type of Orgnization**			
独资企业	Appropratorship	10813654	8041082	2729149
合作、合伙企业	Partnership			
股份有限公司	Corporaton	2597116	1975140	620795
有限责任公司	Limited Liability Company	20248340	15225584	2366175
按控股情况分	**Grouped by Cast strand**			
国有控股	State owned shares	24391207	18244565	3574579
集体控股	Collective shares	790584	655091	135394
私人控股	Private holdings	3504933	2811164	662504
港澳台控股	Hong Kong and Macao Holdings	93614	79299	12404
外商投资	Foreign Investment	4506051	3127126	1283081
其他	Others	372721	324561	48157
按工业行业大类分	**Grouped by Sector**			
煤炭开采和洗选业	Mining and Washing of Coal			
石油和天然气开采业	Extraction of Petroleum and Natural Gas			
黑色金属矿采选业	Mining and Processing of Ferrous Metal Ores			
有色金属矿采选业	Mining and Processing of Non-ferrous Metal Ores			
非金属矿采选业	Mining and Processing of Nonmetal Ores			
开采辅助活动	Mining Auxiliary Activities	175188	174486	697
其他采矿业	Mining of other Ores			
农副食品加工业	Processing of Food from Agricultural Porducts	535359	503730	31629
食品制造业	Manufacture of Foods	237514	225821	11137
酒、饮料和精制茶制造业	Manufacture of Alcohol,Beverages and Tea	562609	437886	123370
烟草制品业	Manufacture of Tobacco			
纺织业	Manufacture of Textile	188504	93607	94897
纺织服装、服饰业	Textile, apparel industry	53924	48754	5170
皮革、毛皮、羽毛及其制品和制鞋业	Manufacture of Leather, Fur, Feather and Related Products, and Shoes	19532	14001	5531
木材加工和木、竹、藤、棕、草制品业	Processing of Timber, Manufacture of Wood,Plam and Straw Products	85422	52635	31235
家具制造业	Manufacture of Furniture	13240	13240	

continued 4

(10 000 yuan)

所有者权益合计 Total Owners' Equities	实收资本 Total Capital Hold	营业收入 Total Revenue	主营业务收入 Revenue from Principal Business	营业成本 Total Cost	主营业务成本 Cost of Principal Business	营业税金及附加 Taxs and Other Changes	主营业务税金及附加 Taxes and Other Charges on Principal Business
6256555	2337689	7584485	7411456	6098149	5956478	44617	39588
9573436	3910308	10481893	10265966	8680454	8517515	42492	41650
4238828	1053761	2783506	2748071	2275655	2254170	12247	11179
12330164	4989491	23188037	22701388	19993032	19488933	150747	145853
17548292	5768376	21882648	21300944	18925571	18365183	116709	111195
1034924	259507	1277693	1250437	1047608	1027247	3768	3768
2504536	697395	7557800	7478181	6490008	6422262	70434	69502
116187	64673	258821	254045	196796	193523	1046	1046
4467272	2909000	4928042	4896983	3841179	3813380	11555	11287
471217	254609	548432	534835	447979	439023	1974	1884
489041	261879	272126	268646	238898	237918	2364	2277
57144	34739	548681	547425	500881	500618	331	330
250554	116527	817078	787656	624402	595963	3653	3653
393528	105852	673492	658609	486242	475480	11470	11383
81839	9556	73213	72394	67372	66884	264	264
18475	7500	33985	33434	26598	26252	821	
27779	15000	59313	58661	52534	51977	281	281
71833	12500	73251	72451	72651	71956	251	242
3717	2200	12500	12500	9559	9559	42	42

12-12 续表5

单位：万元

分　组	Classify	销售费用 Expenses for Sales	管理费用 Expenses for Management	财务费用 Financial cost
中型企业	Medium-size	468479	534732	63908
按经济组织类型分组	**Grouped by Economic Type of Orgnization**			
独资企业	Appropratorship	296537	809227	101523
合作、合伙企业	Partnership			
股份有限公司	Corporaton	132237	183239	34955
有限责任公司	Limited Liability Company	921066	1157943	203324
按控股情况分	**Grouped by Cast strand**			
国有控股	State owned shares	553919	1404351	196846
集体控股	Collective shares	62982	64247	5422
私人控股	Private holdings	339173	248086	50512
港澳台控股	Hong Kong and Macao Holdings	28273	10101	2058
外商投资	Foreign Investment	340806	377556	83026
其他	Others	24687	46068	1938
按工业行业大类分	**Grouped by Sector**			
煤炭开采和洗选业	Mining and Washing of Coal			
石油和天然气开采业	Extraction of Petroleum and Natural Gas			
黑色金属矿采选业	Mining and Processing of Ferrous Metal Ores			
有色金属矿采选业	Mining and Processing of Non-ferrous Metal Ores			
非金属矿采选业	Mining and Processing of Nonmetal Ores			
开采辅助活动	Mining Auxiliary Activities	564	22638	-2962
其他采矿业	Mining of other Ores			
农副食品加工业	Processing of Food from Agricultural Porducts	21517	8743	8114
食品制造业	Manufacture of Foods	115886	30183	-1354
酒、饮料和精制茶制造业	Manufacture of Alcohol,Beverages and Tea	85473	31836	8250
烟草制品业	Manufacture of Tobacco			
纺织业	Manufacture of Textile	527	7200	240
纺织服装、服饰业	Textile, apparel industry	3437	4147	1351
皮革、毛皮、羽毛及其制品和制鞋业	Manufacture of Leather, Fur, Feather and Related Products, and Shoes	1231	1766	138
木材加工和木、竹、藤、棕、草制品业	Processing of Timber, Manufacture of Wood,Plam and Straw Products	451	1956	2451
家具制造业	Manufacture of Furniture		2546	

continued 5

(10 000 yuan)

营业利润 Operating Profit	利润总额 Total Profits	亏损企业亏损额 Total Loss of Deficit Enterprises	利税总额 Total Pre-tax Profits	应付职工薪酬 Salary Payable	本年应交增值税 Value Added Tax Payable
374224	465114	73072	760727	637237	250996
556160	1091055	13101	1408179	1212430	274632
126992	174797	3024	252245	289165	65201
809855	964083	72932	1713228	2222221	598399
742900	926155	33247	1672451	2728198	629586
86588	103453	77	134122	108655	26902
349914	381060	12089	566113	449264	114619
20976	21935		29888	41060	6907
267067	766550	38321	929542	344122	151437
25562	30782	5323	41536	52517	8781
10672	11799	476	19816	97577	5655
7882	16518		22286	16954	5437
43289	45351		78391	56971	29387
50983	62604	2088	100176	73772	26102
-1506	-181	785	1336	25633	1253
-2322	-2231	2231	-349	2990	1061
3446	3536		3885	5457	68
-4510	-3567	3567	-1377	1997	1940
353	357		751	1292	351

12-12 续表6

单位：万元

分 组	Classify	企业单位数（个） Number of Enterprises (unit)	亏损企业 Loss Making Enterprises	工业总产值（当年价格） Gross Industrial Output Value (At Current Prices)
造纸及纸制品业	Manufacture of Paper and Paper Products	1		14073
印刷和记录媒介复制	Printing,Reproduction of Recording Media	7	1	388355
文教、工美、体育和娱乐用品制造业	Manufacture of Articles For Cultural,Educational and Sports Activities			
石油加工业、炼焦和核燃料加工业	Processing of Petroleum, Cokeing,Processing of Nuclear and Nuclear Fuel	1	1	109017
化学原料及化学制品制造业	Manufacture of Raw Chemical Materials and Chemical Products	9		1586202
医药制造业	Manufacture of Medicines	15		1527344
化学纤维制造业	Manufacture of Chemical Fibers			
橡胶和塑料制品业	Manufacture of Rubber and Plastics	2		370317
非金属矿物制品业	Manufacture of Non-metallic Mineral Products	5	1	155777
黑色金属冶炼和压延加工业	Smelting and Pressing of Ferrous Metals	1		8505
有色金属冶炼和压延加工业	Smelting and Pressing of Non-ferrous Metals	7	1	1562202
金属制品业	Manufacture of Metal Products	7		829492
通用设备制造业	Manufacture of General Purpose Machinery	8	1	857829
专用设备制造业	Manufacture of Special Equipment	22	7	1406865
汽车制造业	Manufacture of Motor Vehicle	19	2	7859759
铁路、船舶、航空航天和其他运输设备制造业	Railways,Shipbuilding,Aerospace and Other Transportation Equipment Manufacturing Industry	18	1	4216589
电气机械和器材制造业	Manufacture of Electric Equipment and Machinery	20	7	3037637
计算机、通讯和其他电子设备制造业	Manufacture of Communication Equipment, Computers and other Electronic Equipment	28	2	6228259
仪器仪表制造业	Manufacture of Measuring Instruments and Machinery	6		975421
其他制造业	Manufacture of Other Manufacturing			
废弃资源综合利用业	Recycling and Disposal of Waste			
金属制品、机械和设备修理业	Metal Products,Machinery and Equipment Repair Industry			
电力、热力的生产和供应业	Production and Supply of Electric Power and Heat Power	8	1	2225096
燃气生产和供应业	Gas Mining and Supplying Industry	5	1	389156
水的生产和供应业	Production and Supply of Water	1		99144

continued 6

(10 000 yuan)

工业销售产值（当年价）Value of Industry Products Sales (At Current Prices)	出口交货值 Export Delivery Value	从业人员年平均人数（人）Annual Average Employers (person)	资产总计 Total Assets	流动资产合计 Total Working Capitals	固定资产合计 Total Fixed Assets	固定资产原价 Origing Value of Fixed Assets	累计折旧 Accumulative Total Depreciation
14073		363	9725	5851	900	900	26
377495	1362	4884	451495	245800	159452	372532	213079
109017		4640	130454	14834	115620	112476	43720
1532925	269010	16185	2541547	1296739	693195	1735012	1050001
1419311	3085	11767	1348928	794296	199056	322955	175414
377598	1013	12734	969245	666373	190208	261208	91134
150424		2072	216626	120353	46747	62964	25540
7708		350	14176	5364	7819	10796	2977
1404278	32589	7327	2461660	935961	430802	612778	211030
819823	4118	18002	1604660	929637	426909	739416	337815
843653	25679	10806	2663544	2003449	266727	505016	244865
1332520	90499	18857	3910264	2114567	926921	1218881	438827
7808926	237057	70916	8464130	5267032	1664499	2733443	1149759
4062921	588634	68099	8552713	4596502	1768159	2521146	1173047
2898403	181101	32469	5560347	3756346	1012250	1797830	791290
5771694	2845793	38520	9121390	3189996	5161545	8141949	2919983
957155	45254	11310	1359172	777276	332433	551232	224953
2223357		25508	6199744	765401	4321481	6246121	3566533
388980		4110	834023	307894	253713	339117	99802
99144		2682	216938	103491	113448	251677	163740

12-12 续表7

单位：万元

分 组	Classify	负债合计 Total Liabilites	流动负债合计 Total Working Liabilities	非流动负债 Non-Working Liabilities
造纸及纸制品业	Manufacture of Paper and Paper Products	5630	5553	77
印刷和记录媒介复制	Printing,Reproduction of Recording Media	108480	95423	11057
文教、工美、体育和娱乐用品制造业	Manufacture of Articles For Cultural,Educational and Sports Activities			
石油加工业、炼焦和核燃料加工业	Processing of Petroleum, Cokeing,Processing of Nuclear and Nuclear Fuel	92665	92633	33
化学原料及化学制品制造业	Manufacture of Raw Chemical Materials and Chemical Products	1093205	853302	335006
医药制造业	Manufacture of Medicines	669097	554201	48062
化学纤维制造业	Manufacture of Chemical Fibers			
橡胶和塑料制品业	Manufacture of Rubber and Plastics	791041	560338	230703
非金属矿物制品业	Manufacture of Non-metallic Mineral Products	135594	126657	6276
黑色金属冶炼和压延加工业	Smelting and Pressing of Ferrous Metals	10766	10766	
有色金属冶炼和压延加工业	Smelting and Pressing of Non-ferrous Metals	586577	507030	78366
金属制品业	Manufacture of Metal Products	1051379	788261	263119
通用设备制造业	Manufacture of General Purpose Machinery	1410819	1322382	88437
专用设备制造业	Manufacture of Special Equipment	1754424	1554079	194389
汽车制造业	Manufacture of Motor Vehicle	5404861	4921682	468011
铁路、船舶、航空航天和其他运输设备制造业	Railways,Shipbuilding,Aerospace and Other Transportation Equipment Manufacturing Industry	5014527	3912075	1070043
电气机械和器材制造业	Manufacture of Electric Equipment and Machinery	2625076	2115288	486908
计算机、通讯和其他电子设备制造业	Manufacture of Communication Equipment, Computers and other Electronic Equipment	4734055	3387335	1328188
仪器仪表制造业	Manufacture of Measuring Instruments and Machinery	626337	520594	84220
其他制造业	Manufacture of Other Manufacturing			
废弃资源综合利用业	Recycling and Disposal of Waste			
金属制品、机械和设备修理业	Metal Products,Machinery and Equipment Repair Industry			
电力、热力的生产和供应业	Production and Supply of Electric Power and Heat Power	4990383	1741270	645432
燃气生产和供应业	Gas Mining and Supplying Industry	538926	512299	26627
水的生产和供应业	Production and Supply of Water	143976	96478	47499

continued 7

(10 000 yuan)

所有者权益合计 Total Owners' Equities	实收资本 Total Capital Hold	营业收入 Total Revenue	主营业务收入 Revenue from Principal Business	营业成本 Total Cost	主营业务成本 Cost of Principal Business	营业税金及附加 Taxs and Other Changes	主营业务税金及附加 Taxes and Other Charges on Principal Business
4095	4100	14074	14074	13391	13391	9	9
343015	178798	367154	354745	301525	291504	2630	2621
37789	33000	105422	104050	98150	96988	801	533
1353239	355541	1442823	1402400	1206483	1177085	4565	4563
679831	151158	1424039	1423470	760904	760658	10136	10136
178205	83674	414163	400593	359870	355425	2465	2464
81031	28225	156647	150408	129465	123377	1369	1369
3410	3000	7862	7859	5455	5455	36	36
1875083	470950	1549895	1533819	1433587	1421965	1810	1807
553280	249436	730744	720509	613483	605052	2548	2548
1253385	153158	796851	776824	657867	634786	5726	5461
2155839	737168	1360775	1336603	1036361	1017014	8642	8495
3059269	945019	8393360	8117161	7586510	7318315	66948	66948
3538185	1253447	4354177	4318501	3881080	3772699	11744	10986
2935271	660277	2451990	2360921	1860655	1792855	17287	16490
4387336	2828474	5804572	5783795	4991989	4983040	9535	9518
732835	194741	915436	908445	742025	728604	6221	6221
1209361	807596	3019984	2993027	2726102	2711354	29605	26414
295097	211045	470272	397301	376024	330617	3248	3234
72962	39000	109557	99144	89078	83827	684	357

12-12 续表8

单位：万元

分组	Classify	销售费用 Expenses for Sales	管理费用 Expenses for Management	财务费用 Financial cost
造纸及纸制品业	Manufacture of Paper and Paper Products	203	277	176
印刷和记录媒介复制	Printing,Reproduction of Recording Media	9763	36097	1049
文教、工美、体育和娱乐用品制造业	Manufacture of Articles For Cultural,Educational and Sports Activities			
石油加工业、炼焦和核燃料加工业	Processing of Petroleum, Cokeing,Processing of Nuclear and Nuclear Fuel	4943	7080	943
化学原料及化学制品制造业	Manufacture of Raw Chemical Materials and Chemical Products	29716	100944	11608
医药制造业	Manufacture of Medicines	386215	140236	19184
化学纤维制造业	Manufacture of Chemical Fibers			
橡胶和塑料制品业	Manufacture of Rubber and Plastics	12596	14379	7183
非金属矿物制品业	Manufacture of Non-metallic Mineral Products	9962	6420	-242
黑色金属冶炼和压延加工业	Smelting and Pressing of Ferrous Metals	144	1657	-78
有色金属冶炼和压延加工业	Smelting and Pressing of Non-ferrous Metals	6283	38101	4152
金属制品业	Manufacture of Metal Products	13994	74259	12885
通用设备制造业	Manufacture of General Purpose Machinery	31737	98750	-392
专用设备制造业	Manufacture of Special Equipment	73166	146046	16214
汽车制造业	Manufacture of Motor Vehicle	241644	297841	7736
铁路、船舶、航空航天和其他运输设备制造业	Railways,Shipbuilding,Aerospace and Other Transportation Equipment Manufacturing Industry	58980	274916	47657
电气机械和器材制造业	Manufacture of Electric Equipment and Machinery	157521	285807	10906
计算机、通讯和其他电子设备制造业	Manufacture of Communication Equipment, Computers and other Electronic Equipment	27579	368688	74659
仪器仪表制造业	Manufacture of Measuring Instruments and Machinery	14337	89979	-5423
其他制造业	Manufacture of Other Manufacturing			
废弃资源综合利用业	Recycling and Disposal of Waste			
金属制品、机械和设备修理业	Metal Products,Machinery and Equipment Repair Industry			
电力、热力的生产和供应业	Production and Supply of Electric Power and Heat Power	6083	24746	110305
燃气生产和供应业	Gas Mining and Supplying Industry	31669	22940	2555
水的生产和供应业	Production and Supply of Water	4219	10231	2497

continued 8

(10 000 yuan)

营业利润 Operating Profit	利润总额 Total Profits	亏损企业亏损额 Total Loss of Deficit Enterprises	利税总额 Total Pre-tax Profits	应付职工薪酬 Salary Payable	本年应交增值税 Value Added Tax Payable
18	37		122	1154	76
17223	17823	20	37814	63312	17361
-6495	-6555	6555	-1206	12582	4547
92062	109717		138244	192398	23962
104996	106373		263548	139155	147039
15141	17596		32913	34417	12852
9951	10167	1743	17223	10437	5687
648	808		844	1209	
64362	72370	1792	93423	43794	19244
15596	20866		31337	143261	7923
13419	39241	9	71901	116336	26934
65695	133029	12745	188120	196551	46449
138210	165061	7509	360675	539811	128666
160203	165173	7681	245884	807378	68967
122191	143656	34250	278602	329712	117659
323593	825311	4535	884453	335503	49606
80858	96413		121511	139232	18877
123904	134572	2277	320061	272121	155884
40416	41020	794	56577	34720	12309
2729	3071		6691	28090	2936

12-13 规模以上高技术产业工业企业主要经济指标（2016年）

单位：万元

行　业	Sector	企业单位数（个） Number of Enterprises (unit)	亏损企业 Loss Making Enterprises
总计	**Total**	**263**	**36**
一、医药制造业	**Pharmaceutical Manufacturing**	**53**	**11**
（一）化学药品制造	Chemical manufacturing	18	2
化学药品原料药制造	Chemical raw materials Medicine manufacturing	4	
化学药品制剂制造	Chemical preparations manufacturing	14	2
（二）中药饮片加工	Chinese medicine Pieces processing	1	
（三）中成药生产	Chinese medicine production	23	8
（四）兽用药品制造	Veterinary pharmaceutical manufacturing	2	
（五）生物药品制造	Biopharmaceutical manufacturing	6	
（六）卫生材料及医药用品制造	Sanitary materials and medical supplies manufacturing	3	1
二、航空航天器制造业	**Aerospace & aviation industry**	**46**	**4**
（一）飞机制造	Aircraft Manufacturing	12	1
（二）航天器制造	Spacecraft Manufacturing	2	
（三）航空、航天相关设备制造	Aviation and aerospace-related equipment manufacturing	25	1
（四）其他航空航天器制造	Other aerospace manufacturing	4	
（五）航空航天器修理	Aerospace vehicle repair	3	2
三、电子及通讯设备制造业	**Electronic and communication equipment manufacturing**	**91**	**11**
（一）电子工业专用设备制造	Electronic equipment manufacturing	5	1
（二）光纤、光缆制造	Optical fiber, cable manufacturing	2	
（三）锂离子电池制造	Lithium-ion battery manufacturing	3	2
（四）通信设备制造	Communications equipment manufacturing	17	3
通信系统设备制造	Communications system equipment	15	3
通信终端设备制造	Communication Terminal Equipment	2	
（五）广播电视设备制造	Broadcasting and TV Equipment	2	
广播电视节目制作及发射设备制造	Radio and television program production and transmission equipment		
广播电视接收设备及器材制造	Radio and television reception apparatus and equipment manufacturing	1	
应用电视设备及其他广播电视设备制造	Application television equipment and other radio and television equipment manufacturing	1	
（六）雷达及配套设备制造	Radar and ancillary equipment manufacturers	3	
（七）视听设备制造	Audiovisual equipment manufacturing	1	
电视机制造	TV manufacturing	1	
音响设备制造	Audio Equipment manufacturing		
影视录放设备制造	Video recording equipment manufacturing		
（八）电子器件制造	Electronic device manufacturing	26	2
电子真空器件制造	Electronic vacuum device manufacturing		
半导体分立器件制造	Discrete semiconductor device manufacturing	8	
集成电路制造	Semiconductor Manufacturing	8	1
光电子器件及其他电子器件制造	Optoelectronic devices and other electronic device manufacturing	10	1
（九）电子元件制造	Electronics Manufacturing	23	2
电子元件及组件制造	Electronic components and component manufacturing	21	1
印刷电路板制造	Printed circuit board manufacturing	2	1
（十）其他电子设备制造	Other electronic equipment manufacturing	9	1

Major Economic Indicators of High Technology Industry

Industrial Enterprises above Designated Size (2016)

(10 000 yuan)

工业总产值（当年价格）Gross Industrial Output Value (At Current Prices)	工业销售产值（当年价）Value of Industry Products Sales (At Current Prices)	出口交货值 Export Delivery Value	从业人员年平均人数（人）Annual Average Employers (person)	资产总计 Total Assets	流动资产合计 Total Working Capitals	固定资产合计 Total Fixed Assets	固定资产原价 Origing Value of Fixed Assets	累计折旧 Accumulative Total Depreciation
16031832	**15077665**	**3915676**	**150128**	**24186369**	**11426915**	**8360672**	**13455335**	**5500133**
2061572	**1904933**	**11867**	**16450**	**1881324**	**1091558**	**347087**	**547983**	**266291**
1148858	1043278	4287	8506	997974	598389	139027	237575	129000
28232	19485	1219	419	30283	14707	8404	12418	4014
1120626	1023793	3068	8087	967691	583682	130623	225157	124986
7565	7565	7565	11	570	472	1	1	1
587522	556050	15	4979	486077	307771	83438	110572	45785
6296	6609		889	96700	63699	18893	6765	3498
289367	269553		1713	284659	112988	100237	185902	85666
21964	21878		352	15344	8239	5491	7168	2341
4426931	**4187519**	**651355**	**65398**	**8480293**	**4470897**	**1762782**	**2550561**	**1143977**
3268176	3117892	621402	52618	6550224	3489054	1108432	1836959	820760
359661	358253	3121	4946	904771	411116	363171	290568	136764
719418	638216	26832	6940	866253	440536	270967	407530	180672
66798	60490		703	127081	109614	14355	8393	3887
12878	12668		191	31964	20577	5857	7111	1894
6930396	**6414835**	**2921022**	**47627**	**10169766**	**3851169**	**5359036**	**8428905**	**3013080**
37086	23279	30	549	68211	54355	7080	10693	3613
106982	87798	207	607	60993	48803	8395	25861	17467
70002	68922	4331	1319	336704	124411	120251	141475	21224
2244755	1945617	69730	13138	622944	453414	137298	198965	67715
447558	429891	69730	9891	461845	299322	133217	192645	65476
1797197	1515726		3247	161099	154092	4081	6320	2239
13599	13378	8070	283	23214	21628	1087	2879	1793
4411	4411		52	16326	15210	617	1947	1330
9188	8967	8070	231	6888	6418	470	932	463
464514	375034	38079	5529	1042385	635132	156345	372475	132274
5306	4335	642	95	6025	1612	4413	5130	1131
5306	4335	642	95	6025	1612	4413	5130	1131
3379698	3285855	2727993	14641	7092138	1909028	4803156	7456097	2693438
267856	236419	26519	2410	305467	161474	91679	162807	71202
2888917	2836367	2698609	10300	6695450	1701840	4681963	7253016	2610758
222925	213069	2865	1931	91221	45714	29514	40274	11478
565473	564398	71860	10737	836735	534551	115190	206515	70463
492555	491839	7660	9735	771012	502448	82436	151853	48555
72918	72559	64200	1002	65723	32103	32754	54662	21908
42981	46219	80	729	80417	68235	5821	8815	3962

12-13 续表1

单位：万元

行业	Sector	负债合计 Total Liabilites	流动负债合计 Total Working Liabilities
总计	**Total**	**12830166**	**9725276**
一、医药制造业	**Pharmaceutical Manufacturing**	**946828**	**791278**
（一）化学药品制造	Chemical manufacturing	508400	388168
化学药品原料药制造	Chemical raw materials Medicine manufacturing	17204	16642
化学药品制剂制造	Chemical preparations manufacturing	491196	371526
（二）中药饮片加工	Chinese medicine Pieces processing	456	456
（三）中成药生产	Chinese medicine production	307930	282213
（四）兽用药品制造	Veterinary pharmaceutical manufacturing	30282	30032
（五）生物药品制造	Biopharmaceutical manufacturing	93514	84363
（六）卫生材料及医药用品制造	Sanitary materials and medical supplies manufacturing	6246	6046
二、航空航天器制造业	**Aerospace & aviation industry**	**4844386**	**3764243**
（一）飞机制造	Aircraft Manufacturing	3925662	3080924
（二）航天器制造	Spacecraft Manufacturing	446381	290018
（三）航空、航天相关设备制造	Aviation and aerospace-related equipment manufacturing	413688	321031
（四）其他航空航天器制造	Other aerospace manufacturing	44550	58465
（五）航空航天器修理	Aerospace vehicle repair	14105	13805
三、电子及通讯设备制造业	**Electronic and communication equipment manufacturing**	**5389425**	**3809953**
（一）电子工业专用设备制造	Electronic equipment manufacturing	37877	36769
（二）光纤、光缆制造	Optical fiber, cable manufacturing	31635	31135
（三）锂离子电池制造	Lithium-ion battery manufacturing	223884	89463
（四）通信设备制造	Communications equipment manufacturing	330713	243085
通信系统设备制造	Communications system equipment	239497	156453
通信终端设备制造	Communication Terminal Equipment	91216	86632
（五）广播电视设备制造	Broadcasting and TV Equipment	18297	17907
广播电视节目制作及发射设备制造	Radio and television program production and transmission equipment		
广播电视接收设备及器材制造	Radio and television reception apparatus and equipment manufacturing	13316	12925
应用电视设备及其他广播电视设备制造	Application television equipment and other radio and television equipment manufacturing	4981	4982
（六）雷达及配套设备制造	Radar and ancillary equipment manufacturers	720033	609586
（七）视听设备制造	Audiovisual equipment manufacturing	2621	2621
电视机制造	TV manufacturing	2621	2621
音响设备制造	Audio Equipment manufacturing		
影视录放设备制造	Video recording equipment manufacturing		
（八）电子器件制造	Electronic device manufacturing	3360274	2325673
电子真空器件制造	Electronic vacuum device manufacturing		
半导体分立器件制造	Discrete semiconductor device manufacturing	153520	124911
集成电路制造	Semiconductor Manufacturing	3183090	2177357
光电子器件及其他电子器件制造	Optoelectronic devices and other electronic device manufacturing	23664	23405
（九）电子元件制造	Electronics Manufacturing	638754	429457
电子元件及组件制造	Electronic components and component manufacturing	604662	395850
印刷电路板制造	Printed circuit board manufacturing	34092	33607
（十）其他电子设备制造	Other electronic equipment manufacturing	25337	24257

continued 1

(10 000 yuan)

非流动负债	所有者权益合计		营业收入		营业成本		营业税金及附加	
Non-Working Liabilities	Total Owners' Equities	实收资本 Total Capital Hold	Total Revenue	主营业务收入 Revenue from Principal Business	Total Cost	主营业务成本 Cost of Principal Business	Taxs and Other Changes	主营业务税金及附加 Taxes and Other Charges on Principal Business
2942074	**11354601**	**5421179**	**15082475**	**14999116**	**12487919**	**12338392**	**45423**	**44161**
56892	**934495**	**269536**	**1837375**	**1830014**	**1043808**	**1043558**	**13006**	**13004**
38694	489573	129565	1087267	1086837	623899	623675	7404	7403
562	13079	6180	19486	19486	8745	8745	204	204
38132	476494	123385	1067781	1067351	615154	614930	7200	7199
	114	500	7565	7565	7432	7432	2	2
17170	178147	77099	501089	500972	264652	264642	4325	4324
250	66418	5200	6609	6609	4325	4325	89	89
578	191145	51222	217384	210570	128778	128762	1100	1100
200	9098	5950	17461	17461	14722	14722	86	86
1075001	**3635908**	**1289630**	**4420084**	**4386510**	**3964355**	**3858370**	**9181**	**8422**
812868	2624562	1047740	3341912	3335074	3062677	2977277	6561	6255
156363	458390	18672	404267	391098	333047	323880	362	362
92080	452566	188607	598810	585782	515718	504817	1687	1234
13390	82531	13542	61979	61979	42747	42747	532	532
300	17859	21069	13116	12577	10166	9649	39	39
1551077	**4780339**	**3231147**	**6431464**	**6403556**	**5506034**	**5492569**	**12364**	**12347**
1108	30334	15600	27014	25379	16947	16322	170	170
500	29358	23825	75603	74940	60187	59681	375	375
134421	112820	127900	70200	70078	67441	67441	150	150
85330	292232	187628	1961168	1952377	1794683	1791651	4056	4056
80748	222347	154628	446614	439522	307516	304484	4054	4054
4582	69885	33000	1514554	1512855	1487167	1487167	2	2
390	4917	3600	13475	13378	10061	10048	32	32
390	3011	2400	4506	4411	3782	3769	29	28
	1906	1200	8969	8967	6279	6279	3	4
110447	322352	61335	446792	442811	361327	359484	336	336
	3404	3000	4335	4335	3349	3349		
	3404	3000	4335	4335	3349	3349		
1030822	3731863	2680495	3256039	3252442	2737505	2737047	4084	4084
28608	151947	51459	216709	215513	185819	185593	196	196
1002030	3512359	2585144	2833222	2830888	2374807	2374642	281	281
184	67557	43892	206108	206041	176879	176812	3607	3607
186978	197980	95344	530315	521978	423090	416383	2872	2855
186492	166349	64540	455012	449262	362742	358474	2782	2765
486	31631	30804	75303	72716	60348	57909	90	90
1081	55079	32420	46523	45838	31444	31163	289	289

12-13 续表2

单位：万元

行业	Sector	销售费用 Expenses for Sales	管理费用 Expenses for Management
总计	**Total**	**599190**	**1041443**
一、医药制造业	**Pharmaceutical Manufacturing**	**439716**	**173972**
（一）化学药品制造	Chemical manufacturing	236976	108514
化学药品原料药制造	Chemical raw materials Medicine manufacturing	3273	4758
化学药品制剂制造	Chemical preparations manufacturing	233703	103756
（二）中药饮片加工	Chinese medicine Pieces processing	46	40
（三）中成药生产	Chinese medicine production	157687	49490
（四）兽用药品制造	Veterinary pharmaceutical manufacturing	327	459
（五）生物药品制造	Biopharmaceutical manufacturing	43709	14589
（六）卫生材料及医药用品制造	Sanitary materials and medical supplies manufacturing	971	880
二、航空航天器制造业	**Aerospace & aviation industry**	**55112**	**254337**
（一）飞机制造	Aircraft Manufacturing	45482	176394
（二）航天器制造	Spacecraft Manufacturing	2539	32886
（三）航空、航天相关设备制造	Aviation and aerospace-related equipment manufacturing	5213	36376
（四）其他航空航天器制造	Other aerospace manufacturing	1658	4997
（五）航空航天器修理	Aerospace vehicle repair	220	3684
三、电子及通讯设备制造业	**Electronic and communication equipment manufacturing**	**50363**	**435162**
（一）电子工业专用设备制造	Electronic equipment manufacturing	2216	3826
（二）光纤、光缆制造	Optical fiber, cable manufacturing	2880	4106
（三）锂离子电池制造	Lithium-ion battery manufacturing	2861	19130
（四）通信设备制造	Communications equipment manufacturing	7285	31005
通信系统设备制造	Communications system equipment	7022	25940
通信终端设备制造	Communication Terminal Equipment	263	5065
（五）广播电视设备制造	Broadcasting and TV Equipment	1401	1197
广播电视节目制作及发射设备制造	Radio and television program production and transmission equipment		
广播电视接收设备及器材制造	Radio and television reception apparatus and equipment manufacturing	76	363
应用电视设备及其他广播电视设备制造	Application television equipment and other radio and television equipment manufacturing	1325	834
（六）雷达及配套设备制造	Radar and ancillary equipment manufacturers	3581	50599
（七）视听设备制造	Audiovisual equipment manufacturing	818	79
电视机制造	TV manufacturing	818	79
音响设备制造	Audio Equipment manufacturing		
影视录放设备制造	Video recording equipment manufacturing		
（八）电子器件制造	Electronic device manufacturing	10654	268828
电子真空器件制造	Electronic vacuum device manufacturing		
半导体分立器件制造	Discrete semiconductor device manufacturing	3679	14700
集成电路制造	Semiconductor Manufacturing	2174	240237
光电子器件及其他电子器件制造	Optoelectronic devices and other electronic device manufacturing	4801	13891
（九）电子元件制造	Electronics Manufacturing	16068	49272
电子元件及组件制造	Electronic components and component manufacturing	14154	47596
印刷电路板制造	Printed circuit board manufacturing	1914	1676
（十）其他电子设备制造	Other electronic equipment manufacturing	2599	7120

continued 2

(10 000 yuan)

财务费用 Financial cost	营业利润 Operating Profit	利润总额 Total Profits	亏损企业亏损额 Total Loss of Deficit Enterprises	利税总额 Total Pre-tax Profits	应付职工薪酬 Salary Payable	本年应交增值税 Value Added Tax Payable
150822	**817541**	**1368028**	**52077**	**1745998**	**1612059**	**332548**
23907	**135006**	**138255**	**4745**	**313732**	**163027**	**162470**
19446	88266	87303	902	211109	120211	116401
322	2185	2770		4582	1651	1608
19124	86081	84533	902	206527	118560	114793
42	4	4		7	68	1
3149	21687	24843	3813	66531	28243	37362
293	1115	1131		1331	723	111
865	23244	23959		33061	12293	8003
112	690	1015	30	1693	1489	592
43063	**173949**	**180240**	**9248**	**252519**	**771259**	**63099**
36571	99810	110658	47	155384	619433	38165
1568	34646	26276		29975	69808	3338
4829	29059	32450	7681	52616	68140	18479
169	11635	11946		15110	2886	2632
-74	-1201	-1090	1520	-566	10992	485
81361	**331096**	**841775**	**31237**	**916595**	**401061**	**62458**
234	3190	1810	72	3302	3423	1323
587	7217	7351		10415	5346	2690
3363	-25090	-19173	19621	-19052	10845	-29
-1180	124592	136563	6717	174757	90695	34138
-1466	102822	105559	6717	136754	67562	27142
286	21770	31004		38003	23133	6996
148	530	521		770	1684	217
143	113	129		374	284	217
5	417	392		396	1400	
2987	23345	23488		26866	56610	3042
29	60	60		60	167	
29	60	60		60	167	
62497	167227	656605	1837	663042	164527	2353
2617	9261	12341		15500	17148	2963
59156	151759	637610	1802	636766	135491	-1126
724	6207	6654	35	10776	11888	516
12133	25968	29615	2859	50072	62190	17585
11237	15588	19046	2733	39008	55405	17179
896	10380	10569	126	11064	6785	406
563	4057	4935	131	6363	5574	1139

12-13 续表3

单位：万元

行 业	Sector	企业单位数（个） Number of Enterprises (unit)	亏损企业 Loss Making Enterprises
四、计算机及办公设备制造业	**Computer and office equipment manufacturing**	**4**	
（一）计算机整机制造	Computer machine manufacturing		
（二）计算机零部件制造	Computer parts manufacturing		
（三）计算机外围设备制造	Computer peripheral equipment manufacturing	2	
（四）其他计算机制造	Other computer manufacturing	2	
（五）办公设备制造	Office Equipment manufacturing		
复印和胶印设备制造	Photocopying and offset printing equipment manufacturing		
计算器及货币专用设备制造	Calculator and money and special equipment manufacturing		
五、医疗设备及仪器仪表制造业	**Medical equipment and instrumentation manufacturing**	**66**	**9**
（一）医疗仪器设备及器械制造	Medical equipment and device manufacturing	9	2
医疗诊断、监护及治疗设备制造	Medical diagnosis, monitoring and treatment equipment manufacturing	3	1
口腔科用设备及器具制造	Stomatology manufacture equipment and appliances		
医疗实验室及医用消毒设备和器具制造	Medical laboratory and medical sterilization equipment and equipment manufacturing		
医疗、外科及兽医用器械制造	Medical, surgical and veterinary instruments manufacturing		
机械治疗及病房护理设备制造	Mechanical treatment and ward care equipment manufacturing	1	1
假肢、人工器官及植（介）入器械制造	Prostheses, artificial organs and implantable(interventional) device manufacturing	1	
其他治疗设备及器械制造	Other treatment equipment and equipment manufacturing	4	
（二）仪器仪表制造	Instruments manufacturing	57	7
工业自动控制系统装置制造	Manufacture of industrial automation control system devices manufacturing	11	3
电工仪器仪表制造	Electrical Instruments manufacturing	4	1
绘图、计算及测量仪器制造	Drawings, calculation and measurement equipment manufacturing	1	
实验分析仪器制造	Experimental analysis equipment manufacturing	2	1
试验机制造	Testing Machine Manufacturing		
供应用仪表及其他通用仪器制造	Supply of manufacturing devices and other general instrument Manufacturing	10	
环境检测专用仪器仪表制造	Environmental testing special Instruments Manufacturing	4	
运输设备及生产用计数仪表制造	Transport equipment and manufacturing with the counting instrument manufacturing		
导航、气象及海洋专用仪器制造	Navigation, meteorological and oceanographic special equipment manufacturing	1	
农林牧渔专用仪器仪表制造	Agriculture, forestry, animal husbandry and fishery special Instruments manufacturing	1	
地质勘探和地震专用仪器制造	Geological exploration and seismic special equipment manufacturing	6	2
教学专用仪器制造	Teaching special equipment manufacturing		
核子及核辐射测量仪器制造	Nucleon and nuclear radiation measuring instruments manufacturing	2	
电子测量仪器制造	Electronic Measuring Instruments Manufacturing	1	
其他专用仪器制造	Other special equipment manufacturing	4	
光学仪器制造	Optical Instruments Manufacturing	3	
其他仪器仪表制造业	Other instrumentation manufacturing	7	
六、信息化学品制造业	**Information chemicals manufacturing**	**3**	**1**
（一）信息化学品制造	Information Chemical Manufacturing	3	1

continued 3

(10 000 yuan)

工业总产值（当年价格）Gross Industrial Output Value (At Current Prices)	工业销售产值（当年价）Value of Industry Products Sales (At Current Prices)	出口交货值 Export Delivery Value	从业人员年平均人数（人）Annual Average Employers (person)	资产总计 Total Assets	流动资产合计 Total Working Capitals	固定资产合计 Total Fixed Assets	固定资产原价 Origing Value of Fixed Assets	累计折旧 Accumulative Total Depreciation
37970	**37994**		**387**	**43343**	**33825**	**1512**	**3360**	**1830**
32125	31949		289	38924	32029	1139	2733	1571
5845	6045		98	4419	1796	373	627	259
1404030	**1385368**	**65968**	**17975**	**2092977**	**1297337**	**430061**	**696225**	**281852**
47262	46866	127	949	90955	64217	17537	20126	7079
14811	15547	127	391	50832	33969	11739	10733	3483
2112	2164		132	5475	3669	1368	2910	1542
7340	6284		88	6749	2838	2867	3509	642
22999	22871		338	27899	23741	1563	2974	1412
1356768	1338502	65841	17026	2002022	1233120	412524	676099	274773
355952	350761	3055	1840	272970	131296	79543	101019	28370
23497	21883	1255	366	43099	34863	4124	2904	600
10229	10289	850	170	25563	15549	1362	2543	1191
6981	6072		121	7718	5700	1296	2206	910
63593	60068	641	1297	74725	59332	12224	17092	5266
109764	109249	38716	980	108973	102150	6459	17084	11220
9226	12226		126	10595	9701	849	1807	958
23151	21161		104	12133	6772	2891	3297	1227
31725	30901	1826	763	101869	74062	18592	27749	9238
33553	40130	51	956	82365	48178	3814	10265	6405
3126	2672		110	4786	4056	625	1616	997
50931	49498	12909	516	89189	72586	8550	9997	2815
587114	568838	6538	8914	1087798	615068	258759	458856	198808
47926	54754		763	80239	53807	13436	19664	6768
1170933	**1147016**	**265464**	**2291**	**1518666**	**682129**	**460194**	**1228301**	**793103**
1170933	1147016	265464	2291	1518666	682129	460194	1228301	793103

12-13 续表4

单位：万元

行　业	Sector	负债合计 Total Liabilites	流动负债合计 Total Working Liabilities
四、计算机及办公设备制造业	**Computer and office equipment manufacturing**	**9686**	**7641**
（一）计算机整机制造	Computer machine manufacturing		
（二）计算机零部件制造	Computer parts manufacturing		
（三）计算机外围设备制造	Computer peripheral equipment manufacturing	8380	6335
（四）其他计算机制造	Other computer manufacturing	1306	1306
（五）办公设备制造	Office Equipment manufacturing		
复印和胶印设备制造	Photocopying and offset printing equipment manufacturing		
计算器及货币专用设备制造	Calculator and money and special equipment manufacturing		
五、医疗设备及仪器仪表制造业	**Medical equipment and instrumentation manufacturing**	**986209**	**831856**
（一）医疗仪器设备及器械制造	Medical equipment and device manufacturing	45738	28502
医疗诊断、监护及治疗设备制造	Medical diagnosis, monitoring and treatment equipment manufacturing	33677	16826
口腔科用设备及器具制造	Stomatology manufacture equipment and appliances		
医疗实验室及医用消毒设备和器具制造	Medical laboratory and medical sterilization equipment and equipment manufacturing		
医疗、外科及兽医用器械制造	Medical, surgical and veterinary instruments manufacturing		
机械治疗及病房护理设备制造	Mechanical treatment and ward care equipment manufacturing	920	920
假肢、人工器官及植（介）入器械制造	Prostheses, artificial organs and implantable(interventional) device manufacturing	1116	1116
其他治疗设备及器械制造	Other treatment equipment and equipment manufacturing	10025	9640
（二）仪器仪表制造	Instruments manufacturing	940471	803354
工业自动控制系统装置制造	Manufacture of industrial automation control system devices manufacturing	192248	161900
电工仪器仪表制造	Electrical Instruments manufacturing	25132	25097
绘图、计算及测量仪器制造	Drawings, calculation and measurement equipment manufacturing	10467	10467
实验分析仪器制造	Experimental analysis equipment manufacturing	4106	4106
试验机制造	Testing Machine Manufacturing		
供应用仪表及其他通用仪器制造	Supply of manufacturing devices and other general instrument Manufacturing	29477	28774
环境检测专用仪器仪表制造	Environmental testing special Instruments Manufacturing	27861	26758
运输设备及生产用计数仪表制造	Transport equipment and manufacturing with the counting instrument manufacturing		
导航、气象及海洋专用仪器制造	Navigation, meteorological and oceanographic special equipment manufacturing	3987	3987
农林牧渔专用仪器仪表制造	Agriculture, forestry, animal husbandry and fishery special Instruments manufacturing	2548	2548
地质勘探和地震专用仪器制造	Geological exploration and seismic special equipment manufacturing	48805	45275
教学专用仪器制造	Teaching special equipment manufacturing		
核子及核辐射测量仪器制造	Nucleon and nuclear radiation measuring instruments manufacturing	39414	39211
电子测量仪器制造	Electronic Measuring Instruments Manufacturing	1006	1006
其他专用仪器制造	Other special equipment manufacturing	38451	27434
光学仪器制造	Optical Instruments Manufacturing	484607	397531
其他仪器仪表制造业	Other instrumentation manufacturing	32362	29260
六、信息化学品制造业	**Information chemicals manufacturing**	**653632**	**520305**
（一）信息化学品制造	Information Chemical Manufacturing	653632	520305

continued 4

(10 000 yuan)

非流动负债 Non-Working Liabilities	所有者权益合计 Total Owners' Equities	实收资本 Total Capital Hold	营业收入 Total Revenue	主营业务收入 Revenue from Principal Business	营业成本 Total Cost	主营业务成本 Cost of Principal Business	营业税金及附加 Taxs and Other Changes	主营业务税金及附加 Taxes and Other Charges on Principal Business
2045	**33656**	**21896**	**27517**	**27229**	**15619**	**15543**	**225**	**225**
2045	30543	20396	21226	20990	11169	11146	193	193
	3113	1500	6291	6239	4450	4397	32	32
128732	**1105169**	**396292**	**1342412**	**1329173**	**1045798**	**1025849**	**9254**	**8770**
16995	45217	19283	46255	46150	22059	21991	233	233
16610	17155	12834	14931	14912	9523	9481	77	77
	4555	1000	2164	2164	1228	1228	28	28
	5633	1049	6052	6052	2267	2267	30	30
385	17874	4400	23108	23022	9041	9015	98	98
111737	1059952	377009	1296157	1283023	1023739	1003858	9021	8537
8726	80722	100827	305462	304034	257326	256791	3828	3599
35	17967	17208	22137	22121	17837	17832	138	138
	15096	5900	10258	8617	6690	5468	43	41
	3612	9488	6182	6182	3339	3339	36	36
48	45247	27242	57381	57057	36261	35264	353	353
1104	81112	14375	110081	109463	72736	70077	1148	1148
	6609	1303	12226	12226	8517	8517	74	74
	9584	2000	21161	21161	18631	18631	20	20
3530	53064	31691	33988	31701	25319	24449	511	258
202	42951	9941	40811	40811	36012	27436	567	567
	3781	600	2879	2669	1518	1478	28	28
11016	50738	17070	46159	46159	25089	25089	522	522
87076	603191	118616	573007	566549	472701	467773	1452	1452
	46278	20748	54425	54273	41763	41714	301	301
128327	**865034**	**212678**	**1023623**	**1022634**	**912305**	**902503**	**1393**	**1393**
128327	865034	212678	1023623	1022634	912305	902503	1393	1393

12-13 续表5

单位：万元

行　业	Sector	销售费用 Expenses for Sales	管理费用 Expenses for Management
四、计算机及办公设备制造业	**Computer and office equipment manufacturing**	**1192**	**3608**
（一）计算机整机制造	Computer machine manufacturing		
（二）计算机零部件制造	Computer parts manufacturing		
（三）计算机外围设备制造	Computer peripheral equipment manufacturing	773	2936
（四）其他计算机制造	Other computer manufacturing	419	672
（五）办公设备制造	Office Equipment manufacturing		
复印和胶印设备制造	Photocopying and offset printing equipment manufacturing		
计算器及货币专用设备制造	Calculator and money and special equipment manufacturing		
五、医疗设备及仪器仪表制造业	**Medical equipment and instrumentation manufacturing**	**44440**	**146403**
（一）医疗仪器设备及器械制造	Medical equipment and device manufacturing	8658	6959
医疗诊断、监护及治疗设备制造	Medical diagnosis, monitoring and treatment equipment manufacturing	2346	2967
口腔科用设备及器具制造	Stomatology manufacture equipment and appliances		
医疗实验室及医用消毒设备和器具制造	Medical laboratory and medical sterilization equipment and equipment manufacturing		
医疗、外科及兽医用器械制造	Medical, surgical and veterinary instruments manufacturing		
机械治疗及病房护理设备制造	Mechanical treatment and ward care equipment manufacturing	450	669
假肢、人工器官及植（介）入器械制造	Prostheses, artificial organs and implantable(interventional) device manufacturing	668	1117
其他治疗设备及器械制造	Other treatment equipment and equipment manufacturing	5194	2206
（二）仪器仪表制造	Instruments manufacturing	35782	139444
工业自动控制系统装置制造	Manufacture of industrial automation control system devices manufacturing	7017	12648
电工仪器仪表制造	Electrical Instruments manufacturing	509	1554
绘图、计算及测量仪器制造	Drawings, calculation and measurement equipment manufacturing	1401	1352
实验分析仪器制造	Experimental analysis equipment manufacturing	791	1574
试验机制造	Testing Machine Manufacturing		
供应用仪表及其他通用仪器制造	Supply of manufacturing devices and other general instrument Manufacturing	4866	9493
环境检测专用仪器仪表制造	Environmental testing special Instruments Manufacturing	7331	7596
运输设备及生产用计数仪表制造	Transport equipment and manufacturing with the counting instrument manufacturing		
导航、气象及海洋专用仪器制造	Navigation, meteorological and oceanographic special equipment manufacturing	49	1130
农林牧渔专用仪器仪表制造	Agriculture, forestry, animal husbandry and fishery special Instruments manufacturing	544	681
地质勘探和地震专用仪器制造	Geological exploration and seismic special equipment manufacturing	1761	7346
教学专用仪器制造	Teaching special equipment manufacturing		
核子及核辐射测量仪器制造	Nucleon and nuclear radiation measuring instruments manufacturing	1837	7213
电子测量仪器制造	Electronic Measuring Instruments Manufacturing	348	784
其他专用仪器制造	Other special equipment manufacturing	3336	7190
光学仪器制造	Optical Instruments Manufacturing	2142	75825
其他仪器仪表制造业	Other instrumentation manufacturing	3850	5058
六、信息化学品制造业	**Information chemicals manufacturing**	**8367**	**27961**
（一）信息化学品制造	Information Chemical Manufacturing	8367	27961

continued 5

(10 000 yuan)

财务费用 Financial cost	营业利润 Operating Profit	利润总额 Total Profits	亏损企业亏损额 Total Loss of Deficit Enterprises	利税总额 Total Pre-tax Profits	应付职工薪酬 Salary Payable	本年应交增值税 Value Added Tax Payable
100	**6260**	**6718**		**8711**	**2616**	**1768**
101	5539	5987		7777	2174	1597
-1	721	731		934	442	171
-1420	**108909**	**137942**	**4849**	**178365**	**187619**	**31168**
1083	7244	9447	781	11325	5614	1644
566	-586	225	597	820	2467	518
15	-225	-184	184	78	524	234
58	1918	2241		2360	504	88
444	6137	7165		8067	2119	804
-2503	101665	128495	4068	167040	182005	29524
755	23137	29176	1831	43833	16641	10830
70	2001	2141	64	2618	1789	339
-154	926	1153		1467	1057	271
66	606	713	1040	676	1063	-74
242	5208	5796		9029	6885	2881
-2384	23715	24448		30066	10358	4470
39	2323	2357		2986	2484	555
100	1184	1399		1467	424	48
8	-1048	-331	1133	1978	7361	1798
417	10585	10778		13240	8981	1895
-1	203	268		533	684	237
1549	8379	10215		11505	5109	768
-3731	21404	36450		42748	112419	4845
521	3042	3932		4894	6750	661
3811	**62321**	**63098**	**1998**	**76076**	**86477**	**11585**
3811	62321	63098	1998	76076	86477	11585

12-14 规模以上工业企业主要经济效益指标（2016年）

行业	Sector	总资产贡献率（%） Ratio of Total Assets to Industrial Output Value (%)	资产负债率（%） Assets-Liability Ratio (%)
总计	**Total**	**6.4**	**55.7**
按工业行业大类分	**Grouped by Sector**		
煤炭开采和洗选业	Mining and Washing of Coal		
石油和天然气开采业	Extraction of Petroleum and Natural Gas		
黑色金属矿采选业	Mining and Processing of Ferrous Metal Ores		
有色金属矿采选业	Mining and Processing of Non-ferrous Metal Ores		
非金属矿采选业	Mining and Processing of Nonmetal Ores		
开采辅助活动	Mining Auxiliary Activities	2.7	26.8
其他采矿业	Mining of Other Ores		
农副食品加工业	Processing of Food from Agricultural Porducts	5.3	78.2
食品制造业	Manufacture of Foods	14.1	46.3
酒、饮料和精制茶制造业	Manufacture of Alcohol,Beverages and Tea	11.8	61.0
烟草制品业	Manufacture of Tobacco	13.0	9.1
纺织业	Manufacture of Textile	4.6	66.2
纺织服装、服饰业	Textile, Garments industry	-1.1	61.7
皮革、毛皮、羽毛及其制品和制鞋业	Manufacture of Leather, Fur, Feather and Related Products	7.3	38.4
木材加工和木、竹、藤、棕、草制品业	Processing of Timber, Manufacture of Wood,Plam and Straw Products	0.6	54.0
家具制造业	Manufacture of Furniture	9.1	50.2
造纸及纸制品业	Manufacture of Paper and Paper Products	13.1	49.4
印刷和记录媒介复制	Printing,Reproduction of Recording Media	8.2	27.9
文教、工美、体育和娱乐用品制造业	Manufacture of Articles For Cultural,Educational and Sports Activities	4.4	96.6

Major Indicators of Economic Performance of Industrial Enterprises above Designated Size (2016)

流动资产周转率（次）Rate of Annual Turnover Working Capitals (times)	成本费用利润率（%）Ratio of Profits to Cost (%)	工业产品销售率（%）Proportion of Industrial Products Sold (%)	产值利税率（%）Ratio of Output Value to Profits and Tax (%)	每百元固定资产实现利税（元）Profit and Tax per 100 yuan of Fixed Assets (yuan)	每百元销售收入实现利税（元）Profit and Tax per 100 yuan of Sales Revenue (yuan)
1.3	**6.0**	**96.0**	**8.3**	**19.9**	**8.7**
0.7	4.4	100.2	5.5	14.5	7.4
2.5	2.1	98.8	2.3	18.7	2.7
3.7	5.4	94.6	7.8	44.9	8.6
1.6	8.2	113.8	13.4	28.8	12.5
1.3	17.5	105.6	26.3	85.7	23.3
1.3	4.5	88.7	7.1	8.9	8.3
0.5	-9.4	90.5	-3.2	-17.0	-5.6
1.9	5.7	93.1	5.8	51.3	6.0
1.8	-3.4	92.6	-0.8	-1.8	-1.1
1.3	9.4	94.2	9.2	26.6	11.1
3.3	4.3	98.1	6.3	48.2	6.6
2.1	3.9	97.2	7.3	21.2	7.8
4.7	0.8	96.8	1.2	15.9	1.3

12-14 续表1

行 业	Sector	总资产贡献率（%） Ratio of Total Assets to Industrial Output Value (%)	资产负债率（%） Assets-Liability Ratio (%)
石油加工业、炼焦和核燃料加工业	Processing of Petroleum, Cokeing,Processing of Nuclear and Nuclear Fuel	0.6	66.4
化学原料及化学制品制造业	Manufacture of Raw Chemical Materials and Chemical Products	6.8	47.5
医药制造业	Manufacture of Medicines	17.0	50.3
化学纤维制造业	Manufacture of Chemical Fibers	2.7	64.9
橡胶和塑料制品业	Manufacture of Rubber and Plastics	4.9	75.4
非金属矿物制品业	Manufacture of Non-metallic Mineral Products	6.6	60.6
黑色金属冶炼和压延加工业	Smelting and Pressing of Ferrous Metals	17.1	54.2
有色金属冶炼和压延加工业	Smelting and Pressing of Non-ferrous Metals	4.9	30.7
金属制品业	Manufacture of Metal Products	2.8	49.3
通用设备制造业	Manufacture of General Purpose Machinery	3.8	52.0
专用设备制造业	Manufacture of Special Equipment	5.1	48.7
汽车制造业	Manufacture of Motor Vehicle	4.6	63.3
铁路、船舶、航空航天和其他运输设备制造业	Railways, Shipbuilding,Aerospace and Other Transportation Equipment Manufacturing Industry	4.2	56.2
电气机械和器材制造业	Manufacture of Electric Equipment and Machinery	6.5	48.8
计算机、通讯和其他电子设备制造业	Manufacture of Communication Equipment, Computers and other Electronic Equipment	10.3	52.4
仪器仪表制造业	Manufacture of Measuring Instruments and Machinery	8.8	47.0
其他制造业	Manufacture of Other Manufacturing	8.2	51.7
废弃资源综合利用业	Recycling and Disposal of Waste	1.4	27.6
金属制品、机械和设备修理业	Metal Products,Machinery and Equipment Repair Industry	4.1	54.4
电力、热力的生产和供应业	Production and Supply of Electric Power and Heat Power	6.3	81.2
燃气生产和供应业	Gas Mining and Supplying Industry	7.7	62.1
水的生产和供应业	Production and Supply of Water	1.7	68.5

continued 1

流动资产周转率（次）Rate of Annual Turnover Working Capitals (times)	成本费用利润率（%）Ratio of Profits to Cost (%)	工业产品销售率（%）Proportion of Industrial Products Sold (%)	产值利税率（%）Ratio of Output Value to Profits and Tax (%)	每百元固定资产实现利税（元）Profit and Tax per 100 yuan of Fixed Assets (yuan)	每百元销售收入实现利税（元）Profit and Tax per 100 yuan of Sales Revenue (yuan)
3.0	-4.2	101.6			
1.4	7.2	94.3	8.0	23.5	8.8
1.7	8.2	92.4	15.2	90.4	17.1
1.3	6.1	83.7	0.6	0.9	0.7
0.8	4.5	96.9	7.7	19.5	7.9
2.0	3.2	96.6	5.1	18.8	5.2
2.7	5.5	96.7	7.3	64.0	8.7
1.9	4.6	91.5	5.9	24.3	6.2
1.0	3.3	97.1	4.7	10.9	5.3
0.6	5.5	97.6	8.3	31.4	8.7
0.8	8.6	94.4	11.0	24.5	11.7
1.6	2.2	99.2	4.8	22.6	4.7
1.0	4.9	94.8	7.0	18.3	7.1
1.1	5.3	94.3	7.5	40.4	8.8
1.7	14.5	92.9	13.8	17.8	14.9
1.1	10.7	98.7	12.3	40.5	13.0
1.0	5.8	99.9	10.9	92.9	10.5
28.6	0.7	98.7	2.4	9.1	2.5
0.9	1.0	98.8	11.7	32.8	6.3
2.9	4.5	100.0	13.2	6.9	10.4
1.7	8.3	99.8	11.9	22.5	12.1
0.9	2.5	100.0	6.2	4.9	6.3

12-15 规模以上大中型工业企业主要经济效益指标（2016年）

行 业	Sector	总资产贡献率（%） Ratio of Total Assets to Industrial Output Value (%)	资产负债率（%） Assets-Liability Ratio (%)
总计	**Total**	**6.2**	**56.2**
按国民经济行业分	**Grouped by Sector**		
煤炭开采和洗选业	Mining and Washing of Coal		
石油和天然气开采业	Extraction of Petroleum and Natural Gas		
黑色金属矿采选业	Mining and Processing of Ferrous Metal Ores		
有色金属矿采选业	Mining and Processing of Non-ferrous Metal Ores		
非金属矿采选业	Mining and Processing of Nonmetal Ores		
开采辅助活动	Mining Auxiliary Activities	2.6	26.4
其他采矿业	Mining of other Ores		
农副食品加工业	Processing of Food from Agricultural Porducts	4.8	90.4
食品制造业	Manufacture of Foods	15.8	48.7
酒、饮料和精制茶制造业	Manufacture of Alcohol,Beverages and Tea	12.2	58.8
烟草制品业	Manufacture of Tobacco		
纺织业	Manufacture of Textile	0.7	69.7
纺织服装、服饰业	Textile, apparel industry	1.4	74.5
皮革、毛皮、羽毛及其制品和制鞋业	Leather fur feathers and its products and footwear	8.6	41.3
木材加工和木、竹、藤、棕、草制品业	Processing of Timber,Manufacture of Wood,Plam and Straw Products	0.4	54.3
家具制造业	Manufacture of Furniture	4.4	78.1
造纸及纸制品业	Manufacture of Paper and Paper Products	3.0	57.9
印刷和记录媒介复制业	Printing,Reproduction of Recording Media	8.5	24.0
文教、工美、体育和娱乐用品制造业	Manufacture of Articles For Cultural,Educational and Sports Activities		

Major Economic Indicators of Large and Medium-sized Industrial Enterprises above Designated Size（2016）

流动资产周转率（次） Rate of Annual Turnover Working Capitals (times)	成本费用利润率（%） Ratio of Profits to Cost (%)	工业产品销售率（%） Proportion of Industrial Products Sold (%)	产值利税率（%） Ratio of Output Value to Profits and Tax (%)	每百元固定资产实现利税（元） Profit and Tax per 100 yuan of Fixed Assets (yuan)	每百元销售收入实现利税（元） Profit and Tax per 100 yuan of Sales Revenue (yuan)
1.2	**6.4**	**96.8**	**9.2**	**17.7**	**9.4**
0.6	4.6	100.0	5.4	15.2	7.4
1.2	3.1	99.8	3.1	23.3	4.1
3.5	5.9	96.4	9.1	49.8	10.0
1.2	10.2	121.4	17.2	31.3	15.2
0.9	-0.2	100.3	1.9	0.8	1.8
0.6	-6.3	91.2	-0.6	-2.9	-0.9
2.4	6.4	94.8	6.6	50.6	6.6
1.6	-4.6	92.4	-1.3	-2.7	-1.9
1.4	3.0	104.8	6.8	10.5	6.4
2.4	0.3	100.0	0.7	11.1	0.7
1.5	5.1	97.2	9.7	23.7	10.7

12-15 续表1

行　业	Sector	总资产贡献率（%） Ratio of Total Assets to Industrial Output Value (%)	资产负债率（%） Assets-Liability Ratio (%)
石油加工、炼焦和核燃料加工业	Processing of Petroleum, Cokeing,Processing of Nuclear and Nuclear Fuel	-0.2	71.0
化学原料和化学制品制造业	Manufacture of Raw Chemical Materials and Chemical Products	6.0	43.0
医药制造业	Manufacture of Medicines	19.8	49.6
化学纤维制造业	Manufacture of Chemical Fibers		
橡胶和塑料制品业	Manufacture of Rubber and Plastics	4.1	81.6
非金属矿物制品业	Manufacture of Non-metallic Mineral Products	8.3	62.6
黑色金属冶炼和压延加工业	Smelting and Pressing of Ferrous Metals	6.6	76.0
有色金属冶炼和压延加工业	Smelting and Pressing of Non-ferrous Metals	4.0	23.8
金属制品业	Manufacture of Metal Products	2.8	65.5
通用设备制造业	Manufacture of General Purpose Machinery	2.9	53.0
专用设备制造业	Manufacture of Special Equipment	5.2	44.9
汽车制造业	Manufacture of Motor Vehicle	4.4	63.9
铁路、船舶、航空航天和其他运输设备制造业	Railways,Shipbuilding,Aerospace and Other Transportation Equipment Manufacturing Industry	3.3	58.6
电气机械和器材制造业	Manufacture of Electric Equipment and Machinery	5.3	47.2
计算机、通信和其他电子设备制造业	Manufacture of Communication Equipment, Computers and other Electronic Equipment	10.5	51.9
仪器仪表制造业	Manufacture of Measuring Instruments and Machinery	9.2	46.1
其他制造业	Manufacture of Other Manufacturing		
废弃资源综合利用	Recycling and Disposal of Waste		
金属制品、机械和设备修理业	Metal Products,Machinery and Equipment Repair Industry		
电力、热力生产和供应业	Production and Supply of Electric Power and Heat Power	6.9	80.5
燃气生产和供应业	Gas Mining and Supplying Industry	7.7	64.6
水的生产和供应业	Production and Supply of Water	1.9	66.4

continued 1

流动资产周转率（次）Rate of Annual Turnover Working Capitals (times)	成本费用利润率（%）Ratio of Profits to Cost (%)	工业产品销售率（%）Proportion of Industrial Products Sold (%)	产值利税率（%）Ratio of Output Value to Profits and Tax (%)	每百元固定资产实现利税（元）Profit and Tax per 100 yuan of Fixed Assets (yuan)	每百元销售收入实现利税（元）Profit and Tax per 100 yuan of Sales Revenue (yuan)
7.1	-5.9	100.0	-1.1	-1.0	-1.2
1.1	8.1	96.6	8.7	19.9	9.9
1.8	8.1	92.9	17.3	132.3	18.5
0.6	4.5	102.0	8.9	17.3	8.2
1.3	7.0	96.6	11.0	36.8	11.4
1.5	11.3	90.6	9.4	10.3	10.1
1.7	4.9	89.9	6.0	21.7	6.1
0.8	2.9	98.8	3.8	7.3	4.3
0.4	5.0	98.4	8.4	27.0	9.3
0.6	10.5	94.7	13.4	20.3	14.1
1.6	2.0	99.4	4.6	21.7	4.4
1.0	3.9	96.4	5.8	13.9	5.7
0.7	6.2	95.4	9.2	27.5	11.8
1.8	15.1	92.7	14.2	17.1	15.3
1.2	11.5	98.1	12.5	36.6	13.4
4.0	4.7	99.9	14.4	7.4	10.7
1.5	9.5	100.0	14.5	22.3	14.2
1.1	2.9	100.0	6.8	5.9	6.8

12-16 规模以上工业主要产品生产能力（2016年）

Production Capacity of Major Products of Industrial Enterprises above Designated Size（2016）

指 标	Item	2016
原煤	Coal	
卷烟	Cigarettes	
棉纺锭（锭）	Cotton Spindles （unit）	295209
气流纺锭（头）	Air Spindles（unit）	14467
棉布织机（台）	Cotton Loom （unit）	2604
原油加工能力（吨）	Crude Oil Processing Capacity (ton)	
农用氮、磷、钾化学肥料总计（折纯）（吨）	Chemical Fertilizers (ton)	
初级形态的塑料（吨）	Plastic in Primary Form (ton)	
化学纤维（吨）	Chemical Fibre (ton)	24000
硅酸盐水泥熟料（吨）	Portland Cement Clinker (ton)	1500000
水泥（吨）	Cement (ton)	4316000
平板玻璃（重量箱）	Plate Glass (Weight case)	
生铁（吨）	Pig Iron (ton)	
钢材（吨）	Rolled Steel (ton)	734414
铁合金（吨）	Ferroalloy (ton)	3500
金属切削机床（台）	Metal-cutting Machine Tools （unit）	8340
汽车（辆）	Motor Vehicles（unit）	543500
其中：乘用车（辆）	Passenger Vehicles(unit)	303000
微型计算机设备（台）	Micro Computer Equipment （unit）	
移动通信手持机（台）	Mobile Handset （unit）	23700000
彩色电视机（台）	Color TV Set（unit）	46576
发电设备容量总计（万千瓦）	Installed Capacity of Power Generation （10 000kw）	383.89
其中：火电设备容量（万千瓦）	Thermal Power（10 000kw）	289.03
水电设备容量（万千瓦）	Hydropower（10 000kw）	69.61
风电设备容量（万千瓦）	Wind Power （10 000kw）	

主 要 统 计 指 标 解 释

工业 指从事自然资源的开采，对采掘品和农产品进行加工和再加工的物质生产部门。具体包括：（1）对自然资源的开采，如采矿、晒盐等（但不包括禽兽捕猎和水产捕捞）；（2）对农副产品的加工、再加工，如粮油加工、食品加工、缫丝、纺织、制革等；（3）对采掘品的加工、再加工，如炼铁、炼钢、化工生产、石油加工、机器制造、木材加工等，以及电力、自来水、煤气的生产和供应等；（4）对工业品的修理、翻新，如机器设备的修理、交通运输工具（如汽车）的修理等。

工业统计调查单位为独立核算法人工业企业。

独立核算法人工业企业指从事工业生产经营活动的单位。独立核算法人工业企业应同时具备以下条件：①依法成立，有自己的名称、组织机构和场所，能够承担民事责任；②独立拥有和使用资产，承担负债，有权与其他单位签订合同；③独立核算盈亏，并能够编制资产负债表。

国有及国有控股企业 指国有企业加上国有控股企业。国有企业（即原全民所有制工业或国营工业）指企业全部资产归国家所有，并按《中华人民共和国企业法人登记管理条例》规定登记注册的非公司制的经济组织。包括国有企业、国有独资公司和国有联营企业。1957年以前的公私合营和私营工业，后均改造为国营工业，1992年改为国有工业，这部分工业的资料不单独分列时，均包括在国有企业内。国有控股企业是对混合所有制经济的企业进行的"国有控股"分类。它是指这些企业的全部资产中国有资产（股份）相对其他所有者中的任何一个所有者占资（股）最多的企业。该分组反映了国有经济控股情况。

本篇涉及的其他企业登记注册类型的解释详见综合篇。

轻工业 指主要提供生活消费品和制作手工工具的工业。按其所使用的原料不同，可分为两大类：（1）以农产品为原料的轻工业，是指直接或间接以农产品为基本原料的轻工业。主要包括食品制造、饮料制造、烟草加工、纺织、缝纫、皮革和毛皮制作、造纸以及印刷等工业；（2）以非农产品为原料的轻工业，是指以工业品为原料的轻工业。主要包括文教体育用品、化学药品制造、合成纤维制造、日用化学制品、日用玻璃制品、日用金属制品、手工工具制造、医疗器械制造、文化和办公用机械制造等工业。

重工业 指为国民经济各部门提供物质技术基础的主要生产资料的工业。按其生产性质和产品用途，可以分为下列三类：（1）采掘（伐）工业，是指对自然资源的开采，包括石油开采、煤炭开采、金属矿开采、非金属矿开采等工业；（2）原材料工业，指向国民经济各部门提供基本材料、动力和燃料的工业。包括金属冶炼及加工、炼焦及焦炭、化学、化工：原料、水泥、人造板以及电力、石油和煤炭加工等工业；（3）加工工业，是指对工业原材料进行再加工制造的工业。包括装备国民经济各部门的机械设备制造工业、金属结构、水泥制品等工业，以及为农业提供的生产资料如化肥、农药等工业。

根据上述划分原则，修理业中以重工业产品为修理作业对象的划为重工业，反之划为轻工业。

工业总产值

（1）定义：

工业总产值是工业企业在一定时期内生产的以货币形式表现的工业最终产品和提供工业性劳务活动的总价值量。它反映一定时间内工业生产的总规模和总水平。

（2）计算原则：

工业生产的原则，即凡是企业在报告期生产的经检验合格的产品，不管是否在报告期销售，均包括在内。

最终产品的原则，即凡是计入工业总产值的产品，必须是本企业生产的经检验合格的，不需要再进行任何加工的最终产品。如果企业有中间产品（半成品）对外销售，则对外销售的中间产品应视为企业的最终产品。

工厂法原则，即工业总产值是以下业企业作为基本计算（核算）单位，即按企业的最终产品计算工业总产值。按这种方法计算的工业总产值，不允许同一产品价值在企业内部重复计算，不能把企业内部各个车间（分厂）生产的成果相加，但允许企业间的重复计算。

（3）内容及计算方法：

1995年全国工业普查对工业总产值（原规定）的内容及计算原则和方法做了某些修订，修订后的工业总产值（新规定）包括三项内容：即本期生产成品价值、对外加工费收入、在制品半成品期末期初差额价值三部分。

本期生产成品价值指企业本期生产，并在报告期内不再进行加工，经检验、包装入库的全部工业成品（半成品）价值合计，包括企业生产的自制设备及提供给本企业在建工程、其他非工业部门和福利部门等单位使用的成品价值。本期生产成品价值为按自备原材料生产的产品的数量乘以本期不含增值税（销项税额）的产品实际销售平均单价计算；会计核算中按成本价格转帐的自制设备和自产自用的成品，按成本价格计算生产成品价值。生产成品价值中不包括用定货者来料加工的成品（半成品）价值。

对外加工费收入指企业在报告期内完成的对外承接的工业品加工（包括用定货者来料加工产品）的加工费收入和对外工业修理作业所取得的加工费收入。对外加工费收入按不含增值税（销项税额）的价格计算，可根据会计“产品销售收入”科目的有关资料取得。

对于本企业对内非工业部门提供的加工修理、设备安装的劳务收入，如果企业会计核算基础较好，能取得这部分资料，而且这部分价值所占比重较大，应包括在对外加工费收入中。

自制半成品在制品期末期初差额价值指企业报告期在制品期末减期初的差额价值，本指标一般可以从会计核算资料中取得。如果会计产品成本核算中不计算半成品、在制品的成本，则总产值中也不包括这部分价值，反之则包括。

（4）工业总产值统计范围变化和计算方法修订情况：

1984年以前工业总产值不包括村办工业，村办工业总产值划归农业。1984年以后工业总产值包括村办工业。

1995年工业普查对工业总产值计算方法做了修订，即从1995年始按新修订（新规定）方法计算工业总产值。新规定与原规定的区别如下：

全价与加工费的计算原则不同：新规定为凡自备原材料，不论其生产繁简程度如何，一律按全价计算工业总产值；凡来料加工，允许按加工费计算工业总产值。原规定则视生产加工的繁简程度不同，规定哪些行业按全价，哪些行业按加工费计算工业总产值。

自制半成品、在产品期末期初差额价值的计算原则不同：新规定要求，凡会计产品成本核算时计算了成本的差额价值，总产值中就应包括，否则可不包括；原规定则按生产周期六个月的界限区分，凡生产周期六个月以上的企业，总产值计算中应包括这部分差额价值，否则可不包括。

计算价格不同：新规定按不含增值税（销项税额）的价格计算；原规定则按含增值税（销项税额）的价格计算。

工业增加值 指工业企业在报告期内以货币表现的工业生产活动的最终成果。

工业增加值有两种计算方法：一是生产法，即工业总产出减去工业中间投入加上应交增值税；二是收入法，即从收入的角度出发，根据生产要素在生产过程中应得到的收入份额计算，具体构成项目有固定资产折旧、劳动者报酬、生产税净额、营业盈余，这种方法也称要素分配法。本年鉴中的工业增加值是以收入法计算的。

生产法工业增加值的计算方法为：

工业增加值＝工业总产出-工业中间投入+应交增值税

（1）工业总产出：指工业企业在一定时期内工业生产活动的总成果。工业总产出包括：成品生产价值，对外加工费收入，自制半成品、在产品期末期初差额价值。1995年后用新规定计算的工业总产值代替。

（2）工业中间投入：指工业企业在工业生产活动中消耗的外购物质产品和对外支付的服务费用。服务费用包括支付给物质生产部门（工业、农业、批发零售贸易业、建筑业、运输邮电业）的服务费用和支付给非物质生产部门（如保险、金融、文化教育、科学研究、医疗卫生、行政管理等）的服务费用。工业中间投入的确定须遵循以下原则：必须从外部购入的，并已计入工业总产出的产品和服务价值；必须是本期投入生产，并一次性消耗掉（包括本期摊销的低值易耗品等）的产品和服务价值。

工业中间投入包括直接材料费用、制造费用中的工业中间投入、管理费用中的工业中间投入、销售费用中的工业中间投入和利息支出五部分。

资产总计 指企业拥有或控制的能以货币计量的经济资源，包括各种财产、债权和其他权利。资产按流动性分为流动资产、长期投资、固定资产、无形资产、递延资产和其他资产。该指标根据企业会计“资产负债表”中“资产总计”项目的期末数增列。

流动资产 指企业可以在一年内或者超过一年的一个生产周期内变现或者耗用的资产，包括现金及各种存款、短期投资，应收及预付款项、存货等。

固定资产原价 指企业在建造、购置、安装、改建、扩建、技术改造某项固定资产时所支出的全部货币总额。它一般包括买价、包装费、运杂费和安装费等。

固定资产净值 指固定资产原价减去历年已提折旧额后的净额。计算公式为：

固定资产净值=固定资产原价-累计折旧

负债合计 指企业所承担的能以货币计量，将以资产或劳务偿付的债务，偿还形式包括货币、资产或提供劳务。负债一般按偿还期长短分为流动负债和长期负债。根据会计“资产负债表”中“负债合计”的年末数填列。

所有者权益合计 指企业投资人对企业净资产的所有权。企业净资产为企业全部资产与企业全部负债的差额，包括实收资本、资本公积、盈余公积、未分配利润等。根据会计“资产负债表”中“所有者权益”项的期末数填列。

主营业务收入 指会计“利润表”中对应指标的本年累计数。未执行2001年《企业会计制度》的企业，用“产品销售收入”的本期累计数代替。

主营业务成本 指会计“利润表”中对应指标的本年累计数。未执行2001年《企业会计制度》的企业，用“产品销售成本”的本期累计数代替。

主营业务税金及附加 指会计“利润表”中对应指标的本年累计数。未执行2001年《企业会计制度》的企业，用“产品销售税金及附加”的本期累计数代替。

利润总额 指企业在生产经营过程中各种收入扣除各种耗费后的盈余，反映企业在报告期内实现的盈亏总额，包括营业利润、补贴收入、投资净收益和营业外收支净额。根据会计“利润表”中的对应指标的本期累计数填列。

本年应交增值税 指企业按税法规定，从事货物销售或提供加工、修理修配劳务等增加货物价值的活动本期应交纳的税金。指企业在报告期应交增值税额。计算公式为：

本年应交增值税=销项税额-（进项税额-进项税额转出）-出口抵减内销产品应纳税额-减免税款+出口退税

本年进项税额 指工业企业在报告期内购入货物或接受应税劳务而支付的、准予从销项税额中抵扣的增值税额。

本年销项税额 指工业企业在报告期内销售货物或提供应税劳务应收取的增值税额。

从业人员平均人数 是指报告期内每天拥有的从业人员人数。其计算公式为：

月平均人数=报告月内每天实有人数之和／报告月日历日数

季平均人数=季内各月平均人数之和／3

年平均人数=年内各月平均人数之和／12

总资产贡献率 反映企业全部资产的获利能力，是企业经营业绩和管理水平的集中体现，是评价和考核企业盈利能力的核心指标。计算公式为：

总资产贡献率（%）=（利润总额+税金总额+利息支出）／平均资产总额×100%

公式中：税金总额为产品销售税金及附加与应交增值税之和；平均资产总额为期初期末资产之和的算术平均值。

资产负债率 该指标既反映企业经营风险的大小，也反映企业利用债权人提供的资金从事经营活动的能力。计算公式为：

资产负债率（%）=负债总额／资产总额×100%

资产与负债均为报告期期末数。

流动资产周转次数 指一定时期内流动资产完成的周转次数，反映投入工业企业流动资金的周转速度。计算公式为：

流动资产周转次数：产品销售收入／全部流动资产平均余额

公式中：全部流动资产平均余额为期初和期末的流动资产之和的算术平均值。

成本费用利润率 反映企业投入的生产成本及费用的经济效益，同时也反映企业降低成本所取得的经济效益。计算公式为：

成本费用利润率（%）=利润总额／成本费用总额×100%

公式中：成本费用总额为产品销售成本、销售费用、管理费用、财务费用之和。

产品销售率 该指标反映工业产品已实现销售的程度，是分析工业产销衔接情况，研究工业产品满足社会需求的指标。计算公式为：

产品销售率（%）=工业销售产值／工业总产值（现价）×100%

Explanatory Notes on Main Statistical Indicators

Industry refers to the material production sector which is engaged in the extraction of natural resources and processing and reprocessing of minerals and agricultural products, including (1) extraction of natural resources, such as mining, salt production (but not including hunting and fishing); (2) processing and reprocessing of farm and sideline produces, such as rice husking, flour milling, wine making, oil pressing, silk reeling, spinning and weaving, and leather making; (3) manufacture of industrial products, such as steel making, iron smelting, chemicals manufacturing, petroleum processing, machine building, timber processing; water and gas production and electricity generation and supply; (4)repairing of industrial products such as the repairing of machinery and means of transport (including cars).

In industrial statistics surveys, the units of enquiry are corporate industrial enterprises with independent accounting systems.

Corporate industrial enterprises with independent accounting systems refer to enterprises engaging in industrial production activities, which meet the following requirements: (1) They are established legally, having their own names, organizations, location and able to take civil liability; (2) They possess and use their assets independently, assume liabilities and are entitled to sign contracts with other units; (3) They are financially independent and compile their own balance sheets.

State–owned and State–holding Enterprises refer to state-owned enterprises plus State-holding enterprises. State-owned enterprises (originally known as State-run enterprises with ownership by the whole society) are non-corporate economic entities registered in accordance with the Regulation of the People's Republic of China on the Management of Registration of Legal Enterprises, where all assets are owned by the State. Included in this category are State-owned enterprises, State-funded corporations and State-owned joint-operation enterprises. Joint State- private industries and private industries, which existed before 1957, were transformed into state-run industries since 1957, and into State-owned industries after 1992. Statistics on those enterprises are included in the State- owned industries instead of being grouped them separately. State-holding enterprises are a sub- classification of enterprises with mixed ownership, referring to enterprises where the percentage of State assets (or shares by the State) is larger than any other single share holder of the same enterprise. This sub- classification illustrates the control of the State over a particular industry.

For explanation of enterprises of other types of registration covered in this chapter, please refer to General Survey.

Light Industry refers to the industry that produces consumer goods and hand tools. It consists of two categories, depending on the materials used:

(1) Industries using farm products as raw materials. These are the branches of light industry which directly or indirectly use farm products as basic raw materials, including the manufacture of food and beverages, tobacco processing, textile, clothing, fur and leather manufacturing, paper making, printing, etc.

(2) Industries using non-farm products as raw materials. These are the branches of light industry which use manufactured goods as raw materials, including the manufacture of cultural, educational articles and sports goods, chemicals, synthetic fibre, chemical products for daily use, glass products for daily use, metal products for daily use, hand tools, medical apparatus and instruments, and the manufacture of cultural and office machinery.

Heavy Industry refers to the industry which produces capital goods, and provides various sectors of the national economy with necessary material and technical basis for production. It consists of the following three branches according to the purpose of production or the use of products:

(1) Mining, quarrying and logging industry, which refers to the industry that extracts natural resources, including extraction of petroleum, coal, metal and non-metal ores.

(2) Raw materials industry refers to the industry that provides various sectors of the national economy with raw materials, fuels and power. It includes smelting and processing of metals, coking and coke chemistry, chemical materials and building materials such as cement, plywood, and power, petroleum refining and coal dressing

(3) Manufacturing industry which refers to the industry that processes raw materials. It includes machine-building industries which equip sectors of the national economy; industries producing metal structure and cement products; and industries producing means of agricultural production, such as chemical fertilizers and pesticides.

In accordance with the above principles of classification, the repairing trades, which are engaged primarily in repairing products of heavy industry, are classified as heavy industry while those which are engaged in repairing products of light industry are classified as light industry.

Gross Industrial Output Value

(1) Definition: Gross industrial output value is the total volume of final industrial products produced and industrial services provided during a given period in monetary terms. It reflects the total achievements and overall scale of industrial production during a given period.

(2) Principles for calculation:

Statistics on industrial production follow the principle that all products produced by the enterprises and accepted through quality check during the reference period are to be included no matter whether they are sold or not during the reference period.

Determination of final products follows the principle that all products that are included in the calculation of gross industrial output value are the final products of the enterprise which have been accepted through quality check and require no further processing. If an enterprise has intermediate (semi-finished) products to sell, these intermediate products are considered as the final products of the enterprise.

Gross industrial output value is calculated following the principle of factory approach, i.e. industrial enterprise is used as the basic accounting unit in calculating the gross industrial output value. By this approach, value of the same product is not to be double-counted, and the output value of different workshops (branch factories) within the enterprise should not be added. However, this approach allows the possibility of double counting between enterprises.

(3) Content and method of calculation: The old definition of gross industrial output value was modified during the 1995 National Industrial Census. The revised (new) definition of gross industrial output value consists of 3 components: value of the finished products during the reference period, income from processing for external parties, and value of change in semi-finished products between the end and the beginning of the reference period.

Value of finished products during the reference period: refers to the value of all finished (semi-finished) industrial products that are produced during the reference period without the need for further processing, checked for acceptance, packed and put into the warehouse of the enterprise, including the value of own-produced equipment and the value of products provided to the projects under construction of the enterprise, and to other non-industrial or welfare units. Value of finished products during the reference period is calculated by the quantity of products produced using own materials multiplied by the average unit prices at which products are sold (excluding value-added tax). Own-produced equipment and products produced for own use are valued at cost prices as in the case of enterprise accounting. Value of finished products does not include the value of finished products (semi-finished products) that are produced using the materials from the clients who place the orders.

Income from external processing: refers to income from contracted external processing of industrial products (including processing of industrial products using materials from the clients), and the income from industrial repairing work provided to other parties. Income from external processing is calculated using information from the item "products sales income" in the enterprise accounting at the prices with value-added tax excluded.

For income from services such as processing, repairing and installation of equipment provided to non- industrial units within the enterprise, if the accounting work of the enterprise is good enough to separate it from other records, and the share of such services is significant, it should also be included in the income from external processing.

Value of change in semi-finished products between the end and the beginning of the reference period: refers to the value of change in semi-finished products between the end and the beginning of the reference period, which generally can be obtained from accounting records of enterprises. If the enterprise accounting excludes the cost of semi-finished products, then it should not be included in the gross industrial output value, and the reverse if otherwise.

(4) Changes in the scope and method of calculation of the gross industrial output value

Prior to 1984, the value of rural industry run by villages was classified into agriculture instead of industry Since 1984, it has been included in the gross industrial output value. Method of calculation for the gross industrial output value was modified in the industriaLcensus in 1995. The difference in the new method as compared with the old one is outlined below:

Principle in using full value vs. processing fee: The new method stipulates that all products produced using own materials are to be calculated with full value in reporting the gross industrial output value irrespective of the complexity of production, and for external processing, it allows calculation using processing fee. In the old method, however, the use of full value or processing fee was determined by the degree of complexity of production in different branches of industries.

Principle in determining the value of change in semi-finished products: The new method requires that value of change in semi-finished products should be included in the gross industrial output value if it is included in the accounting record of the enterprise, otherwise it should not be included. In the old method, it is determined by the type of enterprises in terms of production cycle. If the production cycle is over 6 months, the value of change in semi-finished products is included in the gross industrial output value, otherwise it is not.

Difference in prices: The new method uses prices excluding value-added tax in the calculation of gross industrial output value, while the old method used prices including value-added tax.

Value–added of Industry refers to the final results of industrial production of industrial enterprises in money terms during the reference period.

Industrial value-added can be calculated by two approaches: the production approach, i.e. gross industrial output value minus intermediate input plus value-added tax, and the income approach, i.e. income for various factors used in the course of production, including depreciation of fixed assets, remuneration of labourers, net of production tax, and operating surplus. Value-added of industry in the Yearbook is calculated by the income approach as follows:

Value-added of industry = gross industrial output - industrial intermediate input + value-added tax

(1) Gross industrial output: refers to the total achievements of industrial production activities during a given period. Gross industrial output includes value of finished products, income from external processing, and value of change in semi-finished products between the end and the beginning of the reference period. Since 1995, the gross industrial output value obtained by the new method is used in the calculation.

(2) Industrial intermediate input: refers to purchased goods and paid services consumed during the industrial production of enterprises. Fees paid for services include fees paid for the services provided by material production sectors (industry, agriculture, wholesale and retail trade, construction, transport, post and telecommunications) and by non-material production sectors (insurance, banking, culture, education, scientific research, health and medical care, public administration, etc.). The determination of industrial intermediate input follows the principle that the goods and services must be purchased from outside and included in the gross industrial output, and that the goods and services are inputted into production and consumed (include low-value consumables) during the reference period.

Industrial intermediate input includes 5 components, namely direct consumption of materials, industrial intermediate input in manufacturing cost, industrial intermediate input in management cost, industrial intermediate input in marketing cost and expenditure on interest.

Total Assets refer to all economic resources, in monetary term, these are owned or controlled by enterprises, including properties, creditor's equity and other economic rights of all forms. Classified by the degree of liquidity, total assets include working capitals, long-term investment, fixed assets, intangible assets, deferred assets and other assets. Data on this indicator can be obtained by the year-end figures of total assets in the Assets and Liability Table of accounting records of enterprises.

Working Capital refers to capital that an enterprise can cash or use during one year or one production cycle that may exceed one year, including cash and savings deposits of various forms, short-term investment, money receivable and prepaid money, inventories, etc.

Original Value of Fixed Assets refers to the total value, in monetary terms, that an enterprise spent on fixed assets, through construction, purchase, installation, transformation, expansion or technical upgrading. Generally, it covers cost of purchase, packing, transportation and installation, etc.

Net Value of Fixed Assets refers to the original value of fixed assets minus depreciation over the years, i.e.:

Net value of fixed assets = original value of fixed assets - cumulative depreciation

Total Liabilities refer to payable liabilities of enterprises that have to be repaid in terms of money, assets or labour services. In terms of payment, it can be divided into liquid liabilities and long-term liabilities. Data on this item is obtained from the ending figures on total liabilities from the Assets and Liability Table from the enterprises.

Total Equity refers to the ownership of net assets of enterprise by its investors. Net assets equal total assets minus total liabilities of the enterprise, including the paid-in capital, accumulation of capital and operating surplus and non-distributed profits. Data are obtained from the ending figures on "total equity" from the "balance sheets".

Revenue from Principal Business refers to the annual accumulation of the corresponding item in the "profit table" of the accountant. For enterprises that do not follow the 2001 Enterprise Accounting Standards, the year-end accumulation of revenue from the sales of products is used as a substitute.

Cost of Principal Business refers to the annual accumulation of the corresponding item in the "profit table" of the accountant. For enterprises that do not follow the 2001 Enterprise Accounting Standards, theyear-end accumulation of cost for the sales of products is used as a substitute.

Tax and Extra Charges from Principal Bosiness refer to the annual accumulation of the corresponding item in the "profit table" of the accountant. For enterprises that do not follow the 2001 Enterprise Accounting Standards, the year-end accumulation of tax and extra charges from the sales of products is used as a substitute.

Total Profits refers to the balance of various incomes minus various spendings in the course of operation, reflecting the total profits and losses of enterprises in reporting period. It includes: operating profits, income from subsidies, net investment income and net income from activities other than operation. Data are obtained from the annual accumulation of the corresponding item in the "profit table" of the accountant.

Value-added Tax Payable in the Current Year refers to the payable tax of enterprises which engaged in selling of goods or providing services that bring added value to the goods, such as processing, repairing, fitting and other activities should be paid according to Tax Law. It refers to the amount of the value-added tax which should be paid by the enterprises during the reference period. The formula is as tollows:

Value-added Tax Payable in the Current Year = tax on sales-(tax on purchase-transferred tax on purchase)- exports deduct tax payable on domestic sales-tax relief+the export tax rebate.

Tax on Purchase in Current Year refers to goods purchased by industrial enterprises or value added tax that should be paid but being granted the right to deduct from the tax on sales.

Tax on Sales in Current Year refers to value added tax on industrial enterprises from sales of goods or taxable services that should be charged value added tax.

Average number of employed persons refers to the number of employee everyday during the reference period, calculated with the following formula:

$$\text{Monthly average Number} = \frac{\text{sum of actual employees everyday in reference month}}{\text{number of calendar dates in reference month}}$$

$$\text{Quarterly average number} = \frac{\text{sum of monthly average number in reference quarter}}{3}$$

$$\text{Annual average number} = \frac{\text{sum of monthly average number in reference year}}{12}$$

Ratio of Profits, Taxes and Interests to Average Assets reflects the profit-making capability of all assets of the enterprise and is a key indicator manifesting the performance and management and evaluating the profit-making potential of the enterprise. It is calculated as

$$\text{Ratio of Profits, Taxes and Interests toAverageAssets(\%)} = \frac{\text{otal profits+ total taxes+ interest payment}}{\text{average assets}} \times 100\%$$

In the above formula, total taxes is the sum of tax and extra charges on the sales of products and value-added tax payable; and average assets is the arithmetic mean of the sum of beginning assets and ending assets.

Ratio of Debts to Assets reflects both the operation risk and the capability of the enterprise in making use of the capital from the creditors. It is calculated as follows:

$$\text{Ratio of Debts toAssets(\%)} = \frac{\text{total debts}}{\text{total assets}} \times 100\%$$

Both assets and debts are figures at the end of the reference period.

Turnover of Working Capital refers to the number of times of turnover of working capital in a given period of time, which reflects the speed of the turnover of working capital of industrial enterprises, and is calculated as follows:

$$\text{Turnover of Working Capital} = \frac{\text{sales revenue of products}}{\text{average balance of total working capital}}$$

In the above formula, average balance of total working capital refers to the arithmetic mean of the sum of working capital at the beginning and at the end of the reference period.

Ratio of Profits to Total Industrial Costs refers to the ratio of profits realized in a given period to the total costs in the same period, which reflects the economic efficiency of input cost and is calculated as follows:

$$\text{Ratio of Profits to Total Industrial Cost (\%)} = \frac{\text{total profits}}{\text{total costs}} \times 100\%$$

Total costs in the above formula are the sum of cost of products sold, marketing cost, management cost and financial cost.

Sales Ratio of Products is an indicator reflecting the actual sale of industrial products, analyzing the production-selling and supply-demand relations. It is calculated as:

$$\text{Sales Ratio of Products (\%)} = \frac{\text{value of industrial sales}}{\text{gross industrial output value (current prices)}} \times 100\%$$

13 能　源

ENERGY

资料整理：于元英　张　育　李　婷　雷稳强
Data management：Yu Yuanying　Zhang Yu　Li Ting　Lei Wenqiang
数据审核：丁抗玲
Data audit：Ding Kangling

第十三部分　能源

一、简要说明

本章资料包括规模以上工业能源购销存情况、全市单位GDP能耗、规模以上工业企业用水情况等，由西安市统计局能源与环境处提供。

二、主要指标

规模以上工业综合能源消费量（万吨标准煤）	495.28	比上年增长	3.1%
单位GDP能耗（吨标准煤/万元）	0.394	比上年下降	3.83%

13　ENERGY

Ⅰ.Brief Introduction

Data in this chapter reflects energy purchases consumption and inventory of industrial enterprises above designated size,energy consumption per unit of GDP in whole city, and statistics on water use of industrial enterprises above designated size. data in this chapter are provided and compiled by Energy and Environment Division of the Xi'an Bureau of Statistics.

Ⅱ.Major Indicators

		Increase over Preceding Year
Comprehensive Energy Consumption Above Designated Size(10 000 Tons of Standard Coal)	495.28	3.1%
Energy Consumption of GDP per Unit (Tons of Standard Coal /10 000 yuan)	0.394	-3.83%

13-1 全市及各区县单位GDP能耗

Energy Consumption per Unit of GDP by Region

单位：吨标准煤 / 万元 (ton of SCE/10 000 yuan)

地 区 Region		单位GDP能耗 Energy Consumption Per Unit of GDP													
		GDP按2005年价格计算 GDP are calculated at 2005 constant prices						GDP按2010年价格计算 GDP are calculated at 2010 constant prices						GDP按2015年价格计算 GDP are calculated at 2015 constant prices	
		2005	2006	2007	2008	2009	2010	2010	2011	2012	2013	2014	2015	2015	2016
西安市	**Xi'an**	**0.911**	**0.873**	**0.823**	**0.768**	**0.726**	**0.711**	**0.575**	**0.555**	**0.535**	**0.516**	**0.486**	**0.470**	**0.410**	**0.394**
新城区	Xincheng	0.783	0.751	0.708	0.667	0.629	0.621	0.563	0.544	0.525	0.506	0.479	0.463	0.416	0.401
碑林区	Beilin	0.640	0.613	0.580	0.547	0.514	0.510	0.438	0.421	0.406	0.392	0.368	0.356	0.287	0.277
莲湖区	Lianhu	0.766	0.735	0.701	0.646	0.609	0.587	0.521	0.501	0.483	0.466	0.430	0.416	0.372	0.359
灞桥区	Baqiao	1.194	1.163	1.091	1.023	0.964	0.923	0.663	0.638	0.615	0.592	0.562	0.543	0.517	0.497
未央区	Weiyang	1.122	1.078	1.019	0.951	0.894	0.882	0.680	0.655	0.632	0.609	0.563	0.539	0.444	0.427
雁塔区	Yanta	0.884	0.842	0.795	0.749	0.703	0.674	0.512	0.494	0.476	0.459	0.441	0.425	0.362	0.349
阎良区	Yanliang	0.825	0.778	0.740	0.695	0.656	0.652	0.533	0.515	0.497	0.480	0.444	0.430	0.364	0.352
临潼区	Lintong	0.940	0.912	0.860	0.790	0.753	0.717	0.676	0.652	0.629	0.607	0.558	0.541	0.502	0.484
长安区	Chang'an	1.059	0.994	0.939	0.890	0.841	0.824	0.642	0.619	0.596	0.575	0.555	0.532	0.460	0.443
高陵区	Gaoling	0.892	0.848	0.790	0.747	0.704	0.677	0.487	0.467	0.451	0.435	0.403	0.391	0.345	0.333
蓝田县	Lantian	1.727	1.673	1.606	1.517	1.444	1.414	1.083	1.047	1.011	0.978	0.924	0.895	0.771	0.742
周至县	Zhouzhi	1.502	1.465	1.386	1.309	1.237	1.212	0.959	0.928	0.897	0.867	0.801	0.778	0.649	0.626
户 县	Huxian	1.411	1.367	1.287	1.188	1.123	1.089	0.978	0.940	0.906	0.873	0.844	0.811	0.791	0.761

13-1 续表 continude

地 区 Region		比上年增长(%) Growth Rates over Preceding Year(%)										
		2006	2007	2008	2009	2010	2011	2012	2013	2014	2015	2016
西安市	**Xi'an**	**-4.15**	**-5.75**	**-6.65**	**-5.56**	**-2.06**	**-3.56**	**-3.51**	**-3.57**	**-5.89**	**-3.20**	**-3.83**
新城区	Xincheng	-4.15	-5.67	-5.79	-5.80	-1.15	-3.51	-3.50	-3.50	-5.39	-3.27	-3.58
碑林区	Beilin	-4.18	-5.44	-5.65	-5.95	-0.91	-3.89	-3.50	-3.50	-6.06	-3.20	-3.66
莲湖区	Lianhu	-4.07	-4.60	-7.93	-5.65	-3.58	-3.84	-3.60	-3.61	-7.76	-3.14	-3.58
灞桥区	Baqiao	-2.54	-6.20	-6.24	-5.80	-4.20	-3.81	-3.62	-3.64	-5.20	-3.30	-3.75
未央区	Weiyang	-3.97	-5.44	-6.63	-6.05	-1.31	-3.60	-3.60	-3.60	-7.60	-4.16	-3.86
雁塔区	Yanta	-4.71	-5.64	-5.80	-6.08	-4.18	-3.61	-3.61	-3.60	-3.89	-3.58	-3.55
阎良区	Yanliang	-5.77	-4.80	-6.08	-5.62	-0.61	-3.38	-3.50	-3.50	-7.59	-3.00	-3.46
临潼区	Lintong	-3.03	-5.73	-8.16	-4.58	-4.81	-3.52	-3.51	-3.51	-8.07	-3.00	-3.46
长安区	Chang'an	-6.15	-5.53	-5.22	-5.50	-2.08	-3.60	-3.63	-3.63	-3.40	-4.10	-3.56
高陵区	Gaoling	-4.85	-6.85	-5.50	-5.70	-3.82	-3.93	-3.52	-3.54	-7.32	-3.00	-3.52
蓝田县	Lantian	-3.13	-4.01	-5.50	-4.84	-2.06	-3.39	-3.40	-3.30	-5.48	-3.17	-3.84
周至县	Zhouzhi	-2.46	-5.43	-5.51	-5.50	-2.06	-3.30	-3.30	-3.30	-7.63	-2.90	-3.50
户 县	Huxian	-3.07	-5.85	-7.70	-5.50	-2.99	-3.85	-3.60	-3.62	-3.40	-3.82	-3.84

注：能源消耗按等价值计算；2013年以前数据，根据第三次经济普查结果进行了调整。

13-2 主要年份全社会用电量

单位：万千瓦时

行 业	Sector	2000	2007
总 计	**Total**	**732373**	**1482896**
#行业用电量合计	Total of Industry of Electricity	599855	1215799
1. 第一产业	Primary Industry	77579	120134
2. 第二产业	Secondary Industry	354245	700026
3. 第三产业	Tertiary Industry	168031	395639
一、农、林、牧、渔、水利业	Agriculture ,Forestry,Animal Husbandry and Fishery	77579	120134
二、工业	Industry	345175	674990
1. 轻工业	Light Industry	152125	187323
2. 重工业	Heavy Industry	193050	487667
三、建筑业	Construction	9070	25036
四、交通运输、仓储及邮政业	Traffic,Transport, Storage and Post	22904	53825
五、信息传输、计算机服务和软件业	Information Transmission,Computer Service and Software		21938
六、商业、住宿和餐饮业	Commercial,Hotels and Catering Services		107343
七、金融、房地产、商务及居民服务业	Finance,Real Estate,Business Affairs and Households Services		67674
八、公共事业及管理组织	Public Utilities and Management Organization		144859
九、城乡居民生活用电	Electricity Consumption of Urban and Rural Residents	132518	267097
1. 乡村	Rural	31281	38395
2. 城市	City	101237	228702

注：本表数据来源于国网陕西省供电公司西安供电公司。

Electricity Consumption of the Whole Society in Representative Years

(10 000 kw. h)

2008	2009	2010	2011	2012	2013	2014	2015	2016
1605089	**1724067**	**1993751**	**2167453**	**2352571**	**2554679**	**2753213**	**2844836**	**3120582**
1293574	1358483	1499903	1590486	1706859	1854696	2002503	2049492	2216797
127054	99083	108720	117984	109086	110405	95997	89970	87825
724852	766029	883259	910360	932622	991202	1086105	1088866	1147294
441668	493371	507924	562142	665151	753089	820401	870656	981678
127054	99083	108720	117984	109086	110405	95997	89970	87825
696291	724920	838317	859796	875018	920024	998132	997115	1062188
182176	167144	177362	183766	175392	170246	165933	165290	170735
514115	557776	660955	676030	699626	749778	832199	831826	891453
28561	41108	44942	50564	57605	71179	87973	91750	85106
56614	62031	58509	66684	69633	78722	88805	90914	109911
26680	29328	30760	33191	37444	39551	42662	46203	61950
111676	122203	148418	166558	199970	228117	253199	277248	301414
81674	102400	116163	131236	150832	165833	180824	185329	212666
165024	177409	154074	164473	207271	240866	254911	270962	295737
311515	365585	493848	576966	645713	699982	750710	795344	903785
63072	99941	142059	169898	197937	216148	235938	241920	263871
248443	265644	351789	407068	447776	483834	514773	553424	639914

13-3 规模以上工业企业能源购进、消费及库存（2016年）

Energy Purchases, Consumption and Inventory of Industrial Enterprises above Designated Size（2016）

能源名称	Name	年初库存量 Stock (year-beginning)	购进量 Purchases	其中：购自省外 Wherein: purchased from outside the province
原煤(吨)	Raw Coal (ton)	786906	8409880	2311110
洗精煤(吨)	Washed Coal(ton)			
其他洗煤(吨)	Other Washed Coals(ton)	25997	134322	25429
煤制品（吨）	Briquettes(ton)	168	1662	
焦炭(吨)	Coke(ton)	107	340	
其他焦化产品(吨)	Other Coking Products(ton)			
天然气（气态）（万立方米）	Natural Gas(10 000cu.m)	1993	34655	
液化天然气（液态）（吨）	Liquefied Natural Gas (Liquid)(ton)		26	
原油(吨)	Crude Oil(ton)			
汽油(吨)	Gasoline(ton)	394	26860	1892
煤油(吨)	Kerosene(ton)	732	176	
柴油(吨)	Diesel Oil(ton)	1093	52001	3475
燃料油(吨)	Fuel Oil(ton)	7	1337	388
液化石油气(吨)	LPG(ton)	13	623	40
润滑油（吨）	Lubricating Oil (ton)		35	
溶剂油（吨）	Solvent Oil (ton)	2	462	
其它石油制品(吨)	Other Petroleum Products(ton)	63	1748	
热力(百万千焦)	Heat (1 million kilo-joule)		5186159	902220
电力(万千瓦时)	Electricity(10 000kwh)		728455	
生物质废料用于燃料（吨）	Biomass Waste for Fuel (ton)		7332	
其他燃料（吨标准煤）	Other Fuels(ton of SCE)	3	148	
能源合计(吨标准煤)	Total Energy(ton of SCE)			

13-3 续表 continued

能源名称	Name	消费量合计 Consumption Total	工业生产消费 Industrial Production Consume	用于原材料 as Raw Material	非工业生产消费 Non-industrial Production Consume	期末库存量 Stock (year-end)
原煤(吨)	Raw Coal (ton)	8267495	8257948	740	9547	844619
洗精煤(吨)	Washed Coal(ton)					
其他洗煤(吨)	Other Washed Coals(ton)	139751	139751			20568
煤制品（吨）	Briquettes(ton)	1665	1148		518	164
焦炭(吨)	Coke(ton)	451	416		35	8
其他焦化产品(吨)	Other Coking Products(ton)					
天然气（气态）（万立方米）	Natural Gas(10 000cu.m)	34799	34079	1193	720	1831
液化天然气（液态）（吨）	Liquefied Natural Gas (Liquid)(ton)	28	21	8	7	
原油(吨)	Crude Oil(ton)					
汽油(吨)	Gasoline(ton)	27034	23367	83	3667	55
煤油(吨)	Kerosene(ton)	158	158			33
柴油(吨)	Diesel Oil(ton)	52116	48694	31	3422	1005
燃料油(吨)	Fuel Oil(ton)	1264	1255		9	80
液化石油气(吨)	LPG(ton)	623	620		3	
润滑油（吨）	Lubricating Oil (ton)	35	31		4	
溶剂油（吨）	Solvent Oil (ton)	463	463	429		1
其它石油制品(吨)	Other Petroleum Products(ton)	1740	1740			71
热力(百万千焦)	Heat (1 million kilo-joule)	6892804	6776683		116121	
电力(万千瓦时)	Electricity(10 000kwh)	800933	790205		10727	
生物质废料用于燃料（吨）	Biomass Waste for Fuel (ton)	7332	7332			
其他燃料（吨标准煤）	Other Fuels(ton of SCE)	136	131	30	5	17
能源合计(吨标准煤)	Total Energy(ton of SCE)	7920874	7876458		44416	

13-4 规模以上工业企业分行业主要能源品种消费量（2016年）

Major Energy Consumption above Designated Size by Industry（2016）

行业	Sector	原煤（吨）Raw Coal (ton)	天然气（万立方米）Natural Gas(10 000 cu.m)
总计	**Total**	**8267495**	**34799**
煤炭开采和洗选业	Coal Mining and Dressing		
石油和天然气开采业	Petroleum and Natural Gas Extraction		
黑色金属矿采选业	Ferrous Metals Mining and Dressing		
有色金属矿采选业	Nonferrous Metals Mining and Dressing		
非金属矿采选业	Nonmetal Minerals Mining and Dressing		
开采辅助活动	Ancillary activities for mining	256	329
其他采矿业	Other Mining Industry		
农副食品加工业	Agricultural Products and Non-stable Food Processing Industry	213057	438
食品制造业	Food Production	22741	3045
酒、饮料和精制茶制造业	Wine, soft drinks and refined tea industry	62227	658
烟草制品业	Tobacco Processing	25	40
纺织业	Textile Industry	1844	251
纺织服装、服饰业	Textile, apparel industry		
皮革、毛皮、羽毛及其制品和制鞋业	Leather, Fur, Feather (eiderdown) and Their Products Industry	32	
木材加工和木、竹、藤、棕、草制品业	Timber Processing,Bamboo,Cane,Palm Fiber and Straw Products		
家具制造业	Furniture Manufacturing		
造纸及纸制品业	Papermaking and Paper products	5629	389
印刷和记录媒介复制业	Printing,Record Medium Reproduction	64	416
文教、工美、体育和娱乐用品制造业	Culture, education, Craft art, sports and entertainment goods manufacturing industry	22	
石油加工、炼焦和核燃料加工业	Petroleum Refining, Ccoke Making and Nuclear Fuel Processing Industry	831	245
化学原料和化学制品制造业	Raw Chemical Materials and Chemical Products	20057	2203
医药制造业	Medical and Pharmaceutical Products	8490	2426
化学纤维制造业	Chemical Fiber		
橡胶和塑料制品业	Rubber and plastic products industry	66565	1342
非金属矿物制品业	Nonmetal Mineral Products	139021	775
黑色金属冶炼和压延加工业	Smelting and Pressing of Ferrous Metals	5848	
有色金属冶炼和压延加工业	Smelting and Pressing of Nonferrou Metals	341	841
金属制品业	Metal Products	3936	373
通用设备制造业	General Equipment Manufacturing Industry	94	681
专用设备制造业	Special Purpose Equipment	91	495
汽车制造业	Automotive Manufacturing	30196	4842
铁路、船舶、航空航天和其他运输设备制造业	Railroad, marine, aerospace and other transportation equipment manufacturing	438	222
电气机械和器材制造业	Electric Equipment and Machinery	860	2541
计算机、通信和其他电子设备制造业	Communication Equipment, Computer and Other Electronic Equipment Manufacturing Industry		2957
仪器仪表制造业	Instrument manufacturing industry		33
其他制造业	Other manufacturing	178	
废弃资源综合利用	Comprehensive utilization of waste resources		
金属制品、机械和设备修理业	Metal products, machinery and equipment repair industry		6
电力、热力生产和供应业	Electric Power, Heating Power Generating and Supplying Industry	7684652	8787
燃气生产和供应业	Gas Mining and Supplying Industry		205
水的生产和供应业	Water Processing and Supplying Industry	2	259

13-4 续表 continued

行 业	Sector	汽油 (吨) Gasoline (ton)	柴油 (吨) Diesel Oil (ton)	热力 (百万千焦) Heat (million kilo joule)	电力 (万千瓦时) Electricity (10 000 kwh)
总 计	**Total**	**27034**	**52116**	**6892804**	**800933**
煤炭开采和洗选业	Coal Mining and Dressing				
石油和天然气开采业	Petroleum and Natural Gas Extraction				
黑色金属矿采选业	Ferrous Metals Mining and Dressing				
有色金属矿采选业	Nonferrous Metals Mining and Dressing				
非金属矿采选业	Nonmetal Minerals Mining and Dressing				
开采辅助活动	Ancillary activities for mining	654	5207		1872
其他采矿业	Other Mining Industry				
农副食品加工业	Agricultural Products and Non-stable Food Processing Industry	1272	1067	1653645	21204
食品制造业	Food Production	1010	987	384042	14884
酒、饮料和精制茶制造业	Wine, soft drinks and refined tea industry	624	1303	221404	17646
烟草制品业	Tobacco Processing	25		5674	240
纺织业	Textile Industry	59		127380	21459
纺织服装、服饰业	Textile, apparel industry	48	2		132
皮革、毛皮、羽毛及其制品和制鞋业	Leather, Fur, Feather (eiderdown) and Their Products Industry	40		11667	264
木材加工和木、竹、藤、棕、草制品业	Timber Processing,Bamboo,Cane,Palm Fiber and Straw Products	9	12		4333
家具制造业	Furniture Manufacturing	152	115		1107
造纸及纸制品业	Papermaking and Paper products	130	167	41061	4244
印刷和记录媒介复制业	Printing,Record Medium Reproduction	420	194	60600	8611
文教、工美、体育和娱乐用品制造业	Culture, education, Craft art, sports and entertainment goods manufacturing industry	19	26		349
石油加工、炼焦和核燃料加工业	Petroleum Refining, Ccoke Making and Nuclear Fuel Processing Industry	791	476		2108
化学原料和化学制品制造业	Raw Chemical Materials and Chemical Products	494	452	6360	46229
医药制造业	Medical and Pharmaceutical Products	1380	294	192831	11875
化学纤维制造业	Chemical Fiber	13	8	1239864	6109
橡胶和塑料制品业	Rubber and plastic products industry	594	2556	2205	13198
非金属矿物制品业	Nonmetal Mineral Products	1499	26234	1493	32125
黑色金属冶炼和压延加工业	Smelting and Pressing of Ferrous Metals	25	74		5116
有色金属冶炼和压延加工业	Smelting and Pressing of Nonferrou Metals	378	89	916776	59861
金属制品业	Metal Products	743	113	7040	7098
通用设备制造业	General Equipment Manufacturing Industry	935	152	4296	8699
专用设备制造业	Special Purpose Equipment	2206	867	36235	19750
汽车制造业	Automotive Manufacturing	3214	8796	421742	101163
铁路、船舶、航空航天和其他运输设备制造业	Railroad, marine, aerospace and other transportation equipment manufacturing	565	499	92194	14598
电气机械和器材制造业	Electric Equipment and Machinery	2315	638	1000490	55920
计算机、通信和其他电子设备制造业	Communication Equipment, Computer and Other Electronic Equipment Manufacturing Industry	642	81	246288	183357
仪器仪表制造业	Instrument manufacturing industry	511	33	7050	2265
其他制造业	Other manufacturing	96	100		323
废弃资源综合利用	Comprehensive utilization of waste resources		38		106
金属制品、机械和设备修理业	Metal products, machinery and equipment repair industry	178	46		95
电力、热力生产和供应业	Electric Power, Heating Power Generating and Supplying Industry	5224	1147	212467	118725
燃气生产和供应业	Gas Mining and Supplying Industry	452	324		6121
水的生产和供应业	Water Processing and Supplying Industry	315	21		9748

13-5 规模以上工业企业分行业综合能源消费量（2016年）

Comprehensive Energy Consumption by Sector above Designated Size（2016）

单位：吨标准煤 (ton of SCE)

行 业	Scetor	2016	比上年增长(%) Increase over Preceding Year (%)
总 计	**Total**	**4952833**	**3.1**
煤炭开采和洗选业	Coal Mining and Dressing		
石油和天然气开采业	Petroleum and Natural Gas Extraction		
黑色金属矿采选业	Ferrous Metals Mining and Dressing		
有色金属矿采选业	Nonferrous Metals Mining and Dressing		
非金属矿采选业	Nonmetal Minerals Mining and Dressing		
开采辅助活动	Ancillary activities for mining	15447	-26.0
其他采矿业	Other Mining Industry		
农副食品加工业	Agricultural Products and Non-stable Food Processing Industry	180572	11.9
食品制造业	Food Production	90506	-2.4
酒、饮料和精制茶制造业	Wine, soft drinks and refined tea industry	84797	-8.1
烟草制品业	Tobacco Processing	820	126.2
纺织业	Textile Industry	33051	7.0
纺织服装、服饰业	Textile, apparel industry	214	-14.7
皮革、毛皮、羽毛及其制品和制鞋业	Leather, Fur, Feather (eiderdown) and Their Products Industry	803	-9.2
木材加工和木、竹、藤、棕、草制品业	Timber Processing,Bamboo,Cane,Palm Fiber and Straw Products	9770	3.3
家具制造业	Furniture Manufacturing	1731	14.0
造纸及纸制品业	Papermaking and Paper products	16182	21.5
印刷和记录媒介复制业	Printing,Record Medium Reproduction	18553	0.1
文教、工美、体育和娱乐用品制造业	Culture, education, Craft art, sports and entertainment goods manufacturing industry	554	6.8
石油加工、炼焦和核燃料加工业	Petroleum Refining, Ccoke Making and Nuclear Fuel Processing Industry	8781	-20.7
化学原料和化学制品制造业	Raw Chemical Materials and Chemical Products	101969	6.0
医药制造业	Medical and Pharmaceutical Products	60353	27.9
化学纤维制造业	Chemical Fiber	49818	66.6
橡胶和塑料制品业	Rubber and plastic products industry	45835	-1.5
非金属矿物制品业	Nonmetal Mineral Products	185546	-15.7
黑色金属冶炼和压延加工业	Smelting and Pressing of Ferrous Metals	10796	-9.1
有色金属冶炼和压延加工业	Smelting and Pressing of Nonferrou Metals	115991	
金属制品业	Metal Products	18555	0.8
通用设备制造业	General Equipment Manufacturing Industry	18106	1.6
专用设备制造业	Special Purpose Equipment	33706	13.3
汽车制造业	Automotive Manufacturing	198131	1.8
铁路、船舶、航空航天和其他运输设备制造业	Railroad, marine, aerospace and other transportation equipment manufacturing	23088	-28.5
电气机械和器材制造业	Electric Equipment and Machinery	140296	8.8
计算机、通信和其他电子设备制造业	Communication Equipment, Computer and Other Electronic Equipment Manufacturing Industry	273048	36.7
仪器仪表制造业	Instrument manufacturing industry	4066	3.9
其他制造业	Other manufacturing	811	-1.1
废弃资源综合利用	Comprehensive utilization of waste resources	187	
金属制品、机械和设备修理业	Metal products, machinery and equipment repair industry	492	107.1
电力、热力生产和供应业	Electric Power, Heating Power Generating and Supplying Industry	3185974	2.1
燃气生产和供应业	Gas Mining and Supplying Industry	10899	-3.0
水的生产和供应业	Water Processing and Supplying Industry	13386	-0.9

13-6 规模以上工业企业用水情况（2016年）

Statistics on Water Use of Industrial Enterprises above Designated Size（2016）

指 标	Item	取水量（万立方米）Water Use (10 000 cu.m)	外供水量（万立方米）Outward Water Supply (10 000 cu.m)
合 计	**Total**	**63940**	**54024**
地表淡水	Surface fresh water	42218	165
地下淡水	Underground fresh water	11065	927
自来水	Tap Water	9509	52931
陆地苦咸水	Land lake Salt water	6	
矿井水	Mine Water	1	
雨水	Rain Water		
再生水	Reclaimed Water	1141	
其他水	Other Water	1	
外排水量	Efflux capacity	4487	
重复用水量	Repeated water consumption	10280	

13-7 规模以上工业企业分行业用水情况（2016年）

Volume of Water Use of Industrial Enterprises above Designated Size by Industry（2016）

行 业	Sector	取水量（万立方米） Water Use (10 000 cu.m)
总 计	**Total**	**63940**
煤炭开采和洗选业	Coal Mining and Dressing	
石油和天然气开采业	Petroleum and Natural Gas Extraction	
黑色金属矿采选业	Ferrous Metals Mining and Dressing	
有色金属矿采选业	Nonferrous Metals Mining and Dressing	
非金属矿采选业	Nonmetal Minerals Mining and Dressing	
开采辅助活动	Ancillary activities for mining	80
其他采矿业	Other Mining Industry	
农副食品加工业	Agricultural Products and Non-stable Food Processing Industry	248
食品制造业	Food Production	420
酒、饮料和精制茶制造业	Wine, soft drinks and refined tea industry	762
烟草制品业	Tobacco Processing	2
纺织业	Textile Industry	94
纺织服装、服饰业	Textile, apparel industry	19
皮革、毛皮、羽毛及其制品和制鞋业	Leather, Fur, Feather (eiderdown) and Their Products Industry	2
木材加工和木、竹、藤、棕、草制品业	Timber Processing,Bamboo,Cane,Palm Fiber and Straw Products	2
家具制造业	Furniture Manufacturing	11
造纸及纸制品业	Papermaking and Paper products	18
印刷和记录媒介复制业	Printing,Record Medium Reproduction	51
文教、工美、体育和娱乐用品制造业	Culture, education, Craft art, sports and entertainment goods manufacturing industry	3
石油加工、炼焦和核燃料加工业	Petroleum Refining, Ccoke Making and Nuclear Fuel Processing Industry	79
化学原料和化学制品制造业	Raw Chemical Materials and Chemical Products	309
医药制造业	Medical and Pharmaceutical Products	310
化学纤维制造业	Chemical Fiber	58
橡胶和塑料制品业	Rubber and plastic products industry	371
非金属矿物制品业	Nonmetal Mineral Products	302
黑色金属冶炼和压延加工业	Smelting and Pressing of Ferrous Metals	4
有色金属冶炼和压延加工业	Smelting and Pressing of Nonferrou Metals	200
金属制品业	Metal Products	58
通用设备制造业	General Equipment Manufacturing Industry	60
专用设备制造业	Special Purpose Equipment	208
汽车制造业	Automotive Manufacturing	777
铁路、船舶、航空航天和其他运输设备制造业	Railroad, marine, aerospace and other transportation equipment manufacturing	122
电气机械和器材制造业	Electric Equipment and Machinery	619
计算机、通信和其他电子设备制造业	Communication Equipment, Computer and Other Electronic Equipment Manufacturing Industry	1318
仪器仪表制造业	Instrument manufacturing industry	135
其他制造业	Other manufacturing	7
废弃资源综合利用	Comprehensive utilization of waste resources	
金属制品、机械和设备修理业	Metal products, machinery and equipment repair industry	2
电力、热力生产和供应业	Electric Power, Heating Power Generating and Supplying Industry	2822
燃气生产和供应业	Gas Mining and Supplying Industry	23
水的生产和供应业	Water Processing and Supplying Industry	54444

13-7 续表 continude

行 业	Sector	外供水量（万立方米）Outward Water Supply (10 000 cu.m)
总 计	**Total**	**54024**
煤炭开采和洗选业	Coal Mining and Dressing	
石油和天然气开采业	Petroleum and Natural Gas Extraction	
黑色金属矿采选业	Ferrous Metals Mining and Dressing	
有色金属矿采选业	Nonferrous Metals Mining and Dressing	
非金属矿采选业	Nonmetal Minerals Mining and Dressing	
开采辅助活动	Ancillary activities for mining	
其他采矿业	Other Mining Industry	
农副食品加工业	Agricultural Products and Non-stable Food Processing Industry	
食品制造业	Food Production	
酒、饮料和精制茶制造业	Wine, soft drinks and refined tea industry	
烟草制品业	Tobacco Processing	
纺织业	Textile Industry	
纺织服装、服饰业	Textile, apparel industry	
皮革、毛皮、羽毛及其制品和制鞋业	Leather, Fur, Feather (eiderdown) and Their Products Industry	
木材加工和木、竹、藤、棕、草制品业	Timber Processing,Bamboo,Cane,Palm Fiber and Straw Products	
家具制造业	Furniture Manufacturing	
造纸及纸制品业	Papermaking and Paper products	
印刷和记录媒介复制业	Printing,Record Medium Reproduction	
文教、工美、体育和娱乐用品制造业	Culture, education, Craft art, sports and entertainment goods manufacturing industry	
石油加工、炼焦和核燃料加工业	Petroleum Refining, Ccoke Making and Nuclear Fuel Processing Industry	
化学原料和化学制品制造业	Raw Chemical Materials and Chemical Products	
医药制造业	Medical and Pharmaceutical Products	
化学纤维制造业	Chemical Fiber	
橡胶和塑料制品业	Rubber and plastic products industry	
非金属矿物制品业	Nonmetal Mineral Products	
黑色金属冶炼和压延加工业	Smelting and Pressing of Ferrous Metals	
有色金属冶炼和压延加工业	Smelting and Pressing of Nonferrou Metals	
金属制品业	Metal Products	
通用设备制造业	General Equipment Manufacturing Industry	
专用设备制造业	Special Purpose Equipment	3
汽车制造业	Automotive Manufacturing	
铁路、船舶、航空航天和其他运输设备制造业	Railroad, marine, aerospace and other transportation equipment manufacturing	
电气机械和器材制造业	Electric Equipment and Machinery	
计算机、通信和其他电子设备制造业	Communication Equipment, Computer and Other Electronic Equipment Manufacturing Industry	
仪器仪表制造业	Instrument manufacturing industry	
其他制造业	Other manufacturing	
废弃资源综合利用	Comprehensive utilization of waste resources	
金属制品、机械和设备修理业	Metal products, machinery and equipment repair industry	
电力、热力生产和供应业	Electric Power, Heating Power Generating and Supplying Industry	
燃气生产和供应业	Gas Mining and Supplying Industry	
水的生产和供应业	Water Processing and Supplying Industry	54021

13-8 分区县规模以上工业企业综合能源消费量（2016年）

Comprehensive Energy Consumption above Designated Size by Region（2016）

单位：吨标准煤 (ton of SCE)

区 县	Region	综合能源消费量 Comprehensive Energy Consumption	增速（%） Growth Rate (%)
全 市	**Total**	**4952833**	**3.1**
新城区	Xincheng	291251	4.9
碑林区	Beilin	27149	2.2
莲湖区	Lianhu	159914	6.0
灞桥区	Baqiao	864864	0.6
未央区	Weiyang	533840	8.2
雁塔区	Yanta	1290606	1.1
阎良区	Yanliang	49330	22.1
临潼区	Lintong	71245	-10.1
长安区	Chang'an	481644	16.0
高陵区	Gaoling	202916	8.5
蓝田县	Lantian	117818	-17.7
周至县	Zhouzhi	21570	16.7
户 县	Huxian	840686	0.8

主要统计指标解释

能源消费总量 指一定时期内，地区各行业和居民生活消费的各种能源的总和。该指标是观察能源消费水平、构成和增长速度的总量指标。能源消费总量包括原煤和原油及其制品、天然气、电力等，不包括低热值燃料、生物质能和太阳能等的利用。能源消费总量分为终端能源消费量、能源加工转换损失量和能源损失量三部分。

（1）终端能源消费量：指一定时期内，全国生产和生活消费的各种能源在扣除了用于加工转换二次能源消费量和损失量以后的数量。

（2）能源加工转换损失量：指一定时期内，全国投入加工转换的各种能源数量之和与产出各种能源产品之和的差额。该指标是观察能源在加工转换过程中损失量变化的指标。

（3）能源损失量：指一定时期内，能源在输送、分配、储存过程中发生的损失和由客观原因造成的各种损失量，不包括各种气体能源放空、放散量。

工业生产能源消费 指工业企业为进行工业生产活动所消费的能源。

非工业生产能源消费 指在工业企业能源消费中，除“工业生产能源消费”以外的能源消费，即非工业生产用能和工业企业附属的不从事工业生产活动的非独立核算单位用能。

运输工具消费 指在厂区内、外进行交通运输活动的交通运输工具所消费的能源。

能源加工转换投入 能源的加工转换是指为了特定的用途，将一种能源（一般为一次能源），经过一定的工艺，加工或转换成另外一种能源（一般为二次能源）。能源加工转换的投入即能源加工、转换消费。

一次能源 是指自然界中以现成形式存在，不经任何改变或转换的天然能源资源，即从自然界直接取得并不改变其形态和品位的能源。如原煤、原油、天然气、核燃料、植物燃料、风能、水能、太阳能、地热能、海洋能、潮汐能等。

二次能源 是指为了满足生产工艺和生活的特定需要以合理利用能源，将一次能源直接或间接加工转换产生的其它种类和形式的人工能源。如原煤加工产出的洗煤；由煤炭加工转换产出的焦炭，煤气；由原油加工产出的汽油、煤油、柴油、燃料油、液化石油气、炼厂干气等；由煤炭、石油、天然气转换产出的电力。

综合能源消费量 报告期内工业企业在工业生产活动中实际消费的各种能源的总和净值。计算综合能源消费量时，需要先将使用的各种能源折算成标准燃料后再进行计算。

单位生产总值能耗 指一定时期内，一个国家或地区每生产一个单位的生产总值所消耗的能源。计算公式为：

单位生产总值能耗=能源消费总量／生产总值

单位工业增加值能耗 指一定时期内，一个国家或地区每生产一个单位的工业增加值所消耗的能源。计算公式为：

单位工业增加值能耗=工业能源消费量／工业增加值

Explanatory Notes on Main Statistical Indicators

Total Energy Consumption refers to the total consumption of energy of various kinds by the production sectors and the households in the country in a given period of time. It is a comprehensive indicator to show the scale,composition and pace of increase of energy consumption. Total energy consumption includes that of coal,crude oil and their products,natural gas and electricity. However,it does not include the consumption of fuel of low calorific value, bio-energy and solar energy. Total energy consumption can be divided into three parts: end-use energy consumption; loss during the process of energy conversion; and energy loss.

(1) End-use Energy Consumption: It refers to the total energy consumption by the production sectors and the households in the country (region) in a given period of time. It does not include the consumption during the conversion of primary energy into secondary energy and the loss in the process of energy conversion.

(2) Loss During the Process of Energy Conversion: It refers to the total input of various kinds of energy for conversion, minus the total output of various kinds of energy in the country in a given period of time. It is an indicator to show the loss that occurs during the process of energy conversion.

(3) Energy Loss: It refers to the total of the loss of energy during the course of energy transport, distribution and storage and the loss caused by any objective reason in a given period of time. The loss of various kinds of gas due to gas discharges and stocktaking is not included.

Industry Consumption Energy refers to the volume of energy consumed by Industrial enterprises for industrial production activities.

Non–industry Consumption Energy refers to the energy consumed by industrial enterprises except for industrial production activities,means that energy consumed by non-industry production and not independent accounting units which was not engaged in industrial production activities affiliated to industrial enterprises.

Vehicle Energy refers to the energy consumed by vehicles which carried out transport activities in and out of factories.

Energy Processing Conversion Devoted energy processing conversion refers to for specialized application, a source of energy (normally primary energy) , after a certain technology , processed or converted to another kind of energy (normally secondary energy) . The input of energy conversion processing that is energy processing, and conversion consumption.

Primary Energy Source refers to natural energy resources as found naturally in the form of ready-made,without any change or conversion,as energy obtaineddirectly from natural and not change its shape and grade,such as raw coal, crude oil, natural gas, nuclear fuel, plantfuel, wind energy, water energy, solar energy,geothermalenergy, oceanic energy, tidal energy and so on.

Secondary Energy refers to other types and formsof artificial energy which was processed and conversed from primary energy sources directly or indirectly , in order to meet the specific needs in production process and life to use energy more effectively. Such as washing coalprocessed from raw coal; coke and coal gas processed andtransformed from raw coal; gasoline, kerosene, diesel oil, fuel oil, liquefied petroleum gas, dry gas refinery processed from crude oil; electric power conversed from coal, oil and natural gas.

Comprehensive energy consumption refers to the total and net energy actually consumed in industrial production activities by industrial enterprises in the reference period. When calculated the volume of consumption of comprehensive energy, should converted sorts of energy which was used into standards fuel firstly.

Energy Consumption per Unit of GDP refers to the energy consumption per unit of Gross Domestic Product in a country or the Gross Regional Product in a region in the same reference period. The formula is:

$$\text{Energy Consumption per Unit of GDP} = \frac{\text{Total Energy Consumption}}{\text{Gross Domestic Product}}$$

Energy Consumption per Unit of Industrial Value–added refers to the energy consumption per unit of industrial value-added in a country or region in the same reference period. The formula is:

$$\text{Energy Consumption per Unit of Industrial Value-added} = \frac{\text{Total Energy Consumption}}{\text{Industrial Value-added}}$$

14 建筑业

CONSTRUCTION

资料整理：杨雪峰
Data management: Yang xuefeng
数据审核：黄小丹
Data audit: Huang Xiaodan

第十四部分　建筑业

一、简要说明

本章资料主要包括建筑业基本情况、建筑业施工企业生产情况和财务状况，由西安市统计局固定资产投资处提供。

二、主要指标

企业个数（个）	893	比上年增长	26.5%
建筑业总产值（亿元）	2897.55	比上年增长	9.3%
#国有及国有控股企业	2288.23	比上年增长	11.9%
房屋建筑竣工面积（万平方米）	2233.20	比上年下降	17.7%
房屋建筑面积竣工率(%)	18.7	比上年减少	3.9个百分点

14 CONSTRUCTION

Ⅰ.Brief Introduction

This chapter consists of basic situation of the construction industry, production and financial situation of the construction enterprises, provided by Fixed Asset Investment Division of the Xi'an Bureau of Statistics.

Ⅱ.Major Indicators

		Increase over Preceding Year
Number of Enterprises(item)	893	26.5%
Total Output Value of Construction(100 mil. yuan)	2897.55	9.3%
State-owned or State Holding Majority Shares	2288.23	11.9%
Floor Space of Buildings Completed(10 000 sq.m)	2233.20	-17.7%
Rate of Floor Space of Buildings Completed(%)	18.7	-3.9 percentage points

14-1 主要年份建筑业总产值

Total Output Value of Construction in Representative Years

单位：亿元 (100mil. yuan)

年份 Year	单位数（个） Number of Enterprises (unit)	建筑业总产值 Total Output Value of Construction	国有及国有控股 State-owned Or State Holding Majority Shares	集体企业 Collective-owned Enterprises
2000	184	105.93	78.87	14.87
2001	205	114.81	91.82	15.47
2002	223	133.47	85.03	15.35
2003	204	177.11	119.99	13.40
2004	244	244.42	201.68	16.59
2005	235	326.65	276.68	19.61
2006	217	416.48	348.20	23.65
2007	279	604.75	432.63	32.67
2008	328	915.12	676.12	460.14
2009	326	1074.55	875.19	47.15
2010	324	1334.00	1034.04	58.39
2011	336	1619.09	1278.33	79.42
2012	396	1874.23	1364.70	96.83
2013	420	2228.41	1702.08	154.87
2014	539	2586.33	1981.24	95.02
2015	706	2650.41	2044.05	69.73
2016	893	2897.55	2288.23	63.35

注：1、1996年以后建筑业年报统计范围由往年的县及县以上（含县级建制镇）各种经济类型的建筑企业，改为具有建筑业资质等级三级及三级以上的各种经济类型的建筑施工企业；2002年改为具有建筑业资质等级的各种经济类型的建筑施工企业。

2、本表资料含劳务分包企业。

3、由于统计口径变化，对部分年份建筑业总产值相关数据进行了修订。

14-2 全市建筑施工总承包企业基本情况（2016年）

Basic Situation of Construction General Contracting Contractors in Whole City (2016)

指　标	Item	合计 Total	国有及国有控股 State-owned Or State Holding Majority Shares
企业单位数（个）	Number of Enterprises (unit)	577	108
#二级以上企业	Special and First and Second Class Enterprise	482	96
计算劳动生产率的平均人数（万人）	Average Number of Employed Persons in Calculation of Labor Productivity (10000 person)	60.72	43.55
#二级以上企业	Special and First and Second Class Enterprise	58.13	42.20
建筑业总产值（亿元）	Total Output Value of Construction(100 million yuan)	2616.80	2146.11
#二级以上企业	Special and First and Second Class Enterprise	2539.04	2102.72
全员劳动生产率 按总产值计算(万元/人)	Overall Labor Productivity Calculated by Total Output Value(10 000yuan/person)	43.09	49.28

14-3 施工总承包和专业承包建筑企业生产情况（2016年）

分 组	Classify	签订的合同额（万元）Contract Value (10 000 yuan)	建筑业总产值（万元）Total Output Value of Constrution (10 000 yuan)
总计	**Total**	**76666915**	**28975481**
#国有及国有控股	State-Owned and State Holding Majority Shares	66256673	22882335
一、按登记注册类型分	**Grouped by Registion Status**		
内资	Domestic Investment Enterprises	76661445	28967491
国有企业	State-owned Enterprises	3798805	1834771
集体企业	Collective-owned Enterprises	946903	633500
股份合作企业	Share-holding Corperative Enterprises	8531	8320
联营企业	Joint Ownership Enterprises	18454	13319
国有独资公司	State-owned Company	10500708	4856199
其他有限责任公司	Limited Liability Corporations	52034849	16529856
股份有限公司	Share-holding Corperation Ltd.	1480604	547843
私营企业	Private Enterprises	7872591	4543683
其他企业	Others		
港澳台商投资企业	Enterprises with Funds from Hong Kong,Macao and Taiwan	217	217
外商投资企业	Enterprises with Foreign Investment	5253	7773
二、按国民经济行业分	**Grouped by Sector**		
房屋建筑业	Building Engineering Construction	25771792	10631785
土木工程建筑业	Civil Engineering Construction	46349881	15539004
建筑安装业	Installation of Construction	3260735	1916248
建筑装饰和其他建筑业	Architectural decoration and other Construction	1284507	888444
三、按隶属关系分	**Grouped by Administrative Relationship**		
中央	Central	46006915	13808304
地方	Region	30660000	15167177
四、按企业资质等级分	**Grouped by Class of Enterprises**		
1. 施工总承包	Overall Contractor for Construction	72162397	26167955
#特级	Special Class	19297563	5418516
一级	First Class	46455831	17635286
二级	Second Class	4805536	2336642
2. 专业承包	Special Contractor	4504518	2807526
#一级以上	First Class	3350791	1896186
二级	Second Class	846399	679099

Main Indicators on General Constructing Contractors and Professional Contractors（2016）

在外省完成的产值 Output value in other provinces	建筑工程产值 Output Value of Constrution	安装工程产值 Output Value of Installation	其他产值 Others	竣工产值（万元） Completed output value (10 000 yuan)	计算劳动生产率的平均人数（人） Average Number of Employed Persons in Calculation of Labour Productivity(person)
13230955	**25988186**	**2140313**	**846982**	**12028718**	**685938**
12657806	21315777	1068131	498427	9203630	468757
13230955	25985927	2134582	846982	12024739	685650
640290	1644079	167350	23343	669482	37120
10874	491755	123410	18335	430239	24607
	8320				281
	13319			2965	541
2268271	4733105	115452	7642	1907111	107929
9704460	15062949	964609	502297	6775930	323316
180582	511420	36291	132	120232	16531
426478	3520980	727470	295233	2118780	175325
	217			179	8
	2042	5731		3800	280
2137921	9828633	676763	126388	5659995	301954
10106661	14379680	579566	579758	5263883	313022
854339	1124803	721668	69778	682412	36120
132034	655070	162316	71058	422428	34842
10178954	13065623	301736	440945	5060245	283572
3052001	12922563	1838577	406037	6968473	402366
12624936	24053075	1397037	717843	10921474	607240
3201693	5292476	69910	56130	1409006	62181
8760606	16095083	1033563	506640	7945668	421971
409612	2016868	205754	114020	1343897	97160
606019	1935111	743276	129139	1107244	78698
517139	1453471	324427	118287	880918	49377
13699	287437	384129	7533	130711	22727

14-3 续表

分 组	Classify	建筑业企业期末从业人员数（人）The number of employees in construction enterprises at the end of period (person)	工程技术人员 Technical Personnel
总计	**Total**	**588418**	**99584**
#国有及国有控股	State-Owned and State Holding Majority Shares	394411	64435
一、按登记注册类型分	**Grouped by Registion Status**		
内资	Domestic Investment Enterprises	588196	99553
国有企业	State-owned Enterprises	29103	5400
集体企业	Collective-owned Enterprises	26530	3180
股份合作企业	Share-holding Corperative Enterprises	243	33
联营企业	Joint Ownership Enterprises	529	239
国有独资公司	State-owned Company	86048	18382
其他有限责任公司	Limited Liability Corporations	277087	42134
股份有限公司	Share-holding Corperation Ltd.	15963	1398
私营企业	Private Enterprises	152693	28787
其他企业	Others		
港澳台商投资企业	Enterprises with Funds from Hong Kong,Macao and Taiwan	6	4
外商投资企业	Enterprises with Foreign Investment	216	27
二、按国民经济行业分	**Grouped by Sector**		
房屋建筑业	Building Engineering Construction	246749	43002
土木工程建筑业	Civil Engineering Construction	282973	44619
建筑安装业	Installation of Construction	34525	8643
建筑装饰和其他建筑业	Architectural decoration and other Construction	24171	3320
三、按隶属关系分	**Grouped by Administrative Relationship**		
中央	Central	240898	35019
地方	Region	347520	64565
四、按企业资质等级分	**Grouped by Class of Enterprises**		
1. 施工总承包	Overall Contractor for Construction	524699	88171
#特级	Special Class	51976	12766
一级	First Class	360545	54001
二级	Second Class	87592	16070
2. 专业承包	Special Contractor	63719	11413
#一级以上	First Class	34671	6670
二级	Second Class	25067	3672

continued

企业总产值（万元）Gross output value of enterprises (10 000 yuan)	房屋建筑施工面积（平方米）Number of Projects under Constrution (sq.m)	本年新开工 Beginning Projects in this year	房屋建筑竣工面积（平方米）Floor Space of Buildings Completed (sq.m)	房屋竣工价值（万元）Housing completion value (10 000 yuan)	自有机械设备年末净值（万元）The net value of machinery and equipment owned at the end of the year (10 000 yuan)	自有机械设备年末总台数（台）The total number of machinery and equipment owned owned (stand)	自有机械设备年末总功率（千瓦）Total power of machinery and equipment owned at the end of the year (kw)
30891873	**119457289**	**34614927**	**22332035**	**4609391**	**835122**	**78210**	**3155065**
24449858	89980185	22616874	14421061	3210230	612849	45871	2366831
30883793	119457289	34614927	22332035	4609391	834862	77989	3154784
1864375	6699735	541628	833475	159565	30821	5496	137156
667651	3624778	1644041	1973015	334156	17541	6691	37407
8320							
14436	120358	30296	14784	1042	6321	31	1988
5297133	17227032	4577042	3012640	736127	121696	12345	749075
17629313	61139341	17369551	10684061	2331825	474542	29593	1534369
552679	5687218	550240	185766	29927	6952	1260	10903
4849886	24958827	9902129	5628294	1016749	176989	22573	683886
217							
7863					260	221	281
10900322	106609853	31388595	21265730	4368847	183205	25961	624994
17060735	10760864	2730846	860658	185158	592896	44411	2288643
2005117	2061598	477352	194551	54601	39452	4489	107503
925699	24974	18134	11096	785	19569	3349	133925
15013340	33749360	8229210	2439878	613117	477784	30641	1697095
15878533	85707929	26385717	19892157	3996274	357338	47569	1457970
27921611	118776605	34227328	22192973	4586805	755683	70537	2888721
6446394	19328899	6399655	4126228	958257	120492	12558	628293
18142530	88665592	23277243	14956885	3078456	489330	35982	1646086
2545227	9917738	4038135	2590118	473096	126133	18651	477235
2970262	680684	387599	139062	22586	79439	7673	266344
1998207	270399	1356	16000	2600	66451	5325	236925
734943	401639	377597	123062	19986	12091	1950	27507

14-4 施工总承包和专业承包建筑业企业主要指标（2016年）

指　标	Item	企业数（个）Number of Enterprises (unit)	总产值（万元）Total Output Value (10 000 yuan)	直接从事生产经营活动的平均人数（人）Directly engaged in the production and business activities of the average number of people (person)
总计	**Total**	**882**	**28975481**	**685938**
#国有及国有控股	State-Owned and State Holding Majority Shares	147	22882335	468757
一、按登记注册类型分	**Grouped by Registion Status**			
内资	Domestic Investment Enterprises	878	28967491	685650
国有企业	State-owned Enterprises	32	1834771	37120
集体企业	Collective-owned Enterprises	43	633500	24607
股份合作企业	Share-holding Corperative Enterprises	1	8320	281
联营企业	Joint Ownership Enterprises	2	13319	541
国有独资公司	State-owned Company	33	4856199	107929
有限责任公司	Limited Liability Corporations	103	16529856	323316
股份有限公司	Share-holding Corperation Ltd.	11	547843	16531
私营企业	Private Enterprises	653	4543683	175325
其他企业	Others			
港澳台商投资企业	Enterprises with Funds from Hong Kong,Macao and Taiwan	1	217	8
外商投资企业	Enterprises with Foreign Investment	3	7773	280
二、按国民经济行业分	**Grouped by Sector**			
房屋建筑业	Building Engineering Construction	377	10631785	301954
土木工程建筑业	Civil Engineering Construction	233	15539004	313022
建筑安装业	Installation of Construction	129	1916248	36120
建筑装饰和其他建筑业	Architectural decoration and other Construction	143	888444	34842
三、按隶属关系分	**Grouped by Administrative Relationship**			
中央	Central	51	13808304	283572
地方	Region	831	15167177	402366
四、按企业资质等级分	**Grouped by Class of Enterprises**			
1. 施工总承包	Overall Contractor for Construction	577	26167955	607240
#特级	Special Class	6	5418516	62181
一级	First Class	163	17635286	421971
二级	Second Class	313	2336642	97160
2. 专业承包	Special Contractor	305	2807526	78698
#一级以上	First Class	134	1896186	49377
二级	Second Class	124	679099	22727

Major Indicators of General Construction Contractors and Professional Contractors (2016)

建筑业企业期末从业人员数（人） The number of employees in construction enterprises at the end of period (person)	利润总额（万元） Total profit (10000 yuan)	利税总额（万元） Total profits and taxes (10000 yuan)	按总产值计算劳动生产率（万元/人） Productivity by gross output value (10000 yuan/person)	产值利润率（%） Profit rate of output value (%)	产值利税率（%） Profit and tax rate of output value (%)	资产总计（万元） Total assets (10000 yuan)	负债总计（万元） Total liabilities (10000 yuan)	资产负债率（%） Asset liability ratio (%)
588418	**888794**	**1684438**	**42.24**	**3.1**	**5.8**	**37076717**	**29231613**	**78.8**
394411	596485	1130313	48.81	2.6	4.9	28680929	24555696	85.6
588196	888077	1681919	42.25	3.1	5.8	37069064	29227413	78.8
29103	70186	126762	49.43	3.8	6.9	1780142	1409799	79.2
26530	24780	60530	25.74	3.9	9.6	603823	347348	57.5
243	156	610	29.61	1.9	7.3	7014	5860	83.5
529	8698	9409	24.62	65.3	70.6	29701	6558	22.1
86048	97007	227573	44.99	2.0	4.7	5610527	4662699	83.1
277087	445409	819318	51.13	2.7	5.0	22330696	19312628	86.5
15963	12559	23981	33.14	2.3	4.4	751871	614739	81.8
152693	229282	413736	25.92	5.0	9.1	5955290	2867783	48.2
6	540	2014	27.13	248.8	928.1	3716	2469	66.4
216	177	505	27.76	2.3	6.5	3937	1731	44.0
246749	295701	619052	35.21	2.8	5.8	10592941	7539040	71.2
282973	475623	838581	49.64	3.1	5.4	23627903	19749507	83.6
34525	75089	141800	53.05	3.9	7.4	1977273	1394960	70.5
24171	42381	85005	25.50	4.8	9.6	878600	548107	62.4
240898	448873	738508	48.69	3.3	5.3	21314559	18511894	86.9
347520	439921	945930	37.69	0.8	2.2	6233146	5123669	82.2
524699	748086	1436685	43.09	2.9	5.5	33884687	27036726	79.8
51976	225513	387210	87.14	4.2	7.1	13192026	11488253	87.1
360545	408813	802716	41.79	2.3	4.6	16504977	13163006	79.8
87592	111699	210765	24.05	4.8	9.0	3346324	1728867	51.7
63719	140708	247753	35.67	5.0	8.8	3192030	2194887	68.8
34671	83205	150418	38.40	4.4	7.9	2110481	1533157	72.6
25067	50007	81694	29.88	7.4	12.0	817347	493248	60.3

14-5 施工总承包和专业承包建筑业企业财务状况（2016年）

指　标	Item	资产总计（万元）Total assets (10000 yuan)	流动资产合计（万元）Total current assets (10000 yuan)
总计	**Total**	**37076717**	**31027819**
#国有及国有控股	State-Owned and State Holding Majority Shares	28680929	23911543
一、按登记注册类型分	**Grouped by Registion Status**		
内资	Domestic Investment Enterprises	37069064	31020461
国有企业	State-owned Enterprises	1780142	1494903
集体企业	Collective-owned Enterprises	603823	517233
股份合作企业	Share-holding Corperative Enterprises	7014	6694
联营企业	Joint Ownership Enterprises	29701	26586
国有独资公司	State-owned Company	5610527	4563617
有限责任公司	Limited Liability Corporations	22330696	18818881
股份有限公司	Share-holding Corperation Ltd.	751871	669033
私营企业	Private Enterprises	5955290	4923514
其他企业	Others		
港澳台商投资企业	Enterprises with Funds from Hong Kong,Macao and Taiwan	3716	3646
外商投资企业	Enterprises with Foreign Investment	3937	3712
二、按国民经济行业分	**Grouped by Sector**		
房屋建筑业	Building Engineering Construction	10592941	9322563
土木工程建筑业	Civil Engineering Construction	23627903	19245011
建筑安装业	Installation of Construction	1977273	1715937
建筑装饰和其他建筑业	Architectural decoration and other Construction	878600	744308
三、按隶属关系分	**Grouped by Administrative Relationship**		
中央	Central	21314559	17445324
地方	Region	15762158	13582495
四、按企业资质等级分	**Grouped by Class of Enterprises**		
1. 施工总承包	Overall Contractor for Construction	33884687	28286997
#特级	Special Class	13192026	10366498
一级	First Class	16504977	14522741
二级	Second Class	3346324	2761833
2. 专业承包	Special Contractor	3192030	2740822
#一级	First Class	2110481	1854956
二级	Second Class	817347	669987

Financial Status of General Constructing Contractors and Professional Contractors（2016）

固定资产合计（万元）Total fixed assets (10000 yuan)	固定资产原价（万元）Original value of fixed assets (10000 yuan)	累计折旧（万元）Accumulated depreciation (10000 yuan)		负债合计（万元）Total liabilities (10000 yuan)	流动负债合计（万元）Total current liabilities (10000 yuan)	非流动负债（万元）Non current liabilities (10000 yuan)	所有者权益合计（万元）Total owners' equity (10000 yuan)
			本年折旧 Depreciation of this year				
1878527	**3410015**	**1873340**	**306646**	**29231613**	**27311547**	**1518763**	**7845104**
1197388	2557153	1516801	256104	24555696	23021510	1335876	4125233
1878453	3409692	1873091	306625	29227413	27307347	1518763	7841651
78910	153517	86214	15649	1409799	1288360	95656	370343
59391	75853	26683	3921	347348	335221	10028	256474
109	1284	1175	66	5860	5736	124	1154
994	1431	1283	191	6558	5415		23143
325837	792465	516254	92989	4662699	4298419	348974	947828
825641	1680752	953775	151837	19312628	18222631	931490	3018068
27800	49984	23003	1932	614739	602029	12710	137133
559771	654406	264704	40040	2867782	2549536	119781	3087508
61	277	215	14	2469	2469		1247
13	46	34	7	1731	1731		2206
585428	746198	331294	41191	7539040	6932501	321006	3053901
1142166	2427109	1426249	251715	19749507	18542940	1108776	3878396
85402	138289	74575	8858	1394960	1311542	78803	582313
65531	98419	41222	4882	548106	524564	10178	330494
901612	2050697	1230173	215618	18511894	17331895	1025798	2802664
976915	1359318	643167	91028	10719719	9979652	492965	5042440
1653891	3123470	1728460	290498	27036726	25190088	1464820	6847961
288191	542795	285422	47236	11488253	10499700	988553	1703773
979467	2054464	1195455	207348	13163006	12537142	388231	3341971
324986	400152	175574	27621	1728867	1517918	67640	1617457
224636	286545	144880	16148	2194887	2121459	53943	997143
131471	219451	112700	11404	1533157	1488105	29452	577324
70958	56018	27849	3938	493248	469466	20090	324099

14-5 续表

指 标	Item	实收资本（万元）Paid in capital (10000 yuan)	主营业务收入（万元）Main business income (10000 yuan)
总计	**Total**	**5789722**	**35838980**
#国有及国有控股	State-Owned and State Holding Majority Shares	2941758	28855183
一、按登记注册类型分	**Grouped by Registion Status**		
内资	Domestic Investment Enterprises	5786599	35824006
国有企业	State-owned Enterprises	206912	2044416
集体企业	Collective-owned Enterprises	262616	783015
股份合作企业	Share-holding Corperative Enterprises	865	13273
联营企业	Joint Ownership Enterprises	13847	38957
国有独资公司		689669	5117294
有限责任公司	Limited Liability Corporations	2182354	22155054
股份有限公司	Share-holding Corperation Ltd.	77551	596059
私营企业	Private Enterprises	2352785	5075938
其他企业	Others		
港澳台商投资企业	Enterprises with Funds from Hong Kong,Macao and Taiwan	1185	8427
外商投资企业	Enterprises with Foreign Investment	1938	6547
二、按国民经济行业分	**Grouped by Sector**		
房屋建筑业	Building Engineering Construction	2323281	11351697
土木工程建筑业	Civil Engineering Construction	2819964	21427795
建筑安装业	Installation of Construction	404951	2050702
建筑装饰和其他建筑业	Architectural decoration and other Construction	241526	1008786
三、按隶属关系分	**Grouped by Administrative Relationship**		
中央	Central	1997617	20159364
地方	Region	3792105	15679616
四、按企业资质等级分	**Grouped by Class of Enterprises**		
1. 施工总承包	Overall Contractor for Construction	5098996	32728205
#特级	Special Class	1291444	12066654
一级	First Class	2272202	17086638
二级	Second Class	1370134	2760883
2. 专业承包	Special Contractor	690726	3110775
#一级以上	First Class	421824	2194092
二级	Second Class	187020	743589

continued 1

主营业务成本（万元） Main business costs (10000 yuan)	主营业务税金及附加（万元） The main business tax and surcharges (10000 yuan)	管理费用（万元） Management costs (10000 yuan)	税金 taxes	营业利润（万元） Operating profit (10000 yuan)	利润总额（万元） Total profit (10000 yuan)	应付职工薪酬（万元） Payable to employees (10000 yuan)	应交增值税（万元） value added tax Payable (10000 yuan)
33354765	**428012**	**965678**	**32333**	**870309**	**888794**	**4192326**	**353784**
27295004	270417	692103	17585	576432	596485	3310490	265879
33342450	427805	963937	32303	869590	888077	4189661	352221
1885372	30045	52184	2187	69893	70186	314588	24637
583804	23025	28076	1064	26818	24780	116375	9623
12750	239	137	8	156	156	114	207
29126	252	909	80	8705	8698	2854	372
4777204	66716	183049	2400	95881	97007	711401	62576
21012559	189095	504127	13886	427078	445409	2341609	189259
554459	6824	14929	467	12037	12559	37112	4653
4487176	111609	180526	12211	229022	229282	665608	60894
7525	102	267	22	539	540	1455	1351
4790	105	1474	8	180	177	1210	213
10412601	200026	238311	9557	295129	295701	1752617	114340
20208516	167288	610905	19127	458488	475623	2112311	193678
1823850	38221	88793	2255	74172	75089	220969	27152
909798	22477	27669	1394	42520	42381	106429	18614
19109729	134112	501748	12859	431210	448873	2116701	160327
14245036	293900	463930	19474	439099	439921	2075625	193457
30620113	371727	817573	27672	729017	748086	3897660	308269
11614457	72631	217758	1354	215049	225513	761387	98176
15923284	220967	440517	18201	399902	408813	2619754	163646
2339638	59444	109554	7014	110375	111699	387523	33932
2734652	56285	148105	4661	141292	140708	294666	45515
1975124	33243	79333	2411	83673	83205	191169	31091
611361	18581	57365	1899	49923	50007	84423	11291

14-6 劳务分包建筑业企业生产经营情况（2016年）

单位：万元

指 标	Item	固定资产原价 Original value of fixed assets	本年折旧 Depreciation of this year
总计	**Total**	**352**	**91**
#国有及国有控股	State-Owned and State Holding Majority Shares		
一、按登记注册类型分	**Grouped by Registion Status**		
内资	Domestic Investment Enterprises	352	91
国有企业	State-owned Enterprises		
集体企业	Collective-owned Enterprises		
股份合作企业	Share-holding Corperative Enterprises		
联营企业	Joint Ownership Enterprises		
国有独资公司	State-owned Company		
其他有限责任公司	Limited Liability Corporations	3	
股份有限公司	Share-holding Corperation Ltd.		
私营企业	Private Enterprises	349	91
其他企业	Others		
港澳台商投资企业	Enterprises with Funds from Hong Kong,Macao and Taiwan		
外商投资企业	Enterprises with Foreign Investment		
二、按国民经济行业分	**Grouped by Sector**		
房屋建筑业	Building Engineering Construction	292	52
土木工程建筑业	Civil Engineering Construction		
建筑安装业	Installation of Construction	3	
建筑装饰和其他建筑业	Architectural decoration and other Construction	57	39
三、按隶属关系分	**Grouped by Administrative Relationship**		
中央	Central		
地方	Region	352	91

Production and Management Situation of Subcontractor Construction Enterprises（2016）

(10 000yuan)

资产总计 Total assets	负债合计 Total liabilities	实收资本 Paid in capital	营业收入 Total Revenue	主营业务收入 Main business income	营业成本 Total Cost	主营业务成本 Main business Cost
45947	**41287**	**3484**	**120534**	**120534**	**112700**	**112700**
45947	41287	3484	120534	120534	112700	112700
2265	2183		3564	3564	3611	3611
43682	39104	3484	116970	116970	109089	109089
41437	38152	2239	98049	98049	90734	90734
2265	2183		3564	3564	3611	3611
2245	952	1245	18921	18921	18355	18355
45947	41287	3484	120534	120534	112700	112700

14-6 续表

单位：万元

指 标	Item	营业税金及附加 Taxs and Other Changes	主营业务税金及附加 Taxs and Other Changes on Principal Business
总计	**Total**	**2089**	**2089**
#国有及国有控股	State-Owned and State Holding Majority Shares		
一、按登记注册类型分	**Grouped by Registion Status**		
内资	Domestic Investment Enterprises	2089	2089
国有企业	State-owned Enterprises		
集体企业	Collective-owned Enterprises		
股份合作企业	Share-holding Corperative Enterprises		
联营企业	Joint Ownership Enterprises		
国有独资公司	State-owned Company		
其他有限责任公司	Limited Liability Corporations	46	46
股份有限公司	Share-holding Corperation Ltd.		
私营企业	Private Enterprises	2043	2043
其他企业	Others		
港澳台商投资企业	Enterprises with Funds from Hong Kong,Macao and Taiwan		
外商投资企业	Enterprises with Foreign Investment		
二、按国民经济行业分	**Grouped by Sector**		
房屋建筑业	Building Engineering Construction	1747	1747
土木工程建筑业	Civil Engineering Construction		
建筑安装业	Installation of Construction	46	46
建筑装饰和其他建筑业	Architectural decoration and other Construction	296	296
三、按隶属关系分	**Grouped by Administrative Relationship**		
中央	Central		
地方	Region	2089	2089

continued 1

(10 000yuan)

销售费用 Sale Expenses	管理费用 Management costs	税金 taxes	财务费用 Financial Expenses	营业利润 Operating profit	利润总额 Total profit	应付职工薪酬 Payable to employees	应交增值税 value added tax Payable
17	**4277**	**58**	**187**	**1186**	**1168**	**62362**	**1872**
17	4277	58	187	1186	1168	62362	1872
	101	4		-195	-195	3911	74
17	4176	54	187	1381	1363	58451	1799
	3985	48	187	1319	1314	58099	1799
	101	4		-195	-195	3911	74
17	191	6		62	49	352	
17	4277	58	187	1186	1168	62362	1872

14-7 各区县建筑业主要经济指标（2016年）

Major Indicators of Construction Enterprises by Region（2016）

区 县	Region	企业个数(个) Number of Enterprises (unit)	总产值(亿元) Total Output Value (100 million yuan)	计算劳动生产率的平均人数(万人) Average Number of Employed Persons in Calculation of Labor Productivity(10 000person)	全员劳动生产率(万元/人) Overall Labor Productivity (10 000 yuan/person)	利税总额(亿元) Total Pre-tax Profits (100 million yuan)
全 市	**Total**	**882**	**2897.55**	**68.59**	**42.24**	**168.44**
新城区	Xincheng	54	305.67	5.37	56.92	15.23
碑林区	Beilin	141	743.68	12.75	58.33	40.67
莲湖区	Lianhu	70	225.30	5.68	39.67	12.25
灞桥区	Baqiao	35	84.83	3.75	22.62	6.28
未央区	Weiyang	148	585.73	15.80	37.07	33.56
雁塔区	Yanta	300	803.69	18.39	43.70	45.08
阎良区	Yanliang	22	13.26	0.78	17.00	0.73
临潼区	Lintong	25	10.46	0.56	18.68	0.73
长安区	Chang'an	45	59.79	2.24	26.69	7.52
高陵区	Gaoling	10	29.82	1.90	15.69	3.68
蓝田县	Lantian	12	12.60	0.44	28.64	1.17
周至县	Zhouzhi	13	9.50	0.47	20.21	0.92
户 县	Huxian	7	13.22	0.46	28.74	0.62

注：本表数据依据施工总承包和专业承包企业数据加工整理。

14-8 各区县建筑业房屋施工及竣工面积（2016年）

Floor Space of Buildings under Construction & Completed by Region（2016）

区 县	Region	房屋建筑施工面积（万平方米）Floor Space under Construction (10 000sq.m)	本年新开工面积 Newly Started This Year	房屋建筑竣工面积（万平方米）Floor Space of Buildings Completed (10 000sq.m)	竣工房屋价值（亿元）Value of Buildings Completed (100 million yuan)
全 市	**Total**	**11945.73**	**3461.49**	**2233.20**	**460.94**
新城区	Xincheng	1221.74	373.58	293.76	60.74
碑林区	Beilin	3621.70	1078.31	660.97	144.16
莲湖区	Lianhu	1588.44	485.62	337.07	79.46
灞桥区	Baqiao	96.15	28.61	30.74	5.16
未央区	Weiyang	2140.66	548.67	230.30	49.61
雁塔区	Yanta	2676.52	721.71	387.30	77.66
阎良区	Yanliang	54.46	10.32	9.48	1.49
临潼区	Lintong	51.43	23.38	18.18	2.93
长安区	Chang'an	150.62	28.72	51.75	7.95
高陵区	Gaoling	109.24	62.51	67.68	10.09
蓝田县	Lantian	47.66	27.17	29.20	3.87
周至县	Zhouzhi	73.52	37.82	45.52	6.37
户 县	Huxian	113.59	35.07	71.25	11.45

14-9 各区县建筑业企业主要经济效益指标（2016年）

Major Economic Performance Indicators on Construction Enterprises by Region（2016）

区 县	Region	人均利润总额（元/人）Per Profit (yuan/person)	人均利税（元/人）Per Pre-tax Profits (yuan/person)	人均竣工产值（元/人）Per Output Value of Buildings Completed (yuan/person)	人均施工面积（平方米/人）Per Floor Space of Buildings Under Construcyion (sq.m/person)	人均竣工面积（平方米/人）Per Floor Space of Buildings Completed (sq.m/person)
全 市	**Total**	**12957**	**24557**	**175362**	**174**	**33**
新城区	Xincheng	12208	28379	333061	228	55
碑林区	Beilin	17952	31873	226208	284	52
莲湖区	Lianhu	7551	21577	223497	280	59
灞桥区	Baqiao	10519	16737	568716	26	8
未央区	Weiyang	11629	21244	77624	136	15
雁塔区	Yanta	13547	24512	108321	146	21
阎良区	Yanliang	2973	9296	109663	70	12
临潼区	Lintong	4293	13118	113129	92	33
长安区	Chang'an	18726	33582	106738	67	23
高陵区	Gaoling	10808	19367	53704	58	36
蓝田县	Lantian	14554	26439	121261	108	66
周至县	Zhouzhi	9208	19833	155180	158	98
户 县	Huxian	2337	13354	255298	246	154

14-9 续表 continued

区 县	Region	产值利润率（%）Ratio of Profits to Output Value (%)	产值利税率（%）Ratio of Pre-tax Profits to Output Value (%)	资产利润率（%）Ratio of Profits to Assets (%)	资产利税率（%）Ratio of Pre-tax Profits to Assets (%)	资产负债率（%）Ratio of Debts to Assets (%)
全 市	**Total**	**3.1**	**5.8**	**2.4**	**4.5**	**78.8**
新城区	Xincheng	2.1	5.0	2.3	5.4	83.8
碑林区	Beilin	3.1	5.5	2.6	4.6	81.5
莲湖区	Lianhu	1.9	5.4	1.8	5.0	76.7
灞桥区	Baqiao	4.7	7.4	3.6	5.7	79.9
未央区	Weiyang	3.1	5.7	1.8	3.3	84.0
雁塔区	Yanta	3.1	5.6	2.6	4.7	75.3
阎良区	Yanliang	1.8	5.5	1.0	3.3	60.6
临潼区	Lintong	2.3	7.0	2.2	6.8	49.5
长安区	Chang'an	7.0	12.6	3.3	6.0	72.8
高陵区	Gaoling	6.9	12.3	4.5	8.0	13.8
蓝田县	Lantian	5.1	9.3	10.8	19.5	36.6
周至县	Zhouzhi	4.5	9.7	7.2	15.6	37.6
户 县	Huxian	0.8	4.7	1.3	7.4	57.6

主要统计指标解释

建筑业统计单位 指从事房屋、构筑物建造和设备安装活动的法人企业。建筑业法人企业应具有建筑业资质并能够独立核算，同时其应具备以下条件：①依法成立，有自己的名称、组织机构和场所，能够承担民事责任；②独立拥有和使用资产，承担负债，有权与其他单位签订合同；③独立核算盈亏，能够编制资产负债表。

建筑业总产值 是以货币形式表现的建筑业企业在一定时期内生产的建筑业产品和提供的服务的总和。建筑业总产值包括：

（1）建筑工程产值：指列入建筑工程预算内的各种工程价值。

（2）安装工程产值：指设备安装工程价值，不包括被安装设备本身的价值。

（3）其他产值：建筑业总产值中除建筑工程、安装丁程以外的产值。包括房屋构筑物修理产值、非标准设备制造产值、总包企业向分包企业收取的管理费以及不能明确划分的施工活动所完成的产值。

a. 房屋构筑物修理产值：指房屋和构筑物修理所完成的产值，但不包括被修理房屋、构筑物本身价值和生产设备的修理价值。

b. 非标准设备制造产值：指加工制造没有定型的非标准生产设备的加了费和原材料价值（如化工厂、炼油厂用的各种罐、槽，矿井生产统一使用的各种漏斗、三角槽、阀门等）以及附属加工厂为本企业承建工程制作的非标准设备的价值。

建筑业增加值 指建筑业企业在报告期内以货币形式表现的建筑业生产经营活动的最终成果。

从2004年第一次全国经济普查开始，建筑业现价增加值按生产法和分配法（收入法）两种方法计算，以收入法的计算结果为准，即从收入的角度出发，根据生产要素在生产过程中应得的收入份额计算。具体计算方法：经济普查年度建筑业增加值按照《经济普查年度GDP核算方案》计算，非经济普查年度建筑业增加值按照们≥经济普查年度GDP核算方案》计算。

房屋建筑施工面积 指在报告期内施过工的全部房屋建筑面积，包括本期新开工的房屋面积、上期施工跨入本期继续施工的房屋面积、上期停缓建在本期恢复施工的房屋面积、本期竣工的房屋面积及本期施丁后又停缓建的房屋面积。

房屋建筑竣工面积 指在报告期内房屋建筑按照设计要求全部完工，达到了使用条件，经验收鉴定合格，正式移交使用单位的房屋建筑面积。

Explanatory Notes on Main Statistical Indicators

Statistical Unit in the Construction Industry refers to a corporate enterprise engaged in the construction of buildings and structures and in the installation of equipment. A corporate construction enterprise should have qualification certificates with independent accounting system, and should meet the following 3 requirements: a) being set up in line with relevant legal basis, having its full name, organization and location, and capable of taking civil liabilities; b) independently possessing and using its assets and assuming its liabilities, and entitled to sign contracts with other institutions; and c) making independent accounts of its profits and losses, and capable of compiling its own balance sheet.

Gross Output Value of Construction refers to total of construction products and services, expressed in money terms, produced or rendered by construction and installation enterprises during a given period of time. It includes:

(1)Output value of construction projects: the value of projects covered by the project budgets;

(2) Output value of installation projects: the value of the installation of equipment, (excluding the value of the equipment to be installed);

(3)Other output values: the output value of construction industry apart from that of construction projects and installation projects. It includes: output value of repair of buildings and structures; output value of non-standard equipment manufacturing; overhead expenses received by contracted enterprises from the sub-contracted enterprises and the completed output value of construction activities for which there is no clear definition.

a. Output value of repair of buildings and structures: the value created through the repairs of buildings or structures. It does not include the value of buildings or structures being repaired and the value of the repair of production equipment;

b. Output value of manufactured non-standard equipment: the value of non-standard production equipment, including raw materials and manufacturing cost, made for the construction project (i.e., chemical plant; kettles or tanks used by refineries; various fillers, triangle tanks, valves used by mines). It also includes the output value of equipment manufactured by subsidiary workshops.

Value-added of Construction refers to the final result of the activities of production and operation of enterprises of the construction industry in monetary terms during the reference period.

Starting from the 2004 economic census, value-added of construction is calculated by both production approach and income approach, with the figures from the income approach as the final figures. Under the income approach, calculation starts from the perspective of income and is based on the share of income derived from the production process by the relevant factors of production. Specifically, value-added of construction for the Census years is calculated in accordance with the Programme of Compilation of GDP and National Accounts for the Year of Economic Census, and value-added of construction for other years is calculated in accordance with the Programme of Compilation of GDP and National Accounts for the Non Economic Census Years.

Floor Space of Buildings Under Construction refers to floor space of buildings under construction during the reference period, including the floor space of buildings for which construction has newly started; buildings for which construction has started earlier and is continuing during the reference period; and buildings for which construction has been suspended earlier but has restarted during the reference period; buildings completed during the reference period; and buildings under construction but construction has subsequently been during the reference period.

Floor Space of Buildings Completed refers to the floor space of buildings that are completed in the reference period in accordance with the requirements of the design, up to the standard for being put into use, and having been checked and accepted by departments concerned as qualified ones.

15 运输邮电和信息化

TRANSPORT,POSTAL TELECOMMUNICATION SERVICE AND INFORMATIZATION

资料整理：齐昆峰　陈春光

Data management：Qi Kunfeng Chen Chunguang

数据审核：王金桂

Data audit：Wang Jingui

第十五部分　运输邮电和信息化

一、简要说明

本章资料包括交通运输业和邮电通信业的基本情况，主要是交通运输工具、货物和旅客运输量、邮电业务、邮政局所及服务点等基本情况。资料由西安市统计局服务业和社会科技处根据有关部门提供资料整理。

二、主要指标

邮电业务总量（亿元）	383.11	比上年增长	15.6%
全社会车辆数（万辆）	258.85	比上年增长	8.1%
#民用小轿车	146.14	比上年增长	14.0%

15　TRANSPORT,POSTAL TELECOMMUNICATION SERVICES AND INFORMATIZATION

Ⅰ.Brief Introduction

Data in this chapter consists of primarily basic data of communication, transportation and postal service industry, transportation facility, amount of goods and passenger transportation, basic data of postal service, post offices and service establishments of Xi'an City. Data in this chapter is compiled by Tertiary Industry and Social & Science and Technology Division of the Xi'an Bureau of Statistics according to the data provided by department concerned of the municipal government.

Ⅱ.Major Indicators

		Increase over Preceding Year
Amount of Postal and Telecommunication Service(100 mil. Yuan)	383.11	15.6%
Number of Vehides in the whole Sciety(10 000 unit)	258.85	8.1%
Civil Car	146.14	14.0%

15-1 主要年份各种交通线路和桥梁

Transportation Routes and Bridges in Representative Years

年 份 Year	公路里程 （公里） Length of Highways (km)	桥 梁 （座） Bridges (seat)	桥梁长度 （公里） length of Bridge (km)
1978			
1979			
1980			
1981			
1982			
1983			
1984			
1985			
1986			
1987			
1988			
1989	2563		
1990	2586		
1991	2785		
1992	2786		
1993	2801		
1994	2830		
1995	2852		
1996	2877		
1997	3026		
1998	3047		
1999	2789		
2000	3010		
2001	3298		
2002	7862	629	29799
2003	8360	629	29799
2004	8360	629	29799
2005	8500	634	46973
2006	9530	634	46973
2007	9672	1319	91412
2008	11895	1710	151996
2009	12378	1856	154866
2010	12378	1856	154866
2011	12599	1863	149743
2012	13127	2190	214978
2013	13135	2213	224962
2014	13251	2213	224949
2015	13328	2323	250910
2016	13356	2423	256058

注：本表数据来自市交通局、民航通航里程2013年统计口径发生较大变化。

15-1 续表 continued

年 份 Year	永久式桥梁 （座） Permanent Bridges (seat)	永久式桥梁长度 （公里） Length of Permanent Bridges (km)	民航通航里程 （重复航线）（公里） Length of Total Civil Aviation Routes(km)
1978			
1979			
1980			
1981			
1982			
1983			
1984			
1985			
1986			
1987			
1988			
1989			
1990			
1991			
1992			65007
1993			83215
1994			100800
1995			119753
1996			126433
1997			173010
1998			180000
1999			141284
2000			139764
2001			154614
2002	629	29799	211000
2003	629	29799	381800
2004	629	29799	386953
2005	632	46915	485749
2006	632	46915	418852
2007	1275	90716	553355
2008	1657	150980	515524
2009	1803	153850	587904
2010	1803	153850	742375
2011	1811	148810	898628
2012	2138	213985	981450
2013	2161	223970	70643568
2014	2171	224165	78626210
2015	2286	250175	93375419
2016	2386	255322	92561215

15-2 各种交通线路里程和桥梁数（2016年）

Length of Transportation Routes and Number of Bridges（2016）

指　标	Item	2016
公路里程（公里）	**Length of Highways (km)**	**13356**
等级公路	Expressways and Class I to IV Highways	12853
高速	Expressway	553
一级	First Class	323
二级	Second Class	1404
三级	Third Class	1232
四级	Forth Class	9341
等外公路	Highways below Class IV	502
桥梁	Bridges	
永久式桥梁	Permanent	
座（座）	Seat (seat)	2386
长度（公里）	Length (m)	255322
民航通航里程(公里)(重复航线)	**Length of Total Civil Aviation Routes(km)**	**92561215**
民航航线条数（条）	**Length of Civil Aviation routes(Article)**	**313**
国际航线（条）	International routes	46

注：本表数据来自市交通局。

15-3 主要年份全社会车辆数

Possession of Civil Vehicles in Representative Years

单位：辆、台 (unit)

年 份 Year	合计 Total	汽车 Motor	载客汽车 Passenget Vehicles	载货汽车 Ordinary Trucks	摩托车 Motorcycles	拖拉机 Tractors
1999	**279335**	133192	63772	44348		38023
2000	**310252**	138318	89783	44974		37177
2001	**369988**	172436	110744	55453		31355
2002	**454998**	206653	134527	64623	176960	36083
2003	**516719**	242599	163872	70781	191834	34733
2004	**512802**	276012	195524	74557	156709	34755
2005	**544586**	377628	240923	82463	131440	34741
2006	**608155**	393778	296078	89772	131449	33236
2007	**840376**	522616	360081	97614	284594	32028
2008	**875005**	595735	430472	89093	247079	30176
2009	**1012937**	754803	567326	113430	224121	31347
2010	**1253461**	961283	739038	145740	259239	29151
2011	**1445811**	1174874	928669	171649	241132	25600
2012	**1633257**	1380125	1123105	186412	224279	24458
2013	**1862063**	1634885	1372371	207058	200419	21898
2014	**2139024**	1926012	1658714	224409	190625	17484
2015	**2394052**	2191023	1929195	224322	179619	18099
2016	**2588479**	2444000	2191862	226915	119771	19352

注：本表数据来自市车管所。

15-4 全社会车辆数（2016年）

Possession of Civil Vehicles（2016）

指　标	Item	2016
合计（辆）	**Total (unit)**	**2588479**
民用汽车（辆）	Motor(unit)	2444000
#私人汽车拥有量	Possession of Private Vehicles	2221445
载客汽车	Passenget Vehicles	2191862
#大　型	Large	16810
轿　车	Car	1461402
普通载货汽车	Ordinary Trucks	226915
#重、中型	Heavy and Medium	59437
其他汽车	Others	25223
#三　轮	Three Wheelers	8233
拖拉机（台）	Tractors(unit)	19352
# 大中型	Large and Medium	
小　型	Small-sized	
摩托车（辆）	Motorcycle (unit)	119771
普通摩托车	Bicycle Motor	117266
挂车（辆）	Articulated Trailers (unit)	5331
其他类型车（辆）	Others (unit)	25

注：本表数据来自市车管所。

15-5 主要年份交通运输量及周转量

Passenger Traffic and Kilometers and Freight Traffic and Ton-kilometers in Representative Years

年 份 Year	客运量 （万人次） Passenger Traffic (10 000 person-times)	旅客周转量 （万人公里） Passenger-Km (10 000 person-Km)	货运量 （万吨） Freight Traffic (10 000 tons)	货物周转量 （万吨公里） Freight Ton-Km (10 000 ton-Km)
1978	1334		3723	
1979	1420		3919	
1980	1508		3655	
1981	1839		3379	
1982	2340		4067	
1983	3054		4225	
1984	2899		4966	
1985	2404		5681	
1986	2186		5409	
1987	3781		6294	
1988	5721		6968	
1989	6092		8742	
1990	5748		6980	
1991	4193		3389	
1992	4368		8233	
1993	8036		8406	
1994	8321		8754	
1995	9069		9590	
1996	9854		10577	
1997	8922		9358	
1998	9223		9429	
1999	10311	2130383	9766	3452383
2000	10756	2507896	10191	3691963
2001	9078	2658037	7728	4229430
2002	12527	2524444	9484	4544040
2003	11413	2596402	9392	5037684
2004	10832	3112374	14845	5850029
2005	10479	1607568	12051	1249525
2006	11245	1721217	11832	1354318
2007	12466	1753464	15124	1473182
2008	26501	2529007	27560	3490707
2009	28693	2582025	30606	3766806
2010	30294	2942957	34323	4301680
2011	33375	3223544	39239	5212010
2012	36154	3387448	44924	5958742
2013	38289	3634915	50119	6471497
2014	25719	3091147	42039	6234128
2015	26904	3241463	46270	6430083
2016	23671	2909172	23888	5521252

注：本表数据由市交通局、西安铁路局、咸阳机场、长安航空公司、东方航空公司西北分公司提供。
2016年陕西省公路运输统计计算系数变化，因此与往年数据不可比。

15-6 交通运输量及运输周转量（2016年）

Passenger Traffic and Kilometers and Freight Traffic and Ton-kilometers（2016）

指 标	Item	2015	2016
一、客运量合计（万人次）	**Passenger Traffic(10 000 person-times)**	**26904**	**23671**
铁路	Railway	3982	4199
公路	Highway	19625	15773
民航	Civil Aviation	3297	3699
二、旅客周转量合计（万人公里）	**Passenger-Km (10 000 person-Km)**	**3241463**	**2909172**
铁路	Railway	684134	676528
公路	Highway	1088896	908379
民航	Civil Aviation	1468432	1324265
三、货运量合计（万吨）	**Freight Traffic(l0 000 tons)**	**46270**	**23888**
铁路	Railway	848	854
公路	Highway	45401	23011
民航	Civil Aviation	21	23
四、货物周转量（万吨公里）	**Freight Ton-Kin (10 000 ton-Km)**	**6430083**	**5521252**
铁路	Railway	2164003	2270502
公路	Highway	4254824	3240829
民航	Civil Aviation	11256	9920

注：本表数据由市交通局、西安铁路局、咸阳机场、长安航空公司、东方航空公司西北分公司提供。
2016年由于公路统计计算系数变化，与上年数据不可比。

15-7 主要年份邮政电信情况

年份 Year	邮电业务总量（万元） Business Volume of Postal and Telecommunication Services(10 000 yuan)	电信业务总量 Business Volume of Telecommunication Services	邮政业务总量 Business Volume of Postal Services
1978	1420		
1979	1616		
1980	1640		
1981	1713		
1982	2154		
1983	2250		
1984	2484		
1985	2972		
1986	3244		
1987	3911		
1988	5327		
1989	5973		
1990	7843		
1991	5700		
1992	6610		
1993	36581		
1994	54034		
1995	76450		
1996	104566		
1997	124601		
1998	204927		
1999	306457		
2000	461628		
2001	367620		
2002	515259	470492	44767
2003	820943	770673	50270
2004	1027415	975045	52370
2005	1320447	1261033	59414
2006	1867560	1796533	71027
2007	2267633	2191250	76383
2008	2646662	2564524	82138
2009	2989246	2900836	88410
2010	3231059	3167750	63309
2011	2005025	1944329	60696
2012	2162035	2098273	63762
2013	2479430	2313630	165800
2014	2922011	2695332	226679
2015	3315324	2983024	332300
2016	3831119	3299859	531260

注：2002年及以后，邮政电信机构分离；2001—2010年邮电业务总量按2000年不变价格计算；2011年后邮电业务总量按2010年不变价格计算，故与以往年份不可比。

Basic Statistic on Postal and Telecommunication Service in Representative Years

固定电话年末用户数（户） Number of Immobile Telephone at Year-end (subscriber)	农村电话用户数 Number of Telephone in Rural Areas at Year-end	移动电话用户年末数（户） Number of Mobile Phone at Year-end (subscriber)	互联网年末宽带用户数（户） Number of Broad Band Net User (subscriber)
12828	1062		
13487	1052		
14024	1086		
14497	1125		
15357	1129		
16922	1156		
18611	1203		
21624	1239		
26373	1235		
30200	1290		
34265	1357		
39506	1498		
45267	1668		
49516	2479		
60727	2613		
101327	2671		
197398	5067		
299485	8386		
430270	13654		
573244	21202		
736998	37863		
874586	74761		
1242637	170199		
1711500	259374	1277400	17183
2095230	358803	1964200	35230
2538393	415593	2412392	160900
2934424	480276	3500900	243448
3214806	500847	4199570	339280
3159639	467526	5510720	508775
3145819	419446	6645863	586213
3068807	383869	7377575	813987
2891009	358238	11200566	1167916
2617691	335048	14230800	1461804
2703640	320189	16141463	1841027
3110176	335864	18035397	2023059
3191112	330602	21606662	2670473
3066575	372823	20253157	2779458
2920773	306336	17669953	2899714
2843336	314457	17395026	3358343

注：本表数据由市邮政管理局、市邮政局，中国联通、中国电信、中国移动等西安分公司提供。

15-8 邮政业务及服务网点

Postal Service and Branch Post Office

指　标	Item	2011	2012	2013	2014	2015	2016
一、邮政业务总量（万元）	**Business Volume of Postal Services(10 000 yuan)**	60696	63762	165800	226679	332300	531260
二、邮政业务收入（万元）	**Gross Income of Post Services (10 000 yuan)**	65174	71778	177100	213893	307008	439867
其中：快递业务收入（万元）	Express delivery business income (10 000 yuan)			97100	134306	207451	331605
三、函件（万件）	**Number of Letters (10 000 pcs)**	3061	2769	2856	2112	1707	1367
四、包件（万件）	**Parcels (10 000 pcs)**	91	50	89	71	69	51
五、汇票（万张）	**Money Order (10 000 pcs)**	112	90	148	81	48	17
六、报纸订销累计份数（万份）	**Accumulated Newspaper Prescribing and** Sales Volume (10 000 pcs)	12603	13052	14495	14338	14457	14395
七、杂志订销累计份数（万份）	**Accumulated Magazine Prescribing and** Sales Volume (10 000 pcs)	564	613	1628	1572	1285	1155
八、特快专递类业务（万件）	**Express Mail Service Volume (10 000 pcs)**	1901	129	138	107	61	63
九、集邮业务量（万枚）	**Stamps For Collection (10 000 pcs)**	1060	2312	1431	1477	1920	1607
十、邮政营销网点（处）	**Number of Post Office Branch Establishments (unit)**	277	279	269	280	299	297
#设在农村的局所	In it: number of post offices in rural area	50	115	110	123	140	149
十一、邮政信筒信箱（个）	**Number of Mailboxes(unit)**	1108	1108	1108	1170	1170	422

注：本表数据来自市邮政管理局和邮政局，2013年邮政数据统计口径变化。

15-9 电信业务情况

Telecommunication Service

指　标	Item	2010	2011	2012	2013	2014	2015	2016
一、电信业务总量（万元）	**Business Volume of Telecommunication Services (10 000 yuan)**	3167750	1944329	2098273	2313630	2695332	2983024	3299859
二、电信业务总收入（万元）	**Gross Income of Telecommunication Services (10 000 yuan)**	1038865	1029629	1162257	1316435	1356705	1338203	1420708
三、固定电话年末用户数（万户）	**Number of Immobile Telephone at Year-end(10 000 subscribers)**	261.77	270.36	311.02	319.11	306.66	292.08	284.33
#农村电话年末户数	Number of Telephone in Rural Areas at Year-end	33.50	32.02	33.59	33.06	37.28	30.63	31.45
四、电话交换机总容量（万门）	**Capacity (number) of Telephone Switchboard (10 000 lines)**	449.05	441.49	420.38	378.02	230.01	145.08	75.92
五、移动电话用户年末数（万户）	**Number of Mobile Phone at Year-end (10 000 subscribers)**	1423.08	1614.15	1803.54	2160.67	2025.32	1767.00	1739.50
#4G电话用户数	4G Mobile Phone Subscribers							1113.03
六、互联网年末用户数（万户）	**Number of Broad Band Net User (10 000 subscribers)**	146.18	184.10	202.31	267.05	277.95	289.97	335.83

注：本表数据由中国联通、中国电信、中国移动等西安分公司提供。

15-10 一套表单位信息化基本情况（2016年）

单位：个

指　标	Item	企业数 Number of Enterprises	使用计算机的企业 Computer-used Enterprise
总计	**Total**	**5730**	**5713**
按规模分	**By Size**		
大型企业	Large	302	302
中型企业	Medium-sized	1701	1701
小型企业	Small-scale	3037	3037
微型企业	Miniature	690	673
按登记注册类型分	**By Registered Type**		
内资企业	Domestic Capital Enterprises	5426	5410
港澳台商投资	Hong Kong, Macao and Taiwan invested Enterprises	121	120
外商投资	Foreign-invested Enterprises	183	183
按控股类型分	**By Holding Type**		
国有控股	State Holding	1053	1050
集体控股	Collective Holding	167	166
私人控股	Private Holding	3829	3817
港澳台商控股	Hong Kong, Macao AND Taiwan Businessmen holding	96	95
外商控股	Foreign Holding	155	155
其他	Others	430	430
按国民经济门类分	**According To the Categories of National Economy**		
采矿业	Mining Industry	5	5
制造业	Manufacturing Industry	1142	1142
电力、热力、燃气及水生产和供应业	Electricity, Heat, Gas and Water Production and Supply	33	33
建筑业	Construction Business	884	882
批发和零售业	Wholesale and Retail Trade	1005	1005
交通运输、仓储和邮政业	Transportation, Warehousing and Postal Services	168	168
住宿和餐饮业	Accommodation and Catering Industry	565	565
信息传输、软件和信息技术服务业	Information Transmission, Software and Information Technology	168	167
房地产业	Estate	1030	1016
租赁和商务服务业	Leasing and Business Services	232	232
科学研究和技术服务业	Scientific Eesearch and Eechnical Services	211	211
水利、环境和公共设施管理业	Management of Water Wonservancy, Environment and Public Facilities	44	44
居民服务、修理和其他服务业	Services of Households, Repairs and Other Services	52	52
教育	Education	15	15
卫生和社会工作	Health and Social Service	56	56
文化、体育和娱乐业	Culture, Sports and Entertainment	120	120

注：一套表单位包括规模以上工业企业、限额以上批零住餐企业、资质以内建筑业企业、规模以上服务业企业、房地产开发经营企业。

Basic Statistics on Informatization of "One Sheet" Units (2016)

(unit)

有信息技术人员的企业 Enterprises with Information Technology Personnel	有局域网的企业 LAN Enterprises	使用信息化管理的企业 Enterprises Managed by Information Technology	有信息化投入的企业 Enterprises with Informatization Input	使用互联网的企业 Enterprises Using the Internet
4819	**4414**	**5507**	**4409**	**5709**
297	292	302	288	302
1503	1446	1677	1433	1701
2540	2261	2894	2285	3030
479	415	634	403	676
4549	4129	5204	4147	5405
105	109	120	103	121
165	176	183	159	183
888	878	1033	891	1048
133	122	158	119	166
3202	2831	3644	2868	3815
81	87	95	83	96
138	146	154	133	155
377	350	423	315	429
3	4	5	2	5
1069	976	1115	990	1138
32	28	33	30	33
727	604	817	676	881
830	779	978	736	1003
120	113	162	126	168
473	421	536	388	564
166	161	166	158	167
779	745	987	724	1020
188	177	222	178	232
183	177	207	175	211
35	31	43	33	44
44	40	52	42	52
14	14	15	12	15
50	44	53	48	56
106	100	116	91	120

15-11 一套表单位信息化设施及投入情况（2016年）

指 标	Item	期末使用计算机数量（台）Computers Used at the End of Period（unit）
总计	**Total**	**517119**
按规模分	**By Size**	
大型企业	Large	286192
中型企业	Medium-sized	134000
小型企业	Small-scale	87598
微型企业	Miniature	9329
按登记注册类型分	**By Registered Type**	
内资企业	Domestic Capital Enterprises	457600
港澳台商投资	Hong Kong, Macao and Taiwan invested Enterprises	22266
外商投资	Foreign-invested Enterprises	37253
按控股类型分	**By Holding Type**	
国有控股	State Holding	240882
集体控股	Collective Holding	12560
私人控股	Private Holding	174801
港澳台商控股	Hong Kong, Macao AND Taiwan Businessmen holding	14750
外商控股	Foreign Holding	33004
其他	Others	41122
按国民经济门类分	**According To the Categories of National Economy**	
采矿业	Mining Industry	3809
制造业	Manufacturing Industry	125502
电力、热力、燃气及水生产和供应业	Electricity, Heat, Gas and Water Production and Supply	3742
建筑业	Construction Business	64083
批发和零售业	Wholesale and Retail Trade	54808
交通运输、仓储和邮政业	Transportation, Warehousing and Postal Services	19893
住宿和餐饮业	Accommodation and Catering Industry	15494
信息传输、软件和信息技术服务业	Information Transmission, Software and Information Technology	119515
房地产业	Estate	32045
租赁和商务服务业	Leasing and Business Services	12831
科学研究和技术服务业	Scientific Eesearch and Eechnical Services	45476
水利、环境和公共设施管理业	Management of Water Wonservancy, Environment and Public Facilities	3701
居民服务、修理和其他服务业	Services of Households, Repairs and Other Services	1331
教育	Education	2374
卫生和社会工作	Health and Social Service	6227
文化、体育和娱乐业	Culture, Sports and Entertainment	6288

注：一套表单位包括规模以上工业企业、限额以上批零住餐企业、资质以内建筑业企业、规模以上服务业企业、房地产开发经营企业。

Information Technology Facilities and Investment of "One Sheet" Units (2016)

信息技术人员（人）Information Technology Personnel (Person)	拥有网站个数（个）Number of Websites Owned (unit)	信息化投入（万元）Informatization Input (10 000 yuan)	一次性投入（万元）Disposable Input (10 000 yuan)	运营维护投入（万元）Operation and Maintenance Input (10 000 yuan)
28953	**4052**	**425802**	**298228**	**127574**
7213	401	265297	189602	78333
11020	1348	83086	58520	24566
9561	2011	51458	34301	17183
1159	292	25961	15805	7492
24422	3793	362383	267515	94868
1329	97	9956	6378	3578
3202	162	53463	24335	29128
6292	904	131489	93324	38165
861	103	7572	5002	2570
15187	2510	106436	72317	34120
1227	77	8021	5557	2464
3117	136	47224	18692	28532
2269	322	125060	103336	21723
22	3	19	17	2
5088	1106	92015	50653	41361
136	21	3478	3033	445
3059	541	21457	15576	5881
2909	651	34009	21317	12692
1063	77	28385	19356	9029
1035	307	6461	3441	3020
9774	172	172641	133460	39181
2265	571	27684	21081	6604
932	174	9382	6378	3004
1667	191	18667	14009	4658
159	32	634	341	293
82	42	487	327	160
88	14	823	659	164
195	50	3656	3276	380
479	100	6004	5304	700

15-12 一套表单位信息化管理情况（2016年）

单位：个

指 标	Item	企业数 Number of Enterprises	使用信息化管理的企业 Number of Enterprises Managed by Information Technology
总计	**Total**	**5730**	**5507**
按规模分	**By Size**		
大型企业	Large	302	302
中型企业	Medium-sized	1701	1677
小型企业	Small-scale	3037	2894
微型企业	Miniature	690	634
按登记注册类型分	**By Registered Type**		
内资企业	Domestic Capital Enterprises	5426	5204
港澳台商投资	Hong Kong, Macao and Taiwan invested Enterprises	121	120
外商投资	Foreign-invested Enterprises	183	183
按控股类型分	**By Holding Type**		
国有控股	State Holding	1053	1033
集体控股	Collective Holding	167	158
私人控股	Private Holding	3829	3644
港澳台商控股	Hong Kong, Macao AND Taiwan Businessmen holding	96	95
外商控股	Foreign Holding	155	154
其他	Others	430	423
按国民经济门类分	**According To the Categories of National Economy**		
采矿业	Mining Industry	5	5
制造业	Manufacturing Industry	1142	1115
电力、燃气及水的生产供应业	Electricity, Heat, Gas and Water Production and Supply	33	33
建筑业	Construction Business	884	817
批发和零售业	Wholesale and Retail Trade	1005	978
交通运输、仓储和邮政业	Transportation, Warehousing and Postal Services	168	162
住宿和餐饮业	Accommodation and Catering Industry	565	536
信息传输、软件和信息技术服务业	Information Transmission, Software and Information Technology	168	166
房地产业	Estate	1030	987
租赁和商务服务业	Leasing and Business Services	232	222
科学研究和技术服务业	Scientific Eesearch and Eechnical Services	211	207
水利、环境和公共设施管理业	Management of Water Wonservancy, Environment and Public Facilities	44	43
居民服务、修理和其他服务业	Services of Households, Repairs and Other Services	52	52
教育	Education	15	15
卫生和社会工作	Health and Social Service	56	53
文化、体育和娱乐业	Culture, Sports and Entertainment	120	116

注：一套表单位包括规模以上工业企业、限额以上批零住餐企业、资质以内建筑业企业、规模以上服务业企业、房地产开发经营企业。

Information Management Situation of "One Sheet" Units (2016)

(unit)

财务管理 Financial Management	购销存管理 Purchase and Sale Management	生产制造管理 Manufacturing Management	物流配送管理 Logistics Distribution Management	客户关系管理 Customer Relationship Management	人力资源管理 Human Resource Management	其他 Others
4896	**2286**	**837**	**549**	**1673**	**2173**	**1275**
287	167	74	72	112	222	81
1541	760	209	174	551	796	388
2523	1226	522	279	867	941	647
545	133	32	24	143	214	159
4611	2089	730	481	1551	1998	1214
114	71	29	19	41	68	22
171	126	78	49	81	107	39
983	401	182	111	279	506	258
128	48	24	11	47	65	48
3169	1483	481	328	1105	1283	801
90	58	21	14	37	60	19
144	107	64	43	68	91	33
382	189	65	42	137	168	116
5	1	1		1	3	3
1015	686	515	216	377	418	174
31	11	14	3	4	12	4
729	152	76	22	210	360	235
840	664	66	181	352	315	175
147	36	9	43	40	63	46
453	258	29	28	150	170	138
152	64	23	12	67	90	42
890	234	41	20	285	431	254
199	33	7	8	63	95	60
185	47	34	5	52	100	59
39	6	3		7	15	18
42	18	3	2	16	18	13
14	1			4	10	4
45	27	2		14	20	17
110	48	14	9	31	53	33

15-13 一套表单位电子商务交易情况（2016年）

指 标	Item	企业数（个） Number of Enterprises (unit)
总计	**Total**	**5730**
按规模分	**By Size**	
大型企业	Large	302
中型企业	Medium-sized	1701
小型企业	Small-scale	3037
微型企业	Miniature	690
按登记注册类型分	**By Registered Type**	
内资企业	Domestic Capital Enterprises	5426
港澳台商投资	Hong Kong, Macao and Taiwan invested Enterprises	121
外商投资	Foreign-invested Enterprises	183
按控股类型分	**By Holding Type**	
国有控股	State Holding	1053
集体控股	Collective Holding	167
私人控股	Private Holding	3829
港澳台商控股	Hong Kong, Macao AND Taiwan Businessmen holding	96
外商控股	Foreign Holding	155
其他	Others	430
按国民经济门类分	**According To the Categories of National Economy**	
采矿业	Mining Industry	5
制造业	Manufacturing Industry	1142
电力、燃气及水的生产供应业	Electricity, Heat, Gas and Water Production and Supply	33
建筑业	Construction Business	884
批发和零售业	Wholesale and Retail Trade	1005
交通运输、仓储和邮政业	Transportation, Warehousing and Postal Services	168
住宿和餐饮业	Accommodation and Catering Industry	565
信息传输、软件和信息技术服务业	Information Transmission, Software and Information Technology	168
房地产业	Estate	1030
租赁和商务服务业	Leasing and Business Services	232
科学研究和技术服务业	Scientific Eesearch and Eechnical Services	211
水利、环境和公共设施管理业	Management of Water Wonservancy, Environment and Public Facilities	44
居民服务、修理和其他服务业	Services of Households, Repairs and Other Services	52
教育	Education	15
卫生和社会工作	Health and Social Service	56
文化、体育和娱乐业	Culture, Sports and Entertainment	120

注：一套表单位包括规模以上工业企业、限额以上批零住餐企业、资质以内建筑业企业、规模以上服务业企业、房地产开发经营企业。

E-commerce Transactions of "One Sheet" Units (2016)

有电子商务交易的企业（个） Enterprises with Ecommerce Transactions (unit)	有电子商务销售的企业 Ecommerce Sales Enterprises	有电子商务采购的企业 E-Commerce Purchases Enterprises	拥有电子商务交易平台的企业（个） With Ecommerce Trading Platform Enterprises (unit)	全年电子商务销售金额（万元） Sales of Ecommerce (10 000 yuan)	全年电子商务采购金额（万元） Purchases of Ecommerce (10 000 yuan)
795	**518**	**449**	**34**	**4315578**	**3116392**
58	30	35	5	2865847	2783026
209	138	118	14	354327	242218
488	337	262	15	1090307	57099
40	13	34		5097	34049
741	485	418	33	2985554	1986949
19	13	11		28085	1106
35	20	20	1	1301939	1128337
130	87	70	7	2380573	1743151
11	5	8		8410	2499
538	342	316	23	454158	163585
17	12	10		27535	1100
30	17	18	1	1300486	1128270
69	55	27	3	144416	77787
142	90	98	4	173004	362723
1		1			20000
65	6	61	1	8207	401128
122	91	69	14	3017845	2237350
18	11	11	2	34705	2022
246	235	60	3	70090	668
43	14	34	5	75321	18986
51	8	47		451	30644
37	19	27	3	903555	11458
16	2	15		79	30492
6	4	4		139	57
6	4	4	1	128	77
2	2	2		14221	600
5	2	4		283	88
35	30	12	1	17550	99

主要统计指标解释

公路里程 指在一定时期内实际达到《公路工程技术标准JTJ01-88》规定的等级公路，并经公路主管部门正式验收交付使用的公路里程数。包括大中城市的郊区公路以及通过小城镇街道部分的公路里程和桥梁、隧道渡口的长度，不包括大中城市的街道、厂矿、林区生产用道和农业生产用道的里程。两条或多条公路共同经由同一路段，只计算一次，不得重复计算里程长度。它是反映公路建设发展规模的重要指标，也是计算运输网密度等指标的基础资料。

民用航空航线里程 指民航运输定期班机飞行的航线长度的总和。航线长度按机场之间的距离计算，通常有两种计算方法：一是将每条航线长度相加称为重复计算航线里程；一是将两线或两条以上航线经过同一区段里程，只计算一次航线长度称为不重复计算航线里程。一般常用的是后者，它能确切反映民航运输网的规模，是表明民航事业为国民经济服务和方便人民生活程度的主要指标。

货（客）运量 指在一定时期内，各种运输工具实际运送的货物（旅客）数量。它是反映运输业为国民经济和人民生活服务的数量指标，也是制定和检查运输生产计划、研究运输发展规模和速度的重要指标。货运按吨计算，客运按人计算。货物不论运输距离长短、货物类别，均按实际重量统计。旅客不论行程远近或票价多少，均按一人一次客运量统计；半价票、小孩票也按一人统计。

货物（旅客）周转量 指在一定时期内，由各种运输工具运送的货物（旅客）数量与其相应运输距离的乘积之总和。它是反映运输业生产总成果的重要指标，也是编制和检查运输生产计划，计算运输效率、劳动生产率以及核算运输单位成本的主要基础资料。计算货物周转量通常按发出站与到达站之间的最短距离，也就是计费距离计算。计算公式为：

货物（旅客）周转量=∑货物（旅客）运输量×运输距离

民用汽车拥有量 指报告期末，在公安交通管理部门按照《机动车注册登记工作规范》，已注册登记领有民用车辆牌照的全部汽车数量。汽车拥有量统计的主要分类：根据汽车结构分为载客汽车、载货汽车及其他汽车；根据汽车所有者不同分为个人（私人）汽车、单位汽车；根据汽车的使用性质分为营运汽车、非营运汽车；根据汽车大小规格不同载客汽车分为大型、中型、小型和微型，载货汽车分为重型、中型、轻型和微型。

邮电业务总量 指以价值量形式表现的邮电通信企业为社会提供各类邮电通信服务的总数量。邮电业务量按专业分类包括函件、包件、汇票、报刊发行、邮政快件、特快专递、邮政储蓄、集邮、公众电报、用户电报、传真、长途电话、出租电路、无线寻呼、移动电话、分组交换数据通信、出租代维等。计算方法为各类产品乘以相应的平均单价（不变价）之和，再加上出租电路和设备、代用户维护电话交换机和线路等的服务收入。它综合反映了一定时期邮电业务发展的总成果，是研究邮电业务量构成和发展趋势的重要指标。计算公式为：

邮电业务总量=∑（各类邮电业务量×不变单价）+出租代维及其他业务收入

移动电话用户 是指通过移动电话交换机进入移动电话网、占用移动电话号码的电话用户。用户数量以报告期末在移动电话营业部门实际办理登记手续进入移动电话网的户数进行计算，一部移动电话统计为一户。

电话用户 指接入国家公众固定电话网，并按固定电话业务进行经营管理的电话用户。1997年以前，电话用户分为市内电话用户和农村电话用户。“市内电话用户”是指接入县城及县以上城市的电话网上的电话用户；“农村电话用户”是指接入县邮电局农话台及县以下农村电话交换点，以县城为中心（除市活用户外）联通县、乡（镇）、行政村、村民小组的用户。从1997年起，电话用户数分组调整为以用户所在区域划分为“城市电话用户”和“乡村电话用户”，与过去的按市内电话和农村电话划分方法不同。而电话用户总数、电话机总部数统计范围不变。

农村电话用户 指县城关区以下的集镇和农村接入局用交换机的电话用户数。

局用交换机容量 是指安装在本地电信运营商内用于接续本地固定电话的电话交换机容量，有倍增设备按倍增后的数量计数。包括现用和备用的人工或自动交换机的全部容量。

计算机数 指报告期末企业（单位）使用的计算机数量，包括台式机、笔记本电脑和平板电脑。

信息技术人员 指专职从事信息技术系统的制定、设计、开发、安装、操作、维护、管理和评估的人员。

信息化投入 包括企业（单位）一次性投入和运

营维护投入。

一次性投入 包括企业（单位）购置各类硬件和软件的实际支出。

运营维护投入 包括企业（单位）更新维护各类信息通信硬件和软件的实际支出。

互联网 指在世界范围内的公共计算机网络。它提供一系列通信服务（包括万维网）的接入，并传送电子邮件、新闻、娱乐和数据文件等。

全年电子商务销售金额 指报告期内企业（单位）借助网络订单而销售的商品和服务总额。借助网络订单指通过网络接受订单，付款和配送可以不借助于网络。

全年电子商务采购金额 指报告期内企业（单位）借助网络订单而采购的商品和服务总额。借助网络订单指通过网络发送订单，付款和配送可以不借助于网络。

Explanatory Notes on Main Statistical Indicators

Length of Highways refers to the length of highways which are built in conformity with the grades specified by the highway engineering standard formulated by the Ministry of Communications, and have been formally checked and accepted by the departments of highways and put into use. The length of highways includes that of the suburb highways at large and medium- sized cities,highways passing through streets at small cities and towns,and also the length of bridges, tunnel and ferries. It does not include the length of streets in big and medium-sized cities and highways built for the production purpose at factories, mines, forest areas and agricultural areas. If two or more highways go the same section of the way, the length of the section is only calculated for once and no duplication is allowed. The length of highways is an important indicator to show the development of the highway construction and to provide essential information to calculate the transport network density.

Length of Civil Aviation Routes refers to the length of all routes for regular civil aviation flights. There are usually two ways to calculate the distance between airports connected by the route length: one is to put the length of all air routes together, called duplicated calculation of the length of the routes; the other is not to allow the duplication in calculation when two or more routes passing the same section of aviation routes. The latter is usually used, as it can precisely show the size of the civil aviation network and indicate the extent of civil aviation serving the national economy and the people.

Freight (Passenger) Traffic refers to the volume of freight (passenger) transported with various means. Freight transport is calculated in tons and passenger traffic is calculated in the number of persons. Despite the type of freight and travelling distance, the freight transport is calculated in the actual weight of the goods: and despite the travelling distance and ticket price, the passenger traffic is calculated by the principle that one person can be counted only once in one travel. The passenger who travel with a half price ticket or a child ticket is also calculated as one person. The freight (passenger) traffic provides a quantitative measure to show how the transport industry serves the national economy and people, and is also an important indicator for planning the transport industry and for studying the development scale and speed of the transport industry.

Freight Ton–kilometers(Passenger–kilometers) refer to the sum of the products of the volume of transported cargo (passengers) multiplying by the transport distance, usually using ton-kilometer and passenger-kilometer as units for measurement. Normally, the shortest distance between the departure station and the destination station (i.e., the payable distance) is the basis to calculate the freight ton-kilometers. This is an important indicator to show the total results of the transport industry, to prepare and examine the transport plan and to measure the efficiency, the labour productivity and the unit cost of transport.

The formula is as follows:

Freight Ton-kilometers(Passenger-kilometers)=Σ {Freight (Passenger) Traffic × Distance of Transportation }

Measuring unit: ton-kilometer (person-kilometer)

Possession of Civil Motor Vehicles refer to the total numbers of vehicles that are registered and received vehicles license tags according to the Work Standard for Motor Vehicles Registration formulated by the Transport Management Office under the department of public security at the end of the reference period. They are divided into categories. According to the structure of motor vehicles, they are divided into passenger vehicles, trucks and others; according to ownership into private vehicles and vehicles for the unit' s use; according to kind of usage into working vehicles and non-working vehicles; and according to size of vehicles into large passenger vehicles, medium-sized passenger vehicles, small passenger vehicles and mini passenger vehicles, heavytrucks, light-heavy trucks, light trucks and mini-trucks.

Business Volume of Post and Telecommunications refers to the total amount of post and telecommunications services, expressed in value terms, provided by the post and telecommunications departments for the society. Post and telecommunication services can be classified asletters, parcels, remittance, issue of newspapers and magazines, fast mail service, express mail service, savings deposits, stamps for collection, public and individual telegraph service, facsimiles, long-distance telephone service,leasing of telephone lines, urban paging service, mobile telephone service, data transfer

and transmission, etc. The accounting approach is to multiply the service products of all types with their average unit price (constant price) to get sum of business value, plus income from other services such as leasing of telephone lines and equipment, maintenance of telephone switchboards and lines on behalf of customers. This indicator reflects the overall results of post and telecommunications service during a given period, and is important to study the composition of business service and the development of post and telecommunications service.

The formula is as follows:

Business Volume of Post and Telecommunications=Σ (Transaction of Post and Telecommunication Service x Constant Price) + Income from Leasing, Maintenance and other Services

Mobile Telephone Subscribers refer to the persons who own mobile telephone numbers and are connected with the mobile telephone communication network through the mobile telephone switchboards. The number of subscribers is calculated by the subscribers who have completed registration at mobile communication business centers and entered into the mobile telephone network. One mobile telephone is taken as a subscriber.

Telephone Subscribers refer to subscribers that are connected to the public line telephone network provided with telephone services. Before 1997, telephone subscribers were classified as city subscribers and village subscribers. City subscribers referred to those connected

to city telephone networks in county towns and cities, while village subscribers referred to those connected to village telephone stations at and below counties. Since 1997, the classification of telephone subscribers was modified on the basis of physical location of the subscribers as Urban telephone subscribers and rural telephone subscribers , which is different from the previous classification of categorizing local telephones and rural telephones , while the definition of total subscribers and total number of telephones remain unchanged.

Rural Telephone Subscribers refer to telephone subscribers, located at towns under county town and country, that are connected to the public line telephone network.

Capacity of Office Telephone Exchanges refers to the capacity (measured in gate) of telephone exchanges installed in the offices of local telecommunication service providers for communication between fixed telephones. It includes the capacity of both manual and automatic exchanges in use and for stand-by purpose. Equipment with expansion function is to be counted by the expanded capacity.

The number of computer srefers to the number of computers used in an enterprise or a company at the end of the reporting period, including desktops, laptops, and tablet computers.

Information technology personnel refers topeople who is engaged in the formulation, design, development, installation, operation, maintenance, management and evaluation of an information technology system.

Informatization Input includes the One-time investment input and operation maintenance investment of an enterprise or a company.

One-time Investment Input includes the actual expenditure in purchasing all kinds of hardware and software of an enterprise or a company.

Operation and Maintenance Input includesthe actual expenditure inupdating and maintenance of all kinds of information communication hardware and software of anenterprise or a company.

The Internet refers to the public computer network around the world. It provides access to a range of communications services including the world wide web, and transmits e-mail, news, entertainment, and data files,etc.

The amount of E-commerce sales during the whole year the total amount of goods and services sold by means of network orders of an enterprise or a company during the reporting period.By means of network ordersmeans that the orders are received over the network, but the payment and distribution can be made without the network.

The amount of E-commerce purchases during the whole yearrefers to the total amount of goods and services purchased by means of network orders of an enterprise or a company during the reporting period.

By means of network orders means that the orders are sent over the network, but the payment and distribution can be made without the network.

16 国内贸易

DOMESTIC TRADE

资料整理：马晓庆　杨　骏　左　宇　赵琳瑛　胡树建
Data management: Ma Xiaoqing　Yang Jun　Zuo Yu　Zhao Linying　Hu Shujian
数据审核：栾立森
Data audit: Luan Lisen

第十六部分　国内贸易

一、简要说明

本章资料主要包括社会消费品零售总额，批发零售贸易业商品购、销等情况，限额以上批发零售贸易业主要商品销售情况，限额以上批发零售贸易和住宿餐饮企业财务状况、经济效益，以及交易市场情况，由西安市统计局贸易外经处提供。

二、主要指标

社会消费品零售总额（亿元）	3730.70	比上年增长	9.6%
#批发零售贸易业零售额	3436.40	比上年增长	9.4%

16 DOMESTIC TRADE

Ⅰ.Brief Introduction

Content of this chapter consists of total retail sales of consumer goods, sails data on commodity purchasing and sails of wholesale and retail trade, sales data on primary goods exceeds quotation, financial, economic performance and market data on wholesale and retail trade and food services industry exceeds quotation. Data in this chapter is compiled and provided by Trade and Foreign Economy Division of the Xi'an Bureau of Statistics.

Ⅱ.Maior Indicators

		Increase over Preceding Year
Total Retail Sales of Consumer Goods (100 mil. yuan)	3730.70	9.6%
Retail Sales of Wholesale and Retail Enterprises	3436.40	9.4%

16-1 主要年份社会消费品零售额

Total Retail Sales of Consumer Goods in Representative Years

单位：亿元 (100 million yuan)

年 份 Year	社会消费品零售总额 Total Retail Sales of Consumer Goods	城镇 Urban	乡村 Village	批发和零售业 Wholesale Trades and Retail Trades	住宿和餐饮业 Accommodation and Catering Trade	其他行业 Others
1978	12.70	8.82	3.88	11.01	0.53	0.21
1979	13.94	9.88	4.06	11.88	0.60	0.21
1980	15.88	11.53	4.35	13.05	0.80	0.20
1981	17.41	12.85	4.56	14.31	0.80	0.19
1982	18.54	13.79	4.75	15.25	0.88	0.27
1983	20.82	15.14	5.68	16.95	1.03	0.32
1984	24.87	19.13	5.74	19.47	1.29	0.46
1985	32.92	26.09	6.83	25.04	1.69	0.48
1986	37.50	29.25	8.25	28.88	1.97	0.64
1987	43.86	34.62	9.24	33.32	2.50	0.49
1988	59.65	47.74	11.91	44.84	2.97	0.78
1989	68.05	54.60	13.45	54.41	2.98	0.76
1990	72.77	59.42	13.35	57.46	3.79	0.90
1991	81.04	66.93	14.11	60.35	4.43	1.26
1992	100.84	89.17	11.67	71.86	6.13	2.30
1993	115.38	104.41	10.97	75.99	7.49	2.71
1994	144.64	131.56	13.08	89.79	9.12	3.43
1995	186.60	165.98	20.62	115.46	11.97	3.73
1996	222.94	198.19	24.75	145.05	15.83	4.02
1997	264.47	238.17	26.30	169.08	22.12	4.17
1998	291.45	257.39	34.06	183.43	30.97	4.27
1999	323.37	283.32	40.05	207.96	34.78	4.85
2000	360.42	317.12	43.30	232.89	41.42	5.43
2001	406.21	358.97	47.24	265.25	48.87	5.86
2002	459.76	409.86	49.90	309.36	51.42	6.45
2003	502.65	449.62	53.03	440.28	53.30	9.07
2004	578.55	520.89	57.66	509.55	56.87	12.13
2005	670.56	604.63	65.93	592.77	63.59	14.20
2006	784.95	708.31	76.64	694.03	74.77	16.15
2007	936.21	845.59	90.62	828.63	89.32	18.26
2008	1176.58	1063.93	112.65	1033.00	122.90	20.68
2009	1398.37	1336.41	61.96	1250.41	147.96	
2010	1678.01	1610.88	67.13	1497.71	180.30	
2011	2039.24	1968.41	70.83	1825.79	213.45	
2012	2400.67	2326.84	73.83	2156.49	244.18	
2013	2742.89	2657.49	85.40	2494.74	248.15	
2014	3093.89	2996.43	97.46	2830.90	262.99	
2015	3405.38	3292.83	112.55	3140.65	264.73	
2016	3730.70	3598.73	131.97	3436.40	294.30	

注：依据2008年第二次经济普查数据，对2005-2007年数据进行调整。
依据2013年第三次经济普查数据，对2009年—2013年数据进行调整。
2009年以前按经营单位所在地分为市和县及县以下。
2002年以前按行业分组中不包括制造业零售额和农业对非农业居民零售额。

16–2 社会消费品零售总额

Total Retail Sales of Consumer Goods

单位：亿元 (100 million yuan)

分　类	Classify	2015	2016
社会消费品零售总额	**Total Retail Sales of Consumer Goods**	**3405.38**	**3730.70**
（一）按销售单位所在地分	Grouped by Region		
（1）城镇	Urban	3292.83	3598.73
#城区	District	2832.66	3065.98
（2）乡村	Village	112.55	131.97
（二）按行业分	Grouped by Sector		
（1）批发业	Wholesale Enterprises	625.11	629.65
限额以上单位	Enterprises Above Designated Size	401.84	354.53
限额以下单位	Enterprises Below Designated Size and Self-employed Laborers	223.27	275.12
（2）零售业	Retail Enterprises	2515.54	2806.75
限额以上单位	Enterprises Above Designated Size	1855.70	2032.41
限额以下单位	Enterprises Below Designated Size and Self-employed Laborers	659.84	774.34
（3）住宿和餐饮业	Accommodation and Catering Trade	264.73	294.30
限额以上单位	Enterprises Above Designated Size	88.36	82.58
限额以下单位	Enterprises Below Designated Size and Self-employed Laborers	176.37	211.72
（4）其他行业	Others		

16–3 各区县社会消费品零售总额

Total Retail Sales of Consumer Goods by Region

单位：亿元 (100 million yuan)

区 县	Region	2005	2006	2007	2008	2009	2010	2011	2012	2013	2014	2015	2016
西安市	**xian**	**670.56**	**784.95**	**936.21**	**1176.58**	**1398.37**	**1678.01**	**2039.24**	**2400.67**	**2742.89**	**3093.89**	**3405.38**	**3730.70**
新城区	Xincheng	129.00	146.70	169.95	207.01	241.56	285.41	342.48	397.08	446.06	499.78	557.59	607.98
碑林区	Beilin	131.09	149.07	172.55	206.80	241.48	285.45	342.56	395.07	445.11	505.87	561.46	610.53
莲湖区	Lianhu	116.34	128.71	144.57	169.62	198.10	234.84	282.08	325.93	368.62	413.00	451.82	491.72
灞桥区	Baqiao	17.89	20.06	22.79	27.01	36.26	50.18	68.02	95.43	132.26	154.28	173.26	200.82
未央区	Weiyang	64.38	85.21	114.53	164.14	200.54	245.41	301.10	361.75	423.72	480.79	515.21	566.17
雁塔区	Yanta	104.87	131.53	167.18	225.95	272.35	327.95	401.56	472.92	534.30	596.50	656.47	714.37
阎良区	Yanliang	8.25	9.58	11.29	13.85	16.41	19.67	23.91	27.87	31.37	34.93	37.90	41.22
临潼区	Lintong	20.37	22.45	25.04	29.02	34.29	40.95	49.72	57.75	64.08	72.63	77.99	84.66
长安区	Chang'an	37.36	44.13	52.44	64.67	76.80	91.86	111.41	130.09	144.94	164.00	183.37	202.49
高陵区	Gaoling	4.75	5.80	7.24	9.48	11.51	14.09	17.53	22.43	25.01	28.40	31.73	36.04
蓝田县	Lantian	13.53	15.41	17.83	21.44	25.00	29.70	35.64	41.18	45.74	51.57	56.40	62.08
周至县	Zhouzhi	8.54	9.94	11.69	14.38	16.75	19.86	23.84	27.68	30.71	34.63	38.47	42.64
户 县	Huxian	14.18	16.37	19.12	23.21	27.31	32.63	39.38	45.49	50.97	57.52	63.71	69.98

16-4 限额以上批发零售贸易企业财务状况（2016年）

单位：万元

分类	Classify	单位数（个） Number (unit)	资产总计 Total Assets	流动资产合计 Circulating Funds	固定资产合计 Total Fixed Assets
总计	**Total**	**1014**	**22524488.5**	**14443320.0**	**1974122.7**
一、批发企业	**Wholesale Enterprises**	**422**	**10203338.9**	**8014643.1**	**460156.3**
1. 按登记注册类型分组	Grouped by Category of Commodities				
内资企业	Domestic Funded Enterprises	405	9148541.9	7312818.8	432268.9
国有	State-owned Enterprises	22	828400.4	683179.3	81518.1
集体	Collective-owned Enterprises	1	1586.5	1485.0	101.5
股份合作	Corperative Enterprises				
联营	Joint Ownership Enterprises				
国有联营	State Joint Ownership Enterprises				
集体联营	Collective Joint Ownership Enterprises				
国有与集体联营	Joint State-collective Enterprises				
其他联营	Others Joint Ownership Enterprises				
有限责任公司	Limited Liability Corporrations	216	5645975.8	5035410.5	107672.1
国有独资公司	State Funded Corporations	11	1442321.9	1260247.1	13800.2
其他有限责任公司	Other Limited Liability Corporrations	205	4203653.9	3775163.4	93871.9
股份有限公司	Other Limited Liability Corporrations	11	1318858.9	383952.3	167607.9
私营	Other Limited Liability Corporrations	152	1352104.2	1208393.7	74152.7
私营独资	Private-funded Enterprises	1	1231.8	1168.7	63.1
私营合伙	Private Partnership Enterprises				
私营有限责任公司	Private Limited Liability Corporations	148	1240262.6	1115378.2	72683.3
私营股份有限公司	Private Share-holding Corporations Ltd.	3	110609.8	91846.8	1406.3
其他	Other Enterprises	3	1616.1	398.0	1216.6
港澳台商投资	Enterprises with Funds from Hong Kong, Macao &Taiwan	5	121672.5	113183.5	6876.5
外商投资	Foreign Funded Enterprises	12	933124.5	588640.8	21010.9
2. 按国民经济行业分组	Grouped by Sector				

Financial Status of Wholesale and Retail Enterprises above Designated Size (2016)

(10 000 yuan)

固定资产原价 Original Value of Fixed Assets	累计折旧 Accumulated Depreciation	负债合计 Total Liabilities	流动负债合计 Circulating Liabilities	非流动负债合计 Non-Circulating Liabilities	所有者权益合计 Total Owners' Equities	实收资本 Paid in Capital	营业收入 Total Revenue	主营业务收入 Revenue from Principal Business
2844796.9	**870791.6**	**14623206.3**	**13707896.7**	**915309.6**	**7901282.2**	**3477402.9**	**44914772.3**	**44532411.6**
734224.8	**274139.4**	**7915634.4**	**7454429.2**	**461205.2**	**2287704.5**	**1422297.4**	**26716833.1**	**26639497.3**
694359.5	262161.5	7096373.0	6812306.7	284066.3	2052168.9	1254119.3	22170466.9	22097548.9
144738.6	63220.5	390205.8	384452.5	5753.3	438194.6	58553.5	2094574.1	2087767.4
103.2	13.5	1493.1	900.2	592.9	93.4	110.8	2358.1	2358.1
203355.7	95742.7	4668765.6	4479217.2	189548.4	977210.2	580260.7	15737675.3	15711349.3
28920.5	15120.3	1292134.5	1271624.3	20510.2	150187.4	70232.3	3297081.0	3284787.9
174435.2	80622.4	3376631.1	3207592.9	169038.2	827022.8	510028.4	12440594.3	12426561.4
239184.2	71576.3	969742.2	919883.6	49858.6	349116.7	354999.9	2244639.7	2210120.8
105173.4	31020.7	1065792.0	1027478.9	38313.1	286312.2	259114.0	2076235.2	2070968.8
176.7	113.6	1185.0	1185.0		46.8	46.8	3803.0	3803.0
101695.6	29012.3	985832.0	954597.3	31234.7	254430.6	241906.3	1800267.4	1795210.9
3301.1	1894.8	78775.0	71696.6	7078.4	31834.8	17160.9	272164.8	271954.9
1804.4	587.8	374.3	374.3		1241.8	1080.4	14984.5	14984.5
9521.3	2644.8	105892.5	98877.6	7014.9	15780.0	7633.0	328216.9	327838.6
30344.0	9333.1	713368.9	543244.9	170124.0	219755.6	160545.1	4218149.3	4214109.8

16-4 续表1

单位：万元

分　类	Classify	营业成本 Total Cost	主营业务成本 Cost of Principal Business	营业税金及附加 Taxs and Other Changes	主营业务税金及附加 Taxs and Other Changes on Principal
总计	**Total**	**40699158.5**	**40563171.7**	**318515.4**	**316392.2**
一、批发企业	**Wholesale Enterprises**	**24863759.1**	**24814090.4**	**182595.3**	**181866.0**
1. 按登记注册类型分组	Grouped by Category of Commodities				
内资企业	Domestic Funded Enterprises	20427326.9	20379004.0	181220.2	180491.6
国有	State-owned Enterprises	1724149.5	1719679.2	152757.7	152641.3
集体	Collective-owned Enterprises	2193.0	2193.0	2.0	2.0
股份合作	Corperative Enterprises				
联营	Joint Ownership Enterprises				
国有联营	State Joint Ownership Enterprises				
集体联营	Collective Joint Ownership Enterprises				
国有与集体联营	Joint State-collective Enterprises				
其他联营	Others Joint Ownership Enterprises				
有限责任公司	Limited Liability Corporrations	14727988.6	14715217.9	21067.2	20953.6
国有独资公司	State Funded Corporations	2854644.1	2848857.4	3759.3	3657.4
其他有限责任公司	Other Limited Liability Corporrations	11873344.5	11866360.5	17307.9	17296.2
股份有限公司	Other Limited Liability Corporrations	2035700.3	2007578.3	4080.3	3586.7
私营	Other Limited Liability Corporrations	1923496.7	1920536.8	3313.0	3308.0
私营独资	Private-funded Enterprises	3617.5	3617.5	3.5	3.5
私营合伙	Private Partnership Enterprises				
私营有限责任公司	Private Limited Liability Corporations	1667715.0	1664845.2	2543.8	2538.8
私营股份有限公司	Private Share-holding Corporations Ltd.	252164.2	252074.1	765.7	765.7
其他	Other Enterprises	13798.8	13798.8		
港澳台商投资	Enterprises with Funds from Hong Kong, Macao &Taiwan	281458.1	281457.6	877.0	877.0
外商投资	Foreign Funded Enterprises	4154974.1	4153628.8	498.1	497.4
2. 按国民经济行业分组	Grouped by Sector				

continued 1

(10 000 yuan)

销售费用 Sale Expenses	管理费用 Managenment Expenses	财务费用 Financial Expenses	营业利润 Business Profits	利润总额 Total Profits	应付职工薪酬 Salary Payable	应交所得税 Income Tax payable	应交增值税 Value Added Tax Payable
1958157.0	**691736.6**	**200882.1**	**1044443.0**	**1072608.1**	**751786.1**	**157622.7**	**489610.8**
965973.5	**237529.6**	**93371.3**	**353916.0**	**375659.2**	**272594.4**	**71595.1**	**213502.8**
930460.8	220516.9	53981.0	337622.2	359236.1	245024.2	69926.2	204032.4
36391.3	48276.7	3706.7	130659.3	134115.0	37302.6	32694.5	56907.4
62.0	85.5	30.0	-14.4	-14.4	120.5		16.4
664872.1	122992.5	40636.3	142506.2	152513.4	119030.4	23018.0	102997.1
399749.3	19911.1	2824.3	8641.7	10960.7	24073.1	5580.1	37523.3
265122.8	103081.4	37812.0	133864.5	141552.7	94957.3	17437.9	65473.8
152110.7	14472.4	3325.1	30726.6	32038.1	53361.6	10962.5	27025.5
76884.7	34559.9	6232.9	32878.7	39575.2	34569.1	3251.2	17086.0
143.1	20.8	24.9	-6.8	-6.8	60.0		35.0
73174.3	32817.1	4235.4	20894.7	27461.0	25775.1	3042.9	16710.9
3567.3	1722.0	1972.6	11990.8	12121.0	8734.0	208.3	340.1
140.0	129.9	50.0	865.8	1008.8	640.0		
26329.6	9071.6	-470.7	10919.6	10862.7	19700.0	0.9	6770.2
9183.1	7941.1	39861.0	5374.2	5560.4	7870.2	1668.0	2700.2

16-4 续表2

单位：万元

分 类	Classify	单位数（个） Number (unit)	资产总计 Total Assets	流动资产合计 Circulating Funds	固定资产合计 Total Fixed Assets
农、林、牧产品批发	Wholesale of Agricultural,Forestry and Animal Husbandry Products	5	79828.6	34658.2	14979.6
食品、饮料及烟草制品批发	Wholesale of food Beverages and Tobaccos	50	938121.2	788879.5	76271.6
纺织、服装及家庭服务器批发	Wholesale of Textiles, Garments and Daily Articles	29	629990.4	572330.0	32905.1
文化、体育用品及器材批发	Wholesale of Culture, Sports Applionces and Equipments	19	262148.5	163556.7	10736.9
医药及医疗器材批发	Wholesale of Medicines and Medical Appliances	81	1761631.6	1655067.1	32752.8
矿产品、建材及化工产品批发	Wholesale of Mineral Products, Building Materials and Chemical Products	145	5431229.4	3827895.2	222157.9
机械设备、五金产品及电子产品批发	Wholesale of Machinery, Hardware, and Electronic Equipment	85	1074548.1	949739.9	68236.5
贸易经纪与代理	Trade Borker and Agency	2	13308.0	12629.5	336.0
其他批发	Other wholesale not Classified Elsewhere	6	12533.1	9887.0	1779.9
二、零售企业	**Retail Trade**	**592**	**12321149.6**	**6428676.9**	**1513966.4**
1. 按登记注册类型分组	Grouped by Category of Commodities				
内资企业	Domestic Funded Enterprises	545	9723852.9	4852751.6	1099096.9
国有	State-owned Enterprises	10	439752.6	372215.3	47783.3
集体	Collective-owned Enterprises	16	11889.8	3809.7	6773.5
股份合作	Corperative Enterprises				
联营	Joint Ownership Enterprises				
国有联营	State Joint Ownership Enterprises				
集体联营	Collective Joint Ownership Enterprises				
国有与集体联营	Joint State-collective Enterprises				
其他联营	Others Joint Ownership Enterprises				
有限责任公司	Limited Liability Corporations	313	3982443.2	2691150.4	585462.6
国有独资公司	State Funded Corporations	8	163284.4	96783.5	52140.9

continued 2

(10 000 yuan)

固定资产原价 Original Value of Fixed Assets	累计折旧 Accumulated Depreciation	负债合计 Total Liabilities	流动负债合计 Circulating Liabilities	非流动负债合计 Non-Circulating Liabilities	所有者权益合计 Total Owners' Equities	实收资本 Paid in Capital	营业收入 Total Revenue	主营业务收入 Revenue from Principal Business
20712.8	5733.2	67966.6	40232.5	27734.1	11862.0	17357.0	57172.4	57172.4
132774.1	56561.6	336180.9	324165.7	12015.2	601940.3	64307.5	2089727.5	2088008.6
65541.0	32635.9	544933.0	539802.6	5130.4	85057.4	56276.5	2795162.3	2791290.8
19513.3	8776.4	168316.8	145352.8	22964.0	93831.7	46521.0	454281.2	452769.9
52038.7	19285.9	1569951.8	1491796.1	78155.7	191679.8	171193.7	3111216.6	3104923.1
342857.6	120711.5	4271838.5	3972582.4	299256.1	1159390.9	957219.6	16796315.3	16746087.3
97180.8	28944.3	939606.2	924126.9	15479.3	134941.9	101630.0	1366552.6	1352840.4
405.1	69.1	12096.9	11776.5	320.4	1211.1	1251.1	34724.2	34723.8
3201.4	1421.5	4743.7	4593.7	150.0	7789.4	6541.0	11681.0	11681.0
2110572.1	**596652.2**	**6707571.9**	**6253467.5**	**454104.4**	**5613577.7**	**2055105.5**	**18197939.2**	**17892914.3**
1569368.0	470317.6	5233447.8	4909084.6	324363.2	4490405.1	1499280.8	13728470.6	13523351.7
65063.9	17280.6	357866.8	356151.5	1715.3	81885.8	4763.0	774353.4	764671.6
7618.9	891.0	9846.9	9232.8	614.1	2042.9	1623.1	30568.9	30561.5
831108.1	245646.4	2952389.4	2860163.3	92226.1	1030053.8	685090.5	8714523.6	8572276.6
67728.4	15587.5	114447.5	106947.5	7500.0	48836.9	25147.2	215107.0	213054.7

16-4 续表3

单位：万元

分类	Classify	营业成本 Total Cost	主营业务成本 Cost of Principal Business	营业税金及附加 Taxs and Other Changes	主营业务税金及附加 Taxs and Other Changes on Principal
农、林、牧产品批发	Wholesale of Agricultural,Forestry and Animal Husbandry Products	55142.3	55142.3	59.0	59.0
食品、饮料及烟草制品批发	Wholesale of food Beverages and Tobaccos	1649685.7	1648619.5	153069.7	153060.7
纺织、服装及家庭服务器批发	Wholesale of Textiles, Garments and Daily Articles	2672389.0	2671379.0	10100.8	10100.6
文化、体育用品及器材批发	Wholesale of Culture, Sports Applionces and Equipments	372389.3	371681.9	1115.1	1081.7
医药及医疗器材批发	Wholesale of Medicines and Medical Appliances	2955137.8	2955099.8	3898.0	3895.0
矿产品、建材及化工产品批发	Wholesale of Mineral Products, Building Materials and Chemical Products	15835650.8	15796615.0	12628.0	12013.5
机械设备、五金产品及电子产品批发	Wholesale of Machinery, Hardware, and Electronic Equipment	1282362.4	1274551.1	1701.6	1632.4
贸易经纪与代理	Trade Borker and Agency	31422.3	31422.3	2.6	2.6
其他批发	Other wholesale not Classified Elsewhere	9579.5	9579.5	20.5	20.5
二、零售企业	**Retail Trade**	**15835399.4**	**15749081.3**	**135920.1**	**134526.2**
1. 按登记注册类型分组	Grouped by Category of Commodities				
内资企业	Domestic Funded Enterprises	12041741.7	12006024.5	115779.1	115568.1
国有	State-owned Enterprises	707561.0	707139.1	1393.4	1388.5
集体	Collective-owned Enterprises	27318.7	27318.6	657.4	657.4
股份合作	Corperative Enterprises				
联营	Joint Ownership Enterprises				
国有联营	State Joint Ownership Enterprises				
集体联营	Collective Joint Ownership Enterprises				
国有与集体联营	Joint State-collective Enterprises				
其他联营	Others Joint Ownership Enterprises				
有限责任公司	Limited Liability Corporrations	7661022.8	7631620.8	79779.7	79695.6
国有独资公司	State Funded Corporations	187058.5	186982.7	266.8	234.1

continued 3

(10 000 yuan)

销售费用 Sale Expenses	管理费用 Managenment Expenses	财务费用 Financial Expenses	营业利润 Business Profits	利润总额 Total Profits	应付职工薪酬 Salary Payable	应交所得税 Income Tax payable	应交增值税 Value Added Tax Payable
2260.3	596.1	352.9	-562.7	61.6	877.9	2.6	60.0
96511.7	45439.8	-3050.7	152548.4	159853.9	49160.2	35233.1	63128.5
55103.1	25267.4	869.0	31306.2	32114.7	44225.0	2609.8	15372.8
14840.2	8046.8	-345.5	58005.5	58359.3	8400.5	690.5	1276.1
64187.3	45224.4	21247.0	19860.7	20968.5	42265.1	5391.0	27008.0
686718.9	76663.4	76099.1	104326.9	114787.1	96518.1	24870.0	94306.3
43237.4	35284.5	-1702.1	-12944.5	-11970.5	30034.5	2686.4	12189.1
2389.4	481.8	-115.5	543.6	537.7	497.0	3.3	25.2
725.2	525.4	17.1	831.9	946.9	616.1	108.4	136.8
992183.5	**454207.0**	**107510.8**	**690527.0**	**696948.9**	**479191.7**	**86027.6**	**276108.0**
605092.5	358343.8	84537.8	541312.3	544094.3	342733.7	46617.5	230321.5
30682.1	20712.6	2685.7	11317.4	10201.3	17145.8	2281.6	6217.9
641.7	1688.6	55.4	207.1	185.9	1862.9	17.2	212.5
395428.4	220295.3	49584.7	326868.4	324964.2	219004.4	37823.3	157786.3
16170.0	10092.3	164.7	3055.3	5215.9	12536.1	628.2	1644.1

16-4 续表4

单位：万元

分 类	Classify	单位数（个）Number (unit)	资产总计 Total Assets	流动资产合 计 Circulating Funds	固定资产合 计 Total Fixed Assets
其他有限责任公司	Other Limited Liability Corporrations	305	3819158.8	2594366.9	533321.7
股份有限公司	Other Limited Liability Corporrations	10	3801822.7	663005.3	314341.2
私营	Other Limited Liability Corporrations	193	1485492.4	1120845.6	144444.0
私营独资	Private-funded Enterprises	5	3845.1	2384.6	1088.1
私营合伙	Private Partnership Enterprises	2	948.7	760.3	168.2
私营有限责任公司	Private Limited Liability Corporations	179	1365852.8	1050192.2	100357.3
私营股份有限公司	Private Share-holding Corporations Ltd.	7	114845.8	67508.5	42830.4
其他	Other Enterprises	3	2452.2	1725.3	292.3
港澳台商投资	Enterprises with Funds from Hong Kong, Macao &Taiwan	27	1549758.6	1087586.3	127397.7
外商投资	Foreign Funded Enterprises	20	1047538.1	488339.0	287471.8
2. 按国民经济行业分组	Grouped by Sector				
综合零售	Integrated Retail	118	6229275.9	2109543.9	783126.9
食品、饮料及烟草制品专门零售	Food, Beverages and Tobaccos Special Retail Trade	45	590840.1	349515.5	165364.6
纺织、服装及日用品专门零售	Special Retail of Textiles,Garments and Daily Consumer Articles	44	480517.2	267609.1	35859.8
文化、体育用品及器材专门零售	Retail of Culture,Sports Appliances and Equipments	28	359059.0	235200.5	48905.3
医药及医疗器材专门零售	Retail of Medicines and Medical Appliances	27	166841.9	150392.3	7476.6
汽车、摩托车、燃料及零配件专门零售	Retail of Motor Vehicles,Motorcycles, Fuel and Parts	213	3392059.6	2512117.3	296031.9
家用电器及电子产品专门零售	Special Retail of Household Electric Appliances and Electronic Products	53	515832.0	442068.4	48538.1
五金、家具及室内装饰材料专门零售	Special Retail of Hardware,Furniture and Decoration Materials	39	406342.6	235849.3	80767.8
货摊、无店铺及其他零售业	Non-shop and Other Retail	25	180381.3	126380.6	47895.4

continued 4

(10 000 yuan)

固定资产原价 Original Value of Fixed Assets	累计折旧 Accumulated Depreciation	负债合计 Total Liabilities	流动负债合计 Circulating Liabilities	非流动负债合计 Non-Circulating Liabilities	所有者权益合计 Total Owners' Equities	实收资本 Paid in Capital	营业收入 Total Revenue	主营业务收入 Revenue from Principal Business
763379.7	230058.9	2837941.9	2753215.8	84726.1	981216.9	659943.3	8499416.6	8359221.9
448161.5	133820.3	810377.8	659136.5	151241.3	2991444.9	632652.4	1041285.3	1010522.4
216951.0	72507.0	1102369.4	1023803.0	78566.4	383123.0	174426.8	3159407.6	3136987.8
1215.3	127.2	540.9	540.9		3304.2	657.8	11855.2	11854.2
249.9	81.7	1154.8	990.4	164.4	-206.1	130.0	7660.8	7660.8
169514.7	69157.4	1061715.6	984379.3	77336.3	304137.2	170659.0	2863153.5	2842432.1
45971.1	3140.7	38958.1	37892.4	1065.7	75887.7	2980.0	276738.1	275040.7
464.6	172.3	597.5	597.5		1854.7	725.0	8331.8	8331.8
192663.2	65265.5	894701.3	859862.0	34839.3	655057.3	238821.5	1755576.9	1694372.4
348540.9	61069.1	579422.8	484520.9	94901.9	468115.3	317003.2	2713891.7	2675190.2
1026258.5	243131.6	2573584.3	2345017.8	228566.5	3655691.6	1047885.1	3309281.5	3080351.6
240158.0	74793.4	338045.7	258583.1	79462.6	252794.4	96347.5	304510.4	297293.7
64594.3	28780.1	203984.5	175213.6	28770.9	276532.7	107329.2	1187584.1	1180097.2
62299.7	13394.4	229138.4	198507.5	30630.9	129920.6	69117.2	349122.8	347196.5
12875.1	5398.5	133686.6	133296.7	389.9	33155.3	16638.7	252483.8	251233.8
446653.5	150621.6	2543877.0	2486567.1	57309.9	848182.6	564780.3	7475365.5	7433030.8
72931.4	24393.3	290265.5	289800.1	465.4	225566.5	66289.2	2251449.4	2236393.1
131142.2	50375.3	298355.4	270633.2	27722.2	107987.2	65431.4	1696284.7	1695564.8
53659.4	5764.0	96634.5	95848.4	786.1	83746.8	21286.9	1371857.0	1371752.8

16-4 续表5

单位：万元

分 类	Classify	营业成本 Total Cost	主营业务成本 Cost of Principal Business	营业税金及附加 Taxs and Other Changes	主营业务税金及附加 Taxs and Other Changes on Principal
其他有限责任公司	Other Limited Liability Corporations	7473964.3	7444638.1	79512.9	79461.5
股份有限公司	Other Limited Liability Corporations	919320.4	916964.9	5022.5	5022.1
私营	Other Limited Liability Corporations	2720035.9	2716498.2	28860.2	28738.6
私营独资	Private-funded Enterprises	9878.0	9878.0	227.6	227.6
私营合伙	Private Partnership Enterprises	6701.2	6701.2	21.1	21.1
私营有限责任公司	Private Limited Liability Corporations	2510152.4	2507506.8	28000.4	27889.9
私营股份有限公司	Private Share-holding Corporations Ltd.	193304.3	192412.2	611.1	600.0
其他	Other Enterprises	6482.9	6482.9	65.9	65.9
港澳台商投资	Enterprises with Funds from Hong Kong, Macao &Taiwan	1477891.9	1465101.4	10800.4	10677.2
外商投资	Foreign Funded Enterprises	2315765.8	2277955.4	9340.6	8280.9
2. 按国民经济行业分组	Grouped by Sector				
综合零售	Integrated Retail	2666602.3	2616057.3	21404.1	20739.7
食品、饮料及烟草制品专门零售	Food, Beverages and Tobaccos Special Retail Trade	249477.9	241680.8	811.6	811.6
纺织、服装及日用品专门零售	Special Retail of Textiles,Garments and Daily Consumer Articles	1014496.3	1014143.5	10343.4	10323.8
文化、体育用品及器材专门零售	Retail of Culture,Sports Appliances and Equipments	259242.4	259186.7	1996.4	1423.7
医药及医疗器材专门零售	Retail of Medicines and Medical Appliances	195463.4	194866.6	2490.2	2487.0
汽车、摩托车、燃料及零配件专门零售	Retail of Motor Vehicles,Motorcycles, Fuel and Parts	6919640.2	6893744.9	13558.5	13505.0
家用电器及电子产品专门零售	Special Retail of Household Electric Appliances and Electronic Products	1959118.8	1958239.0	31679.5	31674.8
五金、家具及室内装饰材料专门零售	Special Retail of Hardware,Furniture and Decoration Materials	1382040.0	1381883.5	50843.0	50767.4
货摊、无店铺及其他零售业	Non-shop and Other Retail	1189318.1	1189279.0	2793.4	2793.2

continued 5

(10 000 yuan)

销售费用 Sale Expenses	管理费用 Managenment Expenses	财务费用 Financial Expenses	营业利润 Business Profits	利润总额 Total Profits	应付职工薪酬 Salary Payable	应交所得税 Income Tax payable	应交增值税 Value Added Tax Payable
379258.4	210203.0	49420.0	323813.1	319748.3	206468.3	37195.1	156142.2
38264.5	39862.5	18514.3	20928.3	25754.5	14534.0	161.1	15713.0
139734.9	75582.3	13695.1	180754.5	181751.8	89943.9	6334.2	50391.8
716.8	536.8	9.2	486.8	490.0	618.9	18.5	297.4
599.0	245.1		94.4	124.0	482.0	1.8	99.5
132264.8	67708.5	12987.6	111295.1	111991.4	84883.8	6161.7	46563.0
6154.3	7091.9	698.3	68878.2	69146.4	3959.2	152.2	3431.9
340.9	202.5	2.6	1236.6	1236.6	242.7	0.1	
154463.9	62365.0	9880.2	41066.0	46843.3	81412.1	10141.5	23978.1
232627.1	33498.2	13092.8	108148.7	106011.3	55045.9	29268.6	21808.4
351725.6	190356.9	36489.6	47132.0	32544.9	181881.8	17831.2	48722.6
19798.2	15402.7	8690.5	11709.3	15647.4	11104.6	234.7	927.6
71517.7	21383.0	1580.4	69278.6	69457.7	35001.0	9308.0	15759.6
28606.5	21652.2	3719.6	33869.9	40324.7	19647.4	1375.8	785.0
34398.3	10766.8	940.5	8423.6	8543.1	34768.9	677.7	3181.5
256950.6	107276.6	51061.6	124834.1	135536.2	135653.7	36541.0	123456.5
105433.5	46796.7	1738.0	106951.8	106608.2	31960.9	7375.2	36901.9
24828.5	24464.6	3182.3	223721.0	222573.9	13115.2	11701.7	33799.1
98924.6	16107.5	108.3	64606.7	65712.8	16058.2	982.3	12574.2

16-5 限额以上住宿和餐饮企业财务状况（2016年）

单位：万元

分类	Classify	单位数（个） Number (unit)	资产总计 Total Assets	流动资产合计 Circulating Funds	固定资产合计 Total Fixed Assets
总计	**Total**	**568**	**3122122.7**	**966724.2**	**1202286.0**
一、住宿业	**Hotel Services**	**246**	**2415579.2**	**605630.8**	**1026704.9**
1.按登记注册类型分组	Grouped by Type of Registration				
内资	Domestic Funded Enterprises	231	2127712.8	503028.2	870413.4
国有	State-owned Enterprises	26	171407.8	32443.6	122556.4
集体	Collective-owned Enterprises	1	39.9	20.0	19.9
股份合作	Cooperative Enterprises				
联营	Joint Ownership Enterprises				
国有联营	State Joint Ownership Enterprises				
集体联营	Collective Joint Ownership Enterprises				
国有与集体联营	Joint State-collective Enterprises				
其他联营	Others Joint Ownership Enterprises				
有限责任公司	Limited Liability Corporations	122	1232951.0	358611.3	668697.1
国有独资公司	State Sole Funded Corporations	7	83108.0	25573.7	47843.6
其他有限责任公司	Other Limited Liability Corporations	115	1149843.0	333037.6	620853.5
股份有限公司	Share-holding Corporations Ltd.	2	11562.6	316.9	11231.9
私营	Private Enterprises	80	711751.5	111636.4	67908.1
私营独资	Private-funded Enterprises	3	7238.9	3847.8	1256.1
私营合伙	Private Partnership Enterprises				
私营有限责任公司	Private Limited Liability Corporations	76	704484.9	107760.9	66652.0
私营股份有限公司	Private Share-holding Corporations Ltd.	1	27.7	27.7	
其他	Other Enterprises				
港澳台商投资	Enterprises with Funds from Hong Kong, Macao &Taiwan	6	135267.4	43453.3	69531.4
外商投资	Foreign Funded Enterprises	9	152599.0	59149.3	86760.1
2.按国民经济行业分组	Grouped by Sector				
旅游饭店	Tourist Hotel	174	2198410.8	535418.8	945117.3
一般旅馆	Normal Hotel	63	140713.9	57292.9	47813.9
其他住宿业	Others	9	76454.5	12919.1	33773.7

Finacial Status of Catering Eenterprises above Designated Size（2016）

(10 000 yuan)

固定资产原价 Original Value of Fixed Assets	累计折旧 Accumulated Depreciation	负债合计 Total Liabilities	流动负债合计 Circulating Liabilities	非流动负债合计 Non-Circulating Liabilities	所有者权益合计 Total Owners' Equities	实收资本 Paid in Capital	营业收入 Total Revenue	主营业务收入 Revenue from Principal Business
1950940.9	**754966.7**	**2234171.4**	**1729978.2**	**504193.2**	**887951.3**	**983556.9**	**1108580.0**	**1093115.2**
1654233.4	**627528.5**	**1655186.3**	**1195496.8**	**459689.5**	**760392.9**	**698440.1**	**524294.5**	**516631.2**
1348067.2	477653.8	1399050.0	1041318.2	357731.8	728662.8	560405.9	445062.5	439049.9
192289.9	69733.5	117555.1	66425.2	51129.9	53852.7	40343.0	51572.9	50189.5
20.0	0.1	10.0	10.0		29.9	29.9	382.7	382.7
1015601.8	346904.7	1092401.0	824408.6	267992.4	140550.0	408249.2	288352.0	285337.1
136356.7	88513.1	123266.4	65671.0	57595.4	-40158.4	63883.4	28083.3	27319.6
879245.1	258391.6	969134.6	758737.6	210397.0	180708.4	344365.8	260268.7	258017.5
17318.9	6087.0	6129.6	6129.6		5433.0	5433.0	3269.3	3269.3
122836.6	54928.5	182954.3	144344.8	38609.5	528797.2	106350.8	101485.6	99871.3
1742.0	485.9	5994.4	5994.2	0.2	1244.5	2500.0	1849.0	1849.0
121094.6	54442.6	176951.5	138342.2	38609.3	527533.4	103840.8	99192.2	97577.9
		8.4	8.4		19.3	10.0	444.4	444.4
134128.2	64596.8	102029.8	74599.6	27430.2	33237.6	77758.3	28401.3	28401.3
172038.0	85277.9	154106.5	79579.0	74527.5	-1507.5	60275.9	50830.7	49180.0
1541571.5	596454.2	1533646.8	1081882.8	451764.0	664764.0	603960.6	438896.1	432477.7
72530.8	24716.9	82082.6	77157.1	4925.5	58631.3	85529.5	66292.3	65348.3
40131.1	6357.4	39456.9	36456.9	3000.0	36997.6	8950.0	19106.1	18805.2

16-5 续表1

单位：万元

分 类	Classify	营业成本 Total Cost	主营业务成本 Cost of Principal Business
总计	**Total**	**481589.3**	**475326.6**
一、住宿业	**Hotel Services**	**186293.5**	**183932.7**
1.按登记注册类型分组	Grouped by Type of Registration		
内资	Domestic Funded Enterprises	162713.3	160730.3
国有	State-owned Enterprises	18771.9	18526.2
集体	Collective-owned Enterprises	289.7	289.7
股份合作	Cooperative Enterprises		
联营	Joint Ownership Enterprises		
国有联营	State Joint Ownership Enterprises		
集体联营	Collective Joint Ownership Enterprises		
国有与集体联营	Joint State-collective Enterprises		
其他联营	Others Joint Ownership Enterprises		
有限责任公司	Limited Liability Corporations	106684.3	105478.1
国有独资公司	State Sole Funded Corporations	7208.1	7208.1
其他有限责任公司	Other Limited Liability Corporations	99476.2	98270.0
股份有限公司	Share-holding Corporations Ltd.	1771.0	1771.0
私营	Private Enterprises	35196.4	34665.3
私营独资	Private-funded Enterprises	1204.7	1204.7
私营合伙	Private Partnership Enterprises		
私营有限责任公司	Private Limited Liability Corporations	33772.9	33241.8
私营股份有限公司	Private Share-holding Corporations Ltd.	218.8	218.8
其他	Other Enterprises		
港澳台商投资	Enterprises with Funds from Hong Kong, Macao &Taiwan	8224.6	8224.5
外商投资	Foreign Funded Enterprises	15355.6	14977.9
2.按国民经济行业分组	Grouped by Sector		
旅游饭店	Tourist Hotel	155136.7	153022.9
一般旅馆	Normal Hotel	27887.0	27640.0
其他住宿业	Others	3269.8	3269.8

continued 1

(10 000 yuan)

营业税金及附加 Taxs and Other Changes	主营业务税金及附加 Taxs and Other Changes on Principal Business	销售费用 Sale Expenses	管理费用 Managenme Expenses	财务费用 Financial Expenses	营业利润 Business Profits	利润总额 Total Profits	应付职工薪酬 Salary Payable	应交所得税 Income Tax payable	应交增值税 Value Added Tax Payable
30889.4	**30507.7**	**379769.9**	**235874.1**	**29424.8**	**-57435.4**	**-51950.4**	**290925.9**	**5325.9**	**24145.5**
15084.6	**14709.7**	**176261.5**	**166536.8**	**21437.5**	**-48291.3**	**-48314.2**	**150289.9**	**2926.3**	**13560.0**
13249.1	12926.9	151786.0	141362.3	17230.5	-48252.5	-49317.8	128464.1	1359.2	11963.9
1171.0	1030.2	15109.2	15998.7	2319.3	-1794.8	-1817.9	16294.3	349.6	1033.3
7.0	7.0	45.0	45.0		-4.0	-4.0	84.0		6.5
7583.3	7439.4	103052.4	95182.2	11513.1	-42287.0	-43880.0	86313.1	662.3	8541.6
700.3	700.3	11551.5	11182.8	1863.7	-10793.5	-11262.4	10395.3		488.0
6883.0	6739.1	91500.9	83999.4	9649.4	-31493.5	-32617.6	75917.8	662.3	8053.6
73.3	73.3	875.8	252.3	3.8	282.5	280.2	1117.2		96.2
4414.5	4377.0	32703.6	29884.1	3394.3	-4449.2	-3896.1	24655.5	347.3	2286.3
21.7	21.7	297.3	645.5	5.0	-325.0	-323.0	509.8		13.3
4370.0	4332.5	32288.9	29166.3	3389.3	-4137.1	-3586.0	24058.7	347.3	2260.6
22.8	22.8	117.4	72.3		12.9	12.9	87.0		12.4
612.1	612.1	9714.8	10490.2	3373.4	-4027.7	-3001.5	8600.6	56.1	612.8
1223.4	1170.7	14760.7	14684.3	833.6	3988.9	4005.1	13225.2	1511.0	983.3
13136.1	12764.0	145696.3	142178.8	19582.9	-44216.2	-44531.2	129916.0	2649.4	11132.7
1442.9	1440.1	22783.1	15525.4	1284.2	-2220.7	-2017.1	17696.5	246.0	1940.6
505.6	505.6	7782.1	8832.6	570.4	-1854.4	-1765.9	2677.4	30.9	486.7

16-5 续表2

单位：万元

分 类	Classify	单位数（个） Number (unit)	资产总计 Total Assets	流动资产合计 Circulating Funds	固定资产合计 Total Fixed Assets
二、餐饮业	**Catering Trade**	**322**	**706543.5**	**361093.4**	**175581.1**
1.按登记注册类型分组	Grouped by Type of Registration				
内资	Domestic Funded Enterprises	311	627198.5	332763.7	154781.8
国有	State-owned Enterprises	3	5110.2	1693.0	3317.2
集体	Collective-owned Enterprises				
股份合作	Cooperative Enterprises				
联营	Joint Ownership Enterprises				
国有联营	State Joint Ownership Enterprises				
集体联营	Collective Joint Ownership Enterprises				
国有与集体联营	Joint State-collective Enterprises				
其他联营	Others Joint Ownership Enterprises				
有限责任公司	Limited Liability Corporations	160	334982.7	191458.2	100599.9
国有独资公司	State Sole Funded Corporations	1	2416.7	410.7	2005.9
其他有限责任公司	Other Limited Liability Corporations	159	332566.0	191047.5	98594.0
股份有限公司	Share-holding Corporations Ltd.	2	148393.6	68222.5	21154.1
私营	Private Enterprises	144	138418.5	71207.0	29617.7
私营独资	Private-funded Enterprises	12	3466.7	1515.5	1358.4
私营合伙	Private Partnership Enterprises				
私营有限责任公司	Private Limited Liability Corporations	129	134117.7	68997.9	28239.6
私营股份有限公司	Private Share-holding Corporations Ltd.	3	834.1	693.6	19.7
其他	Other Enterprises	2	293.5	183.0	92.9
港澳台商投资	Enterprises with Funds from Hong Kong, Macao &Taiwan	6	25159.4	8273.6	7754.1
外商投资	Foreign Funded Enterprises	5	54185.6	20056.1	13045.2
2.按国民经济行业分	Grouped by Sdctor				
正餐服务	Dinner	311	626389.7	334905.5	136974.3
快餐服务	Fast Food	8	43477.2	22290.3	10880.9
饮料及冷饮服务	Beverages and Cold Drinks				
其他餐饮业	Other Catering Services	3	36676.6	3897.6	27725.9

continued 2

(10 000 yuan)

固定资产原价 Original Value of Fixed Assets	累计折旧 Accumulated Depreciation	负债合计 Total Liabilities	流动负债合计 Circulating Liabilities	非流动负债合计 Non-Circulating Liabilities	所有者权益合计 Total Owners' Equities	实收资本 Paid in Capital	营业收入 Total Revenue	主营业务收入 Revenue from Principal Business
296707.5	**127438.2**	**578985.1**	**534481.4**	**44503.7**	**127558.4**	**285116.8**	**584285.5**	**576484.0**
255187.5	106717.5	517752.2	481185.3	36566.9	109446.3	270438.2	444088.8	443119.7
4549.0	1231.8	3545.7	921.4	2624.3	1564.5	2067.0	7386.0	7386.0
162160.1	67860.0	330239.6	302657.7	27581.9	4743.1	163855.5	223271.8	222518.2
3739.5	1733.6	3032.1	3032.1		-615.4	100.0	1096.6	1096.6
158420.6	66126.4	327207.5	299625.6	27581.9	5358.5	163755.5	222175.2	221421.6
34384.4	13230.3	50181.6	47216.4	2965.2	98212.0	59105.6	60358.6	60358.6
53619.8	24014.1	132471.3	129075.8	3395.5	5947.2	45347.1	152303.8	152088.3
2184.9	826.5	3148.6	3148.6		318.1	1471.4	5586.2	5586.2
51205.8	22978.2	128364.8	124969.3	3395.5	5752.9	43575.7	144731.9	144539.2
229.1	209.4	957.9	957.9		-123.8	300.0	1985.7	1962.9
474.2	381.3	1314.0	1314.0		-1020.5	63.0	768.6	768.6
15510.0	7755.9	28539.3	26073.3	2466.0	-3379.9	6531.0	39359.6	39359.6
26010.0	12964.8	32693.6	27222.8	5470.8	21492.0	8147.6	100837.1	94004.7
239006.3	108343.8	520582.5	480968.8	39613.7	105807.2	268784.8	527564.1	526408.6
21605.0	10724.1	28885.5	24135.5	4750.0	14591.7	5268.7	47495.8	40850.1
36096.2	8370.3	29517.1	29377.1	140.0	7159.5	11063.3	9225.6	9225.3

16-5 续表3

单位：万元

分 类	Classify	营业成本 Total Cost	主营业务成本 Cost of Principal Business
二、餐饮业	**Catering Trade**	**295295.8**	**291393.9**
1.按登记注册类型分组	Grouped by Type of Registration		
内资	Domestic Funded Enterprises	229626.9	227733.0
国有	State-owned Enterprises	6036.1	6036.1
集体	Collective-owned Enterprises		
股份合作	Cooperative Enterprises		
联营	Joint Ownership Enterprises		
国有联营	State Joint Ownership Enterprises		
集体联营	Collective Joint Ownership Enterprises		
国有与集体联营	Joint State-collective Enterprises		
其他联营	Others Joint Ownership Enterprises		
有限责任公司	Limited Liability Corporations	111676.3	110807.9
国有独资公司	State Sole Funded Corporations	709.0	709.0
其他有限责任公司	Other Limited Liability Corporations	110967.3	110098.9
股份有限公司	Share-holding Corporations Ltd.	31025.7	31025.7
私营	Private Enterprises	80498.5	79473.0
私营独资	Private-funded Enterprises	3303.0	3289.4
私营合伙	Private Partnership Enterprises		
私营有限责任公司	Private Limited Liability Corporations	76358.1	75346.2
私营股份有限公司	Private Share-holding Corporations Ltd.	837.4	837.4
其他	Other Enterprises	390.3	390.3
港澳台商投资	Enterprises with Funds from Hong Kong, Macao &Taiwan	19313.1	19313.1
外商投资	Foreign Funded Enterprises	46355.8	44347.8
2.按国民经济行业分	Grouped by Sdctor		
正餐服务	Dinner	269510.6	267561.4
快餐服务	Fast Food	23694.5	21741.8
饮料及冷饮服务	Beverages and Cold Drinks		
其他餐饮业	Other Catering Services	2090.7	2090.7

continued 3

(10 000 yuan)

营业税金及附加 Taxs and Other Changes	主营业务税金及附加 Taxs and Other Changes on Principal Business	销售费用 Sale Expenses	管理费用 Managenme Expenses	财务费用 Financial Expenses	营业利润 Business Profits	利润总额 Total Profits	应付职工薪酬 Salary Payable	应交所得税 Income Tax payable	应交增值税 Value Added Tax Payable
15804.8	**15798.0**	**203508.4**	**69337.3**	**7987.3**	**-9144.1**	**-3636.2**	**140636.0**	**2399.6**	**10585.5**
13062.9	13056.1	155888.2	52874.9	7202.0	-13691.4	-7877.6	115022.5	1584.1	9090.2
388.6	388.6	821.9	594.4	1.2	-456.2	-422.6	720.2		328.1
6547.9	6546.5	82426.1	30143.8	5771.9	-11476.7	-10944.8	54235.6	466.2	5324.6
23.1	23.1	19.4	311.1	3.0	31.0	63.3	259.5		33.2
6524.8	6523.4	82406.7	29832.7	5768.9	-11507.7	-11008.1	53976.1	466.2	5291.4
1630.5	1630.5	18449.7	5580.0	-128.0	3497.4	7989.9	21929.7	945.6	594.0
4478.3	4472.9	53690.4	16532.1	1555.1	-4742.8	-3987.0	37796.0	172.3	2821.0
171.6	171.6	1412.8	649.5	111.6	-30.5	-21.5	1422.3	0.2	94.0
4261.8	4258.5	51220.7	15773.7	1433.3	-4635.0	-3888.2	35801.7	171.0	2687.2
44.9	42.8	1056.9	108.9	10.2	-77.3	-77.3	572.0	1.1	39.8
17.6	17.6	500.1	24.6	1.8	-513.1	-513.1	341.0		22.5
892.3	892.3	15854.6	2135.0	806.4	289.0	182.1	7483.6		702.1
1849.6	1849.6	31765.6	14327.4	-21.1	4258.3	4059.3	18129.9	815.5	793.2
14737.7	14730.9	186726.1	59407.0	7741.5	-12210.6	-6410.6	130094.7	2040.9	9612.0
878.0	878.0	14166.1	5431.4	193.8	3288.1	2994.0	8528.1	358.7	829.9
189.1	189.1	2616.2	4498.9	52.0	-221.6	-219.6	2013.2		143.6

16-6 限额以上批发零售贸易业商品购进、销售、库存总额（2016年）

单位：个、万元

分 类	Classify	单位数 Number of Enterprises	商品购进额 Total Purchases	进口 Exports
总计	**Total**	**1036**	**43492307.4**	**688777.5**
一、批发企业	**Wholesale Enterprises**	**424**	**24954483.6**	**157331.6**
1.按登记注册类型分组	Grouped by Type of Registration			
内资企业	Domestic Funded Enterprises	407	19810498.2	127278.3
国有	State-owned Enterprises	22	1819517.3	3344.8
集体	Collective-owned Enterprises	1	2283.1	
股份合作	Cooperative Enterprises			
联营	Joint Ownership Enterprises			
国有联营	State Joint Ownership Enterprises			
集体联营	Collective Joint Ownership Enterprises			
国有与集体联营	Joint State-collective Enterprises			
其他联营	Others Joint Ownership Enterprises			
有限责任公司	Limited Liability Corporations	216	13524216.8	70107.8
国有独资公司	State Sole Funded Corporations	11	481542.4	9087.4
其他有限责任公司	Other Limited Liability Corporations	205	13042674.4	61020.4
股份有限公司	Share-holding Corporations Ltd.	13	2362357.0	3332.9
私营	Private Enterprises	152	2089774.0	50492.8
私营独资	Private-funded Enterprises	1	3008.5	
私营合伙	Private Partnership Enterprises			
私营有限责任公司	Private Limited Liability Corporations	148	1810096.3	47511.7
私营股份有限公司	Private Share-holding Corporations Ltd.	3	276669.2	2981.1
其他	Other Enterprises	3	12350.0	
港澳台商投资	Enterprises with Funds from Hong Kong, Macao &Taiwan	5	306408.6	
外商投资	Foreign Funded Enterprises	12	4837576.8	30053.3
个体经营户	Individusl Enterprises			
2.按国民经济行业分组	Grouped by Economic Sector			
农、林、牧产品批发	Wholesale of Agricultural,Forestry and Animal Husbandry Products	5	54857.0	

Total Purchases,Sales and Inventories of Wholesale and Retail Enterprises above Designated Size（2016）

(unit，10 000 yuan)

商品销售额			批发额		零售额	期末商品库存额
	公共网络商品销售额	银行卡支付商品销售额		出口		Value of
Sales Value	Public Network Sales	Bank Card Paid Sales	Wholesale Trade	Exports	Retail Trade	Stock at Final goods
52008989.4	**2979299.3**	**7953273.7**	**27749032.9**	**911725.3**	**24259956.5**	**3128236.7**
30141539.3	**1317141.1**	**1505485.3**	**26742675.1**	**758679.8**	**3398864.2**	**1095080.0**
24866226.3	1317141.1	1505485.3	21585835.4	753280.1	3280390.9	1007515.3
2350467.0	1269914.5	1273594.8	2304625.7	25768.8	45841.3	79127.1
2358.1			2358.1			410.0
17479474.0	27721.7	82824.0	15230729.0	384607.0	2248745.0	623255.5
3325803.7		5342.1	2619876.8	61560.0	705926.9	72497.0
14153670.3	27721.7	77481.9	12610852.2	323047.0	1542818.1	550758.5
2723864.9	3040.7	84301.9	1861200.1	149457.3	862664.8	70945.1
2295077.8	16464.2	64764.6	2171938.0	193447.0	123139.8	233667.8
3803.0			3803.0			430.6
2011201.8	16464.2	64764.6	1940080.0	193447.0	71121.8	222869.3
280073.0			228055.0		52018.0	10367.9
14984.5			14984.5			109.8
368739.2			253212.8		115526.4	59359.8
4906573.8			4903626.9	5399.7	2946.9	28204.9
57186.7		1129.5	57186.7			7200.6

16-6 续表1

单位：个、万元

分 类	Classify	单位数 Number of Enterprises	商品购进额 Total Purchases	进口 Exports
食品、饮料及烟草制品批发	Wholesale of Food, Beverages and Tobacco Products	50	1830813.9	650.0
纺织、服装及家庭服务器批发	Wholesale of Textiles, Garments and Daily Articles	30	3596802.0	89.5
文化、体育用品及器材批发	Wholesale of Culture, Sports Articles and Equipments	19	438758.2	
医药及医疗器材批发	Wholesale of Medicines and Medical Appliances	81	2635108.1	10990.5
矿产品、建材及化工产品批发	Wholesale of Mineral Products, Building Materials and Chemical Products	145	14946425.2	67422.1
机械设备、五金产品及电子产品批发	Wholesale of Machinery, Hardwares, Transport Means and Electronic Products	86	1410045.3	77534.7
贸易经纪与代理	Trade Manage and Agent	2	31851.5	644.8
其他批发	Other Wholesales	6	9822.4	
3.按经营形式分组	Grouped by Means of Operation			
独立门店	Independent Shop	268	15153562.3	77801.0
连锁总店	Headquarter of Chain Store	5	1072799.6	
连锁门店	Chain Store	3	157578.3	
其他	Other	148	8570543.4	79530.6
二、零售企业	**Retail Trade**	**612**	**18537823.8**	**531445.9**
1.按登记注册类型分组	Grouped by Registration Status			
内资	Domestic Funded Enterprises	547	13230781.9	401023.5
国有	State-owned Enterprises	12	918814.3	
集体	Collective-owned Enterprises	16	29152.3	
股份合作	Cooperative Enterprises			
联营	Joint Ownership Enterprises			
国有联营	State Joint Ownership Enterprises			
集体联营	Collective Joint Ownership Enterprises			
国有与集体联营	Joint State-collective Enterprises			

continued 1

(unit，10 000 yuan)

商品销售额			批发额		零售额	期末商品库存额
	公共网络商品销售额	银行卡支付商品销售额		出口		Value of
Sales Value	Public Network Sales	Bank Card Paid Sales	Wholesale Trade	Exports	Retail Trade	Stock at Final goods
2314507.4	1270393.8	1294917.5	2165264.5	515.0	149242.9	150260.3
3694270.8	2461.7		2545730.8	245413.0	1148540.0	173965.7
476261.5		4800.0	469509.8	5485.5	6751.7	46306.3
3387426.2	9808.2	27037.9	3118969.1	4491.6	268457.1	234954.5
18614436.5	9170.4	142961.7	16885786.9	58957.1	1728649.6	354782.7
1549623.3	25307.0	34587.7	1452422.7	418048.8	97200.6	121651.6
34724.2			34724.2	25768.8		4892.9
13102.7		51.0	13080.4		22.3	1065.4
19455359.3	41353.2	195973.2	16404516.7	509287.8	3050842.6	633068.6
1477305.2	1269914.5	1273594.8	1428360.3		48944.9	47470.9
187601.6			187280.4		321.2	6745.8
9021273.2	5873.4	35917.3	8722517.7	249392.0	298755.5	407794.7
21867450.1	**1662158.2**	**6447788.4**	**1006357.8**	**153045.5**	**20861092.3**	**2033156.7**
15619915.6	350418.7	3958906.9	898120.3	153045.5	14721795.3	1678203.8
977429.1	68.6	611944.1	236575.9		740853.2	97951.2
31177.8		1421.7	1529.3		29648.5	1539.7

16-6 续表2

单位：个、万元

分 类	Classify	单位数 Number of Enterprises	商品购进额 Total Purchases	进口 Exports
其他联营	Others Joint Ownership Enterprises			
有限责任公司	Limited Liability Corporations	313	8123335.3	210500.4
国有独资公司	State Sole Funded Corporations	8	209446.0	
其他有限责任公司	Other Limited Liability Corporations	305	7913889.3	210500.4
股份有限公司	Share-holding Corporations Ltd.	10	1029248.9	80544.6
私营	Private Enterprises	193	3122696.8	109978.5
私营独资	Private-funded Enterprises	5	13151.3	
私营合伙	Private Partnership Enterprises	2	9121.4	
私营有限责任公司	Private Limited Liability Corporations	179	2814393.0	73978.5
私营股份有限公司	Private Share-holding Corporations Ltd.	7	286031.1	36000.0
其他	Other Enterprises	3	7534.3	
港澳台商投资	Enterprises with Funds from Hong Kong, Macao &Taiwan	27	1566083.4	130182.4
外商投资	Foreign Funded Enterprises	20	3075799.8	240.0
个体经营户	Individusl Enterprises	18	665158.7	
2.按国民经济行业分组	Grouped by Registered Kind			
综合零售	General Retail Sales Trade	122	2436648.1	120.0
食品、饮料及烟草制品专门零售	Retail of Food, Beverage and Tobaccos	47	307307.5	366.2
纺织、服装及日用品专门零售	Retail of Textiles, Garments and Daily Articles	47	1430624.2	
文化、体育用品及器材专门零售	Retail of Culture, Sports Articles and Equipments	28	382111.4	240.0
医药及医疗器材专门零售	Retail of Medicines and Medical Appliances	27	229598.0	64.4
汽车、摩托车、燃料及零配件专门零售	Retail of Motor Vehicles, Motorcycles, Feuls and Parts	219	8317164.2	529726.0
家用电器及电子产品	Retail of Household Electronic Equipments	55	2263318.1	

continued 2

(unit，10 000 yuan)

商品销售额 Sales Value	公共网络商品销售额 Public Network Sales	银行卡支付商品销售额 Bank Card Paid Sales	批发额 Wholesale Trade	出口 Exports	零售额 Retail Trade	期末商品库存额 Value of Stock at Final goods
9769664.2	27062.5	2025553.6	303433.7		9466230.5	1141745.5
232738.7		71168.0	1164.7		231574.0	46228.0
9536925.5	27062.5	1954385.6	302269.0		9234656.5	1095517.5
1244842.7	122400.1	338159.6	260935.6	153045.5	983907.1	140179.5
3588467.0	200887.5	981827.9	95645.8		3492821.2	296451.7
14476.0		658.1			14476.0	1199.1
9127.1					9127.1	508.9
3268521.7	197351.3	813024.1	94494.9		3174026.8	284221.7
296342.2	3536.2	168145.7	1150.9		295191.3	10522.0
8334.8					8334.8	336.2
1982412.8	21371.9	873571.7	51579.9		1930832.9	195072.9
3583821.5	1290367.6	1615309.8	39279.4		3544542.1	139779.4
681300.2			17378.2		663922.0	20100.6
3778656.7	76828.6	1537415.6	21390.5		3757266.2	666436.6
484198.8	4283.2	44851.6	165653.8	136044.0	318545.0	140091.3
1473313.6	5027.4	206352.5	59354.7		1413958.9	166038.3
419109.7	68.6	65242.7	87644.8		331464.9	108677.7
289930.4	587.5	25513.2	12818.7		277111.7	49969.9
9132534.3	73669.7	2128334.2	419802.7	17001.5	8712731.6	779204.7
2697940.4	163815.1	393153.6	221382.1		2476558.3	83159.1

16-6 续表3

单位：个、万元

分　类	Classify	单位数 Number of Enterprises	商品购进额 Total Purchases	进口 Exports
专门零售	and Products			
五金、家具及室内装饰材料	etail of Hardwares, Furniture and Room	42	1742047.0	
专门零售	Decorative Building			
货摊、无店铺及其他零售业	No Fixed Stores and Other Retails	25	1429005.3	929.3
3.按经营形式分组	Grouped by Means of Operation			
独立门店	Independent Shop	492	13953355.1	505676.4
连锁总店	Headquarter of Chain Store	33	997094.8	64.4
连锁门店	Chain Store	8	411305.1	
其他	Other	79	3176068.8	25705.1
4.按零售业态分组	Grouped by Retail Size			
有店铺	Retail of Shop	574	16971549.1	530150.4
食杂店	Grocery Store			
便利店	Convenience Store	8	45082.5	
折扣店	Dime Store			
超市	Supermarket	50	242919.2	
大型超市	Larget Supermarket	17	1049036.7	
仓储会员店	Warehouse Club	4	9545.8	
百货店	Department Store	63	1207736.7	120.0
专业店	Special Store	204	6321486.8	188304.0
专卖店	Monopoly Store	171	4747392.1	341726.4
家居建材商店	Home-building Material Store	22	1283593.7	
购物中心	Shopping Center	16	1825691.6	
厂家直销中心	Factory Outlet Center	19	239064.0	
无店铺零售	Retail of No-shop	38	1566274.7	1295.5
电视购物	TV Shopping	2	180819.4	
邮购	Mail Order	1	954.6	366.2
网上商店	Online Stores	20	1232815.2	929.3
自动售货亭	Vending Machine			
电话购物	Tele Shopping			

continued 3

(unit, 10 000 yuan)

商品销售额 Sales Value	公共网络商品销售额 Public Network Sales	银行卡支付商品销售额 Bank Card Paid Sales	批发额 Wholesale Trade	出口 Exports	零售额 Retail Trade	期末商品库存额 Value of Stock at Final goods
2042906.5		659661.6	3098.8		2039807.7	34620.0
1548859.7	1337878.1	1387263.4	15211.7		1533648.0	4959.1
16696868.2	263430.7	3980527.7	584908.8	17001.5	16111959.4	1506989.5
1095466.2	67827.5	538752.6	6595.8		1088870.4	139058.4
588873.9	1175.4	286730.9	50196.6		538677.3	61680.8
3486241.8	1329724.6	1641777.2	364656.6	136044.0	3121585.2	325428.0
20008196.8	315915.5	5057636.2	862423.8	17001.5	19145773.0	1903191.1
58406.8		2869.6	4671.4		53735.4	4656.0
297266.5	1061.2	53037.2	39335.1		257931.4	30501.3
1277503.6	2204.5	384223.5			1277503.6	572384.2
11012.9	3161.9	202.9	2945.4		8067.5	877.4
2224886.2	66873.4	1081809.6	3620.4		2221265.8	67933.3
7082261.5	159031.7	1820142.5	374756.3		6707505.2	600104.0
5206435.4	66582.8	995920.1	272135.6	17001.5	4934299.8	549758.3
1442344.3		510704.1	2814.0		1439530.3	14863.7
2151692.7		146465.8	136694.0		2014998.7	36154.0
256386.9	17000.0	62260.9	25451.6		230935.3	25958.9
1859253.3	1346242.7	1390152.2	143934.0	136044.0	1715319.3	129965.6
181409.9		168205.7	447.1		180962.8	932.8
1186.3	819.0		367.3		819.0	574.1
1349537.8	1345423.7	1220967.6	4439.7		1345098.1	5045.1

16-7 限额以上住宿和餐饮业经营情况（2016年）

单位：个、万元

分类	Classify	单位数 Number of Enterprises	营业额 Business Revenue	银行卡支付营业额 Bank Card Paid Turnover
总计	**Total**	**604**	**1275340.5**	**250475.0**
一、住宿业	**Lodging Services**	**258**	**600755.6**	**149268.5**
1. 按国民经济行业分组	Grouped by Economic Sector			
旅游饭店	Tour Restaurant	184	508811.9	132920.4
一般旅馆	Common Hotel	65	73410.6	16319.6
其他住宿业	Others	9	18533.1	28.5
2. 按登记注册类型分组	Grouped by Registration Status			
内资企业	Domestic Funded Enterprises	242	505498.4	112072.1
国有	State-owned Enterprises	30	64524.0	9860.0
集体	Collective-owned Enterprises	1	382.7	362.5
股份合作	Cooperative Enterprises			
联营	Joint Ownership Enterprises			
国有联营	State Joint Ownership Enterprises			
集体联营	Collective Joint Ownership Enterprises			
国有与集体联营	Joint State-collective Ownership Enterprises			
其他联营	Other Joint Ownership Enterprises			
有限责任公司	Limited Liability Corporations	126	316716.0	74383.5
国有独资公司	State-funded Corporations	7	28360.3	2439.4
其他有限责任公司	Other Limited Liability Corporations	119	288355.7	71944.1
股份有限公司	Stock Limited Corporation	4	17176.5	33.2
私营	Private Enterprises	81	106699.2	27432.9
私营独资	Private-funded Enterprises	3	1849.0	385.7
私营合伙	Private Partnership Enterprises			
私营有限责任公司	Private Limited Liability Corporations	77	104405.8	27047.2
私营股份有限公司	Private Share Holding Corporations	1	444.4	
其他	Others			
港澳台商投资	Enterprises Funded by Hong Kong, Macao and Taiwan	7	42539.7	14668.6
外商投资	Foreign Funded Enterprises	9	52717.5	22527.8
个体经营	Individual Enterprises			

Statistic on Hotel Services and Catering Services above Designed Size (2016)

(unit, 10 000 yuan)

客房收入 From Hotel Room	公共网络客房收入 Public Network Room Revenue	餐费收入 From Meals	公共网络餐费收入 Public Network Catering Revenue	商品销售收入 From Commodities
360242.5	**35610.1**	**795660.0**	**20205.4**	**47329.2**
319610.1	**32975.9**	**220870.0**	**4590.3**	**13049.6**
264990.1	29420.3	189355.8	4410.9	11416.6
44414.1	3476.8	23949.8	170.3	1598.5
10205.9	78.8	7564.4	9.1	34.5
267002.5	27206.1	189212.7	4294.3	11485.6
29455.6	1967.6	26124.9	47.1	1826.9
138.0		131.8		112.9
160659.9	14831.5	127538.6	3565.5	4600.6
13089.3	1441.5	12977.9	82.5	357.9
147570.6	13390.0	114560.7	3483.0	4242.7
5858.6	31.1	4885.2	1.1	4113.8
70890.4	10375.9	30532.2	680.6	831.4
1141.4	619.3	373.3	1.1	41.6
69304.6	9756.6	30158.9	679.5	789.8
444.4				
23443.6	2928.1	12850.4	219.5	614.9
29164.0	2841.7	18806.9	76.5	949.1

16-7 续表1

单位：个、万元

分 类	Classify	单位数 Number of Enterprises	营业额 Business Revenue	银行卡支付营业额 Bank Card Paid Turnover
二、餐饮业	**Catering Trade**	**346**	**674584.9**	**101206.5**
1. 按国民经济行业分	Grouped by Economic Sector			
正餐服务	Dinner Services	335	616766.0	96122.3
快餐服务	Fast Food Services	8	48209.2	377.1
其他餐饮业	Other Catering Services	3	9609.7	4707.1
2. 按登记注册类型分	Grouped by Registration Status			
内资	Domestic Funded Enterprises	321	498740.0	97527.2
国有	State-owned Enterprises	4	10562.5	
集体	Collective-owned Enterprises			
股份合作	Cooperative Enterprises			
联营	Joint Ownership Enterprises			
国有联营	State Joint Ownership Enterprises			
集体联营	Collective Joint Ownership Enterprises			
国有与集体联营	Joint State-collective Ownership Enterprises			
其他联营	Other Joint Ownership Enterprises			
有限责任公司	Limited Liability Corporations	166	260240.4	35254.4
国有独资公司	State-funded Corporations	1	1147.4	
其他有限责任公司	Other Limited Liability Corporations	165	259093.0	35254.4
股份有限公司	Stock Limited Corporation	2	62236.4	29904.9
私营	Private Enterprises	146	154855.8	32367.9
私营独资	Private-funded Enterprises	12	5614.1	372.2
私营合伙	Private Partnership Enterprises			
私营有限责任公司	Private Limited Liability Corporations	131	147240.7	31661.5
私营股份有限公司	Private Share Holding Corporations	3	2001.0	334.2
其他	Others	3	10844.9	
港澳台商投资	Enterprises Funded by Hong Kong, Macao and Taiwan	6	39748.4	1326.4
外商投资	Foreign Funded Enterprises	5	101290.5	2352.9
个体经营	Individual Enterprises	14	34806.0	

continued 1

(unit, 10 000 yuan)

客房收入 From Hotel Room	公共网络客房收入 Public Network Room Revenue	餐费收入 From Meals	公共网络餐费收入 Public Network Catering Revenue	商品销售收入 From Commodities
40632.4	**2634.2**	**574790.0**	**15615.1**	**34279.6**
37571.4	2153.0	527046.9	10737.6	34109.9
50.0		41144.4	4841.1	169.7
3011.0	481.2	6598.7	36.4	
40214.3	2634.2	410107.6	8641.1	31250.7
992.8		7302.6		1446.5
27906.8	2549.3	215875.2	3721.3	6747.1
490.4		633.1		
27416.4	2549.3	215242.1	3721.3	6747.1
3019.4	20.7	34923.2	1296.0	19148.3
2880.2	64.2	146981.1	3623.8	3859.9
		5217.5	68.7	396.6
2880.2	64.2	139804.1	3555.1	3421.8
		1959.5		41.5
5415.1		5025.5		48.9
367.7		38366.9	6021.1	223.5
		94258.7	952.9	106.6
50.4		32056.8		2698.8

16-8 限额以上批发和零售业主要商品分类销售额（2016年）

Sale Values of Wholesale and Retail Enterprises above Designated Size by Category of Main Commodities (2016)

单位：万元 (10 000 yuan)

分类	Classify	销售合计 Total Sales Value	批发 Wholesale Value	零售 Retail Value
总计	**Total**	**44483853.5**	**24498178.2**	**19985675.3**
其中：通过公共网络实现的商品销售	Sales Achiered through the Prblis Network	2854973.2	1301166.3	1553806.9
粮油、食品类	Cereals, Oils and Foodstuffs	1482092.4	588281.6	893810.8
粮油类	Grain and Oil	497955.0	75164.4	422790.6
肉禽蛋类	Meat, Poultry and Eggs	157835.1	25963.1	131872.0
水产品类	Aquatic Products	39288.1	11190.0	28098.1
蔬菜类	Vegetables	220707.6	167757.0	52950.6
干鲜果品类	Fresh and Dried Fruit Category	336598.1	244808.2	91789.9
饮料类	Beverages	527915.5	229897.3	298018.2
烟酒类	Tobacco and Liquor	1715179.9	1423671.4	291508.5
服装、鞋帽、针、纺织品类	Clothing, Shoes, Hats and Textiles	5608683.2	2804913.3	2803769.9
#服装类	Clothing	4790488.3	2644321.0	2146167.3
鞋帽类	Shoes and Hats	513249.4	118348.9	394900.5
针、纺织品类	Knitwear and Textiles	304945.5	42243.4	262702.1
化妆品类	Cosmetics	401406.9	48912.5	352494.4
金银珠宝类	Gold,Silver and Jewelry	558980.9	165974.4	393006.5
日用品类	Articles for Daily Use	721248.1	94883.2	626364.9
#儿童玩具类	Children's Toys	78385.6		78385.6
五金、电料类	Hardwear and Electrical Materials	271745.7	96498.2	175247.5
体育、娱乐用品类	Sports and Recreation Articles	492559.0	15945.8	476613.2
#照相器材类	Photography Equipment	54231.1	10.0	54221.1
书报杂志类	Newspapers and Magazines	242798.4	144336.5	98461.9
电子出版物及音像制品类	E-journal and Video Products	82851.8		82851.8
家用电器和音像器材类	Household Appliances and Video Products	2115596.6	657321.3	1458275.3
中西药品类	Traditional Chinese and Western Medicine	3209870.4	2952491.5	257378.9
#西药	Western Medicine	2706493.3	2521719.9	184773.4
中草药及中成药	Chinese Herbal Medicine and Traditional Chinese Medicine	206749.5	154924.3	51825.2
文化办公用品类	Cultural and Official Goods	1014585.2	338577.4	676007.8
#计算机及其配套产品	Among Them： Computers and Ancillary Products	357793.3	203008.3	154785.0
家具类	Furniture	976105.4		976105.4
通讯器材类	Communication Appliances	933016.6	212784.3	720232.3
煤炭及制品类	Coal and Related Products	3536762.1	3536684.7	77.4
木材及制品类	Wood and Wooden Products	2890.6	2890.6	
石油及制品类	Petroleum and Related Products	8006863.9	6223307.2	1783556.7
化工材料及制品类	Raw Chemical Materials	428716.4	427644.7	1071.7
#化肥类	Chemical Fertilizers	50728.6	49686.8	1041.8
金属材料类	Metal Materials	2502870.9	2502870.9	
建筑及装潢材料类	Buildings and Decoration Materials	1116896.9	235816.9	881080.0
机电产品及设备类	Mechanical and Electrical Products	686528.6	678100.6	8428.0
#农机类	Agricultural Machinery			
汽车类	Automobile	7105606.5	883155.7	6222450.8
种子饲料类	Seeds and Feedstuff	10072.9	10054.3	18.6
棉麻类	Cotton,Hemp	46197.7	46197.7	
其他类	Others	685811.0	176966.2	508844.8

16-9 亿元以上商品交易市场成交情况（2016年）

Basic Statistics on Commodity Exchange Markets of Transaction Value over 100 Million Yuan（2016）

分 类	Classify	年末出租摊位数（个）Number of Rental Booths at Year-end (unit)	成交额（万元）Turnover (10 000 yuan)
粮油、食品类	Cereals, Oils and Foodstuffs	3998	1956982
#粮油类	Grain and Oil	468	320939
肉禽蛋类	Meat, Poultry and Eggs	753	125695
水产品类	Aquatic Products	500	199248
蔬菜类	Vegetables	1124	65550
干鲜果品类	Fresh and Dried Fruit Category	1125	1244932
饮料类	Beverages	1936	86120
烟酒类	Tobacco and Liquor	213	1754
服装、鞋帽、针纺织品类	Clothing, Shoes, Hats and Textiles	7574	675008
#服装类	Clothing	5136	439562
鞋帽类	Shoes and Hats	1339	159062
针纺织品类	Knitwear and Textiles	1099	76384
化妆品类	Cosmetics	76	1892
金银珠宝类	Gold,Silver and Jewelry	46	843
日用品类	Articles for Daily Use	772	33526
#洗涤用品类	Bathing and Washing		
儿童玩具类	Children's Toys	52	569
五金、电料类	Hardwear and Electrical Materials	905	18916
体育、娱乐用品类	Sports and Recreation Articles	436	17664
书报杂志类	Newspapers and Magazines		
电子出版物及音像制品类	E-journal and Video Products		
家用电器和音像器材类	Household Appliances and Video Products	22	748
中西药品类	Traditional Chinese and Western Medicine	98	200177
#西药	Western Medicine		
中草药及中成药	Chinese Herbal Medicine and Traditional Chinese Medicine	98	200177
文化办公用品类	Cultural and Official Goods	787	215791
#计算机及其配套产品	Computer and Related Products	430	183301
家具类	Furniture	411	31283
通讯器材类	Communication Appliances	1313	234521
煤炭及制品类	Coal and Related Products		
木材及制品类	Wood and Wooden Products		
石油及制品类	Petroleum and Related Products		
化工材料及制品类	Raw Chemical Materials	30	123100
#化肥类	Chemical Fertilizers		
金属材料类	Metal Materials	75	203300
建筑及装潢材料类	Buildings and Decoration Materials	4855	483383
机电产品及设备类	Mechanical and Electrical Products	806	168810
#农机类	Agricultural Machinery		
汽车类	Automobile	1539	552542
种子饲料类	Seeds and Feedstuff		
棉麻类	Cotton,Hemp		
其他类	Others	160	96841

16-10 批发和零售业连锁经营情况（2016年）

Basic Statistics on Chain Business of Wholesale and Retail Trades（2016）

指　标	Item	本年合计 Total	上年合计 Total Last Year	本年直营店 Regular Chain
一、门店总数（个）	**Number of Stores(unit)**	**1209**	**1228**	**1035**
二、年末从业人员数（人）	**Employees at Year-end(person)**	**18800**	**19341**	**18008**
三、年末零售营业面积（平方米）	**Operating Area of Retail at Year-end(sq.m)**	**829784**	**831733**	**814770**
四、连锁门店商品购进额（万元）	**Purchases Value of Chain Stores(10 000 yuan)**	**2677416**	**3099474**	**2647521**
其中：统一配送商品购进额	Centralized Purchases and Delivery	2258224	2791305	2228329
其中：自有配送中心配送商品购进额	Self Centralized Purchases and Delivery	2058438	2578479	2036484
非自有配送中心配送商品购进额	Non-self Centralized Purchases and Delivery	90620	122096	90620
五、连锁门店商品销售额（万元）	**Sales Value of Chain Store(10 000 yuan)**	**3299229**	**3585557**	**3261752**
其中：零售额	Retail Value	1334454	1401769	1296977

16-10 续表 continued

指　标	Item	上年直营店 Regular Chain Last Year	本年加盟店 Franchise	上年加盟店 Franchise Last Year
一、门店总数（个）	**Number of Stores(unit)**	**1075**	**174**	**153**
二、年末从业人员数（人）	**Employees at Year-end(person)**	**18625**	**792**	**716**
三、年末零售营业面积（平方米）	**Operating Area of Retail at Year-end(sq.m)**	**812639**	**15014**	**19094**
四、连锁门店商品购进额（万元）	**Purchases Value of Chain Stores(10 000 yuan)**	**3085360**	**29895**	**14114**
其中：统一配送商品购进额	Centralized Purchases and Delivery	2777191	29895	14114
其中：自有配送中心配送商品购进额	Self Centralized Purchases and Delivery	2565894	21954	12585
非自有配送中心配送商品购进额	Non-self Centralized Purchases and Delivery	122096		
五、连锁门店商品销售额（万元）	**Sales Value of Chain Store(10 000 yuan)**	**3569291**	**37477**	**16266**
其中：零售额	Retail Value	1385503	37477	16266

16-11 住宿和餐饮业连锁经营情况（2016年）

Basic Statistics on Chain Business of Hotels and Catering Services（2016）

指 标	Item	本年合计 Total	上年合计 Total Last Year
一、门店总数（个）	**Number of Stores(unit)**	**202**	**195**
二、年末从业人员数（人）	**Employees at Year-end(person)**	**8919**	**10121**
三、年末餐饮营业面积（平方米）	**Operating Area of Retail at Year-end(sq.m)**	**97026**	**88741**
四、客房总数（间）	**Guest Rooms(room)**		
五、床位数（张）	**Guest Beds(bed)**		
六、餐位数（位）	**Dining Seats(set)**	**61528**	**55906**
七、连锁门店商品购进额（万元）	**Operating Area of Catering Services at Year end(room)(10 000yuan)**	**60018**	**55263**
其中：统一配送商品购进额	Centralized Purchases and Delivery	57750	52661
其中：自有配送中心配送商品购进额	Self Centralized Purchases and Delivery	50090	45413
非自有配送中心配送商品购进额	Non-self Centralized Purchases and Delivery	4655	4242
八、连锁门店商品营业额（万元）	**Sales Value of Chain Store(10 000 yuan)**	**125277**	**123484**
其中：餐费收入	Catering Revenues	124434	122558
商品销售额	Sales Value	843	926

16-11 续表 continued

指 标	Item	本年直营店 Regular Chain	上年直营店 Regular Chain Last Year
一、门店总数（个）	**Number of Stores(unit)**	**197**	**190**
二、年末从业人员数（人）	**Employees at Year-end(person)**	**8596**	**9784**
三、年末餐饮营业面积（平方米）	**Operating Area of Retail at Year-end(sq.m)**	**96326**	**88041**
四、客房总数（间）	**Guest Rooms(room)**		
五、床位数（张）	**Guest Beds(bed)**		
六、餐位数（位）	**Dining Seats(set)**	**61362**	**55806**
七、连锁门店商品购进额（万元）	**Operating Area of Catering Services at Year end(room)(10 000yuan)**	**58994**	**54454**
其中：统一配送商品购进额	Centralized Purchases and Delivery	57750	52661
其中：自有配送中心配送商品购进额	Self Centralized Purchases and Delivery	50090	45413
非自有配送中心配送商品购进额	Non-self Centralized Purchases and Delivery	4655	4242
八、连锁门店商品营业额（万元）	**Sales Value of Chain Store(10 000 yuan)**	**123644**	**122072**
其中：餐费收入	Catering Revenues	122801	121146
商品销售额	Sales Value	843	926

16-12 限额以上住宿和餐饮业经营情况

单位：个、亿元

分 类	Classify	2013 单位数 Number of Enterprises	2013 营业额 Business Revenue
总计	**Total**	**652**	**144.29**
一、住宿业	**Lodging Services**	**232**	**61.02**
1. 按登记注册类型分组	Grouped by Registration Status		
内资企业	Domestic Funded Enterprises	217	50.41
国有	State-owned Enterprises	37	8.02
集体	Collective-owned Enterprises	3	0.33
股份合作	Cooperative Enterprises		
联营	Joint Ownership Enterprises		
国有联营	State Joint Ownership Enterprises		
集体联营	Collective Joint Ownership Enterprises		
国有与集体联营	Joint State-collective Ownership Enterprises		
其他联营	Other Joint Ownership Enterprises		
有限责任公司	Limited Liability Corporations	119	33.15
国有独资公司	State-funded Corporations	4	1.48
其他有限责任公司	Other Limited Liability Corporations	115	31.67
股份有限公司	Stock Limited Corporation	3	0.63
私营	Private Enterprises	54	8.27
私营独资	Private-funded Enterprises	4	0.14
私营合伙	Private Partnership Enterprises	1	0.02
私营有限责任公司	Private Limited Liability Corporations	47	7.99
私营股份有限公司	Private Share Holding Corporations	2	0.12
其他	Others	1	0.01
港澳台商投资	Enterprises Funded by Hong Kong, Macao and Taiwan	6	4.62
外商投资	Foreign Funded Enterprises	8	5.97
个体经营	Individual Enterprises	1	0.02
2. 按国民经济行业分组	Grouped by Economic Sector		
旅游饭店	Tour Restaurant	187	55.43
一般旅馆	Common Hotel	39	4.78
其他住宿业	Others	6	0.81

Statistic on Hotel Services and Catering Services above Designed Size

(unit, 100 million yuan)

2014		2015		2016	
单位数 Number of Enterprises	营业额 Business Revenue	单位数 Number of Enterprises	营业额 Business Revenue	单位数 Number of Enterprises	营业额 Business Revenue
602	**141.65**	**567**	**127.75**	**604**	**127.53**
237	**63.05**	**239**	**57.99**	**258**	**60.08**
220	51.51	221	47.30	242	50.55
32	7.38	29	6.48	30	6.45
2	0.24	2	0.18	1	0.04
119	31.79	119	30.21	126	31.67
4	1.62	4	1.32	7	2.84
115	30.17	115	28.89	119	28.83
4	1.49	5	1.74	4	1.72
63	10.61	66	8.69	81	10.67
3	0.14	3	0.12	3	0.18
1	0.06				
57	10.30	62	8.54	77	10.45
2	0.11	1	0.03	1	0.04
7	5.25	8	5.17	7	4.25
10	6.29	10	5.52	9	5.27
181	55.93	176	50.12	184	50.88
51	5.93	56	6.15	65	7.34
5	1.19	7	1.72	9	1.85

16-12 续表1

单位：个、亿元

分 类	Classify	2013 单位数 Number of Enterprises	2013 营业额 Business Revenue
二、餐饮业	**Catering Trade**	**420**	**83.27**
1. 按登记注册类型分	Grouped by Registration Status		
内资	Domestic Funded Enterprises	313	53.80
国有	State-owned Enterprises	5	1.38
集体	Collective-owned Enterprises	1	0.06
股份合作	Cooperative Enterprises		
联营	Joint Ownership Enterprises		
国有联营	State Joint Ownership Enterprises		
集体联营	Collective Joint Ownership Enterprises		
国有与集体联营	Joint State-collective Ownership Enterprises		
其他联营	Other Joint Ownership Enterprises		
有限责任公司	Limited Liability Corporations	179	32.91
国有独资公司	State-funded Corporations	3	0.40
其他有限责任公司	Other Limited Liability Corporations	176	32.51
股份有限公司	Stock Limited Corporation	4	4.96
私营	Private Enterprises	120	13.88
私营独资	Private-funded Enterprises	13	0.67
私营合伙	Private Partnership Enterprises	1	0.03
私营有限责任公司	Private Limited Liability Corporations	103	12.98
私营股份有限公司	Private Share Holding Corporations	3	0.20
其他	Others	4	0.61
港澳台商投资	Enterprises Funded by Hong Kong, Macao and Taiwan	7	8.13
外商投资	Foreign Funded Enterprises	8	10.02
个体经营	Individual Enterprises	92	11.32
2. 按国民经济行业分	Grouped by Economic Sector		
正餐服务	Dinner Services	396	72.61
快餐服务	Fast Food Services	15	9.69
饮料及冷饮服务	Beverage and Cold Beverage Services		
其他餐饮业	Other Catering Services	9	0.97

continued 1

(100 million yuan)

2014		2015		2016	
单位数 Number of Enterprises	营业额 Business Revenue	单位数 Number of Enterprises	营业额 Business Revenue	单位数 Number of Enterprises	营业额 Business Revenue
365	**78.60**	**328**	**69.76**	**346**	**67.46**
310	53.41	284	50.46	321	49.87
5	1.14	4	1.10	4	1.06
177	33.13	167	31.89	166	26.02
2	0.38	1	0.12	1	0.11
175	32.75	166	31.77	165	25.91
3	4.28	1	3.53	2	6.22
121	14.18	108	12.58	146	15.49
12	0.63	9	0.46	12	0.56
106	13.32	97	11.97	131	14.73
3	0.23	2	0.15	3	0.20
4	0.68	4	1.36	3	1.08
7	6.88	7	4.28	6	3.97
7	10.04	6	9.94	5	10.13
41	8.27	31	5.08	14	3.48
351	69.48	315	63.80	335	61.68
7	7.74	7	4.71	8	4.82
7	1.38	6	1.25	3	0.96

主要统计指标解释

批发业 指批发商向批发、零售单位及其他企事业、机关单位批量销售生活用品和生产资料的活动，以及从事进出口贸易和贸易经纪与代理的活动。批发商可以对所批发的货物拥有所有权，并以本单位、公司的名义进行交易活动；也可以不拥有货物的所有权，而以中介身份做代理销售商。还包括各类商品批发市场中固定摊位的批发活动。

零售业 指百货商店、超级市场、专门零售商店、品牌专卖店、售货摊等主要面向最终消费者（如居民等）的销售活动。包括以互联网、邮政、电话、售货机等方式的销售活动，还包括在同地点，后面加工生产，前面销售的店铺（如前店后厂的面包房）。不包括：谷物、种子、饲料、牲畜、矿产品、生产用原料、化工原料、农用化工产品、机械设备（用车、计算机及通信设备等除外）等生产资料的销售（批发业）；非零售单位附带的零售活动（如汽车修理单位销售汽车零件）；商业零售单位所在商厦的物业管理（物业管理）；商业零售单位所在的商品市场、商业大厦的市场管理活动（市场管理）。

住宿业 指有偿为顾客提供临时住宿的服务活动，不包括提供长期住宿场所的活动（如出租房屋、公寓等）。

餐饮业 指在一定场所，对食物进行现场烹饪、调制，并出售给顾客主要供现场消费的服务活动。

社会消费品零售总额 指批发和零售业、餐饮业、新闻出版业、邮政业和其他服务业等，售予城乡居民用于生活消费的商品和社会集团用于公共消费的商品之总量。社会消费品零售总额包括：

一、批发和零售业企业（单位）售予城乡居民用于生活消费和社会集团用于公共消费的商品。包括：

1. 售予城乡居民的各种生活消费品；

2. 售予入境旅游的外国人、华侨、港澳台同胞的各类商品；

3. 售予行政事业单位、社会团体、军队和武警等机构的商品，以及以零售方式售予各类企业的商品。具体包括：用于非生产和社会交往的办公用品，如通讯设备、计算器具和设备、电讯网络设备、文印设备、音像视听器材和设备、纸张、本册、文具及装订文印材料、家具、日用电器、针纺织品、清洁卫生用品、文体用品、奖品、纪念品、礼品等；供内部人员乘坐的交通工具和燃料；用于办公设施修缮的各类配件、材料、工具等；用于取暖和防暑降温的设备、燃料、材料及食品等；专用于教学的用品和设备；非营利医疗机构的中、西药品、中药材和医疗设备器材；非专用的劳动保护用品；不对外营业的内部食堂用的餐具、炊具、设备、清洁卫生工具和食品、燃料等；军队、武警用于其人员生活的衣着品和个人用品；其他各类非生产性设备和用品。

二、餐饮业出售的主食、菜肴、烟酒饮料和其他商品。

三、新闻出版业、邮政业售予城乡居民、企事业单位、军队和武警等机构的书报杂志、音像制品、邮品等。

四、其他服务业出售的食品、烟酒饮料、服装鞋帽、日常生活用品、医药保健用品、艺术品、工艺美术品、玩具、殡葬用品以及其他消费品。

批发和零售业商品购进、销售、库存总额 指各种登记注册类型的批发和零售业企业（单位）以本企业（单位）为总体的，从国内、国外市场购进的商品总量，销售和出口的商品总量、库存的商品总量等情况。该指标可以反映商品流转过程中商品的购进、销售、库存之间的比例关系和存在的问题。

购进总额 指从本企业（单位）以外的单位和个人购进（包括从境外直接进口）作为转卖或加工后转卖的商品总额。它反映批发和零售业从国内、国外市场上购进商品的总量。商品购进包括：（1）从工农业生产者购进的商品；（2）从出版社、报社的出版发行部门购进的图书、杂志和报纸；（3）从各种登记注册类型的批发和零售业企业（单位）购进的商品；（4）从其他单位购进的商品，如从机关、团体、企业等单位购进的剩余物资，从住宿和餐饮业、其他服务业购进的商品，从海关、市场管理部门购进的缉私和没收的商品，从居民手中收购的废旧商品等；（5）从国（境）外直接进口的商品。不包括企业（单位）为自身经营用和未通过买卖行为而收入的商品以及销售退回、商品升溢等。

销售总额 指对本企业（单位）以外的单位和个人出售（包括对境外直接出口）的商品总额。它反映批发和零售业在国内市场上销售商品以及出口商品的总量。商品销售包括：（1）售给城乡居民和社会集团消费用的商品；（2）售给工业、农业、建筑业、运输邮电业、批发和零售业、住宿和餐饮业、其他服务业等作为生产、经营使用的商品；（3）售给批发和零售业作为转卖或加工后转卖的商品；（4）对国（境）外直接出口的商品。不包括出售本企业（单位）自用的废旧包装用品，未通过买卖行为付出的商品，经本单位介绍、由买卖双方直接结算、本单位只收取手续费的业务，购货退出的商品以及商品损耗和损失等。

库存总额 指报告期末各种登记注册类型的批发和零售业企业（单位）已取得所有权的商品。它反映批发和零售业企业（单位）的商品库存情况和对市场商品供应的保证程度。商品库存包括：（1）存放在批发和零售业经营单位（如门市部、批发站、经营处）仓库、货场、货柜和货架中的商品；（2）挑选、整理、包装中的商品；（3）已记入购进而尚未运到本单位的商品，即发货单或银行承兑凭证已到而货未到的商品；（4）寄放他处的商品，如因购货方拒绝承付而暂时存放在购货方的商品和已办完加工成品收回手续而未提回的商品；（5）委托其他单位代销（未作销售或调出）尚未售出的商品；（6）代其他单位购进尚未交付的商品。不包括所有权不属于本单位的商品、委托外单位加工生产尚未收回成品的商品、外贸企业代理其他单位从国外进口尚未付给订货单位的商品、代国家物资储备部门保管的商品等。

住宿和餐饮业营业额 指住宿和餐饮业法人企业（单位）在经营活动中因提供服务或销售商品等取得的收入。包括：客房收入、餐费收入、商品销售额和其他收入。客房收入指住宿和餐饮业法人企业（单位）在经营活动中因提供住宿服务取得的收入。餐费收入指住宿和餐饮业法人企业（单位）因为顾客提供就餐服务取得的收入，包括经烹饪、调制加工后出售的各种食品，如主食、炒菜、凉拌菜等的收入。商品销售额指住宿和餐饮业法人企业（单位）伴随服务而出售商品所取得的收入（含增值税）。其他收入指营业收入中除客房收入、餐费收入、商品销售额以外的其他收入，包括娱乐、健身和商务服务等。

连锁企业（或称连锁店、连锁公司） 指在核心企业或总店的领导下，由分散的、经营同类商品或服务的企业或活动单位，采取共同方针，实行集中采购和分散销售的有机结合，通过规范化经营，实现规模效益的经济联合组织形式。一般连锁店应由若干个分店组成。其经营特征：（1）经营同类商品；（2）使用统一商号；（3）统一采购配送，采购与销售相分离（部分商品可根据物流合理和保质保鲜原则，由供应商直接送货到门店，其余均由总部统一配送）。

连锁门店的形式分为直营连锁和加盟连锁。

直营连锁也叫正规连锁。指连锁门店均由总部独资或控股开设，在总部的直接领导下统一经营。总部采取纵深似的管理方式，直接下令掌管所有的零售门店，零售门店也必须完全接受总部指挥。这是大型垄断商业资本通过吞并、兼并或独资、控股等途径，发展壮大自身实力和规模的一种形式。

加盟连锁包括特许连锁和自由连锁两种形式。

特许连锁指各连锁门店（被特许人）通过合同形式，取得使用总部（特许人）商标、商号、经营技术和销售总部开发的商品的特许权，各加盟连锁门店为独立法人，在总部指导下统一经营。

自由连锁也称自愿连锁。指连锁公司的门店均为独立法人，各自的资产所有权关系不变，在公司总部的指导下共同经营。各成员店使用共同的店名，与总部订阅有关购、销、宣传等方面的合同，并按合同开展经营活动。在合同规定的范围之外，各成员店可以自由活动。根据自愿原则，各成员店可自由加入连锁体系，也可自由退出。

Explanatory Notes on Main Statistical Indicators

Wholesale Trade refers to the activities of wholesaler selling at wholesale commodities for daily use and capital goods to enterprises of wholesale and retail trades and other enterprises, institutions and government offices, including the activities of wholesaler engaged in import and export and acting as a trade agent. The wholesaler may have the right of ownership over the commodities of wholesale and trade in the name of its own or a company, the wholesaler may not have the right of ownership, only acts an agent. The wholesale trade also include the activities of wholesaler at the fixed stalls of the wholesale market of different commodities.

Retail Trade refers to the activities of department store,supermarket, franchised store, brand store, retail stall and on-the-spot-making-selling store selling commodities to the final consumers (citizens) by any means including internet, post, telephone, sales machine. Retail trade excludes the activities of sales of capital goods such a grain, seed, feed, livestock, mineral products, raw material for production, industrial chemicals, chemical products for farm, machine and equipment (vehicle, computer and communication equipment), and the activities of supplementary sales of non-retailer such as the sales of spare parts of car repair business

Hotel Services refer to the activities of enterprises providing paid services of lodging to the customer, excluding the activities of providing long period of services of lodging (such as leased house and apartments).

Catering Services refer to the activities of enterprises providing on-the-spot services of selling food cooked and prepared to the customer in certain sites

Total Retail Sales of Consumer Goods refer to the sum of retail sales of commodities sold by wholesale and retail trades, catering services, publishing, post and telecommunications and other service industries to urban and rural households for household consumption and to social institutions for public consumption. Retail sales of consumer goods include:

1) Sales sold by wholesale and retail trades to urban~thA and rural households for household consumption and to social institutions for public consumption.

a) of commodities to urban and rural households;

b) of commodities to foreigners, overseas Chinese and Chinese compatriots from Hong Kong, Macao and Taiwan visiting China;

c) of commodities to government agencies, institutions, social organizations, military and armed police units, and commodities to enterprises in the form of retail sales. More specifically, they include: office facilities and articles for non-production purposes such as communications equipment, computing equipment and instruments, TV and network equipment, printing and copying equipment, audio-visual equipment and instruments, paper, notebooks, stationeries, furniture, electric appliances, knitwear, sanitation and cleaning articles, cultural and sport articles, articles for prizes, souvenirs, etc.; transport vehicles and fuels for employees; materials, spare parts and tools for the maintenance of office facilities; equipment, fuels, materials and food for winter heating or summer cooling purposes; articles and equipment for teaching purpose; Chinese and western medicines and medical equipment and facilities purchased by non profit-making medical institutes; non- specialized work safety articles; cooking utensils, tableware, equipment, cleaning articles, food and fuels purchased by in-house cafeterias; clothes and personal articles purchased by military or armed police units for their officials and soldiers; and other equipment and articles for non-production purposes.

2) Sales of stable food, cooked dishes, beverages, tobaccos and other articles by catering units.

3) Sales of books, newspapers, magazines, audio-visual products and post products by publishing, post and telecommunications departments to urban and rural households and to enterprises, institutions, military and armed police units.

4) Sales of food, beverages, tobaccos, clothing, hats, footwear, articles for daily use, medicines, medical and health articles, work of art, handicrafts, toys, funeral articles and other articles by other service industries.

Purchase, Sales and Stock of Commodities by Wholesale and Retail Trades refer to the total volume of commodities purchased, total volume of sales and exports, and the stock of commodities by wholesale and retail enterprises (establishments) of different status of registration from domestic and overseas markets. This indicator reflects the relationship among purchase, sales and stock of commodities in the circulation of goods and reveals the existing problems.

Total Purchases of Commodities refer to the total value of purchases of commodities by enterprises (establishments)from other establishments or individuals (including direct import from abroad) for the purpose of re-selling, either with or without further processing of the commodities purchased. The commodities include: (1) commodities purchased from agricultural and industrial producer, wholesaler, retailer, publishing house and other service business; (2) commodities purchased from institutions and government departments; (3) confiscated goods purchased from the customs authorities or market management agencies; (4) second-hand goods and wastes purchased from residents; The commodities exclude 1 commodities purchased by enterprises (establishments) for use in their own business operation, commodities obtained without buying or selling procedures such as materials, consumable goods of low value, office appliances, etc. 2 received goods without trading, such as goods handed over from others, borrowed goods, preserved goods for others, donated goods from others, processed and retrieved goods, etc. 3. goods of direct settlement between buyer and seller with handling fees introduced by others, 4. goods returned or refused to pay by the buyer, 5. excessive goods.

Total Sales of Commodities refer to value of commodities sold by the establishments to other establishments and individuals (including goods sold for self consumption, including the value-added tax). The commodities include: (1) commodities sold to urban and rural residents and social groups for their consumption; (2) commodities sold to establishments in all industries for their production and operation, including agriculture, industry, construction, transportation, post and telecommunications, catering services, and public utility including commodities sold to wholesale and retail establishments for re-selling, with or without further processing; and (3) commodities for direct export to abroad.Excluded are (1) extended commodities without trading, such as goods handed over to other enterprises and institutions because of the change of organizations, lent goods, returned goods preserved for others, extended processing materials and samples donated to others, (2) goods of direct settlement between buyer and seller with handling fees introduced by others, (3)goods returned after purchase, (4) damaged and spoiled goods, (5) waste and used goods of selfuse,

Total Stock of Commodities refers to total commodities possessed by wholesaler and retailer of various types of registration status at the end of the reference period, reflecting the commodity stock level of various wholesaler and retailer and the potential for market supply. It includes: (1) commodities located in storage, garages, counters, and shelves of operating places (such as sale stores, wholesale centres, and operating offices) ; (2) commodities in the process of being selected, sorted, and packed; (3) commodities not arrived but recorded as purchase in the account, i.e. commodities not arrived but payment receipts for the commodities from the sellers or the banks arrived; (4) commodities deposited in other places rather than places mentioned above, for instance: commodities in the hold of purchasers temporarily due to the refusal of payment and commodities not taken back after going through the formalities; (5) commodities entrusted to other units to sell but not sold yet; (6) commodities purchased for other units but not delivered yet. Commodities not included as stock are those not owned by the enterprises (units), commodities on commission for processing but not yet delivered, imported commodities of agency of foreign trade enterprise but not yet delivered to ordering units and finally those put in stock on behalf of the state material reserves units.

Business Revenue of Hotels and Catering Services refers to revenue received from providing services or selling commodities by corporate enterprises and establishments engaged in hotels and catering services, including income from hotels, from catering services, from selling of commodities and from other services. Income from hotels refers to income of corporate enterprises and establishments engaged in hotels and catering services by providing lodging services. Income from catering services refers to income of corporate enterprises and establishments engaged in hotels and catering services by providing catering services, including selling of cooked or prepared foods such as staple food, cooked dishes or cold dishes. Income from selling of commodities refers to income of corporate enterprises and establishments engaged in hotels and catering services by selling commodities (including value-added tax) that accompany the services they provide. Income from other activities refers to income received other than income from hotels, catering services or selling of commodities, such as income from providing recreation, fitness or business services.

Chain Head Stores (headquarter) refer to the core leading stores responsible for development, allocation, administration and utilization of resources (name of stores, brand of stores, operation model, service standard, management way, ect.) of chain stores. Chain stores refers to the stores engaged in providing homogeneous commodities or services, with the central leadership of head store and guided by common policies, conduct centralized purchase and distributed selling of commodities, in order to gain better efficiency through standardized operation. The chain stores include regular chain stores, franchise chain stores and voluntary chain stores.

Regular Chain store refers to chain stores that are invested or controlled by the headquarters. They operate under direct and unified management from the headquarters.

Franchise chain store refers to the chain stores (franchisees) which are franchised with operation resources such as trade marks, names, patent and operation know-how by the franchisors in form of contract and pay the operation fees to the franchisors.

Voluntary chain store refers the stores operate jointly on the voluntary bases while maintaining their status of independent legal entities with full ownership of their assets. They sell goods of same brand from same channel of resource to the consumers.

17 对外经济贸易和旅游

FOREIGN TRADE AND ECONOMIC COOPERATION TOURISM

资料整理：马晓庆
Data management: Ma Xiaoqing
数据审核：栾立森
Data audit: Luan Lisen

第十七部分　对外经济贸易和旅游

一、简要说明

本章资料包括对外经济贸易、利用外资和旅游等方面资料，由西安市统计局贸易外经处根据西安市商务局、海关和旅游局提供资料整理。

二、主要指标

进出口总值（亿元）	1829.95	比上年增长	3.9%
#出　口	947.31	比上年增长	15.6%
实际利用外商直接投资额（亿美元）	45.05	比上年增长	12.4%

17 FOREIGN TRADE AND ECONOMIC COOPERATION,TOURISM

Ⅰ.Brief Introduction

Data in this chapter consists of data on foreign trade, using of foreign capital and fund and tourism. Data on foreign economy and trade and tourism are compiled and provided by Foreign Economy Division of the Xi'an Bureau of Statistics according to the data from Xi'an Bureau of Commerce, Xi'an Custom Office and Xi'an Bureau of Tourism.

Ⅱ.Major Indicators

		Increase over Preceding Year
Total Imports and Exports (100 mil.yuan)	1829.95	3.9%
#Exports	947.31	15.6%
Total Amount of Foreign Direst zwestment (USD 100 mil.)	45.05	12.4%

17-1 主要年份外资、外贸基本情况

Main Indicators on Foreign Investments and International Trading in Representative Years

指　标	Item	1990	1995	2000	2005	2009	2010
一、利用外资签定协议项目(个)	**Number of Projects of Foreign Capital Used through the Signed Agreements and Contracts (unit)**	**11**	**184**	**135**	**157**	**65**	**82**
利用外资签定协议金额（万美元）	Value of Foreign Capital Used through the Signed Agreements and Contracts(USD 10 000)	415	28956	54123	121499	60027	119689
外商实际直接投资额（万美元）	Value of Foreign Direct Investment (USD 10 000)	1154	18653	15633	57113	121872	156653
二、进出口总值（万美元）	**Total Imports and Exports (USD 10 000)**	**38229**	**137510**	**173696**	**390146**	**724618**	**1039273**
#进口总值	Total Imports	9939	27347	67634	126705	391504	507544
出口总值	Total Exports	28290	110163	106062	263441	333114	531729
进出口差额(出口-进口)	Balance of Imports and Exports	18351	82816	38428	136736	-58390	24185
三、国际旅游者人数总计（万人次）	**Total Number of International Tourists (10 000 person-times)**	**25.88**	**41.35**	**65.03**	**77.56**	**67.29**	**84.18**
#外国人	Foreigners	15.40	37.11	54.65	65.86	59.09	73.21
港、澳、台同胞	Chinese Compatriot From Hong Kong, Macao and Taiwan	10.07	4.16	10.38	11.70	8.20	10.97
四、国际旅游者人天数总计（万人天）	**Total Number of Days of International Tourists (10 000 person/day)**	**55.03**	**84.44**	**162.69**	**224.93**	**195.14**	**241.67**
#外国人	Foreigners	33.48	75.71	131.44	190.99	171.36	211.48
港、澳、台同胞	Chinese Compatriot From Hong Kong, Macao and Taiwan	21.55	8.56	31.15	33.94	23.78	30.19
五、国际旅游收入（亿元）	**Earning of International Tourism (100 millon yuan)**	**1.96**	**10.38**	**22.41**	**33.54**	**31.05**	**42.40**
#商品收入	Income from Mercantile	0.44	2.57	7.71	11.25	8.94	11.87
劳务收入	Income from Labour Service	1.52	7.81	14.70	22.29	22.11	30.53
六、国际旅游者在西安人均停留天数（天）	**Number of Days of Average Tourists Staying in Xi'an (day)**	**2.1**	**2.0**	**2.5**	**2.9**	**2.9**	**2.9**

注：2014年、2015年市旅游局未发布国际旅游统计数据。
本表来源于市商务局、西安海关、市旅游局。

17-1 续表 continued

指 标	Item	2011	2012	2013	2014*	2015*	2016*
一、利用外资签定协议项目(个)	**Number of Projects of Foreign Capital Used through the Signed Agreements and Contracts (unit)**	**99**	**87**	**152**	**103**	**73**	**72**
利用外资签定协议金额（万美元）	Value of Foreign Capital Used through the Signed Agreements and Contracts(USD 10 000)	120083	360264	251874	255321	193684	102103
外商实际直接投资额（万美元）	Value of Foreign Direct Investment (USD 10 000)	200522	247800	312994	370310	400833	450466
二、进出口总值（万美元）	**Total Imports and Exports (USD 10 000)**	**1260179**	**1301446**	**1798534**	**15321514**	**17616896**	18299476
#进口总值	Total Imports	677517	571568	950715	7974693	9418142	8826392
出口总值	Total Exports	582662	729878	847819	7346822	8198754	9473084
进出口差额(出口-进口)	Balance of Imports and Exports	-94855	158310	-102896	-627871	-1219388	646692
三、国际旅游者人数总计（万人次）	**Total Number of International Tourists (10 000 person-times)**	**100.23**	**115.34**	**121.11**			
#外国人	Foreigners	88.63	101.40	106.89			
港、澳、台同胞	Chinese Compatriot From Hong Kong, Macao and Taiwan	11.60	13.94	14.22			
四、国际旅游者人天数总计（万人天）	**Total Number of Days of International Tourists (10 000 person/day)**	**287.09**	**334.44**	**351.11**			
#外国人	Foreigners	254.78	294.90	310.26			
港、澳、台同胞	Chinese Compatriot From Hong Kong, Macao and Taiwan	32.31	39.54	40.85			
五、国际旅游收入（亿元）	**Earning of International Tourism (100 millon yuan)**	**51.28**	**59.89**	**64.16**			
#商品收入	Income from Mercantile	11.38	14.19	14.69			
劳务收入	Income from Labour Service	39.90	45.70	49.47			
六、国际旅游者在西安人均停留天数 （天）	**Number of Days of Average Tourists Staying in Xi'an (day)**	**2.9**	**2.9**	**2.9**			

注：2014年以后进出口数据计量单位为万元。

17–2 主要年份利用外资情况

Utilization of Foreign Capital in Representative Years

单位：万美元 (USD 10 000)

年 份 Year	利用外资签订协议金额 Value of Foreign Capital Used through the Signed Agreements and Contracts	外商实际直接投资额 Direct Foreign Investment
1983	3500	800
1984	8	
1985	8361	1106
1986	19919	4010
1987	3218	5552
1988	2423	6758
1989	1645	11632
1990	415	1154
1991	591	1094
1992	24165	5200
1993	57289	8996
1994	20321	15240
1995	28956	18653
1996	35978	20510
1997	27214	22057
1998	40034	22286
1999	40390	13801
2000	54123	15633
2001	60736	17687
2002	70692	20281
2003	96380	25557
2004	78312	27595
2005	121499	57113
2006	182525	82463
2007	143978	111567
2008	118230	114738
2009	60027	121872
2010	119689	156653
2011	120083	200522
2012	360264	247800
2013	251874	312994
2014	255321	370310
2015	193684	400833
2016	102103	450466

注：本表数据来源于市商务局。

17-3 外商投资情况（2016年）

Foreign Investment Situation（2016）

分类	Classity	新签协议情况 New-signed Agreement Circumstances		外商实际直接投资额（万美元）
		合同数（个） Number of Constracts (unit)	利用外资签定协议金额（万美元） Value of Foreign Captial Used through the Signed (USD10 000)	Value of Foreign Direct Investment (USD 10 000)
合　计	**Total**	**72**	**102103**	**450466**
1.中外合资经营企业	Joint-venture Enterprises	25	35511	48730
2.中外合作经营企业	Cooperation Enterprises			
3.外资企业	Wholly Foreign-owned Enterprises	47	66592	401736
4.外资企业再投资	Re-investment from Foreign-funded Enterprises			

17-4 各区县、开发区外商实际直接投资

Direct Investment by Foreign Entrepreneurs by Region and Development Zone

单位：万美元　　(USD 10 000)

区县及开发区	Region and Economic Zone	2010	2011	2012	2013	2014	2015	2016
区县合计	**Sum of Region**	**38855**	**49726**	**58119**	**45164**	**51423**	**59765**	**67874**
新城区	Xincheng	4900	6765	7800	5012	6500	7775	8768
碑林区	Beilin	5150	6273	7800	5103	5871	6873	9360
莲湖区	Lianhu	5471	7405	7800	5100	5843	6873	7532
灞桥区	Baqiao	5215	6001	7397	6124	6933	8148	9056
未央区	Weiyang	5023	6202	7800	6000	6834	7870	8614
雁塔区	Yanta	5488	6912	8190	6179	6847	8074	8907
阎良区	Yanliang	1208	2070	2200	2200	2346	2555	2801
临潼区	Lintong	1200	2000	2400	2400	2504	2765	3031
长安区	Chang'an	1680	2300	2768	3003	3360	3961	4440
高陵区	Gaoling	950	1089	1100	1100	1182	1478	1621
蓝田县	Lantian	550	600	650	660	707	1283	1401
周至县	Zhouzhi	970	1050	1100	1110	1210	773	864
户　县	Huxian	1050	1060	1115	1173	1288	1339	1479
开发区合计	**Sum of Development Zones**	**117798**	**150797**	**189681**	**267830**	**318887**	**311265**	**381023**
高新区	GaoXin	51130	64935	81776	132632	149387	167112	203870
经开区	JingKai	42608	54201	68202	81423	103009	114538	129186
曲江新区	Qujiang	17187	21002	26433	33870	41436		20588
浐灞生态区	Chanba Eco-District	3070	3856	4837	7266	8453	9800	10833
航空基地	Aviation Industry Base	1239	1701	2072	2640	3082	3636	4186
航天基地	Aerospace Base	1554	2030	2403	3000	3501	3980	4567
国际港务区	International Trade&Logistic Park	1010	1571	2082	3469	5050	6429	7793
沣东新城	FengDongXinCheng		1500	1876	3530	4970	5770	

注：本表数据来源于市商务局。

17-5 主要年份进出口总值

Total Imports and Exports in Representative Years

单位：万美元 (USD 10 000)

年 份 Year	进出口总值 Total Imports and Exports	出口总值 Total Exports	进口总值 Total Imports
1987	13596	7540	6056
1988	36750	24632	12118
1989	32715	21564	11151
1990	38229	28290	9939
1991	55356	41511	13845
1992	70467	53060	17407
1993	93330	62393	30937
1994	104752	76897	27855
1995	137510	110163	27347
1996	143187	91745	51442
1997	150668	107753	42915
1998	180589	100492	80097
1999	172919	94495	78424
2000	173696	106062	67634
2001	169914	87948	81966
2002	186966	112479	74487
2003	230932	140327	90605
2004	309295	203539	105756
2005	390146	263441	126705
2006	415403	272862	142541
2007	536162	347133	189029
2008	704029	447113	256916
2009	724618	333114	391504
2010	1039273	531729	507544
2011	1260179	582662	677517
2012	1301446	729878	571568
2013	1798534	847819	950715
2014*	15321514	7346822	7974693
2015*	17616896	8198754	9418142
2016*	18299476	9473084	8826392

注：本表数据来源于西安海关。2014年以后数据计量单位为万元。

17-6 外贸商品进出口总值分国别和地区（2016年）

Total Value of Imports and Exports by Country and Region（2016）

单位：万元 (10 000 yuan)

国别和地区	Country and Region	进出口总值 Total Imports and Exports	出口 Exports
亚洲	**Asia**	**12557439**	**6073437**
#香港	Hong kong	2282826	2272109
台湾省	Taiwan	4131365	375102
日本	Japan	1187288	399884
菲律宾	Phiilippines	80985	38119
马来西亚	Malaysia	198661	125075
韩国	Korea	3423460	1954848
非洲	**Africa**	**464168**	**243982**
#埃及	Egypt	57969	57674
突尼斯	Tunisia	2755	2661
埃塞俄比亚	Ethiopia	6980	6980
博茨瓦纳	Botswana	116	116
南非	South Africa	226530	40355
欧洲	**Europe**	**1993351**	**1125773**
#德意志联邦国	Germany	360775	132645
法国	France	279176	227182
意大利	Italy	138453	43607
荷兰	Netherland	247262	165592
英国	England	200874	154867
瑞士	Switzerland	78877	7096
西班牙	Spain	31320	26767
俄罗斯联邦	Russia	73690	41378
拉丁美洲	**Latin America**	**419925**	**203865**
#哥伦比亚	Colombia	5522	5494
巴西	Brazil	139875	24911
阿根廷	Argentina	8444	8408
北美洲	**North America**	**2552833**	**1769347**
加拿大	Canada	84803	49419
美国	America	2468019	1719918
大洋洲及太平洋岛屿	**Oceanic and Pacific Islands**	**311726**	**56680**
#澳大利亚	Australia	299561	51214
新西兰	New Zealand	10019	3445

注：本表数据来源于西安海关。

17-7 主要商品分大类出口金额

Export Value of Major Merchandise by Type

单位：万美元 (USD 10 000)

商品分类	HS Section and Division	2000	2001
食用蔬菜、根及块茎	Edible Vegetables, Certain,Roots amd Tubers	1095	1957
蔬菜、水果、坚果或植物其他部分的制品	Vegetables, Fruits, Nuts, or Products Made of Other Parts of Plants	2076	2684
矿砂、矿渣及矿灰	Ores,Slags and Ash	4083	4649
无机化学品；贵金属、稀土金属、放射性元素及其同位素的有机及无机化合物	Inorganic Chemicals,Organic or Inorganic Compounds of Precious Metals,of Rare Earth Metals,of Radioactive Elements or of Isotopes	3714	4141
有机化学品	Organic Chemicals	2367	3279
羊毛、动物细毛或粗毛、马毛纱线及其机织物	Wool ,Fine or Coarse Animal Hair; Horsehair Yarn and Woven Fabric	810	829
棉花	Cotton	3197	2734
化学纤维短纤	Short Staple Chemical' Fibers	5061	3612
针织或钩编的服装及衣着附件	Articles of Apparel and Clothing Accessories, Knitted or Crocheted	6753	1632
非针织或非钩编的服装及衣着附件	Articles of Apparel and Clothing Accessories, not Knitted or Crocheted	7269	3319
其它纺织制成品；成套物品；旧衣着及旧纺织品	Other Made Up Textile Articles;Sets;Worn Clothing and Worn Textile Articles;Rags Articles	1649	1002
鞋靴、护膝和类似品及其零件	Footwear,Gaiters and The Like;Parts of Such Articles Headgear and Parts Thereof	1347	279
玻璃及其制品	Glass and Glassware	3376	3838
钢铁	Iron and Steel	3534	1197
钢铁制品	Articles of Iron or Steel	5535	6401
铅及制品	Lead Areticles Thereof	1371	1363
锌及制品	Zinc Areticles Thereof	4031	1945
其他贱金属、金属陶瓷及其制品	Other Base Metals,Germets;Areticles Thereof	1066	1704
贱金属工具、器具、利口器、餐匙、餐叉及其零件	Tools,Implements,Cutlery,Spons and Forks, of Base Metal;Parts Thereof of Base Metal	2933	2669
核反应堆、锅炉、机器、机械器具及其零件	Nuclear Reactors ,Boilers, Machinery and Mechanical Appliances; and Parts Thereof	10915	11979
电机、电气设备及其零件；录音机及放声机、电视图象、声音的录制和重放设备及其零件、附件	Electrical Machinery and Equipment and Parts Thereof;Sound Recorders and Repreducers, Television Image and Sound Recordes and Repreducers, and Parts and Accessories of Such Articles	8339	8696
光学、照相、电影、计量、检验、医疗或外科仪器及设备、精密仪器及设备；上述物品的零配件、附件	Optical,Photographic,Cinematographic,Measuring, Checking,Precision Medical or Surgical Instruments and Apparatus;Parts and Accessories Thereof	2020	2818
家具、寝具、褥垫、弹簧床垫、软床垫及类似的填充制品；未列名灯具及照明装置；发光标志、发光名牌及类似品；活动房屋	Mattresses,Mattress Supports,Cushions and Similar Stuffed Furnishings;Lamps and Lighting Fittings, not Elsewhere Spcified or Included;Illumihated Signs,Illuminated	2587	2150

注：2014年、2015年、2016年数据计量单位为万元。

17-7 续表1

单位：万美元

商品分类	HS Section and Division	2002	2003
食用蔬菜、根及块茎	Edible Vegetables, Certain,Roots amd Tubers	1275	1379
蔬菜、水果、坚果或植物其他部分的制品	Vegetables, Fruits, Nuts, or Products Made of Other Parts of Plants	3470	4490
矿砂、矿渣及矿灰	Ores,Slags and Ash	8714	11224
无机化学品；贵金属、稀土金属、放射性元素及其同位素的有机及无机化合物	Inorganic Chemicals,Organic or Inorganic Compounds of Precious Metals,of Rare Earth Metals,of Radioactive Elements or of Isotopes	4141	5814
有机化学品	Organic Chemicals	4883	4757
羊毛、动物细毛或粗毛、马毛纱线及其机织物	Wool ,Fine or Coarse Animal Hair; Horsehair Yarn and Woven Fabric	1313	1600
棉花	Cotton	3826	3984
化学纤维短纤	Short Staple Chemical' Fibers	2512	2120
针织或钩编的服装及衣着附件	Articles of Apparel and Clothing Accessories, Knitted or Crocheted	2660	341
非针织或非钩编的服装及衣着附件	Articles of Apparel and Clothing Accessories, not Knitted or Crocheted	3629	4981
其它纺织制成品；成套物品；旧衣着及旧纺织品	Other Made Up Textile Articles;Sets;Worn Clothing and Worn Textile Articles;Rags Articles	1432	2203
鞋靴、护膝和类似品及其零件	Footwear,Gaiters and The Like;Parts of Such Articles Headgear and Parts Thereof	296	585
玻璃及其制品	Glass and Glassware	5542	6667
钢铁	Iron and Steel	2167	2779
钢铁制品	Articles of Iron or Steel	7414	8474
铅及制品	Lead Areticles Thereof	444	232
锌及制品	Zinc Areticles Thereof	1895	2200
其他贱金属、金属陶瓷及其制品	Other Base Metals,Germets;Areticles Thereof	1546	3150
贱金属工具、器具、利口器、餐匙、餐叉及其零件	Tools,Implements,Cutlery,Spons and Forks, of Base Metal;Parts Thereof of Base Metal	2613	3232
核反应堆、锅炉、机器、机械器具及其零件	Nuclear Reactors ,Boilers, Machinery and Mechanical Appliances; and Parts Thereof	16140	21281
电机、电气设备及其零件；录音机及放声机、电视图象、声音的录制和重放设备及其零件、附件	Electrical Machinery and Equipment and Parts Thereof;Sound Recorders and Repreducers, Television Image and Sound Recordes and Repreducers, and Parts and Accessories of Such Articles	8962	15106
光学、照相、电影、计量、检验、医疗或外科仪器及设备、精密仪器及设备；上述物品的零配件、附件	Optical,Photographic,Cinematographic,Measuring, Checking,Precision Medical or Surgical Instruments and Apparatus;Parts and Accessories Thereof	5395	3339
家具、寝具、褥垫、弹簧床垫、软床垫及类似的填充制品；未列名灯具及照明装置；发光标志、发光名牌及类似品；活动房屋	Mattresses,Mattress Supports,Cushions and Similar Stuffed Furnishings;Lamps and Lighting Fittings, not Elsewhere Spcified or Included;Illumihated Signs,Illuminated	2715	3994

continued 1

(USD 10 000)

2004	2005	2006	2007	2008	2009	2010	2011	2012	2013	2014*	2015*	2016*
1386	1190	1136	1232	1374	803	4740	2016	1961	2699	2686	2039	2555
7786	10531	15374	37426	29270	21920	41289	36763	2576	49361	132663	112701	102768
30590	63247	52046	47378	40502	6141	325	4709	1679	1686	14977	96	178
5806	10997	10916	16508	15882	9774	24875	11735	8911	12588	67764	44508	49950
4837	8569	11923	11182	13954	16294	982	20067	17890	28694	109986	109654	117162
1640	903	1400	1065	720	460	10133	796	562	2433	15782	3005	5648
3133	3240	3808	3255	3213	2346	98	2628	2185	5827	9252	14309	6429
1987	1471	1556	1767	1181	2217	479	2586	2375	8245	13685	11581	11178
7465	5736	5332	5345	4371	3617	3209	3366	12316	6491	29551	37030	31646
5543	5068	4078	3875	3623	2919	3394	3262	7050	4861	33872	23610	19393
2667	3000	3342	3090	3187	2813	544	2838	4412	4471	18906	15677	15187
2687	1368	216	348	380	367	150	1003	5252	6293	20186	5032	2292
8083	8576	8272	6246	6538	5574	928	8073	10995	13856	54453	45991	46764
5244	5314	4900	11366	11966	4254	18549	16681	8407	6730	31854	20390	27589
10398	13959	16903	17329	26568	11943	5998	25319	24259	33546	102720	88740	100956
43	12	158	1650	2	1	10	2	4913	16	3		26
522	135	4119	2470	46	78	28545	10	11	59	109	93	20
6419	11233	17695	23414	27576	11276	3556	28092	21397	24030	106691	95442	83309
3406	3052	3607	3917	4083	2777	2893	3641	5176	5992	30653	25321	24868
24696	30832	36174	47381	75911	52372	130296	99631	127795	211009	1929864	2744726	3431041
19812	23605	22801	33393	56758	53355	136	137105	183536	327931	3113155	3625079	4264312
1847	2341	3521	4230	6348	5255	196	11066	14908	17879	112646	119117	107892
4955	4773	5086	8301	8296	4769	5328	3860	25644	23595	52352	42140	40142

17-8 主要商品分大类进口金额

Import Value of Major Merchandise by Type

单位：万美元 (USD 10 000)

商品分类	HS Section and Division	2000	2005	2007	2008	2009	2010
无机化学品；贵金属、稀土金属、放射性元素及其同位素的有机及无机化合物	Inorganic Chemicals,Organic or Inorganic Compounds of Precious Metals,of Rare Earth Metals,of Radioactive Elements or of Isotopes	1467	317	1039	6001	5040	7513
有机化学品	Organic Chemicals	7257	15237	14536	15692	14186	13949
塑料及其制品	Plastic and Articles Thereof	2559	4317	5149	2553	3134	4091
钢铁	Iron and Steel	2467	752	1270	3888	2537	10949
铜及制品	Copper and Articles Thereof	2367	689	22683	11097	41195	43343
铝及制品	Aluminium and Articles Thereof	2652	3627	3223	4767	6505	3116
核反应堆、锅炉、机器、机械器具及其零件	Nuclear Reactors ,Boilers, Machinery and Mechanical Appliances; and Parts Thereof	12990	38050	55243	68504	87493	134753
电机、电气设备及其零件；录音机及放声机、电视图象、声音的录制和重放设备及其零件、附件	Electrical Machinery and Equipment and Parts Thereof;Sound Recorders and Repreducers, Television Image and Sound Recordes and Repreducers,and Parts and Accessories of Such Articles	5911	23337	25164	48008	113034	207937
车辆及其零件、附件、铁道及电车道车辆除外	Vehicles Other Than Railway or Tramway Rolling- and Rarts and Accessories Thereof	1530	1387	1529	3789	1798	3109
航空器、航天器及其零配件	Aircraft, Spacecraft and Parts Thereof	10443	8800	2463	26148	13057	3620
光学、照相、电影、计量、检验、医疗或外科仪器及设备、精密仪器及设备；上述物品的零配件、附件	Optical,Photographic,Cinematographic,Measuring, Checking,Precision Medical or Surgical	3673	10424	17026	17737	24210	37414

17-8 续表 continued

单位：万美元 (USD 10 000)

商品分类	HS Section and Division	2011	2012	2013	2014*	2015*	2016*
无机化学品；贵金属、稀土金属、放射性元素及其同位素的有机及无机化合物	Inorganic Chemicals,Organic or Inorganic Compounds of Precious Metals,of Rare Earth Metals,of Radioactive Elements or of Isotopes	19766	13329	11869	166549	185175	299328
有机化学品	Organic Chemicals	18100	12331	12504	98293	86359	154656
塑料及其制品	Plastic and Articles Thereof	3250	3107	8014	37082	54103	76182
钢铁	Iron and Steel	10643	5928	1802	11893	17403	16093
铜及制品	Copper and Articles Thereof	78482	11857	65170	169061	484480	224287
铝及制品	Aluminium and Articles Thereof	5913	8649	11758	45295	43935	34384
核反应堆、锅炉、机器、机械器具及其零件	Nuclear Reactors ,Boilers, Machinery and Mechanical Appliances; and Parts Thereof	135240	98802	186974	2017587	2021311	990108
电机、电气设备及其零件；录音机及放声机、电视图象、声音的录制和重放设备及其零件、附件	Electrical Machinery and Equipment and Parts Thereof;Sound Recorders and Repreducers, Television Image and Sound Recordes and Repreducers,and Parts and Accessories of Such Articles	230957	257444	444407	3919650	5011437	5272203
车辆及其零件、附件、铁道及电车道车辆除外	Vehicles Other Than Railway or Tramway Rolling- and Rarts and Accessories Thereof	1527	2222	2966	17521	19700	22697
航空器、航天器及其零配件	Aircraft, Spacecraft and Parts Thereof	4654	8516	9179	43191	35164	31933
光学、照相、电影、计量、检验、医疗或外科仪器及设备、精密仪器及设备；上述物品的零配件、附件	Optical,Photographic,Cinematographic,Measuring, Checking,Precision Medical or Surgical	39317	48206	61727	452559	542812	521411

注：本表数据来源于西安海关。2014年以后数据计量单位为万元。

17-9 按贸易方式分外贸出口总值

Total Value of Exports in Foreign Trade by Type of Trade

单位：万元 (10 000 yuan)

指 标	Item	2016	2016年比2015年增长（%） Growth Rate in 2016 over 2015(%)
出口总值	**Total Exports**	**9473084**	**15.6**
1.一般贸易	General Trade	2233162	8.9
2.国家间、国际组织无偿援助	Between Countries, International Organizations	1248	-86.4
和赠送的物资	Aid and Donated Materials		
3.来料加工装配贸易	Assembly Processing Trade	37380	-2.3
4.进料加工贸易	Processing With Imported Trade	6964057	25.2
5.对外承包工程出口货物	Exports Contracted Projects	121775	-12.1
6.租赁贸易	Lease Trade		
7.易货贸易	Barter		
8.出料加工贸易	Material Processing		
9.保税监管场所进出境货物	Inward and Outward Goods of Free	266	87.2
(保税仓库进出境货物)			
10.海关特殊监管区域物流货物	Re-export Goods of Free Trade Zone	113327	-71.5
11.其他	Others	1869	-39.0

17-10 按贸易方式分外贸进口总值

Total Value of Imports in Foreign Trade by Type of Trade

单位：万元 (10 000 yuan)

指标名称	Item	2016	2016年比2015年增长（%） Growth Rate in 2016 over 2015(%)
进口总值	**Total Imports**	**8826392**	**-6.3**
1.一般贸易	General Trade	1973783	6.0
2.国家间、国际组织无偿援助和赠送的物资	Between Countries, Internationals Organization Aid and Donated Materials		
3.华侨、港澳台同胞、外籍华人捐赠物资	The overseas Chinese, Hong Kong, Macao, Taiwan,Chinese of foreign Donated Materials		
4.来料加工装配贸易	Assembly Processing Trade	38234	56.3
5.进料加工贸易	Processing With Imported Trade	5557438	14.5
6.来料加工装配进口的设备	Assembly Processing Trade Equipment		
7.租赁贸易	Lease Trade	25	489.9
8.外商投资企业作为投资进口的设备、物品	Foreign-invested Enterprises as the Import Investment of Equipment, Goods	46017	79.3
9.出料加工贸易	Material Processing		
10.易货贸易	Barter		
11.保税监管场所进出境货物（保税仓库进出境货物）	Inward and Outward Goods of Free	13982	-23.9
12.海关特殊监管区域物流货物（保税区仓储转口货物）	Re-export Goods of Free Trade Zone	343327	-45.2
13.海关特殊监管区域进口设备（出口加工区进口设备）	Export Processing Zones Imported	838470	-57.7
14.其他	Other	15116	-29.6

17-11 主要年份旅游人数及收入

Number of Tourists and Tourism Earnings in Representative Years

年 份 Year	接待旅游者人数（万人次） Number of Tourists (10 000 person-times)	国际旅游人数 Number of International Tourists	旅游总收入（万元） Total Tourism Earnings (10 000 yuan)	国际旅游收入 Earning of International Tourists	国际旅游者在西安人均停留天数（天） Number of Days of Average International Tourists Staying in Xi'an(day)
1980	4.00	4.00	1757	1757	3.8
1985	21.15	21.15	7029	7029	2.2
1990	25.88	25.88	19628	19628	2.1
1991	31.00	31.00	29051	29051	2.3
1992	40.16	40.16	40966	40966	2.2
1993	43.50	43.50	48951	48951	1.9
1994	41.49	41.49	82000	82000	2.2
1995	791.35	41.35	440000	103818	2.0
1996	925.39	45.39	470000	149400	2.6
1997	1010.53	48.53	510000	166359	2.6
1998	1105.80	47.98	560000	160244	2.6
1999	1260.40	55.41	830000	186282	2.5
2000	1567.00	65.03	1050000	224100	2.5
2001	1752.20	67.20	1130000	240700	2.4
2002	1984.13	74.13	1310000	260000	2.2
2003	1647.67	33.66	1064200	121200	2.5
2004	2149.03	65.03	1544000	273900	2.9
2005	2423.60	77.56	1785000	335380	2.9
2006	2738.70	86.73	2043000	378270	2.9
2007	3118.01	100.01	2372000	424263	2.9
2008	3232.20	63.20	2435200	287200	2.6
2009	3929.29	67.29	2974000	310500	2.9
2010	5285.18	84.18	4051800	424000	2.9
2011	6653.23	100.23	5301500	512800	2.9
2012	7978.35	115.35	6543900	598900	2.9
2013	10130.00	121.11	8114400	641600	2.9
2014	12000.00		9500000		
2015	13600.80		10736900		
2016	15012.56		12138100		

注：本表数据来源于市旅游局。2014年以后市旅游局未发布国际旅游统计数据。

17-12 主要年份旅行社及A级景点

Statistics of Travel Agencies and Level-A Scenic Spots in Representative Years

项 目	Item	2009	2010	2011	2012	2013	2014	2015	2016
旅行社数（个）	Number of Travel Agencies (unit)	303	334	365	344	360	385	353	410
旅行社营业收入（亿元）	Revenue of Travel Agencies (100 million yuan)	21.34	31.22	44.31	49.49	57.93	45.7	59.54	66.68
旅游A级景点数（个）	Number of Level-A Scenic Spots(unit)	24	34	43	55	61	67	74	72
旅游A级景点年接待游客人次（万人次）	Number of Tourists Received at Level-A Scenic Spots (10 000 person times)	1504	2726	4295	5306	7163	7462	8553	10454

注：本表数据来源于市旅游局。

主要统计指标解释

进出口总额 指实际进出我国国境的货物总金额。包括对外贸易实际进出口货物，来料加工装配进出口货物，国家间、联合国及国际组织无偿援助物资和赠送品，华侨、港澳台同胞和外籍华人捐赠品，租赁期满归承租人所有的租赁货物，进料加工进出口货物，边境地方贸易及边境地区小额贸易进出口货物（边民互市贸易除外），中外合资企业、中外合作经营企业、外商独资经营企业进出口货物和公用物品，到、离岸价格在规定限额以上的进出口货样和广告品（无商业价值、无使用价值和免费提供出口的除外），从保税仓库提取在中国境内销售的进口货物，以及其他进出口货物。该指标可以观察一个国家在对外贸易方面的总规模。我国规定出口货物按离岸价格统计，进口货物按到岸价格统计。

商品经营单位所在地进、出口额 指在所在地海关注册登记的有进出口经营权的企业实际进、出口额。

商品目的地进口额和商品货源地出口额 目的地进口额指进口货物的消费、使用或最终抵运地的实际进口额；货源地出口额指出口货物的产地或原始发货地的实际出口额。

利用外资 指我国各级政府、部门、企业和其他经济组织通过对外借款、吸收外商直接投资以及用其他方式筹措的境外现汇、设备、技术等。

外商直接投资 指外国企业和经济组织或个人（包括华侨、港澳台胞以及我国在境外注册的企业）按我国有关政策、法规，用现汇、实物、技术等在我国境内开办外商独资企业、与我国境内的企业或经济组织共同举办中外合资经营企业、合作经营企业或合作开发资源的投资（包括外商投资收益的再投资），以及经政府有关部门批准的项目投资总额内企业从境外借入的资金。

旅游人数：

（1）入境旅游人数：指报告期内来我国观光、度假、探亲访友、就医疗养、购物、参加会议或从事经济、文化、体育、宗教活动的外国人、港澳台同胞等入境游客。统计时，外国人、港澳台同胞每入境一次统计1人次。

（2）出境人数：指中国（大陆）居民因公或因私出境前往其他国家、中国香港特别行政区、澳门特别行政区和台湾省观光、度假、探亲访友、就医疗养、购物、参加会议或从事经济、文化、体育、宗教活动的人数，即出境游客。统计时，按每出境一次统计1人次。

（3）国内旅游人数：指在报告期内在中国（大陆）观光游览、度假、探亲访友、就医疗养、购物、参加会议或从事经济、文化、体育、宗教活动的中国（大陆）居民人数，其出游的目的不是通过所从事的活动谋取报酬。统计时，国内游客按每出游一次统计1人次。

国际旅游（外汇）收入 指入境游客在中国（大陆）境内旅行、游览过程中用于交通、参观游览、住宿、餐饮、购物、娱乐等全部花费。

国内旅游收入 又称旅游总花费指国内游客在国内旅行、游览过程中用于交通、参观游览、住宿、餐饮、购物、娱乐等全部花费。

国际旅行社 指经营业务范围包括入境旅游业务、出境旅游业务和国内旅游业务的旅行社。

国内旅行社 指经营范围仅限于国内旅游业务的旅行社。

星级饭店 指设备、设施、服务符合《旅游饭店星级的划分与评定》（CB／T14308—2003），通过相关旅游管理部门评定，并取得星级饭店称号的饭店（含预备星级饭店）。

Explanatory Notes on Main Statistical Indicators

Total Imports and Exports at Customs refer to the real value of commodities imported and exported across the border of China. They include the actual imports and exports through foreign trade, imported and exported goods under the processing and assembling trades and materials, supplies and gifts as aid given gratis between governments and by the United Nations and other international organizations, and contributions donated by overseas Chinese, compatriots in Hong Kong and Macao and Chinese with foreign citizenship, leasing commodities owned by tenant at the expiration of leasing period, the imported and exported commodities processed with imported materials, commodities trading in border areas (excluding mutual exchange goods) , the imported and exported commodities and articles for public use of the Sino-foreign joint ventures, cooperative enterprises and ventures with sole foreign investment. Also included is import or export of samples and advertising goods for which CIF or FOB value are beyond the permitted ceiling (excluding goods of no trading or use value and free commodities for export) , imported goods sold in China from bonded warehouses and other imported or exported goods. The indicator of the total imports and exports at customs can be used to observe the total size of external trade in a country. In accordance with the stipulation of the Chinese government, imports are calculated at CIF, while exports are calculated at FOB.

Import Export Value by Location of China's Foreign Trade Managing Units refers to actual value of imports and exports carried out by corporations which have been registered by the local Customs house and are vested with right to run import export business.

Import Value of Commodities by Place of Destination and Export Value of Commodities by Place of Origin in China The former indicator refers to the value of import commodities of the places of their consumption, utilization or the places of their final destination. The latter indicator refers to the value of export commodities of the places of their origin or the places of the commodities dispatched.

Utilization of Foreign Capitals refers to remittance, equipment and technology financed from abroad, by loans, foreign direct investment and other forms undertaken by the Chinese governments at all levels, by various departments, enterprises and other economic units.

Foreign Borrowings refer to funds borrowed from abroad through formal signing of borrowing agreements with foreign institutions, including loans of foreign governments, loans of international financial institutions, commercial loans of foreign banks, export credit, and funds raised by Chinese bonds (and shares before 1996) issued abroad. It is an important part of China's utilization of foreign capitals.

Foreign Direct Investment refers to the investments inside China by foreign enterprises and economic organizations or individuals (including overseas Chinese, compatriots from Hong Kong, Macao and Taiwan, and Chinese enterprises registered abroad) , following the relevant policies and laws of China, for the establishment of ventures exclusively with foreign own investment, Sino-foreign joint ventures and cooperative enterprises or for co-operative exploration of resources with enterprises or economic organizations in China.

Number of Tourists

(1) Visitor arrivals refer to the number of foreigners,Chinese compatriots from Hong Kong, Macao and Taiwan Chinese (mainland) who come to China (mainland) for sight-seeing,vacation,visiting relatives, medical treatment, shopping, attending conference, or to engage in economic, cultural, sports and religious activities. In compiling statistics, each time of entering China is counted as one person-time.

(2) Number of Chinese residents going abroad refer to the number of Chinese (mainland) residents going to other countries, Hong Kong Special Administrative region, Macao Special Administrative region and Taiwan for on official or private purposes, for sight-seeing, vacation, visiting relatives, medical treatment, shopping, attending conference, or to engage in economic , cultural , sports and religious activities. In compiling statistics, each time of leaving is counted as one person-time.

(3) Number of domestic tourists refers to the number of Chinese (mainland) residents who travel within China (mainland) for sight-seeing, vacation, visiting relatives, medical treatment, shopping, attending conference, or to engage in economic, cultural, sports and religious activities. In compiling statistics, each time of travelling is counted as one person-time.

Foreign Exchange Earnings from International Tourism refer to the total expenditure of foreigners, overseas Chinese,Chinese compatriots from Hong Kong,Macao and Taiwan during their stay in the mainland of China on transportation,sighting,accommodation, food,shopping and entertainment.

Income from Domestic Tourism refer to expenditure of domestic tourists on transportation,sighting, accommodation, food, shopping and entertainment while they travel.

International Travel Agencies refer to travel agencies engaged in tourism entering China, Chinese residents going abroad and domestic tourism.

Domestic Travel Agencies refer to travel agencies only engaged in domestic tourism.

Star-rated Hotels refer to hotels rated with stars as assessed by the relevant tourism authorities according to GB/T14308-2003 standard with reference to their infrastructure, facilities and service levels.

18 服务业

TERTIARY INDUSTRY

资料整理：王家峰
Data management：Wang Jiafeng
数据审核：王金桂
Data audit：Wang Jingui

第十八部分　服务业

一、简要说明

本资料主要包括规模以上服务业（九个门类、四个中类）单位个数及主要经济指标，由西安市统计局服务业和社科处提供。

二、主要指标

单位数（个）	1229		
资产总计（亿元）	7070.61	比上年增长	10.8%
营业收入（亿元）	1769.95	比上年增长	10.4%
利润总额（亿元）	142.28	比上年下降	11.0%

18　TERTIARY INDUSTRY

Ⅰ.Brief Introduction

The data in this chapter consists of the number of service units and main economic indicators of Service enterprises above designated size (Including nine categories, four Class) , data in this chapter is provided by Tertiary Industry and Social Science&Technology Division of Xi'an Bureau of Statistice.

Ⅱ.Major Indicators

		Increase over Preceding Year
Number of Units(units)	1229	
Total Assets (100 mil. yuan)	7070.61	10.8%
Operating Income(100 mil. yuan)	1769.95	10.4%
The total Profit (100 mil. yuan)	142.28	-11.0%

18-1 规模以上服务业按登记注册类型分主要经济指标（2016年）

Main Economic Indicators for Services above the Designated Size grouped by Registration Type（2016）

单位：万元 (10 000 yuan)

指 标	Item	单位数（个） Number of Enterprises (unit)	资产总计 Total Assets	固定资产原价 Original Value of Fixed Assets
总计	**Total**	**1229**	**70706084.2**	**37690984.8**
按登记注册类型分组	**Grouped by Registration Type**			
内资企业	Domestic Funded Enterprises	1167	69347841.2	37376856.1
国有	State-owned Enterprises	97	2795302.6	1242684.5
集体	Collective-owned Enterprises	17	113480.0	30381.5
股份合作	Corperative Enterprises	4	11539.9	3567.2
联营	Joint Ownership Enterprises			
国有联营	State Joint Ownership Enterprises			
集体联营	Collective Joint Ownership Enterprises			
国有与集体联营	Joint State-collective Enterprises			
其他联营	Others Joint Ownership Enterprises			
有限责任公司	Limited Liability Corporrations	637	58334309.9	31437044.3
国有独资公司	State Funded Corporations	68	31889712.2	15714229.4
其他有限责任公司	Other Limited Liability Corporrations	569	26444597.7	15722814.9
股份有限公司	Other Limited Liability Corporrations	59	5627674.7	3997658.1
私营	Other Limited Liability Corporrations	338	2338457.1	632473.7
私营独资	Private-funded Enterprises	10	7882.6	3452.9
私营合伙	Private Partnership Enterprises	9	57656.5	12944.7
私营有限责任公司	Private Limited Liability Corporations	302	2198542.9	605243.2
私营股份有限公司	Private Share-holding Corporations Ltd.	17	74375.1	10832.9
其他	Other Enterprises	15	127077.0	33046.8
港澳台商投资	Enterprises with Funds from Hong Kong, Macao &Taiwan	27	477399.4	162092.6
与港澳台商合资经营	Joint Ventures	16	397440.6	134798.7
与港澳台商合作经营	Cooperation Enterprises	2	30607.4	2771.2
港澳台商独资经营	Enterprises with Sole Investment from Hong Kong Macau and Taiwan	8	45091.3	23907.2
港澳台商投资股份有限公司	Share-holding Corporations Ltd. with funds from Hong Kong, Macao & Taiwan			
其他港澳台投资	Other Hong Kong, Macao and Taiwan Investment	1	4260.1	615.5
外商投资	Foreign Funded Enterprises	35	880843.6	152036.1
中外合资经营企业	Sino-foreign Joint Ventures Enterprises	10	645587.8	20919.7
中外合作经营企业	Sino-Foreign Cooperation Enterprises	2	5525.5	3838.2
外资企业	Foreign Owned Enterprises	20	219578.2	124706.8
外商投资股份有限公司	Limited Company Funded by Foreign Investment	1	1937.0	485.6
其他外商投资	Other Foreign Funded Enterprises	2	8215.1	2085.8

18-1 续表1

单位：万元

指　标	Item	负债合计 Total Liabilities	所有者权益合计 Total Owners' Equities	营业收入 Paid in Capital
总计	**Total**	**44500949.3**	**26205716.2**	**17699509.4**
按登记注册类型分组	**Grouped by Registration Type**			
内资企业	Domestic Funded Enterprises	43770844.7	25577577.8	17147433.6
国有	State-owned Enterprises	1949398.9	845903.7	1945532.4
集体	Collective-owned Enterprises	58386.2	55093.8	66794.2
股份合作	Corperative Enterprises	6769.3	4770.6	3747.7
联营	Joint Ownership Enterprises			
国有联营	State Joint Ownership Enterprises			
集体联营	Collective Joint Ownership Enterprises			
国有与集体联营	Joint State-collective Enterprises			
其他联营	Others Joint Ownership Enterprises			
有限责任公司	Limited Liability Corporrations	38224798.5	20110093.2	11723185.8
国有独资公司	State Funded Corporations	22065849.3	9823863.0	2070384.3
其他有限责任公司	Other Limited Liability Corporrations	16158949.2	10286230.2	9652801.5
股份有限公司	Other Limited Liability Corporrations	1833184.1	3794490.6	2313134.1
私营	Other Limited Liability Corporrations	1616426.5	722030.1	1005012.1
私营独资	Private-funded Enterprises	5163.6	2719.0	7210.8
私营合伙	Private Partnership Enterprises	37811.5	19845.0	57248.1
私营有限责任公司	Private Limited Liability Corporations	1530894.2	667648.2	880187.1
私营股份有限公司	Private Share-holding Corporations Ltd.	42557.2	31817.9	60366.1
其他	Other Enterprises	81881.2	45195.8	90027.3
港澳台商投资	Enterprises with Funds from Hong Kong, Macao &Taiwan	149524.3	327875.1	269627.1
与港澳台商合资经营	Joint Ventures	114828.0	282612.6	196795.3
与港澳台商合作经营	Cooperation Enterprises	21136.1	9471.3	22327.7
港澳台商独资经营	Enterprises with Sole Investment from Hong Kong Macau and Taiwan	13305.6	31785.7	47912.7
港澳台商投资股份有限公司	Share-holding Corporations Ltd. with funds from Hong Kong, Macao & Taiwan			
其他港澳台投资	Other Hong Kong, Macao and Taiwan Investment	254.6	4005.5	2591.4
外商投资	Foreign Funded Enterprises	580580.3	300263.3	282448.7
中外合资经营企业	Sino-foreign Joint Ventures Enterprises	510948.1	134639.7	53701.9
中外合作经营企业	Sino-Foreign Cooperation Enterprises	1413.1	4112.4	3199.4
外资企业	Foreign Owned Enterprises	65319.0	154259.2	199156.7
外商投资股份有限公司	Limited Company Funded by Foreign Investment	1662.3	274.7	10256.0
其他外商投资	Other Foreign Funded Enterprises	1237.8	6977.3	16134.7

continued1

(10 000 yuan)

主营业务收入 Revenue from Principal Business	营业成本 Total Cost		销售费用 Sale Expenses
		主营业务成本 Cost of Principal Business	
17233413.9	**13037904.8**	**12536079.8**	**979373.2**
16709817.5	12691550.1	12200017.7	952169.5
1894138.2	1837732.7	1789067.4	37048.4
66677.8	39837.0	39835.7	7177.4
3500.2	545.9	538.6	80.4
11388793.7	8415237.2	8009063.8	709168.2
2026540.0	1281058.3	1199305.1	61212.5
9362253.7	7134178.9	6809758.7	647955.7
2286948.2	1651591.7	1645200.1	122041.8
980088.2	685044.2	655305.3	71937.2
5985.0	4897.5	4692.2	874.1
54661.5	32408.7	32284.8	1435.4
859077.0	607163.9	577754.2	66199.4
60364.7	40574.1	40574.1	3428.3
89671.2	61561.4	61006.8	4716.1
241884.7	163492.5	156934.5	15938.6
195543.4	137206.6	135749.6	9238.3
1538.1	5101.0		
42211.8	20458.7	20458.7	5024.4
2591.4	726.2	726.2	1675.9
281711.7	182862.2	179127.6	11265.1
52988.0	37164.2	36011.3	1464.7
3199.4	1346.8	1346.8	149.5
199133.6	121291.2	118709.5	9647.9
10256.0	9587.1	9587.1	
16134.7	13472.9	13472.9	3.0

18-1 续表2

单位：万元

指 标	Item	管理费用 Management Expenses	财务费用 Financial Expenses	投资收益 investment income
总计	**Total**	**1806745.9**	**1032444.2**	**382392.0**
按登记注册类型分组	**Grouped by Registration Type**			
内资企业	Domestic Funded Enterprises	1713803.0	1031699.9	382195.8
国有	State-owned Enterprises	232672.4	10049.2	9838.3
集体	Collective-owned Enterprises	17433.3	-171.2	-327.9
股份合作	Corperative Enterprises	3226.8	-54.3	335.6
联营	Joint Ownership Enterprises			
国有联营	State Joint Ownership Enterprises			
集体联营	Collective Joint Ownership Enterprises			
国有与集体联营	Joint State-collective Enterprises			
其他联营	Others Joint Ownership Enterprises			
有限责任公司	Limited Liability Corporrations	1130333.4	954569.5	331905.8
国有独资公司	State Funded Corporations	164944.1	765377.8	203852.9
其他有限责任公司	Other Limited Liability Corporrations	965389.3	189191.7	128052.9
股份有限公司	Other Limited Liability Corporrations	136046.2	37800.8	35884.7
私营	Other Limited Liability Corporrations	180041.8	28476.2	4400.2
私营独资	Private-funded Enterprises	1953.2	25.5	-36.0
私营合伙	Private Partnership Enterprises	14027.2	1475.2	
私营有限责任公司	Private Limited Liability Corporations	154302.0	26869.3	4349.6
私营股份有限公司	Private Share-holding Corporations Ltd.	9759.4	106.2	86.6
其他	Other Enterprises	14049.1	1029.7	159.1
港澳台商投资	Enterprises with Funds from Hong Kong, Macao &Taiwan	47504.3	2926.0	-5.7
与港澳台商合资经营	Joint Ventures	29198.7	1866.0	3.9
与港澳台商合作经营	Cooperation Enterprises	4376.8	818.6	
港澳台商独资经营	Enterprises with Sole Investment from Hong Kong Macau and Taiwan	13573.9	233.7	-9.6
港澳台商投资股份有限公司	Share-holding Corporations Ltd. with funds from Hong Kong, Macao & Taiwan			
其他港澳台投资	Other Hong Kong, Macao and Taiwan Investment	354.9	7.7	
外商投资	Foreign Funded Enterprises	45438.6	-2181.7	201.9
中外合资经营企业	Sino-foreign Joint Ventures Enterprises	7030.7	36.3	131.8
中外合作经营企业	Sino-Foreign Cooperation Enterprises	724.2	6.6	
外资企业	Foreign Owned Enterprises	35271.2	-2095.2	70.1
外商投资股份有限公司	Limited Company Funded by Foreign Investment	918.0	-41.3	
其他外商投资	Other Foreign Funded Enterprises	1494.5	-88.1	

continued2

(10 000 yuan)

营业利润 Business Profits	利润总额 Total Profits	应付职工薪酬 Salary Payable	从业人员平均人数（人） Annual Average Employed Persons (person)
1132716.0	**1422770.3**	**3362254.1**	**359745**
1051611.9	1332562.7	3221892.7	349493
-145796.2	-8604.3	467130.5	53039
2353.3	2625.2	25955.8	7898
236.3	346.0	1338.3	300
814811.3	926154.8	2175664.7	209156
57925.2	89203.0	361408.2	38013
756886.1	836951.8	1814256.5	171143
331355.7	361834.0	323963.5	33117
41989.9	43350.3	203562.8	41512
-572.0	-538.6	2406.0	623
7250.6	2058.6	14743.0	1945
29855.5	35599.7	176277.1	37014
5455.8	6230.6	10136.7	1930
6661.6	6856.7	24277.1	4471
37559.0	40344.8	37393.2	3730
18010.4	20518.2	25488.0	2683
11684.1	11651.2	2468.4	116
8103.9	8414.3	8578.7	746
-239.4	-238.9	858.1	185
43545.1	49862.8	102968.2	6522
8621.1	9775.1	8680.1	858
904.8	904.3	799.0	165
33004.7	37383.0	77405.7	4075
-216.0	-85.2	7277.5	430
1230.5	1885.6	8805.9	994

18-2 规模以上服务业按规模分主要经济指标（2016年）

单位：万元

指标	Item	单位数（个） Number of Enterprises (unit)	资产总计 Total Assets	固定资产原价 Original Value of Fixed Assets
总计	**Total**	**1229**	**70706084.2**	**37690984.8**
按企业规模分组	**Grouped by Size of Enterprises**			
大型企业	Large-size	124	45978316.4	34687074.2
中型企业	Medium-size	383	14070789.0	1902755.4
小型企业	Small-size	634	10317317.3	1004071.9
微型企业	Microenterprise	88	339661.5	97083.3

18-2 续表1

单位：万元

指标	Item	销售费用 Sale Expenses	管理费用 Managenment Expenses	财务费用 Financial Expenses
总计	**Total**	**979373.2**	**1806745.9**	**1032444.2**
按企业规模分组	**Grouped by Size of Enterprises**			
大型企业	Large-size	705034.0	1068100.4	865655.0
中型企业	Medium-size	153875.1	451239.1	98484.8
小型企业	Small-size	108023.0	268789.1	64076.4
微型企业	Microenterprise	12441.1	18617.3	4228.0

Main Economic Indicators for Services above the Designated Size grouped by Size of Enterprises (2016)

(10 000 yuan)

负债合计 Total Liabilities	所有者权益合计 Total Owners' Equities	营业收入 Paid in Capital	主营业务收入 Revenue from Principal Business	营业成本 Total Cost	主营业务成本 Cost of Principal Business
44500949.3	**26205716.2**	**17699509.4**	**17233413.9**	**13037904.8**	**12536079.8**
29191246.9	16787069.5	12539582.9	12234465.3	9242155.6	8936343.1
9132029.5	4939341.2	3360292.6	3240371.4	2535039.7	2375102.6
5939667.8	4377649.1	1702050.5	1662222.5	1198721.0	1162996.6
238005.1	101656.4	97583.4	96354.7	61988.5	61637.5

continued 1

(10 000 yuan)

投资收益 investment income	营业利润 Business Profits	利润总额 Total Profits	应付职工薪酬 Salary Payable	从业人员平均人数（人） Annual Average Employed Persons (person)
382392.0	**1132716.0**	**1422770.3**	**3362254.1**	**359745**
70505.7	609606.5	790176.2	2438928.0	215482
181783.0	362872.7	430601.7	624703.6	87485
130104.8	152875.3	191210.9	287865.8	53317
-1.5	7361.5	10781.5	10756.7	3461

18-3 规模以上服务业按行业分主要经济指标（2016年）

单位：万元

指标	Item	单位数（个）Number of Enterprises (unit)	资产总计 Total Assets	固定资产原价 Original Value of Fixed Assets
总计	**Total**	**1229**	**70706084.2**	**37690984.8**
按国民经济行业大类分组	**Grouped by sector categories**			
铁路运输业	Railway transport industry	3	3983288.4	3999213.9
道路运输业	The road transport industry	100	23204707.4	15245882.1
水上运输业	Water transportation			
航空运输业	The air transport industry	8	3074461.2	1810735.1
管道运输业	Pipeline transportation	2	1092077.9	1036134.3
装卸搬运和运输代理业	Handling and transport industry	19	67853.8	15131.9
仓储业	Warehousing industry	29	753419.8	141863.6
邮政业	The postal service	10	534983.6	450557.4
电信、广播电视和卫星传输服务业	Telecommunication, broadcasting and satellite transmission services	11	8514481.1	11220526.4
互联网和相关服务	The Internet and related services	10	214849.6	9662.0
软件和信息技术服务业	Software and information technology services	147	2063096.7	354191.5
物业管理	Property management	138	707224.2	197566.6
房地产中介服务	Real estate intermediary service	4	11592.9	2316.9
其他房地产业	Other Real Estate	1	7189.0	500.3
自有房地产经营活动	Owned Real Estate Business Activities	7	86732.8	63257.5
租赁业	Leasing industry	11	768038.6	55250.5
商务服务业	Business services	225	13746864.0	926854.0
研究和试验发展	Research and development	20	875716.9	344021.2
专业技术服务业	Professional and technical services	176	4545373.1	633113.9
科技推广和应用服务业	Promotion and application of science and technology services	17	839130.7	132101.8
水利管理业	Water resources management industry	3	5129.4	1286.4
生态保护和环境治理业	Ecological protection and environmental control industries	4	148764.7	73786.5
公共设施管理业	Public facilities management industry	37	1725667.3	290487.1
居民服务业	Resident services	23	165317.3	83051.3
机动车、电子产品和日用产品修理业	Motor vehicles, electronics and household goods-repairing	18	128118.6	19088.6
其他服务业	Other service industries	12	16130.5	3811.4
教育	Education	15	61787.7	9549.2
卫生	Health	57	453149.3	231872.2
社会工作	Social work			
新闻出版业	Press and publishing industry	27	446089.2	99276.9
广播、电视、电影和影视录音制作业	Radio, television, film and video recordings	46	509368.8	72869.6
文化艺术业	Culture and arts	31	1878853.8	135292.0
体育	Physical education	9	44924.9	21774.0
娱乐业	The entertainment industry	9	31701.0	9958.7

Main Economic Indicators for Services above the Designated Size grouped by Industry（2016）

（10 000 yuan）

负债合计 Total Liabilities	所有者权益合计 Total Owners' Equities	营业收入 Paid in Capital	主营业务收入 Revenue from Principal Business	营业成本 Total Cost	主营业务成本 Cost of Principal Business
44500949.3	**26205716.2**	**17699509.4**	**17233413.9**	**13037904.8**	**12536079.8**
2539640.5	1443647.8	404875.4	404387.3	294652.3	294188.4
17666388.1	5538319.3	1491158.5	1450081.3	889330.3	874319.6
1007598.7	2066862.5	366228.8	324076.3	302630.8	267730.2
516883.3	575194.6	759721.0	743729.7	660744.0	659801.3
48618.9	19234.9	82484.8	82385.2	72469.6	72152.0
653876.9	99542.9	528860.0	523967.9	520018.6	515629.2
369526.2	165457.4	573936.4	556002.5	546435.1	528778.8
3492540.5	5021940.6	4077345.3	3906378.0	2789026.4	2607268.4
77118.9	137730.7	250330.6	250330.6	179177.6	177020.5
1110854.0	952142.4	2114409.7	2095021.6	1405120.2	1387617.1
559614.5	148291.3	426722.3	399322.7	325727.0	306694.7
6317.4	5275.5	10941.7	10893.7	2352.4	2352.4
3362.9	3826.1	7514.9	6828.5		
68531.4	18201.4	22178.4	20514.7	13654.4	13446.4
550731.3	217307.4	34788.3	34390.2	25653.5	24490.6
8636515.3	5110348.8	1742928.7	1674364.3	1336448.5	1234619.5
300881.5	574835.3	388896.3	381425.8	272752.2	271291.3
2921144.7	1624228.4	2882264.5	2869684.6	2328977.5	2258048.6
510376.0	328754.7	80341.4	79076.2	56342.2	55983.5
3601.0	1528.4	8226.9	8125.1	3714.9	3657.1
99591.9	49172.8	30031.5	29179.8	15740.5	15605.2
1280379.2	445288.1	415706.1	411746.1	331205.2	327144.0
158206.3	7111.1	52850.2	52733.8	41204.3	39668.8
104226.6	23891.9	27500.7	27393.5	24055.2	23644.5
7119.4	9011.1	19111.6	19097.2	15286.8	14764.8
47577.7	14210.0	73108.0	72844.5	52571.2	51883.3
254675.0	198474.3	289707.8	285721.5	209447.6	195869.4
255137.9	190951.3	253130.0	246651.5	180834.8	173712.8
321121.5	188247.3	167300.1	156206.5	89760.8	86988.9
864903.1	1013950.7	91325.1	85283.4	41910.1	41049.2
35367.0	9557.9	15979.3	15966.2	6680.8	6679.3
28521.7	3179.3	9605.1	9603.7	3980.0	3980.0

18-3 续表1

单位：万元

指 标	Item	销售费用 Sale Expenses	管理费用 Managenment Expenses	财务费用 Financial Expenses
总计	**Total**	**979373.2**	**1806745.9**	**1032444.2**
按国民经济行业大类分组	**Grouped by sector categories**			
铁路运输业	Railway transport industry	0.3	3517.1	123692.4
道路运输业	The road transport industry	5984.1	107849.0	700291.0
水上运输业	Water transportation			
航空运输业	The air transport industry	5385.5	29334.6	22611.3
管道运输业	Pipeline transportation	1104.3	13904.7	14778.9
装卸搬运和运输代理业	Handling and transport industry	3205.4	9901.1	465.8
仓储业	Warehousing industry	11723.6	19421.2	16912.2
邮政业	The postal service	2304.9	94548.2	1903.0
电信、广播电视和卫星传输服务业	Telecommunication, broadcasting and satellite transmission services	522458.6	220017.3	-15960.8
互联网和相关服务	The Internet and related services	2900.5	13435.6	330.4
软件和信息技术服务业	Software and information technology services	72406.4	463557.6	3883.0
物业管理	Property management	14276.6	58717.1	7245.3
房地产中介服务	Real estate intermediary service	1132.5	3879.9	-22.7
其他房地产业	Other Real Estate		6534.6	-4.4
自有房地产经营活动	Owned Real Estate Business Activities		10772.6	87.0
租赁业	Leasing industry	2545.3	4375.0	2005.2
商务服务业	Business services	86189.0	187094.6	106339.0
研究和试验发展	Research and development	8837.1	55330.0	1249.1
专业技术服务业	Professional and technical services	90322.4	286423.6	-6508.4
科技推广和应用服务业	Promotion and application of science and technology services	3782.6	14723.1	5012.5
水利管理业	Water resources management industry	89.4	1059.9	4.4
生态保护和环境治理业	Ecological protection and environmental control industries	6255.1	2286.7	1810.9
公共设施管理业	Public facilities management industry	14817.4	38360.9	21166.6
居民服务业	Resident services	5120.7	8359.9	298.9
机动车、电子产品和日用产品修理业	Motor vehicles, electronics and household goods-repairing	1653.9	2206.5	721.5
其他服务业	Other service industries	631.8	2452.9	-39.5
教育	Education	6391.8	10911.9	667.1
卫生	Health	18484.5	46731.2	3956.4
社会工作	Social work			
新闻出版业	Press and publishing industry	30329.1	36562.9	-571.3
广播、电视、电影和影视录音制作业	Radio, television, film and video recordings	21756.4	27672.1	7305.8
文化艺术业	Culture and arts	31152.8	22348.4	12284.9
体育	Physical education	4115.4	2823.5	296.6
娱乐业	The entertainment industry	4015.8	1632.2	232.1

continued 1

(10 000 yuan)

投资收益 investment income	营业利润 Business Profits	利润总额 Total Profits	应付职工薪酬 Salary Payable	从业人员平均人数（人） Annual Average Employed Persons (person)
382392.0	**1132716.0**	**1422770.3**	**3362254.1**	**359745**
	-16473.3	-19453.5	2190.3	150
19995.6	-220616.2	-87604.4	392228.6	50876
13610.1	16456.6	20911.2	102536.6	7440
722.4	69231.5	69871.5	39386.1	2360
-23.9	-3950.5	-3112.6	12308.4	2342
3429.4	-44306.5	-4937.8	18995.7	3421
	-57756.6	-57952.8	178320.5	24503
935.4	509667.2	497465.8	521361.0	42362
	6912.9	7000.4	21733.6	2451
1797.9	155838.3	205593.7	803514.2	44192
1919.8	17920.9	19333.8	155482.1	40392
680.2	4020.5	4067.5	3443.8	370
	830.2	831.3	767.7	100
46.4	-1207.0	-2634.2	2646.1	507
104.4	-138.9	8632.8	3458.5	518
235743.7	267403.7	280460.7	217401.0	40890
12869.1	56737.8	60928.7	84572.2	6003
61164.9	283133.0	294923.7	489173.5	39989
656.5	-869.1	203.4	21242.1	1670
	319.3	319.2	810.5	133
	3229.9	5424.7	6476.5	822
143.2	55491.7	59610.0	62430.2	11499
-355.4	-3115.1	-2612.8	18979.4	5388
	-851.1	-895.9	2827.7	712
	907.4	1007.3	8060.0	2383
10.6	1522.6	1332.7	22100.8	3806
-253.6	14396.5	9145.4	75866.3	12403
574.4	6058.2	13333.7	42365.9	3980
2923.8	23478.6	34574.5	13904.6	2240
25775.1	-12684.1	5828.9	31226.4	4222
-78.0	1598.4	1689.3	3897.3	934
	-470.8	-515.9	2546.5	687

18-4 规模以上服务业按隶属关系分主要经济指标（2016年）

单位：万元

指标	Item	单位数（个）Number of Enterprises (unit)	资产总计 Total Assets	固定资产原价 Original Value of Fixed Assets
总计	**Total**	**1229**	**70706084.2**	**37690984.8**
按隶属关系分	**Grouped by affiliation**			
中央	Central	66	16490752.8	15630581.0
省（自治州、直辖市）	Province (autonomous prefectures, municipalities)	157	26703739.4	17451736.0
地（区、市、州、盟）	Land (District, municipal, State, Union)	152	13217363.7	2447778.1
县（区、市、旗）	Counties (districts, cities, flags)	78	3720842.0	314457.6
街道	Street	2	21932.0	17310.4
镇	Town	1	402.7	19.4
乡	Township			
（社区）居委会	(Community) neighborhood	1	716.7	48.4
村委会	Village	3	31283.0	6040.3
其他	Others	769	10519051.9	1823013.6

18-4 续表1

单位：万元

指标	Item	销售费用 Sale Expenses	管理费用 Management Expenses	财务费用 Financial Expenses
总计	**Total**	**979373.2**	**1806745.9**	**1032444.2**
按隶属关系分	**Grouped by affiliation**			
中央	Central	572700.9	480195.7	95438.5
省（自治州、直辖市）	Province (autonomous prefectures, municipalities)	106455.8	251432.3	699310.9
地（区、市、州、盟）	Land (District, municipal, State, Union)	94455.0	428570.3	143716.7
县（区、市、旗）	Counties (districts, cities, flags)	12944.0	46626.8	25256.2
街道	Street	709.4	1553.8	-0.6
镇	Town		82.7	0.8
乡	Township			
（社区）居委会	(Community) neighborhood	88.5	86.9	2.0
村委会	Village	1140.5	3467.8	-278.3
其他	Others	190879.1	594729.6	68998.0

Main Economic Indicators for Services above the Designated Size grouped by Affiliation（2016）

（10 000 yuan）

负债合计 Total Liabilities	所有者权益合计 Total Owners' Equities	营业收入 Paid in Capital	主营业务收入 Revenue from Principal Business	营业成本 Total Cost	主营业务成本 Cost of Principal Business
44500949.3	**26205716.2**	**17699509.4**	**17233413.9**	**13037904.8**	**12536079.8**
8562495.0	7928257.8	7269900.1	7063058.3	5462069.0	5217418.7
16283107.8	10420631.7	3745141.8	3644119.8	2612403.7	2476485.7
10355868.4	2862076.6	2268332.5	2225897.7	1792958.6	1773585.6
2341375.9	1379466.1	319799.1	290401.6	271199.1	244503.4
16868.6	5063.4	4677.1	4674.7	898.3	898.3
870.3	-467.6	467.5	467.5	393.5	393.5
444.6	272.1	476.1	476.1	252.9	252.9
31609.8	-326.8	11540.3	11423.9	7412.9	7411.6
6908308.9	3610742.9	4079174.9	3992894.3	2890316.8	2815130.1

continued 1

（10 000 yuan）

投资收益 investment income	营业利润 Business Profits	利润总额 Total Profits	应付职工薪酬 Salary Payable	从业人员平均人数（人） Annual Average Employed Persons (person)
382392.0	**1132716.0**	**1422770.3**	**3362254.1**	**359745**
30037.6	667592.3	681426.8	994874.0	74975
220292.6	276879.9	308870.0	514271.3	63005
19309.2	-167495.9	28557.1	746508.5	87944
8144.7	-6939.6	9154.3	61120.3	16009
	1503.4	1538.2	758.4	212
	-20.4	-20.4	142.7	56
	28.6	28.6	352.7	108
-424.6	-208.7	-289.0	1836.7	329
105032.5	361376.4	393504.7	1042389.5	117107

主要统计指标解释

国家统计局规模以上服务业单位统计标准：辖区内年营业收入1000万元及以上，或年末从业人员50人及以上服务业法人单位。包括：交通运输、仓储和邮政业，信息传输、软件和信息技术服务业，租赁和商务服务业，科学研究和技术服务业，水利、环境和公共设施管理业，教育，卫生和社会工作；以及物业管理、房地产中介服务、自有房地产经营活动和其他房地产业等行业。

辖区内年营业收入500万元及以上，或年末从业人员50人及以上服务业法人单位。包括：居民服务、修理和其他服务业，文化、体育和娱乐业。

固定资产原价 指固定资产的成本，包括企业在购置、自行建造、安装、改建、扩建、技术改造某项固定资产时所发生的全部支出总额。根据会计“固定资产”科目的期末借方余额填报。

资产总计 指企业过去的交易或者事项形成的、由企业拥有或者控制的、预期会给企业带来经济利益的资源。资产一般按流动性（资产的变现或耗用时间长短）分为流动资产和非流动资产。其中流动资产可分为货币资金、交易性金融资产、应收票据、应收账款、预付款项、其他应收款、存货等；非流动资产可分为长期股权投资、固定资产、无形资产及其他非流动资产等。根据会计“资产负债表”中“资产总计”项目的期末余额数填报。

执行《企业会计准则》或《小企业会计准则》的企业：资产总计=流动资产合计+非流动资产合计；执行其他企业会计制度的企业资产包括流动资产、长期投资、固定资产、无形资产和其他资产等。

负债合计 指企业过去的交易或者事项形成的，预期会导致经济利益流出企业的现时义务。负债一般按偿还期长短分为流动负债和非流动负债。根据会计“资产负债表”中“负债合计”项目的期末余额数填报。

执行《企业会计准则》或《小企业会计准则》的企业：负债合计=流动负债合计+非流动负债合计；执行其他企业会计制度的企业负债包括流动负债和长期负债。

所有者权益合计 指企业资产扣除负债后由所有者享有的剩余权益。公司的所有者权益又称股东权益。包括实收资本、资本公积、盈余公积、未分配利润等。根据会计“资产负债表”中“所有者权益合计”项目的期末余额数填报。

营业收入 指企业经营主要业务和其他业务所确认的收入总额。营业收入合计包括“主营业务收入”和“其他业务收入”。根据会计“利润表”中“营业收入”项目的本期金额数填报。

主营业务收入 指企业确认的销售商品、提供劳务等主营业务的收入。根据会计“主营业务收入”科目的期末贷方余额（结转前）填报。执行《企业会计准则》或《小企业会计准则》的企业，如未设置该科目，以“营业收入”代替填报。

营业成本 指企业经营主要业务和其他业务所发生的成本总额。包括企业（单位）在报告期内从事销售商品、提供劳务等日常活动发生的各种耗费。包括“主营业务成本”和“其他业务成本”。根据会计“利润表”中“营业成本”项目的本期金额数填报。

主营业务成本 指企业经营主要业务所发生的成本总额。根据会计“主营业务成本”科目的期末借方余额（结转前）填报。执行《企业会计准则》或《小企业会计准则》的企业，如未设置该科目，以“营业成本”代替填报。

销售费用 指企业在销售商品和材料、提供劳务的过程中发生的各种费用，包括保险费、包装费、展览费和广告费、商品维修费、预计产品质量保证损失、运输费、装卸费等以及为销售本企业商品而专设的销售机构（含销售网点、售后服务网点等）的职工薪酬、业务费、折旧费等经营费用。建筑业企业销售费用指企业从事施工生产活动过程中发生的各项费用，包括应由企业负担的运输费、装卸费、包装费、保险费、维修费、展览费、差旅费、广告费和其他经费。房地产企业销售费用指企业在从事主要经营业务过程中所发生的各项销售费用，包括转让、销售、结算和出租开发产品等。执行《企业会计准则》或《小企业会计准则》的企业，根据会计“利润表”中“销售费用”项目的本期金额数填报。执行其他企业会计制度的企业，根据会计“利润表”中“营业费用（或经营费用）”项目的本期金额数填报。

管理费用 指企业为组织和管理企业生产经营所发生的费用，包括企业在筹建期间内发生的开办费、董事会和行政管理部门在企业经营管理中发生的，或者应当由企业统一负担的公司经费等。根据会计“利润表”中“管理费用”项目的本期金额数填报。

财务费用 指企业为筹集生产经营所需资金等而发生的筹资费用，包括企业生产经营期间发生的利息支出（减利息收入）、汇兑损失（减汇兑收益）以及相关的手续费等。根据会计“利润表”中“财务费用”项目的本期金额数填报。

投资收益 指企业确认的投资收益或投资损失，反映企业以各种方式对外投资所取得的收益。根据会计

“利润表”中“投资收益”项目的本期金额数填报。如为投资损失以“-”号记。

营业利润 指企业从事生产经营活动所取得的利润。执行《企业会计准则》的企业，营业利润为营业收入减去营业成本、营业税金及附加、销售费用、管理费用、财务费用、资产减值损失，再加上公允价值变动收益和投资收益。执行《小企业会计准则》的企业，营业利润为营业收入减去营业成本，营业税金及附加、销售费用、管理费用、财务费用，再加上投资收益后的金额；执行其他企业会计制度的企业，营业利润为主营业务收入减去主营业务成本、主营业务税金及附加，加上其他业务利润后，再减去销售费用、管理费用、财务费用后的金额。根据会计“利润表”中“营业利润”项目的本期金额数填报。

利润总额 指企业在一定会计期间的经营成果，是生产经营过程中各种收入扣除各种耗费后的盈余，反映企业在报告期内实现的盈亏总额。根据会计“利润表”中“利润总额”项目的本期金额数填报。执行《企业会计准则》或《小企业会计准则》的企业，利润总额为营业利润加上营业外收入，减去营业外支出后的金额；执行其他企业会计制度的企业，利润总额为营业利润加上投资收益、政府补助、营业外收入，再减去营业外支出后的金额。

应付职工薪酬 指企业为获得职工提供的服务而给予各种形式的报酬以及其他相关支出。包括职工工资、奖金、津贴和补贴，职工福利费，医疗保险费、养老保险费、失业保险费、工伤保险费和生育保险费等社会保险费，住房公积金，工会经费和职工教育经费，非货币性福利，因解除与职工的劳动关系给予的补偿，其他与获得职工提供的服务相关的支出。执行《企业会计准则》或《小企业会计准则》的企业，根据会计科目“应付职工薪酬”的本年贷方累计发生额填报；执行其他企业会计制度的企业，应将本年上述职工薪酬包含的科目归并填报。

从业人员平均人数 指报告期内(年度、月度)平均拥有的人员数。按“谁用工，谁统计”的原则，包括正式人员，劳务派遣人员和临时聘用人员。

Explanatory Notes on Main Statistical Indicators

Statistical standard of the services unit above the designated size of the National Bureau of Statistics: The legal entitiesof the area whoseannual revenues are10 million yuan and above, or at the end of the service sector whose employees are more than 50 people.Including: transportation, storage and postal services, information transmission, software and information technology services, leasing and business services, scientific research and technological services, water conservancy, environment and public facilities management industry, education, health and social work as well as property management and real estate services industries.The legal entitiesof the area whoseannual revenues are5 million yuan and above, or at the end of the service sector whose employees are more than 50 people.Including: service, repair and other services, cultural, sports and entertainment.

Original value of fixed assets: It refers to the cost of fixed assets, including the enterprise itself costs on the acquisition, construction, installation, alteration, expansion, technological innovation of an asset for all expenditure. Depending on the "fixed assets" account debit balance at the end of filling.

Total assets: It refers to the resourcesformed bypast transactions or events, thatthe enterprise owns or controls, is expected to bring economic benefits to the enterprise. Asset is classified into current assets and non-current assets by its liquidity (realization of assets or spent time). Current assets can be divided into currency, tradable financial assets, notes receivable, accounts receivable, prepayments, other receivables and inventory; and non-current assets can be classified as equity investments, fixed assets, intangible assets and other non-current assets. It depends on the "balance sheet" of "total assets" closing balance number of items.

For business enterprisesthat implemented the 2006 accounting standard: total assets= total current assets +total non-current assets; for those who didn't implement the accounting standards, assets for business enterprises include current assets, long-term investments, fixed assets, intangible assets and other assets.

Total liabilities: It refers tothe present obligations of the enterprisethat formed by past transactions or events and are expected to lead to an outflow of economic benefits. Liability is divided into current and non-current liabilities according to the length of the repayment period. It depends onthe "balance sheets" in the "total" closing balance number of items.

For business enterprises that implemented the 2006 accounting standard: total liabilities = total current liabilities+ total non-current liabilities; for those who didn't implement the accounting standards, liabilities include current liabilities and long-term liabilities.

Totalowners ' equity: It refers to the residual rights and interests enjoyed by the owner after deducting the liabilities of an enterprise. The owner of the company is also called the shareholder's right. It includes the paid in capital, capital reserves, surplus reserves, undistributed profit and so on. According to the accounting "balance sheet", "the owner's equity total", the final balance of the project is reported.

Operating income: It refers to the total revenue recognized by the business and other business operations of the enterprise. Total operating income includes "main business income" and "other business income". It's reported according to the "business income" project of the "business income" in the accounting "profit statement".

The main business income: It refers to the income of the business of the main business, such as the sale of goods, services, etc..It's reported in accordance with the final credit balance of the accounts of the subject's "main business income" (before the transfer). For business enterprises that didn't implement the accounting standard, if not set up the subject, should fill the forms instead of the "operating income".

Operating cost: Itrefers to the total cost incurred by the business and other business of the enterprise. It includes a variety of costsof enterprises (units) in the reporting period to engage in sales of goods, services and other daily activities provided.It includes"the main business costs" and "other business costs". According to the "operating cost" of the "business cost" of the project in accordance with the accounting statement.

The main business cost: Itrefers to the total cost of the main business. It's reported in accordance with the final debit balance of the subject of accounting "main business cost". For business enterprises that didn't implement the accounting standard, if not set up the subject, should fill the forms instead of the "operating costs".

Selling expenses: It refers to the expenses of the enterprisein sales of goods and materials and providing services, including insurance, packing, exhibition fees and advertising fees, maintenance of commodity, expected to ensure product quality loss, transportation, loading and unloading charges and sales of the enterprise products and dedicated sales organizations (including sales network and after-sales service network) employee compensation, business expenses, depreciation charges and operating expenses. Construction enterprises selling expenses refers to expenses occurring in the process of production enterprises engaged in construction activities, including transportation fee shall be borne by the enterprise, handling, packing, insurance, maintenance, exhibition fees, poor travel costs, advertising costs and other expenses. Real estate enterprise sales cost refers to the business in the main business process of the sales costs, including transfer, sales, settlement and rental development products, etc.. According to the "sales expense" in accounting "profit statement", the amount of the item in this period of the project is reported. For business enterprises that didn't implement the 2006 accounting standard, according to the number of "operating expenses (or operating expenses)" of the project in accordance with the "profit statement".

Management expenses: Itrefers to the expenses for the organization and management of enterprise production and management of the enterprises, including costs in construction occurred during the start-up costs, the board of directors and administrative departments in enterprise management, or shall be made by the enterprise unified burden of company funds. According to the "management fee" in the accounting "profit table", the amount of this period of the project is reported.

Financial expenses: Itrefers tothe costsof the enterprise to raise the production and business operation required capital and funding, including occurred during the production and operation of enterprises interest payments (a reduction in interest income), exchange loss (less exchange gains) and related fees. It is reportedaccording to the amount of the "financial expense" in the project of "financial expense" in the accounting "profit statement".

Investment income: Itrefers to the enterprise confirming the investment income or investment losses, reflecting the foreign investment income of the enterprise in various ways. According to the "investment income" in the accounting "profit statement", the amount of this period of the project is reported. Such as investment losses to "-".

Operating profit: Itrefers tothe profits made by the enterprises in the production and operation activities. For business enterprises that implemented the 2006 accounting standard, operating profit is revenues minus operating costs, business taxes and surcharges, sales, management costs, financial costs, asset impairment loss and plus fair value changes in income and investment income. Without executing the "accounting standards for business enterprises" enterprises, operating profit equals the main business income minus the cost of major business, main business tax and surcharges, and plus profit from other operations, then minus the cost of sales and management costs, financial costs. It is reported according to the number of "operating profit" items in the accounting "profit table".

Total profit: Itrefers tothe business results of the enterprise in a certain accounting period, and it is the production and operation of various kinds of income after deducting the cost of earnings, reflecting the enterprise in the reporting period to achieve total profit and loss. According to the amount of the total amount of the total profit of the project in accordance with the accounting profit table. For business enterprises that implemented the 2006 accounting standard, the total profit is operating profit plus operating income, andminus operating expenses; while who didn't execute the " accounting standards for business enterprises", a total profit is operating profit plus return on investment, income subsidies, camp outside the industry income, andminus operating expenses.

Employee compensation: Itrefers tovarious forms of remuneration and other related expenses paid by the company for the services provided by the staff and workers. It includes wages, bonuses, allowances and subsidies, employee welfare benefit expenses, medical insurance, endowment insurance, unemployment insurance, work-related injury insurance premiums and maternity insurance fees social insurance, housing provident fund, the trade union funds and employee education funds, non-monetary benefits, for the solution in addition to give labor relations and workers compensation, and obtain a worker to provide other services related expenditure. For business enterprises that implemented the accounting standard, according to accounting subjects "to deal with workers' compensation" this year, the accumulated credits is filled; those who didn't execute the "accounting standards for business enterprises", it should be the employee compensation including the amalgamative course reportingthis year.

Average number of persons engaged in service

activities: It refers to the number of persons engaged in the service industry in the reporting period (annual, monthly). The principles of statistics is implemented according to the principle that "who labor, who statistics," including the official personnel, labor sent contingent personnel and temporaryemployeeswho take part in the enterprise service activities. And itdon't include employeeswho receive wages, dividends, bonusas well as not participate in the service activities of the enterprise.

19 金融业

FINANCIAL INTERMEDIATION

资料整理：罗延庆
Data management:Luo yanqing
数据审核：陈　英
Data audit：Chen Ying

第十九部分　金融业

一、简要说明

本章资料包括金融、证券和保险业情况，由西安市统计局综合处根据人民银行西安分行营业管理部和市金融办提供资料整理。

二、主要指标

金融机构人民币（含外资）存款余额（亿元）	19073.96	比上年增长	7.2%
金融机构人民币（含外资）贷款余额（亿元）	15282.65	比上年增长	11.4%
保费收入（亿元）	345.85	比上年增长	31.5%

19　FINANCIAL INTERMEDIATION

Ⅰ.Brief Introduction

This chapter includes information of the financial, securities and insurance, compiled by Integration Division of the Xi'an Bureau of Statistics, according to data from Xi'an Branch Management Department of the People's Bank of China, Provincial Banking Bureau and Xi'an Financial Office.

Ⅱ.Major Indicators

		Increase over Preceding Year
Deposits in Financial Institution(100 mil. Yuan)	19073.96	7.2%
Loans in Financial Institutions(100 mil. Yuan)	15282.65	11.4%
Premiums(100 mil. Yuan)	345.85	31.5%

19-1 西安银行系统机构、人员数

Number of Institution and Employed Person in Finance System in Xi'an

机构名称	Name of Institution	2015 机构数（个）Number of Institution (unit)	2015 年末人数（人）Number of Staff and Workers (person)	2016 机构数（个）Number of Institution (unit)	2016 年末人数（人）Number of Staff and Workers (person)
合计	**Total**	**1969**	**38882**	**2095**	**39936**
1. 人民银行西安分行营业管理部	Management Department of the People's Bank of China Xi'an Branch	1	364	1	365
2. 国家开发银行	National Development Bank	1	187	1	189
3. 中国进出口银行	Export Import Bank of China	1	83	1	69
4. 中国工商银行	Industrial and Commercial Bank of China	193	4978	189	4931
5. 中国农业银行	Agricultural Bank of China	174	3306	175	3208
6. 中国银行	Bank of China	127	3488	126	3457
7. 中国建设银行	Construction Bank of China	197	4366	200	4362
8. 交通银行	Bank of Communication	55	1177	57	1221
9. 中国邮政储蓄银行	The Postal Savings Bank of China	281	825	280	873
10. 中国农业发展银行	Agricultural Development Bank of China	11	264	11	281
11. 中信银行	CITIC Bank	29	902	29	926
12. 中国光大银行	China Everbright Bank	24	918	41	954
13. 华夏银行	China Huaxia Bank	18	613	20	789
14. 广发银行	China Guangfa Bank	1	104	1	148
15. 平安银行	Pingan Bank	11	408	12	411
16. 招商银行	China Merchants Bank	54	1510	55	1569
17. 上海浦东发展银行	Pufa Bank	19	702	19	690
18. 兴业银行	Fujian Industrial Bank	18	853	70	870
19. 中国民生银行	China Minsheng Banking	21	1151	21	1090
20. 恒丰银行	Evergrowing Bank	11	384	15	427
21. 浙商银行	China Zheshang Bank	6	329	8	400
22. 渤海银行	China Bohai Bank			1	100
23. 北京银行	Bank of Beijing	18	755	19	815
24. 齐商银行	Qi Commercial Bank	7	245	8	243
25. 成都银行	Bank of Chengdu	5	169	5	184
26. 重庆银行	Bank of Chongqing	4	197	4	256
27. 宁夏银行	Bank of Ningxia	6	217	6	233
28. 昆仑银行	Bank of Kunlun	12	428	13	440
29. 西安银行	Bank of Xi'an	131	2543	145	2587
30. 长安银行	Bank of Changan	31	854	52	765
31. 秦农银行	Qinnong Bank	235	3401	235	3377
32. 农村信用社	Rural Credit Cooperatives	251	2731	251	3091
33. 村镇银行	Village Bank	4	39	11	247
34. 香港汇丰银行	Huifeng Bank of Hong Kong	3	46	3	45
35. 香港东亚银行	Dongya Bank of Hong Kong	7	278	7	256
36. 新加坡星展银行	DBS Bank			1	14
37. 英国标准渣打银行	British Standard Chartered Bank	1	36	1	20
38. 韩亚银行	Hana Bank	1	31	1	33

注：本表数据来源于人民银行西安营管部。

19-2 金融机构（含外资）本外币存贷款年末余额（2016年）

Deposits and Loans of Local Currency and Foreign Currency in Financial Institution (Including Foreign-funded institution)at Year-end（2016）

单位：万元 (10 000 yuan)

指　标	Item	2016	比年初增减额 Increase or decrease compared with the beginning of the Year
一、各项存款	**All Deposits**	**194883848**	**14514853**
（一）境内存款	Domestic Deposits	194572177	14462933
1. 住户存款	Household Deposits	71423426	5019840
（1）活期存款	Demand Deposits	28266871	2847389
（2）定期及其他存款	Time and Other Deposits	43156555	2172451
2. 非金融企业存款	Non Financial Enterprises Deposits	80551390	8848667
（1）活期存款	Demand Deposits	41862345	7657880
（2）定期及其他存款	Time and Other Deposits	38689045	1190787
3. 广义政府存款	General Government Deposits	32397787	3398538
（1）财政性存款	Fiscal Deposits	1946266	762044
（2）机关团体存款	Institution Deposits	30451522	2636494
4. 非银行业金融机构存款	Non Banking Financial Institution Deposits	10199575	-2804112
（二）境外存款	Foreign Deposits	311670	51921
二、各项贷款	**All Loans**	**155423873**	**15767457**
（一）境内贷款	Domestic Loans	155187058	15697387
1. 住户贷款	Household loans	33155391	4577262
（1）短期贷款	Short-term Loans	3828894	-309621
消费贷款	Consumer loans	1382713	122107
经营贷款	Business loans	2446181	-431728
（2）中长期贷款	Medium-term and Long-term loans	29326497	4886883
消费贷款	Consumer loans	26224251	4913693
经营贷款	Business loans	3102246	-26810
2. 非金融企业及机关团体贷款	Non Financial Enterprises and Institution Loans	122029712	11135388
（1）短期贷款	Short-term Loans	26301882	1675616
（2）中长期贷款	Medium-term and Long-term loans	87203855	8184529
（3）票据融资	Bill Financing	8313725	1237505
（4）融资租赁	Financial Leasing	21356	-6545
（5）各项垫款	Various Advance Funds	188893	44282
3. 非银行业金融机构贷款	Non Banking Financial Institution Loans	1955	-15263
（二）境外贷款	**Foreign Loans**	**236815**	**70071**

注：本表数据来源于人民银行西安营管部。

19-3 金融机构（不含外资）本外币存贷款年末余额（2016年）

Deposits and Loans Domestic Funded Financial Institution of Local Currency and Foreign Currency at Year-end（2016）

单位：万元 (10 000 yuan)

指　标	Item	2016	比年初增减额 Increase or decrease compared with the beginning of the Year
一、各项存款	**All Deposits**	**193610947**	**14544631**
（一）境内存款	Domestic Deposits	193325701	14497481
1. 住户存款	Household Deposits	71280222	5028935
（1）活期存款	Demand Deposits	28206429	2848345
（2）定期及其他存款	Time and Other Deposits	43073793	2180590
2. 非金融企业存款	Non Financial Enterprises Deposits	79809679	8984189
（1）活期存款	Demand Deposits	41626997	7682409
（2）定期及其他存款	Time and Other Deposits	38182683	1301781
3. 广义政府存款	General Government Deposits	32296225	3328467
（1）财政性存款	Fiscal Deposits	1946266	762044
（2）机关团体存款	Institution Deposits	30349960	2566422
4. 非银行业金融机构存款	Non Banking Financial Institution Deposits	9939574	-2844110
（二）境外存款	Foreign Deposits	285246	47150
二、各项贷款	**All Loans**	**154169671**	**15621991**
（一）境内贷款	Domestic Loans	153936758	15551694
1. 住户贷款	Household loans	33038819	4608825
（1）短期贷款	Short-term Loans	3828894	-300750
消费贷款	Consumer loans	1382713	123701
经营贷款	Business loans	2446181	-424452
（2）中长期贷款	Medium-term and Long-term loans	29209925	4909575
消费贷款	Consumer loans	26140603	4921768
经营贷款	Business loans	3069322	-12193
2. 非金融企业及机关团体贷款	Non Financial Enterprises and Institution Loans	120895983	10958132
（1）短期贷款	Short-term Loans	26121870	1737882
（2）中长期贷款	Medium-term and Long-term loans	86250180	7820996
（3）票据融资	Bill Financing	8313725	1359390
（4）融资租赁	Financial Leasing	21356	-6545
（5）各项垫款	Various Advance Funds	188852	46409
3. 非银行业金融机构贷款	Non Banking Financial Institution Loans	1955	-15263
（二）境外贷款	**Foreign Loans**	**232914**	**70297**

注：本表数据来源于人民银行西安营管部。

19-4 主要年份金融机构（含外资）人民币存款年末余额

Deposits in Financial Institutions (Including Foreign-funded) in Representative Years

单位：亿元 (100million yuan)

年 份 Year	合计 Total	非金融企业存款 Non Financial Enterprises Deposits	住户存款 Household loans Deposits
1978	12.82		3.72
1980	20.99		5.48
1985	40.68		16.70
1990	112.37	31.10	62.23
1995	359.51	114.54	230.63
1996	619.98	199.85	394.02
1997	602.50	227.61	358.78
1998	799.54	245.44	499.68
1999	1014.27	347.49	586.40
2000	1335.63	540.19	675.83
2001	1629.72	674.49	800.86
2002	2191.47	884.69	988.04
2003	2665.87	1041.43	1210.56
2004	3061.66	1159.98	1432.86
2005	3599.70	1237.37	1716.76
2006	4066.16	1374.91	1950.53
2007	4582.71	1702.12	2002.38
2008	5749.35	2213.67	2513.70
2009	7522.08	3077.99	3084.20
2010	8933.23	3556.78	3641.09
2011	10430.27	5997.60	4155.65
2012	12125.53	6927.84	4787.03
2013	13763.19	7759.61	5357.05
2014	15166.78	8604.03	5698.15
2015	17796.38	7031.75	6571.18
2016	19073.96	7788.07	7035.81

注：本表数据来源于人民银行西安营管部。

19-5 主要年份金融机构（含外资）人民币贷款年末余额

Loans in Financial Institutions (Including Foreign-funded) in Representative Years

单位：亿元 (100 million yuan)

年 份 Year	合计 Total	短期贷款 Short-term Loans	中长期贷款 Medium-term&Long-term Loans
1978	23.56		
1980	26.40		
1985	48.60		
1990	131.67	101.13	23.78
1995	334.50	252.30	73.32
1996	477.97	333.88	90.12
1997	443.76	342.79	87.27
1998	597.34	448.74	118.42
1999	786.20	589.52	150.64
2000	972.51	652.00	241.27
2001	1185.97	666.41	387.82
2002	1598.42	780.69	502.03
2003	1954.18	946.64	743.72
2004	2052.33	950.50	850.01
2005	2158.10	830.68	1013.32
2006	2344.77	812.33	1310.57
2007	2683.77	883.32	1593.37
2008	3275.12	1031.62	1905.08
2009	4482.63	1155.83	2908.75
2010	6482.28	1097.60	5075.98
2011	7564.93	1431.29	5776.48
2012	8635.22	1917.51	6378.88
2013	10023.63	2326.63	7385.37
2014	11668.14	2516.78	8685.74
2015	13714.02	2768.31	10218.90
2016	15282.65	2905.68	11526.21

注：本表数据来源于人民银行西安营管部。

19-6 金融机构（含外资）人民币存贷款年末余额（2016年）

Year-end Balance of RMB Deposits and Loans in Financial Institutionst （Including Foreign-funded） （2016）

单位：万元 (10 000 yuan)

指　标	Item	2016	比年初增减额 Increase or decrease compared with the beginning of the Year
一、各项存款	**All Deposits**	**190739616**	**12775777**
（一）境内存款	Domestic Deposits	190613477	12770557
1. 住户存款	Household Deposits	70358059	4646233
（1）活期存款	Demand Deposits	27671246	2621076
（2）定期及其他存款	Time and Other Deposits	42686813	2025157
2. 非金融企业存款	Non Financial Enterprises Deposits	77880729	7563276
（1）活期存款	Demand Deposits	39961604	6571309
（2）定期及其他存款	Time and Other Deposits	37919125	991967
3. 广义政府存款	General Government Deposits	32375710	3403079
（1）财政性存款	Fiscal Deposits	1946266	762044
（2）机关团体存款	Institution Deposits	30429444	2641035
4. 非银行业金融机构存款	Non Banking Financial Institution Deposits	9998979	-2842031
（二）境外存款	Foreign Deposits	126139	5220
二、各项贷款	**All Loans**	**152826450**	**15686214**
（一）境内贷款	Domestic Loans	152785390	15658214
1. 住户贷款	Household loans	33153309	4577309
（1）短期贷款	Short-term Loans	3826874	-309678
消费贷款	Consumer loans	1380694	122050
经营贷款	Business loans	2446181	-431728
（2）中长期贷款	Medium-term and Long-term loans	29326435	4886988
消费贷款	Consumer loans	26224189	4913798
经营贷款	Business loans	3102246	-26810
2. 非金融企业及机关团体贷款	Non Financial Enterprises and Institution Loans	119630126	11096168
（1）短期贷款	Short-term Loans	25229930	1665429
（2）中长期贷款	Medium-term and Long-term loans	85935638	8204069
（3）票据融资	Bill Financing	8313725	1237505
（4）融资租赁	Financial Leasing	21356	-6545
（5）各项垫款	Various Advance Funds	129476	-4290
3. 非银行业金融机构贷款	Non Banking Financial Institution Loans	1955	-15263
（二）境外贷款	**Foreign Loans**	**41060**	**27999**

注：本表数据来源于人民银行西安营管部。

19-7 金融机构（不含外资）人民币存贷款年末余额（2016年）

Year-end Balance of RMB Deposits and Loans in Financial Institutions（Not Including Foreign-funded）（2016）

单位：万元 (10 000yuan)

指　标	Item	2016	比年初增加额 Increase or decrease compared with the beginning of the Year
一、各项存款	**All Deposits**	**189575525**	**12746077**
（一）境内存款	Domestic Deposits	189454209	12740973
1. 住户存款	Household Deposits	70247778	4661299
（1）活期存款	Demand Deposits	27627286	2624819
（2）定期及其他存款	Time and Other Deposits	42620493	2036481
2. 非金融企业存款	Non Financial Enterprises Deposits	77193304	7628696
（1）活期存款	Demand Deposits	39762161	6542021
（2）定期及其他存款	Time and Other Deposits	37431143	1086674
3. 广义政府存款	General Government Deposits	32274148	3333008
（1）财政性存款	Fiscal Deposits	1946266	762044
（2）机关团体存款	Institution Deposits	30327882	2570964
4. 非银行业金融机构存款	Non Banking Financial Institution Deposits	9738978	-2882030
（二）境外存款	Foreign Deposits	121316	5103
二、各项贷款	**All Loans**	**151594014**	**15545080**
（一）境内贷款	Domestic Loans	151553947	15516978
1. 住户贷款	Household loans	33036738	4608873
（1）短期贷款	Short-term Loans	3826874	-300807
消费贷款	Consumer loans	1380694	123644
经营贷款	Business loans	2446181	-424452
（2）中长期贷款	Medium-term and Long-term loans	29209864	4909680
消费贷款	Consumer loans	26140542	4921873
经营贷款	Business loans	3069322	-12193
2. 非金融企业及机关团体贷款	Non Financial Enterprises and Institution Loans	118515254	10923369
（1）短期贷款	Short-term Loans	25054860	1731687
（2）中长期贷款	Medium-term and Long-term loans	84995879	7841000
（3）票据融资	Bill Financing	8313725	1359390
（4）融资租赁	Financial Leasing	21356	-6545
（5）各项垫款	Various Advance Funds	129434	-2163
3. 非银行业金融机构贷款	Non Banking Financial Institution Loans	1955	-15263
（二）境外贷款	**Foreign Loans**	**40067**	**28102**

注：本表数据来源于人民银行西安营管部。

19-8 保险业务情况

Indicators of Insurance Business

指　标	Item	2012	2013	2014	2015	2016
保险金额（亿元）	**Amount Insured(100 million yuan)**	**35199**	**42596**	**51454**	**62319**	**108296**
保费收入（万元）	**Premiums(10 000 yuan)**	**1732089**	**2024067**	**2194924**	**2630158**	**3458459**
一、财产险（万元）	**Property Insurance(10 000 yuan)**	**521619**	**629947**	**741762**	**835526**	**933181**
（一）财产保险	Property Insurance	484476	576666	668574	746317	833296
1. 机动车辆及第三者责任	Motor Vehicle and Outside Person Liability	431460	513634	602905	674555	738965
2. 企业财产险	Enterprise Property Insurance	41398	41140	41996	49949	64568
3. 货物运输险	Freight Transport Insurance	4312	3944	4427	5497	4814
4. 家庭财产险	Family Property Insurance	323	296	584	754	981
5. 建工及安工保险及其责任险	Construction and Installation Projects Insurance and Related Libility Insurance	5938	16133	16893	12325	18368
6. 其他	Others	1045	1519	1770	3237	5601
（二）责任保险	Liability Insurance	10719	13393	16328	23096	26922
（三）信用保险	Export Credit Insurance	8257	8648	8401	10449	17563
（四）保证保险	Guarantee Insurance	15421	21588	36868	45472	42665
（五）农业保险	Agriculture Insurance	2747	9653	11590	10191	12735
二、人身险（万元）	**Personnel Insurance(10 000 yuan)**	**1210469**	**1394120**	**1453162**	**1794632**	**2525278**
（一）人寿保险	Life Insurance	1077710	1221975	1238142	1506062	2158260
1. 非分红保险	Non Dividend Insurance	99073	109810	444520	681952	1261138
2. 分红保险	Dividend Insurance	967751	1099986	780653	810889	882110
3. 投资连接保险	Insurance Connection Insurance	346	330	316	286	236
4. 万能保险	Universal Insurance	10541	11849	12654	12935	14776
（二）意外伤害险	Unforeseen Injury Insurance	40433	49541	52963	63451	71889
（三）健康保险	Health Insurance	92326	122604	162057	225120	295130
赔款支出和各项给付	**Indemnity and Other Expenditure**	**475483**	**664905**	**807652**	**876182**	**1159143**
一、财产险（万元）	**Property Insurance(10 000 yuan)**	**274285**	**339004**	**372906**	**406530**	**422764**
（一）财产保险	Property Insurance	263917	325128	360384	375449	393905
1. 机动车辆及第三者责任	Motor Vehicle and Outside Person Liability	235665	291390	327319	348185	359288
2. 企业财产险	Enterprise Property Insurance	18805	24870	22257	16753	22038
3. 家庭财产保险	Freight Transport Insurance	66	93	107	112	324
4. 货物运输保险	Family Property Insurance	1148	1224	2429	999	1341
5. 建工及安工保险及其责任险	Construction and Installation Projects Insurance and Related Libility Insurance	7893	6480	6719	8023	9740
6. 其他	Others	340	1070	1551	1377	1173
（二）责任保险	Liability Insurance	4713	5192	5695	6300	11030
（三）信用保险	Export Credit Insurance	5357	5414	1668	7884	3287
（四）保证保险	Guarantee Insurance	-581	1450	2752	13129	10690
（五）农业保险	Agriculture Insurance	878	1820	2406	3768	3853
一、人身险（万元）	**Personnel Insurance(10 000 yuan)**	**201198**	**325900**	**434746**	**469652**	**736378**
（一）人寿保险	Life Insurance	167146	268455	360895	379370	637444
1. 非分红保险	Non Dividend Insurance	50929	48680	44359	56908	82635
2. 分红保险	Dividend Insurance	113557	216911	313706	318993	551206
3. 投资连接保险	Insurance Connection Insurance	327	32	33	48	485
4. 万能保险	Universal Insurance	2334	2832	2797	3421	3118
（二）意外伤害险	Unforeseen Injury Insurance Health Insurance	9013	10685	11438	16795	15577
（三）健康保险	Health Insurance	25039	46760	62414	73486	83357
退保金（万元）	**Withdrawal(10 000 yuan)**	**107665**	**167446**	**405676**	**433227**	**482983**
#人寿保险	Life Insurance	105909	165303	403099	414260	459733
1. 非分红保险	Ordinary Life Insurance	5514	6192	20818	195551	276544
2. 分红保险	Dividend Insurance	100373	159077	382274	218693	183191
3. 投资连接保险	Insurance Connection Insurance		9			
4. 万能保险	Universal Insurance	21	24	7	16	-2

注：本表数据来源于市金融办。

19-9 西安地区证券期货系统机构、人员数

Number of Institution and Employed Person in Securities and Futures System in Xi'an

机构名称	Name of Institution	2015		2016	
		机构数（个）Number of Institution (unit)	年末人数（人）Number of Staff and Workers (person)	机构数（个）Number of Institution (unit)	年末人数（人）Number of Staff and Workers (person)
证券经营机构	**Securities Company and the Sales Department**	**235**	**6446**	**331**	**8444**
一、证券公司	**Securities Company**	**130**	**3375**	**181**	**4464**
西部证券股份有限公司	Western Securities Company Ltd.	80	2180	104	2476
陕西开源证券经纪有限责任公司	KaiYuan Securities Company Ltd.	32	774	54	1440
中邮证券有限公司	China Post Securities	18	421	23	548
二、证券营业部（含外地公司在西安营业部）	**Sales Department (include Xi'an) departments of nonlocal companies.)**	**105**	**3071**	**150**	**3980**
期货经纪公司	**Futures Company**	**3**	**277**	**27**	**492**
迈科期货经纪有限公司	Maike Futures Company Ltd.	1	119	10	216
陕西长安期货经纪有限公司	Shanxi ChangAn Futures Company Ltd.	1	61	9	103
西部期货经纪有限公司	Western Futures Brokerage Co., Ltd.	1	97	8	173

注：1.本表数据来源于市金融办。
2.证券公司包括三家公司及其在西安和外地的营业部。
3.中邮证券有限公司原为西安华弘证券经纪有限责任公司。

19-10 证券期货市场基本情况（2016年）

Basic Facts on Securities and Futures Markets（2016）

指　标	Item	2016
一、上市证券公司情况	**Listed Securities Companies**	
拥有上市股份公司（个）	Number of Listed Share-holding Companies(unit)	33
上市股份公司总股本（亿股）	Total Capital of Listed Share-holding Companies (100 millon shares)	490.08
#流通股(亿股)	Negotiable Shares(100 million shares)	331.68
总市值（亿元）	Total Market Capitalization(100 million yuan)	
累计证券市场筹措资金（亿元）	Accumulated Capital Raised by Securities Markets(100 millon yuan)	1365.40
二、证券经营机构情况	**Securities Trading Organizations**	
拥有证券公司（个）	Number of Securities Companies(unit)	3
证券营业部（个）（含外地公司在西安营业部）	Number of Securities Business Departments(unit)	122
投资者开户数（万户）	Number of Investors Who have Opened an Account(10 000 accounts)	255.38
证券交易总额（亿元）	Total Turnover(100 million yuan)	28920.07
三、期货市场情况	**Futures Market**	
拥有期货经纪公司（个）	Number of Futures Business Management Companies(unit)	3
期货营业部（个）	Number of Futures Business,Departments(unit)	31
期货代理交易额（亿元）	Total Transaction Value in Futures Commissioning (100 million yuan)	64287.47
每个经纪公司平均拥有注册资金（万元）	Average Registered Capital of Each Business Management Company(10 000 yuan)	27600

注：本表数据来源于市金融办。

主要统计指标解释

信贷资金 指金融机构以信用方式积聚和分配的货币资金。金融机构信贷资金的来源有各项存款、金融债券、对国际金融机构负债、流通中现金、其他项目等；信贷资金的运用有各项贷款、有价证券及投资、金银占款、外汇占款、财政借款及在国际金融机构中的资产等。

存款 指企业、机关、团体或居民根据资金必须收回的原则，把货币资金存入银行或其他信贷机构保管并取得一定利息的一种信用活动形式。根据存款对象或性质的不同可划分为企业存款、财政存款、机关团体存款、城乡储蓄存款、农业存款、信托及委托类存款、其他存款等科目。它是银行信贷资金的主要来源。

贷款 指银行或其他信贷机构根据资金必须归还的原则，按一定利率，为企业、个人等提供资金的一种信用活动形式。我国银行贷款分为短期贷款、委托及信托类贷款、其他类贷款等。

保险公司 在中国境内的、经过保险监督管理部门批准设立，并依法登记注册的各类商业保险公司。

保险金额 指保险人承担赔偿或者给付保险金责任的最高限额。

保费 指投保人为取得保险人在约定范围内所承担赔偿责任而支付给保险人的费用。

赔款 指保险人根据保险合同的规定，向被保险人支付的赔偿保险责任损失的金额。

给付 包括死伤医疗给付和满期给付。死伤医疗给付是指保险人根据人寿保险及长期健康保险合同的规定，因被保险人在保险期内发生保险责任范围内的保险事故支付给被保险人（或受益人）的金额。满期给付是指被保险人生存期满，保险人按人寿保险合同规定支付给被保险人的满期保险金额。

Explanatory Notes on Main Statistical Indicators

Credit Funds refer to the monetary funds accumulated and distributed in the means of credit by the financial institutions. The sources of credit funds include various deposits, financial bonds, liabilities to international financial institutions, currency in circulation, other items. The uses of credit funds include loans, securities and investment, position for bullion and silver purchase, position for foreign exchange purchase, advances to treasury, and assets with international financial institutions..

Deposit is a form of credit by which enterprises, institutions, organizations or households can put money into banks and other credit institutions for safekeeping and interest earning under the principle of free withdrawal. According to different depositors, deposits are divided into enterprise deposits, fiscal deposits, deposits of government agencies and organizations, savings deposits of rural and urban households, agricultural savings deposits, entrusted deposits and other deposits. Deposits are major sources of the credit funds of banks.

Loan is a form of credit by which banks and other credit institutions provide funds at certain interest rate to enterprises and individuals in the light of the principle of unconditional repayment. Loans from Chinese banks include short-term loan, medium- term and long-term loans, entrusted loans, and other loans.

Insurance Companies refer to commercial insurance companies of various forms registered by law and established in China with the approval of insurance regulatory agencies.

Amount Insured refers to the maximum that the insurant will get for the claim of the case insured.

Premium is the fee paid by the insurant to the insurer to obtain the obligation of compensation from the insurance within the agreed terms.

Settled Claim is the compensation paid by the insurer to the insurant in accordance with the insurance contract.

Payment includes payment for death, injury or medical treatment and payment at maturity. Payment for death, injury or medical treatment refers to the money paid to the insurant (or the beneficiary) in accordance with the life or health insurance contract when the insurant encounters accidents within the insured period covered in the contract. Payment at maturity refers to the payment to the insurant in accordance with the life insurance contract at the end of the insured period.

20 教育和科技

EDUCATION,SCIENCE AND TECHNOLOGY

资料整理：郝　静　陈春光
Data management：Hao Jing Chen Chunguang
数据审核：王金桂
Data audit：Wang Jingui

第二十部分　教育和科技

一、简要说明

本章资料包括教育事业、科技事业基本情况，由西安市统计局服务业和社会科技处根据西安市教育局等有关部门提供资料整理。

二、主要指标

普通高等学校数（所）	63	与上年	持平
普通高等学校（本专科）在校学生（万人）	73.68	比上年减少	2.07
高等学校研究生在校人数（万人）	9.41	比上年增加	0.33

20　EDUCATION,SCIENCE AND TECHNOLOGY

Ⅰ.Brief Introduction

Data in this chapter consists of primarily data of educational undertakings, science and technology activities of Xi'an city, compiled by Tertiary Industry and Social & Science and Technology Division of the Xi'an Bureau of Statistics according to data from Xi'an Bureau of Education concerned.

Ⅱ Major Indicators

		Increase over Preceding Year
Number of Regular Institutions of Higher Education(unit)	63	essentially on a par with last year's
Student Enrollment of Regular Institutions of Higher Education (Universities and colleges) (10 000 persons)	73.68	-2.07
Postgraduates Enrollment of Regular Institutions of Higher Education (10 000 persons)	9.41	0.33

20-1 主要年份各类普通教育基本情况

Basic Statistics on Regular Education in Representative Years

指　标	Item	2010	2011	2012	2013	2014	2015	2016
学校数（所）	**Number of Schools (units)**							
普通高等学校	Regular Institutions of Higher Educatior	50	61	62	63	63	63	63
普通中等专业学校	Regular Specialized Secondary Schools	28	24	24	22	22	20	20
普通中学	Regular Secondary School	436	423	419	418	421	422	422
小学	Primary Schools	1531	1424	1322	1291	1257	1234	1190
幼儿园	Kindergarten	1004	1122	1239	1295	1343	1417	1475
毕业生人数（万人）	**Graduates (10 000 persons)**							
普通高等学校	Regular Institutions of Higher Educatior	18.3	19.7	20.9	20.2	21.3	23.2	24.1
普通中等专业学校	Regular Specialized Secondary Schools	2.5	2.3	2.1	1.9	1.8	1.3	1.3
普通中学	Regular Secondary School	17.0	16.4	15.6	15.2	14.5	13.9	14
小学	Primary Schools	9.6	8.9	8.9	8.5	8.3	7.9	8.5
幼儿园	Kindergarten		6.4	7.6	8.4	8.9	10.0	9.8
招生数（万人）	**New Enrollment (10 000 persons)**							
普通高等学校	Regular Institutions of Higher Educatior	21.7	23.1	25.2	23.9	23.6	23.4	23.1
普通中等专业学校	Regular Specialized Secondary Schools	2.1	2.0	1.7	1.4	1.3	1.0	0.9
普通中学	Regular Secondary School	16.2	15.4	15.0	14.5	14.0	13.4	13.7
小学	Primary Schools	8.6	8.8	8.9	9.6	10.1	10.5	11.7
幼儿园	Kindergarten	8.4	10.0	11.6	11.0	9.6	12.0	13.7
在校学生数（万人）	**Total Enrollment (10 000 persons)**							
普通高等学校	Regular Institutions of Higher Educatior	73.3	76.6	80.7	83.8	85.4	84.8	83.1
普通中等专业学校	Regular Specialized Secondary Schools	6.8	6.1	5.4	4.7	4.1	3.5	3.1
普通中学	Regular Secondary School	48.9	47.2	45.3	43.7	42.6	41.4	40.7
小学	Primary Schools	51.6	51.4	50.9	52.0	53.8	56.6	59.8
幼儿园	Kindergarten	18.4	24.0	27.1	28.6	29.0	30.9	31.8
教职工数（人）	**Staff and Teachers (persons)**							
普通高等学校	Regular Institutions of Higher Educatior	72247	72739	74041	74993	74954	74857	73686
普通中等专业学校	Regular Specialized Secondary Schools	3249	2868	2733	2599	2315	1991	1917
普通中学	Regular Secondary School	39207	41135	41197	41003	40576	40689	41352
小学	Primary Schools	34118	32457	32208	31863	32162	32585	34646
幼儿园	Kindergarten	18710	23680	27735	31989	33062	36004	39753
专任教师（人）	**Number of Full-time Teachers (persons)**							
普通高等学校	Regular Institutions of Higher Education	42098	42734	44487	46436	46766	47768	47158
普通中等专业学校	Regular Specialized Secondary Schools	1845	1723	1595	1474	1346	1228	1210
普通中学	Regular Secondary School	31506	33122	31526	31419	32615	33014	33962
小学	Primary Schools	29944	28453	29651	29421	28395	28748	30941
幼儿园	Kindergarten	10638	12577	14293	16238	17337	19096	21395

注：本表数据来源于市教育局。

本表中普通高等学校毕业生、招生、在校生数含研究生及普通高等学校中普通本、专科学生数。

本表中小学的学校数是指独立小学个数，其在校生、教职工等指标均为普通初等教育；幼儿园的校数是指独立的幼儿园个数，其在校生、教职工等指标均为学前教育。（下表同）

20-2 各级各类学校校数、教职工、专任教师数（2016年）

Basic Facts on Regular Education Teacher by School Type（2016）

指 标	Item	学校数（所）Number of Schools (units)	教职工数（人）Number of Staff and Teachers (persons)	专任教师数（人）Full-time Teachers (persons)
一、高等教育	**Higher education**	**76**	**76337**	**48554**
（一）研究生培养机构	Postgraduate training institutions	(43)		
1、高等学校	Institutions of Higher Schools	(22)		
2、科研机构	Scientific Research Institution	(21)		
(二)普通高等学校	Regular Institutions of Higher Schools	63	73686	47158
1、本科院校	Universities and Colleges of Undergraduate Course	42	63458	40160
其中：独立学院	Non-university Tertiary	11	6600	4102
2、专科院校	Higher Vocational Colleges	21	10228	6998
其中：高等职业学校	Higher Vocational College	19	8735	6200
(三)成人高等学校	Adult Higher Schools	13	2651	1396
二、中等职业教育	**Secondary Occupation Education**	**166**	**12802**	**9399**
(一)普通中等专业学校	Regular Specialized Secondary Schools	20	1917	1210
(二)成人中等专业学校	Adult Secondary Specialized Schools	4	1390	928
(三)职业高中学校	Vocational Hight Schools	64	3126	2275
其中：市属	Municipal schools	63	3126	2275
(四)技工学校	Technical Schools	78	6369	4986
其中：市属	Municipal schools	34	2029	1639
三、基础教育	**Elementary Education**	**3096**	**116153**	**86577**
（一）普通中等教育	Regular Institutions Education	422	41352	33962
1、高中	Senior High Schools	156		18673
完全中学	Complete Secondary Schools	97	13022	10761
高级中学	Senior Secondary Schools	48	7432	6119
十二年一贯制学校	Twelve-year Consistency Schools	11	2268	1793
2、初中	Junior Middle Schools	266		15289
初级中学	Junior Middle Schools	221	15023	12276
九年一贯制学校	Nine-year Consistency Schools	45	3607	3013
完全中学	Complete Secondary school	(11)		
十二年一贯制学校	Twelve-year Consistency schools	(97)		
附设普通初中班的学校	Senior Secondary Schools with Regular Junior Secondary Classes	(1)		
（二）普通初等教育	Regular Primary Education	1190	34646	30941
独立小学	Independent Primary Schools	1190		30019
教学点	Teaching Points	(161)		922
九年一贯制学校	Nine-year Consistency schools	(45)		
十二午一贯制学校	Twelve-year Consistency schools	(11)		
附设小学班的学校	Schools with Primary Classes	(4)		
（三）特殊教育	Special Education Schools	8	359	246
特殊教育学校	Special Education Schools	8	359	246
附设特教班的学校	Schools with Special Edution Classes	(1)		
（四）工读学校	Reformatory Schools	1	43	33
（五）学前教育	Preschool Education	1475	39753	21395
幼儿园	Kindergarten	1475	39753	21395
附设幼儿班的学校	Schools with Nursery Classes	(86)		
另有：技术培训机构	Technique Training Institution	1642	20470	14226

注：本表数据来源于市教育局。
本表为西安市行政区划内各级各类学校全口径数据（不含军事院校、党校）。
技工学校数据由西安市人力资源和社会保障局提供。
按照事业统计主体校原则，完全中学、十二年一贯制学校的学校数计入普通高中，九年一贯制学校的校数计入普通初中。
教职工数按照办学类型划分，为使用方便，专任教师同时按照办学层次列出。
( ) 内数据不计入总计。(下表同)

20-3 各级各类教育学生情况（2016年）

Basic Facts on Education Student by School Type（2016）

单位：人 (persons)

指 标	Item	毕业生数 Number of Graduates	招生数 New Enrollment	在校学生数 Total Enrollment	女生 Female Students
一、高等教育	**Higher education**	**351989**	**398382**	**1164515**	**564998**
(一)研究生	Postgraduates	24779	30263	94720	44479
1、高等学校	Institutions of Higher Schools	24562	30079	94102	44329
2、科研机构	Scientific Research Institution	217	184	618	150
（二）普通高等教育	Regular Institutions of Higher Schools	216022	200723	736849	367540
1、本科	Universities Course Schools	136989	125153	507185	256961
2、专科	Junior Colleges	79033	75570	229664	110579
（三）成人高等教育	Higher Vocational Colleges	43303	37662	122499	59728
其中：成人高等学校	Contains:Adult Higher Education	4699	4768	16749	8253
（四）网络本专科生	Network Undergraduate and clooege students	67885	129734	210447	93251
1、本科	Universities Course Schools	29193	50684	85760	39615
2、专科	Junior Colleges	38692	79050	124687	53636
二、中等职业教育	**Secondary Occupation Education**	**54312**	**65822**	**158675**	**37042**
1、普通中等专业学校	Regular Specialized Secondary Schools	12542	8819	31074	15504
2、成人中等专业学校	Adult Secondary Specialized Schools	1065	79	1295	192
3、职业高中学校	Vocational high Schools	17773	14305	43576	21346
其中：市属	Municipal schools	17502	14305	43576	21346
4、技工学校	Technical Schools	22932	42619	82730	
其中：市属	Municipal schools	5769	17133	27451	
三、基础教育	**Elementary Education**	**322476**	**390458**	**1324560**	**622634**
(一)普通中等教育	Regular Institutions Education	139560	137156	407014	190601
1、高中	Senior High Schools	55720	51688	158863	77735
完全中学	Complete Secondary Schools	24321	24852	74479	37132
高级中学	Senior Secondary Schools	29740	25126	79142	38099
十二年一贯制学校	Twelve-year Consistency schools	1659	1710	5242	2504
2、初中	Junior Middle Schools	83840	85468	248151	112866
初级中学	Junior Middle Schools	45856	44504	131065	58940
九年一贯制学校	Nine-year Consistency Schools	5549	6382	18046	8305
十二年一贯制学校	Twelve-year Consistency Schools	3216	3565	10334	4586
完全中学	Complete Secondary school	29219	31017	88706	41035
(二)普通初等教育	Regular Primary Education	84603	116460	597920	279299
小学	Pricmary Schools	78460	106948	551047	257638
九年一贯制学校	Nine-year Consistency schools	4425	7210	35585	16472
十二年一贯制学校	Twelve-year Consistency Schools	1718	2302	11288	5189
（三）特殊教育	Special Education Schools	214	327	1604	625
1、特殊教育学校	Special Education Schools	91	131	764	297
2、小学附设特教班	Primary Schools with Special Education Classes			8	3
3、小学随班就读	Elementary Inclusive	83	131	623	245
4、初中随班就读	Junior Mainstreaming	40	65	209	80
（四）工读学校	Reformatory Schools	20	14	26	5
（五）学前教育	Preschool Education	98079	136501	317996	152104
1、独立幼儿园	Independent Kindergartens	96284	134908	315663	150971
2、附设幼儿园	Attached Kindergartens	1795	1593	2333	1133
另有：职业技术培训机构	Vocational and Technical Institutions	451194		541500	287302

注：本表数据来源于市教育局。

20-4 主要年份普通高等学校和科研机构研究生情况

Basic Statistics of Postgraduates on Regular Institutions of Higher Education and Scientific Research Institution in Representative Years

单位：人 (person)

年 份 Year	毕业生数 Number of Graduates	高等学校 Higher Schools	招生数 New Enrollment	高等学校 Higher Schools	在校学生数 Total Enrollment	高等学校 Higher Schools
1978					232	232
1980					651	651
1985					4799	4799
1990	2051	2051	1662	1662	5275	5275
1995	1769	1769	2712	2712	7974	7974
1998	2316	2316	3888	3888	10833	10833
1999	2903	2903	5020	5020	12986	12986
2000	3236	3236	6924	6924	16620	16620
2001	3881	3770	9274	8966	22564	21855
2002	4103	3952	11282	10882	28446	27471
2003	5971	5765	14322	13882	36936	35790
2004	8384	8127	17310	16871	45402	44169
2005	10416	10127	18583	18106	52699	51310
2006	12914	12552	19581	19105	58433	56951
2007	15506	15124	20570	20167	64137	62801
2008	17234	16788	21892	21443	67296	65834
2009	19025	18574	24879	24400	72366	70908
2010	19526	19129	25971	25477	76993	75483
2011	20965	20605	26686	26256	81696	80332
2012	22963	22578	28065	27618	84712	83306
2013	24778	24385	28786	28333	87002	85570
2014	24092	23881	28636	28436	88518	87826
2015	25322	25104	29487	29293	91448	90790
2016	24779	24562	30263	30079	94720	94102

注：本表数据来源于市教育局。

20–5 主要年份普通高等学校基本情况（本专科）

Baisc Statistics on Regular Institution of Higher Education in Representative Years (Colleges and universities)

单位：所、万人 (units 10 000 persons)

年 份 Year	学校数 Number of Schools	毕业生数 Number of Graduates	招生数 New Enrollment	在校学生数 Total Enrollment	教职工数 Number of Staff and Teachers	专任教师数 Full-time Teachers
1978	21	0.60	1.31	2.88	2.24	0.87
1980	24	0.21	1.08	4.17	2.55	0.97
1985	28	1.17	2.28	6.49	3.40	1.28
1990	31	2.11	2.00	7.50	4.15	1.56
1995	32	2.87	3.13	10.07	4.21	1.59
1998	29	2.61	3.30	11.58	3.91	1.50
1999	29	2.84	5.12	13.79	3.95	1.52
2000	25	2.71	6.79	17.75	3.81	1.57
2001	32	3.31	8.31	23.24	4.30	1.75
2002	35	3.82	10.75	30.15	4.67	2.06
2003	37	5.89	12.21	36.42	4.92	2.21
2004	41	7.66	13.17	40.29	5.45	2.69
2005	44	10.08	14.68	47.79	5.73	2.95
2006	47	11.75	15.15	51.40	6.14	3.29
2007	48	14.33	16.96	56.03	6.56	3.67
2008	48	15.82	19.31	60.10	6.90	3.89
2009	49	15.04	18.84	63.22	7.08	4.06
2010	50	16.33	19.16	65.74	7.22	4.21
2011	61	17.68	20.52	68.52	7.27	4.27
2012	62	18.64	22.46	72.40	7.40	4.45
2013	63	17.73	21.05	75.27	7.50	4.64
2014	63	18.88	20.74	76.64	7.50	4.68
2015	63	20.72	20.49	75.75	7.49	4.78
2016	63	21.60	20.07	73.68	7.37	4.72

注：本表数据来源于市教育局。

20-6 主要年份普通中等专业学校基本情况

Baisc Statistics on Regular Specialized Secondary Schools in Representative Years

年 份 Year	学校数（所） Number of Schools (units)	毕业生数（万人） Number of Graduates (10 000 persons)	招生数（万人） New Enrollment (10 000 persons)	在校学生数（万人） Total Enrollment (10 000 persons)	教职工数（人） Number of Staff and Teachers(person)	专任教师数（人） Full-time Teachers(person)
1978	19	0.19	0.45	0.82	3937	1110
1980	31	0.18	0.42	1.50	3895	1474
1985	37	0.43	0.76	1.70	6071	2363
1990	44	0.56	0.68	2.09	7136	2891
1995	46	0.97	1.37	3.74	5903	2533
1996	47	1.15	1.61	4.18	5940	2573
1997	47	1.20	1.65	4.63	6124	2731
1998	47	1.26	1.62	5.08	6181	2840
1999	46	1.42	2.11	5.75	6385	2865
2000	47	1.63	1.90	6.02	6964	3172
2001	47	1.70	1.58	5.63	5252	2467
2002	46	1.60	1.69	5.57	5170	2508
2003	34	1.62	1.80	5.28	4562	2302
2004	35	1.40	2.09	5.71	4676	2388
2005	32	1.44	2.26	6.16	3924	2130
2006	31	1.84	2.61	7.30	3621	2014
2007	30	2.03	2.91	7.97	3548	2011
2008	29	2.58	2.55	8.06	3278	1814
2009	28	2.70	2.15	7.44	2965	1720
2010	28	2.45	2.08	6.75	3249	1845
2011	24	2.34	1.96	6.11	2868	1723
2012	24	2.15	1.67	5.43	2733	1595
2013	22	1.93	1.35	4.66	2599	1474
2014	22	1.76	1.25	4.07	2315	1346
2015	20	1.32	0.95	3.47	1991	1228
2016	20	1.25	0.88	3.11	1917	1210

注：本表数据来源于市教育局。

20-7 主要年份普通中学基本情况

Baisc Statistics on Regular Secondary Schools in Representative Years

年 份 Year	学校数（所） Number of Schools (units)	毕业生数（万人） Number of Graduates (10 000 persons)	招生数（万人） New Enrollment (10 000 persons)	在校学生数（万人） Total Enrollment (10 000 persons)	教职工数（人） Number of Staff and Teachers(person)	专任教师数（人） Full-time Teachers(person)
1978	962			44.16	27380	20660
1980	1002	12.33	14.03	44.08	29867	22530
1985	563	10.72	13.05	38.24	30063	22050
1990	518	9.11	10.49	30.03	30739	22386
1995	485	8.13	12.40	32.32	30423	21984
1996	462	8.67	13.03	35.25	30902	22478
1997	466	9.96	13.83	37.16	31682	23129
1998	467	10.64	15.00	39.79	32371	23884
1999	469	11.21	16.58	43.49	33387	25114
2000	466	12.01	17.88	48.31	34385	26230
2001	470	13.85	18.98	52.50	35442	27190
2002	467	15.76	19.68	55.36	36706	28335
2003	467	16.76	18.78	56.44	38252	29887
2004	461	18.01	18.85	56.54	39121	30600
2005	460	18.82	18.83	55.74	39456	31094
2006	457	18.04	18.61	56.11	39341	31203
2007	453	18.37	17.96	54.68	39171	31373
2008	442	17.99	17.16	52.83	39088	31425
2009	439	17.80	16.57	50.63	39002	31415
2010	436	17.01	16.15	48.89	39207	31506
2011	423	16.44	15.42	47.20	41135	31675
2012	419	15.64	14.98	45.33	41197	31526
2013	418	15.24	14.47	43.73	41003	31419
2014	421	14.54	13.97	42.57	40576	32615
2015	422	13.92	13.41	41.37	40689	33014
2016	422	13.96	13.72	40.70	41352	33962

注：本表数据来源于市教育局。

20-8 各区县普通中学基本情况（2016年）

Baisc Statistics on Regular Secondary Schools by Region（2016）

单位：所、人 (unit, person)

区县	Region	学校数 Number of Schools	毕业生数 Number of Graduates	高中 Senior	招生数 New Enrollment	高中 Senior	在校学生数 Total Enrollment	女生 Female Students	高中 Senior	教职工数 Number of Staff and Teachers	专任教师数 Full-time Teachers
合计	**Total**	**422**	**139560**	**55720**	**137156**	**51688**	**407014**	**190601**	**158863**	**41352**	**33962**
新城区	Xincheng	25	11157	3482	11315	3995	33940	16286	11779	2711	2270
碑林区	Beilin	35	15605	6358	17194	6766	49269	22913	20185	3885	3035
莲湖区	Lianhu	20	11435	3888	10972	3658	32207	15385	10925	2854	2277
灞桥区	Baqiao	26	7731	2461	7929	2105	23304	10966	6546	2563	2075
未央区	Weiyang	32	10028	4455	11544	4193	32396	15560	12678	3819	3132
雁塔区	Yanta	47	16019	5370	16728	5664	48881	23273	17008	5219	4248
阎良区	Yanliang	12	3844	1572	3368	1287	10286	5137	4179	1123	971
临潼区	Lintong	33	10991	4581	9544	4019	29645	14688	12850	3294	2764
长安区	Chang'an	50	14053	6349	14021	5918	40702	18891	17665	4138	3637
高陵区	Gaoling	15	3756	1579	3576	1261	10412	5166	3830	1063	904
蓝田县	Lantian	45	10612	4701	9018	3786	28451	13679	12158	3247	2546
周至县	Zhouzhi	35	10842	4918	9840	4207	29859	12105	13288	3278	2541
户县	Huxian	35	10364	5168	8599	3946	27509	11864	12988	3049	2668
沣东新城	Fengdongxincheng	12	3123	838	3508	883	10153	4688	2784	1109	894

注：本表数据来源于市教育局。

20-9 主要年份职业高中基本情况

Baisc Statistics on Vocational Secondary Schools in Representative Years

单位：所、人 (unit, person)

年 份 Year	学校数 Number of Schools	毕业生数 Number of Graduates	招生数 New Enrollment	在校学生数 Total Enrollment	教职工数 Number of Staff and Teachers	专任教师数 Full-time Teachers
1985	40	1661	8346	17621	1375	868
1990	58	5936	8095	20151	2674	1574
1995	71	8976	12490	32673	2394	1877
1996	67	9235	10563	25955	3098	1735
1997	73	8756	13390	29068	2993	1709
1998	89	7753	13949	31264	3152	1823
1999	91	8480	13062	31973	3217	1908
2000	95	9949	13903	32188	3311	1997
2001	85	10300	15591	34336	3517	2113
2002	78	8659	17231	39428	3461	2192
2003	87	10755	17310	44033	4036	2458
2004	83	12177	17865	46358	4101	2515
2005	91	15092	20603	51766	4750	2892
2006	96	14887	21158	53828	5193	3126
2007	86	14881	24434	56012	4899	3064
2008	84	15813	30201	62963	4878	3008
2009	84	14691	31042	72388	5129	3179
2010	84	18100	30042	78244	5222	3178
2011	78	22493	27641	75108	4849	3173
2012	77	24048	24995	67969	4775	3148
2013	74	21243	23043	61968	4699	3085
2014	81	19156	19508	60024	4860	3186
2015	80	18565	15060	49092	3239	2214
2016	64	17773	14305	43576	3126	2275

注：本表数据来源于市教育局。

20-10 各区县职业高中基本情况（2016年）

Basic Statistics on Vocational Secondary Schools by Region（2016）

单位：所、人 (unit, person)

区县	Region	学校数 Number of Schools	毕业生数 Number of Graduates	招生数 New Enrollment	在校学生数 Total Enrollment	女生 Female Students	教职工数 Number of Staff and Teachers	专任教师数 Full-time Teachers
合 计	**Total**	**63**	**17502**	**14305**	**43576**	**21346**	**3126**	**2275**
新城区	Xincheng	9	3930	3277	11395	5602	546	342
碑林区	Beilin	7	1758	1933	3671	1538	249	143
莲湖区	Lianhu	6	2528	1425	5511	3199	293	188
灞桥区	Baqiao	7	1032	642	1820	1288	168	138
未央区	Weiyang	6	695	557	2226	1156	144	109
雁塔区	Yanta	9	2388	1303	4789	1998	355	270
阎良区	Yanliang	2	742	692	2189	1220	181	124
临潼区	Lintong	5	933	998	2622	1051	245	173
长安区	Chang'an	5	1469	1348	3787	1778	453	363
高陵区	Gaoling	1	564	283	1133	570	86	79
蓝田县	Lantian	1	331	600	1306	534	73	54
周至县	Zhouzhi	3	689	473	1433	751	121	92
户 县	Huxian	2	443	774	1694	661	212	200
沣东新城	Fengdongxincheng							

注：本表数据来源于市教育局。
本表仅包括市属部分。

20-11 主要年份小学基本情况

Basic Statistics on Primary Schools in Representative Years

年 份 Year	学校数（所） Number of Schools (units)	毕业生数（万人） Number of Graduates (10 000 persons)	招生数（万人） New Enrollment (10 000 persons)	在校学生数（万人） Total Enrollment (10 000 persons)	教职工数（人） Number of Staff and Teachers(person)	专任教师数（人） Full-time Teachers(person)
1978	2667	13.07	14.10	74.03	29744	26428
1980	2337	11.91	12.57	73.36	31770	28360
1985	2337	11.21	9.57	62.16	31075	26430
1990	2343	8.67	10.85	61.87	37788	29090
1995	2360	9.93	14.09	79.36	35568	30270
1996	2362	10.48	13.63	81.81	35821	30267
1997	2368	10.98	12.48	82.67	35767	30117
1998	2361	12.18	11.88	82.03	35576	30089
1999	2354	13.65	11.61	79.81	35639	30196
2000	2323	13.83	11.51	77.81	35336	30215
2001	2277	14.20	11.07	74.51	34257	29281
2002	2137	13.89	10.13	70.78	34143	29428
2003	2084	12.97	9.28	66.78	34080	29531
2004	2016	12.37	9.12	63.75	33794	29367
2005	1980	11.92	8.47	60.47	33907	29674
2006	1929	11.53	9.16	59.33	34460	30018
2007	1872	11.38	8.67	56.83	34901	30533
2008	1781	10.58	8.33	54.66	34653	30382
2009	1666	9.96	7.84	52.52	34389	30334
2010	1531	9.61	8.64	51.56	34118	29944
2011	1424	8.92	8.77	51.39	32457	29900
2012	1322	8.88	8.88	50.85	32208	29651
2013	1291	8.51	9.56	51.95	31863	29421
2014	1257	8.29	10.13	53.79	32162	28395
2015	1234	7.85	10.51	56.62	32585	28395
2016	1190	8.46	11.65	59.79	34646	30941

注：本表数据来源于市教育局。

20-12 各区县小学基本情况（2016年）

Basic Statistics on Primary Schools by Region（2016）

单位：所、人 (unit, person)

区 县	Region	学校数 Number of Schools	毕业生数 Number of Graduates	招生数 New Enrollment	在校学生数 Total Enrollment	女生 Female Students	教职工数 Number of Staff and Teachers	专任教师数 Full-time Teachers
合 计	**Total**	**1190**	**84603**	**116460**	**597920**	**279299**	**34646**	**30941**
新城区	Xincheng	35	6226	6084	36618	17071	2127	1911
碑林区	Beilin	43	6625	7820	43978	20450	2473	2070
莲湖区	Lianhu	47	7634	9228	53059	24978	2559	2281
灞桥区	Baqiao	79	5845	10022	47558	22441	2282	1923
未央区	Weiyang	64	8308	16607	74218	34326	3090	2731
雁塔区	Yanta	75	12063	18694	92831	43383	4533	4079
阎良区	Yanliang	23	2221	2802	14972	7303	967	894
临潼区	Lintong	106	6063	7083	37673	17778	2880	2578
长安区	Chang'an	137	8005	12517	59971	28323	3662	3263
高陵区	Gaoling	70	2426	3825	18973	9140	1542	1409
蓝田县	Lantian	212	5233	5024	28411	13326	2668	2472
周至县	Zhouzhi	149	5702	6394	33169	14926	2340	2138
户 县	Huxian	107	4903	5183	30582	13935	2132	1966
沣东新城	Fengdongxincheng	43	3349	5177	25907	11919	1391	1226

注：本表数据来源于市教育局。

20-13 主要年份学前教育基本情况

Basic Conditions of Pre-school Education in Representative Years

年 份 Year	幼儿园（所） Number of Kindergartens (units)	班数（个） Number of Class (unit)	在园幼儿数（万人） Student Enrollment (10000 persons)	教职工数（人） Number of Staff and Teachers(person)	专任教师数（人） Full-time Teachers(person)
1978	363		4	3568	1315
1980	186		10	5525	2657
1985	310	3135	10	6887	2770
1990	256	3816	14	6123	2058
1995	257	4464	16	6173	2659
1996	244	4313	15	5918	2661
1997	228	4243	15	6065	2748
1998	235	4195	13	6272	2910
1999	234	4222	13	6329	2982
2000	367	4142	13	6346	2995
2001	366	4306	12	6224	3069
2002	378	4186	12	6541	3397
2003	610	4470	12	8959	4853
2004	660	4507	12	9870	5577
2005	737	4712	13	10528	5959
2006	863	5037	13	12335	7106
2007	830	5081	14	13468	7951
2008	905	5506	15	14932	8704
2009	896	5710	16	15928	9240
2010	1004	6420	18	18710	10638
2011	1122	8010	24	23680	12577
2012	1239	8729	27.10	27735	14293
2013	1295	9408	28.56	31989	16238
2014	1343	9782	28.95	33062	17337
2015	1417	10457	30.90	36004	19096
2016	1475	11090	31.80	39753	21395

注：本表数据来源于市教育局。
　　幼儿园在园人数中包括学前班。

20-14 主要年份特殊教育基本情况

Basic Statistics on Special Education in Representative Years

单位：所、人 (unit, person)

年 份 Year	学校数 Number of Schools	毕业生数 Number of Graduates	招生数 New Enrollment	在校学生数 Total Enrollment	教职工数 Number of Staff and Teachers	专任教师数 Full-time Teachers
1980	1	48	64	315	66	43
1985	2	14	36	318	94	59
1990	5	35	111	451	142	96
1995	5	27	147	1363	204	141
1996	5	60	164	1520	210	150
1997	5	153	164	1655	210	148
1998	5	266	140	2145	232	157
1999	5	349	115	1912	235	160
2000	5	269	145	1880	230	156
2001	5	237	209	1915	238	162
2002	5	216	148	1661	232	157
2003	5	156	161	1380	237	166
2004	5	137	142	1290	236	167
2005	5	184	182	1445	240	169
2006	6	171	143	1425	254	178
2007	6	169	114	1342	259	190
2008	6	83	96	1286	259	190
2009	7	311	202	1523	335	234
2010	8	214	402	1529	340	235
2011	8	280	222	1393	343	231
2012	8	197	220	1392	352	248
2013	8	194	212	1174	338	243
2014	8	172	222	1225	345	238
2015	8	168	338	1373	352	240
2016	8	214	327	1604	359	246

注：本表数据来源于市教育局。
包括盲、聋、哑、弱智儿童教育。

20-15 基础教育监测评价情况（2016年）

Monitoring and Evaluation of Basic Education（2016）

指　标	Item	2016
入学率(%)	Enrollment Rate(%)	
小学	Primary Schools	99.98
初中	Junior Middle Schools	99.86
巩固率(%)	The Consolidation Rate (%)	
小学(六年)	Primary Schools (six years)	97.93
初中(三年)	Junior Middle Schools (three years)	96.49
毕业率(%)	The Graduate Rate(%)	
小学	Primary school	99.78
初中	Junior middle school	98.67
专任教师学历合格率(%)	Qualified Rate Of Full-time Teacher Education (%)	
小学	Primary Schools	99.92
初中	Junior Middle Schools	99.88
高中	Senior Middle Schools	98.52
幼儿园	Kindergartens	97.86
小学教师专科以上学历达到率(%)	Rate of Primary School Teachers with College degree or Above (%)	96.88
初中教师本科以上学历达到率(%)	Rate of Junior Middle SchoolTeachers with Bachelor degree or Above (%)	90.27
高中教师研究生以上学历达到率(%)	Rate of Senior Middle School Teachers with Postgraduate degree or Above (%)	14.63

注：本表数据来源于市教育局。

20-16　主要年份平均每万人口在校学生数及构成

单位：人、%

年　份 Year	平均每万人 高等学校在校学生 Per 10000 people on average Hight Education Students in the school	平均每万人 高中阶段在校学生 Per 10000 people on average Number of Senior high School Students in the school	平均每万人 初中在校学生 Per 10000 people on average Number of Junior Secondary School Students in the school
1978	58		
1980	84		
1985	117		
1990	123		
1995	168		
1996	177		
1997	180		
1998	189		
1999	224		
2000	282		
2001	366		
2002	470		
2003	560		
2004	618	463	517
2005	715	492	489
2006	760	534	484
2007	817	543	466
2008	863	571	444
2009	901	619	413
2010	939	635	361
2011	1090	576	337
2012	1132	541	319
2013	1146	448	307
2014	1157	414	301
2015	1125	374	286
2016	1080	360	280

注：本表数据来源于市教育局。

The Average Number of Students in the School every 10000 Individuals in Representative Years

(persons,%)

平均每万人 小学在校学生 Per 10000 people on average Number of Primary School Students in the school	普通高等学校在校学生 占学生总数比重 Senior high School Students in the school in accounting for the proportion of the total number of students	中等学校在校学生 占学生总数比重 Junior Secondary School students in the school in accounting for the proportion of the total number of students	小学在校学生 占学生总数比重 Primary School students in the school in accounting for the proportion of the total number of students
1486	2.3	34.9	58.6
1434	3.1	33.2	55.3
1124	5.3	31.3	50.9
1016	6.7	25.1	51.7
1224	7.3	28.0	53.6
1249	7.6	28.8	53.5
1249	7.6	29.8	53.1
1228	8.0	31.3	52.0
1183	9.3	33.2	49.2
1131	11.5	34.8	46.0
1072	14.6	35.9	42.6
1007	18.2	36.4	39.0
932	20.1	33.8	33.5
879	22.2	35.2	31.6
815	26.4	36.2	30.1
788	27.7	37.1	28.7
744	29.3	36.3	26.7
708	30.8	36.1	25.2
672	31.8	36.5	23.7
660	33.0	35.0	23.2
604	29.8	30.1	19.9
595	31.0	28.2	19.5
605	32.6	25.3	20.2
626	33.2	23.8	20.9
650	32.8	22.2	21.9
641	31.4	21.4	22.6

20-17 民办教育情况（2016年）

单位：所、人

指标	Item	学校数 Number of Schools	毕业生数 Number of Graduates
一、民办高等教育(民办高校)	**Private higher Education (Institutions)**	**16**	**85369**
二、民办中等教育	**Private Secondary Education**	**89**	**38814**
民办普通高中	Ordinary High School	26	6245
民办普通中等专业学校	Civilian run ordinary secondary vocational school	1	755
民办职业高中	Vocational hight school	38	8663
民办普通初中	Ordinary Junior middle school	24	19965
民办的附设中职班	Private primary school class	(9)	3186
三、民办普通小学	**Private Primary School**	**64**	**9136**
四、民办幼儿园	**Private kindergarten**	**919**	**67288**
另有：民办培训机构	Private Training Institutions	576	230360

注：本表数据来源于市教育局。
毕业生数中幼儿园为离园人数。
民办高等教育在校生为民办高校普通、成人本专科学生数。
聘请校外教师中，小学、中学、幼儿园为代课教师和兼任教师之和。
民办普通高中含完全中学14所、高级中学5所、12年一贯制7所；民办普通初中含初级中学14所，9年一贯制10所。
按照教育报表制度，民办的附设中职班教职工计入基础教育主体校教职工总数，专任教师为中职层次，故单独统计。

Private Education Situation（2016）

(unit, person)

招生数 New Enrollment	在校 学生数 Total Enrollment	教职工数 Number of Teachers and Staff	专任教师 Full-time Teachers	聘请外校教师 Teachers hired from Outside Schools
73173	**262091**	**19852**	**12915**	
37052	**115765**	**8362**	**6785**	**9**
6135	18654	4069	3197	
637	2759	244	160	
7883	25327	1176	710	9
20836	61944	2873	2406	
1561	7081		312	
17213	**79879**	**3838**	**3313**	
99332	**224287**	**28172**	**14285**	**3**
	315972	9073	4940	6031

20-18 研究与试验发展（R&D）情况（2016年）

Research and Experiment Development Facts（2016）

指　标	Item	2016
一、单位数（个）	**Number of Units(unit)**	1967
#有R&D活动单位数	The Number of R&D active units	594
二、R&D人员（人）	**Personnel Eagaged in R&D(person)**	98974
三、R&D人员折合全时当量（人年）	**R&D Stuff Equivalent to Full Time equivalent (person year)**	69160
四、R&D经费内部支出（万元）	**R&D Internal Expenditure(10000 yuan)**	3255583
五、R&D项目(课题）（项）	**R&D Project(Issue)**	39593

注：本表数据来源于省统计局反馈。

20-19 规模以上企业研究与试验发展（R&D）情况（2016年）

R&D Status of Enterprises above Designated Size（2016）

指　标	Item	2016
一、企业数（个）	**Number of Enterprises(unit)**	**2952**
#工业	Industry	1219
建筑业	Construction Industry	740
服务业	Service Industry	993
#有R&D活动的单位数	The Number of R&D active units	417
#工业	Industry	369
建筑业	Construction Industry	18
服务业	Service Industry	30
二、R&D人员（人）	**Personnel Eagaged in R&D(person)**	**45502**
#工业	Industry	36867
建筑业	Construction Industry	2683
服务业	Service Industry	5952
三、R&D人员折合全时当量（人年）	**R&D Stuff Equivalent to Full Time equivalent (person year)**	**31762**
#工业	Industry	26050
建筑业	Construction Industry	2092
服务业	Service Industry	3620
四、R&D经费内部支出（万元）	**R&D Internal Expenditure(10000 yuan)**	**1284534**
#工业	Industry	1005323
建筑业	Construction Industry	82541
服务业	Service Industry	196670
五、R&D项目（课题）（项）	**Project(Issue)**	**2834**
#工业	Industry	2255
建筑业	Construction Industry	183
服务业	Service Industry	396

20-20 规模以上工业企业研究与试验发展（R&D）基本情况（2016年）

R&D Project Status of Industrial Enterprises above Designated Size（2016）

指 标	Item	企业数（个）Number of enterprises (unit)	有R&D活动的企业数 The Number of R&D enterprises
总计	**Total**	1219	369
按规模分	**Grouped by Size**		
大型企业	Large-size	62	40
中型企业	Medium-size	157	83
小型企业	Small-size	966	242
微型企业	Microenterprise	34	4
按登记注册类型分	Grouped by Registered Status		
内资企业	Domestic Investment Enterprises	1105	339
国有企业	State-owned Enterprises	33	23
集体企业	Collective-owned Enterprise	8	
股份合作企业	Stock Cooperative Enterprises	5	1
联营企业	Affiliated Enterprise		
有限责任公司	Limited Liability Corporations	606	175
股份有限公司	Share-holding Corporation Ltd	105	68
私营企业	Private Enterprise	348	72
其他	Other Domestic Funded Enterprises		
港、澳、台商投资企业	Enterprises with Funds from Hong Kong, Macao And Taiwan	25	6
外商投资企业	Foreign Funded Enterprises	89	24
按国民经济行业大类分组	Grouped by Sector		
采矿业	Mining	5	1
煤炭开采和洗选业	Mining and Washing of Coal		
石油和天然气开采业	Extraction of Petroleum and Natural Gas		

20-20 续表1 continued 1

指 标	Item	企业数（个） Number of enterprises (unit)	有R&D活动的企业数 The Number of R&D enterprises
黑色金属矿采选业	Mining of Ferrous Metal Ores		
有色金属矿采选业	Mining of Non-ferrous Metal Ores		
非金属矿采选业	Mining and Processing of Nonmetal Ores		
开采辅助活动	Mining Other Ores	5	1
制造业	Manufacturing Industry	1181	367
农副食品加工业	Processing of Food from Agriculture Products	47	2
食品制造业	Manufacture of Food	43	8
酒、饮料和精制茶制造业	Manufacture of Beverages	16	1
烟草制品业	Manufacture of Tobacco	1	
纺织业	Manufacture of Textile	14	2
纺织服装、服饰业	Manufacture of Textile Wearing, Apparel	4	
皮革、毛皮、羽毛及其制品和制鞋业	Manufacture of Leather, Furs, Feather, Related Products and Footware	3	1
木材加工和木、竹、藤、棕、草制品业	Processing of Timber,Manufacture of Wood, Bamboo, Rattan, Palm and Straw Products	5	1
家具制造业	Manufacture of Furniture	14	
造纸及纸制品业	Manufacture of Paper And Paper Products	23	
印刷和记录媒介复制业	Printing and Reproduction of Recording Media	23	4
文教、工美、体育和娱乐用品制造业	Education, Art, Sports And Entertainment Products Manufacturing	7	
石油加工、炼焦和核燃料加工业	Processing of Petroleum,Coking and Processing of Nuclear Fuel	7	
化学原料和化学制品制造业	Manufacture of Raw Chemical Materials and Chemical Products	75	31

20-20 续表2 continued 2

指 标	Item	企业数（个）Number of enterprises (unit)	有R&D活动的企业数 The Number of R&D enterprises
医药制造业	Manufacture of Medicines	53	29
化学纤维制造业	Manufacture of Chemical Fiber	3	1
橡胶和塑料制品业	Manufacture of Rubber and Manufacture of Plastic	30	3
非金属矿物制品业	Manufacture of Non-metallic Mineral Products	112	6
黑色金属冶炼和压延加工业	Smelting and Pressing of Ferrous Metals	12	
有色金属冶炼和压延加工业	Smelting and Pressing of Non-ferrous Metals	38	17
金属制品业	Manufacture of Metal Products	64	12
通用设备制造业	Manufacture of General Purpose Machinery	74	24
专用设备制造业	Manufacture of Special Equipment	107	47
汽车制造业	Manufacture of Motor Vehicle	49	15
铁路、船舶、航空航天和其他运输设备制造业	Railways, Ships, Aerospace And Other Transportation Equipment Manufacturing Industry	70	28
电气机械和器材制造业	Manufacture of Electric Equipment and Machinery	128	46
计算机、通信和其他电子设备制造业	Manufacture of Communication Equipment, Computers and Other Electronic Equipment	84	49
仪器仪表制造业	Manufacture of Measuring Instruments and Machinery	58	35
其他制造业	Other Manufacturing	10	3
废弃资源综合利用业	Comprehensive Utilization Of Waste Resources	2	1
金属制品、机械和设备修理业	Metal Products, Machinery and Equipment Repair Industry	5	1
电力、燃气及水的生产供应业	Production and Supply of Electric Power,Gas and Water	33	1
电力、热力生产和供应业	Production and Supply of Electric Power and Heat Power	18	1
燃气生产和供应业	Production and Supply of Gas	11	
水的生产和供应业	Production and Supply of Water	4	

20-21 规模以上工业企业研究与试验发展（R&D）人员和经费支出情况（2016年）

指标	Item	R&D人员（人）R&D personnel（person）	研究人员 Researchers
总计	**Total**	**36867**	**14755**
按企业规模分	**Grouped by Size of Enterprises**		
大型企业	Large-size	25488	9518
中型企业	Medium-size	6253	2968
小型企业	Small-size	5086	2250
微型企业	microenterprise	40	19
按登记注册类型分组	**Grouped by Registion Status**		
内资企业	Domestic Investment Enterprises	34722	13705
国有企业	State-owned Enterprises	10615	4484
集体企业	Collective-owned Enterprises		
股份合作企业	Stock cooperative enterprises	12	6
联营企业	Affiliated companies		
有限责任公司	Limited Liability Corporations	19499	7110
股份有限公司	Share-holding Corperation Ltd.	3175	1487
私营企业	Private Enterprises	1421	618
其他	Other Domestic Funded Enterprises		
港、澳、台商投资企业	Enterprises with Funds from Hong Kong,Macao and Taiwan	95	44
外商投资企业	Foreign Funded Enterprises	2050	1006
按工业行业大类分	**Grouped by Sector**		
采矿业	Mining	716	364
煤炭开采和洗选业	Mining and Washing of Coal		
石油和天然气开采业	Extraction of Petroleum and Natural Gas		
黑色金属矿采选业	Mining of Ferrous Metal Ores		
有色金属矿采选业	Mining of Non-ferrous Metal Ores		
非金属矿采选业	Mining and Processing of Nonmetal Ores		
开采辅助活动	Mining of Other Ores	716	364
制造业	Processing of Food from Agricultural Products	36123	14376
农副食品加工业	Manufacture of Foods	19	6
食品制造业	Manufacture of Beverages	166	52
酒、饮料和精制茶制造业	Manufacture of Tobacco	32	17
烟草制品业	Manufacture of Textile		
纺织业	Manufacture of Textile Wearing Apparel, Footware and Caps	143	76
纺织服装、服饰业	Manufacture of Leather, Fur, Feather and Related Products		
皮革、毛皮、羽毛及其制品和制鞋业	Processing of Timber,Manufacture of Wood, Bamboo,Rattan, its Products and Footwear	51	6

R&D Personnel and Expenditure Conditions of Industrial Enterprises above Designated Size（2016）

R&D经费内部支出（万元） R&D Intramural Expenditure (10000 yuan)	政府资金 Government funds	企业资金 Enterprise funds	境外资金 Foreign funds
1005323	**301821**	**697154**	**15**
777747	288166	489537	
129889	7684	117376	9
97144	5961	89706	6
544	10	534	
846316	301483	538561	
251392	73285	178063	
152		152	
476752	220513	253794	
94876	4436	87625	
23144	3249	18927	
2331	208	2062	
156676	130	156531	15
15129	746	14382	
15129	746	14382	
989984	300960	682676	15
100		100	
3865	37	3649	
459	118	341	
3240		3240	
2523		2523	

20-21 续表1

指标	Item	R&D人员（人）R&D personnel (person)	研究人员 Researchers
木材加工和木、竹、藤、棕、草制品业	Plam and Straw Products and Straw Products	25	3
家具制造业	Manufacture of Furniture		
造纸及纸制品业	Manufacture of Paper and Paper Products		
印刷和记录媒介复制业	Printing,Reproduction of Recording Media	169	81
文教、工美、体育和娱乐用品制造业	Manufacture of Articles For Culture, Education and Sport Activities		
石油加工业、炼焦和核燃料加工业	Processing of Petroleum, Coking, Processing of Nuclear Fuel		
化学原料及化学制品制造业	Manufacture of Raw Chemical Materials and Chemical Products	2318	1033
医药制造业	Manufacture of Medicines	1028	479
化学纤维制造业	Manufacture of Chemical Fibers	15	6
橡胶和塑料制品业	Manufacture of Rubber and Manufacture of Plastics	110	58
非金属矿物制品业	Manufacture of Non-metallic Mineral Products	121	58
黑色金属冶炼和压延加工业	Smelting and Pressing of Ferrous Metals		
有色金属冶炼和压延加工业	Smelting and Pressing of Non-ferrous Metals	857	378
金属制品业	Manufacture of Metal Products	1944	732
通用设备制造业	Manufacture of General Purpose Machinery	773	352
专用设备制造业	Manufacture of Special Equipment	1746	873
汽车制造业	Manufacture of Motor Vehicle	2569	1076
铁路、船舶、航空航天和其他运输设备制造业	Railways,Shipbuilding,Aerospace and Other Transportation Equipment Manufacturing Industry	13171	4164
电气机械和器材制造业	Manufacture of Electric Equipment and Machinery	3614	1429
计算机、通讯和其他电子设备制造业	Manufacture of Communication Equipment, Computers and other Electronic Equipment	4714	2281
仪器仪表制造业	Manufacture of Measuring Instruments and Machinery	2477	1183
其他制造业	Other Manufacturing	49	27
废弃资源综合利用业	Comprehensive Utilization Of Waste Resources	5	2
金属制品、机械和设备修理业	Metal Products,Machinery and Equipment Repair Industry	7	4
电力、热力、燃气及水生产和供应业	Production and Distribution of Electricity,Gas and Water	28	15
电力、热力的生产和供应业	Production and Supply of Electric Power and Heat Power	28	15
燃气生产和供应业	Gas mining and supplying industry		
水的生产和供应业	Production and Supply of Water		

continued 1

R&D经费内部支出（万元） R&D Intramural Expenditure (10000 yuan)	政府资金 Government funds	企业资金 Enterprise funds	境外资金 Foreign funds
4194		4194	
3622		2725	
62575	6045	56530	
53255	548	52284	
636		636	
2767	1950	817	
2785	405	2380	
15667	2508	13012	
40214	16225	23837	
29817	517	28877	
31722	5718	25794	9
71599	659	68295	
348470	237137	111283	6
96477	2849	93455	
168865	7663	161080	
46284	18531	26826	
638	49	589	
6		6	
206		206	
210	115	96	
210	115	96	

20-22 规模以上工业企业新产品开发、生产及销售情况（2016年）

指标	Item	新产品开发项目数（项）Number of new product development projects（item）
总计	**Total**	**2416**
按企业规模分	**Grouped by Size of Enterprises**	
大型企业	Large-size	869
中型企业	Medium-size	681
小型企业	Small-size	856
微型企业	microenterprise	10
按登记注册类型分组	**Grouped by Registion Status**	
内资企业	Domestic Investment Enterprises	2266
国有企业	State-owned Enterprises	534
集体企业	Collective-owned Enterprises	
股份合作企业	Stock cooperative enterprises	1
联营企业	Affiliated companies	
有限责任公司	Limited Liability Corporations	994
股份有限公司	Share-holding Corperation Ltd.	434
私营企业	Private Enterprises	303
其他	Other Domestic Funded Enterprises	
港、澳、台商投资企业	Enterprises with Funds from Hong Kong,Macao and Taiwan	15
外商投资企业	Foreign Funded Enterprises	135
按工业行业大类分	**Grouped by Sector**	
采矿业	Mining	25
煤炭开采和洗选业	Mining and Washing of Coal	
石油和天然气开采业	Extraction of Petroleum and Natural Gas	
黑色金属矿采选业	Mining of Ferrous Metal Ores	
有色金属矿采选业	Mining of Non-ferrous Metal Ores	
非金属矿采选业	Mining and Processing of Nonmetal Ores	
开采辅助活动	Mining of Other Ores	25
制造业	Processing of Food from Agricultural Products	2391
农副食品加工业	Manufacture of Foods	3
食品制造业	Manufacture of Beverages	17
酒、饮料和精制茶制造业	Manufacture of Tobacco	2
烟草制品业	Manufacture of Textile	
纺织业	Manufacture of Textile Wearing Apparel, Footware and Caps	10
纺织服装、服饰业	Manufacture of Leather, Fur, Feather and Related Products	
皮革、毛皮、羽毛及其制品和制鞋业	Processing of Timber,Manufacture of Wood, Bamboo,Rattan, its Froducts and Footwear	9

New Product Development, Production and Sales of Above-scale Industrial Enterprises（2016）

新产品开发经费支出（万元） New Product Development Expenditure （10 000 yuan）	新产品产值 （万元） New product output value （10 000 yuan）	新产品销售收入 （万元） Saies of new products （10 000 yuan）
1129162	**10491752**	**7325297**
861461	8323829	5477255
140540	1182826	926231
126096	981841	918327
1066	3256	3484
950110	10015987	6953937
266146	1427041	1317422
		564
141	2034	2034
562035	6949341	4172349
93013	1541218	1371579
28775	96354	89989
10387	221228	163625
168665	254536	207735
3002	17640	14061
3002	17640	14061
1126160	10471993	7306048
116	486	935
4434	100158	83716
1287	1300	671
3240	10889	10377
2738	32755	33164

20-22 续表1

指标	Item	新产品开发项目数（项） Number of new product development projects（item）
木材加工和木、竹、藤、棕、草制品业	Plam and Straw Products and Straw Products	
家具制造业	Manufacture of Furniture	
造纸及纸制品业	Manufacture of Paper and Paper Products	1
印刷和记录媒介复制业	Printing,Reproduction of Recording Media	7
文教、工美、体育和娱乐用品制造业	Manufacture of Articles For Culture, Education and Sport Activities	
石油加工业、炼焦和核燃料加工业	Processing of Petroleum, Coking, Processing of Nuclear Fuel	
化学原料及化学制品制造业	Manufacture of Raw Chemical Materials and Chemical Products	341
医药制造业	Manufacture of Medicines	136
化学纤维制造业	Manufacture of Chemical Fibers	1
橡胶和塑料制品业	Manufacture of Rubber and Manufacture of Plastics	2
非金属矿物制品业	Manufacture of Non-metallic Mineral Products	12
黑色金属冶炼和压延加工业	Smelting and Pressing of Ferrous Metals	
有色金属冶炼和压延加工业	Smelting and Pressing of Non-ferrous Metals	117
金属制品业	Manufacture of Metal Products	104
通用设备制造业	Manufacture of General Purpose Machinery	119
专用设备制造业	Manufacture of Special Equipment	251
汽车制造业	Manufacture of Motor Vehicle	151
铁路、船舶、航空航天和其他运输设备制造业	Railways,Shipbuilding,Aerospace and Other Transportation Equipment Manufacturing Industry	262
电气机械和器材制造业	Manufacture of Electric Equipment and Machinery	477
计算机、通讯和其他电子设备制造业	Manufacture of Communication Equipment, Computers and other Electronic Equipment	225
仪器仪表制造业	Manufacture of Measuring Instruments and Machinery	132
其他制造业	Other Manufacturing	12
废弃资源综合利用业	Comprehensive Utilization Of Waste Resources	
金属制品、机械和设备修理业	Metal Products,Machinery and Equipment Repair Industry	
电力、热力、燃气及水生产和供应业	Production and Distribution of Electricity,Gas and Water	
电力、热力的生产和供应业	Production and Supply of Electric Power and Heat Power	
燃气生产和供应业	Gas mining and supplying industry	
水的生产和供应业	Production and Supply of Water	

continued 1

新产品开发经费支出（万元） New Product Development Expenditure （10 000 yuan）	新产品产值 （万元） New product output value （10 000 yuan）	新产品销售收入 （万元） Sales of new products （10 000 yuan）
252	193	757
2166	819	28632
64455	1012501	967642
58639	305394	229617
636		
470	15000	12505
3007	77756	73300
	5528	3317
20464	395750	331794
40976	149678	152747
32855	112418	142408
43517	294327	248265
141999	4549516	1789055
382907	1475033	1519595
116583	1107522	981365
183939	574257	456914
20535	247488	235924
946	3227	3350
	2119	5188
	2119	5188

20–23 主要年份企事业单位知识产权情况

Intellectual Property Right of Enterprises and Institutions in Representative Years

指 标	Item	2012	2013	2014	2015	2016
一、科技活动情况	**Science and technology activities**					
科技活动人员（人）	People involved into activities(person)	162232	161004	173320	160629	188267
科技活动机构数（个）	units involved into activities(unit)	616	634	656	646	766
二、知识产权拥有量情况	**Number of IPR**					
1. 专利情况（件）	Patents(item)					
（1）累计申请专利	Accumulated patent applications	139290	186401	233435	294421	340524
当年申请专利	Patent applictions in this year	36983	47111	47034	60986	46103
#发明专利	Invention patents	15029	23534	21189	14024	18569
（2）累计授权专利	Accumulated patents awarded	53118	69368	86639	111742	150021
当年授权专利	Patents awarded in this year	11862	16250	17271	25103	38279
#发明专利	Invention patents	3475	3708	4272	5873	6686
2. 商标情况（件）	Trade marks(item)					
（1）当年注册商标申请	Trade mark registration claimed in this year	18230	12372	10023	23000	30145
（2）累计注册商标	Accumulated trade mark registrations	65733	69915	75515	80150	115541
#当年注册商标	Trade mark registrations in this year	12120	8850	8875	9600	35391
三、民事知识产权维权情况（件）	**IPR controversy(item)**	**631**	**476**	**385**	**813**	**887**
1. 专利纠纷	Patent controversies	107	77	48	130	95
2. 商标纠纷	Trade mark controversies	107	209	173	277	353
3. 著作权纠纷	Copyright controversies	365	141	126	327	404
4. 技术合同纠纷	Technological contract controversies	9	16	7	12	10
5. 其他知识产权纠纷	Others IPR controvers	43	33	31	67	25

注：本表数据由省统计局、市科技局、市工商局、市中级人民法院等提供。

20-24 规模以上工业企业自主知识产权情况（2016年）

The Independent Intellectual Property Rights of Industrial Enterprises above Designated Size（2016）

指 标	Item	专利申请数（件）Number of Patent Applications (piece)	#发明专利 Invention Patent of	期末有效发明专利数（件）Number of Valid Invention Patents At the End of the Term (piece)
总计	**Total**	**4705**	**2010**	**7486**
按规模分	**Grouped by Size**			
大型企业	Large-size	2294	1051	2959
中型企业	Medium-size	864	316	1465
小型企业	Small-size	1531	635	3008
微型企业	Microenterprise	16	8	54
按登记注册类型分	**Grouped by Registered Status**			
内资企业	Domestic Investment Enterprises	4571	1932	7150
国有企业	State-owned Enterprises	1012	556	1681
集体企业	Collective-owned Enterprise			
股份合作企业	Stock Cooperative Enterprises	6	1	26
联营企业	Affiliated Enterprise			
有限责任公司	Limited Liability Corporations	2266	900	3381
股份有限公司	Share-holding Corporation Ltd	715	206	1145
私营企业	Private Enterprise	572	269	917
其他	Other Domestic Funded Enterprises			
港、澳、台商投资企业	Enterprises with Funds from Hong Kong, Macao And Taiwan	18	9	99
外商投资企业	Foreign Funded Enterprises	116	69	237
按国民经济行业大类分组	**Grouped by Sector**			
采矿业	Mining	27	20	69
煤炭开采和洗选业	Mining and Washing of Coal			
石油和天然气开采业	Extraction of Petroleum and Natural Gas			
黑色金属矿采选业	Mining of Ferrous Metal Ores			
有色金属矿采选业	Mining of Non-ferrous Metal Ores			
非金属矿采选业	Mining and Processing of Nonmetal Ores			
开采辅助活动	Mining Other Ores	27	20	69
制造业	Manufacturing Industry	4642	1977	7393
农副食品加工业	Processing of Food from Agriculture Products			
食品制造业	Manufacture of Food			27
酒、饮料和精制茶制造业	Manufacture of Beverages	2		2
烟草制品业	Manufacture of Tobacco			
纺织业	Manufacture of Textile			
纺织服装、服饰业	Manufacture of Textile Wearing, Apparel			
皮革、毛皮、羽毛及其制品和制鞋业	Manufacture of Leather, Furs, Feather, Related Products and Footware	15	4	3

20-24 续表1 continued 1

指 标	Item	专利申请数（件）Number of Patent Applications (piece)	#发明专利 Invention Patent of	期末有效发明专利数（件）Number of Valid Invention Patents At the End of the Term (piece)
木材加工和木、竹、藤、棕、草制品业	Processing of Timber,Manufacture of Wood, Bamboo, Rattan, Palm and Straw Products			
家具制造业	Manufacture of Furniture			
造纸及纸制品业	Manufacture of Paper And Paper Products			
印刷和记录媒介复制业	Printing and Reproduction of Recording Media	5	5	64
文教、工美、体育和娱乐用品制造业	Education, Art, Sports And Entertainment Products Manufacturing			
石油加工、炼焦和核燃料加工业	Processing of Petroleum,Coking and Processing of Nuclear Fuel			
化学原料和化学制品制造业	Manufacture of Raw Chemical Materials and Chemical Products	484	275	718
医药制造业	Manufacture of Medicines	52	39	343
化学纤维制造业	Manufacture of Chemical Fiber			
橡胶和塑料制品业	Manufacture of Rubber and Manufacture of Plastic	11	5	12
非金属矿物制品业	Manufacture of Non-metallic Mineral Products	29	8	131
黑色金属冶炼和压延加工业	Smelting and Pressing of Ferrous Metals	10		9
有色金属冶炼和压延加工业	Smelting and Pressing of Non-ferrous Metals	153	106	477
金属制品业	Manufacture of Metal Products	145	65	362
通用设备制造业	Manufacture of General Purpose Machinery	185	45	258
专用设备制造业	Manufacture of Special Equipment	664	253	797
汽车制造业	Manufacture of Motor Vehicle	594	131	156
铁路、船舶、航空航天和其他运输设备制造业	Railways, Ships, Aerospace And Other Transportation Equipment Manufacturing Industry	690	452	1614
电气机械和器材制造业	Manufacture of Electric Equipment and Machinery	719	243	856
计算机、通信和其他电子设备制造业	Manufacture of Communication Equipment, Computers and Other Electronic Equipment	585	244	735
仪器仪表制造业	Manufacture of Measuring Instruments and Machinery	262	90	753
其他制造业	Other Manufacturing	37	12	76
废弃资源综合利用业	Comprehensive Utilization Of Waste Resources			
金属制品、机械和设备修理业	Metal Products, Machinery and Equipment Repair Industry			
电力、燃气及水的生产供应业	Production and Supply of Electric Power,Gas and Water	36	13	24
电力、热力生产和供应业	Production and Supply of Electric Power and Heat Power	36	13	24
燃气生产和供应业	Production and Supply of Gas			
水的生产和供应业	Production and Supply of Water			

20-25 主要年份高新技术产业开发区情况

Basic Statistics of Hi-Tech Development Zone in Representative Years

指 标	Item	2010	2011	2012	2013	2014	2015	2016
1. 高新技术企业数 （个）	Number of High-tech Enterprises(unit)	672	774	690	802	878	1008	1034
2. 年末从业人员（人）	Number of Persons Employed at year-end (person)	287140	296723	320259	328707	346679	399403	415344
从事技术开发人数（人）	Number of Persons Engaged in Technology Development	67708	78636	81787	88179	101479	117176	130919
3. 技术开发经费支出总额（万元）	Expenditures on Technology Development(10 000 yuan)	1031223	1322923	1768282	1926100	3125766	3841817	4484185
研究与发展支出	Expenditures on Research and Development	669083	831822	1273311	1666389	2049769	1805600	2430000
4. 利润总额（万元）	Total Profits (10 000 yuan)	1707925	2224850	2905877	3539526	3896038	4101017	4590772
5. 上缴税费总额（万元）	Sum of tax (10 000 yuan)	1964820	2586712	3383678	4465587	4640297	5125209	5599041
6. 出口创汇总额（千美元）	Foreign Exchange Earnings of Exports(USD 1 000)	4951265	6447050	6591977	7880206	9488010	12141353	85059382

注：本表数据来源于西安市高新技术开发区。
2016年数据未经科技部评估。
2016年出口创汇总额为人民币（千元）。

20-26 高新技术产业开发区发展规模（2016年）

Development Status of Hi-Tech Development Zone（2016）

指 标	Item	合计 Total	新建区 Newly constructed Zone
累计已开发面积（平方公里）	Accumulated Areas Developed (sq.km)	57.21	57.21
高新区工商注册（个）	Registered Enterprises in Hi-tech Zones (unit)	41124	41124
#工业型技术开发技术服务型企业数	Number of industrial technology developing enterprises	15493	15493
#三资企业数	Enterprises of Joiut Venture,Cooperation and Foreign-funded	1244	1244
已认定的高新技术企业数（个）	Hi-tech Enterprises Designated	1382	1382

注：本表数据来源于西安市高新技术开发区。

20-27 主要年份高新技术产业开发区建设与集资情况

Capital Construction and Funds-Raising of Hi-Tech Development Zone in Representative Years

指　标	Item	2011	2012	2013	2014	2015	2016
一、基建投资（亿元）	**Investment on Capital Construction (100 million yuan)**						
本年基建投资	Investment on Capital Construction of this year	266.51	350.88	432.38	601.01	615.33	653.58
二、开发面积	**Area Developed**						
新建区累计开发土地面积（平方公里）	Accumulated Area Developed in Newly Constructed Zone (sq.km)	35	40	50	55	55.13	57.27
#当年新开发土地面积	Area Developed in this year		5	10	5	1.84	2.14
累计竣工建筑面积（万平方米）	Accumulated Floor Space Completed (10 000 sq.m)	2748.09	3095.09	3433.89	3773.89	4127.39	4533.04
#当年竣工建筑面积	Floor Space Completed in this year	328.22	347	338.8	340	353.5	405.65
三、吸引外资（亿美元）	**Foreign Investment(100million USB)**						
年末累计境外客商协议投资额	Contracted Foreign Investment Accumulated at Year-end	56.71	74.11	150.61	170.61	192.82	215.96
年末累计境外客商实际投资额	Actual Foreign Investment	36.24	45.02	58.28	72.78	89.39	107.7
#当年实际投资额	Actual Investmen in this year	6.49	8.18	13.26	14.5	16.71	18.31

注：本表数据来源于西安市高新技术开发区。

主要统计指标解释

普通高等学校 指按国家规定的设置标准和审批程序批准举办的，通过全国普通高等学校统一招生考试，招收高中毕业生为主要培养对象，实施高等学历教育的全日制大学、独立设置的学院和高等专科学校、高等职业学校及其他机构（独立学院和分校、大专班）。

大学、独立设置的学院主要实施本科层次以上教育。高等专科学校、高等职业学校实施专科层次教育。其他机构是承担国家普通招生计划任务不计校数的机构，包括独立学院、普通高等学校分校、大专班和批准筹建的普通高等学校等。独立学院指由普通本科高校按新机制、新模式举办的本科层次的二级学院，一些普通本科高校按公办机制和模式建立的二级学院，“分校”或其他类似的二级办学机构不属此范畴。

成人高等学校 指按照国家规定的设置标准和审批程序批准举办的，通过全国成人高等教育统一招生考试，招收具有高中毕业或同等学历的人员为主要培养对象，利用函授、业余、脱产等多种形式对其实施高等学历教育的学校。包括职工高等学校、农民高等学校、管理干部学院、教育学院、独立函授学院、广播电视大学、其他机构等。其他机构是承担国家成人招生计划任务不计校数的机构。

小学学龄儿童净入学率 指调查范围内已入小学学习的学龄儿童占校内外学龄儿童总数（包括弱智儿童，不包括盲聋哑儿童）的比重。计算公式为：

小学学龄儿童净入学率（%）=已入学的小学学龄儿童数／校内外小学学龄儿童总数×100%

研究与试验发展（R&D） 指在科学技术领域，为增加知识总量，以及运用这些知识去创造新的应用进行的系统的创造性的活动，包括基础研究、应用研究、试验发展三类活动。国际上通常采用R&D活动的规模和强度指标反映一国的科技实力和核心竞争力。

基础研究 指为了获得关于现象和可观察事实的基本原理的新知识（揭示客观事物的本质、运动规律，获得新发现、新学说）而进行的实验性或理论性研究，它不以任何专门或特定的应用或使用为目的。其成果以科学论文和科学著作为主要形式。用来反映知识的原始创新能力。

应用研究 指为获得新知识而进行的创造性研究，主要针对某一特定的目的或目标。应用研究是为了确定基础研究成果可能的用途，或是为达到预定的目标探索应采取的新方法（原理性）或新途径。其成果形式以科学论文、专著、原理性模型或发明专利为主。用来反映对基础研究成果应用途径的探索。

试验发展 指利用从基础研究、应用研究和实际经验所获得的现有知识，为产生新的产品、材料和装置，建立新的工艺、系统和服务，以及对已产生和建立的上述各项作实质性的改进而进行的系统性丁作。其成果形式主要是专利、专有技术、具有新产品基本特征的产品原型或具有新装置基本特征的原始样机等。在社会科学领域，试验发展是指把通过基础研究、应用研究获得的知识转变成可以实施的计划（包括为进行检验和评估实施示范项目）的过程。人文科学领域没有对应的试验发展活动。主要反映将科研成果转化为技术和产品的能力，是科技推动经济社会发展的物化成果。

R&D人员 指参与研究与试验发展项目研究、管理和辅助工作的人员，包括项目（课题）组人员，企业科技行政管理人员和直接为项目（课题）活动提供服务的辅助人员。反映投入从事拥有自主知识产权的研究开发活动的人力规模。

R&D人员全时当量 指全时人员数加非全时人员按工作量折算为全时人员数的总和。例如：有两个全时人员和三个非全时人员（工作时间分别为20%、30%和70%），则全时当量为2+0.2+0.3+0.7=3.2人年。为国际上比较科技人力投入而制定的可比指标。

R&D经费内部支出 合计指调查单位用于内部开展R&D活动（基础研究、应用研究和试验发展）的实际支出。包括用于R&D项目（课题）活动的直接支出，以及间接用TR&D活动的管理费、服务费、与R&D有关的基本建设支出以及外协加工费等。不包括生产性活动支出、归还贷款支出以及与外单位合作或委托外单位进行R&D活动而转拨给对方的经费支出。

R&D经费内部支出中政府资金 指R&D经费内部支出中来自各级政府部门的各类资金，包括财政科学技术拨款、科学基金、教育等部门事业费以及政府部门预算外资金的实际支出。

R&D经费内部支出中企业资金 指R&D经费内部支出中来自本企业的自有资金和接受其他企业委托而获得的经费，以及科研院所、高校等事业单位从企业获得的资金的实际支出。

R&D项目（课题）数 指在当年立项并开展研究工作、以前年份立项仍继续进行研究的研发项目（课题）数，包括当年完成和年内研究：工作已告失败的研发项目（课题），但不包括委托外单位进行的研发项目（课题）数。

R&D项目（课题）人员全时当量 指实际参加研发项目（课题）活动人员折合的全时当量。

R&D项目（课题）经费内部支出 指调查单位内部在报告年度进行研发项目（课题）研究和试制等的实际支出。包括劳务费、其他日常支出、固定资产购建费、外协加工费等，不包括委托或与外单位合作进行项目（课题）研究而拨付给对方使用的经费。

新产品产值 指报告期企业生产的新产品的产值。新产品是指采用新技术原理、新设计构思研制、生产的全新产品，或在结构、材质、工艺等某一方面比原有产品有明显改进，从而显著提高了产品性能或扩大了使用功能的产品。新产品产值、新产品销售收入既包括经政府有关部门认定并在有效期内的新产品，也包括企业自行研制开发，未经政府有关部门认定，从投产之日起一年之内的新产品。

新产品销售收入 指报告期企业销售新产品实现的销售收入。

专利 是专利权的简称，是对发明人的发明创造经审查合格后，由专利局依据专利法授予发明人和设计人对该项发明创造享有的专有权。包括发明、实用新型和外观设计。反映拥有自主知识产权的科技和设计成果情况。

发明（专利） 指对产品、方法或者其改进所提出的新的技术方案。是国际通行的反映拥有自主知识产权技术的核心指标。

Explanatory Notes on Main Statistical Indicators

Regular Institutions of Higher Education refer to educational establishments set up according to the government evaluation and approval procedures, recruiting graduates from senior secondary schools as the main target by National Matriculation TEST. They include full-time universities, colleges, institutions of higher professional education, institutions of higher vocational education, institutions of higher vocational education and others (non-university tertiary, branch schools and undergraduate classes) .

Universities and colleges primarily provide undergraduate courses; institutions of higher professional education and institutions of higher vocational education primarily provide professional trainings; and others refer to educational establishments, which are responsible for enrolling higher education students under the State Plan but not enumerated in the total number of schools, including: branch schools of universities and colleges, and universities and colleges that have been approved and under plan for construction. Non-university tertiary refers to the regular undergraduate branch college which is running in new mechanism and mode, excluding the branch schools and other similar branches of educational institutions.

Institutions of Higher Education for Adults refer to educational establishments, set up in line with relevant rules approved by the government, enrolling staff and workers with senior secondary school or equivalent education, and providing higher education courses in many forms of correspondence, spare time, or full time for adults. Professionals thus trained receive a qualification equivalent to graduates studying regular courses at regular universities, colleges and professional colleges. Institutions of higher learning for adults include schools of higher education for staff and workers, schools of higher education for peasants, colleges for management cadres, pedagogical colleges, independent correspondence colleges, Radio and TV universities and other educational establishments. Other educational establishments have undertakings to enrol adult students but not enumerated in the schools under the State Plan.

Net Enrolment Ratio of Primary Schools refers to the proportion of school age children enrolled at schools to the total number of school age children both in and outside schools (including retarded children, but excluding blind, deaf and mute children) . The formula is:

$$\text{Net Enrolment Ratio Of Primary Schools} = \frac{\text{Total Primary School-age Children at Schools}}{\text{Total Primary School-age WnerdlihChether or Not Attending School}} \times 100\%$$

Research and Development (R&D) refers to systematic and creative activities in the field of science and technology aiming at increasing the knowledge and using the knowledge for new application. R&D includes 3 categories of activities: basic research, applied research and experimentation for development. The scale and intensity of R&D are widely used internationally to reflect the strength of S&T and the core competitiveness of a country in the world.

Basic Research refers to empirical or theoretical research aiming at obtaining new knowledge on the fundamental principles regarding phenomena or observable facts to reveal the intrinsic nature and underlying laws and to acquire new discoveries or new theories. Basic research takes no specific or designated application as the aim of the research. Results of basic research are mainly released or disseminated in the form of scientific papers or monographs. This indicator reflects the innovation capacity for original knowledge.

Applied Research refers to creative research aiming at obtaining new knowledge on a specific objective or target. Purpose of the applied research is to identify the possible uses of results from basic research, or to explore new (fundamental) methods or new approaches. Results of applied research are expressed in the form of scientific papers, monographs, fundamental models or invention patents. This indicator reflects the exploration of ways to apply the results of basic research.

Experiments and Development refer to systematic activities aiming at using the knowledge from basic and applied researches or from practical experience to develop new products, materials and equipment, to establish new production process, systems and services, or to make substantial improvement on the existing products, process or services. Results of experiment and development activities are embodied in patents, exclusive technology, and monotype of new products or equipment. In social sciences, experiment and development activities refer to the process of converting the knowledge from basic or applied researches into feasible programmes (including conduct of demonstration projects for assessment and evaluation). There are no experiment and development activities in the science of humanities. This indicator reflects the capability of transferring the results of S&T into technique and products, and measures the realization of S&T in spearheading the economic and social development.

R&D Personnel refer to persons engaged in research, management and supporting activities ofR & D, including persons in the project teams, persons engaged in the management of S&T activities of enterprises and supporting staff providing direct service to the research projects. This indicator reflects the size of personnel engaged in R&D activities with independent intellectual property.

Full-time Equivalent of R&D Personnel refers to the sum of the full-time persons and the full-time equivalent of part-time persons converted by workload. For instance, if there are 2 full-time persons and 3 part-time workers (20%, 30% and 70% of working hours respectively on R&D activities), the full-time equivalent are 2+0.2+0.3+0.7=3.2 person-years. This is an internationally comparable indicator of S&T manpower input.

Total Internal Expenditure of Funds on R&D refers to the real expenditure of surveyed units on their own R&D activities (basic research, application study, test and development) including direct expenditure on R&D activities, indirect expenditure of management and services on R&D activities, expenditure on capital construction and material processing by others. Excluding the expenditure on production activities, return of loan, and fees transferred to cooperated and entrusted agencies on R&D activities.

Internal Expenditure of Government Funds refersto the expenditure of funds on R&D activities from government agencies at different levels, including appropriate funds on science and technology from financial departments, scientific funds, operating expenses from education departments and the real expenditure of extra budgetary funds from government agencies.

Internal Expenditure of Funds of Enterprises refers to the expenditure of funds on R&D activities from self-raised funds of enterprises and funds from other enterprises through entrustment, and the expenditure of funds of institutions, such as institution of scientific research and universities, from enterprises.

Number of R&D Projects (subjects) refers to the number of R&D projects (subjects) set up and implemented at the reference year, and the number of R&D projects (subjects) set up in former years and under implementation, including the projects (subjects) finished and failed at the reference year, excluding the projects (subjects) implemented by others through entrustment.

Full-time Equivalent of R&D Personnel refers to the full-time equivalent of persons actually engaged in R&D projects. (subjects)

Internal Expenditure of Funds on R&D Projects (subjects) refers to the real expenditure of internal funds of the surveyed units on research and test of R&D projects (subjects) at the reference year, including service fee, other daily expenditure, cost for capital goods, cost of external process; excluding expenditure of funds transferred to other cooperated and entrusted units of the projects.

Output Value of New Products refers to the output value of new products during the reporting period. The new products refer to brand new products produced with new technology and new design, or product that represent noticeable improvement in terms of structure, material, or production process for improving significantly the character of function of the older versions. The output value and sales income of the new products include those of new products certified by relevant government agencies within the period of certification, as well as new products designed and produced by enterprises within a year without certification by government agencies.

Sales Income of New Products refers to the real sales income of new products of the enterprises at the reporting period.

Patent is an abbreviation for the patent right and refers to the exclusive right of ownership by the inventors or designers for the creation or inventions, given from the patent offices after due process of assessment and approval in accordance with the Patent Law. Patents are granted for inventions, utility models and designs. This indicator reflects the achievements of S&T and design with independent intellectual property.

Patented Inventions refer to new technical proposals to the products or methods or their modifications. This is universal core indicator reflecting the technologies with independent intellectual property.

21 文化、体育、卫生、社会福利和其他

CULTURE,SPORTS,PUBLIC HEALTH,SOCIAL WELFARE INSTITUTIONS AND OTHER SOCIAL ACTIVITIES

资料整理：郝　静
Data management：Hao Jing
数据审核：王金桂
Data audit：Wang Jingui

第二十一部分　文化、体育、卫生、社会福利和其他

一、简要说明

本章资料主要包括文化、卫生、民政、体育、计划生育、共青团、妇联以及公检法等方面的内容，由西安市统计局服务业和社会科技处根据西安市文广新局、卫计委、民政局、体育局、妇联、团市委以及公安局、检察院、法院等部门提供资料整理。

二、主要指标

公共图书馆藏量（千册件）	6957	比上年增加	435
医院数（个）	292	比上年减少	3
医院床位数（万张）	5.15	比上年增加	1678张

21　CULTURE,SPORTS,PUBLIC HEALTH,SOCIAL WELFARE INSTITUTIONS AND OTHER SOCIAL ACTIVITIES

Ⅰ.Brief Introduction

Data in this chapter primarily consists of data of culture, sanitation, civil administration, physical education, family planning, Communist Youth League, the Women's Federation, public security organs, procuratorial organs and people's court, compiled by Tertiary Industry and Social Science & Technology Division of Xi'an Bureau of Statistics according to data from Xi'an Bureau of Cuture, health and Family Planning Commision, Bureau of Civial Adnimistration, Bureau of PE, the Women's Federation, Municipal Committee of Communist Youth League, Bureau of Public Security, Procuratorate, People's Court and other department concerned.

Ⅱ.Major Indicators

		Increase over Preceding Year
Number of Collections in Libraries(1 000 vol.)	6957	435
Number of Hospitals(unit)	292	-3
Number of Beds(10 000 units)	5.15	1678 units

21-1 文化事业机构和人数（2016年）

Number of Institutions and Personnel in Culture and Art（2016）

项　目	Item	机构数（个） Number of Institutions （unit）	人员数（人） Number of Personnel （person）
一、电影事业	**Career of Film**		
制片厂	Studio	1	900
发行放映管理机构	Number of Film Projection and Publication Administrating Institutions	2	8
电影放映单位	Unit of Film shows	206	2813
#电影院	Cinema	74	2600
影剧院	Theaters	5	66
放映队	Film Projection Team	127	147
二、艺术事业	**Art**		
艺术表演团体	Art Performance Troupes	18	2365
艺术表演场所	Art Centers	16	337
三、艺术科研机构	**Art Scientific Research Institution**	**2**	**58**
四、图书馆事业	**Libraries**	**13**	**561**
五、群众文化事业	**Mass Culture**		
群众艺术馆	Activities of Mass Art Centres	2	120
文化馆	Cultural Centers	14	245
文化站	Culture Stations	174	708
农村文化室	Rural Cultural Center	2660	
六、文化部门教育机构	**Educations Institution of Culture Department**	**2**	**120**

注：本表数据来源于市文广新局。

21-2 文化事业发展情况（2016年）

Basic Statistics on Culture Development（2016）

指 标	Item	2016
电影放映场数（千场）	Number of Film Shows (1 000 shows)	980
电影观众人数（千人次）	Number of Spectators (1 000 person-times)	26935
电影票房收入（万元）	Box-office Receipts(10 000 yuan)	83353
艺术表演团体演出场次（场）	Number of Art Performance Troupes Performers (shows)	5172
#国内演出场次	Number of domestic Performance	5089
艺术表演观众人次（千人次）	Number of Spectators(1 000 person-times)	7198
公共图书馆藏量（千册件）	Public Library Reserves	6957
电子图书（千册）	E-books (1 000 volumes)	5119
书刊文献外借人次（千人次）	Books, Journals and Documents Borrowing (1 000 person-times)	1072
书刊文献外借册次（千册次）	Books, Journals and Documents Borrowing (1 000 Volume-time)	2888
县以上公共图书馆购书经费（万元）	Book-purchase Fund of Public Library above the County Level(1 000yuan)	1932

注：本表数据来源于市文广新局。

21-3 主要年份群众艺术馆、文化馆（站）活动情况

Basic Statistics on Activities of Mass Art Centers and Cultural Centers in Representative Years

指 标	Item	2010	2011	2012	2013	2014	2015	2016
机构数（个）	Number of Insititutions (units)	197	196	197	198	199	199	190
举办展览个数（个）	Number of Exhibitions (units)	705	592	652	658	627	606	562
举办展览参观人次（千人次）	Number of Exhibition Visitors(1 000 person-times)		375	416	301	326	289	287
组织文艺活动次数 （次）	Art Performances and Story-telling Sessions (times)	3729	4544	3273	4114	3617	3811	4246
组织文艺活动参加人次（千人次）	Number of Culture Activities attendees (1 000 person-times)		1778	1377	1633	1576	1574	1688
举办训练班班次（个）	Number of Training Courses (units)	3018	2224	1798	1616	1872	2126	1906
举办训练班结业人次（千人次）	Number of Certificate Trained Persons (1 000 person-times)	133	115	143	155	156	207	149
组织各类理论研讨和讲座次数（次）	Number of Theoretical Discussion and Seminars(1 000 person-times)		106	78	122	254	216	189
组织各类理论研讨和讲座参加人次（千人次）	Number of Persons in Theoretical Discussion and Seminars(1 000 person-times)		15	14	19	28	25	18
本年收入（千元）	Income of this year (1 000 yuan)	42937	55367	88475	101365	89520	102567	103706
本年支出（千元）	Expenditure of this year (1 000 yuan)	45160	62368	84522	93485	84827	100749	111942

注：本表数据来源于市文广新局。

21-4 文物保护业基本情况（2016年）

Basic Statistics on Cultural Relics Protection（2016）

指 标	Item	机 构（个）Insititution (unit)	人 员（人）Personnel (person)	文物藏品 实际数量（件）Factual Number of Collections (piece)	一级品（件）Grade One (piece)	举办陈列展览次数(次) Times of exhibition (times)	参观人员（千人次）Number of Visitors (1000 person-times)
文物保护管理机构	Cultural Relics administrative Departments	28	598	28796	36	18	2719
其他文物机构	Other Agencies	7	121	40899			
博物馆	Museums	98	4679	767514	5207	609	26549
#免费开放馆	Museums Open Free	70	1764	658734	2080	362	8852
文物科研机构	Scientific Research of Historical Relics Preservation	3	246	36626	186		

注：本表数据来源于市文物局。

21-5 主要年份广播电台及节目制作情况

Basic Statistics of Broadcasting Stations and Program Production in Representative Years

指 标	Item	2010	2011	2012	2013	2014	2015	2016
省、地广播电台（座）	Broadcasting Stations at the Province and District Level(set)	2	1	1				
省、地广播电视台（座）	Broadcasting Station at Province and District Level(set)		1	1	2	2	2	2
县级广播电视台（座）	Number of Wire Broadcasting Stations and TV Relaying Stations(set)	6	6	6	6	6	6	6
中、短波转播发射台（座）	Medium and Short Wave Broadcast Transmitting Station (base)	55	54	59	57	57	13	13
节目套数（套）	Number of Programs(set)	18	19	20	20	20	20	20
全年播出时间(时：分)	Broadcasting Hours annually(hour)	124100	121723	129856	138278	143873	137075	139159
广播节目综合人口覆盖率（%）	Broadcasts comprehensive population coverage	99.4	99.42	99.45	99.47	99.49	99.55	99.62
制作广播节目(时：分)	Productions of Broadcasting(hour)	110639	83368	104300	106554	104459	116603	119424
#新闻资讯类	News Programs	13786	13821	14025	14355	13208	12208	7590
专题服务类	Special Subject Programs	24451	16318	21891	30181	26884	21864	26957
综艺类	Variety Programs	37720	28679	28096	24516	27148	37885	39735
广播剧类	Literature Programs	2406	2014	1720	3083	3712	6674	3990
广告类	Advertisements	28339	14202	19547	20552	18465	15777	18363
其他类	Service Programs	3937	8334	19021	13867	15042	22195	22787

注：本表数据来源于市文广新局。
中、短波转播发射台2014年之前统计口径为中短波、调频发射台及转播台。数据变化因指标含义变化所致。

21-6 主要年份电视台及节目制作情况

Basic Statistics of TV Stations and Production of TV Program in Representative Years

指　　标	Item	2010	2011	2012	2013	2014	2015	2016
调频电视转播发射台（座）	FM Television Relay Station (base)	10	10	11	11	11	48	48
无线电视节目（套）	Program Productions of Non-cable television Stations (set)	6	6	6	6	6	6	2
有线电视节目（套）	Program Productions of cable television Stations (set)	16	16	16	16	16	16	20
全年播出时间（时：分）	Broadcasting Hours annually(hour)	141856	147003	137936	140927	143000	141839	140312
电视节目综合人口覆盖率（%）	TV shows comprehensive population coverage(%)	98.57	98.60	98.83	98.84	98.96	99.01	99.11
制作电视节目（时：分）	Earth Stations of Satellite TV (set)	29626	43925	30091	46614	35182	43563	54200
#新闻资讯类	News and Information Programs	8930	10656	11169	13360	11797	11839	12891
专题服务类	Special Subject Programs	7762	19192	7689	7751	8289	8073	9346
综艺类	Variety Programs	3942	5202	5458	6508	5014	6242	7883
影视剧类	Film and Television Drama	1729	3781	113	1820	110	462	490
广告类	Advertisement	3313	3200	3663	8066	3491	7921	6198
其他类	Service Programs	3950	1894	1997	9109	6479	9026	17390
有线电视用户（万户）	Users of Cable television Stations (10 000 households)	164.64	179.29	188.71	207.48	216.55	229.00	212.3
有线广播电视干线网总长度(公里)	The total length of cable broadcasting and television arteries of communication(km)		62494	62494	37126	37551	37613	37948
有线电视入户率(%)	The Rate of Cable Television(%)		79.08	80.53	86.62	88.20	91.51	83.87

注：本表数据来源于市文广新局。
调频电视转播发射台2014年之前统计口径为发射台及转播台。数字变化因指标含义变化所致。

21-7 体育事业基本情况（2016年）

The Basic Situations of Sport（2016）

单位：人、枚　　(person, unit)

指　　标	Item	2016
市级体育部门职工人数	**Number of Staffs and Workers in Physical Education System**	**346**
运动员	**Athletes**	2572
教练员	**Coaches**	77
等级裁判员发展人数	**Number of the Development of Grade Referees**	**696**
等级运动员发展人数	**Number of the Development of Grade Athletes**	**252**
全年获得国家级、省级金牌和银牌情况	**Basic Situations of Aquiring National, Provincial Gold and Silver Medals through The Year**	
国家级金牌	National Gold	8
国家级银牌	National Silver	5
省级金牌	Provincial Gold	169
省级银牌	Provincial Silver	121

注：本表数据来源于市体育局。
2016年运动员数据包括市级体育传统项目学校运动员，口径较以前年份大。

21-8 市级体育传统项目学校在校生（2016年）

Students in Municipal Sports Traditional Project School（2016）

单位：人 (person)

指　标	Items	2016
合计	**Total**	**6643**
田径	Track and Field	2480
游泳	Swimming	380
体操	Gymnastics	80
举重	Weightlifting	110
国际式摔跤	Wrestling	58
柔道	Judo	88
射击	Shooting	138
射箭	Archery	88
足球	Football	1800
篮球	Basketball	580
排球	Volleyball	88
乒乓球	Table Tennis	380
拳击	Boxing	38
武术	Wu Shu	95
跆拳道	Kickboxing	130
跳水	Diving	30
棒球	Baseball	80

注：本表数据来源于市体育局。

21-9 群众体育事业（2016年）

Mass Sports （2016）

指　标	Items	2016
社会体育指导员（人）	Social Sports Instructor(persons)	19488
晨晚健身站点（个）	Morning and Evening Fitness sites(units)	1600
社区建有体育组织比重(%)	The community has a sports organization proportion (%)	100
全国、全省体育先进社区（个）	National, provincial advanced sports community (units)	20
体育人口(万人)	Sports population(10 000 persons)	370

注：本表数据来源于市体育局。

21-10 主要年份医疗卫生机构、床位、人员情况

Number of Health Care Institutions, Beds and Personnel in Health Care Institutions in Representative Years

年份 Year	医疗卫生机构数（个）Number of Health Care Institutions（unit）	医院数（个）Number of Health Care Hospital（unit）	医疗卫生机构床位数（张）Number of Health Care Bed（unit）	医院床位数（张）Number of Hospital Bed（unit）	卫生技术人员数（人）Number of Medical Technical Personnel（person）
2008	2239	276	34618	30582	47433
2009	2162	261	36849	32371	51641
2010	2385	258	39407	34274	56579
2011	5554	268	41010	35976	61281
2012	5576	276	44239	39213	66899
2013	5503	281	47867	42753	71134
2014	5554	281	51065	45561	76005
2015	5802	295	54708	49830	81462
2016	5869	292	56332	51508	86258

注：本表数据来源于市卫计委。

21-11 医疗卫生机构、床位及人员情况(2016年)

卫生机构	Health Care Institutions	机构数（个）Number of Institutions (unit)	床位数（张）Number of Beds (unit)
总计	**Total**	**5869**	**56332**
一、医院	**Hospitals**	**292**	**51508**
综合医院	General Hospitals	198	37683
中医医院	Hospitals Specialized in Traditional Chinese Medicine	45	5999
中西医结合医院	Hospitals Integrating Traditional Chinese Medicine with Western Therapeutics in Practice	4	548
民族医院	Nationalities Hospitals		
专科医院	Specialized Hospitals	45	7278
护理院	Nursing Centets		
二、基层医疗卫生机构	**Commuting health care service centre**	**5338**	**3127**
社区卫生服务中心(站)	Community Health Care Center(Station)	215	1594
社区卫生服务中心	Community Health Care Center	119	1586
社区卫生服务站	Community Health Care Station	96	8
卫生院	Health Center	100	1500
街道卫生院	Urban Health-center	5	45
乡镇卫生院	Rural Health-center	95	1455
村卫生室	Village clinics	2951	
门诊部	Outpatient department	225	33
诊所、卫生所、医务室	Clinic, health center, Infirmary	1847	
三、专业公共卫生机构	**College of public health institutions**	**213**	**1467**
疾病预防控制中心	Center for Disease Control and Prevention	16	
专科疾病防治院（所、站）	Specialized disease prevention and cure center (place, station)	1	800
健康教育所（站、中心）	Health Education Institute (station, center)	2	
妇幼保健院（所、站）	Maternal and Child Health Hospital (Station)	13	667
急救中心（站）	Emergency Center	1	
采供血机构	Blood Collection Agencies	1	
卫生监督所（中心）	Health Supervision Agencies (Center)	14	
计划生育技术服务机构	Institutions of Technical Service for Family Planning	165	
四、其他卫生机构	**Other Health Institution**	**26**	**230**
疗养院	Nursing Centres	1	230
卫生监督检验(监测、检测)所(站)	Health Supervision and inspection Agencies		
医学科学研究机构	Medical scientific research institutions	3	
医学在职培训机构	Medical training institutions	5	
临床检验中心（所、站）	Clinical testing center (place, station)	2	
统计信息中心	Statistical information center	1	
其他	other	14	

注：本表数据来源于市卫计委。
本表人员合计中包括乡村医生3229人和卫生员201人。

Number of Health Care Institutions, Beds and Personnel in Health Care Institutions (2016)

人员合计（人）Total Number of Employed Persons (person)	卫生技术人员 Medical Technical Personnel	执业（助理）医师数 Licensed (Assistant) Doctors	#执业医师 Chartered Doctors
107906	**86258**	**27864**	**25023**
78109	**63915**	**18762**	**17899**
59167	48962	14568	13922
7415	6024	1785	1662
405	348	128	117
11122	8581	2281	2198
23701	**18409**	**8034**	**6200**
5728	4811	1534	1182
4872	4046	1251	933
856	765	283	249
2949	2483	632	417
115	99	28	23
2834	2384	604	394
4396	966	818	276
3507	3165	1407	1205
7121	6984	3643	3120
5221	**3490**	**938**	**806**
1116	859	340	309
487	380	87	83
79	27	5	5
1611	1279	327	275
121	56	33	31
143	94	12	10
556	411		
1108	384	134	93
875	**444**	**130**	**118**
91	52	18	15
137	84	43	41
200	82	6	6
165	37		
6			
276	189	63	56

21-11 续表1

卫生机构	Health Care Institutions	人员合计（人）	
		卫生技术人员中	
		注册护士 Registered Nurses	药师（士） Junior Paramedics
总计	**Total**	**37518**	**4075**
一、医院	**Hospitals**	**30293**	**2897**
综合医院	General Hospitals	23128	2123
中医医院	Hospitals Specialized in Traditional Chinese Medicine	2676	416
中西医结合医院	Hospitals Integrating Traditional Chinese Medicine with Western Therapeutics in Practice	175	15
民族医院	Nationalities Hospitals		
专科医院	Specialized Hospitals	4314	343
护理院	Nursing Centets		
二、基层医疗卫生机构	**Commuting health care service centre**	**6196**	**1056**
社区卫生服务中心(站)	Community Health Care Center(Station)	1630	376
社区卫生服务中心	Community Health Care Center	1317	308
社区卫生服务站	Community Health Care Station	313	68
卫生院	Health Center	635	170
街道卫生院	Urban Health-center	25	8
乡镇卫生院	Rural Health-center	610	162
村卫生室	Village clinics	148	
门诊部	Outpatient department	1175	197
诊所、卫生所、医务室	Clinic, health center, Infirmary	2608	313
三、专业公共卫生机构	**College of public health institutions**	**935**	**107**
疾病预防控制中心	Center for Disease Control and Prevention	65	14
专科疾病防治院（所、站）	Specialized disease prevention and cure center (place, station)	194	19
健康教育所（站、中心）	Health Education Institute (station, center)	1	
妇幼保健院（所、站）	Maternal and Child Health Hospital (Station)	558	56
急救中心（站）	Emergency Center	17	2
采供血机构	Blood Collection Agencies	27	4
卫生监督所（中心）	Health Supervision Agencies (Center)		
计划生育技术服务机构	Institutions of Technical Service for Family Planning	73	12
四、其他卫生机构	**Other Health Institution**	**94**	**15**
疗养院	Nursing Centres	17	7
卫生监督检验(监测、检测)所(站)	Health Supervision and inspection Agencies		
医学科学研究机构	Medical scientific research institutions	10	4
医学在职培训机构	Medical training institutions		
临床检验中心（所、站）	Clinical testing center (place, station)		
统计信息中心	Statistical information center		
其他	other	67	4

continued 1

Total Number of Employed Persons (person)					
Among:Medical Technical Personnel			其他技术人员 Other Technical Personnel	管理人员 Administrative Personnel	工勤技能人员 Logistics Technical Workers
技师（士） Technicians	#检验师 Laboratory Technicians	其他 Other			
5058	**3614**	**11743**	**835**	**8470**	**8913**
3725	**2619**	**8238**	**560**	**6462**	**7172**
2814	1996	6329	433	4692	5080
376	205	771	81	621	689
23	20	7	3	36	18
512	398	1131	43	1113	1385
830	**564**	**2293**	**48**	**833**	**981**
357	244	914	16	427	474
310	203	860	9	372	445
47	41	54	7	55	29
212	126	834	3	229	234
10	5	28	1	8	7
202	121	806	2	221	227
210	155	176	29	177	136
51	39	369			137
424	**369**	**1086**	**152**	**962**	**617**
219	211	221	14	135	108
33	23	47	1	59	47
		21	32	19	1
116	87	222	1	172	159
		4		39	26
21	21	30	2	40	7
		411	3	72	70
35	27	130	99	426	199
79	**62**	**126**	**75**	**213**	**143**
4	4	6		17	22
22	15	5	13	22	18
3	3	73	52	47	19
22	22	15	1	61	66
				6	
28	18	27	9	60	18

21-12 各区县医疗卫生机构、床位及人员情况（2016年）

Number of Health Care Institutions, Beds and Employed Persons in Health Care Institutions By Region（2016）

区 县	Region	机构（个）Number of Health Care Institutions (unit)	床位（张）Number of Beds (unit)	人员合计（人）Total Number of Employed Persons (person)	#卫生技术人员 Total Number of Medical Technical Personnel
合 计	**Total**	**5869**	**56332**	**107906**	**86258**
新城区	Xincheng	268	7065	14285	11343
碑林区	Beilin	383	8119	14471	12261
莲湖区	Lianhu	350	7213	13330	11071
灞桥区	Baqiao	448	2825	4953	4056
未央区	Weiyang	406	4948	10002	8267
雁塔区	Yanta	491	8885	18676	15300
阎良区	Yanliang	172	1438	2735	2133
临潼区	Lintong	541	2524	3904	2816
长安区	Chang'an	814	5592	9610	7195
高陵区	Gaoling	210	1702	3244	2676
蓝田县	Lantian	624	1525	3113	2291
周至县	Zhouzhi	549	1470	3853	2672
户 县	Huxian	613	3026	5730	4177

注：本表数据来源于市卫计委。

21-13 各区县农村村级卫生组织情况（2016年）

Village Level Health Organization in the Rural Area by Region（2016）

区 县	Region	村卫生室（个） Village health room（unit）	乡村医生和卫生员（人） Rural doctors and health workers（person）	#乡村医生 Rural doctors	#卫生员 health workers
全 市	**Total**	**2951**	**3430**	**3229**	**201**
新城区	Xincheng				
碑林区	Beilin				
莲湖区	Lianhu				
灞桥区	Baqiao	209	263	261	2
未央区	Weiyang	102	100	100	
雁塔区	Yanta	62	114	105	9
阎良区	Yanliang	80	109	109	
临潼区	Lintong	346	426	381	45
长安区	Chang'an	570	565	562	3
高陵区	Gaoling	122	191	179	12
蓝田县	Lantian	519	423	423	
周至县	Zhouzhi	449	721	595	126
户 县	Huxian	492	518	514	4

注：本表数据来源于市卫计委。

21-14 各区县社区卫生服务中心（站）情况（2016年）

Situations of Community Health Service Center（Station）by Region（2016）

区 县 Region	社区卫生服务中心（站）（个）Community Health Care Center(Station) (unit)	床位数（张）Number of Beds (unit)	人员数（人）Personnel number (person)	卫生技术人员（人）Medical Technical Personnel (person)	执业（助理）医师 Licensed (Assistant) Doctors	注册护士 Registered Nurses
全 市 Total	**215**	**1594**	**5728**	**4811**	**1534**	**1630**
新城区 Xincheng	17		299	238	93	78
碑林区 Beilin	18	60	464	364	146	116
莲湖区 Lianhu	15	140	623	532	205	194
灞桥区 Baqiao	24	153	498	428	139	149
未央区 Weiyang	36	91	778	646	197	254
雁塔区 Yanta	36	35	940	817	255	299
阎良区 Yanliang	8	72	166	147	39	59
临潼区 Lintong	28	540	678	575	136	141
长安区 Chang'an	23	503	1163	959	302	279
高陵区 Gaoling	10		119	105	22	61
蓝田县 Lantian						
周至县 Zhouzhi						
户 县 Huxian						

注：本表数据来源于市卫计委。

21-15 主要年份医疗卫生机构各类人员情况

Number of Personnel in Health Care Institutions in Representative Years

单位：人 (person)

指　标	Item	2010	2011	2012	2013	2014	2015	2016
人员合计	**Total**	**71230**	**79999**	**86096**	**90129**	**95633**	**102684**	**107906**
卫生技术人员	Medical Technical Personnel	56579	61281	66899	71134	76005	81462	86258
执业（助理）医师	Licensed (Assistant) Doctors	18763	21551	23051	23885	24820	26626	27864
#执业医师	Chartered Doctors	16613	18904	20414	21205	22145	23818	25023
注册护士	Registered Nurses	22640	25043	27837	29967	32136	34819	37518
药师(士)	Junior Paramedics	3030	3127	3380	3551	3709	3957	4075
技师（士）	Technicians	4589	3622	3953	4089	4276	4690	5058
#检验师	Laboratory Technicians	2439	2622	2830	2974	3108	3338	3614
其他	Other	7557	7938	8678	9642	11064	11370	11743
其他技术人员	Other Technical Personnel	1156	895	633	590	621	816	835
管理人员	Administrative Personnel	6416	6769	6939	7160	7355	8248	8470
工勤技能人员	Logistics Technical Workers	7079	6789	7555	7437	7944	8326	8913

注：本表数据来源于市卫计委。

本表2011年人员合计中包括乡村医生3856人和卫生员409人；2012年人员合计中包括乡村医生3611人和卫生员459人。

2013年人员合计中包括乡村医生3477人和卫生员331人；2014年人员合计中包括乡村医生3327人和卫生员381人。

2015年人员合计中包括乡村医生3588人和卫生员244人；2016年人员合计中包括乡村医生3229人和卫生员201人。

21-16 医疗卫生机构门诊、住院及病床使用情况（2016年）

指　标	Item	总诊疗人次数 总计 Total
总计	**Total**	**55030338**
一、医院	**Hospitals**	**31956199**
综合医院	General Hospitals	24090767
中医医院	Hospitals Specialized in Traditional Chinese Medicine	2705696
中西医结合医院	Hospitals Integrating Traditional Chinese Medicine with Western Therapeutics in Practice	106031
民族医院	Nationalities Hospitals	
专科医院	Specialized Hospitals	5053705
护理院	Nursing Centets	
二、基层医疗卫生机构	**Commuting health care service centre**	**22034552**
社区卫生服务中心（站）	Community Health Care Center(Station)	3886243
社区卫生服务中心	Community Health Care Center	3091851
社区卫生服务站	Community Health Care Station	794392
卫生院	Health Center	1395033
街道卫生院	Urban Health-center	49990
乡镇卫生院	Rural Health-center	1345043
村卫生室	Village clinics	10207620
门诊部	Outpatient department	1727720
诊所、卫生所、医务室	Clinic, health center, Infirmary	4817936
三、专业公共卫生机构	**College of public health institutions**	**1016127**
专科疾病防治院（所、站）	Specialized disease prevention and cure center (place, station)	45337
妇幼保健院（所、站）	Maternal and Child Health Hospital (Station)	830007
急救中心（站）	Emergency Center	140783
四、其他卫生机构	**Other Health Institution**	**23460**
疗养院	Sanatorium	23460

注：本表数据来源于市卫计委。

Medical and Health Institutions Outpatient, Inpatient and Utilization of Beds（2016）

Total Number of Clinics (person time)				观察室 Observation Room	
门、急诊人次数合计 Total number of people in outpatient and emergency department	门诊人次数(人次) Number of Outpatients (person time)	急诊人次数小计(人次) The number of emergency subtotal (person time)	死亡人数（人） Number of Deaths (person)	留观病例数(人次) Number of Patients Receiving (person time)	死亡人数（人） Number of Deaths (persons)
54373580	**51203351**	**3170229**	**2971**	**28438**	**26**
31830213	**28959219**	**2870994**	**2963**	**28330**	**26**
23993804	21621426	2372378	2865	26868	17
2698459	2614450	84009	54	339	
102566	89421	13145	7	30	8
5035384	4633922	401462	37	1093	1
21512646	**21440667**	**71979**	**5**		
3822976	3772806	50170	5		
3036832	2997602	39230	5		
786144	775204	10940			
1393224	1371415	21809			
49876	49317	559			
1343348	1322098	21250			
9852906	9852906				
1694085	1694085				
4749455	4749455				
1007261	**780369**	**226892**		**108**	
45337	45234	103			
821141	735135	86006		108	
140783		140783			
23460	**23096**	**364**	**3**		
23460	23096	364	3		

21-16 续表1

指　标	Item	急诊死亡率（%）Emergency Mortality (%)	入院人数合计（人）Total Number of Admission Patients (person)
总计	**Total**	**0.09**	**1877938**
一、医院	**Hospitals**	**0.10**	**1785598**
综合医院	General Hospitals	0.12	1409516
中医医院	Hospitals Specialized in Traditional Chinese Medicine	0.06	150570
中西医结合医院	Hospitals Integrating Traditional Chinese Medicine with Western Therapeutics in Practice	0.05	10127
民族医院	Nationalities Hospitals		
专科医院	Specialized Hospitals	0.01	215385
护理院	Nursing Centets		
二、基层医疗卫生机构	**Commuting health care service centre**	**0.01**	**50055**
社区卫生服务中心（站）	Community Health Care Center(Station)	0.01	28412
社区卫生服务中心	Community Health Care Center	0.01	28412
社区卫生服务站	Community Health Care Station		
卫生院	Health Center		21283
街道卫生院	Urban Health-center		141
乡镇卫生院	Rural Health-center		21142
村卫生室	Village clinics		
门诊部	Outpatient department		360
诊所、卫生所、医务室	Clinic, health center, Infirmary		
三、专业公共卫生机构	**College of public health institutions**		**39136**
专科疾病防治院（所、站）	Specialized disease prevention and cure center (place, station)		6159
妇幼保健院（所、站）	Maternal and Child Health Hospital (Station)		32977
急救中心（站）	Emergency Center		
四、其他卫生机构	**Other Health Institution**	**0.82**	**3149**
疗养院	Sanatorium	0.82	3149

continued 1

出院人数合计 (人) Total Number of Discharge Patients (person)	死亡人数 (人) Number of Hospital Csualty (person)	病床周转次数 (次) Nnumber of Bed Rumover (time)	病床使用率 (%) Bed occupancy rate (%)	出院者平均住院日 (天) Average Stay Days in Hospital (day)
1869061	**9394**	**33.6**	**83.77**	**9.0**
1777622	**9368**	**35.0**	**86.94**	**9.0**
1404556	8440	37.5	87.85	8.5
149431	390	25.3	78.72	11.3
10083	54	22.7	61.50	9.7
213552	484	30.7	90.64	10.3
49592	**4**	**16.0**	**37.10**	**8.2**
27967	4	17.5	39.44	8.0
27967	4	17.6	39.59	8.0
21265		14.1	34.63	8.7
140		3.1	5.87	6.9
21125		14.5	35.52	8.7
360				
38680	**21**	**26.3**	**80.69**	**11.1**
6113	20	7.6	85.54	41.0
32567	1	48.7	74.87	5.5
3167	**1**	**13.7**	**31.56**	**8.3**
3167	1	13.7	31.56	8.3

21-17 提供住宿的社会服务机构（2016年）

Social Welfare Insititutions Providing Accommodation（2016）

指 标	Item	机构数（个）Number of Institutions	年末职工人数（人）Number of Staff and Workers at the end of year	#女性 female	床位数（张）Number of Beds	年末在院人数（人）Number of Persons Housed at the Year-end
1、养老服务机构	Pension Service Institutions	130	2628	1571	23484	12557
其中：城市养老服务机构	Among Them:Urban Pension Service Institutions	77	1872	1159	16121	7864
农村养老服务机构	Rural Pension Service Institutions	31	376	229	4023	1712
社会福利院	Social Welfare Homes	3	71	33	1215	803
军干所	Army Cadre Institutions	19	309	150	2125	2178
2、儿童福利院	Baby Welfare Homes	1	71	46	900	661
3、社会福利医院	Social Welfare Hospitals	3	71	33	1215	803
4、救助站	Rescue Station	8	116	43	837	247
5、军事供应站	Military Supply Station	1	20	3		

注：本表数据来源于市民政局。

21-18 主要年份社会福利事业单位机构及人员情况

Number of Social Welfare Institutions and Personnel

单位：个、人 (unit, person)

指 标	Item	2010	2011	2012	2013	2014	2015	2016
一、机构	**Insititutions**							
烈士纪念建筑物管理单位	Institutions Managing Memorial Buildings of Martyrs	2	2	2	2	2	2	2
救助类单位	Units Providing Assistance	8	8	8	8	9	9	9
殡仪服务单位	Funeral Service Units	22	21	22	25	26	26	25
殡仪馆	Funeral Homes	4	5	4	4	3	3	3
公墓	Cemeteries	14	12	12	15	16	16	16
殡葬管理单位	Funeral Management Units	4	4	6	6	7	7	6
二、人员	**Staff**							
烈士纪念建筑物管理单位	Institutions Managing Memorial Buildings of Martyrs	37	38	40	42	44	42	42
救助类单位	Units Providing Assistance	116	119	130	137	139	119	121
殡仪服务单位	Funeral Service Units	1371	1313	1400	1430	1392	1510	1510
殡仪馆	Funeral Homes	375	408	442	491	470	497	481
公墓	Cemeteries	939	838	869	855	838	929	953
殡葬管理单位	Funeral Management Units	57	67	89	84	84	84	76

注：本表数据来源于市民政局。

21-19 社会保障基本情况（2016年）

Basic Situation of Social Security（2016）

单位：万人、万户 （10 000 persons、10 000 households）

指 标	Item	2016
基本养老保险参保人数	Number of Basic Old-age Insurance	605.68
1. 城镇企业职工养老保险参保人数	Number of Town Enterprise Worker Old-age Insurance	330.5
其中：离退休人员	Retired Personnel	65.2
2. 机关事业单位养老保险参保人数	Number of Institution Old-age Insurance	28.47
其中：离退休人员	Retired Personnel	9.61
3. 城乡居民养老保险参保人数	Number of Rural Residents Old-age Insurance	246.71
城镇基本医疗保险参保人数	Number of urban basic medical insurance	435.61
失业保险参保人数	Number of unemployed insurance	152.73
生育保险参保人数	Number of Maternity insurance	121.23
工伤保险参保人数	Number of industrial injury insurance	154.92
城镇居民最低生活保障户数	The Number of Minimum Living Guarantee for Urban Resident Households	2.72
城镇居民最低生活保障人数	The Number of Minimum Living Guarantee for Urban Residents	4.66
农村居民最低生活保障户数	The Number of Minimum Living Guarantee for Rural Resident Households	3.31
农村居民最低生活保障人数	The Number of Minimum Living Guarantee for Rural Residents	9.73

注：本表数据来源于市人社局、市民政局。

21-20 全市及各区县新型农村合作医疗情况（2016年）

Situation of the New Rural Cooperative Medical Care of the Whole City and Area County（2016）

区 县	Region	参加新型农村合作医疗人数（万人）Participate in the new rural cooperative medical Population（10 000 persons）	新型农村合作医疗参合率（%）Participate in the new rural cooperative medical care ration（%）
合 计	**Total**	**381.45**	**99.26**
新城区	Xincheng		
碑林区	Beilin		
莲湖区	Lianhu		
灞桥区	Baqiao	29.77	100
未央区	Weiyang	8.84	100
雁塔区	Yanta	9.71	100
阎良区	Yanliang	17.00	100
临潼区	Lintong	56.80	99.98
长安区	Chang'an	73.15	97.80
高陵区	Gaoling	23.65	100
蓝田县	Lantian	56.69	99.42
周至县	Zhouzhi	58.19	98.54
户 县	Huxian	47.66	100

注：本表数据来源于市卫计委。

21-21 全市及各区县优抚对象人员情况（2016年）

Statistics on Persons Enjoying Favoured Treatment by Region（2016）

单位：人 (person)

区 县	Region	伤残人员 Number of Disabled Veterans	烈军属人员 Number of Family Members of Martyrs and Soldiers	在乡复员军人 Demobilized Soldiers in Hometown	带病回乡退伍军人 Veterans Returning Home in Sick
合 计	**Total**	**4922**	**864**	**2747**	**1754**
市本级	City Level	50			
新城区	Xincheng	612	30	8	
碑林区	Beilin	605	47	5	1
莲湖区	Lianhu	737	53	33	2
灞桥区	Baqiao	271	50	175	230
未央区	Weiyang	204	53	117	3
雁塔区	Yanta	738	70	61	10
阎良区	Yanliang	104	49	189	59
临潼区	Lintong	269	77	434	236
长安区	Chang'an	374	91	359	119
高陵区	Gaoling	137	63	320	172
蓝田县	Lantian	207	70	323	173
周至县	Zhouzhi	300	111	277	212
户 县	Huxian	245	67	275	87
沣东新城	Fengdongxincheng	69	33	171	450

注：本表数据来源于市民政局。

21-22 全市及各区县计划生育和婚姻登记情况（2016年）

Conditions of Birth Control and Marriage Registration by Region（2016）

区 县	Region	计划生育率（%） Family Planning Rate(%)	节育率(%) Birth control Rate(%)	独生子女领证率(%) Only-child Certificate Rate(%)
合 计	**Total**	**98.7**	**90.5**	**42.5**
新城区	Xincheng	99.9	86.2	50.8
碑林区	Beilin	99.9	87.4	54.3
莲湖区	Lianhu	99.9	90.3	54.5
灞桥区	Baqiao	99.4	93.3	50.9
未央区	Weiyang	98.7	91.9	48.0
雁塔区	Yanta	99.5	90.5	51.0
阎良区	Yanliang	98.4	93.5	44.4
临潼区	Lintong	97.2	91.8	29.6
长安区	Chang'an	99.1	93.7	37.5
高陵区	Gaoling	98.8	91.4	42.8
蓝田县	Lantian	97.1	90.7	23.7
周至县	Zhouzhi	98.3	89.2	14.5
户 县	Huxian	96.4	93.3	28.0
沣东新城	Fengdongxincheng	100	93.8	50.2

注：本表数据来源于市计生委、市民政局、市法院。

21-22 续表1 continued 1

区 县	Region	结婚对数（对） Marriages (couple)	再婚人数（人） Remarriages (person)	离婚对数（对） Divorced Couple (couple)
合 计	**Total**	**77371**	**28530**	**25448**
新城区	Xincheng	4288	1963	1788
碑林区	Beilin	8579	2999	2424
莲湖区	Lianhu	5837	2880	2523
灞桥区	Baqiao	5099	2118	1634
未央区	Weiyang	4325	1922	1942
雁塔区	Yanta	8251	3316	2927
阎良区	Yanliang	2721	1313	986
临潼区	Lintong	6151	2373	2094
长安区	Chang'an	9184	3483	3301
高陵区	Gaoling	2905	1427	1161
蓝田县	Lantian	5297	1344	1236
周至县	Zhouzhi	6316	1620	1059
户 县	Huxian	5536	1772	1359
沣东新城	Fengdongxincheng	2882		1014

21-23 全市及各区县妇幼卫生保健情况（2016年）

Care Health Conditions of Women and Child by Region（2016）

区 县	Region	5岁以下儿童死亡率（‰） Mortality rate of Children under 5-year-old（‰）	新生儿死亡率（‰） Infant Mortality Ratio in 2012（‰）	婴儿死亡率（‰） Neonatal Mortality Ratio（‰）
合 计	**Total**	**3.72**	**1.91**	**2.79**
新城区	Xincheng	1.49	1.25	1.25
碑林区	Beilin	2.75	1.00	1.75
莲湖区	Lianhu	6.25	3.68	6.25
灞桥区	Baqiao	1.60	0.80	1.40
未央区	Weiyang	1.39	0.20	0.60
雁塔区	Yanta	2.84	2.27	2.65
阎良区	Yanliang	5.71	4.28	5.35
临潼区	Lintong	2.81	1.32	1.66
长安区	Chang'an	4.79	2.08	3.25
高陵区	Gaoling	6.12	3.19	4.79
蓝田县	Lantian	4.33	2.17	3.07
周至县	Zhouzhi	3.40	1.70	2.55
户 县	Huxian	5.02	1.56	3.12
沣东新城	Fengdongxincheng	4.70	4.03	4.37

注：本表数据来源于市卫计委。

21-23 续表1 continued 1

区 县	Region	孕产妇死亡率（1/10万） Maternal Mortality Ratio (one in hundred thousandth)	产妇住院分娩比例（%） Proportion of maternal Hospital Births (%)
合 计	**Total**	**14.07**	**100**
新城区	Xincheng		100
碑林区	Beilin	25.03	100
莲湖区	Lianhu	36.78	100
灞桥区	Baqiao		100
未央区	Weiyang		100
雁塔区	Yanta	37.88	100
阎良区	Yanliang	35.69	100
临潼区	Lintong	16.56	100
长安区	Chang'an	9.03	100
高陵区	Gaoling	26.6	100
蓝田县	Lantian		100
周至县	Zhouzhi	28.37	100
户 县	Huxian		100
沣东新城	Fengdongxincheng		100

21-24 主要年份律师、公证及调解情况

Basic Statistics on Lawyer, Notaries and Mediation in Representative Years

指　标	Item	2010	2011	2012	2013	2014	2015	2016
一、律师工作	**Lawyers**							
律师事务所（个）	Number of Law Offices (unit)	95	97	105	116	122	149	176
律师（人）	Lawyers(person)	1202	1347	1522	1639	1846	2198	2462
#专职	Full-time	1139	1275	1439	1560	1738	2092	2337
兼职	Part-time	63	68	73	77	88	91	84
刑事诉讼辩护及代理（件）				2438	3267	3118	3524	3260
民事诉讼代理（件）				8848	10754	9985	15308	16743
行政诉讼代理（件）				170	319	374	532	601
非诉讼法律事务（件）				1965	2265	2352	2780	2840
二、公证工作	**Notarization**							
公证处（个）	Number of Notary Offices (unit)	14	14	14	14	14	14	14
公证人员（人）	Notarial Personnel (person)	202	233	235	222	298	307	293
#公证员	Notaries	112	118	116	115	118	121	115
办理公证件数（件）	Number of Notarized Documents Issued (case)	106491	108120	119605	136471	135413	135622	144662
国内	Domestic	72670	68239	79167	98572	90171	86589	95194
涉外	Foreign-related	33410	39545	39888	37444	44773	49033	49468
港澳台	Hong Kong. Macao and Taiwan related	411	336	550	455	469	373	512
三、人民调解工作	**Number of People Mediations**							
已建调委会数（个）	Number of Mediation Committees (unit)	3911	4031	4053	4040	4059	4052	4062
调解人员数（人）	Number of Mediators (person)	15717	12848	15080	15240	15793	14838	14888
调解纠纷数（件）	Number of Civil Disputes Mediated (case)	22247	33851	39230	33651	33641	31696	27455
#调解成功数	Number of Cases Successfully Mediated	22164	32109	37510	32368	32537	30590	26426

注：本表数据来源于市司法局。
2015年开始统计上将港澳台并入国内，表中2015-2016年办理公证件数中港澳台所列数据为其中数，2014年及以前年份港澳台数据与国内、涉外数据为并列关系。

21-25 主要年份共青团组织情况

Basic Facts on Communist Youth League in Representative Years

单位：个、人 (unit, person)

指 标	Item	2010	2011	2012	2013	2014	2015	2016
一、基层团组织	**Grass-root Youth League Organisations**	**7006**	**11248**	**9097**	**10770**	**10152**	**10074**	**10530**
二、共青团员	**Youth League Members**	**308141**	**345682**	**336156**	**344096**	**343121**	**331261**	**251706**
#女团员	Female Youth League Members	142379	159725	157924	158287	153212	146213	110092
三、专职团干部	**Full-time Youth League Cadre**	**311**	**270**	**680**	**737**	**659**	**496**	**165**

注：本表数据来源于共青团西安市委员会。

21-26 妇联组织情况（2016年）

Situation of Women's Organizations（2016）

单位：个 (unit)

指 标	Item	2016
一、妇联组织	**Women's Organizations**	
市级妇联	Municipal Women's Federation	1
街道妇联	Street Women's Federation	108
社区妇联	Community Women's Federation	783
县（区）妇联	County (district) Women's Federation	13
乡（镇）妇联	Township (town) Women's Federation	56
村妇代会	Village Women's Representative Conference	2266
二、非公有制经济组织中妇女组织	**Women's Organizations in Non-public Economic Organizations**	
个体劳动者协会中的妇女组织	Women's Organizations in Association of Individual Workers	5
专业市场中的妇女组织	Women's Organizations in the Professional Market	10
私营企业中的妇女组织	Women's Organizations in the Private Sector	339
三资企业中的妇女组织	Foreign-funded Enterprises in the Women's Organizations	20
三、机关事业单位妇女组织	**Women's Organizations in Government Departments and Institutions**	
直属机关妇委会（妇工委）	Women's Committee of Direct-affiliated Departments	13
部门机关妇委会（妇工委）	Women's Committee of Affiliated Departments	298
事业单位妇委会（妇工委）	Women's Committee of Government Institutions	42
四、民主党派妇女组织	**Women's Organizations of Democratic Parties**	
民主党派妇委会	Women's Committee of Democratic Parties	7
五、团体会员	**Members of Organisation**	
工会女职工委员会	Women Staff Committee of Labor Unions	3246
民政部门登记注册的妇女社团	Women's Communities Registered at Civil Administration Departments	6

注：本表数据来源于市妇联。

21-27 妇联工作情况（2016年）

Basic Facts on Women's Federation（2016）

单位：个、人、户、件 (unit，person，households，case)

指 标	Item	2016
一、双学双比活动	**Double Learning and Double Competition Activities**	
（一）科技培训	Scientific and Technical Training	
接受技术培训人数	Number of People Receiving Technical Training	6269
获得绿色证书人数	Number of People Gaining Green Certificates	300
女农民技术员人数	The number of female farmer technician	308
妇代会主任中农民技术员数	Number of Farmer in Women's Head Technicians	198
（二）巾帼扶贫	Women Aid-the-poor Project	
脱贫户数	Households out of Poverty	1030
扶贫项目数	Number of Poverty Alleviation Projects	13
二、巾帼建功活动	**Women Make Achievements**	
（一）巾帼建功	Women Make Achievements	
评选巾帼建功标兵数	Number of Pacemakes	33
巾帼建功先进工作者数	Number of Advanced Workers	12
巾帼文明示范岗数	Number of Model Workers	44
（二）下岗失业妇女再就业	Re-employment of Laid-off and Unemployed Women	
妇女就业服务机构数	Number of Institutions for Women's Employment Services	13
三、三八红旗手	**Models of Women**	**58**
四、三八红旗集体	**Models of Women Group**	**7**
五、来信来访情况	**Conditions of Letters and Visits**	
女职工劳动保护信访案件	Cases about Labor Protection of Employed Women through Letters and Visits	60
侵犯妇女财产权利信访案件	Cases about Encroachment of Women's Property through Letters and Visits	154

注：本表数据来源于市妇联。

21-28 主要年份交通、火灾及安全生产情况

Transportation, Fire and Safety Production in Representative Years

指　标	Item	2010	2011	2012	2013	2014	2015	2016
道路交通事故	**Road Accidents**							
事故数(起)	Number of Traffic Accident (case)	2323	2264	2446	2252	1970	2392	2943
死亡人数（人）	Number of Deaths (person)	531	531	516	460	483	481	476
受伤人数（人）	Number of Injuries (person)	2520	2260	2486	2217	1832	2318	3012
损失（万元）	Economic Loss (10 000 yuan)	736.6	611.9	1011.1	1143.9	1264.0	1470.2	1653.7
火灾事故	**Fire Accidents**							
事故数(起)	Number of Cases (case)	1825	1920	2568	4062	3199	2590	3434
死亡人数（人）	Number of Deaths (person)	13	8	16	26	17	20	16
受伤人数（人）	Number of Injuries (person)	7	3	4	6	5	7	7
损失（万元）	Economic Loss (10 000 yuan)	2224.2	1587.2	2793.7	3011.9	4381.1	2401.5	1901.1
农机事故	**Farm Machinery Accidents**							
事故数(起)	Number of Cases (case)	5		2	1	24	47	5
死亡人数（人）	Number of Deaths (person)			2	1	1	1	1
受伤人数（人）	Number of Injuries (person)	2				3	7	
损失（万元）	Economic Loss (10 000 yuan)	3.1		12.4	7.0	7.3	5.0	4.5
工矿商贸事故	**Accidents in Industry,Mine,Business and Trade**							
事故数(起)	Number of Cases (case)	20	15	13	14	10	10	33
死亡人数（人）	Number of Deaths (person)	24	27	19	18	15	11	35
受伤人数（人）	Number of Injuries (person)		8	2				38
损失（万元）	Economic Loss (10 000 yuan)	703.0	581.5	707.7	270.0	470.2	418.0	830.0

注：本表数据来源于市公安局及安监局。其中交通、火灾数据2011年及以前年份来自于市安监局，2012年以后数据来自于市公安局。2014年农机及工矿商贸事故发生起数统计口径变化，数据与以前年份不可比。

21-29 主要年份刑事案件情况

Data on Criminal Cases in Representative Years

指 标	Item	2010	2011	2012	2013	2014	2015	2016
一、案件数情况	**Data on Number of Cases**							
立案数（起）	Number of Registered Cases(case)	48566	71499	61071	72611	77051	108955	98056
破案数（起）	Number of Cleared up Cases(case)	18906	17585	20788	26587	25830	28629	30730
破案率（%）	Percent of Cleared up Cases(%)	38.9	24.6	34.0	36.6	33.5	26.3	31.3
抓获作案成员(人)	Number of Criminals Caught(person)	13104	14672	16980	14255	14184	12827	11982
二、查获犯罪集团情况	**Data on Hunted down and Seized Criminal Gangs**							
查获犯罪集团个数（个）	Number of Hunted down and Seized Criminal Gangs (person)	186	209	853	695	359	153	119
查获犯罪集团人数（人）	Number of Members of Hunted down and Seized Criminal Gangs (person)	939	970	3332	2632	1508	680	492
涉及案件（起）	Number of Cases Involved(case)	1172	485	2039	2439	1111	291	242
三、涉枪案件情况	**Data on Cases with Guns Involved**							
立案数（起）	Number of Registered Cases(case)	16	13	30	17	13	9	21
破案数（起）	Number of Cleared up Cases(case)	11	10	25	16	8	6	17
破案率（%）	Percent of Cleared up Cases(%)	68.8	76.9	83.3	94.1	61.5	66.7	81.0

注：本表数据来源于市公安局。

21-30 主要年份治安案件情况

Data on Public Order Cases in Representative Years

指 标	Item	2010	2011	2012	2013	2014	2015	2016
受理数（起）	Number of Accepted Cases(case)	58968	63289	60747	94853	108780	104553	109124
查处数（起）	Number of Investigated and Prosecuted Cases(case)	57151	62647	59949	93546	106811	100954	106999
查处率（%）	Percent of Investigated and Prosecuted Cases(%)	96.9	99.0	98.7	98.6	98.2	96.6	98.1
查处违法人数（人）	Number of Investigated and Prosecuted Law-breakers and Crime Committer(person)	45856	44199	34346	46253	52922	40838	40126

注：本表数据来源于市公安局。

21-31 主要年份西安市人民检察院案件办理情况

Data on Acceptance of Cases of Xi'an People's Procuratorate

指　标	Item	2010	2011	2012	2013	2014	2015	2016
一、贪污贿赂案件立案人数（人）	**Number of Persons Invovled in Case about Corporation and Bribery(person)**	**184**	**166**	**175**	**172**	**207**	**220**	**218**
二、渎职侵权案件立案人数（人）	**Number of Persons Invovled in Case about Misprison and Toetious(person)**	**40**	**33**	**38**	**42**	**56**	**46**	**67**
三、审查逮捕案件受理件数（件）	**Examination and Arresting(case)**	**4229**	**5741**	**5024**	**5748**	**6443**	**6545**	**7381**
四、逮捕各类案件人数（人）	**Arresting of Criminals of each kind(person)**	**6183**	**8787**	**7168**	**7177**	**7534**	**6692**	**7763**
决定逮捕贪污贿赂犯罪嫌疑人（人）	Suspects of Corporation and Bribery to be Arrested (person)	51	34	43	49	64	100	26
决定逮捕渎职、侵权犯罪嫌疑人（人）	Suspects of Misprision and Tortious to be Arrested (person)	2		6		18	4	
批准逮捕刑事犯罪嫌疑人（人）	Suspects of Criminal to be Arrested (person)	6130	8753	7119	7128	7452	6588	7737
五、刑事立案监督、侦查活动监督（件）	**Supervision of Acceptance of Criminal** Cases and Investigation (case)	**623**	**89**	**263**	**368**	**284**	**162**	**118**
六、审查起诉案件受理件数（件）	**Examination and Prosecution (case)**	**4662**	**6298**	**6747**	**6371**	**7278**	**6922**	**8090**
七、起诉各类案件人数（人）	**Prosecution of Criminals of each kind(person)**	**5946**	**8276**	**7307**	**7615**	**8399**	**8018**	**9445**
起诉贪污贿赂犯罪被告人（人）	Prosecution of Criminals of Corruption and Bribery to be Defendants(person)	163	129	157	151	123	153	154
起诉渎职、侵权犯罪被告人（人）	Prosecution of Misprision and Tortious to be Defendants (person)	22	13	29	24	44	17	39
起诉刑事犯罪被告人（人）	Prosecution of Criminal to be Defendants (person)	5761	8134	7121	7440	8232	7848	9252

注：本表数据来源于市检察院。

21-32 西安市中级人民法院案件基本情况（2016年）

Law Cases Basic Data of Xi'an Intermediate People's Court（2016）

单位：件、万元 (case,10 000 yuan)

指 标	Item	合计 Total		中级人民法院theIntermediate People's Court	
		结案 Number of Case	诉讼标的总金额 Subject Matter of Litigation the Total Amount	结案 Number of Case	诉讼标的总金额 The Intermediate People's Court Litigation Total Amount
合 计	**Total**	**137116**	**3989948.17**	**17364**	**2360129.78**
一、刑事	**Criminal**	**8143**	**9475.72**	**921**	**538.34**
二、民商事	**Civil and Commercial Matters**	**91432**	**1881614.86**	**12706**	**889583.85**
三、行政	**Administration**	**1281**	**57.98**	**594**	**57.48**
四、申诉、申请再审	**Appeals, Apply for Retrial**	**3058**		**918**	
五、司法赔偿	**Judicial Indemnification**	**11**	**18.27**	**10**	**18.27**
六、执行	**Execution**	**33191**	**2098781.34**	**2215**	**1469931.85**

21-32 续表 continued

单位：件、万元 (case,10 000 yuan)

指 标	Item	基层人民法院 the Basic People's Court		人民法庭 People's Tribunal	
		结案 Number of Case	诉讼标的总金额 Litigation Total Amount	结 案 Number of Case	诉讼标的总金额 Total Number of Litigation
合 计	**Total**	**119752**	**1629818.39**	**26027**	**174362.13**
一、刑事	**Criminal**	**7222**	**8937.38**		**111.68**
二、民商事	**Civil and Commercial Matters**	**78726**	**992031.01**	**26027**	**174250.45**
三、行政	**Administration**	**687**	**0.50**		
四、申诉、申请再审	**Appeals, Apply for Retrial**	**2140**			
五、司法赔偿	**Judicial Indemnification**	**1**			
六、执行	**Execution**	**30976**	**628849.50**		

注：本表数据来源于市中级人民法院。

主要统计指标解释

艺术表演团体 指由文化部门主办或实行行业管理（经文化行政部门审批并领取营业性演出许可证），专门从事表演艺术等活动的各类专业艺术表演团体，含民间职业剧团。（不包括群众业余文艺表演团队）

艺术表演场馆 指由文化部门主办或实行行业管理（向文化行政部门备案或领取合资（合作）演出场所许可证），有观众席、舞台、灯光设备，公开售票、专供文艺团体演出的文化活动场所。附属于文化部门机构内非独立核算的剧场、排演场，公开营业的也应单独统计。

图书馆 指各类图书馆的管理与服务（对文献和信息的搜集、整理、存储、利用和管理，向社会公众开放并提供科学、文化等各种知识普及教育）。包括公共图书馆和各类机构内部举办的或单独举办的图书馆的管理与服务。不包括部队系统以及文化馆（文化中心、群众艺术馆）、文化站内设的图书室。

群众文化活动 指开展群众文化活动的场所的管理和组织活动。包括文化馆（含综合性文化中心、群众艺术馆）、文化站、文化宫、少年宫等群众文化活动。在本制度中，目前暂不统计文化部门以外的文化宫和少年宫。

文化馆 （含综合性文化中心、群众艺术馆）、文化站：指专门从事群众文化活动的群众文化场馆。不包括临时抽调人员组成、没有编制的农村和街道文化工作队、服务站等。

广播节目综合人口覆盖率 根据国家广电总局制定的《广播电视人口覆盖率统计技术标准和方法》进行统计调查的，分别反映中央、省级、地市级、县级广播节目在本行政区域的综合覆盖情况，反应以无线方式传输的广播节目综合覆盖情况，综合反映广播公共服务覆盖的规模、能力、水平。

电视节目综合人口覆盖率 根据国家广电总局制定的《广播电视人口覆盖率统计技术标准和方法》进行统计调查的，分别反映中央、省级、地市级、县级电视节目在本行政区域的综合覆盖情况，反应以无线方式传输的电视节目综合覆盖情况，综合反映广播公共服务覆盖的规模、能力、水平。

博物馆 指为了研究、教育、欣赏的目的，收藏、保护、展示人类活动和自然环境的见证物，向公众开放，非盈利性、永久性社会服务机构，包括以博物馆（院）、纪念馆（舍）科技馆、陈列馆等专有名称开展活动的单位。

等级运动员人数 指经考核正式批准授予等级运动员称号的人数。运动员等级分为国际级运动健将、运动健将、一级运动员、二级运动员、三级运动员、少年级运动员。

等级裁判员人数 指经考核正式批准授予等级裁判员称号的人数。裁判员等级分为国际裁判、国家级裁判、一级裁判、二级裁判、三级裁判。

医疗卫生机构 指从卫生（卫生计生）行政部门取得《医疗机构执业许可证》、《计划生育技术服务许可证》或从民政、工商行政、机构编制管理部门取得法人单位登记证书，为社会提供医疗服务、公共卫生服务或从事医学科研和学在职培训等工作的单位。包括医院、基层医疗卫生机构、专业公共卫生机构、其他医疗卫生机构。

医院 包括综合医院、中医医院、中西医结合医院、民族医院、各类专科医院和护理院，不包括专科疾病防治院、妇幼保健院和疗养院，包括医学院校附属医院。

基层医疗卫生机构 包括社区卫生服务中心（站）、乡镇(街道)卫生院、村卫生室、门诊部、诊所(医务室)。

专业公共卫生机构 包括疾病预防控制中心、专科疾病防治机构、妇幼保健机构（含妇幼保健计划生育服务中心）、健康教育机构、急救中心（站）、采供血机构、卫生监督机构、取得《医疗机构执业许可证》或《计划生育技术服务许可证》的计划生育技术服务机构。

其他医疗卫生机构 包括疗养院、临床检验中心、医学科研机构、医学在职教育机构、卫生监督（监测、检测）机构、医学考试中心、农村改水中心、人才交流中心、统计信息中心等卫生事业单位。

卫生技术人员 包括执业医师、执业助理医师、注册护士、药师(士)、检验及影像技师(士)、卫生监督员和见习医(药、护、技)师(士)等卫生专业人员。不包括从事管理工作的卫生技术人员(如院长、副院长、党委书记等)。

执业(助理)医师 指《医师执业证》“级别”为“执业（助理）医师”且实际从事医疗、预防保健工作的人员，不包括实际从事管理工作的执业（助理）医师。执业（助理）医师类别分为临床、中医、口腔和公共卫生四类。

提供住宿的社会服务机构 包括养老服务机构、精神疾病服务机构、儿童福利机构以及其他提供住宿机构。

烈士纪念建筑物管理机构 指民政部门管理的、独立核算的褒扬烈士的陵园、纪念馆等单位的总称。

殡葬服务机构 指为殡葬服务的单位总称。殡仪馆（含火葬场）、公墓、独立核算的骨灰堂、殡葬管理机构等。

公证人员 指在国家公证机关依法办理公证事务的司法人员，包括公证员、助理公证员和在公证处工作的其他人员。

办理公证文书 指公证处在一定时期内办结的公证文书件数。公证文书按司法部规定或批准的格式制作，包括国内公证和涉外公证两部分。国内公证分为经济合同公证和民事法律关系公证两大类。

调解人员 指在人民调解委员会担负调解民间一般民事纠纷和轻微违法行为引起纠纷的工作人员，包括调解委员会的委员和调解小组的调解员。

Explanatory Notes on Main Statistical Indicators

Arts Performance Troupes refer to the various professional performing arts groups, which sponsored by the cultural sectors or guided by the cultural society (Receive commercial performance license approved by the cultural administration authority),including non-governmental troupes. (The mass amateur arts performance troupes are not included.)

Arts Performance Places refer to the various sites for cultural activities, which sponsored by the cultural sectors or guided by the cultural society (approved by the cultural market administration, or receive joint/cooperative venues permit), with the facility of auditorium, stage and lighting, and selling tickets in public, including the opera halls and rehearse sites, etc. which are affiliated to the culture sectors without independent financial accounts and open to the public.

Library refers to all types of library management and services(collection, collation, storage, use and management of literature and information, open and provide scientific, cultural and other literacy education to the public). Including the management and services of public libraries and the libraries internally or separately organized by various sectors. Excluding the libraries in troops system and cultural palaces (cultural centers, mass art centers),cultural stations.

Mass Culture Center refers to the management and organization of the places where mass culture activities hold. Including cultural palace (cultural center ,mass art center), cultural stations, cultural palaces ,youth palaces and other mass cultural activities. In this system ,cultural palaces and youth palaces beyond cultural sectors are not counted at present.

Cultural Palaces (Cultural Centers, Mass Art Centers),Cultural Stations refers to the mass cultural venues specialized in mass cultural activities. Excluding rural and street cultural teams, service stations which made up by temporary without authorized strength.

Radio Coverage of Population refers to the comprehensive coverage which respectively reflected central ,province, city, prefecture and county radio programs by wireless in the administrative region, and comprehensively reflect the size, capacity, level of the public broadcasting services, according to Statistical Standard and Method on Television and Radio Coverage of Population established by the State Administration of Broadcasting ,Film and Television

Television Coverage of Population refers to the comprehensive coverage which respectively reflected central, province, city, prefecture and county television programs by wireless in the administrative region, and comprehensively reflect the size, capacity, level of the public broadcasting services, according to Statistical Standard and Method on Television and Radio Coverage of Population established by the State Administration of Broadcasting , Film and Television

Museum refers to the non-profit, permanent society service sectors which collect ,protect ,show human activities and the witnesses of natural environment, including the units that organize activities with the proper name such as museum, memorial hall , science and technology museum, exhibition hall, etc.

Number of Athletes in Grades refers to the number of athletes who have been given titles through examination. The titles of athletes include international masters of sports, masters of sports, first-grade, second-grade and third-grade sportsmen and young athletes.

Number of Referees in Grades refers to the number of referees who have been given titles after examination. They are classified as international referees, national referees and referees of the first, second and third grades.

Medical and health institutions are the organizations that have got thepractice license of medical institutionandfamily planning technical services licensefrom health administrative departments or have obtained legal entity registration certificate from civil, industrial and commercial administration, organization management departments, to provide medical services, public health services or engaged in medical research and medical job training. Itincludes hospitals, primary medical and health institutions, professional public health institutions, and other medical and health institutions.

Hospitals include general hospital, hospital of traditional Chinese medicine, hospital of integrated traditional Chinese and Western Medicine, National Hospital, various specialist hospitals and nursing homes, excluding specialized disease prevention and treatment centers , Maternity and child care centers and sanatorium, including hospitals affiliated to medical colleges and universities.

Primary medical and health institutions include community health service centers (stations), township (street) health centers, village clinics, outpatient department, clinics.

Professional public health institutions include the center for disease control and prevention, specialized disease prevention and treatment centers, maternity and child care centers (including maternal and child health family planning service center), health education institutions, first aid agencies,collecting and supplying agencies, health supervision institutions, andfamily planning technical service institutions which have got the practice license of medical institution and family planning technical services license.

Other medical and health institutions include sanatorium, clinical inspection center, medical research institutions, medical in-service education institutions, health supervision institutions, medical examination center, Rural change water quality center, personnel exchange center, statistical information center and other health institutions.

Health technical personnel include practicing physician, practicing assistant doctors, registered nurses, pharmacists, inspection and imaging technicians, health supervisors and clerksand other health professionals. It does not include health technical personnel engaged in management work such as Dean, vice president, Secretary of the Party committee, etc.

Practicing physician(assistant) refers to the practitioner who is a practitioner (assistant) doctor and actually engaged in medical care and preventive health care, and does not include the practitioner (assistant) practitioner who is actually engaged in the management work. Practitioners (assistants) are classified into four categories: clinical, Chinesetraditional, oral and public health.

Social services providing accommodation include pension services, psychiatric care services, child welfare institutions, and other lodging establishments.

Martyr memorial buildings management organization refers to the floorboard of cemetery, memorial and other units which are independent accounting and managedby civil affairs department to praise the Martyrs

Funeral service agencies refer to the units that serve funeral services. It includesFuneral home (including crematorium), cemetery, independent accounting ashes hall, funeral and interment management organization, etc.

Notary Personnel refers to judicial workers of the state notary offices handling notarization work according to law. They include notaries, assistant notaries, and other people working for notary offices.

Notarized Documents refer to the documents settled by notary offices in a year. The notary documents are drawn up in accordance with the regulations of the Ministry of Justice, including domestic documents and foreign-related documents. Domestic documents are divided into two major categories, documents on economic contracts and documents on civil legal relations.

Mediators refer to workers on peoples mediation committees responsible for mediating in civil disputes and cases of slight infraction of the law. They include members of the mediation committees and mediators of mediation groups.

22 企业调查

ENTERPRISES INVESTIGATION

资料整理：薛　燕
Data management：Xue Yan
数据审核：黄雪冰
Data audit：Huang Xuebing

第二十二部分　企业调查

一、简要说明

本章资料主要包括各行业企业景气调查指数和企业家信心指数等，由西安市统计局社会经济调查中心提供。

二、主要指标

企业景气指数（第四季度）	110.1
企业家信心指数（第四季度）	108.8

22 ENTERPRISES INVESTIGATION

Ⅰ.Brief Introduction

Data in this chapter consists prosperity survey indices of various industries and Entrepreneur Expectation Indicator, provided by Xi'an Municipal Bureau of Statics .

Ⅱ.Major Indicators

Business Climate Index（Fourth Quarter）	110.1
Entrepreneur Expectation Indicator（Fourth Quarter）	108.8

22-1 企业景气指数（2016年）

Business Climate Index（2016）

指　标	Item	一季度 First Quarter	二季度 Second Quarter	三季度 Third Quarter	四季度 Fourth Quarter
企业景气指数	**Business Climate Index**	**103.3**	**101.0**	**105.1**	**110.1**
按行业门类分	**Grouped by Sector**				
工业	Industry	108.9	108.3	110.5	118.7
建筑业	Construction	94.1	90.4	91.0	99.3
批发和零售业	Wholesale and Retail Sales	100.1	95.8	107.6	109.1
住宿和餐饮业	Hotels and Catering Services	88.3	85.8	103.0	100.6
房地产业	Real Estate	90.0	86.3	96.2	103.4
社会服务业	Social Services	107.1	105.0	106.9	109.2

22-2 企业家信心指数（2016年）

Entrepreneur Expectation Indicator（2016）

指　标	Item	一季度 First Quarter	二季度 Second Quarter	三季度 Third Quarter	四季度 Fourth Quarter
企业家信心指数	**Entrepreneur Expectation Indicator**	**103.2**	**101.3**	**105.5**	**108.8**
按行业门类分	**Grouped by Sector**				
工业	Industry	107.7	108.6	111.3	116.7
建筑业	Construction	93.0	88.0	92.3	97.9
批发和零售业	Wholesale and Retail Sales	99.1	96.6	106.0	106.9
住宿和餐饮业	Hotels and Catering Services	91.4	89.5	102.9	102.5
房地产业	Real Estate	91.8	87.1	99.4	101.0
社会服务业	Social Services	108.0	105.5	106.8	108.6

主要统计指标解释

企业景气指数：是根据企业家对本企业综合生产经营情况所作的判断与预期（通常是对“良好”、“一般”、“不佳”的选择）而编制的指数，用以综合反映企业的生产经营状况。企业景气指数也称“企业综合生产经营景气指数”。

企业家信心指数：是根据企业家对企业外部市场经济环境与宏观政策的认识、看法判断和预期（通常是对“乐观”、“一般”、“不乐观”的选择）而编制的指数，用以综合反映企业家对宏观经济环境的感受与信心。企业家信心指数也称“宏观经济景气指数”。

景气指数的表示方式：景气指数的表示范围在0~200之间，其含义：100为景气指数的临界值，表明景气状况变化不大；100~200为景气区间，表明景气状况趋于上升或改善，越接近于200，状况越景气；0~100为不景气区间，表明经济状况趋于下降或恶化，越接近于0，状况越不景气。

Explanatory Notes on Main Statistical Indicators

Business Climate Index it is an index worked out according to the judgment and anticipation (normally a choice from good, ordinary, not good) of entrepreneurs made based on synthetic productive and operational situation of the enterprise. It is used to reflect synthetically the productive and operational situation of the enterprise. It is also referred to as synthetic and productiveoperational prosperity index of enterprise.

Confidence index of entrepreneur it is an index worked out according to the judgment and anticipation (normally a choice from optimistic , ordinary , not optimistic) of entrepreneurs made based on their understandings and views of the market and economic environment outside the enterprise and the macro policies. It is used to reflect synthetically the confidence and feelings of the entrepreneurs to the macro economic environment. It is also referred to as macro-economy prosperity index.

The way to express prosperity index the range of prosperity index is from 0 to 200; 100 is the critical value, and means economic situation didn't change largely; from 100 to 200 is the interval of prosperity; and from 0 to 100 is the interval of not prosperity, meaning economic situation is going down or worse, the closer to 0, the worse the economic situation.

中国统计出版社最新图书简目

（仅供参考，以实际出版为准）

统计资料

中国统计年鉴　中国统计摘要　中国发展报告
中国经济普查年鉴　国际统计年鉴　金砖国家联合统计手册
中国-东盟国家统计手册　中国农村统计年鉴　中国县域统计年鉴
中国城市统计年鉴　中国对外直接投资统计公报　中国地区经济监测报告
中国贸易外经统计年鉴　中国零售和餐饮连锁企业统计年鉴　中国商品交易市场统计年鉴
大中型批发零售和住宿餐饮企业统计年鉴　中国农产品价格调查年鉴　中国住户调查年鉴
中国价格统计年鉴　中国能源统计年鉴　全国农产品成本收益资料汇编
中国环境统计年鉴　中国建筑业统计年鉴　国外资源、能源和环境统计资料汇编
中国工业统计年鉴　中国城乡建设统计年鉴　中国县城建设统计年鉴
中国城市建设统计年鉴　中国科技统计年鉴　中国房地产统计年鉴
中国证券期货统计年鉴　中国劳动统计年鉴　中国第三产业统计年鉴
工业企业科技活动资料　中国社会统计年鉴　中国高技术产业统计年鉴
中国人才资源统计报告　中国教育统计年鉴　中国人口和就业统计年鉴
文化及相关产业统计概览　中国文化及相关产业统计年鉴　中国教育经费统计年鉴
中国民族统计年鉴　中国残疾人事业统计年鉴　中国民政统计年鉴
中国乡镇街道行政区域简册　中国基本单位统计年鉴　中国妇女儿童状况统计资料（英）

省级综合统计年鉴系列

北京 天津 河北 山西 内蒙古 辽宁 吉林 黑龙江 上海 江苏 浙江 安徽 福建 江西 山东 河南 湖北 湖南 广东 广西 海南 重庆 四川 贵州 云南 西藏 陕西 甘肃 青海 宁夏 新疆 新疆生产建设兵团

市(县)级综合统计年鉴系列

滨海新区 石家庄 唐山 邯郸 保定 沧州 邢台 廊坊 承德 衡水 秦皇岛 张家口 太原 大同 阳泉 长治 晋城 朔州 晋中 运城 忻州 临汾 吕梁 呼和浩特 呼和浩特新城区 鄂尔多斯 包头 沈阳 大连 长春 吉林 延吉 四平 通化 松原 哈尔滨 齐齐哈尔 黑龙江垦区 上海浦东新区 南京 无锡 徐州 常州 苏州 南通 连云港 淮安 盐城 扬州 镇江 泰州 宿迁 江阴 丹阳 海门 杭州 宁波 温州 嘉兴 湖州 绍兴 金华 衢州 舟山 台州 丽水 合肥 安庆 马鞍山 福州 厦门 宁德 漳州 龙岩 南昌 九江 上饶 新余 抚州 萍乡 赣州 吉安 景德镇 济南 青岛 潍坊 枣庄 日照 滕州 郑州 洛阳 平顶山 三门峡 商丘 信阳 济源 汝州 武汉 十堰 荆州 宜昌 荆门 咸宁 长沙 广州 深圳 惠州 东莞 汕尾 南宁 柳州 桂林 来宾 河池 防城港 海口 三亚 成都 贵阳 黔南 毕节 昆明 西安 咸阳 延安 宝鸡 安康 铜川 汉中 榆林 兰州 庆阳 银川 乌鲁木齐 兵团一师 兵团十师

调查年鉴系列

天津 山西 内蒙古 辽宁 吉林 上海　福建 江西 河南 湖北 湖南 广西　重庆 四川 云南 甘肃 宁夏 新疆

统计方法应用/实用手册

实用SAS统计分析教程　马克威统计分析与数据挖掘应用案例　统计公文知识问答
乡镇统计人员岗位知识培训系列教材：辅助调查员岗位基础知识　乡镇统计人员岗位基础知识
县级统计人员岗位知识培训系列教材：Excel在统计工作中的应用　简明统计分析
地市级统计人员岗位知识培训系列教材：统计报告与演示　Excel在统计工作中的应用

统计通俗读物/统计科普图书

国家统计局核心统计指标变迁　货架上的统计　账本里的统计

重点图书

砥砺奋进的五年——从十八大到十九大　新编英汉汉英统计大词典　中华医学统计百科全书
新常态下的中国服务业：理论与实践　新动能新产业发展报告-2017
挑大学选专业2018—考研择校指南　挑大学选专业2018—高考志愿填报指南